Macworld®
Mac® OS 9 Bible

Macworld®
Mac® OS 9 Bible

Lon Poole and Todd Stauffer

IDG Books Worldwide, Inc.
An International Data Group Company

Foster City, CA ✦ Chicago, IL ✦ Indianapolis, IN ✦ New York, NY

Macworld® Mac® OS 9 Bible

Published by
IDG Books Worldwide, Inc.
An International Data Group Company
919 E. Hillsdale Blvd., Suite 400
Foster City, CA 94404
www.idgbooks.com (IDG Books Worldwide Web site)

ISBN: 0-7645-3414-9

Printed in the United States of America

10 9 8 7 6 5 4 3 2 1

1B/SX/RS/ZZ/FC

Distributed in the United States by IDG Books Worldwide, Inc.

Distributed by CDG Books Canada Inc. for Canada; by Transworld Publishers Limited in the United Kingdom; by IDG Norge Books for Norway; by IDG Sweden Books for Sweden; by IDG Books Australia Publishing Corporation Pty. Ltd. for Australia and New Zealand; by TransQuest Publishers Pte Ltd. for Singapore, Malaysia, Thailand, Indonesia, and Hong Kong; by Gotop Information Inc. for Taiwan; by ICG Muse, Inc. for Japan; by Intersoft for South Africa; by Eyrolles for France; by International Thomson Publishing for Germany, Austria and Switzerland; by Distribuidora Cuspide for Argentina; by LR International for Brazil; by Galileo Libros for Chile; by Ediciones ZETA S.C.R. Ltda. for Peru; by WS Computer Publishing Corporation, Inc., for the Philippines; by Contemporanea de Ediciones for Venezuela; by Express Computer Distributors for the Caribbean and West Indies; by Micronesia Media Distributor, Inc. for Micronesia; by Chips Computadoras S.A. de C.V. for Mexico; by Editorial Norma de Panama S.A. for Panama; by American Bookshops for Finland.

For general information on IDG Books Worldwide's books in the U.S., please call our Consumer Customer Service department at 800-762-2974. For reseller information, including discounts and premium sales, please call our Reseller Customer Service department at 800-434-3422.

For information on where to purchase IDG Books Worldwide's books outside the U.S., please contact our International Sales department at 317-596-5530 or fax 317-596-5692.

For consumer information on foreign language translations, please contact our Customer Service department at 800-434-3422, fax 317-596-5692, or e-mail rights@idgbooks.com.

For information on licensing foreign or domestic rights, please phone +1-650-655-3109.

For sales inquiries and special prices for bulk quantities, please contact our Sales department at 650-655-3200 or write to the address above.

For information on using IDG Books Worldwide's books in the classroom or for ordering examination copies, please contact our Educational Sales department at 800-434-2086 or fax 317-596-5499.

For press review copies, author interviews, or other publicity information, please contact our Public Relations department at 650-655-3000 or fax 650-655-3299.

For authorization to photocopy items for corporate, personal, or educational use, please contact Copyright Clearance Center, 222 Rosewood Drive, Danvers, MA 01923, or fax 978-750-4470.

Library of Congress Cataloging-in-Publication Data
Poole, Lon.
    Macworld Mac OS 9 Bible / Lon Poole and Todd Stauffer.
        p. cm.
    ISBN 0-7645-3414-9 (alk. paper)
    1. Macintosh (Computer) 2. Mac OS. I. Stauffer, Todd. II.
Title.
QA76.8.M3 P65955   1999
005.4'469–dc21   99-058029
                                                   CIP

ABOUT IDG BOOKS WORLDWIDE

Welcome to the world of IDG Books Worldwide.

IDG Books Worldwide, Inc., is a subsidiary of International Data Group, the world's largest publisher of computer-related information and the leading global provider of information services on information technology. IDG was founded more than 30 years ago by Patrick J. McGovern and now employs more than 9,000 people worldwide. IDG publishes more than 290 computer publications in over 75 countries. More than 90 million people read one or more IDG publications each month.

Launched in 1990, IDG Books Worldwide is today the #1 publisher of best-selling computer books in the United States. We are proud to have received eight awards from the Computer Press Association in recognition of editorial excellence and three from Computer Currents' First Annual Readers' Choice Awards. Our best-selling *...For Dummies®* series has more than 50 million copies in print with translations in 31 languages. IDG Books Worldwide, through a joint venture with IDG's Hi-Tech Beijing, became the first U.S. publisher to publish a computer book in the People's Republic of China. In record time, IDG Books Worldwide has become the first choice for millions of readers around the world who want to learn how to better manage their businesses.

Our mission is simple: Every one of our books is designed to bring extra value and skill-building instructions to the reader. Our books are written by experts who understand and care about our readers. The knowledge base of our editorial staff comes from years of experience in publishing, education, and journalism — experience we use to produce books to carry us into the new millennium. In short, we care about books, so we attract the best people. We devote special attention to details such as audience, interior design, use of icons, and illustrations. And because we use an efficient process of authoring, editing, and desktop publishing our books electronically, we can spend more time ensuring superior content and less time on the technicalities of making books.

You can count on our commitment to deliver high-quality books at competitive prices on topics you want to read about. At IDG Books Worldwide, we continue in the IDG tradition of delivering quality for more than 30 years. You'll find no better book on a subject than one from IDG Books Worldwide.

John Kilcullen
Chairman and CEO
IDG Books Worldwide, Inc.

Steven Berkowitz
President and Publisher
IDG Books Worldwide, Inc.

Eighth Annual Computer Press Awards ≥ 1992

Ninth Annual Computer Press Awards ≥ 1993

Tenth Annual Computer Press Awards ≥ 1994

Eleventh Annual Computer Press Awards ≥ 1995

IDG is the world's leading IT media, research and exposition company. Founded in 1964, IDG had 1997 revenues of $2.05 billion and has more than 9,000 employees worldwide. IDG offers the widest range of media options that reach IT buyers in 75 countries representing 95% of worldwide IT spending. IDG's diverse product and services portfolio spans six key areas including print publishing, online publishing, expositions and conferences, market research, education and training, and global marketing services. More than 90 million people read one or more of IDG's 290 magazines and newspapers, including IDG's leading global brands — Computerworld, PC World, Network World, Macworld and the Channel World family of publications. IDG Books Worldwide is one of the fastest-growing computer book publishers in the world, with more than 700 titles in 36 languages. The "...For Dummies®" series alone has more than 50 million copies in print. IDG offers online users the largest network of technology-specific Web sites around the world through IDG.net (http://www.idg.net), which comprises more than 225 targeted Web sites in 55 countries worldwide. International Data Corporation (IDC) is the world's largest provider of information technology data, analysis and consulting, with research centers in over 41 countries and more than 400 research analysts worldwide. IDG World Expo is a leading producer of more than 168 globally branded conferences and expositions in 35 countries including E3 (Electronic Entertainment Expo), Macworld Expo, ComNet, Windows World Expo, ICE (Internet Commerce Expo), Agenda, DEMO, and Spotlight. IDG's training subsidiary, ExecuTrain, is the world's largest computer training company, with more than 230 locations worldwide and 785 training courses. IDG Marketing Services helps industry-leading IT companies build international brand recognition by developing global integrated marketing programs via IDG's print, online and exposition products worldwide. Further information about the company can be found at www.idg.com. 1/24/99

Credits

Acquisitions Editor
Michael Roney

Development Editors
Kathryn Duggan
Sara Salzmann

Technical Editor
Dennis Cohen

Copy Editors
Richard Adin
Marti Paul

Project Coordinators
Linda Marousek
Joe Shines
Louigene Santos

Cover Design
Peter Kowaleszyn

Graphics and Production Specialists
Mario Amador
Jude Levinson
Michael Lewis
Ramses Ramirez
Victor Varela
Dina F Quan

Quality Control Specialists
Chris Weisbart
Laura Taflinger

Illustrators
Mary Jo Richards
Clint Lahnen

Proofreading and Indexing
York Production Services

About the Author

Lon Poole is the award-winning author or coauthor of over two dozen computer books, including all seven editions of this book, four additional Mac books, and numerous others. He is also the author of the popular "Quick Tips" column in *Macworld* magazine and more than 50 magazine feature articles on Mac topics. He has a B.A. in Computer Science from the University of California, Berkeley. Lon lives in northern California with his wife and two sons. He enjoys hiking, carpentry, and traveling.

Todd Stauffer is the author or coauthor of 20 computer books, including *How to Do Everything with your iMac*, *Macworld Mac Upgrade and Repair Bible*, and *Using Your Mac*. He's the writer and cohost of the Emmy-award winning "Disk Doctors" program on the Knowledge TV network. Todd is also the "Upgrade Guy" columnist and a contributing editor for MacCentral Online, as well as a contributor to *MacAddict* magazine, *CMP TechWeb, and MacTech Magazine,* among others.

Todd has worked as a magazine editor, radio host, feature writer, and advertising copywriter, all in technical fields. He received a B.A. in English Literature from Texas A&M University. Todd lives in New York City.

Preface

According to popular legend, a Mac is so easy to use that you don't need to read books about it. Alas, if only that were true. In fact, discovering all the power that the Mac OS gives your computer would take months of exploring and experimenting. Yes, exploring and experimenting can be fun. But do you really have months to devote to your computer's operating system? Save your time for having fun with games and multimedia, exploring the Internet, or maybe getting some work done. Benefit from the experience of others (in this case, the author and his collaborators). Read this book so that you can put the full power of the Mac OS to work for you without a lot of poking around the Mac desktop.

Maybe you think you don't need this book because you have Apple's manuals and onscreen help. It's true these are good sources of information. But the *Macworld Mac OS 9 Bible* contains a great deal of information you won't find in the manuals or on help screens. This book also provides a different perspective on subjects you may not quite understand after reading the manuals. And because this book describes the Mac OS completely, you can use it instead of Apple's manuals if you don't happen to have them. (They tend to be rather thin these days, anyway.)

Who Should Read This Book

This book is meant for people who already know Mac OS fundamentals such as choosing commands from menus, moving icons on the desktop, and selecting and editing text. If you have spent more than a few days with any Mac OS computer, you know how to do these things and are ready for what's inside this book.

Read this book to learn all about Mac OS 9 — how to use it if you have it, and why you should get it if you don't. Mac OS 9 is a feature-rich upgrade to the venerable Mac OS, touted by Apple as the "Internet OS," and Mac OS 9 definitely has its share of Internet-related upgrades. But there's a heck of a lot more that's changed in Mac OS 9. Whether you're interested in learning the basics or ferreting out every last detail in this latest release, this book will help you get the most from your sessions with Apple's latest OS.

What's Inside

Macworld Mac OS 9 Bible covers all of Mac OS 9's features — new, updated, and existing from previous versions — in six progressive parts:

✦ Part I takes a quick look at the features of the Mac OS. Use it to get started right away or to see the big picture. You get an overview of what's new in Mac OS 9, what "hot" features have been added recently, and what features, even though they've been around for a while, are essential tools in the Mac user's arsenal.

✦ Part II describes in depth what you encounter when you start using the Mac OS. Windows, icons, and menus appear when you start up a Mac, but look closely and you may find some new and useful aspects of these elements. When you go beyond looking around the desktop, you can organize your disks, folders, and files with the Finder. You get right to work by opening programs and documents (including documents from Windows and DOS computers), moving document contents around, and saving documents. You learn to search your computer and the Internet using the much-hyped Sherlock tool. You can modify the Mac OS appearance and behavior, and you can get help onscreen when you need it.

✦ Part III tells you how to use some important Mac OS capabilities. You learn how to fine-tune the system by making changes in the special System Folder and adjusting a multitude of settings in software control panels. You discover how handy aliases can be. You learn to deal with fonts and typography, and also learn to control printing. In this part you find out why the Mac OS deserves its reputation as the multimedia leader among personal computer operating systems. You also learn how the Mac OS makes it easy to explore the Internet, including the Web and e-mail.

✦ Part IV takes you beyond the Mac OS basics — way beyond. You learn to be comfortable with managing your Mac's memory. You learn how to set up a simple network of computers, share your files with others on the network, and use their shared files. You get to know how any Mac can speak and how most can listen. This part of the book also introduces AppleScript and teaches you how to use it to automate repetitive tasks.

✦ Part V presents many ways to make the most of the Mac OS. You'll find that the accessory programs included with the Mac OS come in handy on occasion. If they're not enough, you'll find a chapter devoted to describing low-cost software utilities you can use to enhance the Mac OS. Two more chapters reveal over 100 Mac OS tips and secrets. Another chapter guides you through troubleshooting procedures.

✦ Part VI details how to upgrade or install the Mac OS, including how to install a clean copy. You see how the various recent Mac OS versions compare and what their requirements are, so you can decide whether to stick with the version you have or to upgrade it. You find out how to get ready to install, and you can follow step-by-step instructions for installing everything on your Mac OS 9 installation CD-ROM.

In addition to these six parts, this book includes a glossary filled with those terms you're bound to encounter in a tome like this, including quite a few that Webster hasn't gotten around to, yet.

If you read this book from front to back, you will find that some information appears in more than one place. In particular, everything that Part I covers in summary appears elsewhere in the book in more detail. Also, some of the tips and secrets in Chapters 27 and 28 appear first amidst relevant subject matter throughout earlier chapters. This duplication is intentional and is meant for your benefit.

Conventions Used in This Book

This book makes use of established conventions in an effort to help guide you through the material.

Mac OS version references

As you may have realized from reading this preface, this book uses the term Mac OS to include all versions of the Macintosh operating system, also known as the system software, unless a specific version number is stated (such as Mac OS 9). When you see a range of version numbers, such as Mac OS 8–9, the topic under discussion applies to all versions in the stated range. While all topics discussed pertain to Mac OS 9, we'll occasionally toss in a reference to earlier Mac OS versions to place things in the proper historical context.

Apple named earlier versions of the operating system System instead of Mac OS. You may notice occasional references in this book to System 7.5.5 and earlier. Just remember that Mac OS and System are two terms for the Mac operating system.

Sidebars

Certain discussions in this book are expanded with sidebars. These are shaded boxes that contain background information, expert tips and advice, areas where caution is needed, and other helpful information.

Feedback, Please

The author and publisher appreciate your feedback on this book. Please feel free to contact us, care of IDG Books Worldwide, with questions or comments. (IDG Books Worldwide, Inc.; 919 E. Hillsdale Boulevard, Suite 400; Foster City, CA 94404)

Acknowledgments

When you're going to write a book of this size about a subject as deep and wide as the Mac OS, you can't be shy about asking for help. We have many people to thank for their contributions to this book. Lon Poole, who was sole author of the previous six editions of this book, would like to thank Todd Stauffer for preparing this edition, including writing several new chapters and extensively revising the others. Many other people contributed to earlier editions of the book, and their work lives on in the *Macworld Mac OS 9 Bible*. David Angell and Brent Heslop researched and wrote first drafts of material that appears in Chapters 14, 21, and 22 in this book. Nancy Dunn and Rita Lewis helped reorganize and update an earlier edition of the book, and much of their work survives in Chapters 15, 16, 17, and 23. Tom Negrino compressed information about the entire Internet into what is now Chapter 10. Derrick Schneider applied his AppleScript expertise to Chapter 24. Roxanne Gentile put together the first collection of utility software in Chapter 26. Rob Terrell wrote drafts of material that now appears in Chapters 30 and 31. For the previous edition of this book, Seth Novogrodsky wrote Chapter 29 and revised the material that now appears in Chapters 3 and 24. Katherine Ulrich updated what are now Chapters 12, 25, and 26. And Suzanne Courteau updated the tips in Chapters 27 and 28. We most gratefully acknowledge all their contributions.

We also want to express our appreciation to the editorial and production teams at IDG Books Worldwide, whose diligence made all the difference. In particular, Dennis Cohen as technical reviewer did a great job of filtering out technical impurities. We also want to thank Mike Roney and Sara Salzmann for urging us onward. In addition, we want to thank Kathi Duggan, who for the third time has done a splendid job as development editor. (Believe us, you are glad she went over this book before you did.)

Lon wishes to express his gratitude to his wife, Karin, and sons, Adam and Ethan, for their support of his earlier work on which this book is based.

Todd would like to thank Donna Ladd for putting up with the late nights and annoying alarm clocks while this revision was being written. Also, thanks to Leo and Arno Jakobson for the space, equipment, and moral support that made it possible for Todd to actually sit and write in the midst of a chaotic move to New York.

Contents at a Glance

Contents

Part III: At Work with the Mac OS   255

Chapter 11: Dig into the System Folder 257

Chapter 12: Adjust Controls and Preferences 275

Part IV: Beyond the Basics of the Mac OS   491

Chapter 19: Manage Your Memory   493

Chapter 29: Troubleshoot Problems and Maintain the Mac OS 763

Overview of the Mac OS

What's New about the Mac OS 9?

The update to Mac OS 9 is a significant leap over its predecessor, Mac OS 8.6. After all, it would need to be to get a whole new version number, right? That new number is warranted, because Mac OS 9 sports quite a few new features that might change the way you work with your Mac.

Mac OS 9 doesn't look a lot different—it doesn't include as many tweaks to the appearance of the OS as previous versions—but there are quite a few new utilities and functions to explore. Plus, Mac OS 9 includes many "under-the-hood" updates that fix and augment the innards of the operating system. Hopefully that means more stability and better performance if you're upgrading from an earlier version.

Probably the most obvious new feature in Mac OS 9 is support for multiple users. This makes it possible for different people to log in to a single Mac and customize their desktops, folders, and Mac options and then log out, making the Mac available for others. Along with this comes a new voice authentication system—if you'd like to avoid typing your password, you can opt for a voice password instead.

Other features run the gamut—there are quite a few additions that improve Internet and networking access, as well as the significant addition of Apple Encryption, a method for sending and storing files as secure, encrypted documents. Plus, Mac OS 9 features the return of a Mac OS capability that was left for dead years ago, called the Keychain. With one password you can store all your other passwords, making it easier to remember and sign on to multiple services, Web sites, servers, and so on.

This chapter gives you an overview of all the brand new features included in Mac OS 9. After you've read this one, read the next two chapters to see what features have been *improved* since Mac OS 8.6 (Chapter 2) and which are recent improvements to the overall Mac experience since about Mac OS 8.0 or so (Chapter 3).

Mac OS 9 and Mac OS X: What's the Difference?

The world of Mac OS version numbers has become a bit more complicated over the past few years. Apple offers (or has recently offered) a number of different Mac OS versions, including Mac OS 8.*x*, Mac OS 9, Mac OS X, and even Mac OS X Server. So, what does it all mean?

Apple has essentially a three-pronged strategy (at least, as far as we can tell) that comprises Mac OS 9, Mac OS X, and Mac OS X Server. Essentially an upgrade to Mac OS 8.5 and 8.6, Mac OS 9 is aimed at consumers and professionals who prefer the backward compatibility, familiar interface, and tried-and-true technologies of the current line of Mac OS versions. It's also designed to run on more Power Macintosh machines, including the latest G3 and G4 models. By contrast, Mac OS X will only run on Power Macintosh G3, G4, iMac, and PowerBook G3 models. If you have an earlier Power Macintosh model, then you can't upgrade to Mac OS X.

What makes Mac OS X different?

Mac OS X is considered Apple's "next-generation" operating system because it offers a number of low-level improvements over Mac OS 9. While Mac OS 9 is certainly a robust operating system, Mac OS X has a number of modern features that please the computer scientists to no end, including the following:

✦ **Preemptive Multitasking.** While Mac OS 9 is fully capable of multitasking (running more than one application at a time), its system is called *cooperative multitasking* because it allows the applications to have a lot of say in the matter. For instance, an application can decide how much of the processor's time it would like to take when it's the active application. With Mac OS X's approach, the operating system has more control, telling applications how much processor time they get. That generally proves more efficient and responsive. It also allows Mac OS X to control errant applications that are hogging the processor.

✦ **Multithreading.** Although Mac OS 9 features a form of multithreading, it's an add-on to the OS. Not all applications are written to take advantage of it. With multithreading, different processes within an application are each given threads that are managed individually, which allows parts of the application to be responsive even while another part is busy doing something.

✦ **Memory Protection.** Another advanced feature of Mac OS X is memory protection, which means simply that each application that runs on a Mac OS X system is given its own partition of memory that cannot be written to by another application. While Mac OS 9 offers memory protection, it's not as robust—a poorly written Mac application can sometimes write to or read from another application's memory area. When that happens, the application will generally crash. This crashing can cause corruption in other parts of memory, bringing down many or all of the running applications. In Mac OS 9, this happens less frequently than with older versions, but in Mac OS X, it rarely happens at all.

✦ **Dynamic RAM Allocation.** Mac OS X is able to give applications more or less system RAM as they request it, avoiding some situations in Mac OS 9 where an application runs out of memory because its manual allocation (a number you enter in the Get Info dialog box) isn't high enough.

✦ **Symmetrical Multiprocessing.** Mac OS X features support for Macintosh computers that have more than one processor. This makes it possible for different processes or applications to be running simultaneously on different processors that are installed in the computer. Mac OS 9 includes support for a limited sort of symmetrical multiprocessing, designed specifically to allow certain applications to take advantage of the multiple processors in the Power Macintosh 9600 MP and some non-Apple PowerPC-based Mac OS computers. Mac OS X's foundation is designed so that the OS itself takes advantage of multiple processors, which may very well be built into Power Macintosh G4 workstations by the time you read this.

✦ **Multiuser Support.** Mac OS X allows multiple users to be signed on to and working with a single computer at once. (This is generally achieved using "terminals" or other networked computers that have access to the Mac OS X computer.) While Mac OS 9 also supports multiple users, it only supports one at a time.

Mac OS X features a number of differences from Mac OS 9 and its predecessors, most of which are designed to give it a more modern foundation (see the sidebar "What Makes Mac OS X Different?"). In order to achieve these differences, Mac OS X had to be reworked from the ground up. Mac OS X is based on a variant of Unix, with a Mac OS-style interface and many other additions. Obviously there are advantages to this approach, since it means that the Mac OS of the future will be more reliable, offer higher-end capabilities and better performance. But this change also comes with a downside. First, Mac OS X is essentially a brand-new operating system, meaning there are some bugs to work out. Second, applications need to be updated to take advantage of Mac OS X's unique abilities, something that will take time. Third, the Mac OS X interface is different from the traditional Mac look and feel, including a remarkably different scheme for managing files, system software, updates, networking—the list goes on and on. Even expert users of Mac OS 9 and its predecessors will find they have a lot of learning to do when it comes to Mac OS X.

So, which OS should you use? It generally depends on what you're trying to do. Mac OS 9 is a fully capable operating system that works great for most consumers and professionals. If you're a game player, surfer, checkbook balancer, educator, or business professional, then you'll probably get along just fine with Mac OS 9. Mac OS 9 remains the most advanced OS for Macintosh computers on a number of fronts, including the richest variety of publishing, content creation, and business applications. And, it's familiar to anyone who has used previous Mac OS versions. Plus, if you don't have a PowerPC G3 or higher processor in your Mac, then Mac OS X won't run on your machine, so the best way to get recent advances in the Mac OS is to upgrade to Mac OS 9.

Note   Your Mac must have a PowerPC processor of some kind to use Mac OS 9. This means Macs that were factory-equipped with a 68040, 68030, 68020, or 68000 processor cannot use Mac OS 9. Macs with a 68040 must use Mac OS 8.1 or earlier. Macs with a 68030 must use Mac OS 7.6.1 or earlier. Some Macs with a 68030 (specifically the SE/30, IIx, and IIcx) and all Macs with a 68020 or 68000 processor must use System 7.5.5 or earlier.

Some graphics, media, and Web professionals are the type that will likely gravitate toward Mac OS X, at least in its early iterations. It's a major shift in the way Macs work, so it will take time for the kinks to get ironed out and for all the support to be put into place. Eventually, Apple will probably roll the two together and recommend that everyone update. As of this writing, though, that time is well down the road. Mac OS 9 remains a great choice that offers rich tools, increased stability, and more features than any previous Mac OS version.

Reliability and Performance Improvements

Oddly enough, many "hidden" improvements to the Mac OS were added in Apple's free update, Mac OS 8.6, which was issued in the spring of 1999. Specifically, the Mac OS was ported to a microkernel architecture, giving it some added features and making it a bit more modern in the process. A *microkernel* sits between the Mac hardware and the Mac OS, acting as sort of a traffic cop. Ideally, this improvement has meant less hanging and freezing in Mac OS 8.6 and now in Mac OS 9, since the microkernel can better protect the Mac OS from errant, crashing applications. (The applications will still crash, but the OS can recover more often from those crashes.)

Along with this microkernel architecture comes improvements typical to each new release of the Mac OS — bug fixes, improved stability, and more "native" code. Since the PowerPC processor was introduced in Macintosh computers back in 1993, the Mac OS has been going through a slow evolution, where parts of it have been continually updated to run native PowerPC code instead of code originally designed for the Motorola 680x0 series of processors. (The 680x0 processors were used in pre-Power Macintosh machines like Quadras, Mac IIs, and LCs.) For years some of that old code has run in "emulation" on the PowerPC, where the Mac OS actually pretends it's an older processor so that those instructions can run.

Mac OS 9 also includes rewrites of the Memory control panel and underlying technology to make it a PowerPC native — thus, faster and more efficient. Likewise, there are small improvements to AppleScript, File Exchange (for dealing with Intel-based PC disks and file), and the AppleShare client (for accessing AppleTalk server computers).

Multiple Users 1.0

One of the biggest new features offered by Mac OS 9 is the Multiple Users control panel, finally allowing more than one person to personalize their Mac OS workspace. This technology allows each user to have their own Finder preferences, desktop settings, document folders, applications, and so on. In fact, it's also a way to keep certain applications, documents, or other files secure from others who may use your Mac, whether you're in a shared office setting or you simply don't want your kids throwing out important financial documents. Because Multiple Users requires each individual to have a password, you can keep many different people's data and configurations on one Mac, and still keep all that data safe and secure (see Figure 1-1).

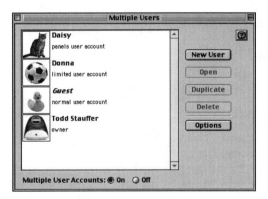

Figure 1-1: If you have Multiple Users active, each individual user must enter a user name and password in order to access the computer.

Once you get past the setup screen, individual users can have their own desktop settings, file folders, organization system — pretty much everything. In fact, this is the perfect solution for many folks who share a single computer without sharing the same sense of, shall we say, fashion (see Figure 1-2).

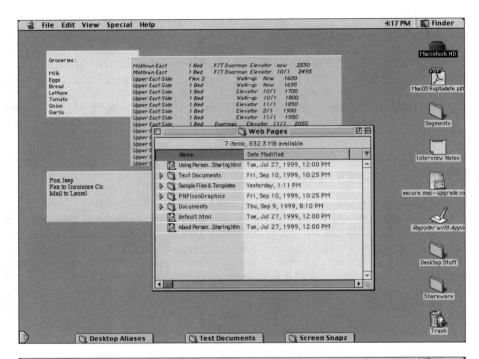

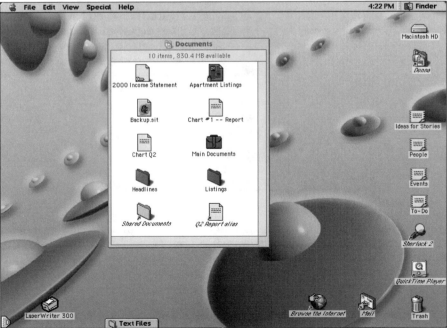

Figure 1-2: Get your own space—when you log in using Multiple Users, you can customize a number of things, like the background, Stickies, and other settings.

The best part is, only the administrator (the "owner" of your computer) has to worry about the Multiple Users control panel — once you've created the accounts, each user can change their own personal settings and preferences without worrying about messing up someone else's desktop.

Types of accounts

The Multiple Users control panel gives you control over each individual user account, allowing you to determine exactly what can be accessed by whom. Using three different kinds of accounts — Normal, Limited, and Panels — you can determine how much access to the Mac each user has.

With Normal accounts, users can change settings, customize their desktop, change the printer, and basically accomplish or configure most anything that a typical Mac user can. In fact, Multiple Users goes deep into the system, allowing you to configure things like Internet settings (e-mail addresses, signatures, Web home pages), default browsers, and e-mail applications — even your monitor's screen resolution can change for each user. Even your preferences *within* applications can be different. That way more than one user can access Netscape Communicator, for example, without stepping on each other's settings or stumbling across each other's e-mail. (Pretty cool, huh?)

With Limited accounts, users have a little less freedom and administrators have a little more power. If you're the one setting up the account, now you have control over some basic configuration issues — things like access to the Control Panels folder, whether or not the user can access CD-ROMs or DVD-ROMs, and whether the limited user can access the Chooser and Network Browser. In fact, you can even decide whether or not a user can print and to which printers they have access. On top of that, you can specifically decide which applications on the system the user can have access to and which are forbidden.

With Panels accounts, users are both limited in what they can access and in what they can see on the screen. Using an interface composed of different tabbed panels, the user can only access exactly what the administrator has made available to them (see Figure 1-3). This is probably best for a lab situation, for young children, or in other circumstances where you not only want to limit what the user can access, but also their ability to move files and folders around on the desktop. With a Panels account, the user is very limited in what they can do.

And just in case you're worried about other people who might need to use the Mac, you can create a guest login that allows anyone to access the Mac — while keeping your personal files, applications, and documents safe. Like any other account, the guest account can be Normal, Limited, or Panels.

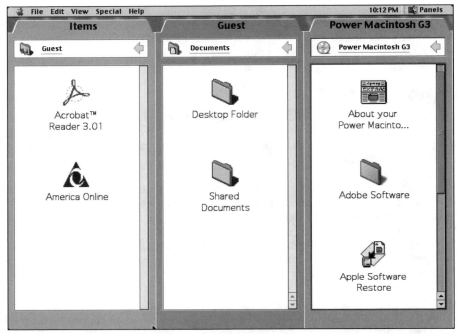

Figure 1-3: The Panels interface makes using the Mac easy and changing anything about the Mac very hard.

Global Multiple User Options

Because Multiple Users gives each user the ability to set their own options (to one degree or another), it then becomes necessary to allow the administrator to set some global options that affect everyone. Right in the Multiple Users control panel is a special button that lets you take a look at those global options (see Figure 1-4).

Global Multiple User Options gives you the opportunity to enter a Welcome message for the log-in screen, choose whether or not Voice Verification is allowed, and specify what happens if a user is idle for a certain number of minutes. Click the tabs at the top of the window and you can control other options, too. For instance, you can set up a list of banned CD-ROMs and DVDs that can't be used or played by anyone whose DVD access you've restricted. This is a great way to keep the kids from watching R-rated DVD movies or playing too much Quake while you're away from the Mac. It's also a way to limit users' access to only certain files or folders on those discs (see Figure 1-5).

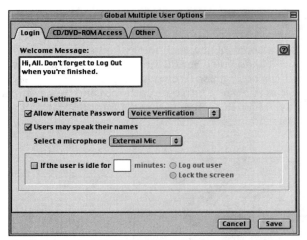

Figure 1-4: The Global Multiple User Options let the administrator make some important decisions.

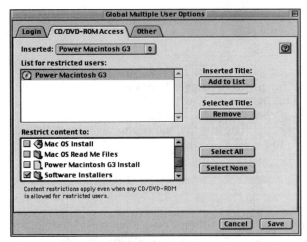

Figure 1-5: The Global Multiple User Options let you limit your users to using only certain files or folders on CD and DVD titles.

Additional features of the Global Multiple User Options include notification when a new application is installed (you'll be told this when you, as the "owner," log out of your account) and whether or not to permit a Guest account, among other things.

Voice Verification

Hand-in-hand with Multiple Users comes a new technology for gaining access to your Mac OS 9-based Macintosh called Voice Verification. This system actually makes a voiceprint of you saying a *passphrase* (which is simply a reference sentence that you speak so the Mac OS can analyze your voice patterns) and then compares it to a stored voiceprint on the system. If it's a match, you get into the Mac. If it's not, you don't get in (see Figure 1-6).

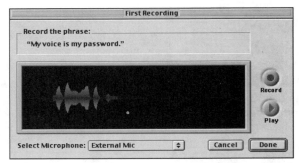

Figure 1-6: Voice Verification compares your voiceprint to the stored password voiceprint.

It's an interesting idea, especially if you're using other voice controls on your Mac with PlainTalk 2.0 (discussed in Chapter 2). You'll need a microphone hooked up to your Mac, and it should be a good one—like the PlainTalk microphone included with most Power Macintosh models. The internal microphone on models that include one should work well, too.

The Keychain

Although technically an existing Apple technology, the keychain hasn't been around since System 7.5.5 (it was part of Apple's PowerTalk technology), and is being reintroduced in Mac OS 9. Put simply, the keychain allows you to store different "keys"—usually user IDs and passwords—and you can automatically supply them as needed so that you don't have to type or even remember them. All you have to remember is one master password that locks and unlocks the whole keychain. If you have trouble remembering all the various passwords you've assigned to documents, Internet sites, or other password-sensitive areas, you can let the keychain handle them for you (see Figure 1-7).

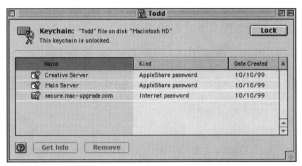

Figure 1-7: The keychain gives you easy access to the user IDs and passwords that you use on the Internet.

Nearly every time you enter a password or try to access a secure Web site, your keychain gets rattled. If your keychain is currently unlocked, then that password can be entered automatically, without you needing to remember it. If the keychain is locked, then you simply enter the password for the keychain. That opens up the keychain, allowing the stored password (the one for the Web site or file you're trying to access) to be accessed automatically. Now, as long as the keychain remains unlocked, other secure sites, files, and network connections can be established automatically.

That does mean, however, that you need to be extra careful with your password — the Mac OS even says as much when you create a password for locking your keychain. After all, this one password could open up all the other passwords you have on your computer, making them available if someone happened by and wanted to access all your stored connections.

Note Whenever you select any password it should be unique, be reasonably nonsensical to others, and include a mix of letters and numbers with no particular pattern. In the case of your Keychain password, you should definitely pick one that isn't the same as your ATM card number or your password for your locker at the gym. Choose a new password that you can remember and no one can guess.

Apple File Security

Another security measure now built into the Mac OS is the ability to encrypt items within the Finder. *Encrypting* a file causes it to be turned into a garbled mess of characters according to a sophisticated algorithm. In this state, it can't be read, launched, or accessed in any way. (Even if someone "broke" into the file and looked around using a text editor or something more sophisticated, they wouldn't be able to read the encrypted mess.) The key to the algorithm is the password (or passphrase) — with the password and the Apple File Security application, you can put the document back in a readable and editable form.

To encrypt a file, you can simply drag it onto the Apple File Security application, located in the Application menu on most Mac OS 9 installations. Once you've dropped a file on it, Apple File Security asks you to enter a password (twice) that will be used for unencrypting the file (see Figure 1-8). You can also choose whether or not to save the password to your keychain.

Figure 1-8: When you choose to encrypt a file, you'll be asked to enter a password to secure it.

If the password matches both times you enter it, the file becomes encrypted. The file's icon changes to show that the file is now encrypted, as shown in Figure 1-9.

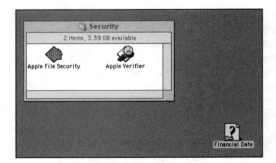

Figure 1-9: Once encrypted, the file shows up in the Finder with an altered icon to show that it's encrypted.

If you do save your password to your keychain, you'll be able to unencrypt the file without remembering the actual password. All you have to do is double-click the file — if your keychain is unlocked, then the file will decrypt itself. If the keychain is locked, you'll have to enter the master keychain password, but then the password for the encrypted file will be accessed automatically, allowing you to open the file without needing to remember your password.

Want another advantage? Encrypted files are also compressed so that they use less hard disk space than the original file. That's great for things like making backup copies for storage on removable disks and archiving files you no longer actively use.

Apple Verifier

Another application that helps in security issues is called the Apple Verifier. This is a quick little program Apple included with Mac OS 9 to help you determine the authenticity and integrity of files that have digital signatures. A *digital signature* is a code that someone has added to an e-mail message, program, or document to prove it came from that person and that it has not been altered since it was signed. You then drag a file to the Apple Verifier, which uses a publicly available certificate stored in your keychain to check the signature. When it gets the result, it will let you know whether or not it has verified the sender as authentic.

Aside from the verifier, Apple has also added into the Mac OS the functionality for digitally signing documents. This means that authors of applications, as they update to Mac OS 9 compatibility, will be able to take advantage of this new feature, if they desire. You'll most likely see this feature used first in e-mail applications, so that you can send digitally signed e-mail messages and attachments. Your recipients will be able to verify that a document or file is really from you and that it hasn't been changed since you signed it.

Software Update

As all computing becomes more and more focused on the Internet, it only makes sense that some new features would pop up that use the Internet to make your life easier. Software Update is a control panel that does just that. It's a pretty simple control panel, too (see Figure 1-10).

Figure 1-10: The Software Update control panel has one main button.

Click the Update Now button and your Mac will connect to the Internet, if it isn't already connected. It will then visit Apple's servers and find out if there have been any updates to any components of the Mac OS. If there have been, those components can be downloaded automatically, then installed and integrated immediately.

Note This doesn't work for third-party updates, which would be a nice idea. It simply updates Apple's own components for the Mac OS.

In addition, you can click the "Update software automatically" button, then create a schedule of days and times when you'd like your Mac to connect to the Internet and check for updates. When an update is found, it can be automatically downloaded or, if you prefer, the Software Update control panel can ask you if it's OK to download the file, and then proceed according to your wishes.

FontSync

FontSync is more of a behind-the-scenes technology, but it's brand-new to the Mac OS. Essentially, this technology makes it easier for you to ensure that two different computers are using the same fonts and font technologies.

Using the FontSync control panel and some AppleScripts included with Mac OS 9, you can create a FontSync profile that precisely identifies the fonts installed on someone else's Macintosh. You can then bring the FontSync profile to your Mac for a comparison of fonts. If the profile matches the fonts on your Mac, then documents created on your computer should display and print correctly on the other Mac.

You can use the FontSync control panel to set any number of characteristics that should be considered in your FontSync profiles, such as whether or not it's a TrueType font, how it's been kerned, the internal font names, and many other characteristics that can make for a better match (see Figure 1-11).

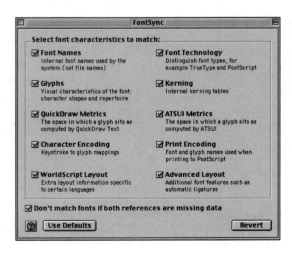

Figure 1-11: The FontSync control panel offers you the chance to choose which characteristics should be matched.

It may take a while before FontSync becomes important for most Mac OS users, but for some involved in high-end graphics and publishing, FontSync is a welcome advance.

Carbon

Like the chemical element, Carbon in Mac OS 9 isn't necessarily something you can see, taste, or touch. Instead, this Carbon is a technology that works together with Mac OS 9 applications to allow them to run simultaneously on both Mac OS 9 and on Apple's next-generation operating system, Mac OS X.

Carbon is a set of *application programming interfaces* (APIs) that have been streamlined to work with both the legacy Mac OS (Mac OS 9 and the Mac OS 8.*x* versions before it) and Mac OS X. (*APIs* are collections of programming commands and functions that are provided by a given operating system.) The Carbon APIs comprise a subset of the possible programming commands that were available in Mac OS 8.x and Mac OS 9, with those that were particularly incompatible with Mac OS X tossed out.

The idea is simple — with a reasonably minor rewrite, many applications that run on Mac OS 8.x can be made Carbon compatible. Then, that same program can run on both Mac OS 9, which is the progeny of those earlier OS versions, and Mac OS X, an entirely new Mac OS. This will make both developers and users happier because the same application will be compatible with both Mac OS versions, thus easing any future transitions to Mac OS X. Plus, Carbon applications take full advantage of the advanced Mac OS X features discussed earlier in this chapter.

Summary

Mac OS 9 is a direct upgrade for Mac OS 8.6 and earlier Mac OS versions. While it doesn't look a lot different from Mac OS 8.6 and 8.5 (which offered some major changes), it does offer a number of new features.

First, it's designed to complement but be different from Mac OS X, the next-generation Mac OS from Apple. Mac OS X will only run on PowerPC G3-based Macs (or higher), whereas Mac OS 9 is designed to run on all Power Macintosh computers. It doesn't offer quite as many modern OS touches as Mac OS X, but Mac OS still holds its own for home users and business professionals.

The new features offered by Mac OS 9 include bug fixes and more "native" code designed specifically to run on PowerPC processors. This speeds up the OS while offering better stability (fewer slowdowns and crashes).

Other new features are more obvious. Mac OS 9 now supports multiple users, allowing different people to log in to the same Macintosh and manage their own individual workspaces. Each user gets a password-protected workspace complete with settings, appearance controls, different Internet accounts, and stored documents. In essence, each user has their own Macintosh that they can sign in to and out of. This feature is great for workgroups, student computers, or home computers where the system owner or administrator would like to set up users with their own protected access.

Other features include security improvements, like voice verification for using a spoken phrase to log in to the Mac. Other security features include the Keychain, which stores passwords and encryption schemes; the Apple File Security application, which allows you to encrypt files; and the Apple File Verifier, which checks the public encryption key "signatures" of a file to make sure it originated from a designated source.

Apple has tossed in still more features, like Software Update, which automatically accesses Apple's Internet servers and checks to see if there are any important Mac OS updates or patches that you don't have on your system. You can even set it to automatically check every so often. And there's FontSync, which allows you to synchronize fonts between different documents, so that font characteristics and nuances can be exactly the same from one Macintosh to another.

Finally, this chapter discusses Carbon, the programming interface that makes it possible for Mac OS 9 and Mac OS X to run the same applications. Carbon is sure to be an important part of the transition from Mac OS 9 (and its predecessors) to Mac OS X in the future.

✦   ✦   ✦

What's Hot in the Mac OS 9?

While Chapter 1 focused on the features that are brand-new in Mac OS 9, this chapter looks at the many technologies that have been updated for Mac OS 9, even though they existed in previous versions. In some cases, existing technologies have been updated in such exciting ways that they're being touted as the most important new features in the upgrade. In other cases, the changes are subtler, although they could significantly affect how you use your Mac.

For instance, Apple has taken flight with its Sherlock search capabilities, which is a strong differentiating feature (and a popular one) for the Mac OS. Sherlock features a new interface and many new choices to make searching on your Mac or on the Internet more productive.

Similar changes have swept QuickTime, which is now at version 4. QuickTime 4 features a new interface, technology improvements, and a couple of new features, including support for new QuickTime streaming technology that enables you to watch video in "real-time" over the Internet.

Other changes are deeper under the surface—things such as improvements to the File Sharing control panel and its newfound capability to share files over an Internet connection. There is also an update to Apple's ColorSync technology, updates to the Help Viewer, additions to PlainTalk speech recognition, and even a tweak to the Connect To application.

We look at all these changes in this chapter. Then, Chapter 3 looks at some of the most exciting features in Mac OS 9, whether they're brand-new or not.

Sherlock 2: The Revenge

One of the most popular features of Mac OS 8.5 was the introduction of Sherlock, the much-improved "find" utility for the Mac OS. With Sherlock, not only was the capability to find documents on the Mac's hard disk improved, but new features were added that hadn't been seen previously in the Mac OS. Sherlock introduced the integrated capability to search *within* many types of documents to find keywords. It also added Internet search capabilities to the Sherlock interface.

Sherlock 2 takes the original concept even further, enabling you to search in new ways using a shiny new interface (see Figure 2-1).

Figure 2-1: Sherlock 2 offers additions to the original Sherlock, plus a snazzy new interface.

File searches

The basic methods for searching haven't changed dramatically, although Apple has put more emphasis on Internet searching in Sherlock 2. The main window is now dominated by picture icons (instead of a tabbed window), with the icons running across the top of the window. Choose the hard disk icon, for example, and your options are to search the hard disk for files by file name, by date, by size, or by content.

To search within the content of documents, Sherlock uses a special database index, which must be created and updated periodically. The index can take a while to update, depending on the number of unique documents you have on your hard disk or network, so it's a process that Sherlock allows you to automatically schedule for slow times (such as nights or weekends). With the hard disk indexed, you can search within plain text, HTML, word processing, and other documents for keywords (see Figure 2-2). Sherlock 2 adds the capability to search within Adobe PDF (Portable Document Format) files.

Figure 2-2: Sherlock 2 enables you to search within many types of documents, including PDF files.

Sherlock can also save individual search criteria, enabling you to quickly reissue searches that you've used in the past. You can even double-click a saved search in the Finder and have it launch Sherlock to perform the search.

Internet searches

The big news for most Sherlock users is the way it enables you to search many different Internet search engines from one interface, thereby exponentially increasing your chances of finding what you were seeking. Sherlock does this using small *plug-ins* that either Apple or the search engine company can write. Plug-ins make it possible for Sherlock to tap into the Web site's databases and return the results in the Sherlock interface. For good will among Internet companies, Sherlock returns results along with any special banner advertising that a particular Web site presents to the traditional visitor.

The key to Sherlock is that you can check any number of these plug-in entries in the Sherlock window, enter your keywords, and click the magnifying glass button. Sherlock heads out to all the databases you've chosen and returns a long list of results from each that responds. This makes it easy to search quite a bit of the Internet in one sitting.

The plug-in approach makes Sherlock very extensible, enabling it to quickly grow past its original role as a mega search engine interface. Because anything can be searched using Sherlock's plug-ins, many Web sites have taken advantage of this and written small plug-ins themselves. (Apple has helped on some, too.) The result is plug-ins that not only search the popular databases such as Yahoo!, Excite, and Lycos, but also those that allow you to search individual sites such as Amazon.com, Barnesandnoble.com, and eBay. This sneaky little capability has quickly turned Sherlock into a potential e-commerce tool, enabling easier searches when you're comparison-shopping on the Web (see Figure 2-3). Apple has helped out by reworking Sherlock so that you can search for sale items easily. When searching the "shopping" sites, Sherlock lets you sort results by price and availability, making it possible to quickly comparison shop at ongoing auctions, prices at the popular online bookstores, and so on.

Figure 2-3: Sherlock's new sorting features make it easy to comparison shop online.

Channels

The Sherlock plug-ins make it possible for Apple to offer all different sorts of searches, resulting in a new approach to the interface. The icons across the top of the Sherlock windows represent "channels," each offering different types of searches. Thanks to the multitude of different online search engines, you can search for a broad range of things, from Web sites to people to reference material and so on.

Sherlock even enables you to create your own channels for grouping plug-ins for the sites that you like to search. For instance, building Sherlock plug-ins is popular among Mac news Web sites, so it's easy to create a channel that enables you to search many different Mac news sites at once.

And while you're creating channels in Sherlock, you can easily move them around and manage them using the desk drawer-like interface that's been added to Sherlock's window in the latest version. Click and drag toward the top of the window and you'll reveal more slots for channel icons, which can be easily dragged and dropped from slot to slot (see Figure 2-4).

Channel icon drawer

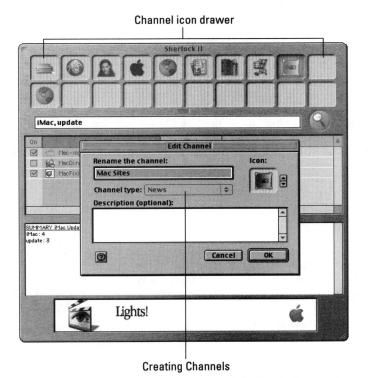

Creating Channels

Figure 2-4: You can create new channels in Sherlock 2, and then rearrange their icons using the drawer-like interface.

QuickTime 4.0: Streaming and Beyond

Although not exclusively a part of the Mac OS 9 installation, Mac OS 9 is the first installation to include the new features of QuickTime 4.0. Along with an interface that's similar to Sherlock 2, QuickTime 4.0 offers a number of improvements on Apple's multimedia technologies.

QuickTime is really a foundation technology — a series of extensions that make it possible for the Mac OS to deal with different types of data that are required to display digital images, sounds, and movies. Basically, the point of QuickTime is to enable active, movie-like media to be a part of the Mac OS and, thus, added to Mac applications. A QuickTime movie works just like a film or television broadcast, by displaying digital images, called *frames*, one after the other, in rapid succession to simulate movement. QuickTime also enables sound, text, and other elements to synchronize with the images, making the movie into an impressively coherent whole.

Apple includes a few QuickTime-enabled applications with QuickTime 4.0, including the QuickTime Player application and the PictureViewer, both of which have been updated to the new "look" of QuickTime 4.0. In addition, many other applications are enabled for dealing with QuickTime, including the ScrapBook and SimpleText, which are built into the Mac OS.

The interface

The QuickTime Player is updated and changed (to mixed reviews) so that the interface looks shiny and metallic — also, perhaps, so that it looks more like a familiar consumer device. You can load a QuickTime movie in the player in a number of different ways, including by choosing the File ⇨ Open menu command or by double-clicking a QuickTime movie file. Doing either of these things loads the movie document into the QuickTime Player and displays the first frame (see Figure 2-5).

Like Sherlock 2, the QuickTime Player offers an interface that features drawer-like elements. Clicking the More Controls button, for instance, reveals a panel of additional controls that allow you to fast forward, rewind, and change the bass and treble levels, among other things.

Otherwise, things should be fairly familiar in the QuickTime Player window. There are Play and Pause buttons, a small dial for controlling the volume level, and a little button that gives you information on the movie being played. The Player also has a typical Mac OS menu bar where you'll find other options, such as commands that let you change the size of the movie window — however, the bigger the movie, the lower the quality of the playback, in most cases.

Figure 2-5: The QuickTime Player is ready to display a movie file.

Play

Volume control   Pause

Information

More controls

Note
The QuickTime Player (along with the PictureViewer) is capable of displaying images in a variety of different image formats such as PICT, JPEG, GIF, and many others. This is thanks to the underlying QuickTime technology, which enables applications to work with and translate between various digital video, audio, and image file formats.

Upgrade to QuickTime Pro (which requires an online transaction at Apple's Web site and about $30) and you can actually use the QuickTime Player to perform some basic editing of QuickTime movies. The interface enables you to cut and paste between movies, add a sound track, or even add text to your movies, overlaying the images. (The text can end up looking like text in a commercial advertisement or the text track for closed captioning on television.) It's not full-fledged video editing, but it starts you in the right direction.

Tip
If you've previously upgraded to QuickTime 3.0 Pro, the same registration number will work for QuickTime 4.0. Just make sure you enter the registration number again whenever you perform a clean installation of the Mac OS. The registration number is entered via the QuickTime Settings control panel, by selecting Registration from the pop-up menu in the control panel.

QuickTime streaming

QuickTime has been playing back movies on Macs for many years now—with each iteration, the quality and size of the images gets better (and, usually, the file sizes required get smaller), but it's no big deal anymore that QuickTime exists and can play movies. What is new and exciting, though (and thus worthy of inclusion in this chapter), is QuickTime 4.0's capability to play streaming media.

Streaming media is a new category of video and audio that allows you to watch (or listen) in "real-time" over the Internet. The video and/or audio is compressed heavily, making the file sizes small enough that they move across the Internet quickly. Then, the streaming QuickTime server software and the QuickTime Player synchronize themselves so that they make sure the stream is as uninterrupted as possible.

All this technology makes it possible for you to view images over the Internet as they take place, in the case of live streaming events, or you can watch TV, movie, or "on-demand" feeds of streaming video from broadcasters around the world (see Figure 2-6).

Figure 2-6: QuickTime's streaming capabilities make it possible to view media streams over the Internet.

Apple is so excited about the streaming technologies in QuickTime that it's put together something called QuickTime TV—actually just a series of QuickTime servers around the world that rebroadcast streams from major broadcast outlets such as BBC World, VH1, HBO, and Fox News.

Streaming technology enables you to do some wonderful things on your computer—we personally like to catch Steve Jobs' keynotes at various tradeshows using the technology—but it's still a young idea that has far to go before it's perfect. Someday soon it may become one of the main ways that video-on-demand and other advanced video services are made available to homes. For now, though, it's fun to play with.

Flash integration

QuickTime 4.0 has another little trick up its sleeve—aside from streaming and other new movie playing technologies, QuickTime 4.0 can now integrate Macromedia Flash controls into movie files. Flash integration enables content creators to add animated buttons in the movie that let the viewer interact with the file. For instance, if you were creating a QuickTime movie, you could use a Flash control to let the user choose from different movies or streams on a particular streaming server (see Figure 2-7).

Figure 2-7: Integrating Macromedia Flash in QuickTime turns QuickTime movies into interactive multimedia files.

Flash makes it possible to turn a basic QuickTime movie into something more like a presentation, multimedia learning tool, or even a standalone demonstration or kiosk. You'll probably see a lot more of this feature popping up in QuickTime movies as the technology unfolds.

PlainTalk 2.0: Talking to Your Mac

For a while, PlainTalk—Apple's speech recognition product—languished without many updates. (In fact, until recently it wasn't even compatible with the iMac.) Apple has once again taken an interest in speech technologies and has refocused its efforts on an update to PlainTalk. While this one doesn't offer too many new features over previous PlainTalk versions, it has been updated for Apple's latest hardware, offers some interesting new advances, and lays the groundwork for some third-party speech applications that are arriving for the Mac.

For the most part, PlainTalk 2.0 is similar to earlier PlainTalk versions, although improvements were made in a few areas. Specifically, PlainTalk features more Speakable Items commands and the ability to integrate with more applications. For example, after installation there are several Application Speakable Item commands available for Internet Explorer, Outlook Express, Netscape Communicator, and others. It's gratifying to have the computer respond to commands such as "Get My Mail" in Netscape Communicator, because PlainTalk in the past has focused on Finder commands (see Figure 2-8).

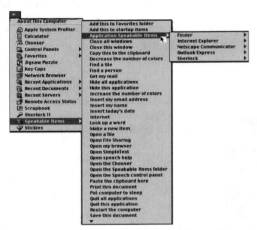

Figure 2-8: The Speakable Items have been augmented in PlainTalk 2.0 to include more application commands.

PlainTalk 2.0 is able to offer these commands because it's been updated to integrate with AppleScript. Thus, applications that support AppleScript can also support Speakable Items. In some cases you may need to create the Speakable Item yourself (or get it prebuilt from someone other than Apple), but many commands in AppleScript-aware applications should be accessible by speech.

Speakable Items is also updated with a few new commands for the Finder, as well as the capability to launch items that appear on the Recent menu (such as recently opened applications and documents). There are also a number of additions for universal commands that draw on settings in control panels. For instance, you can say "Get my mail" and Speakable Items will open your default e-mail application and check for e-mail in that application. Likewise, you can say "Open my browser" or "Search Internet sites" and the appropriate applications (probably Internet Explorer and Sherlock, respectively) will open themselves on your desktop.

PlainTalk 2.0 also automatically pops up an Apple Guide window designed to help you remember all the speakable commands that are available for a given application, the Finder, or in general. This small, floating window can be left open — it will change its contents whenever you encounter a new speakable scenario (see Figure 2-9).

Figure 2-9: When Speakable Items is active, both the Speakable Items feedback window (the little robot or whatever cartoon character you pick) and the Speakable Commands window display.

PlainTalk 2.0 looks to be a promising return to speech recognition technology by Apple, and other companies, such as IBM and Dragon Systems, are promising to add to PlainTalk with third-party applications that allow more control and support for speech dictation.

Better, Easier Networking and Internet Access

Many of the changes in Mac OS 9 are aimed at improving the user's experience while trying to connect to and navigate the Internet. For the last few Mac OS versions, some of the control panels for Internet and network access were confusing. In Mac OS 9, Apple makes them less confusing while, at the same time, adding quite a few features to the networking capabilities of the Mac OS.

File Sharing

The most significant improvement to Mac OS 9's networking capabilities is the addition of File Sharing over TCP/IP connections. Put simply, this means it's now possible for one Macintosh to share files with another Macintosh over an Internet connection without additional software. Until now, it's been necessary to run extra "remote access" software (or AppleShare server software) in order to use File Sharing without physically being on the same network. Now, though, you can perform simple File Sharing over an Internet connection — perfect for logging on to your work computer from home or while traveling.

Sharing over TCP/IP

File Sharing over a TCP/IP connection is really pretty simple. You begin by placing a check mark next to the option "Enable File Sharing clients to connect over TCP/IP" in the File Sharing control panel (see Figure 2-10). Then, you start File Sharing by clicking the Start button.

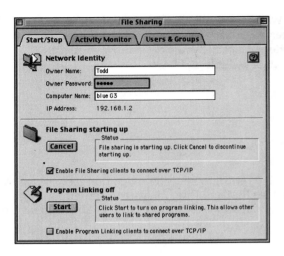

Figure 2-10: The File Sharing control panel in Mac OS 9 includes an option for file sharing over TCP/IP connections.

The File Sharing control panel also includes an entry toward the top that makes a note of the IP address of the machine. Now, from another Mac that needs to share files with this one, you can log on by entering this Mac's IP address in the Chooser after selecting AppleShare (see Figure 2-11).

Note

If your ISP assigned you a dynamic IP address (which is usually the case if you use a modem connection for Internet access), then this new feature is of limited use. You can still enable file sharing over IP, but you'll have to tell your remote users what your IP address is each time you establish a new Internet connection. Users with fixed access (via Ethernet or over some DSL and cable modem connections) can make fuller use of this feature. Likewise, if you have an Internet router in use in your organization, you'll need to provide the router's address instead of the IP address that appears in the File Sharing window. Chapter 22 discusses sharing your files in greater detail.

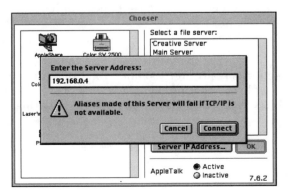

Figure 2-11: Any Mac running Mac OS 8.0 or higher can log on and access files on a Mac OS 9 machine over the Internet.

File Sharing control panel

The File Sharing control panel is revamped with bug fixes and minor performance enhancements. It also includes the Users and Groups information that, in prior Mac OS versions, had been its own control panel. Now logically grouped with the other File Sharing controls (on its own Users and Groups tab control), you can organize and change the permissions for users without leaving the File Sharing control panel.

Remote Access

In Mac OS 8.5, the Remote Access took on double-duty for Mac users, serving as a way to connect to both remote Macintosh networks (AppleTalk over modem connections) and to connect to Internet servers using PPP (Point-to-Point Protocol). So, you use Remote Access whether you're dialing in to your Internet service provider or in to your organization's AppleShare server.

In Mac OS 9, Remote Access is updated even further and now offers an Answer command, which answers incoming Remote Access connections, making it possible for a remote user to dial in to your Macintosh, sign in with a valid password, and begin sharing files. If you're connected to a network of Macs, you can offer the remote user access to those other Macs, too (see Figure 2-12).

Note Don't think this feature is so new? Actually, it's not—Apple Remote Access Personal Server has been available as a premium add-on for the Mac OS for quite some time. In Mac OS 9, it's been bundled with the Mac OS 9 Installer, so now you don't have to pay extra for it.

Figure 2-12: Remote Access includes a newfound capability to answer the phone.

Similarly, remote users can dial in to your Macintosh using PPP, enabling them to share files without using the AppleTalk protocols. This is akin to file sharing publicly over the Internet, except that it allows a direct private connection.

AppleShare Client

The AppleShare component of Mac OS 9 is updated to support Keychain functions and to make it possible to automate AppleShare networking connections in a different way.

The AppleShare Client isn't actually an individual program—it's an extension that affects the different ways through which you can connect to computers over a network. Most of the time you use the AppleShare Client through either the Chooser or the Network Browser. If you see an image similar to the one shown in Figure 2-13, then you're seeing the AppleShare Client.

Figure 2-13: The AppleShare Client screens pop up when you're trying to access another Mac.

With this update, the AppleShare Client now offers the option of adding your password to your keychain. Now, if your keychain is open, you can log on immediately to the remote computer without entering a password each time. If you add all of your various network connections to the keychain, then you won't have to remember each password to log on to any of them—you just have to remember the password for the keychain.

Likewise, the AppleShare Client can be configured to use the keychain to automatically log on to a server computer as the Mac starts up. If you generally logon to the same server computer every time you start up your Mac, you can automate the process by selecting the drive you want to access and placing a check mark next to it. With the new AppleShare Client, you can also decide whether you want to save your password using the keychain to automate the logon (see Figure 2-14).

Figure 2-14: Log on to servers automatically, thanks to your keychain.

Internet improvements

Every iteration of the Mac OS provides an increase in Internet features, and Mac OS 9 is no exception. The major changes aren't apparent in this version, though, except for the File Sharing over IP that's already been discussed. In most other cases, Internet access has only been slightly tweaked in Mac OS 9.

One of the "fix" improvements in Mac OS 9 is better support for DHCP (Dynamic Host Configuration Protocol) thanks to improvements to Open Transport, the underlying networking architecture of the Mac OS. DHCP enables client computers to get their configuration information completely from a server computer, instead of requiring the end user to understand and know the proper number sequences of IP addresses, DNS (Domain Name Service) addresses, and other options. DHCP now behaves better when used in situations where dynamic IP addresses need to be assigned.

Open Transport has also been made a bit more efficient, requiring only two extensions in the System Folder instead of the six that it has used in the past.

Under the Hood: Other Mac OS 9 Updates

A number of the improvements in Mac OS 9 can be considered "under-the-hood" improvements — a catchall of interesting changes to part of the Mac OS that may not change the way you work with your Mac, but that you'll probably come across at some point. Most of these changes are bug fixes and performance tweaks, although you will see the occasional new feature peep through.

Help and guides

Mac OS 9 features revved up versions of both the Help Viewer (now at version 1.5) and the Apple Guide system, which is now version 2.5. These help systems work together to tell you more about the Mac OS and guide you through the steps to accomplish tasks in the Finder and in other applications.

The Help Viewer has gotten mostly bug fixes and speedups. The most notable change, though, is the capability to load external HTML pages over the Internet. Now, when you're looking for an answer, some of the links in the Help Viewer might lead you to Apple's Web sites (or another application vendor's site) for the latest information on a particular help topic (see Figure 2-15). This enables Apple and other application developers to provide the latest possible information on a given feature, bug, or other question that you're trying to get answered through the Help Viewer.

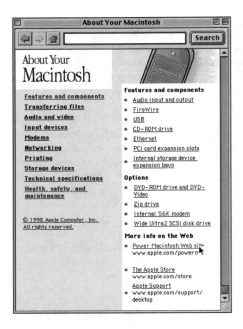

Figure 2-15: The Help Viewer now accesses HTML documents that reside on the Internet.

Along with the Help Viewer, Apple Guide is also updated for bug fixes and minor tweaks. Originally designed as the basic help system for the Mac OS, Apple Guide has been relegated to a more minor role in giving help to Mac users. While Apple Guide was once the dominant form of help in the Mac OS, Apple has since switched its emphasis to the easier Help Viewer documents, which are basic HTML documents like Web pages. It was hoped that more application developers would write documentation as a result, because few have taken time to create the more complex Apple Guide files.

ColorSync

Apple's color-matching technology is updated to ColorSync 3.0 and includes a tweak to the ColorSync control panel and the addition of AppleScript support. ColorSync is a technology built in the Mac OS that enables you to create color profiles for the devices (such as monitors, printers, and scanners) that are attached to your Mac. Once profiles are created (or obtained from your device's manufacturer), the Mac knows how to interpret color on one device and make that color appear on another.

For the most part, this technology is used in high-end publishing applications. For instance, if you have ColorSync properly calibrated, you should be able to choose the colors for an image in an application such as Adobe Photoshop and then print that image to a color inkjet printer that you're using for inexpensive proofs. Then, after any tweaks and fixes (thanks to criticism from the boss) you can turn around and print that document on an expensive color laser printer. Because you have carefully calibrated profiles for each of your relevant peripherals (your video input, your display, your proof printer, and your final output printer), the colors should all be the same from screen to proof printout to final output.

In ColorSync 3.0, the control panel adds the capability to save entire workflow configurations, meaning you can save a particular series of profiles and then switch immediately from one configuration to the next. There may be times when you use a different sequence of printers for proofs and final output, for instance, and you'd like to save the configuration for easy switching (see Figure 2-16). Similarly, if you use different video sources, more than one monitor, different scanners, and so on, then you can create a profile for each of your different sources and outputs and switch quickly between them in the ColorSync control panel.

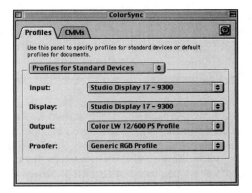

Figure 2-16: The ColorSync control panel now lets you save more than one configuration.

Game Sprockets

Apple's gaming extensions, called Game Sprockets, make it easier for programmers to create games that take advantage of the Mac OS. Instead of requiring the programmer to learn to program in network gaming features, USB device handling, 3D sound, and other special features, Apple provides libraries of prebuilt commands that they can add to their games more easily.

In Mac OS 9, Game Sprockets is updated to version 1.7. It includes four different components, and each is updated somewhat:

   ✦ **DrawSprocket** gives games a little more video speed, about 5 to 10 percent across the board.

   ✦ **InputSprocket** has been updated for more USB support, including the capability to calibrate USB devices such as joysticks and trackballs.

✦ **NetSprockets** is reworked to significantly improve the network gaming features for games that use it. Plus, it now only takes up one file in the Extensions folder.

✦ **SoundSprocket** is completely reengineered to offer new sound code and capabilities. This should result in higher quality 3D sound, along with better performance, taking up only between 2.5 and 5 percent of the CPU for sound.

The Finder and alerts

Minor changes were made in the Mac OS 9 Finder, which is updated to Finder 9. In the new version, a Carbon application package (an application that works on both Mac OS 9 and Mac OS X, thanks to its "Carbon" compliance) looks like a regular application in the Finder. The Get Info window in the Finder also recognizes it as a Carbon package. Although a *Carbon package* appears to be a single application file, it is actually a folder that contains several files that make up a Carbon application (one that can run both in Mac OS 9 and Mac OS X, as discussed in Chapter 1). The Mac OS 9 Finder hides the messy reality of Carbon packages and lets you see and use them exactly the same as conventional, single-file applications. The Carbon package works like any application, allowing you to double-click the icon, drag-and-drop items on the icon, and so on.

Note   Apple notes a problem in Mac OS 9 where regular folders can sometimes suddenly being to look like Carbon applications in the Finder. When you suspect that this has happened, you can use Package First Aid, a new utility tool, that's on the Mac OS 9 installation CD in the Utilities folder. There's also an issue with the standard Open and Save dialog boxes, which allow you to open Carbon packages as if they were files. While that may seem interesting, you certainly don't want to store your files in a Carbon package. This doesn't happen in the newer Navigation Services Open and Save dialog boxes, which Apple is encouraging application developers to use.

Mac OS 9 offers an update to the way alert boxes work—specifically, alert messages from background applications. In the past, alerts could appear from background applications that required you to click an OK button before the frontmost application could continue working. Background alerts don't work that way anymore, however. Instead, there's a new "nonblocking" alert, which appears in a small floating window (see Figure 2-17). Now the alert doesn't block progress in other applications. And, instead of an OK button, you now click the window's close box to dismiss it.

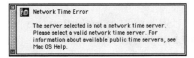

Figure 2-17: The nonblocking alert window keeps things running smoothly in other applications, even if one has complaints.

Other stuff

Most of the other updates to Mac OS 9 are minor, involving a few bug fixes, reworks for newer technology, and some other minor change or two. Here's a quick look at some of the notable changes among them:

✦ **LaserWriter 8.7** — The LaserWriter printer driver (which allows the Mac OS and its applications to print to many PostScript printers) is updated mostly for AppleScript support. Nearly all printing functions are now controllable via AppleScript. The driver also now supports new PostScript plug-ins that can be written by application developers to check the PostScript code as it passes through the driver.

✦ **Memory 8.1** — The Memory control panel is now PowerPC native and it features new AppleScript support enabling you to change memory settings using AppleScript.

✦ **File Exchange 3.0.2** — File Exchange is the software that enables PC-formatted disks to appear on the Mac's desktop. This version includes support for 120MB SuperDisks in PC format and fixes some bugs.

✦ **File Manager** — The underbelly of the Mac's file system is improved to support longer file names and individual files larger than 2GB. (You can't actually use file names longer than 31 characters in the Finder, but files from other systems that use Unicode for naming files can have those names preserved by the File Manager and the Finder.) The number of open files can now be 8169. That may sound like a lot, but the previous limit, 348, was sometimes insufficient for users with many fonts installed, documents opened, and virtual memory turned on.

✦ **OpenGL** — OpenGL is an industry-standard library of graphics commands that developers can use for games, high-end rendering, and other graphics pursuits. OpenGL is now included in the Mac OS and supports 3D acceleration.

✦ **Language Kits** — Language Kits that enable the Mac OS to speak other languages and character sets used to be provided as retail add-ons. They're now included on the Mac OS 9 installation CD.

✦ **UTCUtils Text Utilities and MLTE** — These programming commands enable developers to add international text handling to applications.

Summary

In this chapter, you saw the various parts of the Mac OS that are updated for Mac OS 9. The updates run the gamut from those that simply tweak performance to those that completely change the way the user and Mac OS components interact.

Apple has revved up Sherlock, its searching utility, to Sherlock 2, which sports a new-style metallic interface and more capabilities. Not only can Sherlock search your hard disks, network drives, removable disks, and the Internet, but it can group searches, save searches, and do a whole lot more. A unique feature of Sherlock is its capability to change the sort criteria of the Sherlock window based on things such as price and product availability (or an online auction's closing date), making it possible to comparison shop on popular auction and online store sites.

Similar changes were administered to QuickTime 4, which features a new metallic interface, Macromedia Flash integration, and support for streaming media, which allows you to watch video and listen to audio in "real-time" over the Internet.

Apple also beefed up PlainTalk 2.0, the latest version of its speech recognition software, to include support for more application commands and more basic capabilities. PlainTalk 2.0 can be extended with your own commands more easily, and third-party developers are expected to create commands that can be added to the system.

In addition to these new features and improvements, Apple performed a number of smaller tweaks in the Finder, in various control panels, and throughout the system, including in ColorSync, the Memory control panel, the LaserWriter driver, Help Viewer, and in many others.

Chapter 3 shows some of the most exciting features in Mac OS 9, including both new Mac OS 9 capabilities and those that were added in Mac OS 8 and 8.5 but which make working with a Macintosh even more productive.

✦   ✦   ✦

What's Cool in the Mac OS 9?

Despite all the innovation in Mac OS 9, it has plenty in common with earlier versions of the Mac operating system. This chapter provides an overview of the notable features and the capabilities present since the Mac's major overhaul in Mac OS 8. It takes you through features that have been added over the past few years in Mac OS 8, 8.1, 8.5, and 8.6.

This chapter draws your attention to some of the more powerful capabilities that make the Mac easy to use. Many improved methods make it easier to work with disks and their contents — collapsible windows, pop-up windows, view options for each window, spring-loaded folders, contextual menus, and sticky menus, to name a few.

What's more, versions 8 to 9 of the Mac OS come with more software for accessing the Internet than did previous versions. For starters, a setup assistant program leads you through the confusing process of getting the computer ready to use the Internet for the first time. You also get top-notch programs for sending and receiving e-mail, browsing the Web, and publishing a simple Web site from your own computer.

And, Mac OS 8 began a strong evolution of the Mac's Finder, the main application used for managing files and folders on your Mac. All sorts of cool tricks are possible with the Finder, many of which can be accomplished through simple drag-and-drop.

After reading this chapter, you'll see what's so special, friendly, and easy about the Mac OS in general, and how it all comes together in Mac OS 9.

Ease of Use

The latest releases of the Mac OS have many improved features and innovations that make using the Mac easier and more productive.

Simultaneous operations

The Finder version in Mac OS 8–9 is more responsive than earlier versions. After opening a folder or disk that contains a large number of files and folders, you no longer have to wait for every item to appear in the folder or disk window before you can do anything else. The Finder continues updating the window while you proceed with other work, such as launching a program. What's more, you can do other work in the Finder while it copies files or empties the Trash. Figure 3-1 shows three batches of files being copied at the same time.

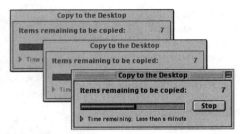

Figure 3-1: You can keep working in the Finder while it copies files or empties the Trash.

Live scrolling

When you drag a scroll box in a folder or disk window in Mac OS 8–9, you see the items in the window scroll past continuously. In earlier versions of the Finder (before Mac OS 8), you see only the scroll box move while you drag it; the items displayed in the window don't change until you release the mouse button after moving the scroll box to a new position.

Mac OS 8.5–9 also include a feature called smart scrolling, which places the window's scroll arrows next to one another instead of on opposite ends of the scroll bar. This behavior can be changed on the Options tab of the Appearance control panel. Click the check box next to Smart Scrolling to place the arrows close together.

Working with windows

Many windows in Mac OS 8–9 have controls not present in versions prior to Mac OS 8. One of these is the collapse box, also known as the windowshade box, which you click to hide all of a window except its title bar, and click again to expand the window. The collapse box sits at the far right end of a window title bar, bumping the zoom box to the left. You still have the option of collapsing and expanding a window by double-clicking its title (as described in Chapter 4).

Another control not present in releases prior to Mac OS 8 is the window frame, which you can drag with the mouse to move the window. It does the same job as the title bar, effectively giving you a bigger handle to grab and drag.

Mac OS 8.5–9 also add a feature called proxy icons, which place a small icon in the title bar of folder and disk windows in the Finder. You can drag that icon from the title bar to the Finder, or move or copy that folder or disk to another location.

Viewing folder and disk contents

You change the view of a folder or disk window with a revamped View menu. You can choose to view files and folders as icons, buttons, or a list of names and other facts. If you're viewing icons or buttons, you can choose View menu commands that clean them up by aligning them to an invisible grid or that arrange them by name, date, kind, and so on. If you're viewing a list, you can sort it by those same criteria. Figure 3-2 shows the View menu for icons and buttons.

Cross-Reference

To learn more about the View menu, see Chapter 5.

Figure 3-2: Choose the view for a folder or disk window from a revamped View menu.

Button views

If you choose "as Buttons" from the View menu, square buttons represent files and folders. Clicking a button once opens it; you drag it by its name; and dragging across multiple buttons selects them. Figure 3-3 is an example of a folder window viewed as buttons.

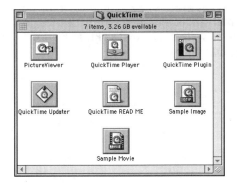

Figure 3-3: View files and folders as buttons, and open one by clicking it once.

Pop-up windows

You can make a pop-up window from a regular window by choosing "as Pop-up Window" from the View menu. This anchors the window to the bottom of the screen and changes its title bar to a tab. Clicking the tab at the top of a window closes it and leaves the tab at the bottom of the screen. Clicking a tab at the bottom of the screen makes the window pop up from there. Figure 3-4 shows an open pop-up window and the tabs of closed pop-ups.

To find out more about pop-up windows, see Chapter 5.

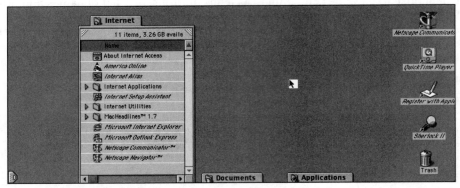

Figure 3-4: Click a pop-up window's tab to open and close it.

View options

By choosing View Options from the View menu, you can adjust several aspects of a window's appearance. Figure 3-5 shows the View Options dialog box for an icon view, a button view, and a list view.

For a window that is viewed as icons or buttons, you can select an icon or button size and a forced arrangement. You can force icons or buttons always to snap to a grid when you move them, or you can keep them arranged by name, date, and so on. If you select any of the forced arrangement options, a small icon in the upper-left corner of the window indicates which arrangement is in force. All these options are available for folder and disk windows, as well as for the Desktop. Figure 3-6 shows the icons that indicate a forced arrangement.

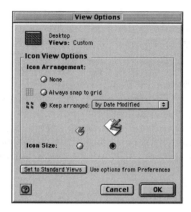

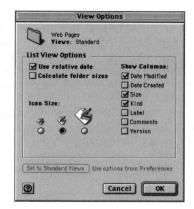

Figure 3-5: Adjust each window's appearance individually with the View Options command.

Figure 3-6: Small icons in a window's header indicate a forced arrangement of icons in Mac OS 8–9.

For a window viewed as a list, you can select an icon size, pick which columns to show, choose whether to take the time to calculate folder sizes, and specify whether to display relative dates such as "today" and "yesterday." You can also display a Date Created column in Mac OS 8–9.

The View Options command adjusts each window or the desktop individually. In Mac OS 8–8.1, you couldn't set view options for all windows or a batch of windows at once. However, Mac OS 8.5–9 lets you change the view options of all windows that adhere to standard view options by changing the standard view options using the Finder's Preferences command (described next). You can make a window adhere to the standard view options by clicking the Set to Standard Views button in the window's View Options dialog box.

You'll find more information about view options in Chapter 5.

Finder preferences

The Finder in Mac OS 8–9 has a Preferences command that you can use to set appearance and behavior options for all Finder icons and windows. You can simplify the menus to see just the essential commands. You can also configure the spring-loaded opening of folders and disks (as described next). Other options replace similar options formerly found in the Views and Labels control panels. The Mac OS 8.5–9 Preferences dialog box has three tabs, one for general preferences, one for views, and one for labels. Figure 3-7 shows the Finder Preferences dialog box in Mac OS 9.

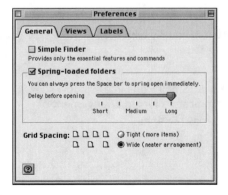

Figure 3-7: Set appearance and behavior options for all Finder icons and windows with the Preferences command.

For more information on Finder Preferences, see Chapter 5.

Spring-loaded opening

You no longer have to do a lot of double-clicking to travel through layers of folders in the Finder. Disks and folders spring open when you pause briefly over them with the mouse button held down. This behavior is handy when you're moving or copying items to a folder that's buried inside other folders. You can also make a disk or folder spring open by clicking it one-and-a-half times (like double-clicking, but hold down the mouse button on the second click). As long as you keep pressing the mouse button, you can open any folder or disk by pausing over its icon. You can adjust the delay factor or turn off the spring-loaded folders feature with the Finder Preferences command.

Contextual menus

Mac OS 8.5–9 bring menu commands closer to hand with contextual menus. You see a contextual menu of commands that can affect an icon, a window, or some text in the Finder when you press Control while clicking the object. What appears in the menu varies depending on the particular item you select. If you Control+click a group of selected items, the contextual menu lists commands that pertain to all of them. You can pop up contextual menus single-handedly with many alternative pointing devices, such as two-button mice and trackballs, made by companies other than Apple. Figure 3-8 is an example of a contextual menu.

Figure 3-8: See a contextual menu by Control+clicking an icon, a window, or some text in Finder.

Sticky menus

When you click once quickly to open any menu on the Mac OS 8–9 menu bar, or any contextual or pop-up menu, it stays open even if you release the mouse button. You can then choose a menu item by clicking it, or you can open a different menu by moving the pointer to the menu title. The menu goes away if you click outside it or if you don't move the mouse for 15 seconds. You can also operate menus the old way (pre-Mac OS 8), by holding down the mouse button.

File menu commands

The Finder's File menu has some additional commands in Mac OS 8–9, several of which have useful keyboard shortcuts. The Move To Trash command disposes of selected items. The Show Original command locates an alias's original item and brings it in view in the window that contains it. You use the items in the Label submenu to apply a colored label to selected items (like the Labels menu prior to Mac OS 8). In addition, the Sharing command's window is improved. Figure 3-9 shows the File menu.

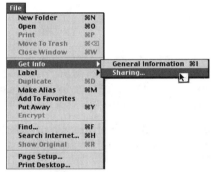

Figure 3-9: Use the additional commands in the Finder's File menu.

You'll find more information on labeling items in Chapter 5, on aliases in Chapter 14, and on sharing in Chapter 22.

The Internet

Mac OS 8–9 goes a lot further than previous system software versions in helping you get connected to the Internet and get access to Internet services after you connect. This section is an overview of what Mac OS 9 provides.

Some new Internet security features are discussed in Chapter 1, and the underlying technology improvements are mentioned in Chapter 2. For the full story of the Internet and the Mac OS, see Chapter 10.

Setting up

Setting up an Internet connection can be an incredible nightmare, but not if you use the Internet Setup Assistant program. It interviews you to get the necessary information and then makes all the control panel settings behind the scenes. You don't have to open the control panels to get started, although you can always tweak them later. Figure 3-10 shows the opening screen of the Internet Setup Assistant.

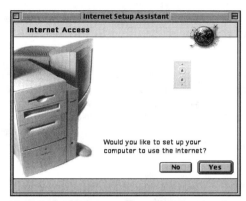

Figure 3-10: Set up an Internet connection with the Internet Setup Assistant program.

E-mail

Exchange electronic mail with people around the world or across the street by using the e-mail programs that come with the Mac OS. More people use the Internet for sending and receiving e-mail than for any other purpose. Microsoft Outlook Express is the standard e-mail program in Mac OS 9, although you can also access e-mail through Netscape Communicator (the Messenger component), which is also bundled with Mac OS 9.

Web browsing

It may not be as utilitarian as e-mail, but the World Wide Web is the flashiest part of the Internet. You can view text, pictures, and movies and hear sounds from Web sites around the world with the Web browser programs that come with Mac OS. Microsoft Internet Explorer is the standard browser installed with Mac OS 9, although it does not replace any other browsers already installed on the computer. Netscape Communicator 8.6 is also installed by default, although you can customize which browsers are installed using the Mac OS 9 installer.

Personal Web Sharing

The Personal Web Sharing software included with Mac OS 9 makes it easy to host a Web site on your computer. You place your prepared Web pages in the Web Pages folder on your startup disk and click the Start button in the Web Sharing control panel. While you're connected to the Internet, anyone with an Internet connection and a Web browser can see your pages. The Web browser that views your site can be running on any kind of computer, or even on an Internet connection device that hooks up to a TV. If you're connected to an intranet (a local TCP/IP network), anyone on the intranet can see your pages with a Web browser running on any kind of computer. This makes it possible to share files (or "publish" Web documents) without enabling File Sharing access to your Mac. Figure 3-11 shows the Web Sharing control panel.

Note　　As with any TCP/IP-based serving, if you have a dynamic IP address (typically, those assigned by ISPs for modem, cable-modem, and some ISDN and DSL connections), then you have to communicate your new IP address to your Web visitors each time you reinitialize the connection. If you'd like your Web server to be a bit more static, then you need to request (and pay for, usually) a fixed IP address and a dedicated connection from your ISP.

Figure 3-11: Share your Web pages on the Internet or an intranet with the Web Sharing control panel.

Mac OS Runtime for Java

Your computer can run programs written in the popular Java programming language with the Mac OS Runtime for Java software that's part of a standard installation of Mac OS 9. Small Java programs, called applets, are often embedded in Web pages to make the pages more interesting or useful. When you view a Web page with an embedded Java applet, the applet runs automatically. You can also run Java applets outside of Web browsers. The Apple Applet Runner is an application program that runs Java applets and is included with Mac OS Runtime for Java.

Essential Maneuvers

The Mac OS has essential features and capabilities to help you with everyday tasks on your computer. This section takes a look at more than a dozen features that you're sure to find useful.

Editing by mouse alone

Instead of using the venerable Cut, Copy, and Paste commands to move text, graphics, or other material in document windows, you can simply drag it from one place to another. You can drag within a document, between documents, and between applications. You can drag material from a document to a Finder window or to the desktop, and the material becomes a clipping file. Conversely, you can drag a clipping file to a document window. This capability, called drag-and-drop editing, works only with applications designed to take advantage of it. Figure 3-12 is an example of drag-and-drop editing.

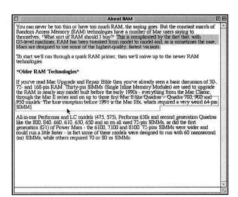

Figure 3-12: Dragging text from place to place within a document

Translucent icon dragging

When you drag an icon, the icon becomes translucent so that you can still identify the icon while you look through it to see where you're dragging. If you drag a group of icons, only the icon under the pointer is translucent; the others in the group are outlines. Figure 3-13 illustrates translucent icon dragging.

Figure 3-13: An icon appears translucent when you drag it.

Dragging to open

You can open a document not only with the application that created it, but also with any compatible application that you have. Drag the document icon to an application icon, and if they're compatible, the application icon becomes highlighted. Release the mouse button and the highlighted application opens the document. For example, you can drag a diverse collection of documents to an application that compresses them so that they consume less disk space. This drag-and-drop capability speeds your work, and you can use it with aliases of documents and applications, as well as with the actual items.

For more information on dragging to open a document, see Chapter 7.

Tooling around with the Apple menu

The Apple menu is like the tool belt a carpenter wears. It doesn't hold all of the tools and equipment, but it holds the things the carpenter needs most often and the special things for the work the carpenter is currently doing. With the Mac OS, you can customize the Apple menu so that it gives you immediate access to programs, documents, folders, and anything else you use frequently or need for a current job. When you choose an item from the Apple menu, it opens right away. You don't have to root around a cluttered desktop or scrounge through folders with the Finder. The Apple menu is available in any program that doesn't hide the menu bar (as some games do, for example). It lists items alphabetically and shows their icons.

You put an item in the Apple menu by dragging its icon into the Apple Menu Items folder in the System Folder. The item becomes instantly available in the Apple menu — there is no need to restart your computer. To remove an item from the Apple menu, drag its icon out of the Apple Menu Items folder. Figure 3-14 is an example of the Apple menu and its special folder.

For more information on the Apple menu, see Chapter 7.

Figure 3-14: Open anything from the Apple menu, which lists whatever you put in the Apple Menu Items folder.

One of the nice additions in Mac OS 8.5–9 is the Favorites folder, in which aliases to your favorite documents, folders, or disks can be kept for easy access. To create a favorite, you just highlight it in the Finder and choose Add To Favorites from the File menu. The Favorites are convenient, and they help you keep your Apple menu a little more organized.

Multitasking

The Mac OS lets you keep more than one program open at a time and switch between the open programs. This capability is known as *multitasking*. You can have as many programs open simultaneously as fit in your computer's memory. You can switch to any open program, including the Finder, by clicking its window or by choosing it from the Application menu at the right end of the menu bar.

You can copy and paste among documents of open programs without closing documents and quitting programs. By switching to the Finder, you can open other programs, find documents, organize folders and disks, and so on. Figure 3-15 shows the Application menu with several programs open simultaneously.

Figure 3-15: Keep multiple programs open at the same time and switch between them with the Application menu.

Having multiple programs open can lead to a confusion of windows. You can eliminate window clutter by using Application menu commands to hide windows temporarily, using that same Application menu.

Because the universal menu bar at the top of the Mac OS screen looks so much alike in many application programs, you can easily get confused about which application is currently active. Often the only surefire sign is the tiny icon that heads the Application menu in the right corner of the menu bar. Mac OS 8.5–9 eliminates all doubt by displaying the name of the active application next to its icon in the menu bar. You can eliminate the name altogether if you prefer.

A bigger change (first seen in Mac OS 8.5) is that you can tear off the Application menu and make it a window called the Application Switcher. You tear off the Application menu by dragging the mouse pointer beyond its last menu item. The Application Switcher floats above ordinary application windows. It displays buttons labeled with miniature application icons and the corresponding application names. You can shrink the window to show just the small icons. To switch to a different application, click the button corresponding to the application you want to use. Figure 3-16 is an example of the Application Switcher.

Figure 3-16: You can tear off the Application Switcher from the Application menu for convenient switching between applications.

Checking the menu bar clock

You can display a digital clock near the right end of the menu bar. Clicking the clock alternates between a display of the time and the date. The format of this clock is set with the Date & Time control panel. You can set the clock to chime on the hour, at quarter past the hour, at half past the hour, and at quarter 'til the hour. Figure 3-17 shows the clock settings in the Date & Time control panel. In Mac OS 8.5–9, you can have the clock automatically check a *network time server* (computers on the Internet that give the correct time) and adjust itself when necessary.

For more information on the clock options, see Chapter 12.

Figure 3-17: Configure the optional menu bar clock to display the time and more.

Printing with desktop printer icons

If you use more than one printer, you can choose one without using Chooser. The Mac OS desktop printing software creates desktop icons for each of your printers. Using the Finder's Printing menu, you make one printer the default printer, which appears when you select a desktop printer icon. Desktop printers queue documents for printing and print them in the background while you do other work. You can open a desktop printer to see and manage the queue. It is also possible to switch between different printers using a Control Strip module or a printer menu in the menu bar. Figure 3-18 shows a desktop printer icon and a desktop printer window.

For more information about desktop printing, see Chapter 16.

Figure 3-18: Use desktop printer icons to choose a printer and manage background printing.

Getting help

Getting assistance onscreen has never been easier than with the Help Viewer. Help Viewer displays short how-to articles that you can search or browse via a table of contents. In addition, the articles contain links that you can click to see related articles, open the programs under discussion, or summon interactive step-by-step help.

The interactive help is provided by Apple Guide, which was first introduced with System 7.5. Help Viewer articles provide detailed information about the Mac OS. Shortcuts and tips, troubleshooting information, and detailed descriptions of Mac OS features and capabilities are all available. Figure 3-19 is an example of the Help Viewer.

Cross-Reference
For more details on all the different types of Mac OS Help, see Chapter 9.

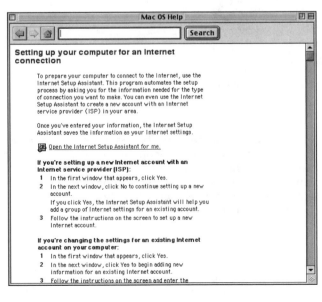

Figure 3-19: The Help Viewer offers Web-like help, with links to interactive Apple Guide lessons.

Outlining in Finder windows

The Finder can display the contents of a folder or disk in a window as a list of item names and other information. Some of the items in a list may be folders, which may contain more folders. You can see the contents of all the enclosed folders as part of one list in an indented outline format. The levels of indentation in the outline clearly diagram the layers of folders listed in the window. You can expand or collapse any level in the outline to show or hide the corresponding folder's contents by clicking a small triangle next to the folder's icon. Expanded folders enable you to select items from more than one folder at a time. Figure 3-20 is an example of the outline structure of a list view.

Cross-Reference   For more information on viewing the contents of folders and disks, see Chapter 5.

Click triangle to expand the
level and see folder contents

🗐 Documents		
39 items, 3.25 GB available		
Name	Date Modified	
🗐 Downloads	Today, 12:45 AM	
📂 Envelope	Thu, May 14, 1998, 5:20 PM	
📂 Exercise Chart	Thu, Oct 23, 1997, 5:25 PM	
🗐 Images for Presentation	Today, 12:45 AM	
🖼 fig0101.pict	Wed, Aug 11, 1999, 9:43 PM	
🖼 fig0106.pict	Thu, Aug 12, 1999, 2:13 AM	
🖼 fig0108.pict	Thu, Aug 12, 1999, 2:11 AM	
🖼 fig0109.pict	Thu, Aug 12, 1999, 2:11 AM	
🖼 fig0110.pict	Thu, Aug 12, 1999, 2:42 AM	
🗐 fig02 Images	Today, 12:44 AM	
🖼 fig0201.pict	Fri, Aug 20, 1999, 2:22 PM	
🖼 fig0202.pict	Fri, Aug 20, 1999, 2:47 PM	
🖼 fig0203.pict	Fri, Aug 20, 1999, 3:11 PM	
🖼 fig0204.pict	Fri, Aug 20, 1999, 3:53 PM	
🖼 fig0205.pict	Fri, Aug 20, 1999, 3:55 PM	
🖼 fig0206.pict	Fri, Aug 20, 1999, 4:38 PM	

Figure 3-20: Expanding and collapsing folder outlines in Finder windows

Tip   The title of a Finder window appears to be static, but when you press ⌘ while clicking the window title, a menu pops up. This pop-up menu reveals the path through your folder structure from the active window to the disk containing it. You can open any folder along the path by choosing the folder from the pop-up menu. To close the active window while opening a folder along the path, press Option while choosing the folder from the pop-up menu.

Using aliases

You can't be in two places at once, but your documents, applications, and folders can be in many places simultaneously. Mac OS aliases make this virtual omnipresence possible. An alias is a small file that points to another file, folder, or disk. When you open an alias, the item it points to opens automatically. When you drag an item to the alias of a folder, the item you drag goes in the folder to which the alias points. You can put aliases anywhere—on the desktop, in the Apple menu, or in other accessible places—and leave the original items buried deep in nested folders. An alias looks like the original item except that its name is in italics, and its name may end with the word *alias*. To further differentiate an alias, Mac OS 8.5–9 display a small badge that looks like a bent arrow on every alias icon. Figure 3-21 shows an alias and its original item.

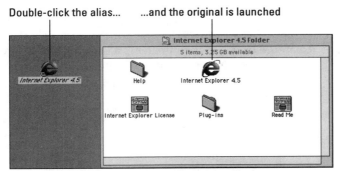

Figure 3-21: Things you do to an alias also happen to its original item.

Aliases have a variety of uses, including:

✦ Opening frequently used programs, documents, and folders from the desktop while the real items remain buried in nested folders.

✦ Adding items to the Apple menu without moving the original items from their folders.

✦ Organizing documents and folders according to multiple filing schemes without duplicating items. For example, you can file documents by project, addressee, date, and topic.

✦ Getting nearly automatic access to your computer's hard disks from another computer on the same network.

To learn to make aliases and to discover more strategies for their use, see Chapter 14.

Sharing files

If your Mac is networked with other computers, the Mac OS makes it possible to share any of your folders, even whole disks, and their contents with other network users. Of course, you can access shared folders and disks on other networked computers as well. The remainder of this section briefly introduces Mac OS file sharing.

Cross-Reference   Chapter 21 details how to access shared files, and Chapter 22 explains how to share your folders and disks.

Using someone else's folders

To use another computer's folder or disk, you can use the Network Browser (in Mac OS 8.5–9) or the Chooser (in all Mac OS versions). Both of these programs list the names of all computers that have shared folders or disks that you can connect to. After you choose a listed computer, the Network Browser or the Chooser asks you to connect as a guest or registered user and then presents a list of items that you may share. Figure 3-22 shows how you connect to shared items using the Network Browser; the Chooser uses a similar procedure.

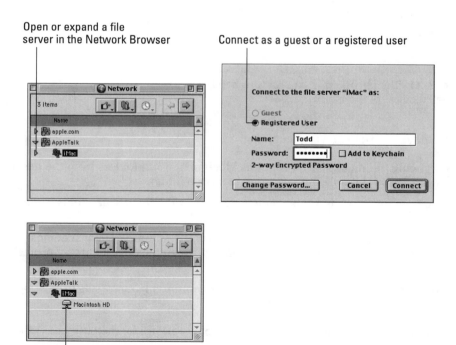

Figure 3-22: Connect to a shared folder or disk using the Network Browser.

Sharing your folders with others

Before you can share your own folders or disks with other network users, you must use the File Sharing control panel to enable file sharing. Your computer then shows up in the Network Browsers and Choosers of other network computers. As discussed and shown in Chapter 2, you can use File Sharing over a local network (using Ethernet or LocalTalk cables), or you can share files over the Internet using File Sharing over TCP/IP. Figure 3-23 shows the File Sharing control panel.

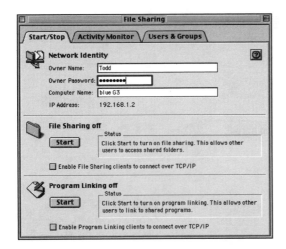

Figure 3-23: The file sharing control panel is where you turn your Mac into a file server.

To share one of your disks or folders, select it and then use the Finder's Sharing command to display the item's sharing information. This information appears in an item's Info window in Mac OS 8.5–9. It is in the Info window that you specify who can see the item's folders, view its files, and make changes to these privileges. You can grant different access privileges to the owner of the item (usually you), to one other registered user or a group of registered users you designate, and to everyone else. Figure 3-24 is an example of sharing information.

You use the Users & Groups control panel to identify registered users, set their passwords, and create groups of users. You can see who is sharing what and how busy they're keeping your computer with the Activity Monitor tab in the File Sharing control panel. You can also use this control panel to disconnect individual users who are sharing your folders and disks. Finally, you can set up the different types of users and groups of users to assign their File Sharing permissions individually by selecting the Users & Groups tab in the File Sharing control panel, shown in Figure 3-25.

Figure 3-24: Use the Sharing command to share an item and set its access privileges in Mac OS 9.

Choose who gets access to the drive down here

Add individuals

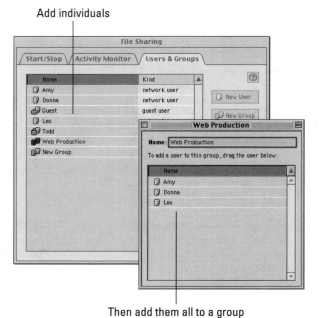

Figure 3-25: Users & Groups is where you set up File Sharing accounts for people (or groups) that access your Mac.

Then add them all to a group

Important Mac OS Features

When you're ready to go beyond the basics, the Mac OS has many powerful features and capabilities to help you work more efficiently. This section looks at organizing the System Folder, fonts and typography, extending memory, managing startup items, and speech capabilities.

Organizing the System Folder

The system software consists of hundreds of files — system extensions, control panels, fonts, preference files, and many other kinds of files. The Mac OS organizes system software files in a number of special folders inside the System Folder. There's a Control Panels folder, a Preferences folder, an Extensions folder, a Fonts folder, and many more. Most of the special folders have distinctive icons. Moreover, the Finder knows which special folder to put many items in when you drag them to the System Folder icon. Figure 3-26 is an example of the System Folder.

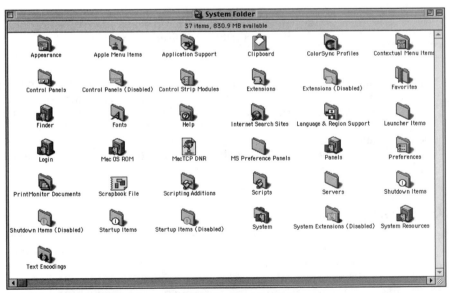

Figure 3-26: Special folders subdivide the System Folder.

In general, you should not move items from one special folder in the System Folder to another, because these files must be in specific locations to function. Likewise, you should not remove items from the System Folder unless you know for sure that an item is not needed.

To learn more about the System Folder's special folders, see Chapter 11. Tackling fonts and typography

The Mac OS works with three basic kinds of fonts: fixed size, TrueType variable size, and PostScript variable size. This section introduces some of the different kinds of fonts and typography.

Chapter 15 covers fonts in detail.

Thanks to the TrueType font technology that is built into the Mac OS, text looks smooth at any size onscreen or on any printing device. TrueType fonts are variable-size outline fonts similar to the PostScript fonts that look so sharp on PostScript printers (and onscreen if you have installed Adobe Type Manager software). The Mac OS smoothly scales TrueType fonts to any size. Fixed-size fonts also look good on the screen at their prescribed sizes, but they appear lumpy when scaled to other sizes. Figure 3-27 shows how much more smoothly TrueType scales 36-point Times text compared with a scaled-up 18-point fixed-size font.

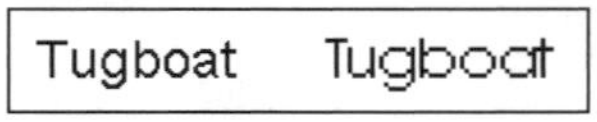

Tugboat   Tugboat

Figure 3-27: The Mac OS scales TrueType fonts (left) more smoothly than fixed-size fonts (right).

Having trouble duplicating this jaggedness? It might be because Mac OS 9 has an option that allows you to "smooth" *every* font that appears on the screen that is over a particular point size. That just makes the Mac display look a little more sophisticated and modern. You can turn this option on or off in the Appearance control panel, under the Fonts tab. There is a check box next to "Smooth all fonts on screen." Click the box to remove the check mark (if it's currently checked) and the feature is turned off. If it's not currently checked, then it's already off.

Extending memory

Application programs are becoming more memory hungry all the time, and the Mac OS has a large memory appetite itself. It seems as if a computer can never have too much memory. The Mac OS can increase the amount of memory available by using part of a hard disk transparently as additional memory. This extra memory, called *virtual memory*, lets you keep more programs open simultaneously and increase the amount of memory each program gets when you open it. Given more memory, programs may enable you to open additional or larger documents. Furthermore, on PowerPC computers, having virtual memory turned on substantially reduces the amount of memory that programs need.

For more information on memory management, see Chapter 19.

Managing startup items

To help manage the large number of items that load when you start up your computer, the Mac OS includes the Extensions Manager control panel. You can use it to disable and enable control panels, extensions, and other startup items either individually or in sets. The Extensions Manager that comes with Mac OS 9 includes improvements first introduced in Mac OS 7.6. For each item, it displays its status (enabled or disabled), name, size, and version, and in some cases, the package it was installed with. You can view items grouped by the folders they're in, grouped by the package they were installed with, or ungrouped. You can enlarge the Extensions Manager window to display detailed information about a particular item. Figure 3-28 is an example of the Extensions Manager.

Caution   Do not use the Extensions Manager to disable extensions unless you know for certain that a particular extension or group of extensions are not needed; some extensions are essential to the proper functioning of your Macintosh.

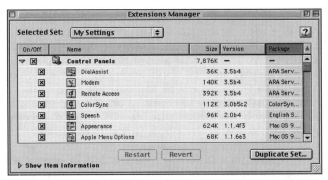

Figure 3-28: Disable and enable startup items with the Extensions Manager control panel.

Cross-Reference   To learn more about the Extensions Manager, see Chapter 11.

Summary

This chapter introduced the features, many of which were introduced in Mac OS 8 or Mac OS 8.5, that make Mac OS 9 easier to use than earlier versions of the system software. The Finder is more responsive thanks to its live scrolling of windows and its capability to perform simultaneous operations. There are additional controls for moving and collapsing windows. The Finder's View menu is revamped, making it simpler to set the view of each folder and disk window, and to keep it arranged. You can view files and folders as one-click buttons, and you can make any disk or folder window into a pop-up window. Many view options that previously applied to all folder and disk windows can now be set for each window separately. The Finder's Preferences command offers a Simple Finder option plus options that were formerly part of the Views and Labels control panels. You can make disks and folders spring open without lifting a finger. You can see a contextual menu of relevant commands by Control+clicking an icon, a window, or some text in the Finder. All menus stay open even if you release the mouse button, and several commands were added to the Finder's File menu.

This chapter also provided an overview of what Mac OS 9 provides for getting connected to the Internet and accessing Internet services. The Internet Setup Assistant simplifies setting up an Internet connection. You can use any of the supplied programs to exchange e-mail. The Personal Web Sharing software makes it easy to publish your own Web pages on the Internet or on an intranet. In addition, you can run Java applets that are embedded in Web pages and run Java programs outside Web pages with the Mac OS Runtime for Java software.

This chapter introduced the special Mac OS features and capabilities that help you with everyday computer tasks, including drag-and-drop editing, translucent icon dragging on a PowerPC computer, and dragging documents to open them with applications that didn't create them. The Mac OS also provides the Apple menu for opening your favorite items quickly and the Application menu for switching between open applications. You can check the time and date with the menu bar clock. Desktop printer icons make it easy to choose a printer and manage background printing. If you need help while using the Mac OS, you can access the Web-like Help Viewer and link to interactive Apple Guide instructions.

Mac OS makes it easier to work with your disks, files, and folders in several ways. You can see indented outlines of your layers of folders. You can categorize items with colored labels. For all practical purposes, you can keep items in more than one place at the same time by making aliases of them. And you can share files with other computer users on a network.

This chapter also showed you other Mac OS features and capabilities that you're sure to find indispensable, including special folders for organizing the contents of the System Folder; virtual memory for reducing program memory needs on PowerPC computers and making more memory available on all computers; and three kinds of fonts that the Mac OS works with — fixed size, TrueType variable size, and PostScript variable size.

Finally, to make the most of the Mac OS, you can manage your startup items with the Extensions Manager control panel.

✦　　✦　　✦

Getting Started with the Mac OS

Start on the Desktop

The desktop, with its menus, windows, and icons, serves as a home base for everything that you do with your Macintosh. Because you use all these things so often, how they look and operate is important. You need to know what all these basic elements are and how to use them: the menu bar, pop-up menus, contextual menus, regular windows, dialog boxes, alert boxes, window controls, other controls, and the active window. You also need to know what different icon shapes mean, how to select one or more icons, and how to rename them. This chapter describes and illustrates all of these basic features of the Mac OS.

Menus

The Mac OS has always used menus to present the commands from which you can choose in a given circumstance. Usually you select something — such as an icon, or a series of words in a document — and then you choose a command from one of the menus in the menu bar at the top of the screen. In a way, those menus are like drawers in your work desk — it's where you keep pens, staplers, scissors, and so on. On the Mac's desktop, the menus are the drawers where you find applications, print commands, formatting options, and so on. And, yes, on the Apple menu you'll even find a Calculator.

At the top of the screen are menu titles in the form of words and icons in a menu bar. The menu bar contains some menu titles that are the same in all applications, as well as menus that are unique to the application program you're using at the time. Menus can also appear outside the menu bar. A menu that pops up from an icon or other object outside the menu bar has an arrow that indicates it is a menu. In addition, Mac OS 9 can display menus in some places based solely on the context of the mouse pointer. This section describes menus in the menu bar, pop-up menus, and contextual menus.

Menu bar

The menus in the menu bar at the top of the screen contain commands that are relevant to the application that you are using at the time. The menus may also contain attributes that apply to objects that you work with in the application. In addition, the menu bar has menus from which you can choose another application that you want to begin using. Menu titles appear in the menu bar, and you can use the mouse to display one menu at a time beneath its title. Figure 4-1 shows the menu bar as it initially appears in Mac OS 9, with one of its menus displayed.

Figure 4-1: The menu bar is a permanent fixture at the top of the screen.

You can change some aspects of the menu bar appearance as described in Chapter 8.

How the menu bar works

To use the menu bar, you position the mouse pointer over a menu title and click or press the mouse button. The menu opens beneath the menu title so that you can see the items in it and choose one, if you like. Figure 4-2 shows an open menu.

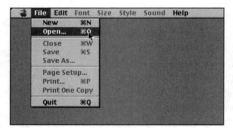

Figure 4-2: Click one of the menu titles and a menu appears.

Why one menu bar?

There are several reasons why the Mac OS has a permanent menu bar at the top of the screen. One reason is that a menu bar at the top of the screen is an easy target to hit with the mouse. You can quickly slide the mouse pointer to the top of the screen, where it automatically stops at the menu bar. If the menu bar were at the top of a window in the middle of the screen (like on a Microsoft Windows computer), you would have to take more time to carefully position the pointer over it.

A second reason is that having a permanent menu bar at the top of the screen gives you a reliable place for every application's commands. If each window on the screen had its own menu bar, you'd have to think about which one you wanted to use.

In Mac OS 9, a menu stays open when you click it. (In Mac OS versions before Mac OS 8, you had to hold down the mouse button or the menu would disappear.) You can leave your finger off the mouse button and move the pointer up and down the menu, highlighting each menu item as the pointer passes over it. The menu disappears if you move the pointer back to the menu bar. Then, you can display the same menu or another menu by moving the pointer over the menu title. You don't have to click again unless it's been more than 15 seconds since you last moved the mouse.

Note   If you're used to the way menus worked pre-Mac OS 8, you can still use them that way. If you click and hold the mouse button while moving up and down a menu, it will disappear immediately after you release the mouse button.

To choose a menu item, position the pointer over it and click. If you click outside a menu, on the menu's title again, or if you don't move the mouse for 15 seconds, the menu disappears and you have to click a menu title again to make menus stick open.

Standard menus

In most Mac OS applications, the menu bar includes these five standard menus:

✦ **Apple menu** is at the left end of the menu and has an Apple logo for its title. This menu usually includes an About item, which describes the application you're currently using, followed by an alphabetical list of programs, documents, and other items that can be opened. For information on using and customizing the Apple menu, see Chapter 7.

✦ **File menu** is next to the Apple menu and contains commands that affect a whole document, such as New, Open, Close, Save, and Print. The last item is usually Quit, which you use when you're done working with an application.

✦ **Edit menu** is to the right of the File menu and contains commands that you can use to change a document's contents, such as Undo, Cut, Copy, Paste, and Clear.

✦ **Help menu** gives you access to onscreen help. In Mac OS 9, the help menu is labeled "Help," and the menu is immediately to the right of the last application menu in the menu bar. (In versions of the Mac OS before Mac OS 8, the help menu is labeled with a question mark icon. It is near the right end of the menu bar and is referred to as the Guide menu.) For more information about onscreen help, see Chapter 9.

✦ **Application menu**, which is located at the right end of the menu bar, displays an alphabetical list of the applications that are currently running on the computer. Choosing a listed application makes it the active application so that you can use it. Find more information about this menu in Chapter 7.

Each application may add its own menus between the Edit menu and the Help menu. In addition, the menu bar normally includes a digital clock near the right end of the menu bar. The clock does not give you access to a menu (it usually just switches between the date and time display).

Pop-up menus

Pop-up menus are special menus that don't appear on the menu bar. Usually they are found in a window in an application, and such menus often ask you to choose from a list of options. When you click a pop-up menu, all those options appear, allowing you to move the mouse up or down to choose one.

Menus outside the menu bar must be marked so that you can tell that clicking one will display a menu. By convention, an arrowhead next to some text or an icon indicates it is a menu title. The arrowhead may point down or to the right. It may also be double-headed and point up and down. Figure 4-3 shows some examples of pop-up menus.

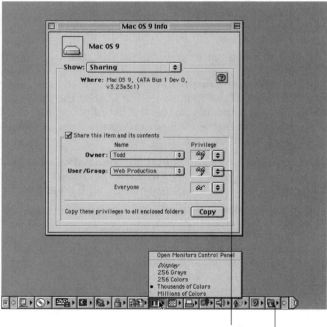

Double-headed arrows suggest a pop-up menu

A single right-facing arrow is another sign

Figure 4-3: Different types of pop-up menus, including those found in preferences windows and in the control strip

Like menus in the menu bar, a pop-up menu stays open after you click it.

Contextual menus

Rooting through menus to find a particular command isn't much fun. Wouldn't it be better if all you saw were relevant commands? That's the point of contextual menus — they offer commands that make sense in a given *context*. You can display a contextual menu by holding down the Control key while clicking an icon, a window, or some selected text for which you want to choose a command or attribute. The contextual menu lists commands that are relevant to the item that you Control+click. Figure 4-4 is an example of a contextual menu for an icon.

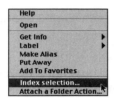

Figure 4-4: Control+clicking an item displays a contextual menu in the Finder.

You can Control+click one icon or a selection of several icons. When several icons are selected, Control+clicking any one of them displays a contextual menu of com-mands that pertain to the whole group. For example, if you Control+click one folder icon in Mac OS 9, the contextual menu includes the command Attach a Folder Action. This command is not included in the contextual menu when you Control+click several folders because the command can only apply to one folder at a time. (For more information on selecting items, see "Icons" later in this chapter.)

Contextual menus are available when you're working with files, folders, and disks in the Finder, although they can be disabled in that context by selecting the Simple Finder option. (More on all this in Chapter 5.) Other applications can adopt contextual menus as well — you'll find that many have, especially Internet applications and others that are updated frequently. In addition, you can extend contextual menus with shareware and freeware add-ons, such as Apple Data Detectors and FinderPop (both of which are described in Chapter 26).

If your Mac has a two- or four-button mouse or trackball, you may be able to display contextual menus by pressing the right button without holding down Control. If your multibutton mouse or trackball does not already work this way, you may be able to program it to simulate a Control+click whenever you press the button on the right. For instructions on programming a multibutton mouse or trackball, see the documentation that came with it. (You may find that the mouse has a control panel that governs this behavior.) These alternative pointing devices are made by Kensington Technology (650-572-2700, http://www.kensington.com), Contour Designs (800-462-6678, http://www.contourdesign.com), and other companies, not by Apple.

Menu symbols

A menu item may be accompanied by a variety of symbols. A triangle pointing to the right indicates the menu item has a submenu. An ellipsis at the end of the item name indicates that choosing the item brings up a dialog box in which you must supply additional information before the command can be completed.

✓ designates an attribute that applies to everything that is currently selected

● also designates an attribute that applies to everything that is currently selected

– designates an attribute that applies only to some things that are currently selected

▶ designates a menu item with a submenu

◆ designates a program that's running in the background and that requires attention; to find out why, make it the active, foreground application

Other symbols are used to specify keyboard shortcuts for menu items. Pressing a specified combination of keys has the same effect as choosing the menu item. For example, pressing ⌘+X is equivalent to choosing the Cut command from the Edit menu. The following symbols represent keys:

⌘   represents the Command key

⇧   represents the Shift key

⌥   represents the Option key

⌃   represents the Control (or Ctrl) key

⌦   represents the Delete key

When you use a keyboard shortcut for a command in a menu, the title of the menu flashes briefly to signal that the command has been issued. You can change how many times the title flashes, or turn off the signal altogether, in the Menu Blinking section of the General Controls control panel (as described in Chapter 12).

Windows

You view and interact with the files stored on your computer in windows. Most windows are rectangular, but some are other shapes. This section describes how different types of Mac OS windows look and work.

Window types

There are several types of Mac OS windows, and each is designed to display a specific kind of information. Some windows display the files and other items stored on disks. Other windows display the contents of files, which may be text, pictures, movies, or other kinds of information. Windows called *dialog boxes* display options that you can set. *Alert boxes* are dialog boxes in which the Mac OS or an application program notifies you of a hazardous situation, a limitation in your proposed course of action, or an error condition. Palettes contain controls or tools, or display auxiliary information for the application program that you're currently using.

Each type of window has a standard structure, and it's basically the same in all versions of the Mac OS. The frame that borders every window looks different for a regular window, a movable dialog box, an immovable dialog box, an alert box, and a palette. Figure 4-5 shows examples of the different types of windows as they initially appear in Mac OS 9.

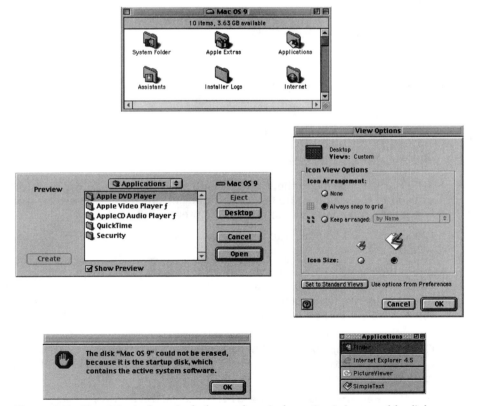

Figure 4-5: Mac OS windows include regular windows (top), immovable dialog boxes (middle left), movable dialog boxes (middle right), alert boxes (bottom left), and palettes (bottom right).

Window controls

The design of a window has as much to do with function as with form. Many parts of a window's frame are actually control surfaces that you can use to move the window, size it, close it, or change the view of its contents. Figure 4-6 shows examples of window controls.

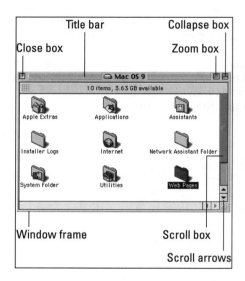

Figure 4-6: Manipulate windows with their many controls

The window controls have these effects:

✦ **Title bar:** Drag to move the window. Double-clicking the title bar may collapse or expand the window, and Option+double-clicking may collapse or expand all windows. (To set up this option, see Chapter 8.)

✦ **Close box:** Click to make the window go away. Press Option+click to close all windows.

✦ **Zoom box:** Click to make the window as large as it needs to be to show all its contents, up to the size of the screen. Click again to make the window resume its previous size and location. Press Option+click to force the window to fill the screen. (The zoom box usually leaves a margin on the right side of the screen.)

✦ **Collapse box:** Click to hide all but the window's title bar, or if the window is collapsed, click to show the entire window. Press Option+click to collapse (or expand) all windows.

✦ **Scroll bar arrow, box:** Click the arrow to scroll the window's contents smoothly; click the gray area to scroll in chunks; drag the box to quickly bring another part of the window's contents in view. The scroll bar controls do not appear if scrolling would not bring anything else in view. In Mac OS, the scroll arrows are bidirectional—placed together near the bottom-right corners of the window—and the scroll box proportional to the window content. (To change this option, which is called Smart Scrolling, see Chapter 8.)

✦ **Size box:** Drag to adjust the size of the window.

✦ **Window frame:** Drag to move the window.

You won't find all the window controls on every kind of window. Document windows have all or most of the available controls, movable dialog boxes have fewer controls, and immovable dialog boxes and alert boxes have no controls built in their borders. Nonblocking alert boxes, new to Mac OS 9, feature a title bar and a close box.

Other controls

Inside many windows are a variety of controls that operate by clicking and dragging with the mouse. Examples include buttons with text or picture labels, check boxes, radio buttons, sliders, little arrows for increasing or decreasing numeric values, disclosure triangles, scrolling lists, and tabs. Figure 4-7 shows examples of some controls in Mac OS 9.

Controls have these effects:

✦ **Buttons** cause an action to take place when clicked. Many dialog boxes have OK and Cancel buttons. Clicking OK accepts all the settings and entries in the dialog box. Clicking Cancel rejects any changes you may have made in the dialog box and restores all settings and entries to their states when the dialog box appeared. One button in a dialog box or alert box may have a heavy border; this is the default button. It represents the action that you'll most often want to take, except that if the most common action is dangerous, a button representing a safer action may be the default button. As a shortcut for clicking the default button, you can press Return or Enter.

✦ **Radio buttons** let you select one setting from a group. They're called radio buttons because they work like the station presets on a car radio. Just as you can select only one radio station at a time, you can select only one radio button from a group. To select a radio button, click it. Although you can't select more than one radio button, several radio buttons in a group may be partly on and partly off because the group indicates the state of more than one thing, such as the right or left alignment of multiple paragraphs.

✦ **Check boxes** let you turn options on or off. When an option is on, a check mark or a cross appears in the check box. When an option is off, the check box is empty. When an option is partly on and partly off because it indicates the state of more than one thing, such as the format of a range of text, a horizontal line appears in the check box. Check boxes are not mutually exclusive like radio buttons. You can turn on check boxes in any combination. Clicking a check box reverses its state.

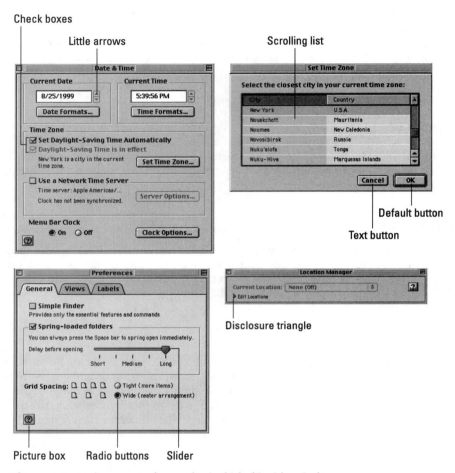

Figure 4-7: Various controls may be included inside windows.

✦ **Sliders** display a range of values or magnitudes. An indicator shows the current setting, and you can drag the indicator to change the setting.

✦ **Little arrows**, which point in opposite directions, let you raise or lower a value incrementally. Clicking an arrow changes the value one increment at a time. Pressing an arrow continuously changes the value until it reaches the end of its range.

✦ **Disclosure triangles** control how much detail you see in the window. Clicking a right-pointing triangle reveals additional detail and may automatically enlarge the window to accommodate it. Clicking a down-pointing triangle hides detail and may automatically shrink the window to fit.

✦ **Scrolling lists** display a list of values in a box with an adjacent scroll bar. If there are more values than can be displayed at once, the scroll bar becomes active and you can use it to see other values in the list. Clicking a listed item selects it. You may be able to select multiple items by pressing Shift or ⌘.

✦ **Tabs** look like the tabs on dividers used in card files and ring binders, and they have a similar function. They divide the content of a window into discrete pages, or sections, with each tab connected to one section of window content. You see one section at a time, and you switch to a different section by clicking its tab.

Active window

When more than one standard window is open, one is active and you can use its controls. You can't use the controls in windows that are open but inactive. In fact, you can't even see controls in the frames of inactive windows. You can tell the active window not only by its visible controls but also because it overlaps inactive windows that touch it. The active window is considered to be in front of inactive windows. Figure 4-8 shows an active window and inactive windows in Mac OS 9.

Note There is an exception to the rule that only one window is active at a time. Palettes are always active when they are open. They float in a layer above other types of windows. If you are using an application with palettes, and switch to another application with palettes, the palettes from the first application should close automatically and any palettes that were previously open in the second application should reopen automatically.

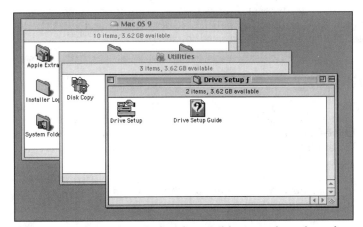

Figure 4-8: The active window has visible controls and overlaps inactive windows that touch it.

Window tricks

Although inactive windows don't have visible controls, you can move and collapse or expand them while they're in the background. If you have more than one program open at the same time, these tricks only work with windows of the program you're currently using.

To move an inactive window, press ⌘ while dragging the window's title bar or its frame.

To collapse or expand an inactive window, press ⌘ while double-clicking the window's title bar. Pressing ⌘ keeps the window from becoming active.

To collapse or expand all windows, press Option while clicking any window's collapse (window shade) box.

To make an inactive window active, click any part of it that you can see. This brings it to the front and moves the formerly active window behind. If a dialog box or alert box is displayed, you must dismiss it before you can make another window active in the same application program. This isn't true of nonblocking alert boxes, which appear to "float" over other windows. You don't have to click the nonblocking alert's close box before manipulating other windows.

Icons

Many entities in the Mac OS are represented by small pictures called icons. The programs, documents, folders, and disks in your computer are used by manipulating icons on the computer screen. This section explains what the look of an icon tells you about it and how you use icons.

Icon appearance

An icon's basic appearance tells you what kind of item it represents. Icons that look like a sheet of paper with a dog-eared corner represent document files, which contain the text, pictures, sounds, and other kinds of data stored on your computer. Icons based on a diamond shape usually represent application programs that you use to work on documents.

Note Many application icons have other shapes, but the diamond shape was the original standard for Mac programs.

Icons that look like folders represent the folders in which programs, documents, and other items are organized on your disks. These are just a few of the icons you learn to recognize on a typical Mac; many other icons are described in other chapters. Figure 4-9 shows examples of document, program, and folder icons in Mac OS 9.

Figure 4-9: An icon's basic appearance indicates the kind of item it represents.

Selecting icons

The look of an icon has no bearing on how you use it. Everyone who uses a Mac quickly learns to select icons by clicking, but even some seasoned veterans don't know that in windows and on the desktop you can select more than one icon at a time. In addition, you can select icons individually by typing instead of clicking.

When you select an icon, the Mac OS highlights it by making it darker and displaying its name in white type on a black (or colored) background. If the icon you select is on a monitor that's set to display black and white, the Mac OS highlights the icon by inverting its colors; white becomes black and black becomes white. Figure 4-10 shows examples of an icon that is highlighted and an icon that isn't highlighted.

Figure 4-10: Icon highlighting on a color or grayscale monitor

Multiple selection by Shift+clicking

Ordinarily, clicking an icon selects it (highlights it) and deselects the icon that was highlighted. You can select a group of icons in the same window or a group of icons on the desktop by pressing Shift while clicking each icon in turn. At any time, you can deselect a selected icon by pressing Shift and clicking it again.

Multiple selection by dragging

In addition to Shift+clicking to select multiple icons, you can select adjacent icons by dragging the mouse pointer across them. As you drag, the Mac OS displays a rectangle, called a selection rectangle, and every icon it touches or encloses is selected. Icons are highlighted one-by-one as you drag over them, not en masse after you stop dragging. All items must be on the desktop or in a single window. Figure 4-11 is an example of selecting several icons with a selection rectangle.

Figure 4-11: Selecting adjacent items by dragging a selection rectangle

You can combine dragging with use of the Shift key. Pressing Shift while dragging a selection rectangle across unselected icons adds the enclosed icons to the current selection. Conversely, pressing Shift while dragging a selection rectangle across selected icons deselects the enclosed group without deselecting other icons (if any).

Selection by typing

When you know the name of an icon that you want to select but aren't sure where it is in a window, you can quickly select it by typing. Typing also may be faster than clicking if the icon you want to select requires lots of scrolling to bring in view.

Open or select the window where the icon is located. To select an icon by typing, simply type the first part of its name. You need to type only enough of the name to uniquely identify the icon you want. In a window in which every icon has a completely different name, for example, you need to type only the first letter of a name to select an icon. By contrast, in a folder where every icon begins with Power, you have to type those five letters plus enough additional letters to single out the icon you want. When selecting by typing, uppercase and lowercase letters are interchangeable.

While typing, pressing Tab selects the next item alphabetically and Shift+Tab selects the previous item alphabetically. Pressing an arrow key selects the icon nearest the currently selected icon in the direction that the arrow key points. To select the icon of the startup disk, press ⌘+Shift+up arrow (↑). Table 4-1 summarizes keyboard selection techniques.

Table 4-1
Selecting Icons by Typing

To Select This	Do This
An icon	Type the icon's partial or full name
Next icon alphabetically	Press Tab
Previous icon alphabetically	Press Shift+Tab
Next icon up	Press up arrow (↑)
Next icon down	Press down arrow (↓)

To Select This	Do This
Next icon left	Press left arrow (←)
Next icon right	Press right arrow (→)
Enclosing folder or disk	⌘+up arrow (↑)
Startup disk icon	Press ⌘+Shift+up arrow (↑)
Multiple icons	Press Shift while clicking each icon or while dragging to enclose them

Renaming icons

Clicking an icon highlights the icon and its name but does not select the icon name for editing. This behavior protects your icons from being accidentally renamed by your cat walking across your keyboard (which has actually happened). If you select an icon and begin typing, expecting your typing to rename the selected icon, you may be surprised to discover that your typing selects another icon whose name most closely matches what you're typing (as described previously).

To rename a disk, folder, program, document, or other item, you must explicitly select its name. Either click the name directly, or click the item's icon and then press Return or Enter. An icon whose name is selected for editing has a distinctive look: The icon is highlighted as usual and the name has a box around it. The box does not appear when you just click the icon. Figure 4-12 shows an icon with its name selected and another icon with its name not selected.

Figure 4-12: A boxed icon name (left) is ready for editing, but a highlighted icon (right) isn't.

For an additional visual cue that you have selected a name on a color or grayscale monitor, make sure the text highlight color is something other than black and white. Then you know that a name highlighted in color (or gray) is ready for editing, whereas a name highlighted in black and white is not. To set the text highlight color, use the Appearance control panel as described in Chapter 8.

Selecting all or part of an icon name

Right after you select an icon name, the whole name is selected. With the whole name selected, you can replace it completely by typing a new name. If you just want to change part of the name, you can select that part and replace or delete it. You can also select an insertion point and type additional text.

To select part of an icon name or an insertion point in one, you must first select the name for editing (as just described). Now position the mouse pointer (which should be shaped something like a capital I) where you want to place an insertion point or begin selecting in the name. Click to place an insertion point, or hold down the mouse button and drag the pointer to select part of the name. As you drag, the Mac OS highlights the text you are selecting. Release the mouse button to stop selecting. If you select an insertion point, you see a thin flashing line that marks its position. Figure 4-13 shows one icon name entirely selected, another name partially selected, and an insertion point in a third name.

Figure 4-13: Select all of an icon name (left), part of an icon name (middle), or an insertion point (right).

To select part of an icon name or an insertion point in the name, be sure to wait until the selection box appears around the name. The Finder may think you're double-clicking an icon and open it if you click the name and then immediately click, double-click, or drag in the name to select part of it. (Opening icons is discussed in greater depth in Chapter 5.)

Copy, Paste, and Undo

While editing a name, you can use the Undo, Cut, Copy, and Paste commands in the Edit menu. These commands are also available in a contextual menu.

To copy all or part of an icon name, select the part that you want to copy and choose Copy from the Edit menu. The Copy command places the selected text on the Clipboard, which is an internal holding area. Then you can paste what you copied by selecting all or part of another icon's name and choosing Paste from the Edit menu. At this point you can make changes to the name that you pasted; you must make changes if the icon whose name you're working on is the same as that of another icon in the same folder. Whatever you copied remains on the Clipboard until you use the Copy command or the Cut command. The Cut command works like the Copy command, but Cut also removes the selected text while placing it on the Clipboard.

Stop waiting for the editing box

After clicking an icon name to edit it, you have to wait and wait for the editing box to appear around the name. To cut the wait short, just twitch the mouse and the name is highlighted for editing. You don't have to wait after clicking an icon's name if you immediately move the pointer.

Another way to avoid waiting after clicking an icon's name is to move the insertion point by pressing the arrow keys. Click the name and immediately press the up arrow (↑) or the left arrow (←) to move the insertion point to the beginning of the name, or immediately press the down arrow (↓) or the right arrow (→) to move the selection point to the end. After the selection point is established, pressing the left arrow (←) moves it left and pressing the right arrow (→) moves it right.

Perhaps the easiest way to immediately edit an icon name is to select the *icon* (not the icon's name) and press Return. This immediately puts you in editing mode with the icon's entire name highlighted.

The length of time you must wait for the editing box to appear around an icon name you clicked depends on the duration of a double-click interval — approximately 1.9 seconds, 1.3 seconds, or 0.9 second, as set in the Mouse control panel. If you have trouble editing icon names without opening the item, try setting a briefer double-click speed with the Mouse control panel (see Chapter 12).

While editing an icon name, you can undo your last change by choosing Undo from the Edit menu. The Undo command works only as long as the icon name remains selected for editing. You cannot undo your changes to a name after you finish editing it.

To finish editing an icon name, press Return or Enter, or click anywhere outside the icon name. You can cancel all the changes you made to an icon name since you began editing it by deleting the entire name (choose Select All from the Edit menu and press the Delete key) and then pressing Return or Enter. Because the icon now has no name when you press Return or Enter (ending the editing of the name), the Mac OS restores the name the icon had when you began editing it.

Besides selecting all or part of a name and copying it, you can copy the entire name of any item by selecting its icon and choosing Copy from the Edit menu. You do not have to select the name to copy it; you can just select the icon. Then you can choose the name of another icon (not just the icon this time) that's not in the same folder and choose Paste from the Edit menu to give it the copied name.

You can copy the names of multiple icons by selecting the icons and using the Copy command. This creates a list of icon names on the Clipboard. You can paste this list in a document such as a Stickies note, a SimpleText document, or the Note Pad, but you can't paste the copied icon names onto a group of selected icons.

Renaming locked items

You can't change the name of a locked item or an item that you are sharing on a network. However, you can copy its entire name as just described. (For information on locking and unlocking items, see Chapter 5. For information on sharing items on a network, see Chapter 22.)

Taking a Screen Picture

You can take a picture of the whole screen — menu bar, windows, and icons — at any time by pressing ⌘+Shift+3. Each picture you take appears at the root level of your startup disk (the main window that appears when you double-click the disk's icon on the desktop) as a file named Picture 1, Picture 2, and so on. You can view the screen pictures with the SimpleText application, which is normally located in the Applications folder of the startup disk.

Rather than taking a picture of the whole screen, you can take a picture of a window or any rectangular portion of the screen. To do so, use these keystrokes:

✦ **Rectangular region:** Press ⌘+Shift+4 and then drag to select a rectangular region that you want to take a picture of (this procedure omits the pointer from the picture).

✦ **Window or menu:** Press ⌘+Shift+4+Caps Lock and then click a window or open menu (you need to click it open before taking the screen shot) that you want to take a picture of (this procedure omits the pointer from the picture).

✦ **Cancel:** Press Space bar (or any other key that normally types a character) to cancel a ⌘+Shift+4 combination.

✦ **Picture on Clipboard:** Add the Control key to any of the screen capture keystrokes to copy the picture to the Clipboard instead of saving it as a picture file on the startup disk. With the ⌘+Shift+4 combinations, you can alternatively press Control while selecting the region or window you want to take a picture of.

Summary

This chapter offered an in-depth look at the interface elements in the Mac OS — controls that make it possible for you to work with documents and applications to get something done on your Mac. The discussion began with menus, where the commands and preferences for your work are set. Menus are found in the menu bar, as pop-up menus, and as special contextual menus.

This chapter also discussed the difference between a regular window, a dialog box, and an alert box. You've seen the function of scroll bars, zoom boxes, buttons, radio buttons, check boxes, and other controls found on window frames and inside windows. You should be able to tell which window is currently active, and you can even manipulate inactive windows using some little-known commands.

Icons are the small pictures on the screen that represent documents, application programs, and folders. You've seen in this chapter how to select one icon or a group of icons. You've also seen how to rename an icon.

Finally, this chapter briefly touched on taking a screen shot, showing you how to take a picture of all or part of the screen by pressing a combination of keys.

✦   ✦   ✦

Get Organized with the Finder

Ask 100 Macintosh users to name the application program they use most often and only a few would come up with the correct answer: the Finder. People don't think of the Finder as a program they use or need to learn to use. In fact, it is a very rich application program that is included with the Mac OS for managing your disks and their contents.

This chapter describes the simple ways in which you can organize the stuff on your computer by using the Finder. You can open and close disks, folders, and files. You can view the contents of each folder and disk as icons, as a list, and, in Mac OS 9, as buttons. You can create folders and you can copy, move, duplicate, and delete folders and files. You can also remove or erase disks, if you have more than one on your desktop. Some of these tasks are time-consuming, but in most cases the Finder can finish them in the background while you work.

Once you've mastered the skills presented in this chapter, you're ready to continue learning about the Finder in other chapters. Chapter 6 discusses the more elaborate ways in which you can organize your disks and their contents. Chapter 7 discusses working with documents and programs. And Chapter 14 teaches you to create aliases in the Finder to expedite your work in almost all applications.

Simple Finder

A quick scan of the Finder's menus gives you an idea of its capabilities. Not all of them are essential. If you'd rather not bother with the Finder's more advanced capabilities, you can simplify its menus using the Finder's Preferences command.

To do this, choose Preferences from the Edit menu to display the Finder's Preferences window. Mac OS 9 has tabs at the top of this window; in this case, click the General tab to see the general preferences. Then click the Simple Finder option to turn it on. (The option is turned on when you see a check mark in the option's check box.) Figure 5-1 shows the Simple Finder option turned on.

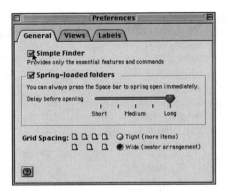

Figure 5-1: Set the Simple Finder option in the Finder's Preferences window in Mac OS 9.

In the interest of simplicity, you can ignore the other options in the Preferences dialog box for now. They're discussed later in this chapter.

Opening and Closing Disks, Folders, and Files

When you want to see what's in a disk, folder, or file, you open it. Opening a disk, a folder, or a file that is a document displays its contents in a window. Opening a file that is a program displays the program's menus in the menu bar and may display a document window for that program (not all programs automatically display a document window). You open a program when you want to use it to view or edit the kinds of documents it can create or read.

There are two basic ways to open a disk, folder, or file. You can select its icon and choose Open from the File menu, or you can double-click the icon. Instead of double-clicking an icon, you click it once if it's part of a square button in a Mac OS 9 window (more about these buttons in the next section). The File menu shows a keyboard shortcut for the Open command, ⌘+O, which means that you can also open an icon by selecting it and pressing ⌘+O. Another keyboard shortcut for the Open command is more of a secret: ⌘+down arrow (↓).

When you don't want to see a window any more, you can close it. There are also multiple ways to close a window. You can choose Close from the File menu (its keyboard shortcut is ⌘+W or ⌘+up arrow (↑)), or you can simply click the window's close box. To close all open windows at once, press Option while closing one of the windows you want to close. This shortcut works with the Close command and the close box.

The Open and Close commands also appear in the contextual menu that pops up when you hold down the Control key and click an icon, as described in Chapter 4. (To see contextual menus, the Simple Finder option must be turned off with the Preferences command in the Finder.)

You can open a folder or file and close the window it's in at the same time. Just press Option while opening the item. This trick works whether you double-click or choose the Open command.

Viewing Folder and Disk Contents

After opening a folder or disk, you'll see its files and folders in a window. You can choose to view those items as *icons*, which you can move around, or as an *ordered list* of item names and other details. You can also choose to see the items as *buttons* that you open by clicking once (instead of double-clicking).

Regardless of a window's view format, you can scroll or size the window to see more of its contents.

Choosing a view

You choose a view format from the View menu. In Mac OS 9, you choose one of three basic formats: icons, buttons, or list. (The View menu has additional commands for choosing variations of the basic formats if the Simple Finder option is turned off in the Preferences dialog box.) Figure 5-2 shows examples of the three basic view formats.

Working with list views

List views can pack a lot of information in a window, and you can use that information to organize the list view. You can sort the list by any of the column headings at the top of the view. You can see the contents of enclosed folders in an indented outline format. Also, you can select items contained in more than one enclosed folder.

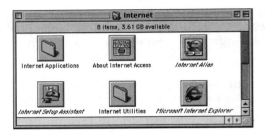

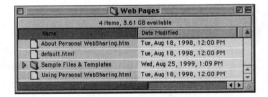

Figure 5-2: Window contents viewed as icons (top), as buttons (middle), or as a list (bottom)

Changing the sort order

When you initially view a window as a list, the items are arranged alphabetically by name. You can sort the list in a different order by clicking one of the column headings near the top of the window. For example, to list the items in the order in which they were last modified, click the Date Modified heading.

A quick glance at the column headings tells you the sort order. The dark heading indicates the sort order in a Mac OS 9 window. You can reverse the sort order by clicking the triangular sort direction indicator (see Figure 5-3 in the next section) at the right end of the column headings.

Rearranging and resizing columns

The columns of a list view are adjustable in Mac OS 9. You can change the size of a column by moving the mouse pointer to the right edge of the column heading, where the pointer shape looks like a sideways pointing arrow. Then press the mouse button and drag left or right. Figure 5-3 is an example of resizing a column in a list view.

Distictive pointer shape ——————   Sort direction indicator

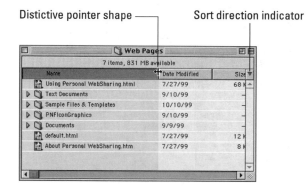

Figure 5-3: Drag a column-heading's borderline to resize the column.

You can also change the order of columns. Simply drag the column heading to the left or right. As you drag, the pointer looks like a hand and you see a pale image of the column you are moving. You can't move the Name column. Figure 5-4 is an example of rearranging columns.

Figure 5-4: Drag a column heading to move the column.

To reset a window's column width and order to the standard configuration, choose Reset Column Positions from the View menu. The Finder asks if you're sure you want to reset the columns. This command affects only one window at a time.

Expanding and collapsing folders

You can open folders to see what's inside, but if you layer lots of folders within folders, windows clutter your screen by the time you reach the innermost folder. There is a faster and easier way. The Finder displays list views in an indented outline format. The levels of indentation in the outline show how folders are nested. The indented outline provides a graphical representation of a folder's organization. You can look through and reorganize folders without opening additional windows. Figure 5-5 is an example of a list view with both expanded and collapsed folders.

Disclosure triangles next to folder names tell you whether the folders are expanded or collapsed. If a triangle points to the right, the folder next to it is collapsed and you cannot see its contents. If the triangle points down, the folder is expanded and you can see a list of the items in the folder indented below the folder name.

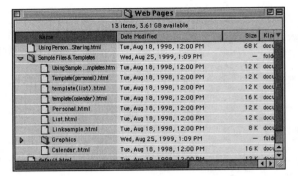

Figure 5-5:
A list view with expanded and collapsed folders

To expand a folder, click the triangle to the left of the folder's icon. When you expand a folder, Finder remembers whether folders nested within it were previously expanded or collapsed and restores each to its former state. Figure 5-6 shows a folder before and after expanding it.

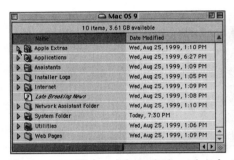

Figure 5-6: Click a right-pointing triangle (Apple Extras on the left) to expand a folder and display its contents (right).

To collapse a folder, click the down-pointing triangle to the left of the folder's icon. It returns to the left-pointing orientation and the contents are no longer displayed.

To collapse a folder and any open subfolders within it, press Option while clicking the disclosure triangle of the outer folder. To expand a folder and all the subfolders within it, press Option while clicking the disclosure triangle.

Selecting from multiple folders

After expanding several folders in a list view, you can select items from more than one of the expanded folders. To select an additional item, press Shift while clicking it. You can also select consecutive items by pressing Shift while dragging a selection rectangle across the consecutive items. If you need to deselect a few items, Shift+click each item or Shift+drag across consecutive items. Figure 5-7 shows a window with items selected from three folders.

Selected items remain selected if you expand other folders in the same window. Selected items also remain selected if you collapse folders in the same window, except that any selected items in a folder you collapse are no longer selected.

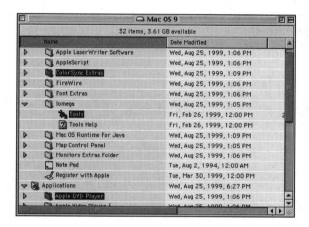

Figure 5-7:
Items selected from
multiple folders

Seeing more contents

If you can't see everything in a window, you can scroll the window or change its size to see more. Each scroll bar becomes active only if using it would bring more into view.

You can scroll a folder or disk window by holding down the ⌘ key and dragging inside the window. While you ⌘+drag, the pointer looks like a gloved hand. You move the window *away* from the direction in which you want to scroll. If you want to scroll down, ⌘+drag *up* to reveal the lower parts of the window.

Smart zooming

A window may not fit its content optimally after you expand or collapse folders in a list view, rearrange icons or buttons in an icon or button view, or simply change from one view to another. You can quickly size a window up or down to fit its contents and view format by clicking the zoom box. The Mac OS makes the window just as large as it needs to be to show as much of the window's contents as will fit on the screen. This smart zooming helps you make best use of your screen's real estate.

If you do want to zoom a window to fill the screen (instead of just large enough to show the window's contents), press Option while clicking the zoom box.

Finder Keyboard Shortcuts

Much of what you do with the mouse you can do with keyboard shortcuts instead. For example, you can select an item in a folder or disk window (or the desktop, if no window is active) without using the mouse by typing the item's name or the first part of its name. Other keystrokes select an item near the currently selected item, open the item, and so on. Table 5-1 gives the details.

Table 5-1 Finder Keyboard Shortcuts	
Objective	**Action**
Icon Shortcuts	
Select an icon by name	Type the icon's full or partial name
Select the next icon alphabetically	Tab
Select the previous icon alphabetically	Shift+Tab
Select the next icon up, down, left, or right	Up arrow (↑), down arrow (↓), left arrow (←), or right arrow (→)
Select the startup disk	⌘+Shift+up arrow (ua)
Select multiple icons	Shift+click each icon or Shift+drag across the icons
Begin editing the selected icon's name	Return or Enter
Insert at the beginning of a selected icon name	Up arrow (↑)
Insert at the end of a selected icon name selected icon name	Down arrow (↓)
Move the insertion point in a selected icon name	Left arrow (←) or right arrow (→)
Align (or don't align) icons or buttons (countermands View Options)	⌘+drag icon or button
Copy an icon to the desktop or another folder on the same disk	Option+drag
Make an alias	⌘+Option+drag
Move selected icons to the Trash	⌘+Delete
Open the selected icon	⌘+O or ⌘+down arrow (↓)
Open the selected icon and close the active window or disk	⌘+Option+O or ⌘+Option+down arrow (↓) or Option+double-click

Objective	Action
Icon Shortcuts	
Open the selected icon's enclosing folder	⌘+up arrow (↑)
Open the selected icon's enclosing folder or disk and close the active window	⌘-Option-up arrow (↑)
Open an enclosing folder or disk of active	⌘+click the window title and window then choose from the pop-up menu
Window Shortcuts	
Zoom a window to its full size	Option+click zoom box
Expand the selected folder in a list view	⌘+right arrow (→)
Expand the selected folder and its enclosed folders	⌘+Option-right arrow (→) or Option+click the triangle
Expand all folders in the active window	⌘+A and then ⌘+right arrow (→)
Expand all folders and their enclosed folders	⌘+A and then ⌘+Option+right arrow (→)
Collapse the selected folder in a list view	⌘+left arrow (←)
Collapse the selected folder and its enclosed folders	⌘+Option+left arrow (←) or Option+click the triangle
Collapse all folders in the active window	⌘+A and then ⌘+left arrow (←)
Collapse all folders and their enclosed folders	⌘+A and then ⌘+Option+left arrow (←)
Close a window	⌘+W
Close all windows	⌘+Option+W or Option+click the close box
Close a pop-up window and remove its tab	⌘+Shift+W
Close all windows and put away all pop-up window tabs	⌘+Shift+Option+W
Close a window while opening the selected item	⌘+Option+O or ⌘+Option+down arrow (↓)
Close a window and make the desktop active	⌘+Option+up arrow (↑)
Collapse all windows	Option+click the collapse box
Move a background window	⌘+drag its title bar

Continued

Table 5-1 (continued)

Objective	Action
Window Shortcuts (continued)	
Collapse a background window ("Double-click" option must be selected in Options tab of Appearance control panel)	Option+double-click its title bar
Hide the active program's windows	Option while making another program active
General Shortcuts	
Switch to the next open application	⌘+Tab*
Switch to the previous application	⌘+Shift+Tab*
Make the desktop active	⌘+Shift+up arrow (↑)
Skip Trash warnings	Option while choosing Empty Trash
Erase a floppy disk	⌘+Option+Tab as you insert the disk
Cancel the operation in progress	⌘+period(.)
Start without extensions	Shift while starting up
Start with Extensions Manager open	Spacebar while starting up
Start up from a disk other than the internal hard disk	⌘+Option+Shift+Delete
Start up from a specific SCSI volume	⌘+Option+Shift+Delete+<*SCSI ID #*>
Start from a CD-ROM (most Macs)	C while starting up
Sleep now (PowerBook only)	⌘+Shift+0 or Control +click menu bar clock
Sleep now (any capable Mac)	Power or ⌘+Option+Power
Restart safely	Power or ⌘+Shift+Power
Shut down safely	Power or ⌘+Option+Shift+Power
Force the active program to quit *and lose unsaved work!*	⌘+Option+Escape
Restart a crashed computer *and lose unsaved work!*	⌘+Control+Power
Rebuild the desktop	⌘+Option during startup or while inserting a disk
Reset Chooser and control panel settings stored in parameter RAM (PRAM)	⌘+Option+P+R while starting up

*Using ⌘+Tab as a shortcut for switching applications in Mac OS 9 conflicts with some application programs, including FileMaker Pro, ClarisWorks, and AppleWorks. See the discussion of the Application Switcher in Chapter 7 for a way to eliminate this conflict.

Working with Files and Folders

There's a lot you can do with the Finder besides fiddling with the way you view the content of folders and disks. You can organize your files in folders, creating new folders as needed and putting files and folders in other folders. You can duplicate a file or folder in the same folder. You can also get rid of files and folders that you don't want to keep.

Creating a new folder

You create a new folder with the New Folder command in the File menu. The new folder is created in the active window or on the desktop if no window is active. This means that you must open a disk or folder before you can create a folder inside it. If the disk or folder is already open but its window is covered by another window, click the window in which you want to create the folder to bring that window to the front. To create a folder on the desktop, click the startup disk icon (or any other desktop icon) to make the desktop active.

If you create a folder in the wrong place, don't sweat it. You can move it as described next.

Moving items

To move an item to a different folder on the same disk, you just drag it to the window or icon of the destination folder. Similarly, you move an item to the root level (main level) of a disk by dragging it to the disk icon or window. To drag an item, you position the pointer over it, press the mouse button, and continue pressing while you move the mouse. The pointer moves across the screen and drags the item you pointed at along with it. You release the mouse button when you get the item positioned over the destination folder icon, disk icon, or window. You can tell when you have the item positioned over the destination because the Finder highlights it. The Finder highlights an icon by making it darker, and it highlights a window by drawing a gray or colored border inside the window frame.

You can move an item in an icon view or list view by dragging its icon or its name. In a list view, you can also drag an item by any text on the same line as the item's icon, such as its modification date or kind. In a window viewed as buttons, you can drag an item only by its name.

If a folder or disk is open, you can move it by dragging the small *proxy icon* in the title bar of its window. To drag a proxy icon, you must place the pointer over it and hold down the mouse button for a second before dragging the icon away. If you don't pause with the mouse button down, you drag the window instead of the proxy icon.

Drag to the main folder

If you're working in a list view and want to move an item from an enclosed folder to the main level of the window, just drag the item to the window header as shown in the figure. A window header is the space just below the title bar where the number of items in the window is reported.

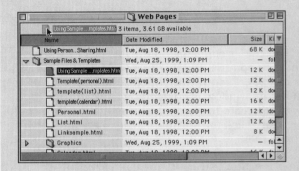

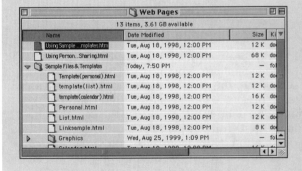

Copying items

To copy an item to another folder on the same disk, press Option while you drag the item to the destination folder. The pointer has a little plus (+) sign to remind you that you're making a copy when you Option+drag.

The Finder always copies an item when you drag it to a folder that's on another disk (or to another disk itself). Again, the Finder displays a little plus (+) sign on the pointer when you drag an item over a folder (or a folder window) of a different disk. When you drag an item to another folder, the Finder figures out whether the destination folder is on the same disk as the source folder. If so, the Finder moves the items you're dragging to the destination folder. If the items you're dragging come from a different disk than the destination folder, the Finder copies the items you're dragging.

Cancel a drag

Oops! Accidentally dragged the wrong icon, or changed your mind while dragging and want to return the item you're dragging to its original location? Just drag it up to the menu bar and release the mouse button as shown in the figure. The Finder returns it to its original location.

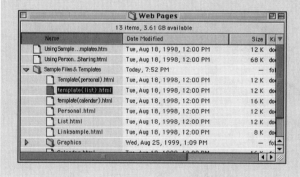

When you copy an item to a disk or folder that already contains an item by the same name, an alert box asks whether you want to replace the item at the destination. The alert tells you which of the like-named items is newer. If you copy a group of items and more than one of them has the same name as items at the destination, the alert doesn't name the duplicates. Figure 5-8 shows examples of the alerts that the Finder displays to verify replacement.

The Finder is also smart about copying an entire floppy disk to a hard disk. It puts the floppy disk's contents in a new folder on the hard disk and gives the folder the same name as the floppy. You can also copy a hard disk to a larger hard disk. You can even copy a whole disk to a folder on another disk (assuming all its contents will fit on the new disk).

Figure 5-8: Confirm imminent replacement of an item (left) or items (right).

Duplicating an item

You can duplicate an item in the same folder by selecting it and choosing Duplicate from the File menu. If the item is a folder, the duplicate contains duplicates of everything in the original folder. You can also duplicate an item by Option+dragging it to another place in the same window. One more way to duplicate an item: choose Duplicate from the contextual menu that pops up when you Control+click the item. (To see contextual menus, the Simple Finder option must be off.)

The Finder constructs the name of a duplicate item you create with the Duplicate command by suffixing the name with the word copy. Additional copies of the same item also have a serial number suffix. Figure 5-9 is an example of several duplicates of an item in the same folder.

Figure 5-9: How the Finder names duplicated items

Note

Icon names can't include colons because the Mac OS uses colons internally to specify the path through your folder structure to a file. A path name consists of a disk name, a succession of folder names, and a file name, with a colon between each pair of names. For example, the path name "Mac OS HD:System Folder:Control Panels:Memory" specifies the location of the Memory control panel on a startup disk named Mac OS HD. Putting a colon in a file name would interfere with the scheme for specifying paths, so the Finder won't let you do it.

Putting stuff back

From time to time you may find that your desktop has become cluttered with files and folders you no longer need to have there. You could drag these items back to some folder, but if you just want to put them back where they came from, there's an easier way. Just select the items you want to put back and use the Put Away command. The Finder returns the selected items to their former locations without opening any folders.

Autoscrolling while moving

You can scroll a window in the Finder without using the scroll bars. Simply place the pointer in the window, press the mouse button, and drag toward the area you want to view, as shown in the figure. Drag the pointer up, down, left, or right past the window's active area to begin scrolling. Dragging past a window corner scrolls diagonally.

As you drag, you can vary the scrolling speed. To scroll slowly, drag just to the window's edge (and continue pressing the mouse button). Increase scrolling speed by dragging beyond the window's edge.

You can use this scrolling technique, known as *autoscrolling*, while performing these operations:

✦ Dragging an icon or group of icons to a new place in any visible window

✦ Dragging an item or group of items to any visible folder or disk icon

✦ Dragging a selection rectangle around adjacent items in the active window to select them all

Be careful when autoscrolling while dragging a selected item or items, especially when autoscrolling to the left. If you accidentally move the pointer completely out of the window and release the mouse button, the Finder places the selected items on the desktop. You can return items from the desktop to their original folder by selecting them and using the Finder's Put Away command.

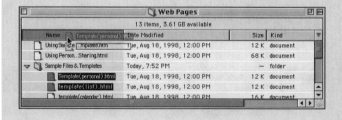

If any suffix results in a name longer than 31 characters, the Finder removes characters from the end of the original item's name. For example, duplicating the item named "June Income and Expense Report" results in an item named "June Income and Expense Re copy."

The Put Away command returns items to the folders they were last in, but does not necessarily return items to their original order in the window.

The Put Away command also works with items in the Trash (discussed in the next section). You can open the Trash, select items you don't want to delete, and use the Put Away command to return them to their former locations.

Deleting files and folders

You get rid of files and folders you no longer want by dragging them to the Trash icon. When you drag a folder to the Trash, everything inside that folder goes to the Trash as well. You can also move an item to the Trash by choosing Move To Trash from the contextual menu that pops up when you Control+click the item.

You don't have to drag things to the Trash with the mouse. Pressing ⌘+Delete moves all selected items to the Trash. (This shortcut doesn't work if the Simple Finder option is turned on.)

Emptying the Trash

Your junk accumulates in the Trash until you explicitly tell the Finder to delete it. You do that by choosing Empty Trash from the Special menu or from the contextual menu that pops up when you Control+click the Trash.

The Finder does not remove locked items. If it encounters one while emptying the Trash, it displays an alert advising you that the Trash contains locked items and asking whether you want to delete the other items or stop deleting. To get rid of locked items in the Trash, press Option while choosing the Empty Trash command.

Trash warnings

When you choose the Empty Trash command, the Finder tells you how many items the Trash contains and how much disk space they occupy. You decide whether to discard them all or cancel. You can disable the Trash warning by pressing Option while choosing the Empty Trash command. Figure 5-10 is an example of the alert that appears when you empty the Trash.

Back from the Trash

When you delete files by emptying the Trash, the disk space occupied by deleted files becomes immediately available for other files. The Empty Trash command removes a file's entry from the disk's file directory. It also changes the disk's sector-allocation table to indicate that the disk sectors the file occupied are available for use by another file.

To save time, the command does not erase file contents in the now-available sectors. Until the system writes a new file over the deleted file's data, the Norton Utilities program from Symantec (408-253-9600, http://www.symantec.com) can resurrect the deleted file. Any blackguard with disk-utility software can retrieve files you deleted — or view any fragment of deleted files' contents — unless you erase their contents with Norton Utilities, SuperTools (described in Chapter 26), or equivalent software. There are actually companies that specialize in sifting through e-mail and other documents that unwary computer users thought they had eliminated by emptying the Trash.

Disable Trash warning

If you always suppress the Trash warning by pressing Option when you choose the Empty Trash command, you may prefer to disable the warnings more permanently. To do that, select the Trash icon and choose Get Info from the File menu. This brings up the Trash Info window. At the bottom of that window, turn off the "Warn before emptying" option by unchecking it and closing the Trash Info window. The figure shows the Trash Info window with the warning turned on.

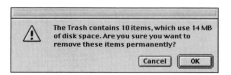

Figure 5-10: Confirm emptying the Trash.

Trash contents

If an item you move to the Trash has the same name as an item already there, the Finder renames the item that's already there. Suppose, for example, that the Trash contains an item named Untitled and you dragged another like-named item there. The Finder renames the item already there to Untitled copy. If you later add another item named Untitled, the Finder changes Untitled copy to Untitled copy 2, changes Untitled to Untitled copy, and leaves the name of the item you just added unchanged. In other words, the item most recently added has the plain name and the least recently added has the highest number suffix.

The Trash contains all the items that you have dragged to it from all the disks whose icons are on the desktop. The Empty Trash command deletes the items from all disks involved. If there's a disk whose trashed items you don't want deleted yet, remove the disk from the desktop as described later in this chapter. The Empty Trash command doesn't affect disks whose icons are not on the desktop. If you can't remove the disk, you have no choice but to open the Trash and drag the items you don't want deleted to the desktop or to a folder. Then use the Empty Trash command.

If you eject a removable disk after dragging items from that disk to the Trash, those items disappear from the Trash, but the Finder does not delete them. They reappear in the Trash the next time you insert that disk. If you insert that removable disk in another Mac, they appear in its Trash.

Sometimes the Trash contains a folder named Rescued Items. This folder contains former temporary files that were found when you started up your Macintosh. The Rescued Items folder appears only after a system crash. Although it's unlikely, you may be able to recreate your work up to the time of the system crash by opening the contents of the Rescued Items folder.

Shared Trash

If you're sharing someone else's disk or folder over a network and you drag an item from the shared disk to the Trash on your desktop, the item goes in your Trash, not in the Trash on the computer where the shared disk or folder resides. The item is removed from that computer if you use the Empty Trash command. From the opposite viewpoint, you do not know when someone sharing your folder drags items from it to his or her Trash. (The owner of a shared disk or folder can set access privileges to keep unauthorized people from dragging items from it to their Trash. Chapter 21 explains how.)

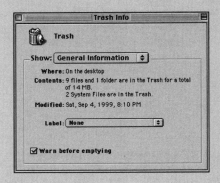

Spring-open folders

You can make a folder or disk spring open when you pause briefly over it. This behavior is normally turned on, but you can use the Finder's Preferences command to adjust the amount of time you must pause until a folder or disk springs open or to turn off spring-loaded opening altogether.

Making folders and disks spring open

A disk or folder springs open automatically if you drag an item to its icon and pause briefly with the pointer positioned over the icon and the mouse button held down. The folder or disk icon flashes twice and opens. This also occurs if you pause while dragging a group of items.

You don't have to pause briefly for a disk or folder to spring open, if you don't want to. To make a disk or folder spring open immediately, drag an item to its icon and press the spacebar.

If you continue holding down the mouse button, you can then drag to a folder icon in the window that just opened and continue deeper into the layers of folders. You may need to travel through a folder that's already open to get into a folder it encloses. Go ahead and drag to the folder's open icon — its open window springs to the front so that you can make a folder in it spring open. If you make the wrong disk or folder spring open by accident, simply drag the pointer out of its window and the window closes automatically.

When you release the mouse button, the Finder moves or copies the item or items you were dragging into the active window. The active window does not close, but all other windows of folders that you made spring open do close automatically. If any of the folders you made spring open were already open, their windows do not close either.

If you change your mind about moving or copying the item you're dragging, just drag it to the menu bar and release the mouse button. The Finder returns the item to the place you got it from.

Actually, folders spring open even if you're not dragging anything but the pointer. To make this happen, begin to double-click the first disk or folder you want to spring open, but don't release the mouse button after pressing it the second time. This gesture is called a *click-and-a-half*, because you make one click and half of a second click. After a brief pause while you continue to hold down the mouse button, the pointer changes to a magnifying glass, the icon flashes twice, and opens. As long as you hold down the mouse button, the pointer remains a magnifying glass and you can continue opening interior folders by pausing over them. Also, after a click-and-a-half you can press the spacebar; the pointer becomes a magnifying glass and the folder or disk opens right away.

Setting spring-open options

To adjust the amount of time you must pause until a folder or disk springs open or to turn off spring-loaded opening altogether, choose Preferences from the Finder's Edit menu. You may need to click the General tab to see the setting for spring-loaded delay time. Figure 5-11 shows the "Spring-loaded folders" option in the Preferences window.

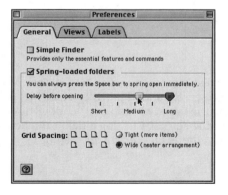

Figure 5-11: Setting options for spring-loaded opening

Finding enclosing folders

Rather than go deeper in your layers of folders, you can go in the other direction and open a folder that encloses an open folder. If the open folder is nested inside several layers of folders, you can quickly open any of those enclosing folders or the disk that encloses them all.

To open any of the nested folders or the disk that encloses an open folder, make the open folder's window active (bring it to the front) and then press ⌘ while clicking the window title. A menu pops up showing the layers of nested folders and the disk that encloses the open folder. You open one of the folders or the disk by choosing it from the pop-up menu. If the outermost folder is on the desktop, the pop-up menu doesn't list an enclosing disk. Figure 5-12 is an example of a folder window's pop-up menu.

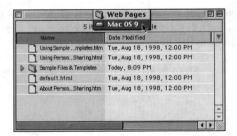

Figure 5-12: Opening an enclosing folder

While opening one of the folders or the disk that encloses an open folder, you can simultaneously close the open folder's window. Simply hold down Option and ⌘, click the menu title, and choose a folder or the disk from the pop-up menu. You must start holding down Option and ⌘ before clicking the window title. If you ⌘+click the window title and then press Option while choosing from the pop-up menu, the window opens for the folder you chose but the previously active window doesn't close.

Using pop-up windows

In the Finder, you can change any folder or disk window to a pop-up window. A pop-up window is anchored to the bottom of the screen, and in place of a title bar, it has a tab labeled with the window title. Clicking the tab at the top of a window closes the window and leaves the tab at the bottom of the screen. Clicking a tab at the bottom of the screen makes the window pop up from there. Figure 5-13 shows both states of a pop-up window.

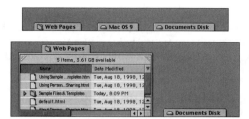

Figure 5-13: Clicking a tab at the bottom of the screen displays a pop-up window, and clicking the tab of an open window closes it and leaves its tab showing.

Pop-up windows are easy to find and open, so they're great places to keep stuff you use often. You can move or copy items to a pop-up window by dragging them to its tab. This works whether the pop-up window is open or closed. When you drag an item to the tab of a closed window, the window pops up. If the window is set for icon or button view, then you can continue dragging inside the window to place the icon or button where you want it.

When you drag something out of a pop-up window, the Finder automatically closes the window when the mouse button is released. If you need to drag several items from a pop-up window to a common destination, select them all and drag them as a group. If you drag them individually, you have to pop up the window for each one.

Making a pop-up window

You can make a regular disk or folder window into a pop-up window by choosing "as Pop-up Window" from the View menu while the window is active. Another method is to drag the window's title bar to the bottom of the screen, where it changes to the tab of a collapsed pop-up window.

If you already have several pop-up windows and you try to make another one whose tab won't fit in the available space at the bottom of the screen, the Finder displays an alert explaining why you can't make another pop-up window. Remember that the length of a pop-up window's name directly affects the size of the window's tab. You can make room for more tabs by abbreviating the names of existing pop-up windows and by moving tabs as close together as possible at the bottom of the screen, as described under the next heading.

To make a pop-up window into a regular window, choose "as Window" from the View menu while the pop-up window is active; the pop-up window must be open to be active. You can also make a pop-up window into a regular window by dragging its tab up toward the top of the screen. As you drag, you see the outline of the window, and eventually the outline changes to the rectangular shape of a regular window. When you see the regular window shape, release the mouse button and you have a regular window.

Moving a pop-up window

You can move a pop-up window left and right by dragging its tab along the bottom of the screen. This enables you to arrange pop-up window tabs in any order you like. Be sure to drag a pop-up window's tab while the window is closed. If you drag the tab while the window is open, it becomes a regular window.

To move a tab as close to its neighbor as possible, drag the tab so that it partially overlaps its neighbor and release the mouse button. When you drag, don't let the pointer touch the neighbor or the tab you're dragging will snap back to its former location when you release the mouse button.

Sizing a pop-up window

While a pop-up window is open, you can change its size by dragging one of the two size boxes at its top corners. The size boxes can adjust the width and height of the window. You can also adjust the height alone by dragging the pop-up window's tab up or down. Remember that if you drag the tab high enough, you make the pop-up into a regular window.

Closing a pop-up window

As mentioned previously, clicking any pop-up window tab closes the pop-up window that's open. You can also close a pop-up window by pressing ⌘+W. You can close a pop-up window and convert it to a regular window (removing its tab from the bottom of the screen) by pressing ⌘+Shift+W. Pressing ⌘+Shift+Option+W converts all pop-up windows to regular windows and closes all Finder windows.

Working with Disks

Every Mac has at least one disk, and its icon appears initially in the upper-right corner of the desktop. It's called the *startup disk* because it contains the software needed to start up the computer, and the startup disk can't be removed from the computer.

In addition, every Mac can use at least one kind of disk that you can remove from the computer. After removing this disk, you can insert another disk of the same kind. These may be floppy disks (also known as *diskettes*), CD-ROMs, DVD-ROMs, Zip disks, or some combination of these, and possibly other kinds of disks as well. Each removable disk can contain different applications and document files. Whenever you insert any kind of removable disk, its icon appears on the desktop and you can open the disk icon to work with the files it contains. Some kinds of removable disks can be erased so that you can reuse them to store different applications and documents.

Removing disks

There are two ways to remove a disk: one is to use the Eject or Put Away menu command and the other is to drag the disk to the Trash.

Eject and Put Away commands

The official way to remove a floppy disk, CD-ROM, or other removable disk from your desktop is to select its icon and choose Eject from the Special menu. You can also Control+click the disk icon to pop up its contextual menu and choose Eject from it. (To see contextual menus, the Simple Finder option must be off.) You can also use the Put Away command to remove a disk.

The Eject and Put Away commands remove the disk's icon from the desktop and make its contents unavailable. If the disk is a floppy disk, CD-ROM, DVD-ROM, Zip disk, or other removable media (optical disk, Jaz, SyQuest, SyJet, and so on), dragging its icon to the Trash ejects the disk from the disk drive. With other types of removable disks, you may have to push a button or flip a lever on the disk drive to remove the disk.

If folders on a removable disk are open when you eject the disk, then, as you might expect, the folders' windows disappear. The same windows appear again the next time you insert the disk (the folders remain open), even if you insert the disk in a different Mac. There is an exception to this behavior: If you eject a disk from a computer that has Mac OS 8–9 and later insert the disk in a computer that has an earlier Mac OS version, the windows are closed.

Dragging a disk to the Trash

The shortcut for removing a disk icon is to drag it to the Trash. Lots of people use this shortcut because it's so convenient, even though it doesn't exactly make sense. If you think about it, dragging a disk to the Trash could just as easily mean that you never want to use that disk again—that is, erase it. By convention, though, dragging a disk to the Trash means that you want to get rid of its icon, not its contents.

If you have more than one hard disk icon, you may be able to remove one that's not your startup disk by dragging the icon to the Trash. The Eject command doesn't work with most hard disk icons, but the Put Away command does. Removing a hard disk from the desktop, which is called *unmounting* the disk, makes its contents unavailable. The reverse process, which is called *mounting* the disk, happens every time you start the computer. You can also mount disks using the Drive Setup utility program that comes with Mac OS 9, or with a disk utility such as Mt. Everything (described in Chapter 26).

Erasing disks

Removable disks that are not read-only or locked can also be erased, or *initialized*. Erasing a disk removes all of the files and folders it contains. When you open a disk after erasing it, you see no folders and no files in its window. Be sure this is what you want *before* you erase a disk.

To erase a disk, you select its icon and choose Erase Disk from the Special menu. The Finder displays a dialog box that asks you to confirm that you really want to erase the disk, and that includes a space to edit the disk name. The capability to change the name is purely for your convenience. You can edit the disk icon's name later, as described in the previous chapter. (However, if file sharing is turned on as described in Chapter 21, you cannot change the name of any disk larger than 2MB.)

Erasing a disk creates a blank disk directory — a process called initialization — which wipes out the means of accessing the existing files on the disk without actually touching the files themselves. The contents of all your old files are still on a disk after you erase it, but there's no easy way to get at them. It's sort of like someone erased the book catalog of a library. The books are still on the shelves, but there is no way to look them up.

In fact, you can recover deleted files after erasing a disk by using the Norton Utilities program from Symantec (408-253-9600, http://www.symantec.com). The same program can erase a disk so that no one can recover files from it.

Mac OS Extended (HFS Plus)

Mac OS versions 8.1 and higher give you the option of erasing (initializing) large disk volumes (32MB or larger) with the Mac OS Extended format, also known as HFS Plus. This format has these advantages over the older Mac OS Standard format, also known as HFS (Hierarchical File System):

✦ The Mac OS Extended format requires less disk space than the Standard Mac OS format to store small files on a large disk. For example, a file that contains 4K or less of data will occupy 64K on a 4GB Mac OS Standard volume, but only 4K on a 4GB Mac OS Extended volume.

✦ The Mac OS Extended format permits a disk to store a far greater number of files (250,000 or more on a 1GB disk).

✦ The Mac OS Extended format allows for extremely large file sizes (up to 2 terabytes, which is 2000 gigabytes).

✦ The Mac OS Extended format reports the creation time and modification time of each file accurately in any time zone. For example, a file last changed at 9 a.m. in San Francisco will have a modification time of 12 p.m. in New York and 6 a.m. in Honolulu. (With Mac OS Standard format, this file would have a modification time of 9 a.m. in all time zones.) Mac OS Extended saves a file's creation and modification times in Greenwich Mean Time (GMT), but reports the adjusted times for the current time zone, whereas the Mac OS Standard format saves the times in local time and cannot adjust for time zone changes.

Offsetting these advantages are these disadvantages:

✦ Mac OS 8 and earlier versions can't access files or folders on a Mac OS Extended disk. People who use Mac OS 8 and earlier cannot share your removable disks that use the Mac OS Extended format. If you want to go back to an earlier Mac OS version, you have to reformat your disks that use the Mac OS Extended format.

✦ Older Macintosh disk utility programs, including old versions of Disk First Aid and Norton Utilities for Macintosh, are incompatible with the Mac OS Extended format and can destroy data stored on a Mac OS Extended disk.

Converting to Mac OS Extended format

You can convert a disk to the Mac OS Extended format by erasing it. Obviously, before you erase a disk you must have an up-to-date backup copy from which to restore the disk's contents after erasing. Instead of erasing, you can also convert a disk to Mac OS Extended format using a utility program such as PlusMaker from Alsoft (281-353-409, http://www.alsoft.com) or SpaceMaker 1.0 from Total Recall (719-380-1616, http://www.spacemaker.recallusa.com). Just to be safe, you should make a backup copy of the disk before converting with a utility program.

To erase a disk using the Mac OS Extended format, select the disk and choose Erase from the Finder's Special menu. Then, in the dialog box that appears, choose Mac OS Extended from the Format pop-up menu, as shown in Figure 5-14.

Figure 5-14: Store more small files on a large disk by erasing it with the Mac OS Extended format.

Do not erase your startup disk with the Mac OS Extended format unless you have a spare Mac OS startup disk (Mac OS version 8.1 or higher, so it can read a Mac OS Extended format disk). In the event you have trouble starting from your regular Mac OS Extended startup disk, you will need the spare Mac OS startup disk to access files on your Mac OS Extended disks. You can use a Mac OS installation CD-ROM as a spare startup disk.

Determining a disk's format

To determine whether a disk has been formatted as Mac OS Standard or Mac OS Extended, look in its Info window. To display a disk's Info window, select the disk icon on the desktop. Then choose Get Info from the File menu. Figure 5-15 shows Info windows of disks that use the Mac OS Extended and the Mac OS Standard formats.

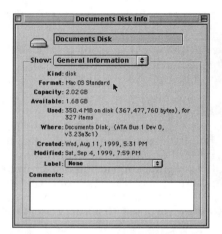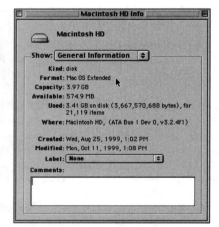

Figure 5-15: A disk's Info window tells you the disk's format: Mac OS Extended (left) or Mac OS Standard (right).

Fine-Tuning Views

You can clean up icons or buttons by aligning them to an invisible grid whenever you want, or you can have the Finder keep them aligned automatically. You can arrange or sort items by name, kind, or another criterion. You can select an icon or button size for any view. In a list view, you can select which columns of information are displayed about items in the view. An additional option lets you force the contents of an icon or button view to stay arranged in a particular order, such as by name.

You can also fine-tune each window individually, or you can make all the windows adhere to standard options.

Cleaning up icons or buttons

When icons or buttons are in disarray, you can have the Finder align them in neat rows and columns. You clean up the active window by choosing Clean Up from the View menu. Figure 5-16 shows a window before and after being cleaned up.

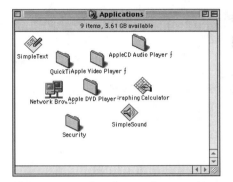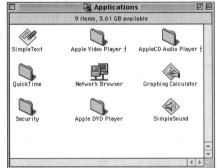

Figure 5-16: Cleaning up icons or buttons: before (left) and after (right) using the Clean Up command

You can clean up individual icons by holding down the ⌘ key while dragging them singly or in groups — unless the Snap to Grid option is turned on (as described later in this section). If that option is turned on, the Finder aligns icons when you drag them normally — without pressing the ⌘ key.

Arranging icons or buttons

While the Finder is cleaning up icons or buttons, you can have it arrange them in a particular order, such as by name or modification date. The Finder arranges icons first by the attribute you choose and second by name if necessary. For example, if you arrange by kind, then all application icons will come before all folder icons; the application icons will be arranged alphabetically by name before the alphabetically arranged folder icons. The first icon goes in the upper-left corner, and remaining icons fill the window from left to right and top to bottom.

You arrange and clean up icons by choosing the order you want from the Arrange submenu of the View menu. You do not need to choose Clean Up as well. Figure 5-17 shows a window before and after being arranged (and simultaneously cleaned up) by icon name.

You can clean up the desktop by clicking any desktop icon to make the desktop active and then choosing the order you want from the Arrange submenu. In this case, the Finder puts the startup disk icon in the upper-right corner and fills the desktop from top to bottom and right to left. No matter which order you choose, the Finder always arranges desktop icons in groups in this order: hard disk volumes, desktop printers, floppy disks and other removable disks, shared disks and folders, and all other icons. The Trash icon always goes in the bottom-right corner of the desktop.

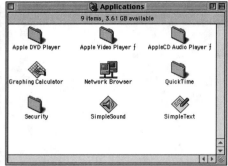

Figure 5-17: Arranging and cleaning up icons or buttons: before (left) and after (right)

Sorting a list view

Much as you can have the Finder arrange icons in a window, you can have it sort a list view. The most direct method is to click the heading of the column by which you want to sort the list, as mentioned in the previous chapter. Alternatively, you can choose a sort order from the Sort submenu of the View menu.

Setting view options

Additional view options let you change the format and contents of folder and disk windows. You can set the icon size for each window, regardless of the type of view. You can have the Finder keep icons arranged automatically. You can set the spacing between icons and buttons. You can determine which columns appear in a list view.

Text font and size

To set the font and font size used in all disk and folder windows, open the Appearance control panel, choose Control Panels from the Apple menu, and then double-click the Appearance control panel in the Control Panels window, or, if you have submenus turned on, just select Appearance from the submenu that pops out. At the top of the Appearance control panel, click the Fonts tab. Then choose a font from the Views Font pop-up menu and choose a font size from the Size pop-up menu. If you want to use a size that isn't listed in the pop-up menu, you can enter any size between 9 and 24 in the space provided (see Figure 5-18).

After changing the font or the font size, use the Clean Up command to adjust the spacing of icons on the desktop and in windows. You must clean up each window individually.

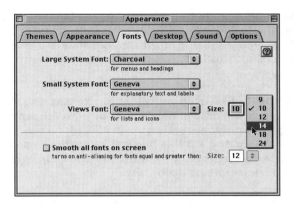

Figure 5-18: Setting a font and size for all icon names and list-view text

Tip   The standard font is Geneva and the standard font size is 10, but you should try Geneva 9. The italic style used for alias names looks better and is easier to edit in Geneva 9 because there is a special italic Geneva 9 font installed in the system. (For more information on aliases, see Chapter 14, and for more information on fonts, see Chapter 15.)

Icon or button view options

You can set the size and automatic arrangement of icons or buttons on the desktop and in each window whose contents you view as icons or buttons. To set these view options for a window, bring it to the front and choose View Options from the View menu. To set these options for the desktop, click any desktop icon to make the desktop active and then choose View Options from the View menu. Figure 5-19 shows the View Options dialog box for icon and button views.

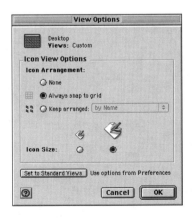
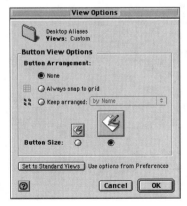

Figure 5-19: Setting view options for an icon view (left) or button view (right) in Mac OS 9

If you customize a window's view options, a button labeled "Set to Standard Views" becomes available in the View Options dialog box. Clicking this button makes all the settings in this particular View Options dialog box match the standard view settings from the Preference command. This button is disabled when the current settings match the standard settings.

Setting the Icon Arrangement or the Button Arrangement option to "Always snap to grid" or "Keep arranged" makes icons you drag in the window align to the same grid as the Clean Up command. When either of these settings is in effect for a window, you see an icon at the left end of the window's status bar, just below the close box. The icon in the window matches the current setting of the Icon Arrangement or the Button Arrangement option in the View Options dialog box.

You can temporarily reverse the state of an "Always snap to grid" or "Keep arranged" setting by pressing ⌘ while dragging icons. If either of those settings is selected, ⌘+dragging temporarily disables forced grid alignment. If neither of those settings is selected, then ⌘+dragging temporarily enables forced grid alignment.

The distance between aligned icons or buttons is determined by the Grid Spacing option of the Preferences command. This option applies to all windows and the desktop, but affects each window only when you next make a change to it.

List view options

You can set the icon size and select what information you want shown in each window viewed as a list. To set these view options for a window, bring it to the front and choose View Options from the View menu. Figure 5-20 shows the View Options dialog box for list views.

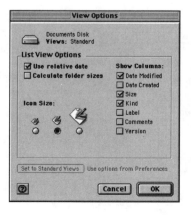

Figure 5-20: Setting view options for a list view

A list view includes an icon and a name for every item in the window. You can select which of seven other columns of information you want displayed. By selecting just the columns you need to see in a window, you can see most or all columns without scrolling the window. Click a window's zoom box to make it just wide enough to show all the columns you selected for display. If the window can't be made wide enough to show all the columns you selected for display, the window fills the screen and you have to scroll horizontally to see some columns. You may be able to reduce or eliminate horizontal scrolling in Mac OS 9 by making columns narrower. To resize columns, drag the lines that separate the column headings.

You can set the icon size in each window to standard (large), small, or tiny. Standard icons are the size you usually see on the desktop. Small icons are the size you see in the Apple and Application menus. Tiny icons are so small that you don't see any unique detail, just a generic folder, application, or document icon.

The Comments column normally shows the first 25 characters of the comments entered in each item's Info window. You can see more or less by dragging the right edge of the Comments header to change the column width. (For details on changing comments, see "Adding Comments" later in this chapter.)

The option "Use relative date" has the Finder display "today" instead of today's date or "yesterday" instead of yesterday's date in the Date Created and the Date Modified columns. For other dates, the Finder uses the date format set in the Date & Time control panel (as described in Chapter 12). If you resize a date column, the Finder automatically changes the date format to fit. For example, a standard-width column that shows "Mon, Aug 27, 2001 12:00 PM" would show just "8/27/01 12:00 PM"; or "8/27/01" in a narrower column; or "Monday, August 27, 2001" in a wider column.

The option "Calculate folder sizes" has the Finder display the size of each folder in the window. It takes a while for the Finder to add up the sizes of items in a large folder. You can keep working on other tasks while the Finder calculates folder sizes, but calculating folder sizes reduces the system's performance for doing other work.

Standard view options

Windows that don't have custom view settings adhere to standard view settings from the Finder's Preferences command. You can change the standard settings by choosing Preferences from the Finder's Edit menu and clicking the Views tab at the top of the Preferences window. You change the standard settings for icon, button, and list views separately. Use the pop-up menu near the top of the Preferences window to choose the type of view whose settings you want to change. Changes you make to standard settings immediately affect all windows that don't have custom settings; windows with custom settings are not affected. Figure 5-21 shows the standard view settings in the Preferences window.

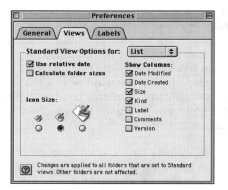

Figure 5-21: Changing standard view settings with the Preferences command

You can make a window adhere to the standard view settings from the Preferences command by clicking the button labeled "Set to Standard Views" in its View Options dialog box (as explained previously in this section).

Labeling Items and Adding Comments

The Finder enables you to add comments to each item's icon. It also enables you to classify folders, programs, and documents by labeling them with a word or phrase. On monitors displaying at least 16 colors, labeling an item also changes its color.

Adding comments

You can attach notes or comments to folders and files in their Info windows. To display an item's Info window, select it and choose Get Info from the File menu. Alternatively, you can Control+click an item to display its contextual menu and then choose Get Info from it. At the bottom of the Info window, you can type anything you want (to a maximum of 199 characters) in the space provided for comments. Although the window has no scroll bar to see lengthy comments, you can scroll by pressing the arrow keys or by dragging the pointer past the borders of the entry box. Figure 5-22 shows comments in an Info window.

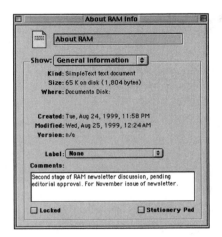

Figure 5-22: Viewing comments in an Info window

Applying labels

To label an item, select the item and choose a label from the Label submenu of the Finder's File menu. Figure 5-23 shows the Label submenu.

Figure 5-23: Specifying a label for selected icons

You can also set an item's label in the item's Info window. Select the item, choose Get Info from the File menu, and use the Label pop-up menu in the Info window.

Using labels

After labeling items, you can view a folder or disk window's contents arranged by label. You can also search for items by label with the Finder's Find command. Label colors also show up in the Apple menu and in the dialog boxes used by many programs' Open and Save commands. Figure 5-24 shows a folder window sorted by label.

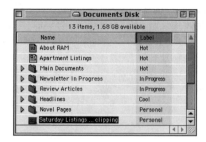

Figure 5-24: Sorting by label

The Finder's Find command actually summons the Sherlock utility program, which is discussed in Chapter 6.

Changing label names and colors

You change the standard label names and colors with the Finder's Preferences command. Figure 5-25 shows the Labels settings in the Preferences window.

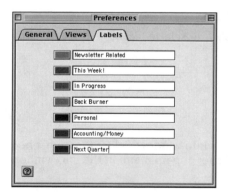

Figure 5-25: Changing label colors or names

If you click a label color to change it, the Finder displays the standard Color Picker dialog box. You can select the type of color picker you want to use from the list on the left side of the dialog box. You pick a new color by clicking a color wheel, adjusting sliders, typing numbers, or clicking a color swatch, depending on the type of color picker you select. For example, the Crayon Picker has swatches that look like crayons. The HLS Picker has a color wheel, which you can use to specify hue (dominant color) and saturation (amount of color); a slider, which you can use to specify lightness (closeness to black or white); and spaces where you can enter hue, saturation, and lightness numerically.

You can also pick up any color displayed on the screen by holding down Option, which turns the pointer into an eyedropper, and clicking the color you want to pick up. Figure 5-26 shows the HLS picker in the Color Picker dialog box, and Table 5-2 lists the HLS settings for the standard label colors (in case you want to reset them after experimenting).

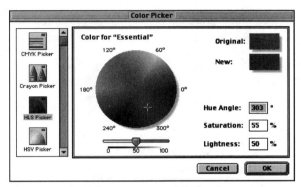

Figure 5-26: Picking a custom label color

Table 5-2 Values for Standard Label Colors			
Label	**Hue Angle**	**Saturation**	**Lightness**
Essential	23°	100%	50%
Hot	1°	97%	86%
In Progress	328°	97%	95%
Cool	196°	99%	92%
Personal	240°	100%	83%
Project 1	131°	100%	39%
Project 2	29°	94%	34%

Tip

Select the Crayon Picker while using the Color Picker and you see a box of 60 crayons in various premixed colors with fanciful names such as Obsidian, Marigold, and Dirt. Instead of clicking each crayon to see a sample of its color and its name on the right side of the dialog box, you can drag across the crayons and watch the color sample and the name change. Hold down Option and click the edge of a crayon to pick up a lighter or darker shade of color, which is appropriately named with the suffix "-ish."

Transparent labels

If you've avoided icon labels because they discolor your beautiful color icons, you need shun them no longer. You can label a color icon without changing its color—provided the label color is white. You can still view the Finder windows by label, find items by label, and so on.

To make a label transparent, display the Finder's Preferences window and click the color of the label that you want to use. The standard Color Picker dialog box appears. On the left side of the dialog box, select the HLS Picker. Then set the Hue Angle to 0 degrees, Saturation to 0 percent, and Lightness to 100 percent. You can type the three values in the spaces provided, or you can click the center of the color wheel and adjust the slider.

Protecting Files, Folders, and Disks

The Mac OS lets you protect files and folders individually so that they can't be changed. You can lock a file with the Get Info command, lock folders with the Sharing command, and specially protect the System Folder and Applications folder with the General Controls control panel. In addition, you can lock some disks so that their contents can't be erased and their contents can't be changed. If you want even more protection, consider setting up your Mac for multiple users as described in Chapter 13.

Locking a file

To lock a file, select its icon and use the Get Info command to display the file's Info window, as shown in Figure 5-27. At the bottom of the Info window is a Locked option. If you turn it on, you can open the file and copy its contents, but you can't change its contents or its name. In addition, the Finder does not delete locked files that are in the Trash unless you press Option while choosing the Empty Trash command (as discussed earlier in this chapter). You can tell a file is locked by the small lock-shaped badge on its icon.

Locking a folder

You can protect against moving, renaming, or deleting a folder by using the Finder's Sharing command. Normally, the Sharing command is used to control who has access to your folder over a network (as described in Chapter 21), but the Sharing command is also useful for simple folder protection.

To lock a folder, select its icon and choose Sharing from the Get Info submenu of the Finder's File menu to display the folder's sharing information. Turn on the option labeled "Can't move, rename, or delete this item (locked)." You don't have to actually share the folder or change any other sharing settings for the folder. A locked folder has a small lock-shaped badge. Figure 5-28 shows the sharing information of a locked folder.

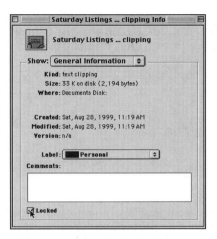

Figure 5-27: Locking a file with the Get Info command

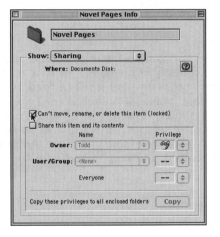

Figure 5-28: Locking a folder with the Sharing command

The Sharing command only locks folders while file sharing is turned on in the File Sharing control panel. In fact, you can't even bring up a Sharing window while file sharing is off. If you try, the Sharing command displays an alert saying you must turn on file sharing and offers to open the appropriate control panel so that you can turn it on. If you lock some folders while file sharing is on and later turn file sharing off, the folders are unlocked until you turn file sharing on again.

Protecting the System Folder and Applications folder

The Mac OS can protect the contents of two special folders in the startup disk, the System Folder and the Applications folder. You set this protection with the option "Protect System Folder" and the option "Protect Applications folder" in the General Controls control panel. You can use these options only if file sharing is turned off (as detailed in Chapter 21). Figure 5-29 shows the General Controls control panel.

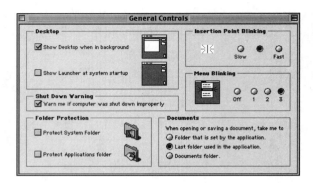

Figure 5-29: Setting folder protection with the General Controls control panel

Turning on folder protection prevents anyone from moving, renaming, or deleting items directly enclosed by the protected folder. The protection does not extend to items in folders enclosed by the protected folder. For example, with System Folder protection turned on, you cannot move, rename, or delete the Control Panels folder, but you can do all those things to individual control panels inside the Control Panels folder.

Note   At the time of writing, System Folder and Applications folder protection in the General Controls panel was not working correctly in prerelease versions of the Mac OS 9. This is a known issue, but it's not clear whether it will be fixed in the Mac OS 9's general release or in a later update. If General Controls doesn't work as described for you (for instance, if the Protect System Folder and Protect Applications folder items are gray and can't be selected), check Apple's Support site (http://www.apple.com/support/) and make sure that you're using the Software Update feature (described in Chapter 12) to keep current with Apple's bug fixes and new releases.

Locking a disk

You can lock floppy disks and some other disks. After locking a disk, you can't erase it, change its name, copy files to it, duplicate files on it, or move files and folders it contains to the desktop or the Trash. A locked disk is said to be *write protected*.

To lock a floppy disk, you slide the tab in the corner of the disk so that the square hole is open. You unlock a floppy disk by sliding the tab so that the square hole is closed.

Some other removable disks have locking mechanisms on their cases. Check the instructions that came with your removable disks or disk drive for specific information about locking them.

You may be able to lock or write-protect your hard disk using the setup program that came with it. For example, you can write-protect an Apple hard disk with the Drive Setup program.

Doing Background Work

The Finder can perform most of its time-consuming work in the background, while you continue doing other work in the Finder or other programs. For example, you can copy files or empty the Trash while opening folders, renaming icons, setting view options, or editing notes with Stickies. You can open control panels and applications (as described in Chapter 7) while the Finder works in the background. You can even start copying a batch of files before an ongoing copy operation finishes. Figure 5-30 shows two copy operations under way simultaneously while the Get Info command is about to be used.

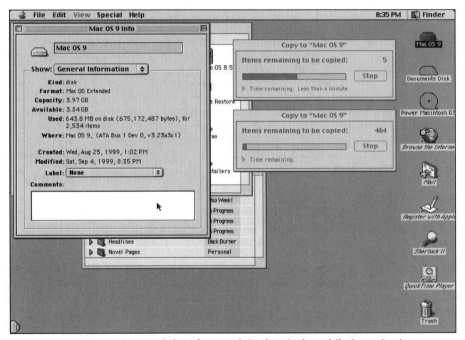

Figure 5-30: Use menus and do other work in the Finder while it copies items or empties the Trash.

The performance of your computer suffers while the Finder works on a task in the background. Furthermore, a background task proceeds more slowly than it does in the foreground. If the computer gets really busy with the background task, the mouse and keyboard may seem to stop working for a few seconds. If you type faster than the screen can display the characters, the system remembers the most recent 20 characters you type (about 5 seconds of typing at 40 words per minute). The system can also remember one click or double-click and can catch up with your dragging as long as you don't release the mouse button.

Summary

This chapter showed you how to boil down the Finder to its essential commands by turning on the Simple Finder option with the Preferences command. Double-clicking or using the Open command with a disk, folder, or file displays its contents in a window. Conversely, the Close command or close box puts a window away when you don't want to see it any more. While a folder or disk window is open, you can use the View menu to see the window's contents as icons, buttons, or a list. In a list view, you can change the sort order by clicking a column heading. You can rearrange columns by dragging their headings, and you can resize columns by dragging the borderlines of their headings. Also, you can expand and collapse folders in a list view by clicking the disclosure triangles next to their names. With enclosed folders expanded, you can select items from multiple folders at the same time.

You can do more with the Finder than just view the contents of your disks and folders. You can create a new folder with the New Folder command; drag items to copy or move them; duplicate items with the Duplicate command; drag items to the Trash to delete them; and to empty the Trash with the Empty Trash command. If there's more than one disk on your desktop, you can remove a disk by dragging it to the Trash or by using the Eject command. You can erase a disk with the Erase disk command using either the Mac OS Extended format or the older Mac OS Standard format. Aside from erasing disks, the Finder can do most of its time-consuming work in the background while you do other work with it or another program at the same time.

Thanks to spring-loaded folders, it's not necessary to do a lot of double-clicking to traverse layers of folders. You can zip through folder layers toward the enclosing disk; you can make folders spring open as you delve deeper through layers of folders.

This chapter also showed you how to make a pop-up window with the View menu or by dragging any window to the bottom of the screen. You can move a pop-up window by dragging its tab and change its size with its two size boxes. You also know how to fine-tune folder and disk windows. You can choose a font and a font size for the text in all windows. You can clean up or arrange windows viewed as icons or buttons. You can sort a window viewed as a list and determine the columns it displays. You can resize and rearrange the columns in a list view.

In this chapter, you also learned to attach comments to items and to lock files with the Get Info command. Likewise, you can classify folders, programs, and documents by applying labels. You can arrange a list view by label, and you can search for items by label with the Finder's Find command. Plus, you can change label names or colors.

Finally, you learned to lock folders with the Sharing command, protect the System Folder and the Applications folder with the General Controls control panel, and lock disks with locking mechanisms on their cases or with their disk setup programs.

✦   ✦   ✦

Searching with Sherlock

In Mac OS 8.5, Apple renamed the Find File utility "Sherlock" and, along with its clever name, offered a more robust tool, one that could perform two new tricks: it could search inside documents for content as well as search the Internet. In Mac OS 9, Sherlock is upgraded to Sherlock 2 and adds to that feature set, including a new interface and more features for performing searches.

Sherlock performs two basic functions: It searches for files on your hard disk or it searches the Internet using keywords. Within those types of searches, it can get pretty sophisticated. For instance, for file searches, you can search by name, by the contents of the file (if the file has text in it), or by any number of other Mac OS criteria, such as the file creation date, the file size, and so on. For Internet searches, you can search all different types of sites, including popular Web search engines (Yahoo!, HotBot, Excite, and so on), people-search sites, references sites, auction sites, and many others.

This chapter begins by discussing the basics of the Sherlock 2 interface — why it looks the way it does. Then, I cover all three major types of searches, and take a look all the new customization features that make Sherlock a full-blown application that you're likely to spend some time using.

The Sherlock Interface

Sherlock 2 sports a new shiny, metallic interface that seems to be the direction Apple is headed with new features it's creating. The first application with this look was the new QuickTime Player included with QuickTime 4.0 (and, hence, with Mac OS 9). Now Sherlock is also updated with this brushed-metal scheme. Whether or not you like the look is up to you.

New Feature

Sherlock 2 is new to Mac OS 9. Aside from its updated appearance, it adds the capability to customize the type of Internet searches you perform (offering different types of searches for Web sites, shopping items, and people, for example) and the results window. (By the way, throughout this chapter we just refer to it as "Sherlock" to keep things simple.)

Launching Sherlock

Before you can judge its shiny new interface for yourself, you need to open up Sherlock. There are several ways to do that, including:

✦ From the Finder, choose File ➪ Find. You can also choose File ➪ Search Internet to load Sherlock and have it automatically open to Internet searching.

✦ Again, while in the Finder, type ⌘+F to search for files or ⌘+H to search the Internet.

✦ From any application, select the Apple menu and choose Sherlock 2.

Using the Sherlock window

More important than Sherlock's appearance (at least for our purposes) is that the redesign of Sherlock also works against some of the conventions we're used to seeing in Mac OS applications. Although the difference isn't dramatic, you may still need to spend a little time getting used to the way Sherlock operates. Figure 6-1 offers a quick look at the Sherlock window.

At the top of the Sherlock window are the channels, which enable you to switch between different types of searches. Each icon represents a different grouping of search criteria—most of them are actually groupings of Internet search sites. Click a channel and the Sherlock window may animate a bit as it changes to another configuration.

The channels area is actually larger than appears on the screen by default. To expand the number of channels you can see on the screen, click and drag the handle that appears beneath the row channels. Drag it down to reveal more channel icons, if you have them—otherwise, you'll see blank spaces where you can add more channels, if you like. (Creating channels is discussed later in the section "Build your own channels.") Figure 6-2 shows an expanded channels area.

Below the channels is the keyword box, where you enter keywords for your various types of searches. Click in the box to place an insertion point, then type the keywords for your particular search. After entering your keywords, press Return or click the magnifying glass icon to begin searching.

Below the keyword box you may have an area of radio buttons and menu items, depending on the type of search you're doing. A file search, for instance, allows you to choose the type of search and the criteria for that search. Internet searches, on the other hand, won't have these options.

The list area features a listing of whatever is relevant for your search. Before you've performed a search, the list area shows you either the disks or the Internet sites you can search, depending on the type of search you're trying to implement. Once you've completed a search, the list area will change to show the results, as shown in Figure 6-3.

Figure 6-1: The Sherlock 2 window is a little different from the typical Mac OS application.

Figure 6-2: Click and drag to see more channels.

Figure 6-3: A successful search turns up possible results that are displayed in the list area.

The bottom pane of the Sherlock interface is an information area, which displays information about whatever is selected in the list area. If you select an Internet site, for instance, information about that site is displayed. If you select a document in the list area, the path to that document (its folder, enclosing folder, and ultimately the disk it's stored on) is displayed in the information area. Figure 6-4 shows a path.

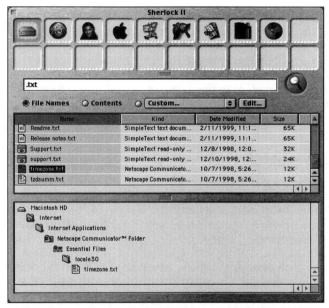

Figure 6-4: Information about an item selected in the list area appears in the information area.

The list area and information area are also separated by another bar with a handle that you can drag to resize the areas relative to one another if you can't see enough of an area's contents.

Finally, you'll notice that the Sherlock window itself is different, failing to follow some Mac OS conventions for typical windows. The title bar doesn't feature a collapse box or a zoom box. Also, double-clicking the title bar will not collapse the window, even if that feature is activated in the Appearance control panel.

At the bottom-right corner of the Sherlock window there is a size box; you can click and drag that box to resize the overall Sherlock window. And, as with any Mac OS window, you can grab any edge of it (except the size box) and drag the window to another location on the screen.

Note   Clicking the close box in Sherlock closes the application, not just the window.

Finding Items

No matter how carefully you organize your folders and disks, there comes a time when you can't find a file or folder without a lot of digging through layers of folders. Sherlock's Find command fetches lost or buried items with less effort. When you choose Find from the Finder's File menu, you see the Sherlock window, which opens automatically to the Files channel. There, you can specify search parameters for finding files. You can set the parameters in this channel to enable you to search by File Names, by Contents, or by a combination of file names and other Finder criteria, such as file size or creation date.

Simple file name search

The simplest form of the Sherlock search lets you specify where to search and the file name or parts of a file name to match. To perform this type of search, set Sherlock to the Files channel by clicking the hard disk icon in the channels area. (It should be in the top-left slot, unless someone has moved it.) Now, make sure the File Names radio button is selected.

Sherlock is preset to look on all disks for items whose names contain the text you specify. You can change where Sherlock looks for items by selecting the disk where Sherlock should search in the list area. Place a check mark next to each disk that Sherlock should search. Sherlock lists all mounted disks, including removable disks and currently mounted network disks. Basically, any disk or network resource that appears on the desktop will appear in Sherlock's list area.

Tip   If you'd like to search only in a particular folder (including all the files and folders enclosed by that folder) you can drag that folder from the Finder to the list area in Sherlock. That folder is added to the list of volumes to search. If that folder is the only item checked, your search is limited to the folder's contents. You can drag more than one folder, too, and select them so that Sherlock searches in multiple folders at once.

Once you've chosen the disks to search, click once in the keyword box and type the file name or part of the file name that you'd like to find. This entry is not case-sensitive, so you can enter file name fragments in uppercase, lowercase, or a combination of cases and Sherlock will find all possible permutations. After you've entered a partial file name, click the magnifying glass icon or press Return. Sherlock begins its search, altering the list area to reveal any results it comes up with, as shown earlier in Figure 6-3. (If it doesn't find results, an alert box appears to tell you that.)

Now you can scroll through the results list to find the file you are seeking. If you come to a good match, click it once to see its path appear in the Information window at the bottom of the Sherlock interface; double-click the file in the list area to launch it. (If it's an application, it will start up; if it's a document, it will attempt to launch its associated application so that the document can be displayed.) If the item is a folder, double-clicking it reveals that folder in the Finder.

You can also click the file's folder or any of the other folders in the path displayed in the information area (see Figure 6-5). Double-clicking a folder in the information area reveals that folder in the Finder.

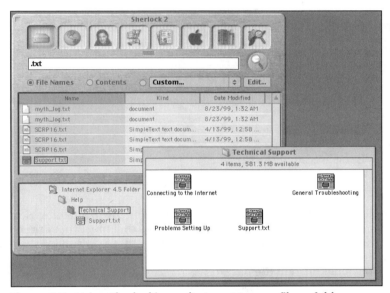

Figure 6-5: Using Sherlock's results to get to your file or folder

You can do other things with the found files and folders, such as summarize a document's contents to the Clipboard or find other files that are similar to one of the found files or folders. Those options are discussed later in the section "Working with Sherlock's results."

Custom search

Sometimes searching for a file name just isn't enough. In some cases, you may need to differentiate between files with the same name. In others, the name isn't as important to you as other details, such as how old the file is, how large it is, or what its Finder label is. That's when you need to create a custom search. You can do that in the Files channel by simply choosing criteria from the Custom pop-up menu.

Sample searches

By default, Sherlock offers some basic custom searches. You can search for applications, for files larger than 1MB, and for files modified "today" or "yesterday." Actually, these are just sample custom searches that Apple includes to show you the sort of searches that are possible (see Figure 6-6).

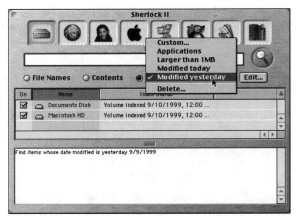

Figure 6-6: Some sample custom searches are already added to the Custom menu.

With one of these custom searches selected, you can click the magnifying glass and begin your search—Sherlock will find all files or folders that meet that criteria on the disks that you've selected in the list area. Of course, that's only mildly useful, because you're unlikely to want to find *every* application, for example, or every file or folder that's been modified in the past day.

That's why custom searches can work in conjunction with a keyword to help narrow things further. So, after selecting Modified Today from the Custom menu, you can enter a partial or complete file name in the keyword box. Now click the magnifying glass and you'll get a search that shows you everything that is similar to the file name you've entered that has been modified recently, as in Figure 6-7. This could be very convenient for gathering project files, backing up recent changes, or transferring the files you've worked on from your desktop to a notebook computer to take home with you.

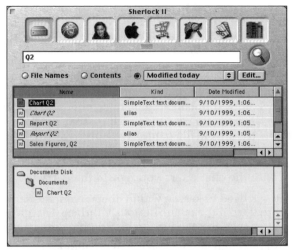

Figure 6-7: A custom search, in conjunction with keywords, can make for a useful search.

Building a custom search

If the custom searches don't match up with what you need, you can dig in further and create new searches. You do that by pulling down the Custom menu and actually choosing Custom from it. (Alternatively, you can click the Edit button next to the Custom menu.) Doing that displays the More Search Options dialog box, which offers the opportunity to create very sophisticated searches based on many more criteria. Figure 6-8 shows the More Search Options dialog box.

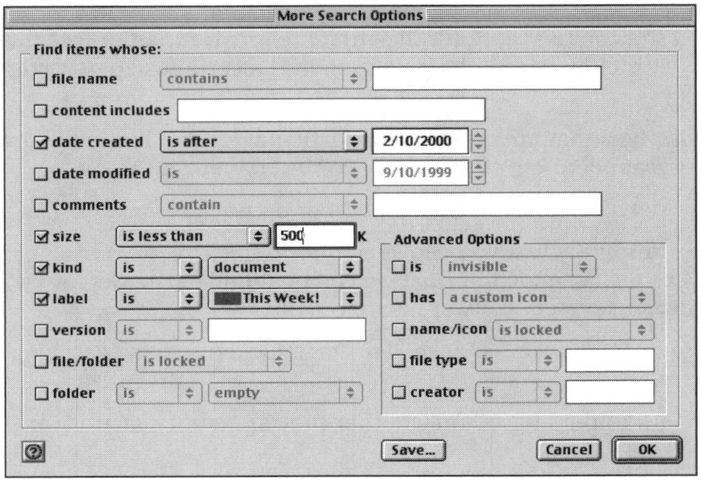

Figure 6-8: The More Search Options dialog box offers you more ways to search for files on your hard disks and network disks.

To build your search, place a check mark next to each criterion that you want included in your overall search attempt. You can add as many as you like, helping you narrow the focus as much as possible. Let's take a look at the different criteria to give you a better sense of how to use this dialog:

✦ **File name**: This entry enables you to perform a keyword search similar to the file name search in the main Sherlock window. Using the pop-up menu, however, you can search in a more sophisticated manner, choosing different ways — such as "contains," "starts with," or "ends with" — that Sherlock will use to compare the file name (or partial file name) you enter to actual files on your disk. You can use "is," for example, to make sure Sherlock only finds files that have exactly the file name you've type — use "starts with" if you want to search for files that begin with the characters you type in the entry box.

✦ **Content includes**: This entry is used to search within documents, the same way that you can search for content from the main Sherlock interface. Searching for contents is discussed in a later section called "Searching within documents."

✦ **Date created**: Open the pop-up menu and you've got many different ways to compare files against a particular date, with options such as "is before," "is after," or "is within 1 month of." You can then, in most cases, choose the actual date to compare against files on your hard disk. If, for example, you want all files created within one week of January 2000, enter that date (1/1/2000) in the date box, then choose "is within 1 week of" from the pop-up menu.

✦ **Date modified**: This works the same as "date created" except that you're searching for the date a file was modified — if it's been edited and resaved since it was created, this date will be different from the Date created.

✦ **Comments**: You can use keywords to search within the Comments field of the file's Get Info window. If you use comments extensively, this can be a great way to find a particular file. You can also use the pop-up menu to find files whose comments *don't* contain a particular keyword.

✦ **Size**: Use this criterion to search for files that are greater than or less than (according to your choice from the pop-up menu) a certain size that you enter in kilobytes.

✦ **Kind**: Search for files that are or are not a particular kind of file, such as an alias, stationery, application, clipping file, control panel, and so on.

✦ **Label**: This one let's you look for files that do or do not have a particular label.

✦ **Version**: Using this entry box you can search for items that do or do not have a particular version. (Version information can be found in the Get Info window for applications and system software components.)

✦ **File/Folder**: You can choose "is locked" or "is unlocked" when searching for files and folders.

✦ **Folder**: Search for folders based on whether they are empty, shared, or mounted.

File type and creator

File type and creator are four-character codes that the Mac OS uses to determine two things: what type of file a particular item is and what application created it. These codes are what make it possible for Mac files to appear as intelligent as they do — enabling you, for instance, to double-click a document and have its application load automatically. Unfortunately, the codes tend to be obscure, but they're also easy to discover using Sherlock. With the More Search Options dialog box open, drag any file from the Finder to the More Search Options window. Drop the file on the window and suddenly its criteria appear in any relevant entry boxes, including those for file type and creator. Now, armed with this knowledge, you can set up a search that finds similar files.

The More Search Options dialog box also offers some advanced options for users who know a little more about how Mac files store information. For example, you can search for hidden files, or you can search for files that have a custom icon or those that have their name and icon locked (through Sharing setup). You can also search for files that have a certain file type and/or creator code.

You may have already noticed something about the More Search Options dialog box — it's basically combing through information you see in the Get Info window for Finder items, along with the criteria you view in a Finder List view. All of this information is fair game when it comes to building a custom Sherlock file search.

Once you've set the criteria the way you want them, click either OK or Save. If you click OK, you return to the Sherlock window and click the magnifying glass to begin your search. If you click Save, you can give your search a name and click Save again. That search is now added to the list of searches in Sherlock's Custom menu. Back in the Sherlock window, click the magnifying glass to begin the search.

Search contents

Aside from basic and custom file searches, there's another way to find documents on your disks: searching by contents. Sherlock has the capability to look in documents on your disks and search them for keywords, just as it searches the names of files. This feature is very useful because you don't need to know the name of the file — just some text that is inside the document.

By necessity, Sherlock can only search documents that have text in them, and it can't get at every type of textual document. In general, you'll have success searching plain text documents (like those edited in SimpleText or BBEdit), HTML documents (the plain text documents, with codes, that are used to create Web pages), word processing documents (AppleWorks, Microsoft Word, WordPerfect), and e-mail (Eudora, Claris Emailer, Outlook Express). Sherlock can also look in Adobe Portable Document Format (PDF) files.

Note By default, Sherlock 2 indexes PDF format version 1.2 and earlier (Acrobat 3.0). Sherlock does not index PDF 1.3 files created by Acrobat 4. Both HTML and PDF searching are enabled by plug-ins in the Find By Content Plug-Ins folder, located in the Find folder of the Extensions folder. If additional plug-ins become available, you can add them to enable Sherlock 2 to search more types of documents by content. See Chapter 11 for more on working with the Extensions folder and the System Folder.

Search within documents

An example of a good reason to search the contents of documents on your disks might be a letter you've written and misplaced, perhaps something to your boss. Enter your boss's name as a keyword and click the radio button next to Contents in the Sherlock File channel. Now, click the magnifying glass to search, and Sherlock sifts through text files on your disks to find files that contain the keywords, as shown in Figure 6-9.

Note If your disk(s) hasn't yet been indexed, your content search won't net any results. See the section "Indexing volumes" for more on indexing.

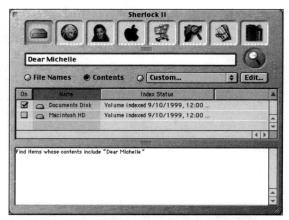

Figure 6-9: Sherlock can search inside documents for keyword text.

You can also search within documents using the Custom menu and the More Search Options dialog box discussed previously in the section called "Custom search." In the More Search Options dialog box, place a check next to "content includes" and enter keywords that Sherlock should search for within documents on your disks.

When you enter keywords to search for within documents, your best bet is to choose words that are as unique as possible. You can enter individual keywords or you can enter an entire phrase that Sherlock can search for. The more often those words appear in a particular document, the higher the relevance of that document, as discussed in the next section.

Find-by-contents results

Unlike regular File Name and custom file name searches, a find-by-contents search offers results (if anything is found) ranked by relevance. Sherlock, in digging through the files, judges which files have the most occurrences of your keywords, and which files offer those keywords in close proximity to one another. If you enter phrases, it looks for keywords that fit those phrases as closely as possible.

The result is a listing of possible matches that includes a column of relevance rankings, shown using a blue bar, as shown in Figure 6-10. The longer the bar, the more relevant Sherlock judges the result to be. That's not always accurate — Sherlock can make mistakes in this respect — but it's a decent indicator of a document that seems to offer many of the search keywords you're seeking.

Figure 6-10: The search results when you find by Content offer a relevance ranking.

Otherwise, the listing works pretty much as the File Names results listing described earlier in the chapter. You can single-click a document to see information about that document, double-click a document to launch it, or double-click a folder (in the path shown in the information area) to open that folder in the Finder. Sherlock results are discussed in more depth later in the section "Working with Sherlock's results."

Indexing volumes

Searching within documents isn't quite magic — there's some work that has to go in it. To search within documents, Sherlock has to create an index of your hard disk. The index is a special database of the content of searchable documents on your disk(s). The index must be maintained for Sherlock to effectively search all of your files for keywords. You can index manually or you can set Sherlock to automatically index your disks at regular intervals. It can take a while to fully index your disk, so it is useful to set it indexing at regular intervals when you're likely to be away from your Mac.

Note   Server volumes can be searched by content, but you can't index server volumes from your Sherlock window. Instead, you need to have the server administrator (or the owner of the Macintosh, if you're using file sharing) create an index from the server computer's version of Sherlock.

To index a disk manually, choose Index Volumes from Sherlock's Find menu. The Index Volumes dialog box shown in Figure 6-11 appears.

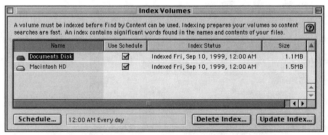

Figure 6-11: The Index Volumes dialog box allows you to create indexes for Content searches.

To manually index a disk:

1. Select the disk you want to index (or use Shift while clicking to select multiple disks) in the Index Volumes dialog box, and click the Create Index button. If you don't see a Create Index button, then an index was created previously. In that case, click the Update Index button to manually update the index to include files added since the index was last updated.

Note You can select a disk and choose Delete Index if you'd like to begin the indexing process over again from scratch. This is recommended if you've made major changes to your disks since the last update or if you've noticed Sherlock becoming noticeably slower in its Content searches. After months or longer of indexing, the index can become large and inefficient. Deleting and starting again may improve performance.

2. Once you've clicked Create Index or Update Index, an alert box warns you that creating the index can be time-consuming. If you're ready to create the index, click Create or Update, depending on the message you receive.

Sherlock then begins creating or updating the index. An Indexing Progress dialog box appears, showing the status of the indexing process (see Figure 6-12).

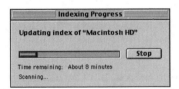

Figure 6-12: The Indexing Progress dialog box shows how much time remains to complete updating the index.

You can also choose to schedule indexing for regular intervals:

1. First, in the Index Volumes dialog box, make sure you've placed a check mark in the Use Schedule column for each disk that you'd like to schedule for indexing.

2. Now, click the Schedule button. This brings up the Schedule dialog box, shown in Figure 6-13.

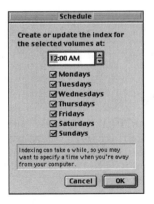

Figure 6-13: The Schedule dialog box enables you to choose the time of day and the days on which the index(es) are to be updated automatically.

3. Choose the time of day and the days on which you'd like Sherlock to update the indexes for the selected disks.

4. Click OK to put the schedule in force.

In either case, you can continue working while Sherlock creates or updates an index in the background. This may slow down your computer somewhat, making it more difficult to work with. Indexing while you're away from your computer is recommended.

Tip A great time to have Sherlock index your disks is at night, when you're not using the computer. This doesn't mean you must leave your computer on all night. When you're finished using the computer for the day, manually start the indexing or index updating process in Sherlock. Now if you shut down the computer (for example by choosing Shut Down from the Finder's Special menu), an alert box asks if you want to finish indexing before shutting down. When indexing is complete, the Mac will shut down automatically.

Saving a search

You've already seen that you can save a custom search, but there's more that you can save. If you'd like to save the exact criteria you used for a particular search, including the disks selected, the keywords entered, and other criteria chosen, you can do that. Choose File ➪ Save Search Criteria. A Save dialog box displays, allowing you to save the criteria. Give the criteria a unique name and click the Save button. Now, you can use File ➪ Open Search Criteria or you can double-click the criteria document in the Finder to open Sherlock and prepare it to perform the same search.

This works for Internet searching as well, as discussed later in the section "Search the Internet."

Multiple searches

You can have more than one search going at a time. Choose File ➪ New Window to create a new Sherlock window. After you've put one search into action, you can switch to the new window and build another search.

Working with Sherlock's results

When a search ends, Sherlock displays all the found items in the list area. This window works somewhat like a List view window in the Finder, offering a familiar interface for sorting through the files that have been found. You can also see a found file's folder location, move files around, send files to the Trash, and even summarize their content (in some cases) to the Clipboard.

Sorting found files

You can sort the list of found items by name, size, kind, or modification date. To change the sort criterion, click the column heading you'd like to sort by in the list area, as shown in Figure 6-14.

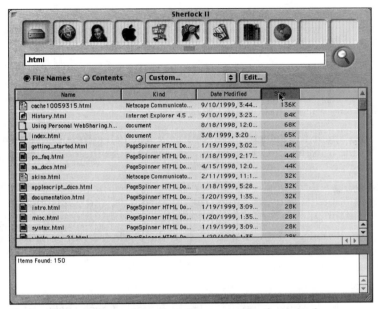

Figure 6-14: Click a column heading to sort by that criterion.

You can also sort in reverse order. Click the triangular sort-direction control at the right end of the column headings in the list area.

If you want to see more columns in the list area, you can make the Sherlock window larger by dragging its size box. You can also resize the columns by dragging the lines that separate the column headings.

Seeing a found item's folder location

While the list area displays items that match your search parameters, the information area displays a folder location (path) for one found item. To see a found item's folder location, select the item (by clicking it) in the list area, and its folder location appears in the information area.

You can select multiple items at the top of the list area as you do in the Finder: by Shift+clicking or dragging a selection rectangle across them. To select all items, use the Select All command in Sherlock's Edit menu or press ⌘+A. When you select more than one item in the list area, no folder location is displayed in the information area.

Moving, copying, and deleting found items

In addition to seeing folder locations of found items, you can also drag items from the list area to the desktop or to any folder or disk that you can see in the Finder. If the destination is on the same disk as the found item you drag, the found item moves to the destination. If the destination is on a different disk, the found item is copied to it. Note that you can drag files and folders from the information area as well.

The Trash is another place to which you can drag one or more found items. You can drag multiple items as a group from the list area to the Trash.

Doing more with found items

In addition to dragging found items, you can use these File menu commands to manipulate the items you selected in the list area:

✦ **Open Item(s)** opens the selected item or items. You can also open an item by double-clicking it in the List or information area. If more than one item is selected, double-clicking one of them opens all of them.

✦ **Open Enclosing Folder** opens the folder that contains the selected item. The Finder automatically becomes active, the folder opens, and the Finder scrolls to and selects the item in the folder window.

✦ **Print Item** prints selected documents just as the Finder's Print command does (see Chapter 17 for details). You can also print documents by dragging them to a desktop printer icon that you can see in the Finder.

✦ **Move To Trash** puts the selected items in the Trash.

✦ **Get Info** ⇨ **General Information** displays the Info windows of selected items.

✦ **Label** classifies the selected items with a color and text label.

✦ **Show Original** displays the selected alias's original item in the Finder.

✦ **Get Info** ⇨ **Sharing** enables you to share selected folders. (File Sharing must be turned on as described in Chapter 22.)

These commands can act either on items selected in the list area or in the information area. You can alternate between the two windows by pressing Tab.

Tip   You can quit the Sherlock program (or close the current Sherlock window, if more than one is open) while opening a found item by holding down Option while choosing Open from the Find menu (or while double-clicking an item in the list or information areas). This trick saves you the trouble of switching back to Sherlock to quit it.

Special Sherlock commands

Aside from the basics just outlined, there are a few other things you can do with results in Sherlock. Most of these are accessed through Sherlock's contextual menu, which appears when you point to an item and Control+click on that item. Figure 6-15 is a typical contextual menu.

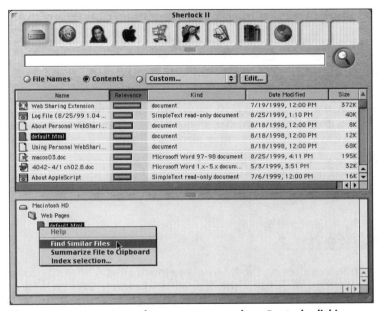

Figure 6-15: A contextual menu appears when Control+clicking a result in the Sherlock window.

Here are the commands that you may encounter:

✦ **Find Similar Files**: This command enables you to perform another search, this time using the selected item as a model for the second search. The second search focuses on content, switching Sherlock to a find by Content mode (if necessary) and then finding documents that have similar content to the one you've selected. This sort of search is less useful if you select application or folder icons.

✦ **Summarize File to Clipboard**: This option takes text documents that Sherlock can read and quickly summarizes them by pulling key sentences from the document. That summary is placed on the Mac OS clipboard (see Figure 6-16). You can either choose Edit ➪ Paste in a text application to see the summary, or you can switch to the Finder, where the Clipboard Viewer should appear on its own. If it doesn't, choose Edit ➪ Show Clipboard in the Finder.

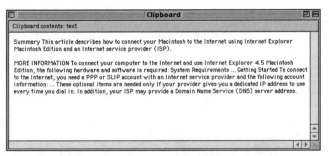

Figure 6-16: Sherlock includes the capability to summarize text documents to the Mac OS Clipboard.

✦ **Index Selection**: This command enables you to update the disk's Find by Content index with the particular document, folder, or disk you've selected. This is a quick way to add to the index manually if you've indexed recently.

✦ **Add a Folder Action**: If the selection is a folder, the contextual menu includes the option of adding a Folder Action to it. Folder Actions are described in Chapter 24.

Search the Internet

Some of the most popular sites on the Internet are index sites. These sites, such as Yahoo!, HotBot, and Lycos, offer users the capability to search through millions of other Web sites to find content of interest to them. But each of these sites has its own mechanisms, its own interfaces, and its own databases of Web documents that don't always offer every possibility. To find what you're looking for, you either need to visit multiple search sites, or you need to find a way to search multiple sites from one interface. In fact, there are Web sites, such as the Search-It-All site (http://www.search-it-all.com), that enable you to do this.

In Mac OS 9, you can conduct a fairly comprehensive search of the Web with Sherlock. Sherlock is designed to search multiple Web sites simultaneously and return the results in the Sherlock window. You can see a brief summary of each found site in the Sherlock window, or you can double-click an entry to have it load in your Web browser.

Sherlock gains access to individual Web search sites through plug-in files, called Internet search sites, written by Apple and other companies. This makes it possible for Sherlock to search not only Web search engines (Yahoo!, Excite, HotBot, and so on), but other searchable Web sites, such as Amazon.com, eBay, and similar e-commerce sites. News sites and Web magazines can also supply plug-in software that enables you to search those sites, too.

New Feature Sherlock 2 offers new features for Internet searches, including the capability to group Internet search sites in different channels—Apple starts you off with channels for e-commerce sites, people (phone and address) searches, reference sites (encyclopedia and dictionary), and news sites. You can also search Apple's Web sites using Sherlock, and you can add more Internet sites and channels to customize Sherlock's search capability.

With certain types of sites, Sherlock can change its interface to offer more useful information. For instance, Sherlock can show pricing information and availability dates for e-commerce sites, making it easy to shop multiple Internet auction sites simultaneously without leaving Sherlock.

Note Although the Internet hasn't been discussed in-depth yet, this discussion of Sherlock's Internet searching capabilities fits in this chapter because Internet searching is similar to file searches on your hard disks. Many of the interface elements are the same for any type of search. To search the Internet, however, you need an active Internet connection. See Chapter 10 for information on using the Internet Setup Assistant to create a connection. Chapter 10 also tells you how to manually create an Internet connection, if necessary.

Web page search

After opening Sherlock, click the Internet channel button—the one that looks like a globe with wired connections on it—and you'll see Sherlock's interface shift to accommodate a Web search. The keyword box remains, but the list area changes to show a list of Internet search sites. In this list, you can place a check mark next to sites you'd like to include in your search. Now, enter keywords for your Internet search and click the magnifying glass icon. If your Internet connection is active, Sherlock will send the search keywords to each of the chosen search sites (see Figure 6-17).

Although different Web search sites vary in the way they handle keywords, Sherlock sends your keywords to the search sites exactly as you format them in the keyword box. In general, you can simply enter a series of keywords that you think might generate results, such as "olympic bobsled trials" or "outdoor camping information." You can also try Boolean keywords, such as **and**, **or**, and **not** between search words. For best results, experiment with different keyword constructs.

Note If you use a modem to connect to the Internet, you should make sure the Internet connection is active by selecting the Remote Access control panel and clicking the Connect button. You can also set up Remote Access to automatically dial your Internet Service Provider whenever Sherlock or another Internet application requests a connection. See Chapter 10 for more details.

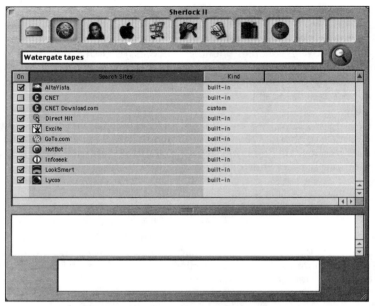

Figure 6-17: Search the Web with multiple search engines using Sherlock.

Getting better results

Different search sites prefer to have keywords formatted in different ways, but there are some general rules that you can follow to help your Internet searches in Sherlock turn up the results you want:

✦ Boolean searches use the words **and**, **or**, and **not** to distinguish between different types of searches. For example, searching for **Steven and Jobs** will generally limit results to documents that include both terms. If you search for **Steven or Jobs**, you'll get a lot more results, because your results will include documents that match either or both terms. Search for **Steven not Jobs** and you'll get results that include the first term but don't include the second term. Most Internet search sites support Boolean searches.

✦ Use commas between words. Many search sites don't require commas, but some work better if you separate each keyword or phrase with a comma. That way the search site won't assume that you're looking for one big phrase such as "cat dog mice toys" when you're actually trying to search for each as a keyword.

✦ Some Internet search sites (but not all) notice whether you capitalize words. If you don't capitalize, they ignore capitalization while searching; if you do capitalize, they look for the same capitalization.

✦ Finally, some Internet search sites prefer that you put phrases or proper names between quotation marks, such as **"Rocky and Bullwinkle"** or **"One for My Baby"**.

Sherlock begins displaying search results as soon as one of the search sites returns them. As other search sites return their results, the Sherlock program merges them in its list area. For each Web page that matches your search request, the list area displays the name, address, and relevance. You can sort the list by clicking a column heading in the list area. To sort in reverse order, click the triangular sort direction indicator at the right end of the column headings.

If you select one of the listed items, a summary appears in the information area. To see the whole page in your Web browser, double-click its name in the list area. That page's Web address is sent to your Web browser, which attempts to load the page over your Internet connection. Figure 6-18 is an example of the results listed from an Internet search.

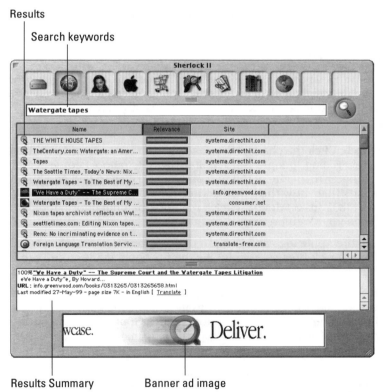

Figure 6-18: A Web search results in a number of different Web documents from different search sites.

Note You may notice that another small area appears at the bottom of the Sherlock window. This window is designed to show banner ads that appear on the Web search site's own Web site. Because most major search site companies rely on Web advertising revenue to make their search sites worthwhile, Apple has made it possible for their advertising to appear within Sherlock. If an ad happens to interest you, you can click the ad and your Web browser will attempt to load the corresponding Web page for that advertisement.

You can also drag Web site listings to an open Web browser window to display them; the Web browser takes over and accesses the page via the Internet. If you'd like to save the site for later access, you can drag a listing from the list area to the desktop or a folder in the Finder. It then becomes a Web Page Location file, which you can store on your hard disk. You can then double-click the Web Page Location file to direct your Web browser to attempt to access that Web document at a later time.

Switching channels

Aside from basic Web searches, Apple's predefined channels offer the opportunity to switch between different types of Internet searches. Here's a quick overview of some of the channel options (channels are the buttons at the top of the Sherlock window):

✦ **People Search**: Click the channel with a woman's face on it and you'll get options for searching "people" servers like Bigfoot, Yahoo! People Search, and Four11. Enter the name of the person you're trying to find and Sherlock returns results that show the e-mail address and phone number of that person, if listed. You can double-click a result to load full information about that person in your Web browser.

✦ **Apple**: Click the Apple logo and you can perform keyword searches in different parts of Apple's Web presence, including their product guides, the Tech Info Library (for troubleshooting articles), and the full Apple.com Web site.

✦ **Shopping**: Select the Shopping channel (which looks like a shopping cart) and you can search Amazon.com, Barnesandnoble.com, and eBay.com, among others. Enter the name of a product you're looking for and click the magnifying glass. The results include pricing information, availability, and other important criteria to help you shop for items (see Figure 6-19).

✦ **News**: The News channel (which looks like a folded newspaper) lets you search recent headlines for topics defined by your keywords.

✦ **Reference**: This channel (which looks like a shelf of books) enables you to search sites that offer reference material, such as Dictionary.com and Encyclopedia.com.

✦ **My Channel**: The My Channel (the Sherlock Holmes hat and magnifying glass) option enables you to move or add your favorite search plug-ins to one channel so you don't have to flip through the others to search sites you use often.

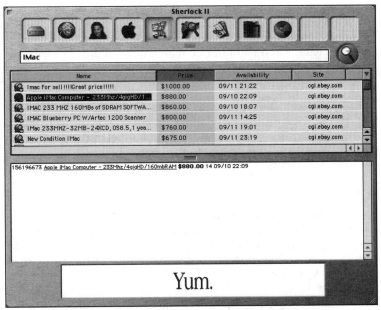

Figure 6-19: Sherlock features the unique capability to recognize a shopping search and organize the results using pricing and product availability.

You can move the channels around on the Sherlock interface if you like. Just click and drag a channel from its current spot in the channels area to an open channel slot.

Build your own channels

If you'd like to create your own channel, it's easy to do. And, once you've created the channel, you can add search sites to it by dragging them from another channel, or by dragging search site files from the Finder, so as to make your channel worth using.

To create a new channel, just choose Channels ➪ New channel. The New Channel dialog box appears, as shown in Figure 6-20.

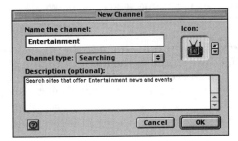

Figure 6-20: The New Channel dialog box helps you build your own channel.

Give the channel a name in the "Name the channel" entry box, then choose the type of channel from the "Channel type" pop-up menu. The type determines how results are displayed: shopping channels include price and availability information; people channels include e-mail and phone number columns; news channels include headlines, relevance, and dates; and search channels include page name, relevance, and site information.

Now you can choose an icon for the channel by clicking the up or down arrow next to the current icon. You can also enter a description for your channel, which will appear in the information area when you select that channel in the Sherlock window. When you're done, click OK to create the channel.

Adding search sites

You can add new search sites to existing channels or to channels you create yourself. The easiest way to do that is to drag search sites from one channel to another. Select a channel in Sherlock's channel area, then drag search sites from that channel area to the icon that represents the destination channel. Those search sites now appear in the new channel.

You can also add search sites to a channel by dragging them from the Finder. The problem is, you need to get them *to* the Finder, first. You generally do that by downloading Internet search site files (often called *plug-ins*) from the Internet. You can get Internet search site files in two different ways. First, you can visit `http://www.apple.com/sherlock/` and look for a link to Internet search site files or search site plug-ins. Apple keeps track of many of the new search site files created by both Apple and by third parties.

Second, you can find Internet search site files on other Web sites that offer Sherlock compatibility. Look for a link that enables you to download the search site file to your Mac. Then, you can add it to Sherlock.

A search site file generally has the three letter extension ".src" at the end of its file name. If you've downloaded such a file, you can simply drag it from the Finder to the Sherlock window, and it's added to the currently active channel (see Figure 6-21). Likewise, you can drag sites *from* the Sherlock window to the Finder, where a duplicate of the search site file is made.

 Tip   Once you have a search site file in the Finder, you can duplicate it before you move it into Sherlock. That way you can have the same search site in two different channels, if you like.

You can also add search site files to Sherlock by dragging them to the appropriate folder in the System Folder. Search site files are stored in the Internet Search Sites folder in the System Folder. Each channel has its own folder within the Internet Search Sites folder; to add a search site file to a particular channel, drag its .src file to that channel's folder.

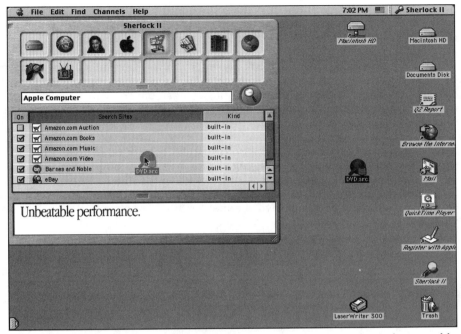

Figure 6-21: Drag a search site file from the Finder to the Sherlock window to add it to the active channel.

Summary

In this chapter, you saw that Mac OS 9 includes an update to the Sherlock program, which was introduced in Mac OS 8.5 and that is now called Sherlock 2. Sherlock 2 features a new interface that not only looks different, but also acts different from the way most other Macintosh applications (and Mac OS windows) function. The interface includes a number of different windows and areas that enable you to manage the different types of searches that Sherlock can perform.

After you get the hang of Sherlock's interface, you can search for files on your hard disks, removable disks, and disks attached to your Mac via a network. The basic File Name search enables you to enter a file name or partial file name and find files that match.

A more advanced search is possible by choosing the Custom menu, which opens the More Search Options dialog box. Here you can create a search that looks at all the different criteria associated with Macintosh files, including date created, the size of the file, the label, the version, and so on. You can also use advanced criteria to search for invisible files, files with custom icons, or files created by a particular application.

Beyond these searches, Sherlock can also look into text-based files and find content within them. To perform a content search, you need to index the files on your hard disk, which you can do manually or according to a preset schedule.

After any of these searches, Sherlock presents you with a results listing that can be organized and manipulated in a number of ways. You can sort the listing, get information about individual files, print files, and so on. You can also use contextual menus to search for similar files, summarize text files to the Clipboard, and add folder actions to folders.

Finally, Sherlock 2 offers the capability to search the Internet in many different ways. You can search major search engines for Web pages on particular topics. You can also search for people, products, or news using the different channels built into Sherlock, which changes its results pages to show you information relevant to your search. You can also add your own channels or augment channels with new search sites that you download from the Internet.

✦   ✦   ✦

Work with Programs and Documents

I t may seem reasonable that once you open a program or a document, you've left the Mac OS behind. True, the Mac OS does pretty much hand over control of the computer to a program when you open it, but many of the functions and capabilities of application programs are actually provided by the Mac OS. The Finder handles opening application programs, and the Mac OS manages to let you have morethan one program open at the same time. You can also use the Finder to open documents, and you can open them from applications using standard dialog boxes provided by theMac OS. Similar dialog boxes appear when you save a document from any application.

Many programs rely on the Mac OS for basic document editing commands, such as Cut, Copy, and Paste. You don't need those editing commands as much in programs that adopt the Mac OS drag-and-drop editing technology, which lets you move material around in a document and between documents by dragging the material with the mouse.

The Mac OS also makes it possible for you to open documents created by programs you don't have, including Mac programs and programs on Windows, DOS, and Apple II computers. You can even use removable disks from those foreign systems in your Mac.

Opening Programs, Documents, and More

You open a program when you want to work with it — this action is sometimes called *launching* a program. You open a document when you want to view or edit its contents. For example, you open SimpleText when you want to view, create, or edit a text document. (You can also work with text documents using other programs.) There are many ways to open programs, documents, other kinds of files, and folders. This section describes how to open items with the Finder, the Apple menu, the Launcher control panel, the Startup Items folder, the Shutdown Items folders, and any application.

Opening items with the Finder

Chapter 5 discussed the basic methods for opening a program or document with the Finder: you either double-click the program or document icon or, in a button view, click the program or document button. If you prefer a more formal approach, you can select the icon by clicking it once and then use the Open command. The Open command is in the File menu; it also appears in the contextual menu that pops up when you Control+click a program.

Opening a document using one of these methods automatically opens the application that created the document. The Finder figures out which application created it, opens that application, and tells the application to open the document. It's quite a chain of events that starts when you double-click a document.

Suppose you want to open a bunch of documents. No problem, just select them all and then double-click one of the selected icons or use the Open command. If the documents were created by different applications, the Finder doesn't get ruffled. It opens each application and gives it a list of the documents you want opened.

Opening a document with any compatible application

Instead of opening a document with the application that created it, you can open it with any compatible application. For example, any word processing application can open plain text documents created by other applications.

To open a document with any compatible application, drag the document's icon to the icon of the application that you want to use. In most cases, if the application is compatible with the document, the application's icon becomes highlighted. Release the mouse button while the application icon is highlighted, and the application opens the document. If the application is not already open, the Finder opens it automatically. If an application can't open a document you drag to it, nothing happens — no highlighting, no opening. (If you miss slightly, you might drop the document in the application's folder by accident.) Figure 7-1 shows how an application icon looks if it can open a document that you drag to it.

Figure 7-1: This is how an application icon looks when opening a document by dragging it to a compatible application.

Opening the unknown

If you try to open a document by double-clicking its icon, clicking its button, or using the Finder's Open command but you don't have the application that created it, you see an alert. Normally, this alert displays a list of alternate applications that can handle the kind of document you tried to open. You select the alternate application you want to open the document and click the Open button in the dialog box. The alternate application then opens the document. The Mac OS remembers which alternate application you selected and uses it to open the same document, or any other like it (same type of document and same creator application), in the future. You don't see the alert box asking you to select an alternate application again for the same kind of document. Figure 7-2 shows the alert box in which you select an alternate application to open a document created by an application you don't have.

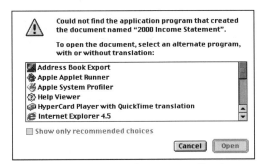

Figure 7-2: Select an alternate application to open a document created by an application you don't have.

Sometimes none of your applications can handle a document that you try to open. In this case, an alert tells you the document could not be opened because the application that created it could not be found. Usually the alert tells you the name of the creator application. Knowing the creator application, you may be able to obtain translator software that will enable you to open the document (see "Translating Documents" later in this chapter). Figure 7-3 is an example of the alert you see when you don't have an alternate application to open a document.

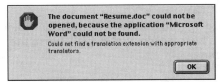

Figure 7-3: The application that created the document you want to open is not available and neither is an alternate.

If you'd rather not see alerts asking about alternate applications for opening documents, you can turn them off. Use the File Exchange control panel, as explained in "Translating Documents" later in this chapter. Another way to stop these alerts is to disable or remove File Exchange, as discussed in Chapter 11.

After turning off automatic file translation, you see a different alert when you try to open a document created by an application that you don't have. In this case, the alert tells you that the document could not be opened because the application that created it could not be found, but the alert does not name the missing application. If the document is a type that SimpleText can open, the Finder asks whether you want to have SimpleText open it. SimpleText can open documents saved in plain-text format by another program (but not word processing documents saved in a proprietary format). In addition, SimpleText can open pictures saved in the PICT format, movies saved in the QuickTime format, and 3D graphics saved in the QuickDraw 3D format (for details on viewing movies and 3D graphics, see Chapter 18). The PICT, QuickTime, and QuickDraw 3D formats are all standard Mac OS formats. Figure 7-4 is an example of the alert that you see when automatic file translation is turned off and you try to open a document created by an application you don't have.

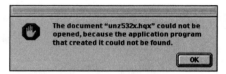

The document "unz532x.hqx" could not be opened, because the application program that created it could not be found.

OK

Figure 7-4: This is the alert shown when the application that created the document you want to open is not available and automatic file translation is turned off.

Opening with the Apple menu

The Apple menu expedites opening items that you use frequently. Anything you can double-click in the Finder, including documents, application programs, desk accessories, folders, control panels, fonts, and sounds, can also be put in the Apple menu and opened by choosing it there. Figure 7-5 is an example of the Apple menu.

Adding and removing Apple menu items

You put an item in the Apple menu by dragging it to the Apple Menu Items folder, which is inside the System Folder. The item becomes instantly available in the Apple menu (no need to restart your computer).

To remove an item from the Apple menu, drag its icon out of the Apple Menu Items folder to the desktop or to another folder.

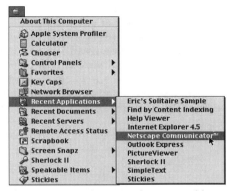

Figure 7-5: An item can be opened by choosing it from the Apple menu.

Making submenus in the Apple menu

If your Apple menu has so many items that you must scroll to see them all, consider consolidating the less-used items in a folder or two within the Apple Menu Items folder. You can make the contents of folders within the Apple Menu Items folder appear as submenus of the Apple menu by using the Apple Menu Options control panel. You can also use this control panel to create submenus that list the items you have used recently. Figure 7-6 shows the Apple Menu Options control panel.

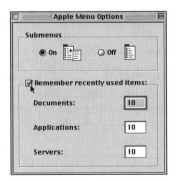

Figure 7-6: Turn on the features to add submenus to the Apple menu and track recently used items.

Turning on the Submenus option creates a hierarchy of submenus in the Apple menu. After turning on the Submenus option, submenus appear whenever you highlight a folder listed in the Apple menu. A submenu lists the contents of the highlighted folder. Highlighting a folder listed in a submenu displays another submenu, up to five levels deep.

Turning on the option to remember recently used items creates folders in the Apple menu for tracking the documents, applications, and servers that you most recently used. You can set the number of documents, applications, and servers to track. The control panel tracks recent items by creating aliases of those items and placing the aliases in the Recent Applications folder, Recent Documents folder, or Recent Servers folder (where appropriate) in the Apple Menu Items folder (inside the System Folder). If you wish to suppress tracking of one type of item, set the number to be remembered to 0 (zero) and discard the appropriate recent items folder if it exists.

Cross-Reference   See Chapter 14 for more information on aliases.

Organizing the Apple menu

The Apple menu always lists items alphabetically, regardless of their order in the Apple Menu Items folder. You don't affect the Apple menu when you rearrange the contents of the Apple Menu Items folder by dragging icons in its window or clicking column headings in a list view.

You can change the order of Apple menu items by beginning their names with certain characters. To make an item appear at the top of the Apple menu, begin its name with a blank space. You can group different types of items by prefixing different numbers of blank spaces to their names. The more blank spaces, the higher on the Apple menu the item appears. For example, you can prefix two blanks to the name of the most important item in your Apple menu, one blank to names of less important items, and none to other items. To make items appear at the bottom of the Apple menu, begin their names with a hollow diamond (◊) or a bullet (•). Press Shift+Option+V for the hollow diamond or Option+8 for the bullet.

Note   Rather than carefully prefixing icon names to arrange them in the Apple menu, you can install the shareware system extension AMICO, which stands for Apple Menu Items Custom Order, by Dennis Chronopoulos. With this extension installed, you determine the order of items in the Apple menu by arranging icons in the Apple Menu Items folder. In addition, you can add gray dividing lines like the ones you see in other menus. (See Chapter 26 for more information on shareware.)

Opening with the Launcher

Another way to open items is with the Launcher control panel. The Launcher displays a window of large buttons, and clicking a button (once) opens the item it represents. The Launcher is similar to a folder window viewed as buttons, but the Launcher has features a folder window doesn't have, as described in the following paragraphs. Figure 7-7 is an example of the Launcher window.

Forcing order invisibly

Forcibly reordering items in the Apple menu by putting spaces or special symbols at the beginning of the items' names has side effects that you may dislike. The spaces or symbols visibly alter the names and conspicuously shift the names to the right. Here's how to invisibly force the order you want:

1. Open the Note Pad or a new document in SimpleText.

2. Press Return to create a blank line, select the blank line, and copy it to the Clipboard.

3. Switch to the Finder. Open the Apple Menu Items folder, and click the name of the item that you want to appear at the top of the Apple menu to select the name for editing.

4. Press the up arrow (↑) key to move the insertion point to the beginning of the selected name and paste. The whole name goes blank, but don't fret.

5. Press Enter or click outside the name, and the name springs back in view. The renamed item jumps to the top of the window if you're viewing by name.

To increase an item's alphabetic buoyancy, paste the blank line two or more times at the beginning of the item's name.

Warning: Some applications don't work properly with files or folders whose names contain blank lines (blank spaces are okay). Specifically, some versions of QuarkXPress and PageMaker generate an undefined PostScript error if you try to print a document that's in a folder whose name begins with a blank line (not a blank space). If you encounter problems after pasting blank lines at the beginning of file or folder names, use blank spaces instead.

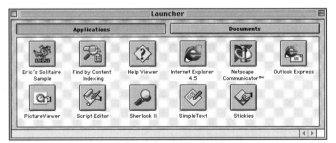

Figure 7-7: Clicking an item's button in the Launcher control panel can open it.

Items in the Launcher window are actually aliases in the Launcher Items folder inside the System Folder.

For detailed information on aliases, see Chapter 14.

Launcher categories

You can categorize items in the Launcher by placing them in specially named folders within the Launcher Items folder. The name of a category folder must begin with a bullet (press Option+8 to type a bullet). The names of up to eight category folders appear as button names in a panel at the top of the Launcher window, and clicking a category button displays the items in the corresponding category folder.

There is a shortcut for opening a category folder: press Option and click the folder's button in the Launcher window. To open the Launcher Items folder itself, Option+click the Applications button in the Launcher window.

Adding, moving, and removing Launcher buttons

You can choose one of three sizes for icons in the Launcher window. You can also drag icons to, from, and within the Launcher window (without opening the Launcher Items folder or its subfolders) and open a document by dragging it to a compatible application in the Launcher. Specifically, you can

✦ Add an item by dragging its icon to the Launcher window, including to a category button in the Launcher window.

✦ Move an item in the Launcher by pressing Option and dragging the item.

✦ Open a document by dragging its icon to a compatible application's icon in the Launcher. (An application icon becomes highlighted when you drag a document icon over it in the Launcher if the application is able to open the document.)

✦ Move or copy an item to a folder in the Launcher — drag the item's icon to the folder's button in the Launcher.

✦ Remove an item from the Launcher by pressing Option and dragging the item to the Trash.

✦ Change the icon size for the visible Launcher category by pressing ⌘, clicking inside the Launcher window, and choosing from the menu that pops up.

Opening at startup and shutdown

If you want to have a program, document, or anything else open every time you start your computer, or every time you shut it down, the Finder can do that for you. Just put the items you want to open during startup in the Startup Items folder, which is inside the System Folder. Put the items you want to open during shutdown in the Shutdown Items folder, which is also inside the System Folder. Actually, to avoid disorganizing your disk you should generally put aliases (not original items) in the Startup Items and Shutdown Items folders.

For more information on these special folders, see Chapter 11. For information on creating aliases, see Chapter 14.

Opening from applications

In most applications, yet another way to open items is with the Open command. Choosing the Open command from any application's File menu (except the Finder's) displays a dialog box that shows a view of your files, folders, and disks that's more or less like a list view in the Finder.

Most applications display a standard Open dialog box, but some display the newer Navigation Services dialog box (introduced in Mac OS 8.5 and updated in Mac OS 9). Figure 7-8 shows examples of Open and Navigation Services dialog boxes.

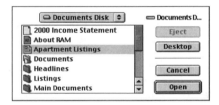

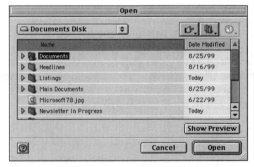

Figure 7-8: An item can be opened using a standard Open dialog box (top) or a Navigation Services dialog box (bottom).

Open dialog box

An Open dialog box shows items from the desktop, the main level of one disk, or one folder at a time in a scrolling list. The Open dialog box also has buttons and a pop-up menu for opening disks, folders, and, ultimately, the document you want. In some applications, the Open dialog box includes a place to display a preview of the document that's currently selected in the dialog box. Each application can also add its own unique controls to assist in opening documents. You can't move an Open dialog box on the screen, you can't change its size, and you can't switch to another application (as described later in this chapter) while an Open dialog box is displayed.

Navigation Services dialog box

The Navigation Services dialog box does the same job as the Open dialog box but eliminates many of its shortcomings. The scrolling list of files, called the browser, looks and operates a lot like the list view of the Finder. You see the icon, name, and modification date of every item in the folder or disk volume named at the top of the list. For each listed item, the modification date automatically expands from the longest date format (Monday, January 1, 2001) to the shortest format (1/1/01) depending on the space available. You can click the column headings to sort the list by name or date. You can also reverse the sort order by clicking the triangular sort direction indicator at the right end of the headings (above the scroll bar).

Next to each folder and disk volume icon is a disclosure triangle. Clicking this triangle expands the folder or volume to display the items inside it.

As you can tell from the title bar, the Navigation Services dialog box is movable. You can drag it by its title bar or its frame. In addition, you can switch to another open application (including the Finder) while the Navigation Services dialog box is displayed.

Look closely at the bottom-right corner of a Navigation Services dialog box. The textured area there is a size box that you can drag to resize the dialog box.

You may occasionally encounter a Navigation Services dialog box that you can't move or resize. If this happens, the application program you are using is restricting the Navigation Services dialog box because the application can't handle the screen updating that would be required if you were to move or resize the dialog box.

Opening a document

You open a document that's listed in an Open or Navigation Services dialog box by selecting it (click it once) and clicking the Open button. In some cases, especially in Navigation Services dialog boxes, the button may have a different name such as Choose or Select. You can also double-click a document to open it. Either way, the dialog box goes away and the document appears in a window.

You can select more than one document in a Navigation Services dialog box if the application program you're using allows this. To select additional documents, just press Shift while clicking them. You can even select multiple items from different folders. To select additional items in another folder, click the folder's disclosure triangle to expand the folder, and then Shift+click the items in it that you want to open.

If you realize while double-clicking an item in an Open or Navigation Services dialog box that you are pointing at the wrong item, you can cancel the operation as long as you have not released the mouse button. To cancel, hold down the mouse button on the second click and drag the pointer outside the dialog box before releasing the mouse button.

Instead of canceling a double-click in an Open dialog box, you can continue pressing the mouse button and drag the pointer to the item that you want to open. When you release the mouse button, the currently selected item opens. This trick does not work in a Navigation Services dialog box, which lets you do other things by dragging items (more on this subject shortly).

Opening a folder

The only way to see documents in a folder that's listed in an Open dialog box, and one of the ways in a Navigation Services dialog box, is to open the folder. To open a folder, either select it and click the Open button or double-click it. When you open a folder, its contents take over the scrolling list and its name appears at the top of the list. The other way to see a folder's contents in a Navigation Services dialog box is to click the folder's disclosure triangle so that it points down. This method doesn't make the folder's contents take over the scrolling list or change the name above it.

The pop-up menu above the scrolling list in an Open or Navigation Services dialog box identifies the folder whose contents you see in the scrolling list. You can use the pop-up menu to go back through the folder layers toward the desktop. At the end of the pop-up menu is the desktop, and just ahead of it is the disk that contains the folder that you currently see in the dialog box. Choosing an item from the pop-up menu takes you to that item and displays its contents in the dialog box. As a shortcut in the Open dialog box, you can move back one folder to the folder that contains the currently listed folder by clicking the name of the disk where it is displayed above the Eject button in the dialog box. This shortcut is not available in a Navigation Services dialog box.

You can quickly show a folder's contents in a Navigation Services dialog box if you can see the folder's icon outside the dialog box on the desktop or in a Finder window. All you do is drag the folder icon to the dialog box. This shortcut does not work in an Open dialog box.

Changing disks

If you use more than one disk, you may want to see folders and files from a different disk in an Open or Navigation Services dialog box. You can do this by showing the desktop in the dialog box and opening the disk there. One way to show the desktop in the dialog box is to choose it from the pop-up menu above the scrolling list in the dialog box. You can also show the desktop in an Open dialog box by clicking the Desktop button. A Navigation Services dialog box has no Desktop button; instead, you use the Shortcuts button as described next.

You can eject a CD-ROM, DVD-ROM, floppy disk, or other removable disk in an Open or Navigation Services dialog box. When you insert a different disk, you see its contents in the dialog box. To eject a disk from an Open dialog box, click the Eject button. In a Navigation Services dialog box, use the Shortcuts menu (described next) to eject a disk. You don't have to go to the desktop before ejecting a disk in either kind of dialog box.

Shortcuts, Favorites, and Recent menus

At the top of a Navigation Services dialog box are three picture buttons that can speed your way through the dialog box. Each of these buttons displays a pop-up menu when you click the button. Figure 7-9 shows examples of these menus.

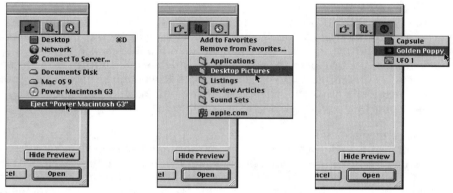

Figure 7-9: The Shortcuts (left), Favorites (middle), and Recent (right) pop-up menus speed your way through a Navigation Services dialog box.

The *Shortcuts* button looks like a pointing finger and displays a menu that lists every disk volume that has an icon on the desktop. Choosing a disk from this menu displays the disk's contents in the dialog box. The Shortcuts menu gives you easy access to the desktop, to your local network, and to file servers. In addition, the Shortcuts menu has an Eject command for every removable disk that you're currently using.

The *Favorites* button looks like a folder with a bookmark ribbon on it and displays a menu of your favorite files, folders, and volumes, based on the contents of the Favorites folder in the System Folder. (The application you're using can filter out all but the kind of items you're opening.) Choosing an item from the Favorites menu displays it in the dialog box. The Favorites menu also includes commands for adding and removing items on the menu. You can add an item by selecting it in the dialog box and choosing Add to Favorites from the Favorites menu. As a shortcut, you can simply drag the item from the scrolling list in the dialog box to the Favorites button. You can remove items by choosing Remove From Favorites on the Favorites menu. This displays a scrolling list of your favorites in a dialog box — select one or more on the list (Shift+click or ⌘+click to select multiple items) and click Remove. Your favorite items are also available in the Apple menu.

The *Recent* button looks like a clock face and displays a menu of documents that you recently opened. Choosing an item from this menu displays it in the dialog box. In some applications, the Recent menu also lists folders and volumes that you recently opened. Furthermore, the application that you're using can restrict the Recent menu to showing only the kind of item that you're opening. Navigation Services keeps track of recent items by storing aliases of them in a folder inside the Navigation Services folder in the Preferences folder, which is in the System Folder. (For details on aliases, see Chapter 14.)

Note
The Shortcuts, Favorites, and Recent buttons are not available in Open dialog boxes, but you can endow Open dialog boxes with similar functionality by installing software such as Default Folder from St. Clair Software (`http://www. stclairsoft.com`), which is described in Chapter 26.

Navigating by keyboard

You can move through folders and open items by using the keyboard as well as the mouse. In an Open or Navigation Services dialog box, typing an item's full name or the first part of it selects the item. For example, pressing M selects the first item that begins with the letter *M* or *m*. Typing several letters quickly specifies a longer name to be selected, but pausing between keys starts the selection process all over again. The Key Repeat Rate setting in the Keyboard control panel determines how long you must pause to make a fresh start. After you have selected an item in an Open or Navigation Services dialog box (by any means), pressing Return or Enter opens the item. These dialog boxes recognize many other keyboard shortcuts. Table 7-1 has the details.

Table 7-1
Keyboard Shortcuts for the Open and Navigation Services Dialog Boxes

Objective	Keystroke
Select a listed document, folder, or disk	Type the item's full or partial name
Scroll up in the list of items	Up arrow (↑)
Scroll down in the list of items	Down arrow (↓)
Open the selected item	Return, Enter, ⌘+down arrow (↓), or ⌘+O
Open the enclosing folder or disk	⌘+up arrow (↑)
Expand the selected folder	⌘+right arrow (→)*
Collapse the selected folder	⌘+left arrow (←)*
Go to the next disk	⌘+right arrow (<right arrow)**
Go to the previous disk	⌘+left arrow (←)**

Continued

Table 7-1 *(continued)*	
Objective	*Keystroke*
Go to the desktop	⌘+Shift+up arrow (↑) or ⌘+D
Eject the current disk	⌘+E**
Eject the floppy disk in drive 1	⌘+Shift+1
Eject the floppy disk in drive 2	⌘+Shift+2
Click the Open button	Return or Enter
Click the Cancel button	Escape or ⌘+period(.)
Show the original of an alias (instead of opening it)	Option+⌘+O, Option+double+click, or Option+click Open button

*Works in Navigation Services dialog box but not in Open dialog box.

**Works in Open dialog box but not in Navigation Services dialog box.

Managing Multiple Open Programs

With the Mac OS, you can have more than one program open at a time. When you open a program, the Finder remains open in the background. You can switch to the Finder without quitting the program you just opened. If your computer has enough memory, you can open additional programs without quitting. You can have as many programs open simultaneously as fit in your computer's memory. Figure 7-10 shows a desktop with windows from several programs open at the same time.

The capability to have multiple programs open simultaneously, which is called *multitasking*, is very convenient. For example, you can copy and paste among documents of open programs without closing documents and quitting programs.

Multitasking's convenience has disorienting side effects. For example, a stray mouse click may make another open program active, bringing its windows to the front and covering the windows of the program you were using. If this happens unexpectedly, you may think that the program you're using has crashed when it is actually open and well in the background. You must get used to having multiple layers of open programs like piles of paper on a desk. Fortunately, you can hide program layers on the Mac — unlike layers of paper on your desk — as discussed later in this section under "Reducing window clutter."

No matter how many programs you have open, only one has control of the menu bar. The program currently in control is called the *active program*. Its icon appears at the right end of the menu bar, and normally its name also appears there. You can tell which open program is currently active by looking at that icon and icon name (if present), and at the titles of the other menus on the menu bar.

Figure 7-10: You can have multiple programs open at the same time.

Switching programs

When you have more than one program open, there are several ways you can switch from one to the other. You can use the Application menu, the Application Switcher window, or the windows and icons that you can see that belong to open programs.

Application menu

Not only do the program icon and name at the right end of the menu bar tell you which program is active, but it also marks the Application menu. The Application menu lists all open programs by name and small icon. You can use the Application menu to switch from one open program to another. Figure 7-11 is an example of the Application menu.

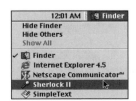

Figure 7-11: Switch applications with the Application menu.

To make a program in the Application menu the active program, choose it from the menu. When you do, that program takes over the menu bar and the program's windows come to the front. The program that was active becomes inactive. Its windows drop back but remain visible except for the parts covered by other open programs' windows.

Although the title of the Application menu initially includes both the icon and the name of the active program, you can shorten the title to show only the icon. To resize the Application menu title, you drag the textured bar on the left side of the title. As you drag to the right, the Mac OS abbreviates the program name more and more in the menu bar. When you stop dragging, the name disappears and just the icon remains. If the Application menu title is only an icon, you can lengthen it to include the name by dragging the textured area to the left.

Note Occasionally, the Mac OS has to shrink the Application menu title to an icon even though you didn't set it up that way yourself. This happens when the active application has so many menus on the menu bar that there isn't room to show the name as part of the Application menu title.

Program windows and icons

You can switch to a program by clicking any of its windows that you can see. All of the program's windows come to the front together, the program's menus take over the menu bar, and the program becomes the active program. Another way to accomplish this is by opening its icon or any of its document icons in the Finder.

Clicking the desktop or a Finder window makes the Finder active. On one hand, being able to bring the Finder to the front with a single mouse click can be very handy. On the other hand, it can be disorienting to have the application you're using suddenly disappear behind the Finder's windows due to a misplaced click on the desktop. If you find this behavior annoying, you can suppress the display of the desktop while you use other applications, as described under "Reducing window clutter" later in this section.

Application Switcher

You can switch among open programs using a window that you get by tearing off the Application menu. This window, called the *Application Switcher*, has a button for each open program. Clicking a program's button in the Application Switcher makes it the active application. The Application Switcher initially displays the icons and names of all open programs, as shown in Figure 7-12, but you can change its size and orientation.

Figure 7-12: Switch to another open application by clicking it in the Application Switcher.

Besides switching programs with the Application Switcher, you can also open a document by dragging its icon to the button of a compatible application in the Switcher. You'll know an application is compatible with a document you're dragging because its button becomes highlighted in the Application Switcher.

To tear off the Application Switcher, drag all the way to the bottom of the Application menu and then drag beyond it. When you see an outline of a window, release the mouse button.

The Application Switcher floats above other windows so it's always accessible. As a result, it can get in your way. You can move it like any other window, by dragging its title bar or window frame. In addition, you can move it by ⌘+dragging any part of it. To indicate this function, the mouse pointer looks like a gloved hand when it is over the Application Switcher and you are pressing ⌘.

There are several ways to make the Application Switcher smaller or larger. You can alternate between the maximum button width (icon and full program name) and minimum button width (icon only) by clicking the zoom box. To adjust the widths of all buttons between these extremes, drag the right edge of any button. You can also alternate between large and small icons by Option+clicking the zoom box.

To alternate between vertical and horizontal orientation, Option+Shift+click the zoom box.

The Application Switcher normally has two keyboard shortcuts that you can use to switch programs. Press ⌘+Tab to switch to the next open program. Press ⌘+Shift+Tab to switch to the previous program. If necessary, you can disable or change these keyboard shortcuts. The simplest way to modify the Application Switcher's keyboard shortcuts is to use the onscreen help that comes with the Mac OS. First, make sure the Finder is the active application and then choose Mac Help from the file menu. On the left side of the Mac Help window, click "Files and programs." Then on the right side of the window, click "Switching between open programs." Scroll down until you see the underlined text "Help me modify the keyboard shortcuts" next to a large diamond and click this text. A series of dialog boxes leads you through the process of modifying the shortcut keys.

 Cross-Reference For more information on using onscreen help, see Chapter 9.

The Application Switcher has advanced features that you can control only through AppleScript. One feature is the capability to hide the title bar and window frame. You can also have programs listed in the order in which you opened them instead of alphabetical order. To give you an idea of the possibilities, the Mac OS comes with three AppleScript scripts for changing the Application Switcher. You can run these scripts by clicking underlined text in the "Using the Application Switcher" topic of the "Switching between open programs" help document in Mac Help. Clicking the text "Open the Application Switcher in a horizontal row..." runs a script that spreads the Application Switcher across the bottom of the screen, without a title bar, window frame, or close box. Clicking the text "Open the Application Switcher in icon view..." runs a script that makes the Application Switcher an icon bar in the lower-right corner of the screen, with programs listed in the order in which they were opened. Clicking "Restore the default display settings..." resets the Application Switcher to its standard appearance.

Cross-Reference   For a detailed introduction to AppleScript, see Chapter 24.

Reducing window clutter

With many programs open, the desktop quickly becomes a visual Tower of Babel. You can eliminate the clutter by choosing the Application menu's Hide Others command. It hides the windows of all programs except the currently active one. The icons of hidden programs are dimmed in the Application menu and the Application Switcher, if you've torn it off and made it visible. To make the windows of all programs visible, choose Show All from the Application menu.

You can hide the active program's windows and simultaneously switch to the most recently active program by choosing the first command from the Application menu. The command's name begins with the word Hide and ends with the name of the currently active program.

To hide the active program's windows as you switch to another program, press Option while choosing the other program from the Application menu or from the Application Switcher. Or press Option while clicking the other program's window. You can hide the application you're using and switch to the Finder by pressing Option while clicking the desktop, a Finder icon, or a Finder window.

You can have the Mac OS hide the Finder's desktop automatically whenever you are working in another program. With the Finder's desktop hidden, you can't accidentally activate the Finder by clicking the desktop. To keep the Finder hidden, turn off the "Show Desktop when in background" option in the General Controls control panel, as shown in Figure 7-13.

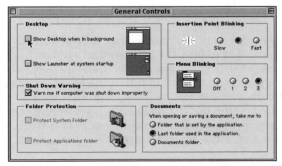

Figure 7-13: Keep the Finder hidden with the General Controls control panel.

Memory partitions

Every application program and desk accessory you open has its own layer on the desktop and its own part of memory. You can see how your computer's memory is partitioned at any time. Just switch to the Finder and choose About This Computer from the Apple menu. Figure 7-14 is an example of the About This Computer window.

Cross-Reference

Chapter 19 explains how to manage your computer's memory.

Figure 7-14: About This Computer lets you check the amount of memory that is being used by open programs.

Background operations

Some programs can operate in the background by using Mac OS multitasking capabilities. Background programs run during the intervals (typically less than one-eighth of a second long) when the active program isn't using the computer. They usually work while the active program waits for you to do something. For example, Chapter 5 explained that the Finder can copy files and empty the Trash in the background.

Moving Document Contents Around

While a document is open, you can generally move its contents to different places in the same document or other documents. The classic way to move contents is with the Edit menu's Cut, Copy, and Paste commands. Many programs also let you drag content from one place and drop it in another.

Interacting with background programs

A background program can't use the menu bar and shouldn't interact directly with you in any way. It can, however, ask you to activate it by some or all of these means:

✦ Displaying a diamond symbol next to its name in the Application menu

✦ Flashing its icon on top of the Application menu's icon or the Apple menu's icon

✦ Playing the system alert sound (commonly a beep)

✦ Displaying a nonblocking alert message

In addition, a program in the background can interact with other open programs by sending them Apple Events messages (as described in Chapter 24).

Cut, Copy, and Paste

Everyone quickly learns to use the Cut, Copy, and Paste commands to transfer material within a document and between documents. First, you select the content to move—some text, a picture, a movie, or whatever kind of data the document contains. Then you choose Cut or Copy from the Edit menu to place the selected data on the Clipboard, which is a holding area for data in transit. The Cut command removes the selected data from its original location, but the Copy command doesn't. Next, you select the location where you want to place the contents of the Clipboard and choose Paste from the Edit menu to put it there.

The Paste command does not empty the Clipboard. After pasting the contents once, you can paste the contents again. The Clipboard doesn't change until you copy or cut again (or until you shut down the computer).

You can copy-and-paste or cut-and-paste within the same document, between documents in the same application, or between documents in different applications. With a little practice, cut-and-paste and copy-and-paste become second nature, especially if you use the keyboard shortcuts (⌘+X for Cut, ⌘+C for Copy, and ⌘+V for Paste).

Drag and drop

The Mac OS provides a more direct way to copy text, graphics, and other material within a document, between documents, and between programs. This capability, called *drag-and-drop editing*, works only with programs that are designed to take advantage of it. Several programs that come with the Mac OS work with drag-and-drop editing, including SimpleText, Stickies, the Note Pad, and the Scrapbook.

To move material within a document, open the document and select the text, graphic, or other material that you want to move. Then position the mouse pointer over the selected material, press the mouse button, and drag to the place where you want to move it. As you drag, an outline of the selected material follows the pointer, and if you're dragging text, an insertion point shows where the material will appear when you stop dragging. If you want to copy rather than move selected material within a document, press Option before releasing the mouse button. Figure 7-15 shows some text being moved within a document.

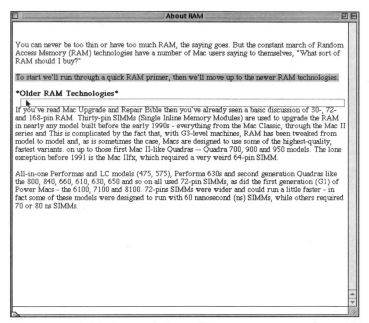

Figure 7-15: With drag-and-drop editing, you can move data within a document.

To copy material between documents, first open both documents and position them so that you can see the source material and the place where you want to drop a copy of it. Select the text, graphic, or other source material and then drag the selected material to the place in the second document where you want the copy. As you drag, an outline of the selected material follows the mouse pointer. When the pointer enters the destination window, a border appears around the content area of the window, and if you're dragging text, an insertion point shows where the copy will appear when you stop dragging. Note that you do not have to press Option to make a copy when dragging between documents. You can use the same method to copy between two documents in the same application or between docu-ments in different applications. Figure 7-16 shows some text being copied from one application to another.

Some people prefer drag-and-drop to cut-and-paste editing because they find it easier to use. Drag-and-drop has one clear advantage: It doesn't wipe out the contents of the Clipboard, so it's a good method to use when the Clipboard contains important material that you're not ready to replace.

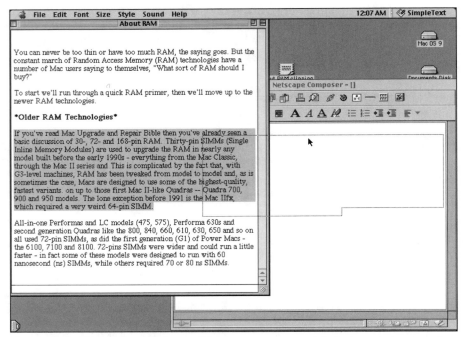

Figure 7-16: With drag-and-drop editing, you can move data between documents.

Clipping files

You can also drag selected material from a document to the desktop or a folder window, where the Finder creates a clipping file that contains a copy of the dragged material. You can open a clipping file to see it in the Finder, but you can't select anything in a clipping file. You can copy the contents of a clipping file to a document by dragging the clipping-file icon to the open document's window. Clipping files can contain text, pictures, QuickTime movies, and sound.

You can use a clipping file over and over. For example, you can keep handy clippings that contain your letterhead, the company logo, a list of your e-mail addresses, and any other element that you use frequently.

Creating Documents

You can't always be opening documents that already exist. Sometimes you need to create new ones. Many application programs automatically create a brand-new, untitled document when you double-click the application icon. Most applications let you create a new document any time you want one by choosing New from the File menu.

You can also create a document by making a copy of an existing document. This method is especially useful if the existing document contains something you want to include in a new document, such as a letterhead or some boilerplate. To make a copy of a document, use the Finder's Duplicate command or one of the other methods described in Chapter 5.

Rather than duplicating a document each time you want a copy of it, you can make it a stationery pad. Opening a stationery pad—whether from the Finder directly, from the Apple menu, from the Launcher, or with the Open command in many applications—is like tearing a page from a pad of printed forms: you get a new document with a preset format and contents. Stationery pads generally have a distinctive icon that looks like a stack of document icons, although some types of stationery have generic (blank) stationery pad icons. Figure 7-17 shows some examples of stationery pad icons.

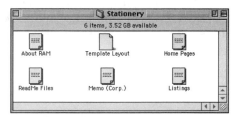

Figure 7-17: Stationery pad icons usually resemble pads of paper.

You can make any document a stationery pad by selecting the document in the Finder, choosing the Get Info command, and setting the Stationery Pad option in the Info window. Some applications enable you to directly save a document as a stationery pad (more about that in the next section, "Saving Documents"). Figure 7-18 shows the Stationery Pad option in an Info window.

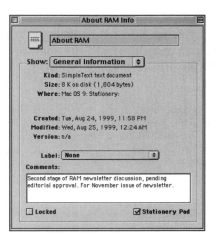

Figure 7-18: You can make a stationery pad with the Finder's Get Info command.

What happens when you open a stationery pad depends on whether the application that opens it knows the difference between stationery pads and regular documents. What happens may also depend on how you open the application. If an application knows about stationery pads, it always creates a new untitled document with the format and content of the stationery pad. In this case, it doesn't matter how you open the stationery pad. If you use the Finder, the Apple menu, or the Launcher, the Mac OS figures out which application creates the type of stationery you're opening and tells that application to open the stationery. If you use the application's Open command, the application opens the stationery directly.

If you open a stationery pad for a type of document created by an application that doesn't know about stationery, the Mac OS creates a new document by making a copy from the stationery pad and has the application open the new document. The Finder automatically names the new document.

If you open a stationery pad with the Open command of an application that doesn't know about stationery, the application opens the stationery pad itself, not a copy of it. A message warns you that you are opening a stationery pad. If you make changes, they are saved in the stationery pad itself.

Saving Documents

After creating a new document or making changes to a document you opened, you need to save the document on disk so that the changes persist. Make sure the document's window is active (in front of other document windows) and choose Save or Save As from the File menu. For a new document, either of these commands brings up a dialog box in which you name the document and select the folder where you want it saved. For a previously saved document, the Save command does not bring up a dialog box; the application automatically saves the changed document in place of the previously saved document. The Save As command always brings up a dialog box so you can save a copy of a previously saved document.

In some applications, the Save and Save As commands display a standard Save dialog box, but in many applications, these commands display the Navigation Services dialog box. These dialog boxes look and work much like the ones for opening documents (described earlier in this chapter). Figure 7-19 shows examples of Save and Navigation Services dialog boxes.

A Save dialog box shows the contents of the desktop, the main level of one disk, or one folder at a time and has controls for opening a different disk or folder in the dialog box. In addition, the Save dialog box has a space where you enter a name for the document. The Save dialog box may have other controls for setting document format options.

When locks are better than stationery

Opening a stationery pad creates a new document file. If you want to make a template that doesn't create a new file every time you open the template, don't make the template a stationery pad. Instead, make the template an ordinary document, but lock it by using the Finder's Get Info command. You may want to use this method with templates for single envelopes and mailing labels, for example. Then you can open the locked template, type or paste the recipient's address, print, and close without saving. (Note that this won't work in all cases—some applications won't allow you to open locked documents, while others may not allow you to edit them once opened.)

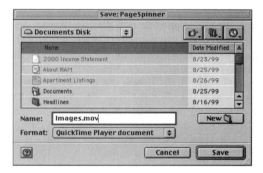

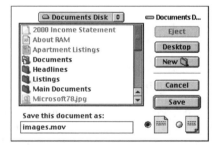

Figure 7-19: Saving a document using a standard Save dialog box (top) or a Navigation Services dialog box (bottom)

Like a Save dialog box, a Navigation Services dialog box for saving a document shows the contents of the desktop, the main level of one disk, or one folder at a time. You cannot see the contents of multiple folders in the same list, because the folders do not have disclosure triangles. In this regard, the Navigation Services dialog box for saving is different than the one for opening files.

Although the Navigation Services dialog box for saving documents is similar to the Save dialog box, it is improved nonetheless. The scrolling list of files and folders shows item names and modification dates, like a list view of a folder window in the Finder. You can sort the list by clicking a column heading in the dialog box, and you can reverse the sort order by clicking the triangular sort direction indicator at the right end of the column headings (above the scroll bar). Moreover, you can usually move a Navigation Services dialog box, change its size, and switch to another application while the dialog box is displayed. (Applications, however, can suppress these abilities to move, resize, or switch applications.)

Specifying a name and location

The first time you save a document, and every time you use the Save As command, you need to type a name for the document in the space provided in the dialog box. You also need to specify where you want the document saved. You do that by opening a folder, the main level of a disk, or the desktop in the dialog box. All the methods described earlier in this chapter for opening folders, disks, and the desktop in dialog boxes for opening documents also work in dialog boxes for saving documents. You can open folders and disks by double-clicking them or by selecting one and clicking the Open button. You can use the pop-up menu (or click the disk name in a Save dialog box) to go back through the folder layers toward the desktop. You can eject a removable disk with the Eject button in a Save dialog box or the Shortcuts menu in a Navigation Services dialog box. You can also use the Favorites and Recent menus in a Navigation Services dialog box to open folders or disks quickly.

When you select a folder or disk in the Save or Navigation Services dialog box, there is an Open button but no Save button. To change the Open button to a Save button so you can save the document, select the document name in the dialog box by clicking it or by pressing Tab.

Tip   While you are entering a name for the document to save in a Save or Navigation Services dialog box, the Cut, Copy, and Paste commands may be available from the Edit menu. This means you can copy a name for a document from within the document before choosing the Save command, and then paste the copied name into the dialog box. When pasting a document name, only the first 31 characters are used; the rest are omitted. In some programs, you must use the keyboard equivalents: ⌘+X for Cut, ⌘+C for Copy, and ⌘+V for Paste.

Saving a stationery pad

In many applications, you can designate in a Save or Navigation Services dialog box whether to save a document as a stationery pad or a regular document. Some applications offer this choice with two radio buttons, one labeled with a regular document icon and the other labeled with a stationery pad icon. Other applications offer more document format options in a pop-up menu in the dialog box.

Creating a new folder

A Save or Navigation Services dialog box usually includes a button that you can click to create a new folder. Clicking the New Folder button displays a small dialog box in which you type the name of the folder you want to create and click. The new folder is created in the folder, disk, or desktop whose contents are currently displayed in the Save dialog box. Figure 7-20 shows the dialog box in which you enter a new folder name.

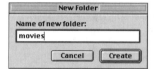

Figure 7-20: Make a new folder while saving in a Save dialog box (top) or in a Navigation Services dialog box (bottom).

Navigating with the keyboard

You can use the same keyboard shortcuts in dialog boxes for saving documents (previously listed in Table 7-1) as in dialog boxes for opening documents. You can also press ⌘+N to create a new folder. However, there is a trick to navigating with the keyboard in dialog boxes for saving. You must select the scrolling list in the dialog box so that your keystrokes don't end up as part of the document name. You can alternate between the scrolling list and the name entry area by pressing Tab. Clicking in either area also makes it the keyboard target. The Mac OS indicates that your typing will affect the scrolling list by outlining it with a heavy black border. If, instead, you see a flashing insertion point or highlighted text in the document name, you know that your typing affects it.

Translating Documents

As the Mac OS has evolved, it has gradually simplified the process of opening documents created with programs you don't have. Someone else may have created the documents on another Mac OS computer or a PC, which uses the Windows or DOS operating system. You may have created the document with an application you don't have any more. In any case, you need to open the document with an application you do have. You may be able to use an application that can open foreign documents itself, or you may need translation software to convert the foreign document to a format your application can open.

PC disks

One of the ways you get PC files on your Mac in the first place is from PC disks. The File Exchange control panel enables the Mac OS to recognize PC floppy disks and SCSI disks. When you insert a PC floppy, a Zip disk formatted for PCs, a PC-formatted CD, or another removable PC disk, its icon appears on the desktop just like a Mac disk. If you attach a PC-format SCSI hard disk to your Mac and then start up the computer, an icon appears on the desktop for the PC hard disk.

You can open a PC disk and see its files and folders (which are also called *subdirectories* in DOS and Windows). You can open folders by double-clicking them, and you can open document files if you know which Mac applications can open them (more on this subject is found under the next heading).

If the Mac OS does not recognize a SCSI hard disk or removable disk, open the File Exchange control panel and click its Mount Now button. If you want PC SCSI disks to automatically appear on your desktop when you start up your Mac, select the "Mount at startup" option at the bottom of the control panel.

PC file mapping

If you have a file that came from a PC, the Mac OS can't use its standard method for determining which application should open it. Where a Mac file has internal codes that tell the Mac OS which applications can open it, a PC file has a code you can see in its name. This code, called a *file name extension* or *file name suffix*, comes at the end of the file name following a period. (File name extensions don't always appear on a computer that uses Windows 95/98 because it is possible, and common, to conceal them there. Windows 95/98 keeps track of file name extensions in a table called the Registry.)

Basically, the Mac OS (like Windows) uses a table to map file name extensions to applications. Mac OS 9 has a sizable table of file extension mappings built in. You can also configure file name extension mappings yourself, as explained next. Table 7-2 lists some common PC file name extensions and their corresponding applications.

Configuring file mapping

To configure the mapping of file name extensions to applications in Mac OS 9, you use the PC Exchange section of the File Exchange control panel (see Figure 7-21).

Table 7-2
PC File Name Extensions

Extension	Application and Document Type
.AI	Adobe Illustrator document
.BMP	Windows or OS/2 bitmap graphic
.CDR	CorelDraw document
.COM	A program
.DBF	Database file (originally dBase, but supported by various spreadsheet and database applications)
.DOC	Microsoft Word document
.DOT	Microsoft Word template
.EPS	Encapsulated PostScript file
.EXE	Self-extracting compressed file (PKzip format) or an application
.GIF	GIF graphic
.HTM	Web page (HTML file)
.IL5	Illustrator document (number is the application version)
.JPG	JPEG compressed graphic
.P65	Adobe PageMaker 6.5 publication file
.PCT	PICT graphic
.PCX	PC Paintbrush graphic
.PDF	Adobe Acrobat document
.PM6	PageMaker 6 document (number is the application version)
.PPT	Microsoft PowerPoint document
.PRN	Any print-to-disk file from many applications, including PostScript, PCL (HP LaserJet), or ASCII (for line printers)
.PS	PostScript file
.PSD	Adobe Photoshop document
.PT6	PageMaker 6 template (number is the application version)
.PUB	Microsoft Publisher document
.QXD	QuarkXPress document
.RTF	Rich Text Format word processing document (which can be opened in a word processor or placed in PageMaker or other desktop publishing programs)
.SAM	AmiPro document

Continued

Table 7-2 *(continued)*	
Extension	**Application and Document Type**
.T65	Adobe PageMaker 6.5 template file
.TBL	Adobe table editor document
.TIF	TIFF graphic
.TXT	Plain-text document
.WK1	Lotus 1-2-3 spreadsheet (the number is the application version)
.WKS	Microsoft Works document
.WMF	Windows Metafile graphic
.WP	WordPerfect document
.WPD	WordPerfect document (version 6.1 and higher)
.WPG	WordPerfect graphic
.WQ1	Quattro Pro spreadsheet (the number is the application version)
.WRI	Microsoft Write document
.WS2	WordStar document (the number is the application version)
.XLS	Microsoft Excel spreadsheet
.ZIP	Compressed file (PKzip format)

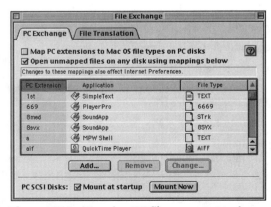

Figure 7-21: Mapping PC file name extensions to Mac applications

You can change the mapping of a PC file name extension by selecting one of the mappings listed in the PC Exchange control panel and clicking the Change button.

You can also add a new mapping of a file name extension by clicking the Add button. These actions bring up a dialog box in which you type an extension, select a Mac application, and choose a document type, as shown in Figure 7-22.

Figure 7-22: Assigning a PC file extension to a Mac application and file type

Clicking the Remove button in the control panel removes the currently selected extension mapping from the list. Before clicking Remove, you can select multiple items in the list by ⌘+clicking them (to select them individually) or Shift+clicking (to select a range).

Note   If the QuickTime Exchange option is turned on in the QuickTime Settings control panel, its mappings for graphics, sound, video, and other media files take precedence over the PC Exchange mappings.

File mapping options

You can turn PC file mapping on or off in the PC Exchange section of the File Exchange control panel. Turn off the first option in the control panel, "Map PC extensions to Mac OS file types on PC disks." If you turn off file mapping, then the files on PC disks are not mapped to Mac applications, and the PC files have generic PC icons. If you turn on file mapping, then PC files on PC disks are mapped; they take on Mac OS file types and have icons that look like Mac file icons.

File mapping happens only to PC files located on PC disks whose icons are on your desktop. The disks can be PC floppy disks, PC Zip disks, PC SCSI disks connected to your Mac's SCSI port (if it has one), and so forth. If you copy a PC file from a PC disk to a Mac disk, the copy on the Mac disk keeps the file mapping of the original on the PC disk.

If you have any unmapped PC files on a Mac disk, they will not be mapped to Mac applications; they must be on PC disks to be mapped. Unmapped files have generic PC icons, not the icons of Mac files. You can get unmapped PC files from many sources. They can come attached to e-mail. You can download them from the Web or FTP sites on the Internet. You can copy unmapped PC files from other computers on your local area network. You can also copy them from PC disks while file mapping is turned off.

File Exchange can determine which Mac application should open any unmapped PC file according to its file name extension. The unmapped file still has a generic PC icon, but at least File Exchange helps you open it. The unmapped file can be on a PC disk or a Mac disk. To enable this feature, turn on the second option at the top of the control panel.

File translation

The Mac OS can help you open files created by applications you don't have. The File Translation section of the File Exchange control panel handles this. This control panel steps in when you try to open a file created by an application that you don't have. It suggests alternative applications of yours that may be able to translate and open the file, as explained in detail under the next two headings.

You may have files that none of your applications know how to open. In this case, software that comes with the Mac OS may be able to translate the files so that your applications can open them. Mac OS 9 comes with QuickTime 4.0, which can translate many types of graphics, sound, and video files.

Note   Earlier versions of the Mac OS included a copy of MacLinkPlus, a program that translates between common word processing and other formats. It doesn't come with Mac OS 9, but you can still buy it and add it to your Mac OS 9 installation if you like. It's available from DataViz (www.dataviz.com).

Translation choices

File Exchange goes to work whenever you open a document that wasn't created by any of the applications you have. It doesn't matter how you open the document — by double-clicking its icon in the Finder, choosing it from the Apple menu, or using the Open command in an application.

When you try to open a document created by an application you don't have, File Exchange displays an alert box that lists your alternatives for opening the document. Each alternative identifies an application you have and may also specify an available translator that can translate the document you're opening for that application. A program may be listed more than once, each time with a different translator. For example, if you try to open an old PICT (picture) document created by MacDraw, which you no longer have, the alert might list ClarisWorks three times, once with no translator (ClarisWorks can open PICT documents directly), once with MacLinkPlus translation, and once with QuickTime translation. Figure 7-23 is an example of the translation choices alert box.

Long file names

Mac and PC file names are not the same length. Mac file names can be as long as 31 characters. Windows 95/98 and NT 4.0 allow file names as long as 253 characters, but for compatibility with earlier Windows versions and DOS, these operating systems also store a truncated version of each file name. The truncated names can be as long as 12 characters and typically consist of up to eight characters that identify the file, followed by a period and a three-character file name extension. This short file name form is known as a DOS file name or an 8.3 file name.

PC Exchange takes care of file name length differences. When you copy a Mac file to a PC disk or save a file directly to a PC disk from a Mac, File Exchange makes up an 8.3 version of the Mac file name. You still see the full Mac file name when you use the PC disk on a Mac. Someone using the same disk on a PC sees either the 8.3 name or the full name, depending on the Windows version installed on the PC.

When you look at PC files on a Mac, you may see 8.3 file names or long file names. PC Exchange can display the first 31 characters of a long PC file name. Of course, if the PC file was saved with an 8.3 name, that's what you see on a Mac.

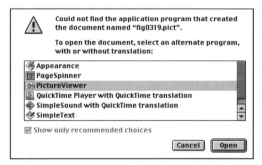

Figure 7-23: Selecting a program and a translator to open a document created by an application you don't have

In the translation choices alert box, you select a translation alternative that looks promising (ideally a translation for a program closely related to the document) and click the Open button. You can alternatively just double-click a translation alternative. File Exchange applies the selected translator (if any) and has the selected application open the translated document.

You can see more choices in the translation choices alert box by turning off the "Show only recommended choices" option. With this option turned off, a list of all the applications you have that can conceivably open the file is displayed. If you choose an alternative that's not on the short recommended list, the file probably won't translate well. For example, America Online can open a Word for Windows document, but the document comes across as unformatted text with a bunch of extraneous box characters. Some of the applications in the long list won't even open the file, so in general you save time when you stick with the recommended translations.

File Exchange keeps track of the application and translator that you choose to open each type of document. If you subsequently open another document of the same type, File Exchange automatically selects the same application and translator for you.

File Exchange setup

You can set several options in the File Exchange control panel, as shown in Figure 7-24, that affect automatic file translation.

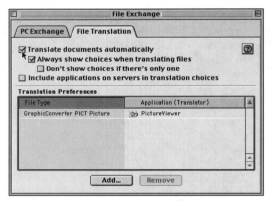

Figure 7-24: Setting automatic file translation options

You can turn off automatic file translation altogether. In the File Translation section of the File Exchange control panel, turn off the option "Translate documents automatically."

You can set File Exchange to display the translation choices alert box only the first time that you open a particular type of file. In the File Exchange control panel, turn off the option "Always show choices when translating files." Turn on the option if you want the alert to appear every time you open a document that wasn't created by an application you have.

Another option lets you suppress the alert when there is only one translation choice. In the File Exchange control panel, turn on the option "Don't show choices if there's only one."

A fourth option controls whether the alert lists applications from file servers, which operate more slowly than applications on your local disks. In the File Exchange control panel, turn on the option "Include applications on servers in translation choices."

Encrypting Files

Mac OS 9 adds a new option to your arsenal for dealing with documents. Not only can you create, open, save, and translate them, but you can also encrypt and compress documents (and other files) using Apple's new Apple File Security technology.

Encrypting documents does two things, at least in Apple's implementation. First, it makes the document unreadable to applications and utilities by garbling the contents so that they are unrecognizable, similar to an encrypted message sent by spies during wartime. Only your password, along with the Apple File Security application, can make the file readable again. Second, the file is compressed, so that it takes up less space on your hard disk. That can be convenient when you'd like to secure documents for storage on your hard disk or backup on removable disks.

New Feature Mac OS 9 adds this new capability to encrypt and compress documents using the Apple File Security application. Integration with the keychain is also new, because the keychain is a feature that was added to Mac OS 9 as well. (The keychain and Keychain Access control panel are covered in Chapter 12.)

Encrypting the file

Creating an encrypted file is easy. You can encrypt a document, application, or system component (if you can come up with a reason to), but you can't encrypt an entire folder. To encrypt a file, drag the file to the Apple File Security icon, which is located in the Security folder in your Mac's Applications folder, as shown in Figure 7-25.

Note Files in the System Folder must be dragged out of the System Folder (or its subfolders) before they can be encrypted. If you attempt to do so, you'll see an alert telling you that items in the System Folder can't be compressed (and, by extension, they can't be encrypted, either).

Figure 7-25: Encrypt a file by dragging it to the Apple File Security application.

When you drop the file on the Apple File Security icon, the Apple File Security application launches, allowing you to enter a password or passphrase for encryption. Enter it once, press Tab, then enter it again. Note the check box, which you can use to decide whether or not to save the password to your keychain. (By default, the option is selected and your password is saved to your keychain.) Adding the password to your keychain enables you to unlock the file without remembering the password, as long as you remember your keychain's main password (discussed later in the section "Using your keychain"). When you're ready to encrypt, click the Encrypt button (see Figure 7-26).

Tip   You can also encrypt a file in the Finder by Control+clicking its icon. In the contextual pop-up menu, choose Encrypt.

Figure 7-26: Enter the password you'd like to use for the encrypted file.

The file is encrypted (and compressed to take up less disk space). In the Finder, you can tell the encrypted file by its icon—the item's regular icon now includes a small gold key as part of it. This means the file cannot be opened unless you have the password.

Caution   If you encrypt a file and send it to a person who is using an older version of the Mac OS (or someone using a different computing platform), it will not appear with a special icon, and the user will not be able to open the document or launch the file. At the time of writing, it wasn't clear whether Apple would release the Apple File Security application for download to users of older Mac OS versions. Also, if you choose not to use the keychain to store your password or passphrase, be sure not to forget it. If you forget your password, you will not be able to use the file in the future.

Opening an encrypted file

To open an encrypted file to view or edit its contents, simply double-click it in the Finder or launch it some other way (by choosing File ⇨ Open, selecting it from the Favorites menu, and so on). If you didn't add this file's password to your keychain, or if you're opening the file on a Mac OS 9 computer that wasn't used to encrypt it, then you'll see the Apple File Security dialog box. Enter the password for the encrypted file and click Decrypt. When the decryption process is finished, the file is opened or launched.

Tip You can also drag the encrypted file to the Apple File Security application to decrypt it.

Using your keychain

If you have saved the encrypted file's password to your keychain, then you may, or may not, see one or more dialog boxes. If your keychain is currently locked, then you'll see a dialog box asking for the password for your keychain. Enter your keychain password and click Unlock. Once the keychain is unlocked (or if it wasn't locked in the first place), you may see the Keychain Access Confirmation dialog box asking whether you want to allow Apple File Security to access the keychain. If you do, click Allow. (You can also choose one of the check box options to alter the keychain's behavior in the future.) Your password is accessed from the keychain and the file is decrypted and opened.

If you've previously decrypted a file and told the keychain to "Allow Apple File Security to access items without warning while running" then you won't see the Keychain Access Confirmation dialog box. The file is simply decrypted and opened. Likewise, if you've used your keychain to access any keychain resource and selected "Allow access without warning when using keychain," you won't see the Keychain Access Confirmation dialog box, and the file is decrypted immediately and opened.

Cross-Reference The Keychain is discussed in more detail in Chapters 12 and 21.

Summary

This chapter began with a discussion of how to open documents in the Finder by dragging the documents to any compatible program. It showed you how to open anything from the Apple menu and the Launcher control panel, and how to have items opened during startup or shutdown. It also covered the dialog boxes used by all applications for opening documents and with the similar dialog boxes used by applications for saving new documents and document changes.

When you have more than one program open at the same time, you can make any of them active using the Application menu and other options. The Mac OS offers a number of options for dealing with window clutter and choices for how multiple programs share your computer's memory and work in the background.

This chapter described several ways to create new documents. You can duplicate existing documents or create new ones from scratch with an application's New command. You can also make and use stationery pads for creating new documents.

Also discussed was how the Mac OS helps you open documents created by applications that you don't have. The File Exchange control enables your computer to use removable disks from Windows and DOS computers, and you can configure the control panel to have your applications automatically open compatible foreign documents according to their DOS file extensions.

Finally, you saw how to encrypt files to securely store them on your disk or on backup media. And, you saw how you can use the Finder, Apple File Security, or the keychain to decrypt files and make them usable again.

✦   ✦   ✦

Modify Appearance and Behavior

If you don't like the way icons, windows, and menus look and act, there are several things that you can do about it. In the looks department, you can choose the accent and highlight colors that are used in menus, windows, and text. You can choose the system font that Mac OS 9 uses in menus and titles, and choose a font for icon names and list views in the Finder. You can smooth fonts on the screen. You can pick a desktop pattern or a desktop picture and you can replace individual icons with your own pictures.

In the behavior department, you can change what action makes the Mac OS collapse or expand a window and you can change the way scroll bars look and work in your windows. Plus, you can add a soundtrack to your Mac's interface, attaching sound effects to system actions.

Overall Look

Mac OS 9 inherits its overall look, which Apple calls the *platinum appearance,* from Mac OS 8. The platinum look features gray menus with color accents and 3D shading. Many windows are also gray, and all have a lot of 3D detail. In addition, the icons that represent folders, disks, and some files have the illusion of depth.

Although Mac OS 9 is theoretically capable of displaying appearances other than platinum, it does not include alternate appearances, and Apple has never officially released any. (An alternate appearance consists of a set of files that you put in the Appearance folder by dragging the files to the System Folder icon.)

Note When Mac OS 8.5 was released it looked as if Apple might include some other appearances with the OS, enabling you to switch between the platinum appearance and a few others that made the entire Mac OS look more futuristic (in one iteration) or kid-like (in another). Unfortunately, enough bugs couldn't get worked out of the way the appearances worked, and too many inconsistencies appeared, so Apple didn't include the additional appearances in the final version.

If you had a choice of appearances, you could pick one in the Appearance control panel. At the top of this control panel, you would click the Appearance tab and then choose the look you wanted from the Appearance pop-up menu. Figure 8-1 shows the location of this pop-up menu.

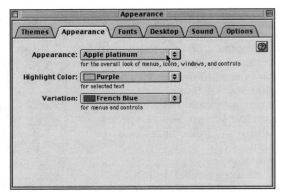

Figure 8-1: Choose an overall look for Mac OS 9 in the Appearance section of the Appearance control panel.

Even though you can't choose an alternate appearance, there are still many changes you can make to the default platinum appearance. Those changes include colors, fonts and font characteristics, background patterns and images, scroll bar behavior and sound effects, and window behavior.

Accent and highlight colors

The Mac OS uses color to accent menus and some window controls, and it uses color to highlight selected text. If you'd like to give your Mac a little splash of color (or if you're having trouble seeing selected text), you can change the highlight color for text in the Appearance control panel. You can also choose a *variation* color for window and menu accents.

To set these colors, click the Appearance tab at the top of the Appearance control panel. The Highlight Color pop-up menu lists nine colors and the option to mix your own color (Other). The Variation pop-up menu lists colors that are defined for the Apple platinum appearance. Figure 8-2 shows the location of these pop-up menus.

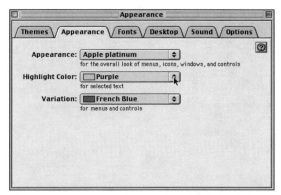

Figure 8-2: You can choose the Highlight Color or Variation in the Appearance section of the Appearance control panel.

System fonts

You have a choice of system fonts in Mac OS 9. You can choose the large system font used for window titles, menus, buttons, and dialog boxes. You can also choose the small system font, which is used for explanatory text and labels. In addition, you can choose the font that the Finder uses for icon names and list views, as described in Chapter 5.

Caution

There are some older programs that won't open when the large system font is set to anything other than Chicago. (This happens rarely, but it's possible if you use older programs.) Because Mac OS 9 defaults to Charcoal as the large system font, you may occasionally encounter this error. If it happens, change the system font to Chicago in the Appearance control panel. Contact the publisher of the program about whether an updated version is available that works with system fonts other than Chicago.

To change your system fonts, click the Fonts tab at the top of the Appearance control panel. Then, use the pop-up menus to choose fonts for each different system font type. Figure 8-3 shows the Fonts section of the Appearance control panel, which contains the pop-up menus for each font type you can set.

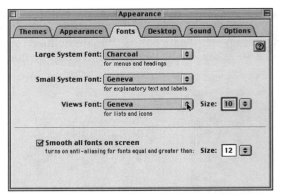

Figure 8-3: Set the Large System Font, Small System Font, and Views Font in the Fonts section of the Appearance control panel.

Font smoothing

Mac OS 9 can improve the look of text displayed on screen by smoothing the edges of fonts. Font smoothing works by blending the edges of text with the background, a technique known as *antialiasing*. To set font smoothing, click the Fonts tab of the Appearance control panel and turn on the option "Smooth all fonts on screen" (see Figure 8-3). The adjacent Size pop-up menu lets you choose a minimum font size for font smoothing. Font smoothing may make small font sizes blurry. In this case, increase the minimum font size for font smoothing.

Font smoothing can affect system performance. If you notice that it takes longer to display text on the screen and the slowdown bothers you, try increasing the minimum font size for smoothing, or turn off font smoothing altogether in the Appearance control panel.

Font smoothing may disfigure text in some applications. You may notice blemishes in highlighted text, especially when the text highlight color is set to black. You may see text alternate between smoothed and not. Or you may find text drawn incorrectly on a background that is not white. If you think font smoothing makes text unsightly or harder to read in one of your programs, turn off font smoothing and ask the publisher of the program if there is an update that fixes the problem.

Desktop background

When it comes to the overall appearance of the screen, nothing has more impact than changing the desktop's background. In addition to changing the background pattern, Mac OS 9 gives you the option of covering the pattern with a picture. You set the desktop background with the Appearances control panel.

Desktop pattern

To change the desktop pattern, click the Desktop tab in the Appearance control panel. Select a pattern by name from the scrolling list on the right side of the control panel and look at the sample displayed on the left side of the control panel. If you can't see a pattern because a picture is covering it, there will be a Remove Picture button, which you can click to reveal the pattern sample. When you see a pattern you like, click the Set Desktop button to make that pattern the desktop pattern. Figure 8-4 shows a desktop pattern in the Appearance control panel.

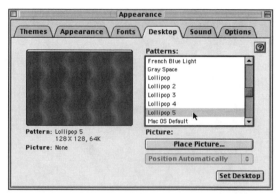

Figure 8-4: Set a desktop pattern in the Desktop section of the Appearance control panel.

You can remove the currently selected pattern from the control panel by choosing Cut or Clear from the Edit menu. After cutting a pattern, use the Paste command to store it in the Scrapbook, if you'd like to hold on to it for posterity.

To modify one of the patterns, first copy it by choosing Copy from the Edit menu. Then open a paint program and paste the copied image in it by choosing Paste from the Edit menu. Make changes to the pasted pattern with the program's painting tools and commands. Select the modified pattern in the paint program and use the Copy command to make a copy of it. Return to the Background section of the Appearance control panel and use the Paste command to add the copied pattern to the set of available desktop patterns.

You can create a new desktop pattern with a graphics program, a scanner, or other graphics source. Select the image you want to use as a desktop pattern, copy it, switch to the Background section of the Appearance control panel, and paste it.

After pasting a pattern in the Background section of the Appearance control panel, you can name it by choosing Pattern Name from the Edit menu. (You can't use this command to change the name of a preinstalled pattern.)

Desktop picture

To set or remove a picture as the desktop background, click the Desktop tab in the Appearance control panel. Then use the Place Picture or Remove Picture button and the pop-up menu near the bottom of the control panel. The control panel shows a reduced view of the current desktop picture or a sample of the current desktop pattern if there is currently no desktop picture. Figure 8-5 is a sample picture in the Appearance control panel.

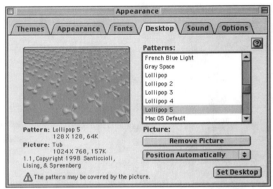

Figure 8-5: Set a desktop picture in the Desktop section of the Appearance control panel.

If the control panel shows a desktop picture that you don't want to use, click Remove Picture. The Remove Picture button then changes to a Place Picture button, and the control panel displays a sample of the desktop pattern that's currently set.

When the control panel shows a sample of the current desktop pattern, you can select a picture to overlay it by clicking Place Picture. The control panel displays a Navigation Services dialog box in which you select a picture file that you want to use as a desktop picture. The button labeled Show Preview or Hide Preview controls the display of picture previews on the right side of the dialog box. Figure 8-6 is an example of the dialog box in which you select a desktop picture file.

Cross-Reference   For more information on the Navigation Services dialog box, see Chapter 7.

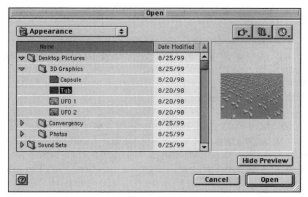

Figure 8-6: Selecting a desktop picture file

The position of the currently selected picture on the screen can be adjusted by using the pop-up menu below the Remove Picture button in the control panel. This setting compensates for any difference between the size of the screen and the size of the selected picture. The Position Automatically setting uses optional alignment and positioning information stored in the picture file by the person who created the picture. If the picture doesn't have that information, the control panel scales the picture to fit the screen without changing the picture's aspect ratio. If you choose a different setting, you can see the effect by looking at the reduced view in the control panel.

Mac OS 9 comes with a collection of pictures for the desktop background. They're located in the Desktop Pictures folder that is inside the Appearance folder in your System Folder. You can also use picture files from other folders and disks.

To have the Mac OS randomly choose a different desktop picture each time you restart the computer, drag a folder of pictures to the sample desktop area of the control panel.

If the picture you select for a desktop picture is on a CD or other removable disk that is not available the next time you start or restart the computer, the desktop pattern is displayed instead. If you want your desktop picture to always be available, copy it to your hard disk and select that copy with the Appearance control panel.

Tip If you have selected a desktop picture and your computer runs low on memory, you may notice the screen redrawing slowly after you close a window. If this happens, try removing the desktop picture and using just a desktop pattern for your background.

Scroll bar controls

Scroll arrows and the scroll box are little things — too little and not as useful as they could be, some people say. That's why Mac OS 9 is preset to put double scroll arrows at one end of every scroll bar. With double scroll arrows, you can scroll in either direction without moving the mouse pointer to the opposite end of the scroll bar. This is what Mac OS 9 calls Smart Scrolling.

In addition, the size of the scroll box indicates how much of a window's contents the window is displaying. A long scroll box means you can see most of the window's contents without scrolling, and a short scroll box means you need to scroll a lot to see all of the window's contents. A scroll bar with this type of scroll box is called a proportional scroll bar.

If you want single scroll arrows (one on each side of the scroll bar) and a scroll box that's always the same size, click the Options tab of the Appearance control panel and turn off the Smart Scrolling option. Figure 8-7 shows this option in the Appearance control panel.

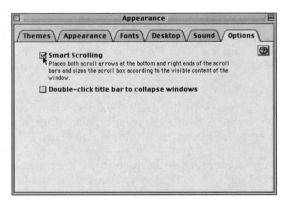

Figure 8-7: Set up the scroll bars in the Options section of the Appearance control panel.

Sound effects

Not only can you make Mac OS 9 look different, you can make it sound off when you do things with menus, windows, controls, and the icons of files, folders, and disks. Different sounds may accompany various actions in each of these categories. An entire set of related sounds is called a sound track. You can choose a sound track from among those installed on your computer, and you can turn sound effects on or off for the various action categories. (Mac OS 9 comes with only one sound track, Platinum Sounds. If Apple ever releases other sound track files, they go in the Sound Sets folder that is in the Appearance folder inside your System Folder.)

If your computer has stereo speakers, the sound effects are heard in stereo. The stereo sounds actually emanate from different locations as the mouse pointer moves from one side of the screen to the other while performing an action that has a sound effect.

To set sound effects, click the Sound tab in the Appearance control panel, choose a sound track from the pop-up menu, and use the check boxes to turn sound effects on or off for each sound category. To turn off all sound effects, choose None from the pop-up menu. Figure 8-8 shows the Sound section of the Appearance control panel.

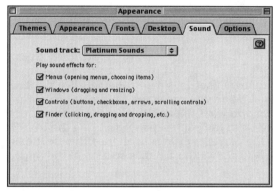

Figure 8-8: Set sound effects for various actions in the Sound section of the Appearance control panel.

Collapsing windows

It's up to you whether windows expand and collapse when you double-click their title bars. To control the collapsing window behavior, click the Options tab of the Appearance control panel and set the option "Double-click title bar to collapse windows" (see Figure 8-9).

Themes

Put together all the appearance and behavior options discussed so far and you have a group of settings called a *theme*. You can add your own themes to the preconfigured themes that come with Mac OS 9 and switch themes any time you like. Switching to a different theme puts in effect all of the new theme's settings for overall look (appearance), variation color, text highlight color, system fonts, font smoothing, desktop background, scroll bars, sound effects, and collapsing windows.

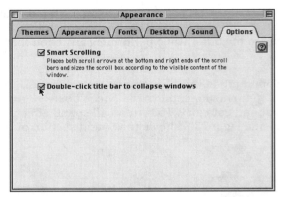

Figure 8-9: Set up window collapsing with the window shade option.

To switch themes or to make your current settings a new theme, click the Themes tab in the Appearance control panel. Then you can scroll through previews of the available themes and click one that you want to put into effect. A theme goes into effect as soon as you click its preview in the control panel. Clicking the Save Theme button creates a new theme from the current settings in all the other sections of the Appearance control panel. Figure 8-10 shows the Themes section of the Appearance control panel.

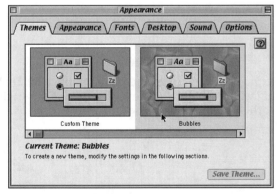

Figure 8-10: Select a theme or create a new one in the Themes section of the Appearance control panel.

If you click Save Theme, the Appearance control panel displays a dialog box in which you can type a name for the theme you're creating. You can change the name of any theme that you created by selecting its preview and choosing Theme Name from the Edit menu. You can't change the names of preconfigured themes.

To remove a theme, select its preview in the Appearance control panel and choose Clear from the Edit menu.

Custom Icons

Would you like to see dinosaurs, humming birds, file cabinets or even a picture of your face on your desktop — instead of ordinary icons? The Mac OS lets you replace the icons of individual documents, programs, folders, and disks with your own pictures. Figure 8-11 shows some examples of custom icons.

Figure 8-11: Icons your way

There are free icon collections available on the Internet, from online information services such as America Online, and from user groups. (For example, the icons shown are from a collection called Dan's icons, designed by Dan Mikel, and distributed as freeware on popular download servers.) You can also make icons from clip art that you get from those sources or on disk. You can even create your own icons with a graphics program.

Installing a custom icon

To replace an icon with a picture, first select the picture that you want to use for the icon and copy it with the Copy command (in the Edit menu). Then go to the Finder and find the icon you want to replace. Select the icon (click it once) and choose Get Info from the File menu. In the Info window, click the icon to select it and use the Paste command (in the Edit menu) to replace it with the picture you just copied. You can also copy an icon from an Info window and paste it into a different Info window. Figure 8-12 shows an Info window with a custom icon.

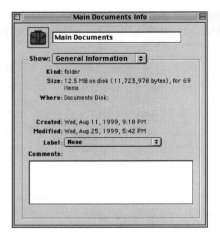

Figure 8-12: A custom icon pasted into an item's Info window

For best results, the picture you use for a custom icon should measure 32 × 32 pixels (dots). Multiples of this size, such as 64 × 64, 128 × 128, or 256 × 256, may also yield acceptable results. If your picture is larger than 32 × 32, the Finder reduces it proportionally to fit that amount of space when you replace an icon with it. Reducing a picture distorts it, especially if the original size is an odd or fractional multiple of the final size. If your picture is smaller than 32 × 32, the Finder centers it in the 32 × 32 icon space.

If you duplicate or make an alias of an item with a custom icon, the duplicate or alias inherits the custom icon

 To learn about duplicating items, see Chapter 5. To learn about making an alias, see Chapter 14.

You cannot replace the icon of a locked item, open document, or open program. Nor can you replace system software icons such as the System Folder, the Finder, Control Panels folder, and Trash. (You can replace individual control panel icons, however.)

Reverting to a standard icon

To revert to an item's standard icon, select the icon in the item's Info window and either press Delete or choose Clear or Cut from the Edit menu.

Summary

This chapter showed you how to modify the appearance and behavior of the Mac OS. The Appearance control panel in Mac OS 9 is "customization central" for changing the way your Mac looks. You can choose accent and text highlight colors as well as change the desktop pattern or a desktop picture that appears beneath your icons and windows. You can also choose system fonts, set up font smoothing, configure scroll arrows and scroll boxes, and select sound effects. And, the Appearance control panel enables you to group all of your design decisions into a single Theme. In addition, you can replace almost any icon with a custom picture.

✦   ✦   ✦

Get Help Onscreen

CHAPTER

◆ ◆ ◆ ◆

In This Chapter

Seeing balloon help

Browsing and searching Help Viewer articles

Following Apple Guide interactive help

◆ ◆ ◆ ◆

If you have a question about something displayed on your computer, or if you aren't sure how to accomplish a task, the Mac OS provides three onscreen help systems. One help system briefly describes objects when you point at them on the screen. Another help system explains how to perform common tasks. You can search the text of this help system and you can follow live cross-references in it by clicking them. A third help system interactively guides you step-by-step through tasks. In addition to the help you can get from the Mac OS, many application programs also provide onscreen help.

Help Menu and Help Buttons

The Mac OS provides onscreen help through the Help menu. This menu lists the kinds of help that are available in the program you are currently using. The kind of help that you can get varies from program to program. You can always get balloon help (described in the next section), although it may be very limited. Additional commands in the Help menu may provide help through the Help Viewer program or through Apple Guide (each described in later sections of this chapter). Figure 9-1 is an example of the Help menu.

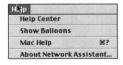

Figure 9-1: Get help onscreen with the Help menu.

As a convenience, some control panels and other programs include a Help button that you can click to get help specifically about the part of the control panel or program that you are currently using. The Help button is a square button with a distinctive question mark on it. Clicking a Help button displays help that is relevant to the context in which the Help button appears. The help may be provided in the Help Viewer program or by Apple Guide; both are described in later sections of this chapter. Figure 9-2 is an example of the Help button.

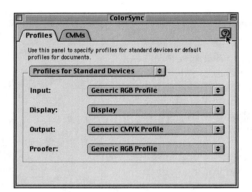

Figure 9-2: Get help by clicking a Help button.

Balloon Help

When you need immediate information about objects that you see onscreen, you can turn on Mac OS *balloon help*. With balloon help on, you position the pointer over an object and a concise description of it appears in a cartoon-style balloon. The balloon points to the object and tells you what the object is, what it does, what happens when you click it, or some portion of this information. You do not have to press any keys or click anything to make help balloons appear. Figure 9-3 is an example of balloon help.

Figure 9-3: A help balloon describes the object under the pointer.

The Mac OS provides balloon help capability, but not all objects have help balloons. Many applications provide no balloon help at all (more on that shortly).

Turning balloon help on and off

You turn on balloon help by choosing Show Balloons from the Help menu. That command then changes to Hide Balloons, and choosing it again turns off balloon help. You can display balloon help by pressing keys if you install the shareware program Helium from Tiger Technologies (http://www.tigertechnologies.com/, described in Chapter 26).

Working with balloon help on

Everything works normally when balloon help is on. Using balloon help does not put the Mac OS in help-only mode. It's similar to someone standing over your shoulder and describing onscreen objects to you.

Help balloons appear whether or not you press the mouse button. You click, double-click, and otherwise use programs normally, except that you may perceive a slight delay as help balloons come and go when you move the pointer slowly across items that have balloon help descriptions.

The object that a help balloon describes may be large or small and individual or collective. For example, the Close box in the active window's title bar has its own help balloon. In contrast, an inactive window has one balloon for the whole window. Sometimes a help balloon describes a group of items. For example, one balloon tells you about all the scrolling controls in a scroll bar. Figure 9-4 shows the help balloons for a close box and a scroll bar.

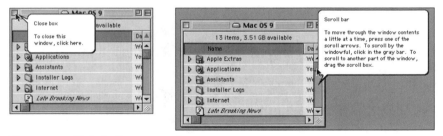

Figure 9-4: Help balloons vary in scope.

Moving the pointer slowly over several objects that have help balloons opens and closes balloons in sequence. To prevent excessive flashing of help balloons, they do not appear when you move the pointer quickly. For a help balloon to appear, the pointer must be in the same area for about one-tenth of a second or longer. You cannot change this timing.

What balloon help knows

Balloon help knows about all standard objects in the Mac OS, including windows in general; system software icons; the Apple menu; the Help menu; the Application menu; standard parts of Open, Save, and Navigation Services dialog boxes (all of which are described in Chapter 7); and the Page Setup and Print dialog boxes (which are described in Chapter 17). Balloon help cannot describe a specific program's menu commands, window contents, dialog boxes, and so on unless the program's developer or publisher has included the necessary information. For example, Apple has provided complete balloon help for the Finder, many control panels, and many of the accessory and utility programs that come with the Mac OS.

Help Viewer

When you need more information than balloon help provides, you can use the *Help Viewer* program to find and read short how-to articles. You can find help by browsing a table of contents or by searching for words that describe the help you need. Most of the articles you read have links that you can click to see related material. These links are familiar to people who browse the Internet's World Wide Web, although you don't need to know how to use Web links to use the Help Viewer.

The Help Viewer is the main means of providing system-level how-to help. You can also get help on AppleScript, QuickTime, and other Apple technologies via the Help Viewer. And, the Help Viewer is updated to enable you to view pages directly from the Internet.

 For details on AppleScript, see Chapter 24.

Displaying the Help Viewer

You can display the Help Viewer by choosing Help Center or Mac Help from the Help menu while you are using the Finder. Choosing Help Center displays a list of all the help sections available in the Help Viewer. Choosing Mac Help displays a list of system-level help categories. If these commands are not in the Help menu, choose Finder from the Application menu at the right end of the menu bar. Figure 9-5 shows what you see when you choose Help Center or Mac Help.

Browsing Help Viewer links

If you've used a Web browser, you should be familiar with the way the Help Viewer works. All the underlined words in Help Viewer are links that you can click to see related material. For example, if you choose Mac Help from the Help menu and then click an underlined help category, you see a list of relevant topics. Clicking an underlined topic displays the article in the Help Viewer. Articles may also contain underlined links. Figure 9-6 is an example of browsing links in the Help Viewer.

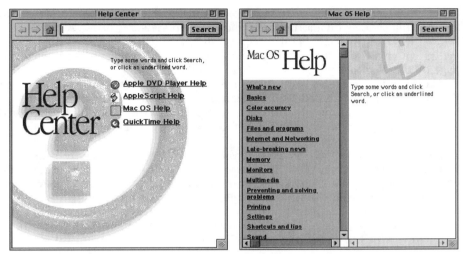

Figure 9-5: From the Help menu, choose Help Center to see a list of help sections (left) or choose Mac Help to see a list of system-level help categories (right).

Click a link

Click a category

Read the article

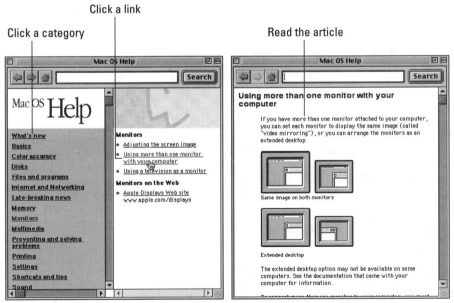

Figure 9-6: Click an underlined link to see related material in the Help Viewer.

Links in articles can take you to many places inside the Help Viewer and outside it. A link may show you another article in the Help Viewer window. A link that begins "Open..." probably opens the program that the article describes. A link that includes an Internet address probably connects to the Internet and shows you a page on the Web (after first asking whether you want to do this). A link may also display interactive, step-by-step help in an Apple Guide window (described later in this chapter). A link labeled "Table of contents" invariably shows you the list of help categories and topics that the article is part of. If the author of the help article writes clearly, you'll have a good idea about where the link will take you.

Besides clicking links, you can go places by clicking the picture buttons in the Help Viewer. Click the left-arrow (←) button to go back to the previous page in the Help Viewer. After going back, you can click the right-arrow (→) button to go forward. Click Home to go to the Help Center page.

If you go back to a page you have seen previously during your current session with the Help Viewer, the links that you previously visited are green instead of blue.

Searching Help Viewer

If you're looking for help on a specific subject and don't want to browse through links until you find it, you can have the Help Viewer search all its articles for the help you need. To search, type some words that describe the subject and click Search. After a few seconds, the Help Viewer displays a list of topics that may help you. It ranks the topics according to their relevance, from five stars (most relevant) to one star (least relevant). Figure 9-7 is an example of a search in the Help Viewer.

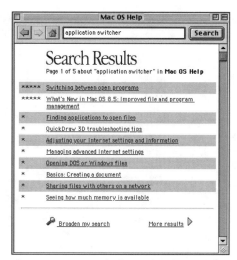

Figure 9-7: Search the Help Viewer for words that describe the help you need.

When typing words to search for, you can include special characters to more precisely describe the subject. Table 9-1 describes these special characters.

Table 9-1 Special Characters for Help Viewer Searching			
Character	*Meaning*	*Search Example*	*Search Results*
+	and	picture + pattern	This example finds articles that include both "picture" and "pattern."
|	or	picture | pattern	This example finds articles that include either "picture" or "pattern."
!	not	picture ! pattern	This example finds articles that include "picture" but exclude "pattern."
( )	grouping	background + (picture | pattern)	This example finds articles that include "background" and either "picture" or "pattern."

Apple Guide

Apple Guide is another form of how-to help that is available for some programs. Apple Guide shows and tells you how to get things done while you actually do them. Step-by-step instructions appear in a guide window, which floats above all other windows. As you move from step to step, Apple Guide may coach you by marking an object onscreen with a circle, arrow, or underline. Figure 9-8 is an example of an Apple Guide instruction and coaching mark.

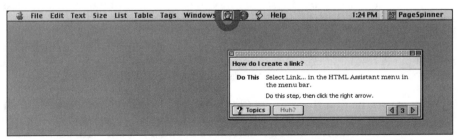

Figure 9-8: Apple Guide displays step-by-step instructions in a floating window and draws coaching marks to point out objects onscreen.

Apple Guide watches what you do and can adjust its steps if you work ahead or make a mistake. In some cases, Apple Guide will actually perform a simple operation for you, such as opening a control panel.

Notice that the Apple Guide window has a zoom box and a collapse box. You can use these controls to temporarily shrink the window so that you can see what's underneath it, and then use them again to restore the window.

Although Apple Guide was the help option of choice in earlier versions of the Mac OS, Mac OS 9 relies more heavily on the Help Viewer program (described previously). These days the Help Viewer is generally the primary help system, sometimes calling upon Apple Guide for step-by-step instructions.

Some programs from companies other than Apple also use Apple Guide, but many do not. Program developers and system administrators can create additional Apple Guide help, which can cover tasks that involve multiple applications. Apple Guide's usefulness depends greatly on how well crafted the help procedures for individual tasks are. Apple has set a good example with its system-level help procedures.

Displaying Apple Guide

In programs that use Apple Guide for their primary help system, you generally display an Apple Guide topics window by choosing a command from the Help menu. For example, while you are using SimpleText you can choose SimpleText Guide from the Help menu to display an Apple Guide topics window for SimpleText.

In programs that provide help primarily through the Help Viewer, you can click a descriptive underlined link to display an Apple Guide window that begins step-by-step instructions for a specific task. For example, the Mac Help article "Sharing your files with other users" has links to Apple Guide help for specifying users and groups, sharing a file, and setting access privileges. These links typically begin with the phrase "Help me...," but there's no way to tell for sure which underlined words are linked to Apple Guide.

It's also possible to display an Apple Guide window by clicking a help button in a control panel or dialog box. For example, clicking the help button in the Location Manager displays an Apple Guide topics window for this control panel.

In many cases, the first thing Apple Guide displays is a topics window. A title at the top of the window tells you what software the help covers. For example, SimpleText Guide covers only topics related to SimpleText, and Location Manager Help lists topics related to the Location Manager control panel.

The Apple Guide topics window generally includes three large buttons labeled Topics, Index, and Look For. You click one of those buttons to choose how you want to find help — by scanning a list of topics, by browsing an index, or by looking for words in the Guide. One of the three methods probably suits you best, but try them all if you have trouble finding the help you need using your favorite method.

The Apple Guide help that comes with some programs may not include the Topics, Index, and Look For buttons. An example is the Location Manager control panel, which offers only scanning by topic.

Browsing Apple Guide topics

To see a list of help topics, click Topics at the top of the Apple Guide topics window. Clicking a topic on the left side of the topics window displays a list of specific tasks and terms on the right side. If the list on the right includes headings in bold, you can show and hide a heading's subordinate phrases by clicking the disclosure triangle next to the heading. Figure 9-9 is an example of scanning Apple Guide topics with some headings expanded and others collapsed.

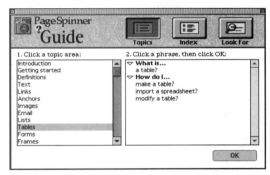

Figure 9-9: Scanning the list of topics in Apple Guide

Browsing the Apple Guide index

To browse an Apple Guide index, click Index in the Apple Guide topics window. Apple Guide displays an alphabetical list of key terms used in the guide. You can scroll through the index with the scroll bar. You can type the first part of a term you want to look up in the index, and the index instantly scrolls to the index entry that most closely matches what you typed. You can also scroll the index to entries starting with a particular letter of the alphabet by dragging the pointer at the top of the index list to that letter or by simply clicking that letter. You can't see all 26 letters of the alphabet at the top of the index list, but you can see more by clicking and dragging the pointer slightly past the last letter you can see. Clicking an entry in the index displays a list of tasks in which that entry appears. Figure 9-10 is an example of browsing an Apple Guide index.

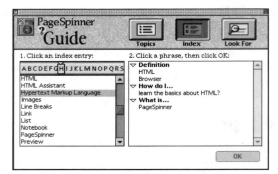

Figure 9-10: Browsing an index in Apple Guide

Searching Apple Guide for key words

To have Apple Guide look for words that you specify, click Look For in the Apple Guide topics window. Then, on the left side of the window, click the arrow button and type a key word or two that describe the step-by-step instructions that you want to see. When you click Search (or press Return or Enter) a list of relevant tasks appears. Figure 9-11 is an example of searching Apple Guide for a key word.

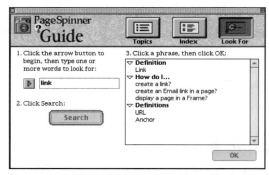

Figure 9-11: Searching for help in Apple Guide

Following step-by-step instructions

When you double-click an item on the right side of the Apple Guide topics window (or select the item and click OK), the topics window goes away. After a brief pause, another Guide window appears with an introduction to the task or a definition of the term you selected in the topics window. Figure 9-12 is an example of the step-by-step window.

Figure 9-12: The first Apple Guide step describes the task or defines the term.

Read the information in the Guide window and follow any instructions it gives you. To go to the next step in a multiple-step task, click the right-pointing arrow at the bottom right of the Guide window. To back up one step, click the left-pointing arrow.

If you decide that you have selected the wrong task or term, you can return to the topics window by clicking the Topics button at the bottom of the Guide window. The Topics button may be labeled with an up-pointing arrow, a question mark, or the word Topics. You can also put away Apple Guide altogether by closing all guide windows.

At each new step, the guide may draw a circle, line, or arrow onscreen to point out a menu title or other object that you must use to complete the step. These coaching marks appear in red or another color on a color monitor. If the step calls for you to choose from a menu, Apple Guide colors the menu item you should choose as well. On a black-and-white screen, the menu item is underlined.

If the Guide window mentions something you don't understand, try clicking the Huh? button at the bottom of the Guide window for clarification. (This button may be labeled I'm Stuck.) Clicking this button brings up another Guide window that may contain a definition of a term or begin step-by-step instructions for accomplishing a task related to the task you initially chose. For example, clicking Huh? in Step 2 of the task "How do I copy text?" in the SimpleText Guide brings up the task "How do I select part of a document?" The Huh? button is dimmed when additional information is not available.

If you work ahead of the step currently displayed in the Guide window, Apple Guide can adjust itself to catch up. When you click the right-pointing arrow to go to the next step, Apple Guide skips ahead to the next step that matches your location in the task.

While you're following the steps in Apple Guide, you can still use your computer normally. If the Guide window is in your way, you can drag it somewhere else or click its zoom box to make it smaller; click again to make it larger. You can collapse a Guide window into its title bar by clicking its collapse box.

If you have not properly completed a step when you click the right-pointing arrow at the bottom of the Guide window, Apple Guide explains what you need to do to get back on track.

Other Help

Many programs add how-to help, onscreen reference material, or other items to the Help menu. For example, many applications published by Claris (now Apple), FileMaker, and Microsoft list onscreen help commands in the Help menu. The help may appear in Apple Guide windows or the Help Viewer, but most applications use different help systems to display their onscreen help. For instructions on an application's own help system, check the documentation that came with the application.

Summary

This chapter showed you the different kinds of help that the Mac OS makes available in the Help menu. Balloon help briefly describes the object under the mouse pointer, using cartoon-like "thought balloons." The Help Viewer program, Mac OS 9's main mechanism for help, displays short how-to articles. You can search for articles, browse a table of contents, and click links in an article to go to a related article. In addition, Apple Guide, which can work both on its own and in conjunction with the Help Viewer, shows and tells you how to complete a task as you do it. Your applications may use the Apple Guide and/or Help Viewer to display help topics, or they may use a different help system.

✦   ✦   ✦

Get on the Internet

The Internet is an amazing resource for work, play, education, or hobbies. Using the Internet, you have access to an incredible variety of information and entertainment resources, from online newspapers and encyclopedias to the latest research data to stage and film reviews, and much more. Electronic mail (e-mail) connects people all around the world, bringing words from faraway lands to your screen just seconds after they're sent. Mac OS 9 makes it easy to get on the Internet; it includes a setup assistant to get you connected easily and many applications that help you surf the Net.

Setting Up an Internet Connection

Before you can tap the wealth of information and services on the Internet, you need to set up your computer so that it can make an Internet connection. To assist you in configuring an Internet connection, Mac OS 9 includes a special program that is aptly named the Internet Setup Assistant. It leads you step-by-step through a series of decisions and questions to gather your Internet information, and it enters that information in the various control panels and applications that the Mac OS uses for Internet access. An alias to the Internet Setup Assistant is in the Assistants folder on your startup disk.

Getting started

You can use the Internet Setup Assistant any time that you want to configure a new Internet connection. You automatically get an opportunity to use the Internet Setup Assistant when you first start your computer after installing Mac OS 9. At other times, you can double-click the Internet Setup Assistant's alias, located in the Assistants folder in the main window of your startup disk. When you open the Internet

Setup Assistant, it immediately asks you to confirm that you want to set up your computer to use the Internet. If you click the Yes button, the Internet Setup Assistant then asks whether you already have an Internet account. Figure 10-1 shows this window.

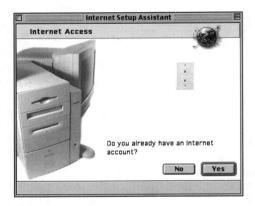

Figure 10-1: The Internet Setup Assistant's first major question: "Do you already have an Internet account?"

Signing up for a new account

If you don't already have an Internet account, click No. The Internet Setup Assistant helps you get a new account with an *Internet Service Provider* (ISP), which is the company that provides you with modem access to the Internet. The Internet Setup Assistant makes a toll-free call through your modem to a registration service and gives you the opportunity to sign up with an ISP. You'll need a credit card to use this service, and it's only available in the United States and Canada.

Be aware that this service offers only a fraction of the ISPs that are doing business in metropolitan areas. For more options, check your Yellow Pages or ads in the local papers, or ask your friends and family for recommendations. You can always switch to a different ISP if you find a deal you like better. However, if you change ISPs then you will probably have to change your e-mail address and have to notify all your e-mail correspondents of your new address. If you receive lots of e-mail, you will probably need to keep your old account open for a while so that you don't miss any e-mail from people who don't send to your new address right away.

Configuring an existing account

If you already have an Internet account with an ISP or via a network at work or school and you just need to set up for that account, click the Yes button. An introduction explains what you need to know to configure an Internet connection. Read the information and then click the right arrow at the bottom of the Internet Setup Assistant window to add an Internet configuration.

Note The information you need to set up your Internet account is all pretty standard stuff. You can take this list in the Internet Setup Assistant and consult your ISP's customer service staff to get the exact answers. Or, if you received printed materials from your ISP, you'll likely find answers to all these questions.

You begin a new configuration by giving the configuration a name. The name of your ISP is a good choice. If you're going to connect to an ISP via a modem or an ISDN modem (technically, an ISDN terminal adapter), select the Modem setting at the bottom of the window and click the right arrow. Now, go to the next section of this chapter, "Setting up a modem connection."

If you have an Internet connection through a network, select the Network setting and click the right arrow. Now, skip to the subsequent section in this chapter, "Setting up a network connection." Cable modems or ADSL modems, despite their names, demand a network connection because the cable modem connects to your Mac's Ethernet network port. An ISDN router also connects via Ethernet and requires a network connection. Figure 10-2 shows the settings for a configuration name and type of connection.

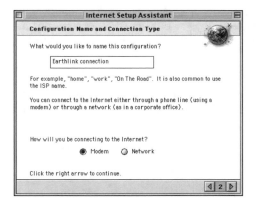

Figure 10-2: Enter the configuration name and select the type of connection.

Setting up a modem connection

If you're setting up a connection to an ISP via modem, the Internet Setup Assistant next asks what kind of modem you're using. Choose your modem model from the Modem pop-up menu. Use the Port pop-up menu to choose the port to which your modem is connected, probably the modem port. If you have an internal modem, you may not need to set the port, especially if your modem is in an iMac or Power Macintosh G3 that has USB connections.

You'll most likely want to set the Tone/Pulse option to Tone, which most phone lines in the United States and Canada use. Figure 10-3 shows the modem settings. Click the right arrow to continue the assistant.

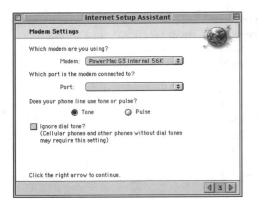

Figure 10-3: Enter your modem settings.

The next step is especially important because it's where you enter the phone number for your ISP, your account name, and your password. Your account name is usually the same as the first part of your e-mail address. Figure 10-4 shows these settings.

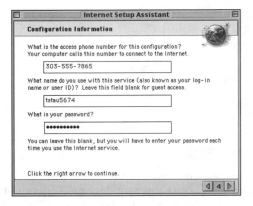

Figure 10-4: Enter your ISP account phone number, your name, and your password.

The Assistant next asks whether your computer must use a PPP Connect Script to establish a connection with your ISP. This script specifies a conversation your computer must have with the ISP's computer, in which the ISP's computer prompts your computer to send items of information in a prescribed order. Your ISP will probably provide a PPP Connect Script file if it requires one. If you select Yes in this step, you then get to choose a PPP Connect Script from a pop-up menu. This pop-up menu lists all the PPP Connect Script files in the PPP Connect Scripts folder inside your Extensions folder. This pop-up also has a Select Other choice, which displays a standard Open dialog box where you can select a PPP Connect Script from a different folder. If you select a PPP Connect Script file from outside the PPP Connect Scripts folder, the Assistant puts a copy of the file in the folder and actually chooses this copy. If you don't require a PPP Connect Script, select No and click the right arrow.

Next, the Assistant asks whether you have been assigned your own permanent IP address, which is a numerical address such as 206.117.213.011 that identifies one machine on the Internet. Because you're connecting by modem, you probably don't have a permanent IP address; instead, your ISP assigns your computer an IP address dynamically, which is to say, temporarily, and only for the length of time you're connected. Don't confuse IP addresses, which identify machines, with e-mail addresses, which identify people. If you don't have a permanent IP address, select No and click the right arrow to move on.

The remaining steps in configuring an Internet connection are the same for a modem connection and a network connection. Go to the section "Finishing setup" to finish setting up your Internet connection.

Connecting via Modem and Network

You might reasonably think that if you connect to the Internet via modem, you should invariably select the Modem setting in the Internet Setup Assistant. In fact, you can also use a modem to connect to a local area network (LAN) that provides your Internet access. In this case, you must select the Network setting. If you use a modem, how do you know which setting to select? If you use a modem to connect to an Internet Service Provider, select the Modem setting. If you use a modem to connect to a network at work, school, or other organization, and you get your Internet access via that network, select the Network or LAN setting.

On a technical level, each setting connects to the Internet using a different protocol, or language. The Modem setting uses PPP (point-to-point protocol), the de facto standard protocol for dial-up connections to TCP/IP networks like the Internet. The Network or LAN setting uses ARAP (Apple Remote Access Protocol) to make a dial-up connection to an AppleTalk network, and then uses the MacIP protocol to make a connection to the Internet over the AppleTalk network. For more information on configuring your computer for a remote connection to an AppleTalk network or the Internet, see Chapter 20.

Setting up a network connection

If you have an Internet account at work, school, or other organization rather than through an ISP, your computer is probably connected to a LAN such as an Ethernet network. You may also be able to connect to the Internet by calling a remote LAN via modem. In either case, your computer connects to the Internet via a local network, not through an ISP. You also connect via network if you have a cable modem or DSL.

Some of the steps for configuring a network connection to the Internet are different than for configuring an ISP connection. The first part of the configuration is the same and is described under the heading "Getting started" earlier in this section. When you come to the step where you indicate how you'll be connecting to the Internet, select the Network setting and forge on by clicking the right arrow at the bottom of the window.

The Internet Setup Assistant will ask whether you've been assigned a permanent IP address such as 206.117.213.011. An IP address uniquely identifies your computer on the Internet. Because your computer is connected to a network, it may well have a permanent IP address. If so, select Yes and click the right arrow. The Assistant asks you to enter the numerical IP address that your network administrator gave you. Figure 10-5 shows the IP address setting.

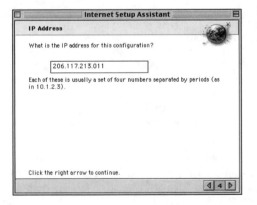

Figure 10-5: Enter your computer's IP address.

After the Assistant asks for an IP address, it asks for a subnet mask and router address. You don't need to know what these settings mean — just enter the numbers exactly as your network administrator gives them to you. Figure 10-6 shows the subnet mask and router address settings.

Figure 10-6: Enter the mysterious subnet mask and router numbers.

Finishing setup

The remaining steps are the same for setting up a modem connection through an ISP or a local area network connection to the Internet. The next information you must supply is the address(es) of your Domain Name Service (DNS) server. A DNS server converts the hard-to-remember numerical IP addresses, such as 17.254.3.62, into something easier for humans to remember such as www.apple.com.

Every ISP or local area network has a DNS server, and whenever you enter any kind of Internet address, the DNS server converts it into its numerical equivalent and sends the address on its way (and in the right direction, too). Your ISP or network administrator will probably give you the IP addresses of two DNS servers (primary and secondary). Enter these numerical addresses in the space provided, pressing Return after each address to separate them. You can skip the DNS addresses if your ISP or network supplies them automatically each time you connect. You can skip the host name for this configuration. Figure 10-7 shows the DNS settings.

Figure 10-7: Enter your DNS servers' IP addresses.

In the next step, the Internet Setup Assistant asks for the e-mail address and e-mail password that your ISP or network administrator has given you. Figure 10-8 shows the e-mail address and password settings.

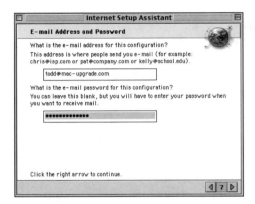

Figure 10-8: Enter your e-mail address and password.

The next step asks for additional information about your e-mail account. You need to enter the e-mail account (sometimes called the POP account). This is different from your e-mail address in that it includes both your user name and the name of the mail server, as in todd@pop.mac-upgrade.com. You also need to enter the mail server name (also known as the SMTP host or the outgoing mail server), as in smtp.mac-upgrade.com. Figure 10-9 shows the e-mail account and mail server settings.

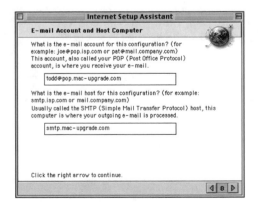

Figure 10-9: Enter your e-mail (POP) account and e-mail server (SMTP host).

Next, the Assistant asks you to specify the name of the host computer for newsgroups, which provides access to discussion groups on the Internet. The newsgroup host is also known as the Usenet host or NNTP (Network News Transfer Protocol) host. If you're connecting through an ISP, it probably has a newsgroup host whose name is the ISP's domain name preceded by the word "news" or "nntp" as in news.mac-upgrade.com. Figure 10-10 shows the newsgroup host setting.

Figure 10-10: Enter your news server address.

Now, the Assistant next asks whether your connection to the Internet goes through proxy servers. Your company, school, or organization may use proxy servers to provide security. If you select Yes, then the Assistant asks you to enter the host and port for each proxy server you use: HTTP (the Web), Gopher, FTP, or SOCKS. Don't worry about what these acronyms stand for. Just get this information from your network administrator.

The last step in setting up an Internet connection gives you an opportunity to review the settings you've entered before the Assistant puts them into effect. To review, click Show Details. If any of the settings are wrong, you can click the left arrow to go back to the steps where you entered them, make corrections, and then click the right arrow to return to this step. To make the settings effective, click Go Ahead and wait a few minutes while the Assistant stores your settings in various control panels. You also have the option of clicking Cancel to quit the Internet Setup Assistant without making any of your settings effective. Figure 10-11 shows the last step in setting up an Internet connection.

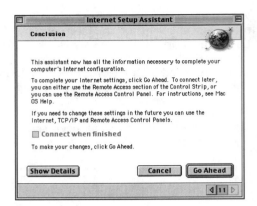

Figure 10-11: Click Go Ahead to make the Internet configuration effective.

After finishing the last step in the Internet Setup Assistant, you can make a connection in a variety of ways, as described later in "Making an Internet Connection."

Managing Internet Settings

Although the Internet Setup Assistant helps you set up a connection to the Internet, you may need to set additional options or change settings later. The Mac OS comes with an assortment of software for managing your Internet settings.

Adjusting network settings

When you connect your computer to the Internet, you are actually connecting it to a very large TCP/IP network. The Internet Setup Assistant gets basic network settings from you and places them in several control panels: TCP/IP, Modem, and Remote Access. You can work directly in these control panels to modify existing settings and to set additional options that the Internet Setup Assistant ignores. You can also use these control panels to set up an Internet connection from scratch. These control panels have these settings:

✦ **TCP/IP** has settings for the method of connecting to the Internet (such as PPP or Ethernet); your computer's permanent IP address, subnet mask, and router address if it has these; the DNS addresses; and the domain name.

✦ **Modem** has settings for the type of modem, the port it's connected to, and the type of phone line (tone or pulse). An additional option that you can't control via the Internet Setup Assistant is whether the modem makes audible dialing and connecting sounds.

✦ **Remote Access** has settings for your Internet account name, password, and phone number. If you use a PPP Connection Script, you set it here. Other options you can set here that you can't set with the Internet Setup Assistant include redialing of the phone number or an alternate number; connection reminders and provisions for automatic disconnection; whether to connect automatically when starting an Internet application; and more.

Cross-Reference

For detailed information on all these control panels, see Chapter 20.

Adjusting Internet application preferences

The variety of application programs that you use to get information and services on the Internet have many preference settings in common. For example, your e-mail application certainly needs to know your e-mail address, but so do your Web browser and the application you use to participate in newsgroups. The makers of many Internet applications have agreed to share common preference settings so that you don't have to enter or change them redundantly in each application. You set some of these common preferences when the Internet Setup Assistant is used. You set all the common preferences and many more using the Internet control panel.

Note

The Internet control panel has its foundation in another program that was bundled with the Mac OS prior to version 8.5, called Internet Config. Internet Config is public domain software written by Peter N. Lewis and Quinn "The Eskimo" (http://www.stairways.com/ic/). While Internet Config is not necessary in Mac OS 9, you may occasionally find references to Internet Config in settings windows or documentation for your Internet software. If you see a setting for Internet Config, select it and the Internet control panel will be used; if you see a reference to Internet Config in documentation, you'll find the same functionality in the Internet control panel.

The Internet control panel is used for changing common Internet preferences shared by many Internet applications. The control panel stores these preference settings in the Internet Preferences file in the Preferences folder inside the System Folder. Your Internet applications may also let you change some of the same preference settings. For example, you can change your e-mail password in your e-mail application or the Internet control panel. The most recent change takes precedence.

You can also use the Internet control panel to save all the current settings as a group, and you can choose a saved group that you want to be in effect. Figure 10-12 is an example of the Internet control panel.

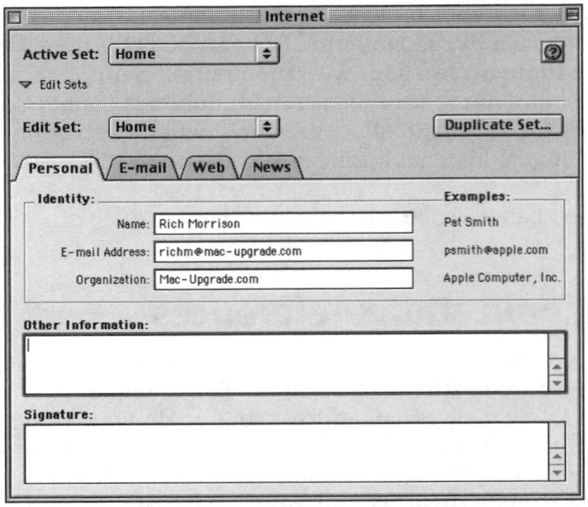

Figure 10-12: Use the Internet control panel to change shared Internet preferences.

Basic settings

The Internet control panel organizes preference settings by category. To see the settings for each category, click its tab in the control panel. The Internet control panel has four basic categories: Personal, E-mail, Web, and News. These categories have settings as follows:

✦ **Personal** has settings for your name, e-mail address, and organization. You can add information that you want displayed by a Finger server, such as your title, mailing address, and phone number. You can also enter the signature text you want added to the bottom of e-mail messages and newsgroup messages that you create.

✦ **E-mail** has settings for your account name, the server names for mail you receive (POP server) and send (SMTP server), and e-mail password. You can also select how you wish to be notified when you receive e-mail. In addition, you can choose a default e-mail application.

✦ **Web** has settings for home page, search page, and the folder for files you download. You can also set the color of linked text, whether it should be underlined, and the color of the background. In addition, you can choose a default Web browser.

✦ **News** has the name of your news server. In addition, you can select whether to connect to the news server as a guest or with a name and password that is set here. You can also choose your default newsgroup application.

Advanced settings

Besides the basic categories, the control panel has seven advanced categories that are normally hidden. To see them, choose User Mode from the Edit menu and select Advanced mode in the dialog box that appears. You can also select Administration mode, which reveals the same settings and lets you lock settings individually. When you select Advanced or Administration mode, an Advanced tab appears in the Internet control panel.

A scrolling list of seven categories appears on the left side of the control panel when you click the Advanced tab. Figure 10-13 shows one of the categories in the Advanced section of the Internet control panel.

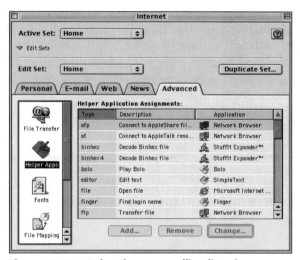

Figure 10-13: Select from a scrolling list of seven preference categories in the Advanced section of the Internet control panel.

The advanced categories have these settings:

✦ **File Transfer** has settings for the default FTP servers and an option to use passive mode for file transfers. Passive mode doesn't work with all FTP servers, but may be required if you connect through a firewall, which is part of a local area network designed to prevent Internet users from getting into the local network and to stop local network users from sending sensitive information out.

✦ **Helper Apps** assigns each type of URL to an application that can handle it. For example, "http" is assigned to a Web browser and "mailto" is assigned to an e-mail application. In this section you can also add or edit MIME types (a specification for nontext documents to be sent over the Internet) so that a particular type launches the assigned helper application. For instance, the type x-macbinary is preset to launch StuffIt Expander.

✦ **Fonts** has settings for the font and size of text displayed in a list, displayed in a message, and printed in a message.

✦ **File Mapping** specifies which Mac applications open various types of Internet files. A table maps each type of Internet file to a Mac application that can open it. The type of file is determined by its file name extension, which is the last part of its name following a period.

✦ **Firewalls** has settings for a SOCKS firewall and for proxy servers for Web, Gopher, and FTP. These settings are required by some organizations to shield their local networks from intrusion by Internet users. You can also list domain names of servers that you do not want to access through a firewall.

✦ **Messages** specifies the character or symbol that marks quoted text in e-mail reply messages. You can also enter text that you want added at the top of outgoing e-mail and text that you want added at the top of outgoing newsgroup messages.

✦ **Hosts** specifies default servers for these Internet services: Ph (finds e-mail addresses inside an organization); Finger (finds information about a specific user on the Internet); Whois (finds e-mail addresses on the Internet); Telnet (remote terminal); FTP (file transfer); Gopher (menu-based information retrieval); WAIS (query-based information retrieval); and LDAP server and search base.

Groups of settings

If you use your Internet applications with more than one Internet connection, you may need different settings for each connection. For example, you may need one group of settings when you connect through your personal ISP and another group of settings when you connect through the local area network at work. You can save groups of settings and switch between them using the Internet control panel.

To save the current settings as a new group, choose New Set from the File menu. To make a copy of the current group, click the Duplicate Set button or choose Duplicate Set from the File menu. To rename a group, choose Rename Set from the File menu. To delete a group, choose Delete Set from the File menu.

To switch groups, choose one from the Active Set pop-up menu at the top of the control panel.

Making an Internet Connection

Setting up your computer to connect to the Internet makes it ready to access e-mail, Web pages, and other Internet services. If you have a network connection to the Internet, you can access its services at any time by using the applications described in subsequent sections of this chapter. A network connection (and again this includes a cable modem or DSL connection) gives you full-time access to the Internet.

A modem connection (and this includes an ISDN modem connection) generally does not give you full-time access to the Internet. When you want to use Internet services through a modem, you must make a connection to your ISP. You can make a manual connection or an automatic connection. When you finish using Internet services, you can disconnect from the ISP. You'll probably want to disconnect if your ISP charges for the amount of time you are connected or the phone company charges for the time you use the phone line. You'll have to disconnect if you need to use the phone line or the modem for something else.

Connecting manually

To make an Internet connection with the Remote Access control panel, just open it, make sure that the information entered there is correct, and then click its Connect button. Your modem will dial your ISP and the control panel will negotiate a connection with your ISP by supplying your account name and password. When a message tells you the connection is OK, you can use an Internet application such as Netscape Communicator or Microsoft Internet Explorer (as described later in this chapter). Figure 10-14 shows the Remote Access control panel.

Figure 10-14: Manually connecting to the Internet with the Remote Access control panel

You can also make a connection using the Control Strip if it's available on your computer. Simply choose Connect from the Remote Access module's menu. Alternatively, you can connect using the Remote Access Status program, found in your Apple menu. Open the program and click the Connect button.

Connecting automatically

You can have the Remote Access control panel automatically dial and connect to the Internet whenever you open an application that requires an Internet connection. For example, when you open Netscape Communicator and it looks for the home Web page, Remote Access will dial the modem and connect to your ISP; then Communicator can go to the home Web page.

To make automatic connections happen, you turn on the "Connect automatically when starting TCP/IP applications" option in the Options dialog box of the Remote Access control panel. You get at this dialog box by clicking the Options button in the control panel. Then to see this option, click the Protocol tab and choose PPP from the pop-up menu in the Remote Access Options dialog box, as shown in Figure 10-15.

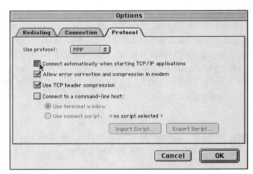

Figure 10-15: Turn on automatic Internet connection in the Remote Access control panel.

There is a disadvantage to connecting automatically. During an automatic connection, the Mac OS displays a dialog box to indicate connection progress, and this dialog box blocks you from doing anything else until the connection is made. The dialog box doesn't appear if you connect manually with the Remote Access control panel or the Remote Access module of the Control Strip, freeing you to get ready for an Internet session while the connection is in progress.

Disconnecting

To disconnect from your ISP, click the Disconnect button in the Remote Access control panel, choose Disconnect from the Remote Access module's menu on the Control Strip, or open the Remote Access Status program and click Disconnect. After a moment, your modem will hang up and the connection will end.

You can also set the Remote Access control panel to disconnect automatically. You can have it disconnect after a period of inactivity you specify. In addition, you can have the control panel prompt you periodically with a dialog box and disconnect if you fail to respond to the dialog box (because you have left your computer and forgotten to disconnect manually). You set up these options in the Connections section of the control panel's Options dialog box.

Sending and Receiving E-Mail with Microsoft Outlook Express

Although not as flashy as the Web, electronic mail is the most popular reason people use the Internet. E-mail lets you communicate with people all over the world. Unlike regular mail, your correspondents can be reading your messages within minutes after you send them, no matter whether the recipients are across the street or halfway around the world.

Microsoft Outlook Express is set to be the default e-mail application in Mac OS 9. Outlook Express handles multiple Internet e-mail accounts. If you have more than one e-mail account, you can see mail from all of them in one place, organize all your mail in one set of folders, and use one unified address book. Another feature is the capability to set up rules that automatically process your mail. For example, you can set up rules that look at the sender of a message and label the message with a color, move it to a specific mail folder, and send a reply, all automatically.

Outlook Express preferences

The first time you open Microsoft Outlook Express, it gives you the opportunity to import from an e-mail program that you used previously. If you want Outlook Express to import your mail, addresses, and settings from another e-mail program, click Yes. If you haven't used any other e-mail program or you don't want to import from another e-mail program, click No. In this case, Outlook Express picks up some of the e-mail settings that you made previously with the Internet Setup Assistant or the Internet control panel. Whether you import from another e-mail program or not, Outlook Express displays its preference settings so that you can make any changes necessary, as shown in Figure 10-16.

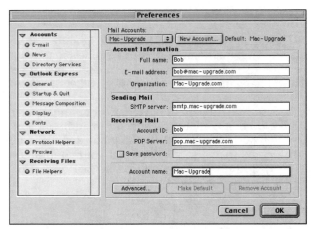

Figure 10-16: Check your e-mail settings in the Outlook Express Preferences dialog box.

The first time you open Outlook Express, it may change some of the settings that you made previously in the Internet Setup Assistant or the Internet control panel. It may clear the e-mail password, which is in the E-mail section of the Preferences dialog box. It also may change the newsgroup server setting (which is in the News section of the Preferences dialog box) to msnews.microsoft.com. Be sure to change these settings to your liking (you can click the check box to have Outlook Express remember your password once you've entered it) and click OK to dismiss the Preferences dialog box.

Tip   Want to use another program as your default e-mail application? Open the Internet control panel and choose the E-mail tab. At the bottom of the control panel is a pop-up menu that lets you select a different e-mail program. Choose the e-mail program that you'd like to use as your default. If you don't see its name, choose Select from the menu and you'll get an Open dialog box you can use to seek out the e-mail application.

Outlook Express main window

The main Outlook Express window has buttons across the top, a list of mail folders on the left, and a list of messages and a message preview on the right. You can hide any of these windowpanes, except the list of messages, by clicking the small icons in the lower-left corner of the window or choosing from the View menu. Figure 10-17 is an example of the Outlook Express main window.

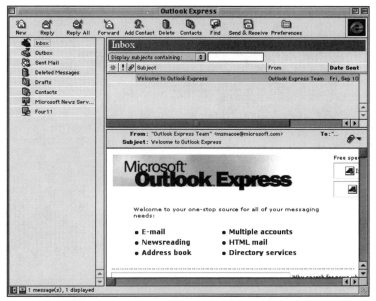

Figure 10-17: See a list of mail folders, a list of messages in the selected folder, and a preview of the selected message in Outlook Express.

To see a list of the messages in any folder, select it by clicking its icon on the left side of the window. To see a preview of a listed message, select it by clicking it in the list. You can also open mail folders and messages in separate windows by double-clicking them.

You can sort the messages in a mail folder by clicking a column heading in the folder's list of messages. Option-click a column heading to sort in reverse order. Most people prefer to have mail sorted by Date or Subject.

You can rearrange and resize the headings in a list of messages. To move a column left or right, drag its headings. To resize a column, drag the borderline of its heading. To add or remove columns, use the Columns submenu of the View menu.

Receiving mail

To get your mail, click Send & Receive at the top of the Outlook Express window or choose a command from the Send & Receive submenu of the Tools menu. A progress window appears to show messages being received. Received mail goes in the In Box. The number of unread messages appears in parentheses after the In Box (or other folder) name on the left side of the window, and unread messages are listed in bold. Although you can read a message in the preview pane of the main Outlook Express window, you won't have to scroll as much if you open the message in its own window. To read a message in its own window, double-click it in the list of messages. Figure 10-18 is an example of an e-mail message window.

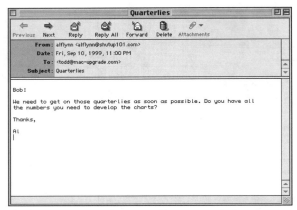

Figure 10-18: Read an e-mail message in its own window in Outlook Express.

The row of buttons atop the message window lets you act on the message. Most of the buttons are self-explanatory. Previous and Next display the message that comes before or after the message that you're reading. Reply and Reply All both create a new message, but Reply addresses the new message only to the sender, whereas Reply All addresses the new message to the sender and to everyone else who received the original message.

You can adjust the amount of space used to display the message header below the buttons. Simply drag the border that separates the header from the body up or down.

If Outlook Express does not connect to your ISP and get your mail when you click Send & Receive or choose from the Send & Receive submenu, then you may not have set the Remote Access control panel for automatic connection (as described in "Making an Internet Connection" earlier in this chapter). In this case, you must first make an Internet connection manually and then use the Send & Receive button or submenu.

After getting your mail, you may want to disconnect from the Internet if you connect via modem. You can disconnect manually or set the Remote Access control panel to disconnect automatically after a period of inactivity. Alternatively, you can use AppleScript to automate connecting, getting and sending mail, and disconnecting (as described in Chapter 24).

Replying to and sending mail

Clicking Reply in a message window brings up a new message window with the subject and the recipient already entered. If you select some text in the message window before you click Reply, Outlook Express copies the text into the new message window and normally marks all this quoted text with a > symbol at the beginning of each line. This is the standard e-mail convention for marking quoted text. (Although you can set a different quote symbol in the Internet control panel, Outlook Express 4.5 ignores your setting and uses the > symbol regardless.) Figure 10-19 is an example of the Outlook Express reply message window.

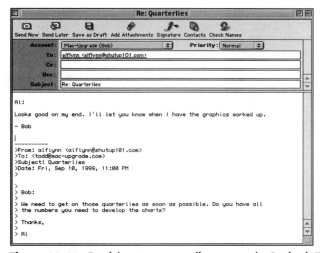

Figure 10-19: Replying to an e-mail message in Outlook Express

After typing the text of your reply, click the Save button or the Send button. The Save button places the message in the Drafts folder. The Send button either sends the message immediately or places it in the Out Box depending on the setting of the option "Send messages immediately" in the General section of the Preferences dialog box.

To start an entirely new message, click New in the main Outlook Express window or choose Mail Message from the New submenu of the File menu. For a new message, you have to type a subject and specify one or more recipients in the spaces provided.

When you're ready to send all your replies and new messages, click Send & Receive or choose a command from the Send & Receive submenu of the Tools menu. If Outlook Express does not connect to your ISP and send your mail, then you may not have set the Remote Access control panel for automatic connection (see "Making an Internet Connection" earlier in this chapter). In this case, you must first make an Internet connection manually, and then use the Send & Receive button or submenu. After Outlook Express sends your mail, you may wish to disconnect from your ISP using the Remote Access control panel. (See "Making an Internet Connection" earlier in this chapter for more information on modem connections.)

E-mail attachments

In addition to text messages, you can send other files with your e-mail messages. Documents, archives of multiple files (created using DropStuff from Aladdin Systems, for instance), and other programs and files can be sent as attachments to an e-mail message using special protocols. This can be useful if you'd like to send an AppleWorks document to a friend or colleague, for example, or even if you'd care to send a shareware or freeware application to an e-mail recipient.

Adding an attachment is easy to do in Outlook Express. With your new e-mail (or reply e-mail) open in its window, click Add Attachments in the button bar. In the Open dialog box that appears, find the document you'd like to send with your e-mail and click Add. You can add more than one attachment, if desired. When you're finished adding attachments, click Done (see Figure 10-20).

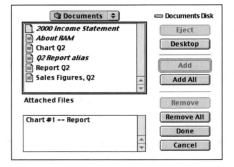

Figure 10-20: Adding an attachment to your e-mail message

Now, when you send the e-mail message, the attachment will go with it.

Note   It's generally considered good "netiquette" (etiquette on the Internet) to only send attachments to receiving parties that expect or would want the file. A large attachment may require your recipient to wait some time before it's downloaded; if you send the file without permission, you may upset your recipient.

Choosing an attachment method

To send an attachment, the file must be converted from a *binary file* — a file that uses a computer's ones and zeros — into a text-based file, because the Internet's e-mail protocols can only handle text-based transmissions. This is done automatically by Outlook Express, which, by default, converts attachments into the appropriate text format using the AppleDouble format. You can select other formats as well, by choosing Edit ➪ Preferences and selecting the Message Composition option in the Preferences dialog box (see Figure 10-21).

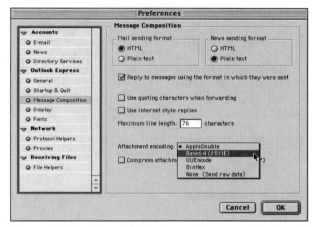

Figure 10-21: Choosing the format for your attachments

The possible formats for attachments are:

✦ **AppleDouble**: Enables you to send files to any computer (Windows-based, Unix, Macintosh) while maintaining the special qualities of Macintosh files.

✦ **Base64**: Can be sent to any MIME-compliant e-mail program (Windows, Unix, Macintosh), but doesn't maintain the special qualities of Macintosh files.

✦ **UUEncode**: Works for most platforms, but is generally best for sending to Unix users. This format doesn't maintain special qualities of Macintosh files.

✦ **BinHex**: Best for sending to other Macintosh users. This format maintains the special qualities of Macintosh files.

Notice the mention of the "special qualities" of Macintosh files. Files created on the Macintosh include two *forks* in which data is stored: a data fork and a resource fork. Other operating systems don't recognize the resource fork, which is used by the

Mac OS to identify the icon, creator application, type of file, and other extended information about a Macintosh file.

If you're sending a file that is intended for ultimate use on a Macintosh, then it's best to send it using AppleDouble or BinHex, so that the two forks are maintained intact. If you're sending to a Microsoft Windows or a Unix computer, it isn't necessary to maintain the resource fork; instead, you simply need to make sure you're sending a document that the Windows or Unix user can either use directly or translate on their computer. For instance, Microsoft Word for Windows can generally translate a Microsoft Word document created on your Mac, even if you send the document using Base64. When in doubt, use AppleDouble. (That's why it's the default in Outlook Express.)

You can also choose the Compress Attachments option in the same Preferences window. This uses the StuffIt Engine to create a StuffIt archive automatically before you send the document. This is a nice touch, because it makes the attachment(s) smaller so that they transmit over the Internet faster. However, only other Macintosh computers are generally equipped with StuffIt Expander, which is required to decompress the attachments and make them useful again. So, only send compressed files to Macintosh users or Microsoft Windows users that you know have Aladdin Expander for Windows on their computers. Aladdin Expander for Windows is available free from Aladdin Systems (`http://www.aladdinsys.com/expander/`).

Cross-Reference   See Chapter 21 for more on compressing files.

Receiving attachments

It's usually pretty easy to tell when you have an attachment in your e-mail. In Outlook Express, a small paperclip appears in the e-mail's entry in the Inbox listing. If you select the e-mail message, the small paperclip in the top-right corner of the e-mail message becomes activated, instead of its usual gray. (Other e-mail programs often have document icons or hyperlinks that represent the attached file.) You can usually do a few different things with an attachment.

In Outlook Express, select the active paperclip icon and a menu appears. You can select the name of the attachment to launch it. Or, choose All... and a Save dialog box appears, enabling you to save the attachment to your hard disk. If you prefer, you can also select the message in the Inbox and choose Message ➪ Save Attachments ➪ All.

Once saved, the attachment can be double-clicked like any other document. In some cases, if the file is encoded or compressed (with a .hqx, .bin, .sit, or .zip file name extension) you may need to drag the file to the StuffIt Expander icon (located in the Aladdin folder inside the Internet Utilities folder in the Internet folder) for it to be expanded.

Browsing the World Wide Web

The World Wide Web is the 800-pound gorilla that shook the Internet to public prominence, so much so that many people think that the Web is the Internet. Not so; the Web is just one of the many services available over the Internet. It happens to be the most interesting because it lets you easily access text and pictures from places all over the world. You access the Web with a program called a *Web browser*, two of which are installed with Mac OS 9 (Microsoft Internet Explorer and Netscape Communicator). You can open the default Web browser by double-clicking the Browse the Internet icon on the desktop.

To use the Web, you first need to know a bit of its terminology. Web browser programs display information in *Web pages*, which can contain text, pictures, and animation, as well as audio and video clips. On a Web page, there is usually underlined text known as *links* or *hyperlinks*. Clicking a link takes you to another Web page. The machines that store all of this information and that serve it to you on request are called *Web servers*. The intriguing thing about hyperlinks is that the Web page that they take you to can be another page on that same server or a page on any other Web server on the planet. So, it's possible to click your way around the world and not even know it!

Note

At the time of writing, Web browser applications were not available that support the keychain features of Mac OS 9. However, they will likely be updated to do so in the future, allowing you to store the user names and passwords for password-protected Web sites in your keychain. For instance, Anarchie Pro, discussed in this chapter and in Chapter 21, allows you to add FTP user names and passwords to your keychain. Check your Web browser's documentation for instructions on adding user names and passwords to your keychain.

Using Netscape Communicator or Internet Explorer

When Netscape Communicator or Internet Explorer opens, it displays a browser window and goes to a Web page that has been previously designated as the home page. With Mac OS 9, the home page is initially set to the Apple Excite page (http://apple.excite.com). Figure 10-22 shows the Apple Excite page in Internet Explorer 4.5; Figure 10-23 shows it in Netscape Communicator 4.6.

You can change the home page setting to a different Web page or to no page at all. In Internet Explorer, you set the home page in the Home/Search section of the Preferences dialog box (accessed from the Edit menu). In Communicator, you set the home page in the Navigator section of the Preferences dialog box (accessed from the Edit menu).

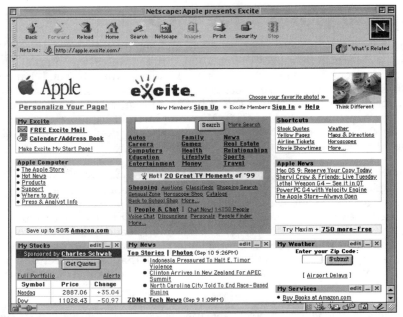

Figure 10-22: Browsing the Web with Netscape Communicator
(Web page courtesy of Apple Computer, Inc.)

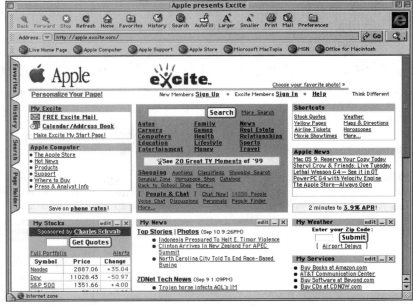

Figure 10-23: Browsing the Web with Internet Explorer
(Web page courtesy of Apple Computer, Inc.)

Choosing a Web browser

Want to use a different default browser? The easiest way to use a different Web browser is to install it and open it by double-clicking its icon. But you can also change the default browser using the Internet control panel.

To change the default browser in the Internet control panel, click the Web tab and use the Default Web Browser pop-up menu. Technical note: This pop-up menu changes the assignment of the "http" helper application, but not the "https" or "file" helpers. To change these as well, click the Advanced tab and then click the Helper Apps icon on the left side of the control panel. In the scrolling list of helper application assignments, select one that is still assigned to the old default browser and click the Change button. In the Edit Helper dialog box, click the Select button and select the new default browser. Repeat this procedure for all other helper assignments that need updating. (If you don't see the Advanced tab in the control panel, choose User Mode from the Edit menu and select Advanced mode.)

Note   With some Web browsers, especially if you've upgraded from an earlier OS version, you may need to specifically set the home page to http://apple.excite. com/ for the Apple Excite home page to load quickly. Older settings (such as http://livepage.apple.com/) still work, but they build in delays as your browser starts up.

From the home page, you can go to other places on the Web by clicking an underlined link on the page. Graphics on the page can also be links. To determine whether something is a link on a Web page, move the mouse over the area; if the pointer turns from an arrow to a pointing hand, it's a link.

Clicking links is a good way to browse the Web, but you should also know how to use the browser's other navigation features, which include toolbar buttons, location or address box, Bookmarks or Favorites menu, Go menu, and multiple browser windows. Internet Explorer also has Favorites buttons and a tabbed Explorer bar.

Toolbar buttons

The toolbar at the top of the browser window contains a set of buttons that you can use to navigate the Web. These navigation buttons help you move from one page to the next, move to your home page, or get around the Web page that you're currently viewing. Each browser has a slightly different complement of navigation buttons; the buttons may even vary from one version of a browser to the next. Here's what the most common toolbar buttons do:

✦ **Back** takes you to the page you were just viewing. You can keep clicking the Back button to go to previous pages. This is useful when you're browsing and want to get back to a place that you want to read again. In Internet Explorer 4.5 and Communicator 4.6, a pop-up menu of recently visited Web pages appears when you click the Back button and hold the mouse button.

✦ **Forward** returns you to a subsequent page after you've used the Back button. Most times, this button is grayed out (which means it's unavailable) because you are at the front of your browsing session.

✦ **Stop** tells the browser to stop loading a page and to display as much of the page as it has loaded.

✦ **Home** takes you back to the home page — the page that loads automatically when the browser starts up. (If you have no home page entered in Internet control panel or in your browser's preferences, this button may either be inactive or it may take you to the browser publisher's preset home page.)

✦ **Reload** or **Refresh** tells the browser to get the current Web page from the Internet again and redisplay it. This reloading is useful with pages that have constantly changing content, such as online news.

✦ **Search** takes you to a page that helps you locate Web pages that contain information that you want to see. You can also search the Web using Sherlock, as detailed in Chapter 6.

✦ **Favorites** displays a window of links to Web pages that you have added to your Favorites list in Internet Explorer.

✦ **Larger** and **Smaller** increase and decrease the size of text in the Internet Explorer window.

✦ **Images** tells Communicator to reload all the graphics on a page (unlike Reload, which reloads the entire page). People with slow connections seem to use this the most, because they don't always let all the graphics from a page finish loading before they press the Stop button.

✦ **Print** prints the current Web page on the printer you have selected. Be aware that many Web pages are wider or taller than real sheets of paper, so one Web page may take several pages to print out. You may be able to make a Web page fit on one sheet of paper by using the Page Setup command to change the page orientation or reduction factor.

As useful as the toolbar buttons are, they take up a fair amount of space. You can make them smaller by eliminating their icons and displaying just their text labels. In Internet Explorer, you change the toolbar settings in the Browser Display section of the Preferences dialog box. In Communicator, you change the toolbar settings in the Appearance section of the Preferences dialog box. You can alternately hide and show the toolbar altogether by choosing from the View menu in Internet Explorer or Communicator.

Understanding URLs

You've probably seen Web addresses in advertisements—they're the ones that look like `http://www.paramount.com`. These Web addresses are one example of a type of address called a *URL*, which stands for Uniform Resource Locator. The nice part about URLs is that they can point you directly to any Web page, or to any file on an FTP site. In fact, there's a URL for everything that you can get to on the Internet.

A URL begins with a code that specifies a kind of Internet protocol. (Protocols also exist for local networking protocols, such as afp:/ for AppleTalk Filing Protocol.) The remainder of the URL specifies a location in terms of a server or account name, a *domain name* (the name of the organization or company that owns the server), and, in some cases, a file directory. In the `http://www.paramount.com` example, `http://` specifies that the address is for a Web page, `www` is the name of a computer that serves Web pages, and `paramount.com` is the domain name.

Address or location box

Below the toolbar buttons is a box labeled Address or Netsite. You can use it to identify the URL of the current page and to enter the URL of a page you want to see. To go to another page whose URL you know, click the old URL to select it, type the new URL, and press Return. You can also select all or part of the URL and copy it to the Clipboard.

When you type a URL in the address box or location box, you don't have to type in the entire URL of a site you want to visit. You can omit the http:// part of the URL because the browser assumes it and puts it in for you when you press Enter or Return. In fact, you don't even have to type in the www. or .com parts of a URL that has them. Because most of the places on the Web start with www. and end with .com, if you type a one-word URL in the location box, the browser adds www. to the beginning and .com to the end. For example, if you type apple in the location box and press Enter or Return, you'll end up at `http://www.apple.com`, the main Apple Web site.

Bookmarks or Favorites menu

Rather than remembering the URL for a page, you can add a *bookmark* for it to the Favorites menu in Internet Explorer or the Bookmarks menu in Communicator. A bookmark keeps track of the URL and the name of a Web page.

To create a bookmark for the current Web page, choose Add Bookmark from the Bookmarks menu or Add Page to Favorites from the Favorites menu. The browser adds the name of the page to the bottom of the menu. You can go back to that Web page later by choosing its name from the Bookmarks menu or Favorites menu.

Go menu

The Go menu keeps a list of the recently visited pages in the current browsing session. To go back to a page, choose it from the Go menu.

Internet Explorer keeps a record of pages that you have visited, including pages from previous browsing sessions. To see this list, choose History from the Go menu. You can revisit a page by double-clicking it on the list. The number of pages that Internet Explorer remembers is set in the Advanced section of the Preferences dialog box.

Opening multiple browser windows

You can have more than one browser window open at a time. This is useful because sometimes you want to read one page while another page loads from the Internet. Browser windows are independent, and you can have as many Web pages open as the browser program has the memory to handle. To open another browser window, choose New Window (New Web Browser in Communicator 3) from the File menu. If you regularly keep many browser windows open, it's a good idea to increase the browser program's memory size by 2000K or more with the Finder's Get Info command (see Chapter 19).

Searching the Internet

As mentioned previously, you can search for specific information on the Web by clicking the Search button at the top of a browser window in Netscape Communicator or Microsoft Internet Explorer. This button takes you to one of many Internet search sites, which are also known as search engines. You can go to another search site by typing its URL in the address box or location box in the Web browser window. Here are the URLs of several popular Web search sites:

✦ Yahoo! — `http://www.yahoo.com`

✦ Excite — `http://www.excite.com`

✦ InfoSeek — `http://infoseek.com`

✦ HotBot — `http://www.hotbot.com`

✦ Lycos — `http://www.lycos.com`

✦ AltaVista — `http://www.altavista.digital.com`

Each Internet search site has a unique index of the Web, so an identical search at each site could produce different results. It stands to reason that the most comprehensive search would entail using several of the search sites. Web sites, such as the Search-It-All site (`http://www.search-it-all.com`), enable you to do this.

In Mac OS 9, you can also conduct a comprehensive search of the Web with Sherlock. Sherlock is discussed in Chapter 6.

Storing Internet Locations

When you see a Web page or a link that you want to keep track of, you can add it to the Bookmarks or Favorites menu in Netscape Communicator or Microsoft Internet Explorer. You can also drag a link to the Scrapbook or to a text document to put its URL there. Later, you can drag a URL from a text document or the Scrapbook to a Web browser window to see the Web page at that location.

You can also keep track of Internet locations by dragging URLs to the desktop, a folder, or a disk. The Finder creates an Internet location file, which points to the URL you dragged. When you open an Internet location file, your Web browser or other Internet application opens and connects to the URL specified by the document.

You can make Internet location files for several types of locations on the Internet or your local area network, and each type of location file will have a unique icon. Figure 10-24 shows examples of several kinds of location files.

Figure 10-24: Each type of location file has a unique icon in Mac OS 9.

You can create these kinds of location files:

✦ Web page location such as `http://www.conglomerated.com`

✦ E-mail address such as `mailto:zap@conglomerated.com`

✦ Newsgroup location such as `news:news.conglomerated.com`

✦ FTP location such as `ftp://ftp.conglomerated.com`

✦ AppleShare file server location such as `afp:/at/Silver Server: White Zone`

✦ AppleTalk network zone such as `at://White Zone`

✦ File location such as `file:///Mac%200S%20HD/Web%20Pages/default.html`

Sharing Your Own Web Site

Ever wanted to host your own Web site? Mac OS 9 has a Web server built in. The Web Sharing control panel is a snap to set up and use and lets you put a Web site on the Internet or on your company's intranet in about a minute (not counting the time it takes to actually create your Web pages). There are, however, some limitations.

A Web server needs a fixed IP address and name so that people can point their browser to the Web site. If you connect to the Internet by modem, your ISP assigns your computer a temporary IP address, also called a dynamic address, which isn't very useful for a Web server. Because a dynamic address changes every time you connect to the Internet other people won't be able to find the address of your Web server. But if your computer happens to have a fixed IP address, which is likely if you have a network connect to the Internet, you can take advantage of Web Sharing to make Web pages and files on your computer available to any computer that has a Web browser and an Internet connection. (Other computers connecting to your Web site do not need fixed IP addresses.)

Because Web Sharing is intended for personal use, it's not especially high-powered. On the one hand, you shouldn't try to use Web Sharing to host a Web site getting thousands of hits per day. On the other hand, it's perfect for sharing information within your company with your coworkers. And it can even run CGIs (Common Gateway Interfaces), which are scripts (often written in Perl, AppleScript, or UserLand Frontier) that can do things such as take the output from a Web form and send it to a database such as FileMaker Pro.

You use the Web Sharing control panel to specify which folder contains your Web pages and to specify which of those pages is your site's home page. You also use the control panel to select the type of security you want and to start or stop Web sharing. Figure 10-25 shows the Web Sharing control panel.

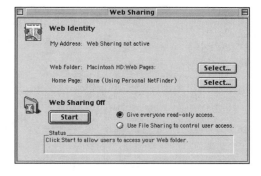

Figure 10-25: Set up your Web site and start Web sharing in the Web Sharing control panel.

In the control panel, you use the first of two buttons labeled Select to specify the folder that contains your Web pages. Initially, this is set to the Web Pages folder on the startup disk. You use the second Select button to bring up a dialog box that lists the Web pages in that folder, and you select one to be your Web site's home page. Figure 10-26 shows the dialog box in which you select a home page.

Figure 10-26: Choosing your home page

In the home page dialog box, you can click the None button (instead of selecting a home page and clicking the Select button) to turn on an interesting feature called Personal NetFinder. When Personal NetFinder is active, visitors to your Web site don't see a regular home page; instead, they see a listing of the files and folders that are found in the Web Pages folder (similar to the list view of a folder window). Figure 10-27 is a sample of a Personal NetFinder listing as viewed in Netscape Communicator. This makes it easy to display file names (instead of Web pages) for your visitors to download.

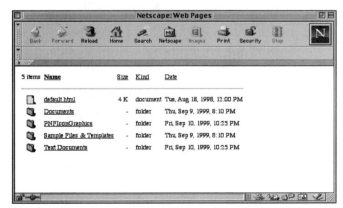

Figure 10-27: If your Web site has no home page, visitors see a listing of files that are found in your Web Pages folder.

After specifying the folder that contains your Web pages and selecting a home page (or not), all you need to do to get your server on the air is to click the Start button. You can also use the two radio buttons to the right of the Start button to enable all users read-only access, or to have Web Sharing apply the security and require passwords that you've set up using the Users & Groups control panel (as described in Chapter 22).

When Web Sharing is on, your Web site's address appears in the Web Sharing control panel next to the heading My Address. Your Web site has a numeric IP address such as `http://192.0.0.2`. Depending on the type of Internet connection you have, your Web site may also have a name address, such as `http://mac1.mac-upgrade.com`. Give this name or number to people who want to connect to your Web site so that they can type the name in their Web browsers.

If your network only assigns numeric IP addresses, put a note on your home page telling people who connect to add a bookmark for your page so that they don't have to type in those numbers again.

Participating in Newsgroups

In addition to e-mail and the Web, there's another part of the Internet — the Usenet. You can think of Usenet as a worldwide bulletin board system, where people from everywhere can post messages and join discussions about subjects that interest them. Each subject is called a newsgroup. There are more than 25,000 newsgroups covering virtually every subject imaginable. To find a newsgroup that interests you, you have to know a little about the structure of newsgroup names. A newsgroup name has several parts separated by periods. The first part specifies the general subject, the next part narrows the subject, and subsequent parts narrow the subject still further. Table 17-1 shows the most common top-level newsgroup names, and Table 17-2 shows examples of full newsgroup names.

Table 17-1 Common Top-Level Newsgroup Names	
Identifier	*Included Subjects*
alt	Subjects that don't fit into one of the other "official" categories
biz	Business
comp	Computers
misc	Miscellaneous subjects
news	News and other topical information

Identifier	Included Subjects
rec	Recreational hobbies and arts
sci	Scientific
soc	Social
talk	Debates

Table 17-2
Sample Full Newsgroup Names

Newsgroup Name	Subject
alt.fan.gill-anderson	The pictures are out there
comp.sys.lang.java	Java programming language
rec.arts.music.folk	Folk music and musicians
sci.nanotech	Nanotechnology discussions

Using Outlook Express to read news

You can find the newsgroup of your dreams using a variety of programs. In addition to sending and receiving e-mail, Microsoft Outlook Express can read and post messages to newsgroups. Outlook Express lists news servers among the folders in the left pane of the main window. Click a news server to see a list of available newsgroups in the right pane of the main window. The first time you do this, don't be surprised if it takes several minutes to retrieve all the newsgroup names from the news server. Outlook Express remembers the newsgroup names, so the next time you click the same news server the names appear right away. You can check for new newsgroups by choosing Get New Newsgroups from the View menu.

You can scroll through groups to find the ones that interest you. When you see a likely group, you can subscribe to it to make it easier to find again. To subscribe to a newsgroup, select it and choose Subscribe from the Tools menu. After subscribing to all of the groups that look good to you, choose Subscribed Only from the View menu to list only your groups. To see all groups, choose Subscribed Only again so there is no check mark next to it in the View menu.

To see a list of messages in a newsgroup, double-click its title. The list of messages appears in the top pane of a new window. If no messages are listed, click More at the top of the window. Select a listed message to see a preview of it in the bottom pane of the same window. You can also open the message in its own window by double-clicking its title in the list. If there are replies to a message, you can see them by clicking the disclosure triangle next to the original message title.

If you wish to reply to a message and join the discussion, click Reply To Newsgroup above the list of messages, and type your message in the new message form that appears. Click Post to send your message.

Using other news clients

Besides Outlook Express, you can use Netscape Communicator (also included with Mac OS 9) to read and post Usenet messages. Communicator's Messenger component is used for reading news groups.

Two other popular newsreaders are MT-NewsWatcher (by Brian Clark) and YA-NewsWatcher (by Simon Fraser). Both are freeware applications that are based on the public domain source code of the original NewsWatcher by John Norstad (see Chapter 26). While Norstad has stopped updating the original, the other two programs have many tools to make subscribing to newsgroups, as well as reading and replying to messages, easy. If you get serious about Usenet, be sure to check out one of these versions of NewsWatcher.

Summary

Getting on the Internet with Mac OS 9 is pretty simple — all it takes is a quick walk through the Internet Setup Assistant's steps. Once you've got your connection entered, you can tweak its settings, along with other Internet preferences, in the Internet control panel. With the housecleaning complete, you're ready to sign on to the Internet, either manually or automatically, according to your preference.

Once online, you can use Outlook Express or Netscape Communicator to read, write, and respond to e-mail messages. It just takes a little setup and pushing the right buttons. From there, it's on to the World Wide Web, which you can surf with Netscape Communicator or Internet Explorer, both of which are installed with Mac OS 9. You can also take advantage of the Mail icon and Browse the Internet icons on the desktop, as well as the Connect To . . . program that appears on Mac OS 9's Apple menu.

There are other things to do online. You can create your own Web site, for example, and turn your Mac into a Web server or a file server, enabling friends to download files from your machine. Likewise, you can get on the Usenet and participate in the thousands of discussion groups that are available on nearly any topic imaginable.

✦   ✦   ✦

At Work with the Mac OS

Dig into the System Folder

Your computer has a special folder that contains all the essential software that gives the Mac OS its unique appearance and behavior. That folder is normally named System Folder, although the name is not mandatory. You can always spot the System Folder by its distinctive icon, which looks like a folder emblazoned with a miniature Mac OS icon.

The Mac OS uses additional special folders and files, several of them invisible, to keep track of items in the Trash, items on the desktop, and temporary files used by application programs. A desktop database matches documents with the applications that created them so that they all have the right icons and you can open documents from the Finder.

Exploring the System Folder

The System Folder contains several special folders, each with a distinctive icon, a unique name, and particular contents. The System Folder also contains a few files, such as the System file, which you can open like a folder, and the Finder. In addition, there may be some ordinary folders in the System Folder. Figure 11-1 is an example of a System Folder.

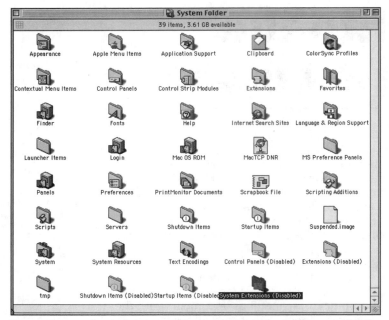

Figure 11-1: A basic System Folder contains essential files and folders.

Here's a brief rundown on some of the more common items found in the System Folder:

✦ **Appearance**, which contains files that can change the look and sound of Mac OS 9: desktop pictures, themes, and sound sets (see Chapter 8).

✦ **Apple Menu Items**, which contains items listed in the Apple menu (see Chapter 7).

✦ **Application Support**, which contains items used by some application programs.

✦ **Clipboard**, which temporarily stores what you copy or cut (see Chapter 7).

✦ **ColorSync Profiles**, which contains color-matching profiles for specific scanners, monitors, and printers (see Chapters 12 and 16).

✦ **Contextual Menu Items**, which contains plug-in software modules that add commands to contextual menus. These modules require the SOMobjects for Mac OS file in the Extensions folder.

✦ **Control Panels**, which contains small programs for setting options and preferences (see Chapters 7, 8, 10, 12, 13, and 18 to 23). This folder is normally listed in the Apple menu.

✦ **Control Strip Modules**, which contains the modules that appear in the Control Strip (see Chapter 12).

✦ **Extensions**, which contains software that extends the capabilities of the Mac OS and application programs (see "Managing Startup Items" later in this chapter).

✦ **Favorites**, which contains the alias files that determine which items are listed in the Favorites pop-up menu of the Navigation Services dialog boxes (see Chapter 7).This folder is normally listed in the Apple menu.

✦ **Finder**, which is the application for organizing files, folders, and disks (see Chapter 5).

✦ **Fonts**, which contains fixed-size, TrueType, and PostScript fonts (see Chapter 15).

✦ **Help**, which contains the pages of the Mac OS Help and AppleScript Help that you see onscreen through the Apple Help Viewer (see Chapter 9).

✦ **Internet Search Sites**, which specifies the means of searching that you can use in the Sherlock program's Search the Internet (see Chapter 6).

✦ **Language & Region Support**, which stores files that make it possible to change the Mac OS to support different languages and lettering systems.

✦ **Launcher Items**, which contains items to be displayed in the Launcher window (see Chapter 7).

✦ **Login**, which is a file that the Mac OS uses to bring up the log-in window when you have set up Multiple Users (see Chapter 13).

✦ **Mac OS ROM**, which contains essential parts of the Mac OS that are loaded in the memory of newer Mac models (such as iMac, iBook, and the G4 desktop) as the computer starts up.

✦ **MacTCP DNR**, which is mostly obsolete, but which some applications that use a TCP/IP network (as described in Chapter 20) may require.

✦ **MS Preference Panels**, which contains preference settings for Microsoft Internet Explorer and other Microsoft applications (see Chapter 10).

✦ **Note Pad File**, which stores the text you write in the Note Pad, discussed in Chapter 25. (The Note Pad File only appears after you've launched the Note Pad, which is stored in the Apple Extras folder on your startup disk after a clean install of Mac OS 9.)

✦ **Panels**, which is a file used by the Mac OS to display the limited Panels interface (instead of the Finder) when a user has been given that sort of access in the Multiple Users control panel (see Chapter 13).

✦ **Preferences**, which contains settings, status, and other information used by various programs (see "Investigating Preferences" later in this chapter).

✦ **PrintMonitor Documents**, which temporarily holds pending requests for background printing (see Chapter 16).

✦ **Scrapbook File**, which stores the text, pictures, and other items that you can add to and can copy from the Scrapbook (see Chapter 25).

✦ **Scripting Additions**, which contains files that extend the AppleScript language (see Chapter 24).

✦ **Scripts**, which contains AppleScript scripts, such as those used for folder actions (see Chapter 24).

✦ **Servers**, which contains aliases to file sharing servers that you've chosen to connect to at startup time.

Note   At the time of writing, we found that the Servers folder was located in the System Folder in late test versions of Mac OS 9. Apple's technical documentation suggests that it will be moved to the Startup Items folder, so you may find it there in the shipping version of Mac OS 9. See Chapter 13 for more on this issue.

✦ **Shutdown Items**, which contains items to be opened as the computer shuts down (see Chapter 7).

✦ **Startup Items**, which contains items to be opened as the computer starts up (see Chapter 7).

✦ **Suspended.image**, which is a file created on Mac models that support the option to Preserve memory contents on sleep in the Advanced settings of the Energy Saver control panel.

✦ **System**, which contains much of the Mac OS as well as sounds, keyboard layouts, and language script systems (as described in the next section, "Probing the System File").

✦ **System Enabler**, which has additional system software required by your Mac model. Most models with Mac OS 9 don't need a System Enabler, so you may not find one in your System Folder.

✦ **System Resources**, which contains additional system software used by Mac OS 9.

✦ **Text Encodings**, which contains software that translates between different methods of encoding text, such as ASCII for Western European languages and Unicode for worldwide languages.

The names of most of these items can't be changed.

Your System Folder may contain items not listed here. For example, it may contain folders whose names end with "(Disabled)" but that are otherwise the same as the names of folders listed here. Those folders contain items that you have deactivated using Extensions Manager, Conflict Catcher, or another program that manages startup files (see "Managing Startup Items" later in this chapter). Furthermore, additional items may appear in your System Folder after you install applications or other software.

Conversely, your System folder may not contain all of the items listed here. For example, if you have never used the Note Pad, you will not have a Note Pad file. Likewise, if your Mac model doesn't support Apple's new sleep scheme, you may not see the Suspended.image file.

Probing the System File

The System file, which is one of the most important files in the System Folder, is unusual because you can open it like a folder. You can see some of the system resources it contains, and you can remove some or add more of the same.

Of all the items in the System Folder, there are two that must be present for the computer to start. One is the Finder and the other is the System file. The System file has long been terra incognita to all but the most intrepid resource-hacking Mac OS users. Although a large part of it remains an uncharted wilderness of basic system software, the Finder lets you see and work with some of the System file's contents.

Seeing System file contents

You can open the System file as if it were a folder and see which alert sounds, keyboard layouts, and script systems for foreign languages it contains. Several of these kinds of items do not appear when you open the System file because they are permanently installed in every computer that can use the Mac OS. These items include the simple beep sound, the U.S. keyboard layout, and the Roman script system for Western languages. Figure 11-2 shows examples of the items you can see by opening a System file.

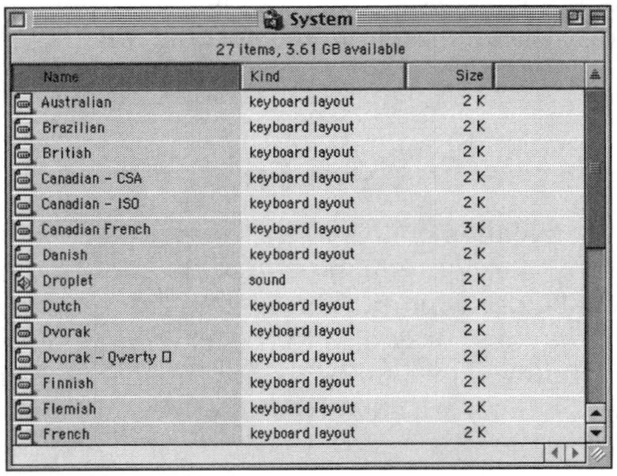

Name	Kind	Size
Australian	keyboard layout	2 K
Brazilian	keyboard layout	2 K
British	keyboard layout	2 K
Canadian – CSA	keyboard layout	2 K
Canadian – ISO	keyboard layout	2 K
Canadian French	keyboard layout	3 K
Danish	keyboard layout	2 K
Droplet	sound	2 K
Dutch	keyboard layout	2 K
Dvorak	keyboard layout	2 K
Dvorak – Qwerty □	keyboard layout	2 K
Finnish	keyboard layout	2 K
Flemish	keyboard layout	2 K
French	keyboard layout	2 K

System — 27 items, 3.61 GB available

Figure 11-2: The System file contains sounds and keyboard layouts.

Working with System file contents

Not only can you see the contents of the System file, you can also drag items in and out of it as if it were a folder. Changes to sounds take effect as soon as you close the System file, but changes to other items require restarting your computer first. The Finder doesn't allow you to drag items in or out of the System file when other programs are open. You must quit all open programs except the Finder, make your changes to the System file contents, and then open the programs again.

Items that you drag out of the System file become independent files. You can move them to any folder or the desktop and copy them to other disks. You can rename sounds but not other items in the System file. Opening a sound that's in or out of the System file makes the computer play it.

Installing sounds in the System file makes them candidates for the system alert sound, which you choose with the Monitors & Sound control panel or the Sound control panel (see Chapter 12). There are many kinds of sound files that exist, but you can put only one kind of sound file in the System file — a *System 7 Sound* (it has an internal type code of sfil). Specifically, you can't put MP3 music clips or AIFF sounds in the System file.

The keyboard layouts that you install appear as choices in the Keyboard control panel. Selecting a different keyboard layout there changes your Mac's arrangement of the keys on your keyboard. Selecting the Español (Spanish) layout, for example, makes the semicolon key on a U.S. keyboard produce a ñ (for details on foreign-language keyboard arrangements, see Chapter 12).

Adding Items to the System Folder

Most of the items in the System Folder are placed there for you when you install the Mac OS, applications, and other software. Nevertheless, from time to time you may need to add items to the System Folder. Most items must go in a special folder or the System file inside the System Folder. The Finder can automatically route many kinds of items to the proper place, or you can drag items to specific folders yourself.

Automatic routing inside the System Folder

The Finder can automatically route many kinds of files to the proper place in the System Folder. To take advantage of this service, you must drag the files to the System Folder icon, not to the System Folder window. The System Folder icon can be open (its window displayed), but you must drag files to the icon nonetheless. If you drag files to the System Folder window, they simply go into the main part of the System Folder, where some kinds of items are effective but others are not.

When you drag the items to the System Folder icon (not the System Folder window), the Finder recognizes items that go in many of the special folders or the System file and asks whether you want the items put in their proper places. If you consent, the Finder automatically routes the items to special folders as enumerated in Table 11-1. Figure 11-3 is an example of the alert that appears if the Finder recognizes items that you drag to the System Folder icon.

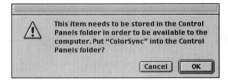

Figure 11-3: The Finder knows where to put some of the items that you drag to the System Folder.

Table 11-1
Automatic Routing to Special Folders in the System Folder

Kind of Item	Routed to
Apple Guide document	Extensions folder
Chooser extension	Extensions folder
ColorSync Profile	ColorSync Profiles folder
Communications tool	Extensions folder
Contextual menu plug-in	Contextual Menu Items folder
Control panel	Control Panels folder
Control Strip module	Control Strip Modules folder
Desk accessory program	Apple Menu Items folder
Font or Font suitcase	Fonts folder
Internet Search Site	Internet Search Sites folder
JPEG picture	Desktop Pictures folder (inside Appearance)
Keyboard layout	System file
Library	Extensions folder
Location Manager module	Location Manager Modules folder (inside Extensions folder)
Modem script	Modem Scripts folder (inside Extensions folder)
PostScript Font	Fonts folder
Preference files of type "pref"	Preferences folder

Continued

Table 11-1 *(continued)*	
Kind of Item	**Routed to**
Script system	System file
Scripting addition	Scripting Additions folder
Sound (alert)	System file
Sound Set file	Sound Sets folder (inside Appearance)
System extension	Extensions folder
Text Encoding Converter document	Text Encodings folder
Theme file	Theme Files folder (inside Appearance)

Manual routing inside the System Folder

Some kinds of items can't be routed automatically to special folders because they are not a unique kind of item. For example, the Finder can't tell where to put a particular alias file — it may belong in the Apple Menu Items folder, Launcher Items folder, Favorites folder, Recent Applications folder (inside the Apple Menu Items folder), Recent Items folder (inside the Navigation Services folder), Startup Folder, or another special folder. Likewise, the Finder doesn't know it should put items like printer descriptions into the Printer Descriptions folder because that kind of file is nothing more than plain text.

If you know where items belong inside the System Folder, you can drag them directly to the proper special folder or, if appropriate, to the System file. Many items belong in folders you can see when you open the System Folder. Other items belong in folders located inside the folders at the main level of the System Folder. For example, most system extension files belong in the Extensions folder, but text-to-speech voices and printer descriptions belong in folders inside the Extensions folder. You need to be careful when putting items directly into folders inside the System Folder. You're not likely to damage anything by putting an item in the wrong place, but the item may not function if put in the wrong folder.

Removing Items from the System Folder

Before you can remove an item from the System Folder, you must know which inner folder contains it. If you're not sure where the item is, use Sherlock to locate the item (see Chapter 6). Be sure to drag items from the special folders to the desktop or to an ordinary folder. Some items you drag out of special folders remain effective if you merely drag them to the System Folder window.

How to spot and fix routing mistakes

The Finder sometimes makes mistakes when it puts items in special folders for you. It may put some items in the correct places and incorrectly leave others in the System Folder itself. For example, the Finder correctly puts many preference files in the Preferences folder, but it incorrectly puts others in the System Folder.

You know that the Finder made a mistake if you don't see the expected alert when you drag items to the System Folder icon. If the Finder doesn't recognize items you drag to the System Folder icon, it doesn't put them in special folders. Of course, the System Folder is the right place for some items, such as a replacement Scrapbook File or Note Pad File.

You know that the Finder is about to make a mistake if you drag items to the System Folder icon and see an alert saying that *some* of the items need to be put in special folders. The key word here is some. In this case, you may want to cancel the alert and drag the items one at a time. This procedure takes a little longer than dragging a group of items, but you know more precisely which items do not go in special folders.

When the Finder makes a mistake and puts an item in the System Folder itself rather than in the special folder where it belongs, you must open the System Folder and drag the misplaced item to the proper special folder yourself.

Don't remove items from the System Folder unless you're sure your system doesn't need them. Sometimes a file name may sound like the item is used for one specific feature that you don't care about while it is actually required by the Mac OS or is used by other features that you don't want to deactivate. For example, the Text Encoding Converter library in the Extensions folder may sound like you don't need it unless you want to read or write foreign languages. While you do need this library file to use foreign languages, you also need it to see the contents of a disk that uses the Mac OS Extended format.

If you happen to discard a special folder, you can make a replacement by using the Finder's New Folder command (in the File menu). After creating a new folder, change its name to that of the special folder you discarded. Wait a few seconds and you'll see its icon get the distinctive look of the special folder you discarded. If you've lost important Mac OS or other system files, you may need to reinstall those files from your Mac OS 9 CD, from the software that comes from your peripherals, or from backup disks.

Managing Startup Items

Files from several places in the System Folder are loaded in the computer's memory when you start or restart the computer. Files from the Extensions folder, Control Panels folder, and the System Folder itself extend the capabilities of the Mac OS.

Startup files are also known as *extensions* because many of them extend some part of the Mac OS. An extension used to be called an *INIT*, which is a common internal type code for a system extension, and you still hear this term applied to all startup files.

You can manage startup files so that some of them take effect but others don't. There are several reasons for doing this. For example, you may want to deactivate some startup files to reduce the amount of memory that the Mac OS uses and make more memory available for opening applications (see Chapter 19); or you may want to deactivate other startup files to improve system performance for special tasks such as digitizing movies (see Chapter 18); or you may want to activate or deactivate startup files required for an application that you only use occasionally; or you may want to deactivate startup files to troubleshoot a problem (see Chapter 29).

The most direct way to manage startup files is to drag them in and out of folders. You can more easily activate and deactivate startup files with a startup management utility such as the Extensions Manager control panel installed with Mac OS 9 or the Conflict Catcher (version 8 or later) program from Casady & Greene (831-484-9228, `http://www.casadyg.com`).

These programs can also manage items in the Startup Items and Shutdown Items control panels. In addition, Conflict Catcher can manage Control Strip modules, fonts, Internet plug-in software, and more.

Adding and removing startup files

Most startup files are placed in the proper folder as part of installing the Mac OS, an application, or utility software. As a result, you generally don't have to drag startup files into the Extensions folder or Control Panels folder. However, you can drag files out of these folders if you neither want nor need the capabilities they provide. For example, if you don't have an AudioVision 14 monitor, you don't need the PowerPC Monitors Extension file in your Extensions folder. After removing or adding startup files, you typically must restart your computer for the changes to take effect.

The best place to drag a startup file that you want to deactivate is to a specially named folder inside the System Folder. Drag files from the Extensions folder to the Extensions (Disabled) folder; from the Control Panels folder to Control Panels (Disabled) folder; and from the main level of the System Folder to the System Extensions (Disabled) folder. These folders may already exist in your System Folder, because Extensions Manager and Conflict Catcher create them automatically, or you may have to make new folders and name them yourself. If you use the specially named folders, you can switch back and forth between dragging startup files directly to them and using Extensions Manager or Conflict Catcher.

If you drag a startup file out of the Extensions folder or Control Panels folder, do not drag it to the main level of the System Folder. Startup files are still active there.

Startup file loading sequence

Startup files may be in the Extensions folder, the Control Panels folder, or the System Folder itself. During startup, the Mac OS loads files from each of these folders in turn. First, it goes through the Extensions folder in alphabetical order. Then it loads startup files from the Control Panels folder, again alphabetically. Finally, the Mac OS checks the main level of the System Folder and alphabetically loads the startup files it finds there. This loading sequence can cause problems for a few combinations of startup files.

Some startup files in the Extensions folder, Control Panels folder, or System Folder need to be loaded before or after other files in the same folder. These files have peculiar names that put them first or last in the loading sequence. Names of files meant to come first usually begin with blank spaces or a character that has no visible symbol, so the Mac OS displays a hollow box (□). Names meant to come last often begin with a tilde (~) or a diamond (◊).

If a startup file from one of the special folders needs to load before or after startup files in another special folder, name prefixes alone won't suffice. You must also move the file into another folder. For example, to have a file from the Control Panels folder start before files in the Extensions folder, you must prefix its name with a blank space and put it in the Extensions folder. To have a file from the Control Panels folder load after startup files in the System Folder, you must prefix its name with a tilde or diamond and put it in the System Folder. For convenient access to control panels that you move out of the Control Panels folder, make aliases of the control panels, and put the aliases in the Control Panels folder. (See Chapter 14 for instructions on making aliases.)

You can also change the loading order of startup files without renaming them by using Conflict Catcher 8 or later from Casady & Greene, or another startup file manager program that offers this feature.

Using Extensions Manager

The Extensions Manager control panel can individually deactivate startup files in the Control Panels folder, the Extensions folder, and the main level of the System Folder, as well as items in the Startup Items and Shutdown Items folders. The Extensions Manager window has a scrolling list of these items. For each listed item, the Extensions Manager displays its status (on or off), name, size, version, and the package it was installed with. You can also display each item's type and creator codes by selecting options with the Preferences command (in the Edit menu). Figure 11-4 is an example of the Extensions Manager.

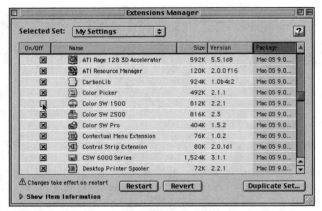

Figure 11-4: Deactivate and activate startup items with Extensions Manager.

Reorganizing the Extensions Manager list

You can reorganize the Extensions Manager list as follows:

✦ View items grouped by the folders they're in, grouped by the package they were installed with, or ungrouped through the View menu.

✦ Collapse and expand a group by clicking the disclosure triangle next to the group name or by double-clicking the name.

✦ Sort the list within each group by clicking any column heading to set the sort order.

✦ Adjust the widths of the Name and Package columns by dragging the right boundary line of the Name column heading or the left boundary line of the Package column heading. (You can't adjust the other column widths.)

Seeing detailed information about an item

To see more information about a particular item, click its name to select it and then click the disclosure triangle labeled Show Item Information at the bottom-left corner of the Extensions Manager window. You can also select an item and choose Get Info from the Extensions Manager's File menu to open the item's Get Info window in Finder, or choose Find Item to open the folder that contains the item and select the item. If you want more information about any startup file in your System Folder, get the InformINIT shareware by Dan Frakes — the latest version is available on the Internet through a link at http://cafe.AmbrosiaSW.com/DEF/InformINIT.html. Figure 11-5 is the Extensions Manager expanded to show item information.

The Missing Extensions alert

Sometimes when you open the Extensions Manager, it displays an alert asking if you'd like to save information about missing extensions. If you agree, Extensions Manager saves a text file with the name Missing Extensions (or another name you specify) in the folder you indicate. Do not be alarmed.

The Missing Extensions report itemizes startup files that the Extensions Manager expected to find in the folders it tracks — Control Panels, Extensions, Startup Items, Shutdown Items, and System Folder — but didn't. You probably dragged something from one of these folders since the last time you opened Extensions Manager. Another possibility is that you used a software installer to remove startup files or to install software that removed startup files.

Go ahead and save the missing extensions report. Switch to the Finder, open the report with SimpleText, and check it over just in case a startup file vanished mysteriously and you need to replace it by installing the software it came with.

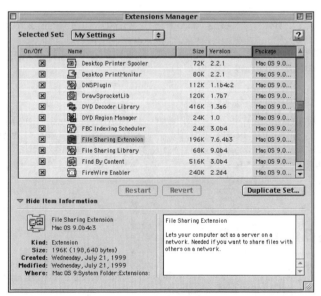

Figure 11-5: The Extensions Manager is expanded to show item information.

Activating and deactivating items

You deactivate or activate an extension or other item by clicking the check box next to the item's name. Activating or deactivating a group affects all the items in the group. You can save the current configuration of the Extensions Manager as a named set by choosing New Set from the File menu. Your named sets appear in the Selected Set pop-up in alphabetical order, and choosing a set from that pop-up changes Extensions Manager to the configuration saved for that set. To activate or deactivate all items, use the All On or All Off commands in the Edit menu.

Extensions Manager comes with two preconfigured sets: Mac OS All and Mac OS Base. Choosing the Mac OS All set turns on all the startup items that are installed by the Mac OS Installer. Choosing the Mac OS Base set turns on only the most essential startup items.

Changes you make to the status of any items take place when you restart. To restart immediately, click the Restart button. To restart later, quit Extensions Manager and press Power or use the Restart command in Finder's Special menu when you are ready to restart. To cancel the changes you've made, click Revert in the Extensions Manager window.

Extensions Manager puts deactivated items from the Extensions folder in a folder named Extensions (Disabled). Deactivated control panels are stored in a folder named Control Panels (Disabled). Deactivated items from the System Folder go into a folder named System Extensions (Disabled).

Using Extensions Manager during startup

You can activate or deactivate startup items while your computer is starting up. To bring up the Extensions Manager control panel at the beginning of the startup process, hold down the Spacebar. Holding down Shift at the beginning of the startup process temporarily deactivates all extensions, without affecting settings in the Extensions Manager control panel.

Investigating Preferences

What you see in your Preferences folder depends on what you have installed on your hard disk. Many application programs save files of preference settings in the Preferences folder. Also, the Mac OS saves a plethora of preference files in the Preferences folder.

It's generally pretty easy to figure out which preferences file goes with what program by looking at the name of the preferences file. See if you can guess which control panels save settings in these preferences files: Date & Time Preferences, Keyboard Preferences, and Launcher Preferences. Here are descriptions of some of the items found in the Preferences folder, excluding files that by their names obviously contain settings you make with like-named control panels:

✦ The **File Sharing** folder contains file-sharing access privileges for your disks and folders (as described in Chapter 22). You don't have this folder if File Sharing has never been turned on.

✦ **Finder Preferences** contains many of the settings you make with Finder's Preferences command in Mac OS 9 (as described in Chapter 5).

✦ **Navigation Services** contains a folder of the items listed in the Recent pop-up menu in Navigation Services dialog boxes in Mac OS 9 (described in Chapter 7).

✦ **Internet Preferences** stores settings that you make with the Internet control panel in Mac OS 9.

✦ **AppSwitcher Prefs** specifies the current configuration of the Application Switcher (covered in Chapter 7). Remove this file to reset the Application Switcher to its standard configuration.

✦ **Users & Groups Data File** contains names and privileges for registered users and groups to whom you have given access to your computer (as described in Chapter 22).

✦ **Keychains** is a folder that contains individual keychain files. It's a good idea to back up your keychain files often so that you don't lose login and password information for your keychain resources. Likewise, you can copy your keychain file to other Macs running Mac OS 9 or higher and use it to access your secure resources. (This is discussed in depth in Chapter 12.)

✦ **Multi-User Items** is a folder that stores the preferences files for your users if you've set up Multiple Users (discussed in Chapter 13). If you need to move your Multiple Users files to a clean installation of the Mac OS, copy the Multi-Users Prefs document, Multi-User Items folder, and the Client Prefs document to the new Preferences folder. If you've set up Voice Verification for your users, you should copy the Voice Verifications Prefs file to the new Preferences folder as well.

✦ **AppleCD Audio Player Prefs** and **CD Remote Programs** contain album and song titles that you enter for individual audio CDs together with other settings for the AppleCD Audio Player program (as described in Chapter 18).

✦ **Stickies File** contains the text of notes that you post on your screen with the Stickies program (covered in Chapter 25).

Revealing More Special Folders

The Mac OS further organizes your disks with additional special folders outside the System Folder. The Finder creates these special folders as needed on each disk:

✦ The invisible **Temporary Items folder** contains temporary files created by the programs that you are using. A program normally deletes its temporary files automatically when you quit it.

✦ The **Trash folder** contains the items you drag from the disk to the Trash icon. Your disks' Trash folders are invisible, but you see their consolidated contents when you open the Trash icon. A visible Trash folder in a shared disk contains items from the disk that are located in the owner's Trash.

✦ The **Network Trash folder** contains items from your shared disk or folder that network users have dragged to the Trash — but have not yet permanently removed — on their computers. The discarded items appear in the network users' Trash, not yours.

✦ The **Rescued Items folder** contains items the Finder finds in the Temporary Items folder when you restart after a system crash (or after switching off the power without using the Shut Down command — tsk! tsk!). You may be able to reconstruct your work by opening them. If a Rescued Items folder exists, you can always see it by opening the Trash.

✦ **TheFindByContentFolder** is a hidden folder that stores files created by the Find by Content option of Sherlock in Mac OS 9.

✦ The **Desktop folder** contains items located on the desktop. Although it is invisible on your disks, the Desktop folder of a shared disk is visible to others and contains items from the disk that are on the owner's desktop.

✦ The **Users folder** stores various items for each user (each in a folder named for that user) that are *mirrored* in the System Folder when that user logs in to the Mac. For instance, you'll find individual folders for Apple Menu Items, Favorites, Preferences, and so on, as well as that user's Documents folder. Each user also has a hidden Trash folder in his or her user folder. Most of the contents of these folders can be altered by the owner to customize each user's experience, as discussed in Chapter 13.

Checking the Desktop Database

Something you don't see in the System Folder is the invisible desktop database that Finder uses to track:

✦ Which icons to use for documents created by all your applications (unless you have customized them, as described in Chapter 8)

✦ What kind of file each icon refers to

✦ Where programs are located

✦ What comments you enter with the Finder's Get Info command

The Mac OS keeps this database hidden so users can't alter it inadvertently, but you can see some of the information the database contains by selecting a file in the Finder and choosing Get Info from the Finder's File menu.

The Finder creates and maintains a desktop database on every disk. On disks larger than 2MB, the desktop database consists of two invisible files named Desktop DB and Desktop DF. On smaller disks, the desktop database is kept in one file named Desktop. Finder creates these files automatically on new disks and updates them with new information whenever you install an application.

You can force the Finder to rebuild the desktop database by holding down the Option and ⌘ keys when starting the computer or anytime while the Mac's extensions are loading. (If you have Multiple Users active, you can hold down the key combination immediately after entering your password, just before your desktop begins to appear.) After the Mac OS has loaded all startup files, the Finder displays an alert asking whether you want to rebuild the desktop file on the startup disk. After rebuilding the startup disk, the Finder asks whether you want to rebuild the next disk on the desktop, if you have more than one disk. The Finder asks about each disk on the desktop separately, even if you stop holding down the ⌘ and Option keys (so give your fingers a rest). See Chapter 29 for more information about rebuilding the desktop as a preventive measure and as a solution to some problems.

Summary

This chapter showed you the files in the System Folder and told you why they're there. The Finder file is in the System Folder along with the System file, which contains much of the basic system software as well as sounds, keyboard layouts, and script systems for foreign languages. The Apple Menu Items folder contains items listed in the Apple menu, and the Favorites menu contains items listed in the Favorites pop-up menu in Navigation Services dialog boxes. The Startup Items folder contains items that are to be opened as the computer starts up, and the Shutdown Items folder contains items to be opened as the computer shuts down. The Extensions folder contains software that extends the capabilities of the Mac OS. Control Panels and Control Strip modules have their own folders. The Fonts folder contains fixed-size, TrueType, and PostScript fonts. The Preferences folder contains settings, status, and other information used by various programs. The System Folder contains many other items as well.

You can add items to and remove from the System Folder using a number of different methods, including the Extensions Manager and a manual drag-and-drop operation. You learned how to manage startup files in the Extensions, Control Panels, and main level of the System Folder.

This chapter also revealed other special folders that the Mac OS uses to keep track of items in the Trash, items on the desktop, Multiple User items, and temporary files used by application programs. In addition, the Finder maintains a desktop database to match documents with the applications that created them so that they all have the right icons and you can open documents from the Finder.

✦   ✦   ✦

Adjust Controls and Preferences

Your computer is highly configurable. You can set numerous options that affect various aspects of its operation, including the keyboard and mouse sensitivity, the screen resolution and color depth, the way the computer uses energy, and the alert sound you hear. All these options and many, many more are set with various control panels and the Control Strip.

This chapter delves into ten types of customization that can adapt the Mac OS to fit your circumstances, making it easier to use and helping you become more efficient.

General Preferences

The General Controls control panel sets a number of system options. Figure 12-1 shows the options that you can set in the General Controls control panel.

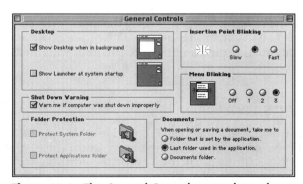

Figure 12-1: The General Controls control panel

On the left side of the General Controls window, you can show or hide the Finder's desktop when the Finder is not the active application, and you can have the Launcher control panel open automatically during startup. You can have the Mac OS display a warning during startup if the computer crashed or was not shut down properly. In addition, you can individually protect the System Folder and the Applications folder on the startup disk, preventing items in them from being renamed or removed; to use these options, however, file sharing must be turned off in the File Sharing control panel.

On the right side of the General Controls window, you can set blinking rates for the text insertion point and menus. Another option determines which folder you see first in a dialog box for opening or saving a document. The first setting, "Folder that is set by the application," specifies the folder that contains the document you opened to launch the application, which is the application's folder if you opened the application directly instead of opening one of its documents. The second setting specifies the most recent folder used in the application. The third setting specifies the Documents folder on the startup disk.

Keyboard and Mouse Adjustments

Although you might think of the Mac OS as something you look at, there are also parts of it that you touch, namely, the keyboard and the mouse, trackpad, or trackball. Like many aspects of the Mac OS, the behavior of the keyboard and the mouse, trackpad, or trackball is adjustable to allow for differences among users. If you find yourself becoming frustrated or impatient as you use one of your input devices, you may be able to solve the problem by changing its sensitivity. Similarly, if you type a character repeatedly when you mean to type it only once, you can adjust the keyboard sensitivity. You make these adjustments using the Keyboard, Mouse, and Trackpad control panels.

If you have difficulty typing, moving the mouse, or clicking the mouse button, you can set up alternative methods of using them. These alternatives are especially helpful for people with disabilities. You configure these alternatives with the Easy Access control panel.

Setting keyboard sensitivity

When you press almost any key on the keyboard and hold it down, the computer types that character repeatedly as long as you keep the key pressed. (The ⌘, Option, Control, Caps Lock, and Esc keys don't repeat.) In the Keyboard control panel, you can change how quickly the characters repeat and how long you must hold down a key before the repeat feature kicks in. If you find repeating keys annoying rather than handy, you can disable the repeat by selecting Off in the Delay Until Repeat section of the keyboard control panel. Figure 12-2 shows the Keyboard control panel.

Figure 12-2: Set keyboard sensitivity in the Keyboard control panel.

The Keyboard control panel also enables you to choose a keyboard layout. You use this option when you want to type in a different language. These adjustments are covered in "Language Preferences," later in this chapter.

Setting mouse, trackpad, or trackball sensitivity

You can change the way the Mac OS responds to your manipulation of your computer's mouse or trackball by setting options in the Mouse control panel. On a PowerBook with a trackpad, you adjust its responsiveness with the Trackpad control panel. Figure 12-3 shows the Mouse and Trackpad control panels.

Figure 12-3: Set mouse or trackball sensitivity in the Mouse control panel and trackpad sensitivity in the Trackpad control panel.

The Mouse Tracking option (Mouse control panel) or Tracking Speed option (Trackpad control panel) determines the tracking speed — how fast the pointer moves as you glide the mouse, trackpad, or trackball. This setting is a matter of personal taste. If you feel that the pointer doesn't keep up, try a faster setting. If you often lose track of the pointer as you move it, try a slower one. Often, when you switch from a small monitor to a large one, you need to switch to a faster tracking speed because the pointer has a longer distance to travel from the menu bar to the Trash.

The Double-Click Speed option determines how quickly you must double-click for the Mac OS to perceive your two clicks as one double-click rather than two separate, unrelated clicks. When you select a double-click speed, the mouse button pictured in the Mouse control panel or the trackpad button pictured in the Trackpad control panel flashes to demonstrate the selected double-click interval.

In addition, the Double-Click Speed option determines how long you can hold down the mouse, trackpad, or trackball button when you click a menu title and still have Mac OS 9 interpret the gesture as a click so that the menu stays displayed after you release the mouse button. The shorter the double-click speed, the more quickly you must press and release. If you don't release within the allotted time, Mac OS 9 interprets the gesture as a press instead of a click and puts away the menu when you release.

Many PowerBook models have three additional options under "Use Trackpad for" in the Trackpad control panel. These options let you configure the trackpad so that you can click and drag without using the trackpad button. If you turn on the Clicking option, you can click by tapping on the trackpad as well as by pressing the trackpad button. The Dragging option lets you drag without pressing the mouse button. To drag an object when this option is turned on, begin to double-tap the object, but don't lift your finger on the second tap. Now move your finger across the trackpad to drag the object across the screen. If your finger reaches the edge of the trackpad and you need to drag farther, you can lift your finger briefly, put it down again on the opposite edge of the trackpad, and continue dragging. Dragging ends when you keep your finger off the trackpad for a few seconds, unless you turn on the "Drag lock" option in the Trackpad control panel. With this option on, you can leave your finger off the trackpad indefinitely, and you stop dragging an object by tapping it again.

Easy Access

The Easy Access control panel sets up three alternative methods of using the keyboard and mouse. The first, called *Mouse Keys*, lets you use the numeric keypad portion of the keyboard to move the pointer on the screen and to click as if you were using the mouse button. The second, called *Slow Keys*, filters out accidental keystrokes. The third alternative keyboard behavior, called *Sticky Keys*, lets you type combination keystrokes such as ⌘+Z one key at a time.

Easy Access gives an audible warning when one of its features is turned on or off. You hear an ascending scale when you turn a feature on, and you hear a descending scale when you turn one off. You can eliminate the warning by turning off the audio-feedback option at the top of the Easy Access control panel.

To work, Easy Access must be in the Control Panels folder at startup time. Easy Access is not installed automatically with the rest of the control panels. You may find Easy Access in the Universal Access folder inside the CD Extras folder on your Mac OS 9 installation CD. You can drag the control panel from there to your Control Panels folder. You can also install Easy Access by doing a custom installation of the Mac OS module and selecting the Universal Access component group of this module (as described in Chapter 31). Figure 12-4 shows the Easy Access control panel.

Figure 12-4: The Easy Access control panel

Mouse Keys

The Mouse Keys feature of the Easy Access control panel enables you to click, drag, and move the pointer with the numeric keypad instead of the mouse, trackpad, or trackball. Mouse Keys is very handy for moving graphic objects precisely. Mouse Keys can be turned on by pressing ⌘+Shift+Clear instead of using the Easy Access control panel and turned off by pressing Clear. When Mouse Keys is on, the 5 key in the keypad acts like a mouse button. Press once to click; press twice to double-click; or hold it down. The eight keys around 5 move the pointer left, right, up, down, and diagonally. Pressing 0 locks the mouse button down until you press the period key in the keypad.

PowerBook Mouse Keys

You can't use the Mouse Keys feature of the Easy Access control panel to point and click on a PowerBook because PowerBooks have no numeric keypad. To use this feature on a PowerBook, install the system extension called Mouse Keys, which Apple distributes free via the Internet (`ftp://ftp.info.apple.com/Apple_Support_Area/disability-solutions/Mouse_Keys_-_PowerBook_1.0-.sit.bin`). This extension modifies the Easy Access control panel to recognize different keys instead of the numeric keypad. It substitutes the K key and the keys next to it for the 5 key and the keys next to it on the keypad. The Esc key substitutes for the Clear key. Thus, after installing the Mouse Keys extension, you turn on Mouse Keys by pressing ⌘+Shift+Esc, and you turn it off by pressing Esc. Be careful not to press ⌘+Option+Esc, which, instead of activating the Mouse Keys feature, brings up a dialog box that asks whether you want to force the active program to quit.

When Mouse Keys is on, the K key acts like the button on a trackball or trackpad. Press once to click; press twice to double-click; or hold it down. The eight keys around K move the pointer left, right, up, down, and diagonally. Pressing the spacebar locks the mouse button down until you press Enter.

Slow Keys

The Slow Keys feature of the Easy Access control panel makes the Mac OS wait before it accepts a keystroke, thereby filtering out accidental keystrokes. You can turn Slow Keys on or off from the keyboard by holding down Return for about 10 seconds. No icon indicates whether Slow Keys is on or off, but about five seconds after you begin pressing Return, the computer makes three short, quiet beeps. About four seconds after that, the computer plays an ascending scale to confirm that Slow Keys is being turned on or a descending scale to confirm that it's been turned off. You don't hear these sounds if you use the Easy Access control panel, however, and some applications (such as Microsoft Word) may mute the sounds.

Sticky Keys

The Sticky Keys feature of the Easy Access control panel enables you to type combination keystrokes, such as ⌘+Shift+3 (which puts a snapshot of your screen in a picture document that SimpleText and most graphics programs can open), one key at a time. Sticky Keys also enables you to lock down any modifier key by pressing it twice. You can turn on Sticky Keys by pressing Shift five times in succession. You can turn Sticky Keys off by pressing Shift five times again or by pressing any two modifier keys simultaneously. When Sticky Keys is on, an icon at the right end of the menu bar shows its status. Figure 12-5 shows the four states of the Sticky Keys status icon.

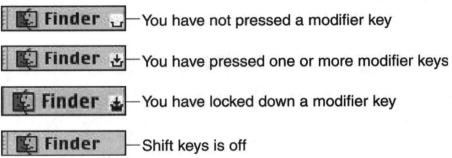

Finder —You have not pressed a modifier key

Finder —You have pressed one or more modifier keys

Finder —You have locked down a modifier key

Finder —Shift keys is off

Figure 12-5: Checking the status of Sticky Keys (enlarged to show detail)

Sound Adjustments

There are many adjustments that you can make to the sounds your computer generates itself or plays from external sources. You can set the sound level and a source for audio input. Depending on how your computer is equipped, you may also be able to set sound output options. In addition, you can select an alert sound and set its loudness.

In past Mac OS versions, sound was controlled from a joint-function control panel called Monitors & Sound. In Mac OS 9, they've been split up and you now set sound options using the Sound control panel.

Alert Sounds

You set the system alert sound and its volume separately from the other sounds played by your computer. To set these options, you click the Alert Sounds entry listed on the left side of the Sound control panel.

You can always add and remove alert sounds by dragging them in and out of the System file (as described in Chapter 10). If you get sound files in a format that can't be used as alert sounds, such as .wav format files from the Internet, you can convert them to the proper format for alert sounds using Norman Franke's free SoundApp program (described in Chapter 26). You can also record new alert sounds from within the Sound control panel. Figure 12-6 shows the system alert options in the Sound control panel.

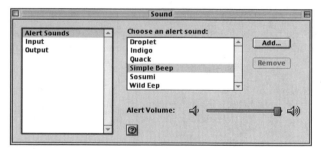

Figure 12-6: The Alert Sounds options

You select an alert sound simply by clicking its name in the menu. If you don't like any of the sounds offered, you can record your own by clicking Add. This action brings up a dialog box that has buttons for controlling recording and playback, and a gauge that measures the duration of the recorded sound. Click Record to record or rerecord up to ten seconds of sound from the computer's microphone or another audio source. (You set the sound input source in the Input section of this control panel.) Then click Play to hear your recording. When you're satisfied with your recording, click Save, and type a name for the new alert sound when you're asked. Figure 12-7 shows the dialog box in which you record an alert sound from the Sound control panel.

Figure 12-7: The dialog box for recording an alert sound

There are two ways to add and remove system alert sounds in the Alert Sounds section of the Sound control panel. One way is to use the Edit menu's Cut, Copy, and Paste commands. For example, you can copy a sound from the Scrapbook (described in Chapter 25) and paste it in the Sound control panel. You can also record a new system alert sound by clicking Add, or remove an alert sound by selecting it and clicking Remove.

Sound input

Click Input in the list on the left side of the Sound control panel and you can change the device that your Mac uses for listening to or recording sounds. For instance, if you wish to record sounds from a CD or DVD, you can select that device for sound input by clicking it in the device list at the top of the control panel.

Note   If you don't see the specific device listed (for example, your CD-ROM drive) you may need to choose Built-in from the device list and then select the input source from the Input Source menu.

After the device is selected, you can choose from the Input Source menu to set the specific input source (if the selected device has more than one) to use for sound input. Now, the Mac will "listen" to that device whenever you use an application to record sound. Figure 12-8 shows the Sound input options.

Note   Some input sources may offer additional options. Click the Options button to set these if the button is active (not gray). The Options aren't always useful, by the way—sometimes the dialog box simply offers the same choices as the Input Source pop-up menu. If that's the case, just select the same Input Source that you've already specified in the menu.

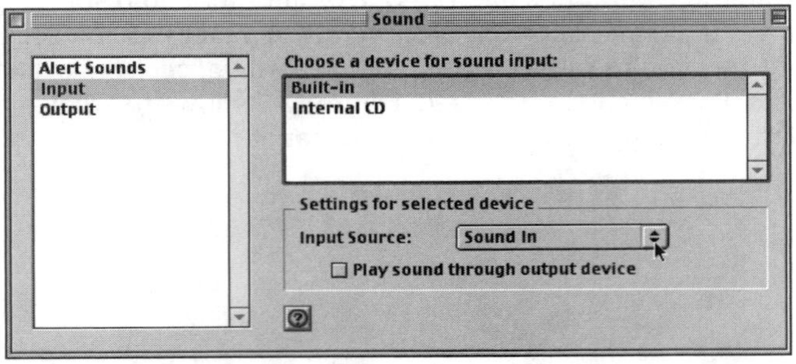

Figure 12-8: Choose the device from which you'll capture sound in any recording applications.

With some input sources, you can also turn on the option "Play sound through output device," which enables sounds to go straight from the input device (say, a CD) to the output device (say, external speakers). If you don't have this option selected, then the sound won't be played externally when you're recording from the input device using a sound application.

Sound output

As with input, you can select the device for your Mac to use for sound output. When the Mac generates a sound, it will send that sound to the selected device. On the left side of the Sound control panel, choose Output. Now, your choices change to enable you to select a sound output device, as shown in Figure 12-9.

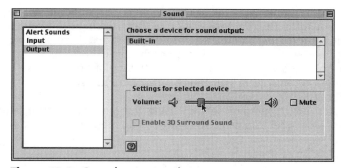

Figure 12-9: Sound output options

The Sound output options also enable you to choose the volume for output sound using a simple slider — drag the slider control to the right to make sounds louder and to the left to make them softer. You can mute all sound by selecting the Mute option. On certain Macs (or those with particular external speakers and other optional equipment) you can activate 3D Surround Sound, which uses surround sound to make the sounds coming out of your Mac richer and more engrossing. This option tends to work better with games than with music.

Control Strip sound

The Control Strip also offers modules for adjusting sound input and output. The Sound Volume module lets you change the volume of the computer's sound output. Clicking the speaker icon in the Control Strip pops up this module's volume slider. The Sound Strip module enables you to change the sound input source; for example, to switch to an audio CD or external microphone as your sound source. Clicking the microphone-plus-CD icon displays a menu of sound input sources. Figure 12-10 shows these two control strip modules. The Sound Strip module doesn't work on all Mac models, and doesn't appear in the Control Strip unless it will work.

Figure 12-10: The Control Strip gives you quick access to sound options.

Monitor Adjustments

If you stare at your monitor for hours on end (like many of us do), you want the view to be crisp and easy on the eyes. If you work with color, you want your monitor to display colors as accurately and consistently as possible. If you work with more than one monitor on your computer you need to have control over how the two work together.

In this section, you learn about changing the screen resolution, number of colors, and magnification; making multiple monitors work together; making onscreen color as accurate as possible by adjusting gamma and white points; matching onscreen color to the colors created by other input and output devices; calibrating your monitor to keep those colors consistent over time; and finding out the precise color of a pixel on your monitor, so that you can recreate it on the Web.

 New Feature With Mac OS 9, you adjust monitor settings using the Monitors control panel regardless of your Mac model. You can also change some monitor options via the Control Strip.

Screen resolution and color depth

The two most basic adjustable monitor settings are color depth and resolution. *Resolution* is the size of the rectangular screen image—the number of pixels (picture elements or dots) wide by the number of pixels high. *Color depth* is the number of colors available for each pixel of the screen image. Color depth is sometimes referred to as *bit depth*, which is a measure of the amount of memory it takes to store each pixel.

The higher the color depth, the more realistic the screen image can look. However, increasing the color depth doesn't necessarily make the screen display better, because the picture displayed onscreen may not make use of all of the available colors. For example, a black-and-white photograph will still be black, white, and shades of gray when displayed on a screen capable of displaying millions of colors.

The possible settings for color depth range from black and white to millions of colors, depending on the capabilities of your monitor and your computer's video-output circuitry. Typical settings include black-and-white, 16 grays or colors (4-bit grayscale or color), 256 grays or colors (8-bit grayscale or color), thousands of colors (16-bit color), and millions of colors (32-bit color). Most video circuitry cannot use color settings below 256 grays or colors.

The settings for resolution depend on the monitor and the computer's video-output circuitry, but in general range from 512 × 384 pixels (the size of the original Mac's 9-inch monitor) up to 1600 × 1024 pixels (the size of a 22-inch Apple Cinema Display). Some monitors can display only one resolution, while most recent monitors can display multiple resolutions.

Resolution and color depth are related because increasing either requires more video memory. If you increase the resolution, the Mac OS may have to automatically reduce the color depth. Conversely, you may be able to set a higher color depth by decreasing the resolution. On some Mac models you can make higher resolutions and color depths available by installing more video RAM (VRAM). To learn how much VRAM your computer can accommodate, use the free GURU program (described in Chapter 26).

Resolution and color depth with Monitors

One place you can adjust resolution and color depth is the Monitors control panel. Click the Monitor button at the top of the control panel to see the current settings. If your monitor can display more than one resolution, you can select one from the scrolling list on the right side of the control panel. On the left side of the control panel you can set the computer to display colors or grays. In addition, if your computer's video circuitry can display more than one color depth at the current resolution, you can select a color depth from the scrolling list on the left side of the control panel. Figure 12-11 shows the resolution and color depth options in the Monitors section of the Monitors control panel.

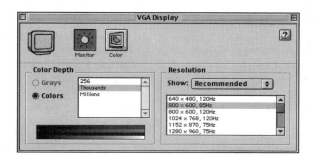

Figure 12-11: Set resolution and color depth in the Monitors control panel.

On a computer with more than one monitor, the Monitors control panel displays a separate window on each monitor. Each window has a Monitor button to adjust color depth and resolution on the monitor on which the window is displayed.

Resolution and color in the Control Strip

Another place where you can change your monitor's resolution and color depth is in the Control Strip. The Monitor Resolution module's icon looks like a monitor displaying a checkerboard pattern. Clicking this module displays a menu that lists the available resolutions of all monitors connected to the computer, and the current setting is marked with a bullet. The Monitor BitDepth module's icon looks like a monitor displaying a striped pattern. Clicking this module displays a menu that lists all the available color depths for each monitor connected to the computer. The bullet-marked menu item indicates the current color depth settings. Figure 12-12 shows the Control Strip modules and menus for setting the monitor's color depth and resolution.

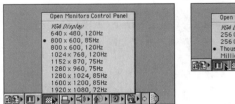

Figure 12-12: Use the Control Strip to set the monitor resolution (left) or color depth (right).

Multiple monitor setup

If your computer has two or more monitors, you can arrange them in an extended desktop, or you may be able to set them up to do video mirroring. In video mirroring, which is available on PowerBooks with external video ports and on some desktop Macs with two monitor ports, all monitors display exactly the same image — you get duplicate desktops. In the extended desktop mode, each monitor displays a different part of the desktop — as you move across the desktop, the pointer moves from one monitor to another. Some PowerBook models can use two monitors only for video mirroring, not for an extended desktop.

You can configure an extended desktop or set up video mirroring using the Monitors control panel. You can also turn video mirroring on and off using the Control Strip.

To configure an extended desktop or set up video mirroring using the Monitors control panel, click the Arrange button at the top of the control panel. Figure 12-13 shows the Arrange section of the Monitors control panel.

You can adjust the relative positions of the monitors by dragging the little images of them in the control panel. You can set which monitor has the menu bar by dragging the little menu bar to the appropriate little monitor in the control panel. You can also designate which monitor displays startup messages and icons. Turn on the option "Identify the startup screen" to display a tiny Macintosh icon that indicates the startup monitor. Then drag this icon to the little monitor image that you want to use during startup.

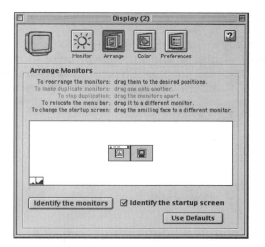

Figure 12-13: The Monitors control panel can configure an extended desktop or you can set up video mirroring.

To turn on video mirroring, drag the little image of one monitor over the little image of the other monitor. To turn off video mirroring, drag the little monitor images apart.

If your Mac supports two monitors, you'll also see changes in the Monitor Bit Depth and Monitor Resolution control strip modules in your Control Strip. From there, you can change resolutions and color bit depths for each monitor individually. Figure 12-14 shows the control strip modules and their menus.

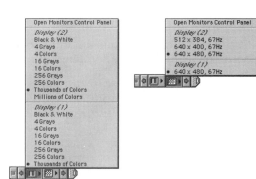

Figure 12-14: Use the Control Strip to change the number of colors (on the left) or the resolution (on the right) for either of your monitors.

On PowerBooks and other Macs enabled for video mirroring, you can also use the Video Mirroring control strip module to set the second monitor to mirror the main monitor.

Color accuracy

There's an inherent problem with the way we use digital equipment to produce color output: monitors, scanners, digital cameras, and so on create color with light, whereas any tangible output that you create (from color laser printouts to four-color offset lithography) creates colors with pigment, and the two methods create slightly (or sometimes vastly) different sets of colors. In addition, each individual device has a specific range of colors that it can handle.

The ColorSync software built in the Mac OS can improve color accuracy by matching a color profile for your monitor to color profiles for printers, scanners, and other color equipment you use. Each profile specifies the range of colors that a particular type of monitor can display, printer can print, scanner can scan, and so on. The ColorSync software uses the profiles to shift colors so that they look as alike as possible on all compatible devices.

You specify the profile for your monitor with the Monitors control panel. You also need to specify ColorSync color matching when you print a color document, as described in Chapter 16. In addition, take advantage of any ColorSync options that are available in application programs you use for scanning, image creation, image editing, page layout, and printing.

The ColorSync software, including the ColorSync control panel and profiles for several Apple monitors, is part of a standard installation of Mac OS 9. Profiles for other devices come with the devices themselves. You can create a custom ColorSync profile for your monitor using the Monitors control panel.

Choosing a monitor profile

You can choose a ColorSync profile for your monitor using the Monitors control panel. Click Color at the top of the control panel to display a scrolling list of the available monitor profiles, as shown in Figure 12-15.

Figure 12-15: The Color section of the Monitors control panel

The Calibrate button in the Color section of Monitors control panel provides access to the Monitor Calibration Assistant. (You'll find detailed information about using the Monitor Calibration Assistant later in this section.)

Another place you can work with monitor profiles is the ColorSync control panel. In addition, you can use this control panel to choose profiles for RGB and CMYK colors, and to specify a color-matching method. Figure 12-16 shows the ColorSync control panel.

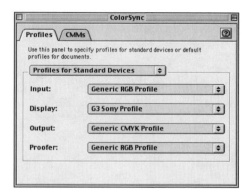

Figure 12-16: The ColorSync control panel

Creating a custom monitor profile

All monitors change over time—the brightness of the CRT dims, the phosphors that make your monitor display color shift and fade. The Monitor Calibration Assistant helps you account for these changes so that you will see consistent onscreen colors by creating a ColorSync profile tailored for your monitor. Before you use Calibration Assistant for the first time, you should adjust your monitor's brightness and contrast settings. Depending on the monitor model, you may find contrast and brightness controls in the Monitors section of the Monitors control panel or in your monitor's own controls. You want the brightness to be at a level that is comfortable and clear for your viewing. Set the contrast to the highest setting. Also, set the height, width, resolution, and position of the screen image as you want it. (The height, width, and position can't be changed on some monitors.)

Tip You should always avoid putting your monitor at its highest brightness setting, which could limit the life of the monitor. Instead, back off a few notches and set the contrast higher (or at its limit).

To calibrate your monitor, click the Color button at the top of the Monitors control panel. At the bottom of the control panel, click the Calibrate button to display the Monitor Calibration Assistant. The assistant walks you through a six-step process for adjusting your monitor and creating and saving a ColorSync profile. Figure 12-17 shows the introductory screen of the Assistant.

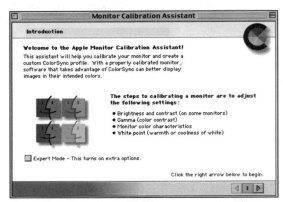

Figure 12-17: The Monitor Calibration Assistant's introductory screen

The introductory screen gives you one option — you can choose to use Expert settings instead of the basic calibration settings. There isn't much difference to the casual user, but professionals who use ColorSync for important projects may find it useful to place a check next to Expert Mode before moving on to the next screen of the Assistant. (Expert mode gives you a little more control over the settings in the Assistant, although it doesn't change the Assistant dramatically.)

In the Monitor Calibration Assistant's first step, you set your monitor to its highest contrast setting and then adjust the brightness. A test image helps you find the proper setting.

In the second step, you give Assistant information about the monitor's current gamma. *Gamma* refers to the relationship between intensity of the computer's video signal and the resulting luminance of color on a display. In regular mode, you make adjustments to a gray image; in Expert mode, you determine the current gamma by adjusting sliders until red, green, and blue test images look right.

The third step lets you specify a gamma setting that you want the monitor to use: 1.0 is linear gamma; 1.8 is the standard gamma setting for Mac OS computers; 2.2 is the standard gamma for television monitors and Windows computers. A low gamma setting makes colors appear more washed out. A high gamma setting makes colors appear more brilliant and with higher contrast. In this step, Expert mode allows you to use a slider to choose a very specific gamma setting.

Gamma options

Gamma options in the Monitors control panels provide alternative color balancing for a video display. Color balancing is necessary because the intensity with which a monitor actually displays colors may not correspond uniformly to the intensity of the electronic signals that generate the colors. For example, on a monitor with a picture tube, a video electron beam traces the video picture on the phosphor coating inside the tube, but the phosphors are not equally luminous for all levels of light. The computer's video circuitry adjusts the strength of the electron beam to provide the most accurate color possible.

This compensation is commonly called gamma correction. Changing the gamma correction has no effect on video performance, only on color balance and luminance.

In step four, you select your monitor type from a scrolling list. If your monitor's specific make and model are not listed, choose a generic description that fits your monitor, such as Generic LCD Color, Generic sRGB Monitor, or Generic Trinitron Monitor.

In step five, you select your target white-point: D50 is used mainly for graphic arts and attempts to match the white seen in printed matter; 6500 is a white that is the same as the sun at midday; 9300 is the white point used by most computer monitors and is the brightest white setting. You can also choose to make no white-point correction. In Expert mode, you can use a slider to choose a specific white point number.

In step six, you create and name the custom profile for future use. You can create a number of profiles if you use your monitor at different resolutions or for different purposes.

For ColorSync Profiles to be most effective, you should repeat the calibration process on a regular basis (monthly for graphics professionals) or when you change resolutions.

Geometry options

Some monitors have additional options that you can adjust via the Monitors control panel. For example, the Geometry button appears at the top of the Monitors control panel for many AppleVision and Apple Studio Display monitors, as well as for the iMac.

The Geometry section, if present in the Monitors control panel, includes options for changing how the monitor draws the screen picture. You can expand the display area, so that there is less of a black border around the visible area. You can also change the pincushion (how concave the sides of the picture are) and the rotation of the display. A Recall Factory Settings button resets the monitor to its presets.

Screen magnification

You can use the CloseView control panel to magnify your screen 2 to 16 times and to invert the displayed colors. Several of the control panel options have keyboard shortcuts. The keystrokes are displayed in the control panel. Figure 12-18 shows the CloseView control panel.

Figure 12-18: The CloseView control panel

CloseView is not installed automatically with the rest of the control panels. You may find CloseView in the Universal Access folder inside the CD Extras folder on your Mac OS 9 installation CD. You can drag the control panel from there to your Control Panels folder. You can also install CloseView by doing a custom installation of the Mac OS module and selecting the Universal Access component group of this module (as described in Chapter 31).

Date, Time, and Location Settings

In addition to displaying a clock on your menu bar, your computer uses date and time information for a variety of operations. For example, your computer uses date and time information to provide files with creation and modification dates and to time-stamp e-mail. You use the Date & Time control panel to set the current date, time, time zone, and daylight-saving time status for your system.

Setting the date and time

You set your computer's current date and time at the top of the Date & Time control panel. Through the Date Formats and Time Formats buttons, you can also choose how the date and time are displayed and the language of display. Figure 12-19 shows the Date & Time control panel.

Figure 12-19: The Date & Time control panel

The Date & Time control panel offers a choice of preset formats for the language script system used by your version of the Mac OS, which for North American and Western European users is the Roman script system. Installing Apple language kit software so that you can write in additional languages does not add any preset formats to the Date & Time control panel, but you can set your own custom format. (For more information on using multiple languages, see "Language Preferences" later in this chapter.)

Setting the time zone

In the Time Zone area of the Date & Time control panel, you can see and set the time zone in which you are using your computer. Even if you never move your computer, you should set its location so that people receiving your e-mail in a different time zone can tell what time you sent the e-mail.

To set the time zone, click the Set Time Zone button. This displays a list of city names; select one in your time zone. (You can find out what time it is in a different zone by selecting a city in that time zone.)

Setting daylight-saving time

The Date & Time control panel lets you adjust the computer's clock for daylight-saving time. Turning on the Daylight-Saving Time option sets the Mac's clock ahead one hour; turning off this option sets the Mac's clock back one hour, returning it to standard time. The first time you set this option, you may have to adjust the hour displayed at the top of the control panel. You can also choose to have daylight-saving time applied automatically by turning on the Set Daylight-Saving Time Automatically option.

Using the menu bar clock

In the Menu Bar Clock area of the Date & Time control panel, you can turn on and off an optional digital clock near the right end of the menu bar. Clicking the Clock Options button in this section brings up a dialog box in which you can set the display format of the clock and set the clock to chime on the hour, half-hour, and quarter-hour. On a battery-powered Mac, you also can turn on or off a battery-level indicator, which appears next to the clock. You can also choose to show the seconds, day, and AM/PM, and you can change the color of the clock, if desired.

You can see the date instead of the time in the menu bar by clicking the clock in the menu bar. After a few seconds, the clock shows the time again. You can hide the menu bar clock by Option+clicking it. To see the clock again, Option+click its usual location on the menu bar.

Using a network time server

You can set your computer to get the time from a time server on the Internet or your local network (if your local network has a time server). You set this up in the Date & Time control panel. First, turn on the option Use a Network Time Server. Then click the Server Options button. In the dialog box that appears, choose a time server from the pop-up menu and choose how to update the time. You can choose to synchronize your clock manually, have it updated whenever there is a discrepancy between it and the server's clock, or have it updated on a regular schedule.

If you select either of the automated options, the Date & Time control panel automatically connects to the server when it's time to update your computer's clock. If the time server is on the Internet and you have a dial-up account, the Date & Time control panel automatically tries to establish a dial-up connection. Neither of the automated time update options can occur more than once every 12 hours.

Control Strip Adjustments

The modular Control Strip control panel provides quick access to commonly adjusted features. Clicking a button in the Control Strip pops up a menu of related settings. Each button in the Control Strip corresponds to a module in the Control Strip Modules folder (inside the System Folder). Figure 12-20 shows the Control Strip.

Figure 12-20: The Control Strip provides quick access to commonly adjusted features.

This section explains how to resize and move the Control Strip, rearrange modules in it, and remove modules from it. To use the Control Strip, you need to make sure it's turned on — choose Control Strip from the Control Panels entry in the Apple menu to see the Control Strip control panel. In the control panel, you can choose to show or hide the Control Strip, or you can designate a hot-key sequence for making the Control Strip appear. You can also make some basic font settings for the Control Strip's modules.

Manipulating the Control Strip

To open the Control Strip, click the small tab at the end of the strip and it pops open to reveal its contents. You can drag the end of the Control Strip to lengthen or shorten it to show fewer modules. If there are more modules than can be displayed at once on the Control Strip, the small arrows at each end are activated.

When the Control Strip pops open, modules initially appear in alphabetical order, from left to right. You can change a module's position by dragging it in the Control Strip while pressing Option.

The Control Strip floats above all application windows. You can collapse and expand the strip by clicking or dragging the tab at the end nearest the center of the screen. To collapse the strip to its smallest size, click the box at the opposite end. You can move the strip by pressing Option and dragging the tab, but the strip must touch the left or right edge of the screen.

Adding and removing modules

You add modules by dragging their files to the System Folder icon or to the Control Strip Modules folder. You can also add modules by dragging Control Strip module files to the Control Strip itself. Option+dragging a module from the strip makes a copy of the module where you drag it on the desktop or in a folder. To remove modules, you must drag their files from the Control Strip Modules folder.

Groups of Settings

Originally designed for PowerBooks, the Location Manager provides an easy way to save a group of settings for your computer. As its name implies, the Location Manager is useful for computers that are often transported to different locations. If you have a PowerBook that you use at home and at the office, for example, you may need to change the settings for your printer, network connection, or Internet connection each time you move the computer to a new location. The Location Manager takes care of that by saving a group of settings for each location and letting you switch to any group of settings simultaneously.

You can also use the Location Manager to create groups of settings for different work activities. For example, you might have one group of settings that opens your word processor and memo templates and connects you to the printer that's stocked with your company's letterhead, while another group opens your graphics programs, switches your monitor's color depth to display more colors, and connects you to a color printer.

Sound volume, default printer, Extensions Manager configuration, file sharing on or off, AppleTalk and TCP/IP network configurations, time zone, and one or more items to be opened automatically are among the settings that can be saved with Location Manager. In addition, you can save settings for remote access, Internet connections, and QuickTime download speeds. Figure 12-21 is an example of the Location Manager control panel.

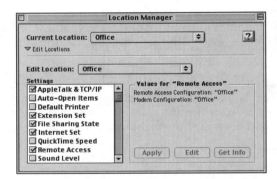

Figure 12-21: The Location Manager control panel lets you change a multitude of settings with one quick menu.

Changing to a different settings group

To switch to a different group of settings, simply choose the group's name from the Current Location pop-up menu at the top of the Location Manager control panel. When you switch groups, a dialog box reports which settings were changed and tells you whether you need to restart to make any of the changes take effect. Figure 12-22 shows where you can change the settings group.

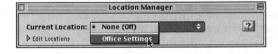

Figure 12-22: Switch to a different settings group using the Location Manager control panel.

You can also change the settings group in the Control Strip by choosing the Location Manager's module and selecting the group you'd like to make active.

Choosing a settings group during startup

If you want to choose a location when you start up the computer, you can set the Location Manager to display a pop-up menu of available locations in a dialog box during startup. You can have the Location Manager display this dialog box every time you start the computer, only when you hold down a special hot key (which you can assign), or never. You select one of these options in the dialog box displayed by the Preferences command in the Location Manager's Edit menu. Figure 12-23 shows the Preferences dialog box for Location Manager.

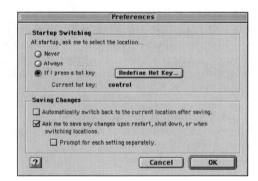

Figure 12-23: Startup preferences for the Location Manager control panel

Creating a new settings group

To create a new group of settings, choose New Location from the Location Manager's File menu. Name the new group in the dialog box that appears and click Save. The control panel window expands to full size (if it was not already) and displays a list of settings modules. You can include any settings module in your new group by selecting the module's check box. To remove a module from the group, deselect the check box.

When you've selected all the modules you want remembered for the new group, choose Save Location from the File menu. Figure 12-24 is an example of a new settings group.

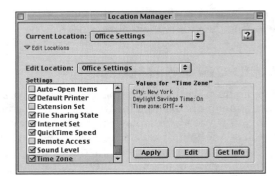

Figure 12-24: Select the settings that are to be part of a group in the Location Manager.

What Location Manager remembers

When you add settings to a group, the Location Manager stores their current values as part of the group. For instance, if the computer's sound volume is set to 3 when you add Sound Level, then the Location Manager stores a sound volume of 3 for that group, and whenever you switch to that group, your computer's sound volume will be set to 3.

If you add an Auto-Open Item to a group, the Location Manager displays a standard Open dialog box in which you select the program or document that you want automatically opened whenever you switch to the group. You can add more than one Auto-Open Item to a group.

Changing settings used for a group

You can change a group by adding, removing, or changing settings. You start by selecting the group you want to change from the Edit Location pop-up menu in the expanded Location Manager control panel. (To expand the control panel, click the disclosure triangle labeled Edit Locations.) To add a settings module, select its check box. To remove a settings module, deselect its check box.

To change the values stored in a settings module, select it in the Location Manager control panel and click the Edit button there. Because you must change the actual system settings, the Location Manager displays a dialog box that tells you which other control panels you must use to make the changes. You can open the necessary control panels by clicking buttons in this dialog box.

Note

You can also open the necessary control panels by double-clicking them in the Finder, choosing them from the Control Panels submenu of the Apple menu, and so on.

After making changes in a control panel, close the control panel or use the Application menu to switch back to the Location Manager. In the dialog box that's still open, click Apply to update the settings group with the change you just made. For example, if you select Time Zone and click Edit in the Location Manager dialog box, a dialog box that contains a button for opening the Date & Time control panel, where you actually change the time zone, opens. After changing the time zone, you close the Date & Time control panel (or switch to the Location Manager using the Application menu), and then click Apply in the dialog box that's still open.

If you need more help with changing a settings module in the Locations Manager, select it in the list on the left side of the Locations Manager window and click Get Info. You do not have to select a settings module's check box to use Get Info; you can simply select a settings module's name.

The Location Manger's Preferences dialog box (previously shown in Figure 12-23) includes several options that affect saving changes. One option determines whether Location Manager automatically switches or asks before switching back to the group that was active when you started editing a new or different group. Another option determines whether Location Manager offers to update the current settings group if you make changes to it outside the Location Manager.

The Location Manager will offer to update the current settings group when you switch settings groups, restart, or shut down your Mac. Say, for example, that the current settings group includes a setting for sound level and you change the system's sound level. Now, the Location Manager will ask whether you want to update the current settings group the next time you shut down or restart the computer, or whenever you change to another settings group that has a setting for the sound level.

A related option determines whether your computer asks you to save each settings module individually or to save all changes simultaneously.

Removing a settings group

To remove a settings group, choose Delete Location from the Location Manger's File menu. This command displays a list of groups. A group is deleted by selecting it in the list and clicking Delete.

Sharing settings groups

You can share groups of settings by importing and exporting them as Location Manager files. Choose Import Location or Export Location from the Location Manger's File menu. The Export Location command displays a standard Save dialog box in which you can name the exported location file and select a place to save it. The Import Location command displays a standard Open dialog box in which you can select a Location Manager file to import.

Sleep, Startup, and Shutdown Settings

All Macintosh PowerBooks and many Mac desktop models can go to sleep or automatically shut down to save energy while they are inactive. In the sleep state, the computer uses very little power. Shutting down the computer conserves even more energy, but there are advantages to making your computer sleep instead of shutting it down. The sleep state preserves your open programs, documents, and control panel settings so that when you "wake" the computer, you can start work from where you left off.

You can adjust how much energy your computer saves by setting how long it waits after becoming inactive before putting itself to sleep or shutting itself down. You may also be able to schedule times for a PowerBook to sleep and wake automatically or a desktop computer to shut down and start up automatically.

With Mac OS 9, you use the Energy Saver control panel to set the various sleep, startup, and shutdown options on a Mac that is capable of sleep or scheduled shutdown and startup. This one control panel works on both desktop computers and PowerBooks that use Mac OS 9.

Setting sleep options

You can set sleep options that control how long your computer will remain idle before going to sleep. The sleep options are somewhat different for desktop computers and PowerBooks because the purpose of sleep is different on the two kinds of computers. A PowerBook sleeps to conserve battery power, and to achieve this goal it needs to go to sleep after a few minutes of inactivity. A desktop computer sleeps to save energy on a larger scale, and it can accomplish this without cycling in and out of sleep as frequently as a PowerBook.

Sleep or shutdown options on a desktop computer

If your desktop computer has the Energy Saver control panel, you can use it to set the amount of time before your computer goes to sleep or shuts down. To control these options, click the Sleep Setup button at the top of the control panel. You may see a single conservation-performance slider or you may see three sliders that enable you to set separate sleep timings for the whole system, the display, and the hard disk. You can alternate between these two views by clicking Show Details or Hide Details at the bottom of the control panel. In both views, you can select an option that makes your computer shut down rather than sleep. Figure 12-25 shows the full Show Details view of Energy Saver's sleep timings for desktop computers.

If you have configured sleep options on a PowerBook, you may wonder why desktop Macs have no provision for automatically reconnecting to network file servers and remounting shared folders and disks on wake-up. These actions are not necessary because shared disks and other network volumes remain mounted while a desktop computer sleeps.

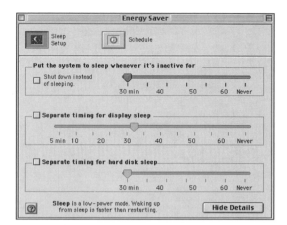

Figure 12-25: The Sleep Setup section of Energy Saver controls basic or detailed sleep timings for all desktop computers.

Energy Star savings

When you make an Energy Star computer and monitor sleep with the Energy Saver control panel, you reduce their power consumption to 60 watts or less (30 watts for the computer and 30 watts for the monitor). For example, a 150-watt Energy Star computer and monitor that sleeps half of each 10-hour weekday costs $62 less per year to operate (at $0.10 per kWh) than a conventional system. Turning off an Energy Star computer nights and weekends saves another $42 per year. (Energy Star is a designation that the U.S. Environmental Protection Agency gives to computers, monitors, and other office equipment that meet its guidelines for energy conservation.)

Even more important than the cost savings is the reduction in air pollution that's a byproduct of generating electricity. According to the Rocky Mountain Institute (970-927-3851, http://www.rmi.org), "Computers and other electronic office equipment represent the fastest-growing electrical load in the United States, keeping at least a dozen 1000-megawatt power plants fully occupied." In an office, using the Energy Saver control panel and turning off your computer at night and over weekends also decreases the demand for air conditioning, which saves even more energy and reduces pollution.

Sleep options on a PowerBook

In the Energy Saver control panel, you set sleep options by clicking the Idle Sleep button at the top of the control panel. You may see a single conservation-performance slider or you may see three sliders that enable you to set separate sleep timings for the whole system, the display, and the hard disk. You can alternate between these two views by clicking Show Details or Hide Details at the bottom of the control panel. Figure 12-26 shows the Energy Saver's sleep timings for PowerBooks.

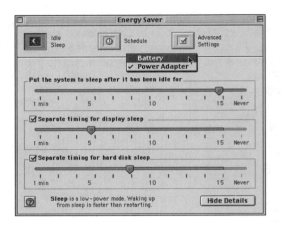

Figure 12-26: The Idle Sleep section of Energy Saver controls basic or detailed sleep timings.

In the Energy Saver control panel, you can set the timings differently for battery operation than for operation with the power adapter plugged into the computer. You choose the power mode from the pop-up menu in the control panel.

Advanced sleep options on a PowerBook

With a PowerBook, you can click the Advanced Settings button to optimize energy use and control network connections on wake-up. The Power Cycling option lets the processor switch to a reduced-power mode when it is idle. The Reduced Processor Speed option makes the processor run at a slower speed, which may affect your PowerBook's performance.

The option "Turn off the PowerBook Display instead of dimming it" conserves additional battery power by turning off the display back lighting altogether. The option "Turn off power to inactive PC Cards" forces all inactive PC cards to stop draining battery power, even those that normally require power when not in use. The Advanced section of the Energy Saver control panel also has options for reconnecting to file servers automatically on wake-up. Figure 12-27 shows the advanced options in the Energy Saver control panel.

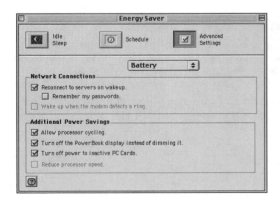

Figure 12-27: The Advanced Settings section of Energy Saver controls network connections and optimizes power use for PowerBooks.

Note On the iBook (and perhaps future PowerBook models), you may have an additional option in the Advanced Settings dialog box called "Preserve memory contents on sleep." When this option is selected, the Mac OS saves the contents of RAM to a file in the System Folder called Suspended.image whenever you put the iBook to sleep. This is an additional safeguard that preserves your open documents and applications in case the iBook loses battery power while sleeping. Because the iBook has no backup battery, this option should be selected if you attempt to switch batteries while the iBook is sleeping.

Control Strip energy savings

Instead of using the Energy Saver control panel to set sleep option on a PowerBook, you can set the basic power conservation level using the Control Strip. Figure 12-28 shows the control strip module to use.

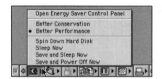

Figure 12-28: The Control Strip can set the basic power conservation level.

The Control Strip module may also enable you to trigger sleep mode, spinning down the hard disk. This control strip module is designed to handle the immediate power-reduction needs of PowerBooks, and it does not work on most desktop Macs.

Triggering sleep manually

Although the Mac OS will put your computer to sleep after a user-specified period of inactivity, you gain additional energy savings by putting it to sleep manually if you know you won't use it for a while. You can choose Sleep from the Special menu to make the computer sleep immediately. This command is available only while using the Finder.

You can make your computer sleep from any program by pressing the Power key on the keyboard. A dialog box appears asking whether you want to restart, sleep, cancel, or shutdown. Click Sleep.

PowerBook users have other options for inducing sleep. Closing the lid puts many PowerBook models in the sleep state. Also, any PowerBook sleeps when you press ⌘+Shift+0.

Waking up your computer

To make your Mac wake up, press Power or any other key on the keyboard. (On some models, the Caps Lock and function keys may not work for this purpose.) You may hear a distinctive sound to let you know the computer is waking up, not restarting.

Scheduling wake up and sleep

You can schedule a PowerBook to wake itself up and, in some cases, to put itself to sleep. In the Energy Saver control panel, you can set a recurring time or one time for wake-up and another recurring time or one time for sleep. You select these settings in the Schedule section of the control panel, which is shown in Figure 12-29.

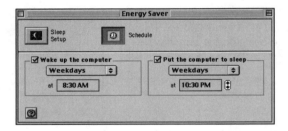

Figure 12-29: Schedule automated wake-up and sleep.

Scheduling startup and shutdown

On most desktop Macs, you can use the Energy Saver control panel to schedule automated startup and shutdown times. This is a handy feature, especially if your computer takes a while to start. You could set your Mac to turn on automatically so that it's ready when you get to work in the morning, or to shut down automatically to make sure it's off at night in case you forget. To see Energy Saver's scheduling options, click Schedule at the top of the Energy Saver control panel window.

To set a time for the computer to start up or shut down, turn on the "Start up the computer" option or the "Shut down the computer" option and enter a time in the space provided. Use the pop-up menu to choose the day or days you want the schedule to be effective: a specific day of the week, weekdays only, weekends only, or every day.

Language Preferences

The Mac OS puts all languages on an equal footing. It works with English, Spanish, French, German, and other languages that use the Roman alphabet and works equally well with Asian, Middle Eastern, and other languages that use different alphabets. The Mac OS deals with the differences in language structure, writing direction, alphabetical sorting, calendar, date and time display, and currency. You're not limited to working in one language at a time. You can work in multiple languages and switch languages while you work. However, you may need to install additional software to use some languages, particularly languages that have a different alphabet than your system's primary language (the language used by the Finder).

To switch languages, select a keyboard layout for a particular language and country, as described in this section. This section also explains how to change the text behavior and number format for a particular language and country. To change the date and time format, use the Date & Time control panel (see "Date, Time, and Location Settings" earlier in this chapter). Finally, this section describes the language kits included with Mac OS 9 that you can install to add more languages to your Mac.

Language script systems and keyboard layouts

The world's languages have many different alphabets and methods of writing (vertical or horizontal, left-to-right, or right-to-left). The software that defines a method of writing is called a language script system, or simply a script. Do not confuse this kind of script with the kind of script you create with AppleScript (as described in Chapter 24).

A language script system tells the Mac OS which character in the specified language each keystroke produces, as well as how the characters should behave—for example, the direction in which text flows. The script also specifies sort order, number and currency formats, and date and time formats.

Multiple languages can use one language script system. For example, the Roman script is used in most Western languages, such as English, French, Italian, Spanish, and German.

Associated with each language script system are one or more keyboard layouts. A keyboard layout defines the relationship between keys you press and characters entered. For example, the keyboard layout for U.S. English produces a # symbol when you press Shift+3, but the same keystroke produces a £ symbol with the British English keyboard layout.

Selecting a keyboard layout

There are several ways to designate which keyboard layout you want to use of the ones installed on your computer. You can use the Keyboard control panel, a keyboard shortcut, or the Keyboard menu. You can also synchronize the keyboard layout with the currently selected font. Remember, however, that only one keyboard layout matches the printed key caps on your keyboard. If you change to a different layout, some keys no longer generate the characters printed on the keyboard.

Keyboard control panel

You can select a keyboard layout by opening the Keyboard control panel and clicking the name of the layout to use. You can also select more than one keyboard layout and you can choose a language script system in the Keyboard control panel. If you select more than one keyboard layout, the Keyboard menu appears near the right end of the menu bar (as described shortly). Figure 12-30 shows the Keyboard control panel.

Figure 12-30: Select a keyboard layout from the Keyboard control panel.

Keyboard layout shortcut keys

The Keyboard control panel includes an option for enabling a keyboard shortcut. By default, you can switch between layouts in the active script using ⌘+Space, whether or not you enable the option.

If you prefer, you can click Options in the Keyboard control panel, and then turn on the option Use Command+Option+Space to change the keyboard shortcut.

Keyboard menu

If you regularly switch keyboard layouts, you can list the layouts you use in the Keyboard menu. You can then choose the layout from this menu while working in any application. To make the Keyboard menu appear, select more than one keyboard layout in the Keyboard control panel and then close the control panel. The Keyboard menu is located near the right end of the menu bar next to the Application menu. The Keyboard menu's icon is a flag that indicates which keyboard layout is currently selected. Figure 12-31 is an example of the Keyboard menu.

Figure 12-31: Switch keyboard layouts with the Keyboard menu.

If your computer has more than one language script system, switching keyboards may also change script systems. Each keyboard implicitly designates a script system because a keyboard layout can only be part of one script system. Switching from the U.S. keyboard layout to the Hebrew keyboard layout, for example, implicitly switches from the Roman script system to the Hebrew script system.

The Keyboard menu always appears if your computer has more than one language script system installed because there must be at least one keyboard layout selected for each script system.

English and other Western languages typically provide only one way to enter text, and U.S. keyboards are based on that text input method. But in languages that are based on ideograms, such as Japanese and Chinese, text can be input in multiple ways. The Japanese language kit comes with an input method called Kotoeri that enables entering Kanji, Katakana, Hiragana, and Romaji. Other input methods are available. (Input methods are listed in the Keyboard menu.) The Chinese language kit is equipped with Pinyin, Zhuyin, Cangjie, and Wubi input-method software, as well as two character sets: simplified and traditional.

Setting text behavior

Each language has its own rules of behavior, even though it may use the same script as another language. You teach the Mac OS the rules to use by setting the language behavior in the Text control panel. The options in this control panel tell the Mac OS how to produce text from characters. For languages that flow right-to-left, the control panel provides additional options. You can split the flashing vertical line that marks the insertion point so that you can see where your next typing will appear for left-to-right writing as well as for right-to-left writing.

In the Text control panel, you also specify a set of rules for alphabetizing, capitalizing, and distinguishing words. First you choose among the installed language-script systems, such as Roman, Cyrillic, Arabic, Japanese, and Chinese. Then you choose among the regional rules for text behavior that the selected script system supports. For example, the Roman script system has text behavior rules for Brazilian, Canadian French, Danish, Dutch, English, Finnish, French, German, Italian, Norwegian, Spanish, and Swedish. Figure 12-32 shows the Text control panel options for the Roman script.

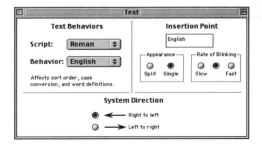

Figure 12-32: Use the Text control panel to set behavior options for each installed language.

Setting number formats

The Numbers control panel sets the number format — decimal separator, thousand separators, and currency symbol. You can choose a preconfigured number format for a region of the world that corresponds to one of the languages installed on your system, or you can specify a custom format by entering the punctuation marks to use as separators and the currency symbol. Figure 12-33 shows the Numbers control panel.

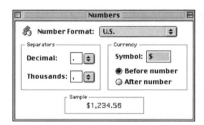

Figure 12-33: The Numbers control panel sets the format for numbers.

Installing multilingual software

To read or write in a language that uses a different alphabet than your system's primary language, a language kit must be installed. A language kit includes a language script system, one or more keyboard layouts, and fonts.

New Feature

Eleven language kits that Apple had sold separately are bundled with Mac OS 9, but installation is optional. The 11 kits are Arabic, Central European, Cyrillic, Devanagari, Gujurati, Punjabi, Hebrew, Japanese, Korean, Simplified Chinese, and Traditional Chinese. To install these languages, do a custom installation of Mac OS 9 (as described in Chapter 31) and select the Language Kits module.

Besides language kits, you need applications that can use the languages installed on your computer. You get two such applications: Microsoft Internet Explorer and Netscape Communicator. You can use either to browse foreign language Web pages on the Internet. (Web browsing is covered in Chapter 10.) In addition, you can buy applications that let you create multilingual documents as well as applications whose menus and dialog boxes are in a foreign language. For example, if you have English, Spanish, and Hebrew installed on your computer, you might use applications that are exclusively Spanish or Hebrew. You might also use a word processor that has English menus but lets you write documents in any combination of languages.

Software Update

One of Mac OS 9's new Internet-integration features is the Software Update control panel, which enables automatic searching for updates to the Mac OS that Apple makes available for downloading. The control panel is simple to use — just open it and click Update Now. A control panel confirms your choice; click OK to continue. If you're connected to the Internet, the control panel will contact Apple's software servers and find out whether there are any updates available for your Mac. If the control panel finds any available updates, it will list them. Place a check mark next to the updates you'd like to download, and then click Install.

You can also schedule updates automatically using the control panel. If you'd like to schedule updates, turn on the "Update software automatically" option. Now, set a schedule. Click the Set Schedule button to open the Set Schedule dialog box. Choose a time of day for the update, and then click the days on which you'd like Software Update to perform its check. When you're done, click OK.

The Software Update control panel has another option if you've enabled scheduled updates: "Ask me before downloading new software." Turn this option on if you'd like to be notified when new system software is found during a scheduled check.

Configuring Keychain Access

One of the centerpieces of the Mac OS 9 upgrade is the *keychain*, a technology that enables you to save your login names and passwords for file-sharing services, Internet locations, and encrypted files, among other things. Your keychain holds a number of different keys, metaphorically speaking. Each key is really a username and password (or sometimes just a password) for a network, Internet, or encryption resource. When your keychain is locked, none of these keys can be used. When your keychain is unlocked, then all of the keys can be used — meaning you only have to remember your keychain password to access all of the resources for which you have keys.

It's a fairly useful system because it enables you to create unique and secure passwords for the various logons you have, but you only have to remember one password. And, in the sense that you'll be less inclined to jot all of your passwords down in the Note Pad or on Stickies, the keychain approach is more secure.

It's less secure than memorizing all your login names and passwords, though, because if your keychain is unlocked, anyone who sits at your computer can gain access to all of the passwords and logons you've added to the keychain. Of course, it's tough to memorize all those login names and passwords, which is why the keychain is a nice feature. If you use it, you need to remember to lock your keychain whenever you get up from your machine — or, better yet, have it lock itself automatically.

Chapters 7and 21 discuss using the keychain for your encryption passwords and file-sharing connections, respectively. In this section, the discussion focuses on using the Keychain Access control panel to manage your keychain items.

Accessing your keychain

When you first access the keychain by choosing Keychain Access from the Control Panels menu, one of three things will happen:

✦ If you haven't created a keychain, an alert box will ask if you'd like to create a keychain. Click Create in the alert box to create your keychain. The Create Keychain dialog box will appear. Enter a name for the keychain and a password and then type the password again to confirm it (see Figure 12-34). Click Create to access your new keychain.

Note

If your password is shorter than Apple recommends, an alert box warning you that the password should be more secure appears. To return to the Create Keychain dialog box and change your password, click No. Keychain passwords are important, because the keychain can hold quite a bit of information about you. You should select a password at least six characters long (preferably longer), ideally with a mix of numbers and letters that's difficult to guess or nonsensical to anyone but you.

Figure 12-34: The Create Keychain dialog box appears when you choose to create a new keychain.

✦ If your keychain is locked, a dialog box asking whether you'd like to enter a password for your keychain to unlock it will appear. Choose the keychain from the pop-up menu, and then enter your password. You'll see the Keychain window with its contents revealed.

✦ If your keychain is already unlocked, it is unlocked either because you recently used the keychain to access a password, or because you recently logged in to your Multiple Users account. By default, your Multiple User's password is the same as your keychain password, and both are opened when you log in.

Locking and unlocking your keychain

If your keychain is unlocked, you can lock it by clicking Lock in the Keychain Access control panel. This immediately locks the keychain. Now, to access the items on the keychain, you either need to specify your keychain passwords as you're logging in (or decrypting) or you need to unlock the keychain.

If your keychain is locked but the Keychain Access control panel is still open, you can unlock the keychain by clicking Unlock. Choose the keychain you want to unlock from the Unlock Keychain pop-up menu, and then enter the appropriate password. Click Unlock.

Tip   If you have more than one keychain open, you can choose File ⇨ Lock all keychains to lock them simultaneously.

Managing keychain items

Most of the time you add keychain items through other applications or utilities. For instance, Internet sites are generally added through the Internet applications you use to access those sites, as discussed in Chapter 10. Likewise, the Network Browser or Chooser is generally how keychain items are added for file sharing access, as discussed in Chapter 21.

Get Info

Once items are on the keychain, you can learn more about them by selecting them in the Keychain Items listing and clicking Get Info. This brings up a special Get Info window that tells you a little about the keychain item, as shown in Figure 12-35.

Figure 12-35: The Get Info window for a keychain item shows the details on that item.

If you'd like to view the password for this item, click the View Password button. You'll be asked to re-enter your keychain password. After you've done that, the password for that item is revealed.

If the item you're viewing is an Internet location or an AppleShare password, you'll also see a Go There button in the Get Info window. You can use this button to load the Internet location in the associated Internet application or to mount the network volume. In the case of a Web Internet location, for instance, a secure Web site would be loaded in the default Web browser that's specified in the Internet control panel.

Remove items

From the Keychain Items list you can also remove an item. Removing an item doesn't make it impossible to access the associated resource; it simply means that your keychain won't remember the username and password for that resource. If you remove an item from your keychain, then you need to make sure that *you* remember the username (if applicable) and password for that item. The next time you try to access the item, you'll have to manually enter the username and password.

To remove an item, simply select it in the Keychain Items list and click Remove. An alert box will appear asking whether you're sure you want to remove the item. Click OK.

> **Tip** You can also drag items from the Keychain Items list to the Trash to remove them.

Changing keychain settings

Your keychain offers a few settings that enable you to customize its behavior. You can also change the keychain password. To do those things, choose "*Keychain*" Settings from the Edit menu, where *Keychain* is the name of the currently selected keychain.

To edit settings, you need to enter your keychain password again. Enter the password and click the View button. The Change Settings dialog box appears (see Figure 12-36).

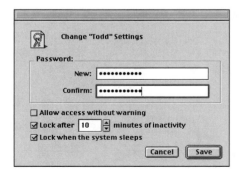

Figure 12-36: The Change Settings dialog box enables you to change your password as well as change how the keychain is accessed and locked.

At the top of the dialog box, you can enter a new password and then type it again to confirm the password. When you click Save, the password change will be made.

Place a check mark next to any other options in this dialog box that you would like to have active:

✦ **Allow access without warning.** If you activate this option, access to your keychain will be allowed automatically, without asking for confirmation in an alert box. This makes it more convenient if you access a lot of secure resources that consult the keychain, but it cuts down on security because you won't be warned if and when unauthorized access (by an application or AppleScript, for instance) to the keychain takes place.

✦ **Lock after minutes of inactivity.** If you'd like the keychain to automatically lock itself after a period of inactivity, activate this item and enter the number of idle minutes you'd like the keychain to wait before it locks itself.

✦ **Lock when the system sleeps.** Activate this item if you'd like the keychain to lock when this Mac is put to sleep (by you or by the Energy Saver control panel).

Creating more than one keychain

You can create a new keychain by selecting New Keychain from the File menu. Give the keychain a name, enter a password, and confirm the password, and the new keychain will appear in the Keychains menu.

You can also add a keychain by simply dragging it from a removable disk or from a network volume. If you'd like you use your own keychain from another computer, for example, you can do that by copying the keychain file (which is located in the System Folder, in the Preferences folder, in a folder called Keychains) to a removable disk or over a network drive. Copy it to the new machine and you can access it through the Keychain Access control panel as follows:

1. Lock all keychains and close the Keychain Access control panel.

2. Reopen the Keychain Access control panel from the Control Panels menu.

3. In the Unlock Keychain dialog box, choose Other from the pop-up menu.

4. In the Choose a Keychain dialog box, locate the keychain you'd like to use and click Open.

5. Enter a password for the keychain and click Unlock.

The keychain opens in the Keychain Access control panel. Now, to switch between two or more keychains, you can select them from the Keychains menu. To make a particular keychain the default keychain (where most new passwords will be added) choose Make "*Keychain*" Default from the Keychains menu, where *Keychain* is the name of the selected keychain.

Summary

This chapter showed you how to use control panels to customize various aspects of your computer's operation to make your work more comfortable and productive. General preferences can be set to determine the preferred location for opening and saving documents, and the blinking rates for the insertion point and menus. You can also adjust the responsiveness of the keyboard and mouse.

In addition, this chapter discussed how to change sound levels and alert sounds; how to adjust the way your monitor looks; and how to set the current date, time, and location for your computer. You saw how to use and modify the Control Strip. You saw how to use the Location Manager to create groups of settings and what control panels allow you to set sleep, startup, and shutdown times. You also saw how to set foreign language preferences and adjust compatibility settings. And, you saw a new control panel that enables you to automatically search for updates to the Mac OS over the Internet.

Finally, this chapter discussed the Keychain Access control panel, which can be used to manage one or more keychains on your Mac. You can add keychains, lock and unlock keychains, get information on keychain items, delete keychain items, and set preferences. You can also copy keychains between different Macs and manage more than one keychain at a time.

✦ ✦ ✦

Set Up for Multiple Users

Mac OS 9 offers a new built-in feature that could prove to be a boon for users of many Macs. Called Multiple Users, it's actually an updated implementation of software that Apple has sold for some time as a separate add-on for the Mac OS called At Ease. What this feature enables you to do is create separate accounts for each user on your Mac — whether they're members of your family, coworkers, or different users in a lab setting.

Each user gets his or her own login name and password. Once logged in, what each user sees can be very different. You have your own storage space, access to private documents and a set of applications you can use. Moreover, preferences for your applications and the Mac OS can be tailored to your needs. Your Internet preferences, application preferences, Appearance settings, and even your keychain can all be set up so that the Mac OS interface you use is completely different from that of others who share this one Macintosh.

For the administrator (or "owner") of the machine, your options are extensive, too. You can assign different levels of interface to your users, giving some more control over their environment than others. You can restrict access to network volumes, CD-ROM, and DVD drives, and control what in the Mac OS each user sees. If you've ever tired of setting and resetting preferences or customization options after other people have worked with a particular Mac, you'll probably find Multiple Users a boon for the power it gives you to control access.

This chapter discusses setting up multiple users, accessing individual accounts, and setting preferences for individual users. You'll also see how to set up Voice Verification, Apple's new system for allowing users to sign in to their account by simply speaking a passphrase instead of remembering a password.

How Multiple Users Works

Multiple Users is an extension to the Mac OS that enables you to create multiple user accounts on a single Mac OS 9 computer. Each user account is given its own set of preferences files, documents, and access to a subset of the applications that are available on the Mac. In essence, nearly the entire experience—the desktop, documents folder, application preferences, and more—can be customized and controlled for each individual user.

There are a number of situations where this can be handy. As the "owner" or administrator of a particular Mac, you can create accounts that only have access to applications that you authorize. For instance, you might want to restrict access to an FTP application on a lab-based Macintosh to keep users from downloading software over the Internet. Or, you might determine that you have users who shouldn't have access to certain Control Panels so that they don't make system-level changes to the setup of the Mac (such as changing TCP/IP or File Sharing settings). You can also determine factors such as whether the user can print and which printer the user can choose.

Multiple Users also enables you to set up the Finder differently for each user. For trusted users, you can give them pretty much full access to the Finder, even enabling them to manage other user accounts, if desired. A more limited Finder enables you to add the customizations noted previously, such as restricted access to Control Panels or the Network Browser. To place even more restrictions on a user, you can choose the Panels interface, which basically gives the user access to only selected applications, personal documents, and, if you so choose, removable media.

The log-in process

Once Multiple Users is activated, a new interface is added to the Mac OS. Near the end of the startup process, after extensions loading has occurred (but before Startup Items are opened), the Login screen appears, complete with usernames and custom icons for each user (see Figure 13-1). This window enables a user to select his or her username and click Log in or press Return. Then, the user is prompted for a password. If the password is correct, that user's Preferences and settings are loaded and the user's personal Startup Items are opened. The desktop appears (unless the user has been assigned the special Panels interface), complete with that user's custom settings.

Now, depending on his or her configuration, this user will have access to a subset of the applications and control panels that you've installed on the Mac. (You can select that subset using the Multiple Users administrative tool, as discussed later in the section "Enable Multiple Users and Create Accounts"). Likewise, all of the user's application preferences, Internet preferences, and other settings are customized for them. And, the user will have his or her own storage space on the desktop that offers an area where he or she can save files and folders for personal use. In addition, a shared folder might also be accessible to the user, allowing files and folders to be stored that all other users on the Mac can access.

Figure 13-1: With Multiple Users, each user has his or her own log-in account.

Multiple Users also adds another command to the Finder's Special menu: Logout (see Figure 13-2). When selected, this command tells all open applications to quit. (Technically, it sends the Apple Event "Quit" to all applications in the Application menu, as described in Chapter 24, so that they all go through a clean quit process.) Then, any items in the user's personal Shutdown Items folder are performed and, finally, the user is logged out of his or her account. The Login window reappears and another user is now free to access the Mac.

Cross-Reference Apple Events are discussed in Chapter 24; Startup and Shutdown items are discussed in Chapter 11.

Figure 13-2: With Multiple Users active, a new Logout command appears in the Finder's Special menu.

The nuts and bolts

From the user's point of view, Multiple Users is seamless. To make it happen, though, requires a bit of magic — especially to ensure that it can't be easily defeated.

On a Mac that isn't enabled for Multiple Users, the Mac generally goes through its startup routine until it's loaded all extensions, then it calls on the Finder to start up and create the desktop, Apple menu, and mount drives, and otherwise create the user interface. When Multiple Users is activated, the Mac OS actually loads a different application before it loads the Finder, called *Login*. This is what displays the Login screen where users can select their account names and enter passwords.

Once a user has logged in correctly, Login is then responsible for setting up the user's personal environment. In some cases, that simply means redirecting the Preferences folder (as far as applications are concerned) so that the user's applications all load the appropriate Preferences folder for that user. It also means setting permissions for the user's access to applications and folders on the system. Then, Login loads either the Finder or the Panels program, depending on which is enabled for the user.

Note Another change in Mac OS 9 can affect what your users see at startup. If you or any user with access to the Chooser elects to have volumes mounted at startup (see Chapter 21 for more on how this works), then the Finder will attempt to mount those volumes regardless of which user has logged in. The reason this happens is that network volume aliases to be mounted are now stored in the Servers folder instead of in the Startup Items folder in the System Folder. The Servers folder is not swapped in and out for a given user (unlike the Startup Items folder), so those items are accessed regardless of the user. To work around this issue, you can remove any aliases in the Servers folder and place aliases to network volumes in selected users' Startup Items folders. Of course, if you'd like to have a network volume login appear regardless of the user, the Servers folder is the way to go.

Login isn't finished, however. It actually sits in the background (you won't see it on the Application menu or the Application Switcher window, but it's still running) where it acts to redirect requests from applications so that the application itself doesn't need to know that it's being run in the Multiple Users environment. Instead, it "sees" the Preferences folder and other system items in the correct places so that it can continue to function normally.

Owners, users, and administrators

In Multiple Users parlance, there are two basic types of users: regular users and the owner. The owner is the first account created on the Mac, and it's the one that has the most power. As the owner, you can create accounts, change user access levels, and configure the overall Mac to your liking.

The owner also has the ability to give certain users administrator privileges, enabling them, for example, to create and alter user accounts. In general, this still doesn't give the user as much power as the owner, because even an administrative user can have his or her access privileges managed by the owner. And, in the case where the Mac is started up with extensions off, the owner password is still required to gain access to the machine and make changes.

The Users folder

So where are all these settings saved? Multiple Users creates a new folder on the startup disk called *Users*, where each user's files, preferences, Favorites, and other settings are stored. When a user logs in, those are the settings that are redirected to the appropriate places in the System Folder and elsewhere on the system. As the owner you can access these settings for individual users by double-clicking the Users folder on your startup disk (see Figure 13-3).

Figure 13-3: The Users folder window opens to reveal the files of your users.

Here you'll find a folder for each user, including a number of settings that you'd normally find in the System Folder for a non-Multiple Users system—Favorites, Apple Menu Items, Startup and Shutdown items, and so on. As the owner, you can make changes in these folders that will be reflected when the user next logs in to the system (see the section "Administration and Troubleshooting").

The Users folder also includes a Shared Documents folder where users can store documents that are accessible to most other users on the system. (You can choose to limit an individual user's access to the Shared Documents folder.) The Users folder is also where each individual user's personal files are saved, in a special Documents folder that's found inside the user's folder. These documents are generally only accessible to the user and owner, although you can enable users to see other user's documents and have read, write, or read and write access to them.

Note   If you have a folder named Documents on your startup disk, it becomes the owner's personal documents folder. If you don't, a Documents folder is created when you start up Multiple Users and subsequently log in as the owner.

Enable Multiple Users and Create Accounts

Multiple Users is enabled and managed using the Multiple Users control panel. To use Multiple Users, you must first activate it in the control panel, and then create a user account for each user who will be accessing this Mac. You can also create a guest account that enables users who don't have a username and password on the system to access the Mac.

Note   To enable Multiple Users and use it for the first time, you must have an owner's name and password entered in the File Sharing control panel (you'll generally set this in the Mac OS Setup Assistant, discussed in Chapter 31, or you can set it up through the File Sharing control panel, as discussed in Chapter 22). This name and password are used to create the owner account in Multiple Users. If you don't have these specified, Multiple Users will open the File Sharing control panel when you attempt to turn on Multiple Users or create a new user.

Enabling Multiple Users

To enable Multiple Users, choose Multiple Users from the Control Panels menu in the Apple Menu. This will bring up the control panel shown in Figure 13-4.

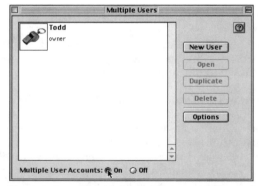

Figure 13-4: The Multiple Users control panel

At the bottom of the Multiple Users control panel are two radio buttons that enable you to turn Multiple Users on and off. Select On to activate Multiple Users. At any time, you can choose Off to disable Multiple Users. When Multiple Users is off, the Login window doesn't appear and anyone who accesses the Mac has access to the entire system.

Creating a user

When you have Multiple Users active, you already have one user, the owner. You don't actually have to create another user if you don't want to — Multiple Users can be used with just the owner account to enable you to password-protect the login process. With Multiple Users active and only one account, you can easily disallow anyone who doesn't know the owner's password (or doesn't match the owner's voiceprint, as discussed later in the section "Create Your Voice Verification Password") from accessing this Mac.

Note   Multiple Users enables you to create up to 40 user accounts and 1 guest account.

To enable more than one user to have access, you need to create a user account for each user. To begin creating a new user, click New User in the Multiple Users control panel. This brings up the Edit "New User" window, as shown in Figure 13-5.

Figure 13-5: The Edit "New User" window

You begin by entering a name for the user in the User Name entry box. This name can be up to 31 characters long and follows the same requirements as creating a folder name in the Finder. (In fact, creating a folder is part of what happens when you create the user.) You can simply enter a user's first and last name, or you can use some other naming system that you prefer.

When you've entered a username, press Tab to move to the Password dialog box. Now, enter a password for this user. Again, it can be up to 31 characters long. Passwords are not case sensitive, so the password "longitude393quack" is the same as "LongiTude393Quack" or other permutations of upper- and lowercase.

Note The username and password are actually optional. If you don't mind giving users access to the system without a username and/or password, you can leave these fields blank. This isn't recommended, but it is possible. Also, creating a user automatically creates a keychain for that user, which is assigned the same password as his or her account password. The keychain is opened automatically as the user logs in, unless the user changes his or her keychain password using the Keychain Access control panel. (For more on the keychain, see Chapter 12.)

Once the password is entered, you can select the type of user account to assign to this user. There are three basic options:

✦ **Normal**. A Normal user account gives the user access to most features in the Finder. These users can access all applications, AppleScripts, and most folders that are available to the owner. By default the users cannot access other user's documents and are restricted from using some of the control panels that are reserved for the owner account.

✦ **Limited**. These users still see the typical Finder interface, but you have more customization options. Specifically, you can customize which applications, AppleScripts, and control panels the users can access. You can also determine whether the users have access to CD-ROMs or DVD-ROMs, other removable media, the Chooser, and the Network Browser, and other features of the OS.

✦ **Panels**. This user doesn't see the Finder interface, but is instead shown the more limited Panels interface. Panels basically enables users to manage their applications and documents from a simplified interface that uses tabbed windows and button icons for access. These users cannot see disk icons on the desktop or open them to find items.

If you select Normal, you don't have to do anything else, if you don't want to — you can simply close the Edit window and the new user is created. For Limited and Panels interfaces, you need to do a bit more customization, which is covered in the next sections.

To reveal the details for this particular setup, you can click the Show Details Setup disclosure triangle at the bottom of the Edit window. This displays four tabs, which you may or may not be able to access, depending on the type of account you're creating. They are: User Info, Applications, Privileges, and Alternate Password.

User Info

On the User Info tab (which is available regardless of the type of account being set up), are a number of options that let you make basic decisions about this user, including the icon used for that particular user in the log-in window, whether the user can change his or her own password, and how other users will access this user's documents. If you've selected a Normal account, you can also decide whether this user will have the privileges required to alter other users' accounts and create new users. Figure 13-6 shows the User Info tab of the Multiple Users control panel.

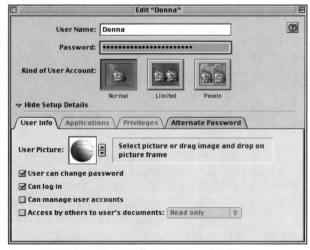

Figure 13-6: Setting basic User Info options

Here's a look at each option:

✦ **User Picture**. Using the up and down arrows, you can select the picture that will appear next to this user's name in the login window. You can add images to use by dragging them from the ScrapBook, an application, or a Web browser window.

Tip

If dragging-and-dropping an image to the User Picture doesn't work, try to copy and paste it. Select an image in another application and choose Edit ➪ Copy in that application. Now, click once on the picture box labeled User Picture and choose Edit ➪ Paste. You should see the image appear. Images that are perfectly square look best as User Pictures.

✦ **User can change password**. Turn on this item if you'd like to enable this user to change his or her own login password. Users can do this from the login window by selecting the Change Password option before logging in to the Mac.

✦ **Can log in**. You may want to temporarily disable a user without deleting his or her user account. If that's the case, turn off this item. The user will not be able to log in, but his or her settings and documents will be preserved for future use.

✦ **Can manage user accounts**. If the user has a Normal user account, you can decide to enable the user to manage other user's accounts. If you turn on this option, the user will have access to the Multiple Users control panel, allowing them to create, modify, and delete other user accounts (except the owner account).

✦ **Access by others to user's documents**. This setting enables you to determine how other users will view this user's documents. If you want to allow this user to keep his or her documents from being seen by others, turn off this option. Otherwise, use the pop-up menu to determine how this user's documents will appear to others — Read Only, Write Only, or Read & Write.

Applications

By default, Normal users have access to all applications and AppleScripts on the Macintosh, with the exception of the Multiple Users control panel and some other restricted control panels discussed later in the section "Limits on User Accounts."

Limited and Panels accounts, however, require that you set up the individual applications that the user has access to. You do this on the Applications tab, which you access by clicking the Applications tab of the Edit window. Figure 13-7 shows the Applications tab.

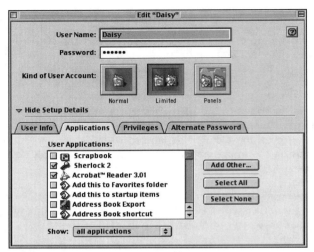

Figure 13-7: Choosing which applications a Limited or Panels account can access

To designate which applications this user can access, simply scroll through the list and turn each application on or off by clicking its check box. By default, you'll see not only ordinary applications that are installed on the Mac, but AppleScripts and Speakable Items as well. Unlike regular applications that have distinctive icons, most AppleScripts have the standard AppleScript application icon, which looks like a diamond with a scroll on top of it, although some, such as the Mail and Browse the Internet applets, have custom icons. (AppleScript applications are described in Chapter 24.) Including all AppleScripts in the list gives you increased flexibility but can make the list lengthy and difficult to manage. If you'd prefer to simply view the available applications, choose "all but AppleScripts" from the Show pop-up menu. If you'd like to see just the items you've already selected as accessible, you can choose "selected items only" from the Show pop-up menu.

Note If you have a CD or DVD in your drive or other removable disks mounted, you may see applications in the User Applications list that are on those removable disks. To avoid confusion, you may want to eject those disks so that you're only adding local applications (those actually stored on this Mac) via this list.

If you don't see an application that you want to give this user access to, you can find it by clicking Add Other. Now, using the Open dialog box, locate the application to which you'd like to give this user access. Once you've found it, select it and click Open. It's added to the list of applications; you can find it in the list (in alphabetical order) and click its check box to turn it on. You can also select all applications in the window by clicking Select All, or you can turn off access to all listed applications by clicking Select None.

Setting application privileges for a user affects whether the user can see and open applications. A Limited user can see all applications in the Finder but can open only the ones to which you have enabled access. If the user tries to open an application to which he or she doesn't have access, an alert box appears telling the user that he or she cannot open that application.

Limited and Panels users are also given a special way to launch applications to which they have access. For the Limited user, this is a special folder that appears on the desktop called Items for *username*, where *username* represents the name of the user (for example, the folder might be named "Items for Daisy Smith"). For a Panels user, a panel called Items appears on the screen. This panel includes the applications to which this user has access. For more on how this looks and works, see the section "The User Experience" later in this chapter.

Note   If you want to add access to control panels for individual users, but you don't want them to see the entire Control Panels menu in the Apple Menu, you can add some control panels individually in the User Applications list. The user will then be able to open the control panels from his or her personal items folder or Items panel.

Privileges

If you're configuring a Limited or Panels account, you can set additional options by clicking the Privileges tab in the Edit window (see Figure 13-8). These options don't apply to a Normal account, because they are all enabled by default for such users.

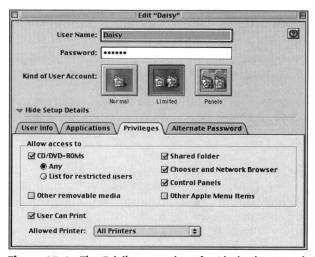

Figure 13-8: The Privileges options for Limited or Panels accounts

The Privileges options determine whether the user has access to CDs and DVDs, other removable media, the shared folder for all users, and the Chooser and Network Browser. You can also determine whether the user has access to Control Panels and other Apple Menu Items and whether the user can print. If you enable the user to print, you can limit the user to access to a particular printer.

Privileges are organized in two different sections. Here are the options in the section labeled Allow access to:

✦ **CD/DVD-ROMs**. You can choose to allow or disallow a user from accessing the CD-ROM or DVD-ROM drive in the Macintosh by turning this option on or off. If turned off, the user cannot access any CDs or DVDs placed in the drive (they're automatically ejected). If turned on, then you have two other options—you can choose to enable the user to access any CDs or DVDs placed in the drive, or you can choose to have the user's access compared against a list of restrictions for particular CD and DVD titles. (Creating this list is discussed in the section "Global Multiple User Options" later in this chapter.)

✦ **Other removable media**. You can select this item to enable this user to access other removable media to which your Mac has access, including floppy drives, Zip drives, or any other removable device that's connected to the Macintosh.

✦ **Shared Folder**. Each Mac set up for Multiple Users has a shared folder that can be used to exchange files between users. By default the owner and all Normal users have access to this folder. For Limited and Panels users, you can determine whether they, too, have access to the shared folder. If they do, it appears in a Limited user's personal items folder and in a Panels user's Items panel.

✦ **Chooser and Network browser**. If you'd like to give users access to the Chooser and Network Browser for connecting to file sharing servers, turn on this option.

Note   A user that has access to the Chooser but doesn't have print privileges can change the printer to which he or she is connected. But, when that user attempts to print from an application, the user will be asked for the owner's password in order to complete the printing process.

✦ **Control Panels**. If you'd like this user to have access to the Control Panels submenu in the Apple menu, turn on this option. This gives the user access to many of the appearance and behavior-related control panels on the machine, but still limits the user's ability to access the restricted control panels, which are outlined in the section "Limits on User Accounts" later in this chapter.

✦ **Other Apple Menu Items**. If you'd like to restrict this user's access to Apple menu items other than the Chooser, Network Browser, and the Controls Panels menu, check this option. This denies the user access to accessories such as the Apple System Profiler, Calculator, ScrapBook, and Stickies, among other items.

At the bottom of the Privileges screen you can choose whether this user can print. If you enable printing for the user, you can either enable the user to print to any available printer (which the user can select in the Chooser) or limit that user to a particular printer. If limited to a particular printer, the user can still change printers in the Chooser (if the user has access to it). Printing to an unauthorized printer, however, requires the owner's password.

Alternate Password

If you've enabled the Alternate Password global option (discussed in the section "Global Multiple User Options" later in this chapter), then you can set additional options by clicking the Alternate Password tab. Figure 13-9 shows the Alternate Password options.

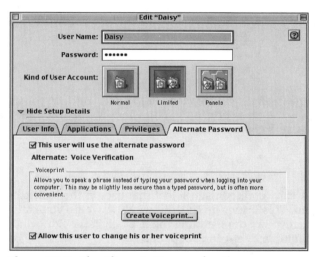

Figure 13-9: The Alternate Password options screen

In the Alternate Password tab, you can enable this user to use a password method other than a typed password. By default, Mac OS 9 supports Voice Verification as its sole alternate scheme. However, developers can create other alternate schemes (for example, thumbprint identification) which can then be added as an option for your users.

To enable this user to use an alternate password scheme, turn on the option This user will use an alternate password. Below this option is the alternate scheme that's available. (The alternate password scheme is selected elsewhere, as described later in the section "Global Multiple User Options.")

The Alternate Password tab includes options for the alternate scheme that's been selected. For instance, with Voiceprint Verification, you can click the Create Voiceprint button to create a voiceprint password for this user. (See the section "Create Your Voiceprint Passphrase" later in this chapter.) There is also an option that enables the user to change his or her voiceprint password during login.

Note   You shouldn't create a voiceprint for another user, because, by definition, it won't work. If you select Create Voiceprint, then the user needs to be available to create his or her own voiceprint. Otherwise, simply avoid creating a voiceprint and turn on the option that enables the user to change the voiceprint. The user can then set his or her own voiceprint password by selecting Change Password from the Login window.

If you select an alternate password scheme for your users, you should still assign them regular passwords. If the alternate password scheme fails, the user can use his or her regular password to gain access. Also, the regular password is used to verify that the users have the privilege to change their alternate password, when they elect to do so.

Saving the user

After you're satisfied with the changes you've made in the Edit window, you can save a user simply by clicking the close box in the Edit window. You'll see the new user's entry in the Multiple Users control panel.

Editing a user

To change settings for an already created user, select that user in the Multiple Users control panel and click Open. This brings up the Edit window, where you can make any changes you'd like. When you're done editing the user, click the Edit window's close box to return to the Multiple Users control panel.

Note   If you change a user's password, you may also be asked to enter that user's keychain password. That's because creating a user also creates a keychain for that user, which is given the same password as the user's password. (The keychain is opened automatically when users log in as long as they don't change their password.) After you've unlocked the user's keychain, you can then enter that user's keychain password again and click View. (This button doesn't make much sense — it's a glitch in Mac OS 9.) The keychain password is automatically changed so that it's the same as the user's login password. Now, the keychain will still be opened automatically when the user logs in.

Duplicating a user

One quick way to add users to your system is to select a user who has privileges and settings similar to those that you'd like for the new user. Select the existing user and click Duplicate. Now you'll see an Edit window that includes the name of the existing user and an empty password entry box (see Figure 13-10). Enter a user name and password for the new user.

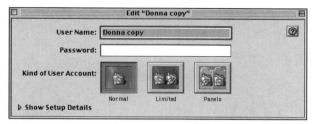

Figure 13-10: Creating a user by duplicating an existing user

You can change settings and privileges as before, but they'll default to the settings that you've already given the existing user that you used as a template. That should make it easier to set up this user if you only want to make minor changes.

Deleting a user

You can delete a user from the Multiple Users control panel. You have the option of deleting the user and maintaining the user's files on the system or deleting the user outright.

To delete a user, select the user in the Multiple Users control panel. Now, with the user highlighted, click Delete. An alert box asks if you're sure; there's no way to recover a user's settings once that user is deleted. Click Delete to delete the user or click Don't Delete to leave the user on the system.

The next alert box gives the choice of keeping the user folder for this user. (It's the folder that's stored in the Users folder on your system's hard disk. This folder contains the user's personal files.) Click Keep to maintain the folder, Delete to delete the folder, or Cancel to stop the deletion process and leave the user on the system. Once deleted, a user's folder can't be recovered (except via a disk utility program).

Tip   If you keep a user's folder but delete the user, you can reinstate the user by adding the user with exactly the same username. Multiple Users will ask whether you want to keep the existing user folder or delete it and create a new folder for this user. If you choose to keep it, that user can have access to his or her existing documents and settings.

Limits on user accounts

One of the biggest limitations placed on users is their access to control panels. No user except the owner can access the following control panels, most of which deal with networking and managing the Mac computer itself:

✦ AppleTalk

✦ DialAssist

✦ Energy Saver

✦ Extensions Manager

✦ Memory

✦ Modem

✦ Multiple Users

✦ Remote Access

✦ TCP/IP

Perhaps the biggest limitation is the Remote Access control panel. Users cannot switch between Remote Access configurations and they can't open the control panel to initiate a remote access connection. While this may seem like a huge limitation on Macs that only have modem-based access to the Internet, there is one work around — users that can access the control strip can use it to connect using Remote Access. These users cannot, however, switch between Remote Access configurations; they are locked in to whatever choice you last selected as owner.

If your user doesn't have control strip access, then you should set Remote Access so that its Connect automatically when starting TCP/IP applications option is turned on. That way, when the user starts a Web browser, e-mail application, or another Internet application that you've made available to them, the Remote Access connection will be made automatically.

Cross-Reference   See Chapter 10 for more on Remote Access options.

Global Multiple User Options

Aside from activating Multiple Users and creating individual user accounts, the Multiple Users control panel offers some global options. These options enable you to set behavior for all of your user accounts, as well as some settings for how Multiple Users operates in general. These settings include an opportunity to customize the login prompt and to automate the logging out of inactive users. You can also set up the restriction for CD and DVD titles, and you can establish some other general settings, such as whether to have a Guest User account, how users enter the username, and whether Multiple Users should work in conjunction with the Macintosh Manager software to establish user accounts.

To display the global Multiple User options, click Options in the Multiple Users control panel. The Global Multiple User Options dialog box appears. Its settings are organized on tabs: Login, CD/DVD-ROM Access, and Other. Click a tab to access each set of options.

Login

The Login options under Global Multiple User Options enable you to customize the login prompt, determine whether users can use an Alternate Password scheme (and which one) and whether users are allowed to speak their names instead of selecting them from the Login list. You can also determine whether users will be logged out or the screen will be locked (requiring their password again) if they are inactive for a specified amount of Time. Figure 13-11 shows the Login options screen.

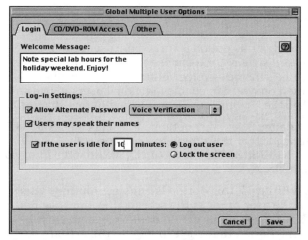

Figure 13-11: Login options enable you to customize login and logout behavior for the system.

Here are the options:

✦ **Welcome Message**. In the Welcome Message text box you can type a message that will appear in the Login window whenever a user accesses the system. This message appears near the top of the window, welcoming them to the system and providing any additional instructions or notifications that you'd like to add. Figure 13-12 shows a customized Welcome Message.

Figure 13-12: The login screen with a custom Welcome Message

✦ **Allow Alternate Password**. If this option is turned on, users can log in with an alternate password scheme. You choose the scheme from the pop-up menu. By default, only one scheme — Voice Verification — is available. After this option is turned on, you can enable individual users to use an alternate password. (See the "Privileges" section earlier in this chapter.)

✦ **Users may speak their name**. Select this option and users can speak their names aloud when logging in. For this option to work correctly, Speakable Items must be enabled in the Speech control panel. (See Chapter 23 to learn more about Speakable Items.)

✦ **If user is idle for . . . minutes**. If this option is enabled, Multiple Users automatically logs out the user or locks the screen after the specified number of minutes. Enter the number of minutes the system must be idle, and then choose the option that corresponds to the action you'd like taken after the system has been idle. If you select Log out user, the login window will be displayed and any user can log in. If you choose Lock the screen then the user must enter his or her password or log out before anyone can access the computer again. It's a good idea to choose one of these options, especially if security is a priority, to ensure that other people can't use the current account to access the computer — either accidentally or on purpose — if the current user gets up and walks away from the machine.

CD/DVD-ROM Access

The CD/DVD-ROM Access tab of the Global Multiple Users dialog box enables you to customize access for specific CD or DVD-ROM titles. This can be a time-consuming process because you need to insert each CD or DVD-ROM in your CD/DVD-ROM drive that you wish to allow restricted users to access. In some cases, you can restrict access to specific parts of a disc. Figure 13-13 shows the CD-DVD-ROM Access tab.

Note
You can't restrict a specific disc for one user but not another user. All users with limited CD/DVD access share the same list of restricted discs and items. In the Edit User window, you can restrict the user from all discs or just those in the common list, or you can give the user unfettered access to discs.

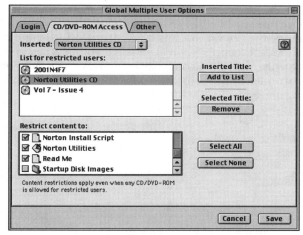

Figure 13-13: The CD/DVD-ROM Access tab lets you determine which discs (and what content on those discs) are restricted.

To add a disc to the list that restricted users can access, place it in the CD/DVD-ROM drive. When it's mounted, it will appear in the Inserted pop-up menu on the CD/DVD ROM Access tab.

To add the title, click the Add to List button. The title appears in the List for restricted users and any folders on that disc appear in the Restrict content to list. By default, all folders and files can be accessed. To deny access to a particular folder, click to remove the check next to that folder in the list. You can also click Select None to deny access to all folders or Select All to enable access to all folders.

To add another disc, switch to the Finder and eject the current disc. Now, insert another disc that you'd like to set up access privileges to. Repeat the process for any discs that you'd like to enable your restricted users to access, or any disc that contains folders or files that you want to prevent them from using.

> **Note** You can't selectively enable users to listen to audio CDs. If you disable a user's access to the CD/DVD-ROM drive overall, the user can't play audio CDs. Although you can enable access only to CD-ROM titles on your list for restricted users, you can't add audio CDs to this list, meaning users can't play them at all. For users to play audio CDs, you have to enable unrestricted access to the CD/DVD-ROM. (Don't forget to give users access to the AppleCD Audio Player as well.)

Other

In the Global Multiple User Options window, the Other tab includes a number of unrelated options. These include the option to allow guest users to log in and the option to notify the owner when a new application is installed so that you can allow or restrict access to it. You can also establish some basic settings regarding how users log in and whether the user account is stored locally or on a network that uses the Macintosh Manager. Figure 13-14 shows the Other tab.

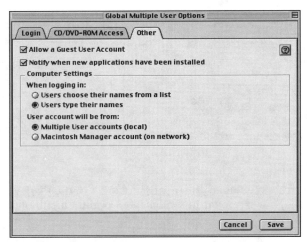

Figure 13-14: The options on the Global Multiple User Other tab

Here's what each option does:

✦ **Allow a Guest User Account** creates a new login account that can be used by *guest users* (users who don't have their own usernames and passwords). This account doesn't require a password. You can edit the Guest user in the Multiple Users control panel to restrict that user's access just as you would any other user account.

Caution   The default setting for the Guest user account is Normal, which gives the user quite a bit of access to your system. You should immediately edit the Guest user account to restrict its access if you'd prefer that Guests not have many privileges on your system.

✦ **Notify when new applications have been installed** displays an alert message that tells the owner that a new application has been installed if either the owner or a Normal user installs an application. (This alert appears at the end of the next owner's session.)

✦ **When logging in** lets you specify whether users choose a name from a list or type in their username. Forcing users to type their names offers additional security, because the user has to know both his or her username and password to gain admittance to the machine. Allowing users to choose a name from a list makes it easier on your users, but offers less security.

✦ **User account will be from** lets you specify the source of user accounts. If you have a Macintosh Manager server set up on your network, you can use it to create the user accounts for this machine. Otherwise, choose Multiple User accounts to use the accounts you set up through the Multiple Users control panel.

The User Experience

After you've activated and created accounts for your users, they can log in to the computer, customize their settings, and access the resources you've made available to them. This section walks you through the login and logout process, showing you the different items a user can customize and how the interface will appear to different users.

Login

When you start up the Mac (or after another user logs out) the Login window displays. This window is where you select your account from a list or type the account name (if the owner has set options so that the account name must be typed) and move on to the verification step. You may also have the option of changing your password and changing your Voice Verification passphrase. Figure 13-15 shows the Login windows for choosing a user account or entering a user name.

Figure 13-15: When you log in, you are asked to choose your username (on the left) or to enter it yourself (on the right).

Enter a password

After selecting or typing your username, click Log in. Now verify your account by entering a password. There are a number of things that can happen at this step:

✦ If the Enter Password dialog box appears, enter your password in the Password entry box and click OK. If the password is correct, your desktop appears. If your password is incorrect, the Enter Password dialog box shakes (sort of signifying a shake of the head "No") and the password is deleted. Try again to enter the password. If you don't get it right, click Cancel to return to the Login window.

✦ If Voice Verification is active and you have a Voice Verification passphrase established, the Voice Verification dialog box displays. As the line scrolls across the dialog box, speak your passphrase (see Figure 13-16). If your voiceprint matches, the dialog box disappears and your desktop appears. If the voiceprint doesn't match, an alert box tells you so. Click Try Again to speak the passphrase again. If you click Cancel in the Alert box, or if you click Cancel in the voiceprint dialog box, you'll see an alert box that asks you for your regular password. Type it and click Continue to enter the system.

✦ If you have another alternative method of access, a corresponding dialog box will appear after you've entered your username.

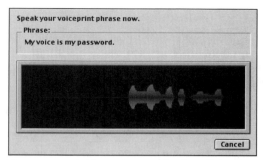

Figure 13-16: The Voice Verification dialog box has heard me speak my passphrase.

Change your password

Before logging in, you can choose to change your password. You can do this at any time if you feel you've been using your current password long enough and that changing it would enhance the security of your user account. You can also choose to change your password if you know that Voice Verification (or another alternate password system) has been activated for your account, but you haven't yet recorded your voiceprint.

After selecting your account or typing your username in the login window, click Change Password. (This button is grayed for users who don't have the privilege to change the password.) In the Change Password dialog box, enter your current password in the Current Password entry box. Everything you type in this dialog box is displayed as a string of bullet characters so that no one can read your password over your shoulder. Figure 13-17 shows the Change Password dialog box.

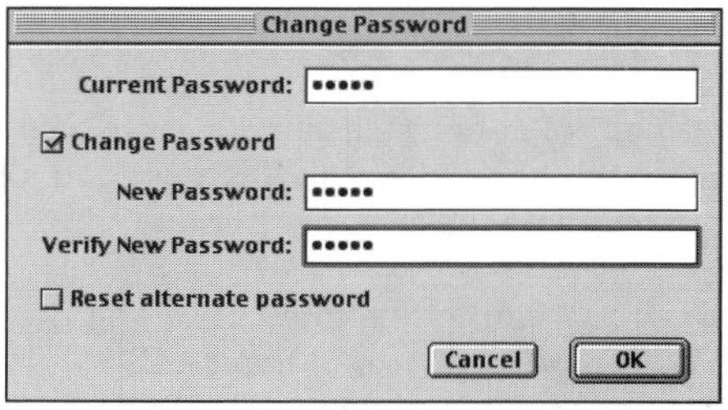

Figure 13-17: Changing your password

Now you have two choices:

✦ With the Change Password option selected, you can enter your new password. Type it once in the New Password entry box, and then retype it in the Verify New Password entry box. These two must match before the password is set. Click OK to see whether your password is successfully changed.

Note If you haven't ever changed your keychain password, it is the same as your login password for Multiple Users. In that case, changing your login password will automatically change your keychain password. The Unlock Keychain dialog box will appear. If you'd like to change your keychain password, enter the new password now. Then confirm it in the next dialog box. Otherwise, click Cancel for both dialog boxes.

✦ With the option Reset alternate password selected, you can change your Voice Verification password (or other alternate password scheme). This enables you to create a new passphrase for voice verification, as described in the next section.

Note You can choose to select both Change Password and Reset alternate password in the Change Password dialog box. If you do, enter your new password twice in the New Password and Verify New Password boxes and click OK. Your typed password will change right away, and then you go through the process of creating a new Voice Verification passphrase (or other alternate password).

Create your Voice Verification passphrase

If you are logging in as a user, you can create or edit your voiceprint by following the steps that enable you to reset your alternate password as detailed in the previous section, "Change Your Password." If the owner of your machine has designated Voice Verification as the alternate password scheme, you can now create your Voice Verification passphrase.

Note If you're the owner or an administrator, you can help a user to create his or her voiceprint by opening the Multiple Users control panel, selecting the user account, and clicking Edit. In the Edit user dialog box, click the Alternate Password tab. Click Create Voiceprint and the user can begin to create his or her voiceprint.

You'll see the Voiceprint Setup dialog box. In this dialog box, click Change Phrase to enter a new phrase. In the Change Phrase dialog box (shown in Figure 13-18), type the phrase you'd like to use, then select the option Hide phrase at login if you don't want to be prompted with the phrase. (This adds additional security.) Click OK after you've edited your phrase.

Note The passphrase wording doesn't matter to your Mac, because it does not attempt to recognize the words in the passphrase using voice recognition. Instead, it simply analyzes your voiceprint by comparing your stored values against what you say (and how you say it) at log in. You don't even have to say the passphrase that's displayed on screen, if you remember to say the same thing when you're subsequently logging in. For instance, the displayed passphrase could be "My voice is my password" and you could create your voiceprint by saying "Log me in, please" as long as you remember to say "Log me in, please" again when you're logging in. It's best to use only one sentence — it's more difficult for the verification software to understand two sentences because you're likely to vary the pauses between sentences.

Figure 13-18: Type your new passphrase and decide whether it will be displayed as you log in.

Now, in the Voiceprint Setup dialog box, click Continue to begin recording your voiceprint. You'll record it four times — these are the voiceprints against which your subsequent log-in voiceprints will be compared. To begin recording, click Record First.

The First Recording dialog box displays. In this dialog box, select the microphone to use from the Select Microphone pop-up menu. Then, when you're ready to record, click Record. Now, speak your passphrase, and click Stop when you've finished. Click Play to hear yourself, Record to start over again, or Done if you're satisfied.

Note This is a sophisticated algorithm that's not easy to trip up. That said, you should avoid speaking much faster, slower, or in a tone or accent that you don't usually use. Again, it's not voice recognition, so you don't need to enunciate words or even speak in English. You simply need to speak your passphrase in the same manner as you're likely to speak it when you log in.

Now, repeat the recording until you've recorded all four versions.

After completing the fourth, you may see a message that warns you that there's too much variation between your recording attempts. If the message appears, it's best to click Record Again to repeat the process of creating all four versions again. Try to speak naturally and at the same pace each time.

If the software determines that all four of your voiceprints are close matches, you'll see the voiceprint processed. Now you can try the voiceprint. To do so, click Try It. You'll see the voiceprint dialog box; speak your passphrase. If it's accepted, a dialog box displays saying as much. If it isn't accepted, an alert displays that lets you try again. Your try must be successful before the voiceprint can take effect.

Logout

As a user, you can log out at any time by choosing Special ➪ Logout or by pressing ⌘+Q in the Finder. This brings up an alert box that asks whether you want to log out. If you do, click Yes; if not, click No. If you don't click anything, the message is automatically accepted after 90 seconds and you are logged out. The Multiple Users software tells all applications listed in the Applications menu to quit, activates any items in your Shutdown Items folder, and then quits the Finder. When the Finder has quit, the Mac returns to the Login window.

Note   Some background applications have no menu bar or other user interface and are not listed in the Applications menu; these *faceless background applications* are not told to quit when someone logs out.

You can also log out by choosing Restart or Shut Down from the Special menu. In this case, you won't see an alert asking you to confirm the logout. In addition, all open applications must quit at this time, including the faceless background applications. When the Mac restarts (or is started up at a later time) the Login dialog box appears after the startup process.

Customize your workspace

Depending on your access as a user, you may have quite a few customization options at your disposal and the Multiple Users software keeps your personal settings for many of these options separate from similar personal settings made by other users of the same Mac. Most any application you have access to has its own preferences file, enabling you to customize it using the application's Options or Preferences command without worrying about affecting other users' settings. If you have access to Internet applications, your settings in the Internet control panel can also be kept private.

Cross-Reference   Actually, applications that don't store their preferences file in the Preferences folder may still share preferences with other users. See the section "Troubleshooting" later in this chapter for more details.

Your settings in all of these standard Mac OS control panels can be kept private (assuming you have access to control panels): Appearance; Apple Menu Options; ColorSync; Control Strip; Date & Time; File Exchange; File Sharing; General Controls; Keyboard; Keychain Access; Launcher; Location Manager; Monitors; Mouse; Numbers; QuickTime Settings; Sound; Speech; Startup Disk; Text; and Web Sharing.

For the most part, any settings changes you make won't affect other users. For instance, you can change the Appearance control panel to give your workspace a different look and feel, or you can change the Monitors settings to alter the resolution of your screen or the number of colors displayed.

If you're a Normal user, you can even change the contents of the System Folder. Limited and Panels users don't have enough access to change these settings.

Personal and items folders

Each user on the system gets his or her own personal folder in which documents and other items can be stored. Access to these folders is governed by the settings in the Edit user window, as discussed in the section "Creating a User" earlier in this chapter. The owner or a Normal user who has access to the Multiple Users control panel can hide a user's folder from all other users.

For a Limited user or a Normal user, the personal folder appears in the form of an alias icon on the desktop with the user account name as its name. That alias, when double-clicked, opens the user's personal folder. (The folder itself is stored inside the Users folder in a folder with the user's name. The folder itself is called Documents.) Figure 13-19 shows the icon and folder for a personal folder.

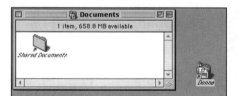

Figure 13-19: Double-clicking the personal folder icon opens the Documents folder.

If you have a Limited user account, you must store all your documents inside your personal folder or panel. If you have a Normal account, you should store most of your documents in your personal folder, even if you have the option of saving documents elsewhere on the system. If you do store your documents elsewhere, those documents may be accessed by other Normal users and seen by Limited users. If you store files in your personal folder and the owner or administrator denies other users access to your personal files, then your files will be hidden from other users except the owner.

Note   You can also encrypt files to keep them from being accessed or viewed by anyone else on the system. See Chapter 7 for more on Apple File Security and file encryption.

If you have a Limited user account, then you also have an Items folder. It appears on the desktop in the form of an alias with the username as its name, as in Rhonda's Items. It gives you quick access to any applications that have been designated for your use by the owner or administrator. This is a handy way to quickly open any of the applications to which you have access without browsing through folders trying to find them all.

Note   Panels users also have personal folders and Items folders, but items in these folders are displayed in panels, as described later in the section "Panels."

Shared Documents

If your account has access to the Shared Documents folder, the Shared Documents folder will also appear in your Personal folder in the form of an alias. This folder can be used to share files between all users on the system who have access to the Shared Documents folder. Simply save or copy items to the folder and others with access will be able to use those items.

Panels

If your account was set up to use Panels, you'll see a much more restricted interface. First, the Finder doesn't load; instead, Panels serves as your entire interface. By default two different panels display—your Items panel and your Documents panel (see Figure 13-20). If you have access to CD/DVD discs, you may also see a panel that shows any mounted discs.

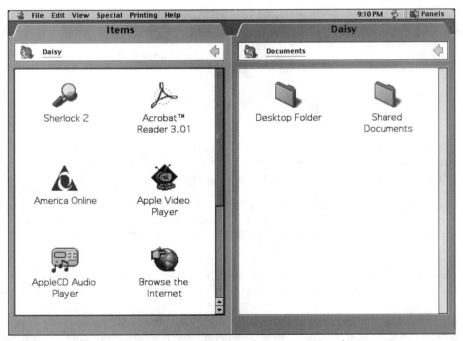

Figure 13-20: The Panels interface offers much more restricted access.

Working with Panels

Panels works fairly simply. To access an item in a Panel, click on the application or document. This launches the application (or launches the associated application and opens the document if you click the document). You can then work normally in the application. The panels shrink to the bottom of the screen, displaying only tabs that name the panels (this works a little like the pop-up windows described in Chapter 5).

To return to the Panels interface, you can click one of the panel tabs, or you can switch using the Application menu.

Clicking a folder in one of your panels opens a new panel that shows the contents of that folder. To close the folder, click its tab. The panel disappears and the remaining panels fill the screen. You can't close your Items or Documents panel — if you click their tabs, they simply move to the bottom of the screen.

You can customize the view in each individual panel. To do that, select a panel, then choose View ➪ View Options to see the View Option dialog box (shown in Figure 13-21). In that dialog box you can choose whether to show the desktop pattern in the background, how large the icons in your panels should be, and what font and point size the names of items should display in.

Figure 13-21: View Options for the Panels interface

You can also select an individual panel and choose View ➪ As Icons or View ➪ As List from the menu.

The Panels interface gives you access to the Apple Menu (along with Control Panels and accessories if the owner has made them available to you). Likewise, there are options in the Special menu of Panels that let you Restart or Shut Down the machine. You can also choose Logout if you'd like to log out and return the Mac to its Login window.

Preferences

The Panels interface has a Preferences command that lets you make some
other changes. Choose Preference from the Edit menu while Panels is active.
The Preferences dialog box appears (as shown in Figure 13-22), enabling you
to change sound settings, apply label colors, choose to smooth the display
of icons, and change the way the Tabs behave in the Panels interface.

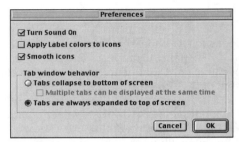

Figure 13-22: The Preferences dialog box
for the Panels interface

Here's what you can do in the Preferences dialog box:

✦ **Turn Sound On**. Use this option to turn sound on or off for this Mac. If you
  don't have access to the Control Panels, this is the only way to enable or
  disable sound.

✦ **Apply Label colors to icons**. To be able to use the File ➪ Label command
  in the Panels interface, enable this option.

✦ **Smooth icons**. If you'd like the Mac to antialias the appearance of icons so
  that they seem to have smooth edges at larger sizes, enable this option.

✦ **Tabs collapse to the bottom of the screen**. If this option is selected, clicking
  an individual panel's tab collapses that panel to the bottom of the screen. If
  the Multiple tabs can be displayed at the same time option is turned off, then
  each panel collapses to the bottom of the screen as another tab is expanded.

✦ **Tabs are always expanded to the top of the screen**. If you select this option,
  then each panel works more like a file folder in a file drawer. Each tab is seen
  at the top of the screen, but only one panel is displayed at a time. Clicking a
  tab brings its panel to the front, as shown in Figure 13-23.

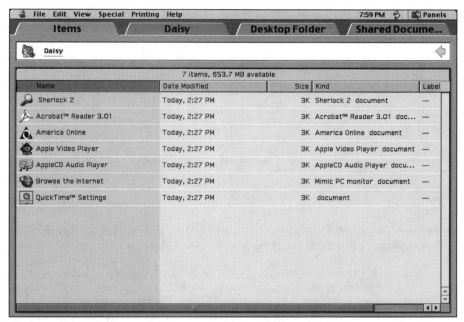

Figure 13-23: When tabs are always expanded to the top of the screen, the effect is more like a drawer full of file folders.

Administration and Troubleshooting

This section looks at some administrative issues that fall to you as the owner of a Mac set up for Multiple Users, including Users folder maintenance tasks, as well as some troubleshooting issues that can crop up with Multiple Users.

The Users folder

The information for user's preferences, along with their files, is stored in the Users folder on your Mac's startup volume. This folder contains quite a bit of information, including the items on that user's Desktop, items in that user's Apple Menu, that user's Favorites, Internet Search Sites, Launcher Items, and so on. Significantly, this is also where the user's Preferences files, Startup Items, and Shutdown Items are all stored. Figure 13-24 shows a particular user's folders.

Figure 13-24: Viewing an individual user's folder in the Users folder

As the owner or system administrator, these folders give you an opportunity to further customize the items for each of your users. Here are some possible scenarios:

✦ **Desktop folder.** If you'd like to place an item on a user's desktop, you can add that item to his or her Desktop folder. Note that the arrangement of icons in the desktop folder mirrors their position on the user's desktop, so you must scroll the window to its right side to place icons where they normally appear on a typical desktop.

✦ **Apple Menu Items.** You can place aliases, folders, or other items on a given user's Apple menu by adding it to his or her Apple Menu Items folder. That user can access anything you add as long as the user's account privileges enable access to other Apple Menu items and to specific applications that you add.

✦ **Favorites.** You can add Internet Location files to each user's Favorites folder; for example, if you'd like them all to have quick access to certain sites.

✦ **Startup and Shutdown Items**. If you'd like a particular user — or all users — to have certain items launch when they login and logout, you can place items in these folders. You could place AppleScripts in these folders, for instance, that offer them reminders, automatically launch other applications, or otherwise automate tasks.

You get the idea. There's quite a bit that you, as the owner, can do to customize these files because you have access to them.

Tip

Having most of your users' documents and other items in the Users folder makes it easier to back up all your users documents and preferences.

New applications

If you or other Normal users add applications to the system, a notification to that effect (if you've set the option for notification in the Global Options) displays. This happens as you log *out* of your owner account, at which time you'll see a dialog box that tells you that applications were installed (see Figure 13-25).

Note   An application dragged from a removable disk or network volume to the startup disk may not show up as an installed application. Generally, only a new application that is installed using an installer program will cause the owner to be alerted to the new application.

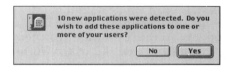

Figure 13-25: If new applications are installed, this alert displays as you log out of the Owner account.

If you want to add all or some of the applications that have been installed to users' accounts, click Yes in the dialog box. You'll then see an Add Application dialog box for each application that's been installed, as shown in Figure 13-26. In this dialog box, you can pick the user accounts to which you want to add access to this application. Place a check mark next to each user who should get access to the application, and then click Add.

Figure 13-26: Add each application to the selected users' accounts.

To pass on a particular application you can either leave no users selected or click Cancel. If you'd like to stop adding applications, click Stop. If you click Stop, you'll need to add the applications manually to each account; the Add Application dialog box will not be displayed again for any skipped applications.

Troubleshooting Multiple Users

A couple of issues can crop up with Multiple Users, including some kinks that still need to be worked out of the software, as well as some trouble that you can have with applications that aren't aware that they're in the Multiple Users environment.

Here's a quick list of some potential issues and how you can fix them:

✦ **Applications give user errors in Limited and Panels accounts.** Apple notes that you need to open applications at least once as the owner before some of them will work for users who have limited access to the system. If the application's errors persist past the initial launch, then it's possible that the application is attempting to write preferences or other needed data to the disk in a nonstandard way. (For instance, an application that attempts to write data to its own application folder may not have enough access to do so under Limited or Panels accounts.) If that's the case, you need to either upgrade the application or change the user's access to Normal.

✦ **Limited users open items they don't have access to.** Limited users can work around your limitations by opening applications through the Script Editor (or using AppleScripts created with the Script Editor). If this is a problem, deny those users access to the Script Editor.

Caution

Some applications allow you to import options or settings from other applications or data files. Some of these applications (Outlook Express 5.0, for example) can gain access to settings, documents, and preferences in other applications, even if you haven't given the user access to the other applications. The only answer may be to move sensitive data or applications to the owner's Documents folder or delete that information (such as old e-mail accounts) from the Mac.

✦ **You aren't notified when an application is installed.** The owner should be notified whenever a new application is installed. Make sure you log in as owner before installing applications. If another user installs an application, you won't be notified until you log out of the owner account.

✦ **The User Applications list doesn't refresh correctly.** To remove aliases that point to applications that have been deleted, click Select None, and then choose All Applications from the Show menu. Now, click Select All.

✦ **Anyone can gain access to private folders if a different startup disk is used.** If you start up using an older version of the Mac OS on a different startup disk, a removable disk, or a CD, then all user folders, including the owner's Documents folder, can be accessed. The solution is to avoid allowing other drives or removable disks to be attached to the Mac and to disallow access to the Startup control panel for your users. Unfortunately, there's no way to keep users from restarting the Mac and starting up from older Mac OS CDs (by holding down the C key at startup) or starting up from older Mac OS versions on attached disks (by holding down ⌘+Option+Shift+Delete). The best defense against this is to use Apple File Security to encrypt sensitive files.

Note If you attempt to start up from the Mac OS 9 CD and Multiple Users is activated, you must enter the owner's password.

Summary

This chapter showed what Multiple Users does and how it can help you organize a Macintosh that is used by more than one person. You then saw how to start up Multiple Users and create individual users. You can give users Normal, Limited, or Panels accounts, customize their user information, specify the applications to which each Limited or Panels account has access, and set the user's privileges regarding CD/DVD access, Control Panels access, and whether the user sees additional Apple Menu Items. If you enable support for alternate passwords, you can give a user an alternate password (such as Voice Verification) while you're creating that user's account. Editing and deleting users is also simple, because it's done from the Multiple Users control panel.

Multiple Users also offers a number of Global Multiple User Options, which you can use to set up how your system works for all users. You can determine whether alternate passwords can be used, if users can speak their names in the Login window (assuming your Mac supports speakable items), and what the Welcome Message will be. Also, the Global Multiple User Options lets you determine which CDs and DVDs restricted users can access and what items they can access on those discs. In addition, you can create a Guest account and you can choose to be notified when new applications are installed. You can also determine how users identify themselves (by selecting a username or typing it) and whether the Multiple Users accounts should be accessed locally or from a Macintosh Manager account.

You then saw how different users see the Mac environment based on their settings and what's possible while you're logged in as a user on a Multiple Users system. You saw how to log in, log out, change passwords, set up a Voice Verification password, and work with the Panels interface.

Finally, you read some tips for administering a Multiple Users-enabled Mac as the owner by accessing the Users folder, adding new applications when they are installed, and troubleshooting some common Multiple Users errors.

✦　　✦　　✦

Make Aliases Hop

Did you ever wish a file or folder could be in more
than one place? You want to keep the contents of
your disk organized by putting programs and documents
in folders, and putting those folders in other folders, but
when you want to open an item, you end up digging through
folders to find what you want to open. Aliases cut through the
organizational red tape. Think of an alias as a stand-in or an
agent for a real program, document, folder, or disk. Aliases act
like real items when you open them or drag items to them. You
can place these agents at your disposal in any handy location,
such as on the desktop or in the Apple menu. Aliases even
look a lot like the items they represent.

Understanding Aliases

Like the documents, programs, and other files on your disks,
aliases are files that contain information. Aliases just contain
a different kind of information than do the other files. Where
a document file contains text, pictures, or other data and a
program file contains code, an alias file contains a pointer
to a document, program, other file, folder, or disk.

By analyzing the information in an alias, the Mac OS can locate
the alias's *original item*. This process is called *resolving* an alias.
The Mac OS can successfully resolve an alias to locate the
alias's original item, even if you move or rename the original
item or move the original item to a different folder.

When you open an alias, the Mac OS uses the information in
the alias to locate the original item and then opens the original.
Dragging an item to the alias of a folder or disk in the Finder has
the same effect as dragging it to the original folder or disk: The
Finder uses the information in the alias to locate the original

folder or disk and places the item you dragged there. Likewise, dragging a document to an alias of a compatible program opens the document. You can even drag an alias of a document to an alias of a compatible application; the Finder uses the information in both aliases to have the application open the document.

Remember, though, that moving an alias to a new folder, to a new disk, or to the Trash moves just the alias, not the original file. That includes moving an alias to a network volume or removable disk. Only the alias is moved. To move the original item, you must select the original item's icon.

If you move an alias to a new location that no longer has access to the original file, the alias can break. One way to break the connection between an alias and its original item is to drag the original item to the Trash and empty the Trash. The Mac OS cannot successfully resolve an alias whose original item no longer exists. Similarly, if you move the alias to a removable disk or network volume, and the alias is later accessed while the original item isn't available (for instance, the removable disk is used in another computer or the remote volume no longer has access to your machine over the network), the alias can't be used to access the original item.

Making an Alias

You can make an alias for any item that you can open from the Finder. That means you can make aliases for documents, application programs, desk accessories, folders, disks, control panels, and even fonts and sounds. Making an alias is a simple procedure. In the Finder, select the item for which you want to create an alias and choose Make Alias from the File menu. A new item appears with the same icon as the original item, except that in Mac OS 8.5 and later the icon has a small curved arrow superimposed to indicate it is an alias. Every alias has an italicized name that matches that of the original item plus the suffix *alias*. Figure 14-1 illustrates the procedure.

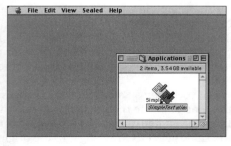

Figure 14-1: The Make Alias command (left) creates an alias that looks a lot like the original item (right).

In addition to the File menu, you can Control+click an item to pop-up its contextual menu and choose Make Alias from there.

Cross-Reference For more information on using contextual menus, see Chapter 4.

Mac OS 9 provides a convenient shortcut for making an alias. Just drag the original item to the place you want the alias, and then press ⌘+Option before releasing the mouse button. You can start pressing those keys any time while dragging, but you must hold them down while you release the mouse button to make an alias. The pointer changes shape when you ⌘+Option+drag an item to a place where the Finder can make an alias, such as a folder, a disk, or the desktop. The pointer acquires a small right-pointing arrow in addition to its normal large left-pointing arrow. If you press ⌘+Option to make an alias at a location that is different from the original—for example, in another folder or on another disk—then the alias does not have the word "alias" at the end of its name. Figure 14-2 shows the pointer shape that means "make alias."

Figure 14-2: The pointer has a special shape when you press ⌘+Option+drag to create an alias.

Note Aliases vary in size from 1K to 17K or more, depending on the capacity and format of the disk they're on. For example, an alias takes up 1K of a floppy disk, a 20MB hard disk, or a 40MB hard disk. On a 100MB disk, an alias takes up 2K. On a 1GB disk in Mac OS Standard format, an alias occupies 17K. The same aliases occupy 4K or less each on a disk in Mac OS Extended format. If a hard disk is partitioned into multiple volumes (each having its own icon on the desktop), the volume capacity determines the size of the aliases on it.

Changing an Alias

After you make an alias, you can manipulate it as you would any other item. You can move it, copy it, and rename it. You can change its icon, comments, or locked status in its Info window.

Moving and copying an alias

If you move an alias to another folder on the same disk or to the desktop, the alias still knows where to find its original item.

You can copy an alias by using the Finder's Duplicate command or by dragging the alias to another disk or to a folder on another disk. To copy an alias or other item to another folder on the same disk, press Option while dragging. All copies of the alias point to the same original item.

Renaming an alias

You rename an alias as you would any other item on the desktop or in a Finder window. Immediately after you create an alias, its name is selected for editing. You can change the name by typing a replacement or by using other standard text-editing techniques (see Chapter 4). For example, you might want to shorten "Microsoft Word alias" to "Word" before adding the alias to the Apple menu or the Launcher. To keep the name as is, click anywhere outside the name or press Return or Enter.

If you want an alias to have exactly the same name as its original item, the two cannot be in the same folder. You must move one out. For example, if you make an alias with the idea of moving it to another folder and you don't want the alias to have the suffix "alias," you have to move the alias before editing its name. Of course, an alias and its original can be in the same folder if their names are very similar but not identical. For example, the alias name could have an extra blank space at the end.

Deleting an alias

Like any item, you remove an alias by dragging it to the Trash. Remember that throwing away an alias doesn't affect the original item. You're only throwing away the alias, not the item to which it points.

Removing the suffix "alias"

To remove the word *alias* quickly from the end of an alias's name, click the name once to select it for editing. Pause briefly (or avoid the pause by moving the mouse slightly to the right after you click the alias name). Double-click the last word of the name. Then press Delete twice (once to delete the selected word *alias* and a second time to delete the space before that word). If you double-click too soon after selecting the name, the Finder opens the item to which the alias points rather than selecting the last word of the name.

Alternatively, you can select the name for editing, press the down-arrow (↓) key or right-arrow (→) key to move the insertion point to the end of the name, and press Delete six times to erase the last word and the space preceding it. To conclude your name editing, click anywhere outside the name or press Return or Enter. If you want the Finder never to add the word *alias* as a suffix, you can modify the Finder with the free ResEdit utility program (see Chapter 27).

Changing an alias's icon

An alias inherits its icon from the original item. An alias's icon normally looks like the icon of its original item with a small curved arrow superimposed. If you subsequently change the original item's icon, the alias icon is updated automatically the next time you open it.

Like most other icons, you can customize an alias icon in its Info window. Use the Finder's Get Info command (see Chapter 8) to bring up the Info window. The alias's custom icon isn't affected by changes to the icon of the original item.

Locking an alias and entering its comments

Although an alias initially inherits the icon of its original item, the alias does not inherit the comments or the locked attribute of its original item. Every new alias is initially unlocked and has no comments. You can type comments about an alias and lock the alias in its Info window, which you display by using the Finder's Get Info command. The Info window has a space where you can enter comments (see Chapter 5). The Info window also has a Locked option that you can turn on and off (see Chapter 5). Locking an alias prevents changing the name or icon of the alias — the same as locking any file. Locking an alias does not lock its original item.

Tip

You can create multiple aliases for the same original item so that you can access the original from different locations. Only disk space limits the number of aliases that you can create. To make aliases for several items in the same window at once, select them all and ⌘+Option+drag the group where you want the aliases or use the Make Alias command. An alias appears for each item that you selected. All the new aliases are automatically selected so that you can immediately drag them to another place without having to manually select them one by one.

Keeping Track of Original Items

Aliases are truly amazing at keeping track of their original items. Not only can you rename and move an alias's original item, but you also can replace it with another file that has the same name — all without breaking the link to the alias. You may wonder how the Mac OS can find an alias's original item after you rename or move the original item. If the Mac OS cannot find an item that has the same name and folder location as the original, it searches for the original item's unique *file ID number*, which the Mac OS internally assigns to each file. Once the Mac OS finds the item by using this ID number, it updates the alias with the original item's current name and folder location.

When you copy the original item referenced by an alias, the alias still points to the original item (not to the copy you just made). Sounds reasonable, but it doesn't feel reasonable when you want to move an alias's original item to a different disk. That's because moving and copying involve basically the same action — dragging an item. If you drag to a folder on the same disk, the Finder moves the item and the item's alias knows where to find the moved item. If you drag to a folder on another disk, the Finder copies the item. The alias knows where the original item is, but not the copy. If you then delete the original item (on the alias's disk), you break the alias's link to the item, even though a copy of the item exists on another disk.

Tip   There are (at least) two different ways that you can create an alias of an item on a remote volume over a network, but one method is less reliable than the other. The first method is to log into the remote volume from your computer, find the item you want to make an alias of, and then create the alias on your Mac. The second way is to go to the remote computer, mount your Mac's disk over the network, and then create the alias of the item on the remote computer and drag it to your Mac's disk. Both aliases will work in the future while your Mac is connected to the remote volume. But the alias created using the second method may end up orphaned when you're no longer connected to the remote volume. The alias created using the first method, on the other hand, will always attempt to connect to the remote volume over the network.

Fixing Orphaned Aliases

If you use an alias whose original item was deleted, the Mac OS tells you that it can't find the original item. Figure 14-3 shows the alert that you see in the Finder if the system can't resolve an alias.

Figure 14-3: Finder displays an alert when it can't find an alias's original item.

You see a somewhat different alert when you try to open an orphaned alias in a standard Open or Save dialog box. This alert is smaller and does not name the alias. Moreover, this alert simply tells you that the alias' original item can't be found, and doesn't allow you to fix the alias.

The Finder's alert has a Delete button and a Fix Alias button. Clicking Delete deletes the alias; clicking Fix Alias brings up a Fix Alias dialog box in which you can choose a new original for the alias. Figure 14-4 shows the Fix Alias dialog box in which you choose a new alias.

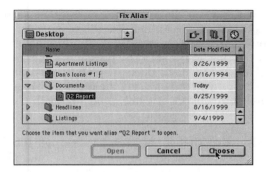

Figure 14-4: Choosing a new original for an orphaned alias

You can also use utility software to connect an orphaned alias to its original file or to a copy of the original. For example, Spring Cleaning from Aladdin Systems (http://www.aladdinsys.com) can list the orphaned aliases on a disk and help you delete or fix them. The shareware programs Alias Crony by Rocco Moliterno and AliasZoo by Cliff McCollum have similar capabilities (see Chapter 26). But it's often easier just to create a new alias and throw out the broken one.

Finding an Original Item

You can find an alias's original item by choosing Show Original from the Finder's File menu. The Show Original command brings up the window that contains the original item, scrolls the original item into view, and selects it. The Get Info command displays the alias's Info window. An alias's Info window reports the disk and folder path to the original. Figure 14-5 is an example of a Get Info window.

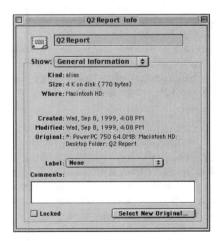

Figure 14-5: Checking alias information in the Get Info window

If you try to find an original item on a removable disk that's not currently inserted, the Finder usually asks you to insert that disk. The Finder also ejects any currently inserted disk of the same type (floppy disk, Zip disk, and so forth). This can lead to a vicious bout of disk swapping, which you can cut short by pressing ⌘+period (.) repeatedly until the Finder stops asking you to insert disks. Then put away the currently inserted disk (by dragging it to the Trash or using the Move To Trash command), insert the disk that contains the alias's original item, and try the Show Original command again.

Instead of asking you to insert a missing disk that contains an alias's original item, the Finder may display a message saying the original item couldn't be found. That happens with some types of removable hard disks unless another disk of the same type has been inserted since you started or restarted your computer.

Selecting a New Original Item

If desired, you can change an alias so that it opens a different item. Select the alias and use the Get Info command to display the alias's Info window. In the Info window, click the Select New Original button. This brings up a Fix Alias dialog box (shown in Figure 14-4), in which you select the item that you want to become the alias's new original item.

Discovering the Many Uses of Aliases

There are many useful applications for aliases. The most common is quick access to programs and documents with which you work frequently. For example, you can make an alias of a spreadsheet that you use regularly to update sales figures and place the alias in a convenient location, such as the desktop. Some of the most important uses of aliases include adding items to the Apple menu, Favorites,or the Startup Items folder; adding desktop convenience for accessing items; accessing archived information from removable disks; and streamlining access to shared items. The following sections provide a collection of scenarios to leverage the power of aliases, providing express service to a wide range of items.

Aliases in the Apple menu

The most convenient place from which to open application programs, desk accessories, control panels, documents, folders, and other items is the Apple menu. Because the Apple menu is always on the menu bar, items in the Apple menu are never more than a mouse click away. You can add to the Apple menu any item that you can open by using the Finder, including aliases.

Placing an alias in the Apple menu is as easy as dragging the alias icon to the Apple Menu Items folder, which is in the System Folder. The name of the alias appears instantly in the Apple menu in plain (not italic) text. Choosing the alias from the Apple menu opens the alias's original item. You don't have to restart your computer for changes to the Apple Menu Items folder to occur.

You can add as many aliases as you want to the Apple Menu Items folder. However, it's a good idea to keep the number within a reasonable range to avoid having to scroll through an extra-long menu. To remove an alias from the Apple menu, drag its icon out of the Apple Menu Items folder.

One way to shorten the Apple menu is to put some related aliases in a submenu. You do this by putting the aliases in a folder inside the Apple Menu Items folder, or by putting the alias of a folder (or a disk) in the Apple Menu Items folder. For example, during installation of the Mac OS, an alias of the Control Panels folder is placed in the Apple Menu Items folder, making all the control panels appear in a Control Panels submenu of the Apple menu. Another example: The Finder places folders named Recent Applications, Recent Documents, and Recent Servers in the Apple Menu Items folder and puts aliases of recently used items in those folders. What's more, you can get universal access to your entire hard disk (up to the first five levels of nested folders) by putting an alias of your hard disk in the Apple Menu Items folder. However, don't be surprised if the overhead of keeping all the resulting submenus up-to-date slows your system somewhat.

Note To see submenus in the Apple menu and to track recent items in submenus, you must have the options for submenus and recent items turned on in the Apple Menu Options control panel (as described in Chapter 7).

Adjusting an alias's position in the Apple menu

Items in the Apple menu appear alphabetically by name. You may want to change the name of your alias to adjust its position in the Apple menu. You can force an item to the top of the menu by putting a blank space at the beginning of its name or force it to the bottom of the list by beginning its name with a bullet (•).

Cross-Reference These and other techniques for organizing the Apple menu are described in more detail in Chapter 7.

Fast access to the Apple Menu Items folder

One useful alias that you can add to the Apple menu is an alias of the Apple Menu Items folder. Adding this alias enables you to quickly open the Apple Menu Items folder and to easily customize the Apple menu.

A frequent items menu

You can organize your frequently used items in the Apple menu by putting aliases of them in folders inside the Apple Menu Items folder. For example, you might have folders named Applications, Utilities, and Documents. (The folders create submenus in the Apple menu if you have the Submenus option turned on in the Apple Menu Options control panel.) The problem with this scheme is the time it takes to make aliases and place them in the appropriate folders.

An efficient way to manage favorite items in the Apple menu is to create a folder named Frequent Items and leave it open as a pop-up window. Put an alias of the Frequent Items folder in the Apple Menu Items folder. Now the contents of the pop-up window appear as a submenu in the Apple menu. You can easily add and remove items from this submenu by dragging the corresponding items (preferably aliases) in and out of the pop-up window.

Universal Show Clipboard

Some application programs lack a Show Clipboard command and others that have one use a private clipboard whose contents may look different when pasted in another program. With an alias, you can put a Show Clipboard command in your Apple menu for reviewing the standard Clipboard contents from any application program. First, make an alias of the Clipboard file, which is in the System Folder. Then place the alias in the Apple Menu Items folder and rename the alias Show Clipboard. Now, choosing Show Clipboard from the Apple menu switches to the Finder and opens the Clipboard.

Aliases on the desktop

Other than the Apple menu, the desktop is the most accessible place for opening items and the most accessible place for folders to which you want to drag items. Rather than drag frequently used programs, control panels, documents, and folders themselves to the desktop, make aliases of them and put the aliases on the desktop. Aliases on the desktop give you immediate access to items buried deep within nests of folders.

Putting aliases of programs on the desktop avoids the problems that can occur when you move the programs themselves to the desktop. Some programs depend on support files being with them in the same folder (or on the desktop). For example, a word processor may also need a dictionary file on the desktop in order to check spelling. Aliases save you the hassle of guessing which support files a program needs to run correctly and avoid the mess that may result when you place those support files on the desktop. By creating an alias for an application, the alias accesses the original application in its folder, saving you from moving the application and its supporting files to get full access to the application.

By making aliases of documents and programs that you use frequently and putting the aliases on the desktop, you don't have to always remember where you put the original items. Also, you can open several related items at the same time, even if the original items happen to be in different folders or on different disks, by opening aliases on the desktop.

Getting at buried desktop aliases

When windows of background applications cover desktop aliases, you can hide those windows by choosing Hide Others from the Application menu.

When windows of the foreground application cover desktop icons, you can collapse the windows. Click each window's collapse box, or Option+click any window's collapse box to collapse all the active application's windows. You can also collapse a window, or Option+double-click to collapse all windows, if the Double-click title bar to collapse option is turned on in the Appearance control panel. When this option is turned on, you can collapse a background window of the active application (but not a window of a background application) by ⌘+double-clicking its title bar.

You can also close all the active application's windows at once by Option+clicking the close box of any window.

Clearing the desktop of alias clutter

If your desktop becomes too cluttered with aliases, you can put related aliases together in folders on the desktop. You can make these folders even more accessible by putting them (or aliases of them) in the Apple Menu Items folder. Choosing a folder from the Apple menu opens it and brings its window to the front even if the Finder was not the active application.

You can also put a folder full of aliases anywhere, open it, and drag its window to the bottom of the screen to make it a pop-up window. To see how this works, try opening the Favorites folder (choose it from the Apple menu) and drag its window to the bottom of the screen to make it a pop-up window.

Multiple trash cans

If you have a big monitor, put aliases of the Trash in the upper-left and lower-left corners of the desktop. The extra Trash icons expedite discarding items when you're working on the left side of the desktop. Extending this idea, if you have two monitors, put a Trash alias on the desktop of the second monitor. That way, you never have to drag icons across two screens to throw them away.

"Eject disk" icon

In a few minutes you can solve a problem that has bothered Mac OS users since day one — the customary but dumb method of removing a disk from the Mac by dragging the disk icon to the Trash. You simply make an alias of the Trash, change the alias's name to Eject Disk, and paste a custom icon in the alias's Get Info window. Make the custom icon look like a hand removing a disk or a disk with an arrow pointing in the direction of ejection. Figure 14-6 is an example of an "eject disk" icon.

Figure 14-6: For removing disks, try an alias of the Trash with a custom icon.

Open, Save, and Navigation Services shortcuts

Alias names appear in italics in dialog boxes that list folder and disk contents. These dialog boxes include the Open and Save dialog boxes as well as the Navigation Services dialog boxes. Opening an alias in these dialog boxes (by double-clicking it, for instance) opens its original item. Instead of opening an alias's original item, you can quickly select the original item in an Open, Save, or Navigation Services dialog box by pressing Option while opening the alias. In this case, the system opens the folder containing the original item and selects the original item (but does not open the original item). Figure 14-7 is an example of an alias in Open and Navigation Services dialog boxes.

Figure 14-7: Alias names are italicized in an Open dialog box (top) and in the Navigation Services Open dialog box (bottom).

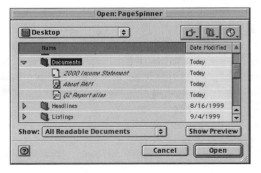

To make an alias appear near the top of the list in Open, Save, and Navigation Services dialog boxes, put a blank space at the beginning of the alias's name. Items having initial blank spaces in their names float alphabetically to the top of the list in an Open, Save, or Navigation Services dialog box. (When you view the desktop level in an Open or Save dialog box, disks always appear at the top of the list above all other items. Navigation Services dialog boxes intermingle disks with other desktop items.)

If you don't like how initial spaces look, you can paste a blank line at the beginning of each name that you want to appear at the top of the list. Create the blank line by pressing Return in the Note Pad or any word processor.

 For step-by-step instructions and a caveat, see Chapter 7.

Aliases as startup items

Every time you start (or restart) your computer, or when you log in using your Multiple Users name and password, the Finder automatically opens everything in your Startup Items folder. If you regularly use a particular program, you may want it ready to go immediately after you start your computer. But some programs must remain in a folder with other auxiliary files and won't work correctly if you move their icons to the Startup Items folder. Furthermore, returning items to their previous locations when you no longer want them opened at startup time can be a drag.

Moving an alias of a program, document, or other item to your Startup Items folder causes the original item to open during startup. To remove an alias from the startup sequence, drag it out of the folder.

Application programs in your Startup Items folder open in alphabetical order, so you can rename the alias of an application program to determine when it starts relative to other application programs in that folder. Aliases of applications, desk accessories, control panels, and folders open alphabetically after all application programs and other non-alias items have opened.

 For more information about the Startup Items folder, see Chapter 7.

Startup messages

Do you like to have reminders at startup, but don't want to use the Stickies program? Create a clipping file of your notes, and place an alias of it in the Startup Items folder. Rename it to be alphabetically last (for example, "zzNotes") so that it opens after other startup items. At startup, the Finder does not have to launch an application to display the note, which you can easily dismiss by pressing ⌘+W. If you keep the clipping on your desktop, you can view it anytime you want, within seconds. You can use a startup clipping in a lab setting to display general notes, update information, disclaimers, warnings, and so on.

Quick access to favorite folders

For quick access to a favorite folder in Open and Save dialog boxes, put an alias of the folder on the desktop. In an Open or Save dialog box, you can quickly get to aliases of favorite folders at the desktop level by clicking the Desktop button. Instead of working your way down through one branch of your folder structure and then working your way up another branch to the folder you want, you zip to the desktop level and there open the alias of the folder you want. It's as if you can jump from one branch of a tree to root level and then jump to a spot on another branch on another tree without having to crawl up the trunk and along the other branch.

Chances are you will only use aliases of favorite folders in Open and Save dialog boxes, never in the Finder. You also don't need to use desktop aliases of favorite folders in Navigation Services dialog boxes, where you can use the Favorites button instead (see Chapter 7).

The specially named folder alias doesn't have to clutter your desktop to appear at the desktop level of Open and Save dialog boxes. Simply drag the alias to the bottom of the screen so that the alias name and most of its icon are out of view below the edge of the screen. Then cover up the remaining visible part of the icon by placing a pop-up window over it. (If you try to put an icon too low on the screen, the Finder automatically moves the alias back up to the desktop. Try again, but don't drag the icon quite so low this time.)

 Cross-Reference   For information on creating clipping files, see Chapter 7.

Audio CD autoplay

Would you like to have an audio CD play when you start your Mac? Putting an alias of any track from any audio CD into the Startup Items folder has the Finder automatically launch AppleCD Audio Player during startup and begin playing whatever CD is in the drive at that track. The track alias works with any audio CD, not just the one used to make the alias. If there's no CD in the drive, the Mac requests one. You can get a similar effect with the Enable Audio CD AutoPlay option in the QuickTime Settings control panel (see Chapter 18). The control panel option always starts at track 1, but you can make an alias to start with any track.

Abridged System Folder

Aliases can help you quickly find folders in the System Folder whose contents you need to get at, such as the Startup Items folder and the Fonts folder. Here's how: Make aliases for the System Folder items you access often — including the System Folder itself — and put all those aliases in a new folder. You can open and find an item in that new folder faster than in the System Folder. To make the new folder look like a System Folder, copy the icon from the System Folder's Info window and paste it in the new folder's Info window.

Aliases of items on removable disks

You can use aliases to keep track of and to quickly open items on removable disks — even the ones that aren't currently inserted. For example, you can keep the installation software for applications that you download from the Internet on removable hard disks and make an alias of each installation folder or installer program in a folder named Installers on your main hard drive. Then when you need to reinstall some software, you can quickly open the appropriate alias in your Installers folder. The system tells you the name of the disk to insert so that it can open the alias's original item.

> **Tip** A single floppy disk or a folder on a removable disk can use aliases to store hundreds of interesting icons for later use as custom icons for any file, folder, or disk. Just make aliases of files, folders, or disks having icons that you want to save and copy the aliases to a floppy named Personal Icon Library. Whenever you want to use one of the custom icons from the floppy disk, copy the icon from the alias's Info window. Then paste it in the Info window of the file, folder, or disk whose icon you want to customize (as described in Chapter 4).

Be sure to make aliases of archived items *after* copying them to removable disks, not before. If you make aliases of the items while they are still on the hard disk, the aliases stop working when you delete the original items from the hard disk after copying them to a removable disk. (Remember, aliases point to the original items, not to copies of the originals on other disks.)

Aliases of shared items

The file-sharing capabilities of the Mac OS enable you to share items from someone else's computer if it is connected to the same network as yours. But getting access to shared items involves wading through a fair amount of bureaucracy in the Chooser or Network Browser.

Aliases cut through the red tape. Here's how: You access a shared disk or folder once by using the Chooser or Network Browser (see Chapter 21). Next, select the shared item or any folder or file in it and make an alias of it on your hard disk. An alias keeps track of its original item even when the original item is on another networked Mac. Figure 14-8 shows some aliases of shared items.

Figure 14-8: Aliases of a shared disk, a shared folder that you can't access, and a shared folder

Once you make an alias of a shared item, you can get to the shared item by opening the alias. Dragging something to the alias of a shared disk or folder also automatically accesses that shared item. You still must enter a password unless you initially access the original item as a guest. (If you've added this password to your keychain, you won't need to enter the password.) If the shared item is not available—for example, because the Mac on which it resides is turned off—then the Finder tells you that it cannot find the item on the network.

Sometimes when you try to open an alias of a shared item, an alert tells you that the alias's original item can't be found. An alias of a shared item may stop working for many reasons. Your Mac may be disconnected from the network, or the AppleTalk control panel may be set incorrectly (see Chapter 20). The file server where the original shared item is located may be shut down or disconnected from the network. If the file server is someone's personal computer, that person may simply have turned off Mac OS file sharing (see Chapter 22). If the computer is a PowerBook, it may be in sleep mode (sleep mode does not disable file sharing on a desktop Mac).

An alias of a shared item may not work correctly if the shared item is located on a file server that does not use the Mac OS. For instance, file servers in some organizations use the Windows NT operating system. Windows NT's Services for Macintosh feature enables Macs to connect to and use files on a Windows NT computer, but some versions of Windows NT have trouble with aliases. Updating Windows NT to the latest version usually clears up this trouble.

Server access from the Save dialog box

Don't you hate it when you get into a Save dialog box only to realize that you want to save on a server volume that you're not connected to? You don't have to cancel the Save dialog box, mount the server volume, and choose Save again if you take the time to make an alias of your Recent Servers folder and put it on your desktop. You can open that alias and get at recently used servers quite easily from within any Save dialog box. (Click Desktop in the Save dialog box for fast access to the Recent Servers alias.) If you find that the server you want to use is not included in the Recent Servers folder because you have not accessed it as recently as the servers that are included, you need to increase the number of servers that the Finder keeps track of in this folder. To do that, use the Apple Menu Options control panel (see Chapter 7).

Aliases of remote shared items

Not only do aliases work across a local network, they also work across a remote network connection made with Apple Remote Access (ARA, which is described in Chapter 20). If you create an alias of a remote file, folder, or disk, disconnect the remote network, and then open the alias, the Mac OS tries to make the remote network connection again automatically.

Instead of locating the alias's original item on the remote network as it should, the Mac OS may locate another item that coincidentally has the same name on your local network. Sound far-fetched? Suppose the alias's original item is a shared disk with a common name, such as "Macintosh HD," on a remote Mac with a common name, such as "Power Mac 7600." Further suppose that your Mac is connected to a local network on which someone is sharing a hard disk named "Macintosh HD" from a Mac named "Power Mac 7600." If you double-click the alias, your system will open the Macintosh HD on your local network, not the one on the remote network. A similar situation can occur if you sometimes connect to two remote Macs that are named alike and have shared hard disks with the same names.

Situations like these can develop unexpectedly when someone changes the name of a Mac or a shared disk; suddenly you discover that double-clicking an alias opens the wrong item. What's worse, the Mac OS updates the alias so that it now points to the wrong item. Even after you fix the conflicting aliases by changing one of the original item's names, the alias will continue representing the wrong item.

If an alias starts referring to an item on the wrong network or the wrong computer, delete the alias and make a new one. To prevent future problems, suggest to the owners of the computers with identical names that they give their computers and their hard disks unique names.

Your office on disk

Aliases can give you nearly automatic access to your computer's hard disks by using a removable disk in any other computer on the same network. To set up access to your office from a removable disk, follow these steps:

1. Make sure that file sharing is turned on (see Chapter 22).

2. Select all your hard disk icons. Then choose Sharing from the Get Info submenu of the File menu. The Sharing command displays sharing privileges in a separate window for each selected disk.

3. In each sharing privileges window, set the options as shown in the figure. These settings restrict access to your disks so that only you can make changes or see files or folders.

Continued

(continued)

4. Make an alias of each hard disk and copy the aliases to a removable disk.

Now you can use that removable disk to access your hard disk from any Mac on your network, as long as file sharing is active on your Mac. You simply insert the disk, open the alias for the disk you want to use, and enter your password when asked. Correctly entering your password gives you access to all applications, folders, and documents on your disk from any remote computer. You don't have to open the Chooser or Network Browser on a borrowed computer, select your computer, and type your name as the registered user.

An alias's alias for network administrators

When you move a drive from one AppleShare file server to another, network users have to tediously search all servers (by using the Chooser or the Network Browser) for the moved drive unless you inform them of its new location. That may happen if, for example, you have to move a shared drive from a busy server to an idle server or from a server needing repair to a temporary substitute.

You can solve this problem by creating an alias of an alias of every shared hard disk by following these steps:

1. Working from a shared hard disk that is always available to everyone, create an alias of every shared hard disk on the network.

2. Create aliases of those hard-drive aliases and copy the second set of aliases to each user's Mac.

With the double aliases in place, a shared hard disk named Crown Jewels, for example, can be accessed by double-clicking the alias named "Crown Jewels alias alias" on any user's Mac. That alias points to the alias "Crown Jewels alias" on the always-available shared drive, which in turn points to Crown Jewels itself.

Now, if you move Crown Jewels to a different file server, you merely make a new alias to replace the old Crown Jewels alias on the always-available shared drive. You do not have to update users' copies of "Crown Jewels alias alias," and users do not need to know that Crown Jewels was moved.

This example uses the initial alias names that the Mac generates, but you can rename aliases freely. For example, both the alias and the alias's alias could be named Crown Jewels like the hard disk.

Aliases keep shared documents current

Besides providing easy access to shared items from other computers, aliases can help make sure that others who share your documents have the latest versions.

Suppose, for example, that you create a letter template that you want the rest of your group to use. By making an alias of the template and copying it to a shared folder, other users can copy the alias to their disks and use the alias to open the original template. If you later replace the original template with a version having the same name, the aliases that people already copied will open the new version. Users who share the alias always get the newest version of the original item it represents, even when the original frequently changes.

The only drawback to using an alias to share a template is that unless you're using a program that allows more than one person to open the same document, only one person can access the template document at a time. However, anyone who opens the template can quickly and easily save it with a different name and then close it to free it for someone else to open.

Summary

This chapter showed you many different things that can be done with the Mac OS's capability to create aliases. An alias is a file that represents another item, such as a program, document, folder, or disk. Opening an alias or dragging something to an alias in the Finder has the same effect as opening or dragging to the alias's original item. But you can rename, move, or copy an alias or give it a custom icon without affecting its original item and without breaking the link between the alias and its original. An alias stays linked to its original item even if you move or rename the original. To see an alias's original item, use the Finder's Show Original command.

Aliases have a multitude of uses, some of which this chapter described. You can use aliases to add items to the Apple menu and Startup Items folder. You can use an alias to make a universal Show Clipboard command. An alias can be an "eject disk" icon on the desktop and can provide shortcuts in Open, Save, and Navigation Services dialog boxes. Aliases are also useful for archiving files on removable disks and for easily accessing shared disks and folders. This chapter also described many other uses and tricks for using aliases.

✦   ✦   ✦

Take Charge of Your Fonts

With the original Mac OS font technology, text looked great when displayed or printed as long as you stuck to a half-dozen font sizes — usually 9, 10, 12, 14, 18, and 24 points. Apple's TrueType font technology, a standard part of Mac OS 9 (introduced in System 6.0.8), makes odd sizes and big sizes like 11, 13, 36, 100, and 197 points look just as good. PostScript fonts are generally used in professional settings to get the highest print quality. Whatever your project, though, it's easy to set up the Mac OS to make fonts look good.

Introducing Fonts

Your computer can display and print text in three types of fonts: fixed-size, TrueType, and PostScript. Which looks best depends on the font size and the output device (display screen or type of printer).

Fixed-size fonts

Originally, all Macs used fixed-size fonts to display text onscreen and to print on many types of printers. A *fixed-size* font contains exact pictures of every letter, digit, and symbol for one size of a font. Fixed-size fonts often are called *bitmap fonts* because each picture precisely maps the dots, or *bits,* to be displayed or printed for one character. Figure 15-1 shows the dots in an enlarged view of a couple of fixed-size letters.

Figure 15-1: Courier capital A and G bitmaps at fixed sizes 12, 14, and 18 points (enlarged to show detail)

Each fixed-size font looks great in one size only, so fixed-size fonts usually are installed in sets. A typical set includes 9-, 10-, 12-, 14-, 18-, and 24-point sizes. If you need text in a size for which no fixed-size font is installed, the Mac OS must scale a fixed-size font's character bitmaps up or down to the size you want. The results are lumpy, misshapen, or blocky, as shown in Figure 15-2.

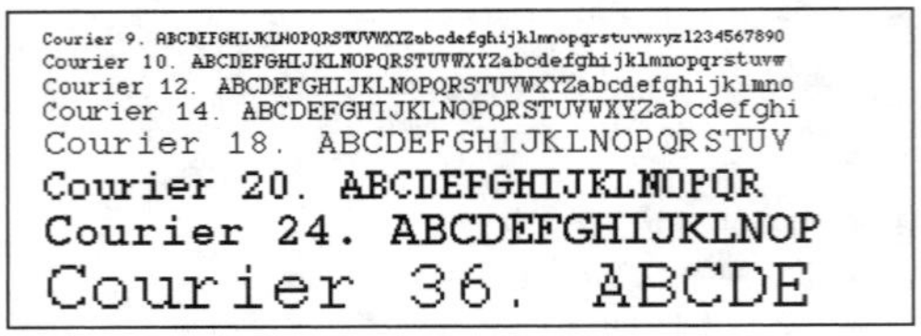

```
Courier 9.  ABCDEFGHIJKLMNOPQRSTUVWXYZabcdefghijklmnopqrstuvwxyz1234567890
Courier 10. ABCDEFGHIJKLMNOPQRSTUVWXYZabcdefghijklmnopqrstuvw
Courier 12.  ABCDEFGHIJKLMNOPQRSTUVWXYZabcdefghijklmno
Courier 14.  ABCDEFGHIJKLNOPQRSTUVWXYZabcdefghi
Courier 18.  ABCDEFGHIJKLNOPQRSTUV
Courier 20.  ABCDEFGHIJKLMNOPQR
Courier 24.  ABCDEFGHIJKLNOP
Courier 36.  ABCDE
```

Figure 15-2: Fixed-size fonts look best at installed sizes — note the blockiness of the 20- and 36-point font sizes.

TrueType fonts

TrueType is a variable-size font technology. Instead of fixed-size bitmaps, TrueType fonts use curves and straight lines to outline each character's shape. Because TrueType fonts are based on outlines, they sometimes are called *outline fonts*. Figure 15-3 is the outline of an example TrueType letter.

Figure 15-3: TrueType Times New Roman capital G

TrueType fonts look good at all sizes. They work with all Mac OS applications and all types of printers, including PostScript printers. The Mac OS smoothly scales a TrueType font's character outlines to any size on a display screen and on printers of any resolution, all with equally good results. The Mac OS also lets you mix TrueType fonts with fixed-size and PostScript fonts. Figure 15-4 is an example of TrueType font scaling.

```
Times 9. ABCDEFGHIJKLMNOPQRSTUVWXYZabcdefghijklmnopqrstuvwxyz1234567890
Times 10. ABCDEFGHIJKLMNOPQRSTUVWXYZabcdefghijklmnopqrstuvwxyz123
Times 12. ABCDEFGHIJKLMNOPQRSTUVWXYZabcdefghijklmnopq
Times 14. ABCDEFGHIJKLMNOPQRSTUVWXYZabcdefgh
Times 18. ABCDEFGHIJKLMNOPQRSTUVW
Times 24. ABCDEFGHIJKLMNOP
Times 36. ABCDEFGH
```

Figure 15-4: TrueType fonts scale smoothly to all sizes and resolutions.

PostScript fonts

TrueType fonts look great in any size displayed onscreen or output on any printer, but they are not alone. *PostScript* fonts were the first to look great at any size and any resolution. They use an outline font technology invented by Adobe Systems. It's similar to TrueType but differs in how it mathematically specifies font outlines and how it adjusts the outlines for small font sizes and low resolutions.

There are actually two main types of PostScript fonts, imaginatively called Type 1 and Type 3. Most of the PostScript fonts you see nowadays are Type 1 because they yield better results at small font sizes and low resolutions. Although Type 1 fonts generally look better, Type 3 fonts can be more elaborate. The characters in Type 3 fonts can have variable stroke weights and they can be filled with something other than a solid color, such as shades of gray or blends that go from white to black.

Although PostScript fonts originally were designed for printing on LaserWriters and other PostScript output devices, Adobe Type Manager (ATM) software smoothly scales PostScript fonts to any size for non-PostScript printers and the display screen, just like TrueType. With ATM and PostScript fonts, you don't need a set of fixed-size or TrueType fonts for the screen display. ATM is included with Adobe Acrobat Reader, which is available on the Mac OS 9 CD-ROM, as described in "Setting Font Options," later in this chapter.

To make use of ATM, you must buy (or download, if you find some freeware or shareware Type 1 fonts) PostScript fonts for your System Folder — fonts built into your printer don't help. The Adobe Type Basics package includes the 11 standard LaserWriter font families — Avant Garde, Bookman, Courier, Helvetica, Helvetica Narrow, New Century Schoolbook, Palatino, Symbol, Times, Zapf Chancery, and Zapf Dingbats — along with 15 other font families. You'll find information on using ATM in the next section, "Managing Fonts." For more sources of fonts, see "Obtaining Fonts" at the end of this chapter.

TrueType fonts cannot replace PostScript for a number of reasons. For one, PostScript fonts include a lot of information in the font itself that TrueType doesn't, such as kerning information and hints that help the font look better at different sizes. In addition, PostScript offers more than outline fonts. It's a *page description language* that precisely specifies the location and other characteristics of every text and graphic item on the page.

PostScript or TrueType?

Which type of outline font should you use, TrueType or PostScript? Many longtime Mac OS users have invested thousands of dollars in PostScript fonts, and for them it makes sense to stick with PostScript and ATM. But PostScript fonts are messier than TrueType fonts. With PostScript fonts, each style of a font — bold, italic, bold italic, plain, and so on — is a different file on your hard disk. Moreover, PostScript font file names can be hard to figure out because they're a contraction of the full font name plus style name. For example, Helvetica Bold Italic has the file name HelveBolIta, and Garamond Demi Book comes out GaramDemBoo. So, just to have the basic four font styles of a font you must have four PostScript font files.

But that's not all. In addition, for each PostScript font family such as Times or Helvetica, you must also have at least one size of the same fixed-size font installed. ATM can't jigger the system without that fixed-size font. For example, to go with the four PostScript fonts AGarBol, AGarBolIta, AGarIta, and AGarReg you must also have at least one Adobe Garamond fixed-size font such as AGaramond 12.

In contrast, with most TrueType fonts you have just one item to deal with, a *font suitcase*. (Font suitcases are covered in the "Managing Fonts" section.)

If you don't already have a collection of PostScript fonts, and especially if you don't print on PostScript printers, it is preferable to use TrueType fonts. More PostScript fonts are available than TrueType, but TrueType fonts sometimes cost less, and some are even free. For example, every version of the Mac OS from 7.0 onward includes TrueType versions of at least the Times, Helvetica, Courier, and Symbol fonts. Also, many applications from Apple (and its former subsidiary Claris) and Microsoft come with an assortment of TrueType fonts. You can even find free TrueType fonts available for downloading from Microsoft's (http://www.microsoft.com/truetype/) and Apple's (http://asu.info.apple.com/) Web sites.

In fact, you will probably end up with a mixture of TrueType and PostScript fonts. This situation is perfectly acceptable. You can even use TrueType and PostScript fonts in the same document. However, it's best to avoid having TrueType and PostScript fonts with the same name on your computer. If you do, the Mac uses TrueType to display the document and PostScript to print it (on a PostScript printer), and you may notice differences in line lengths, line breaks, and page breaks between the displayed TrueType and the printed PostScript.

How to recognize the best font sizes

You can usually tell which font sizes will look good onscreen by inspecting the Font menu of a program that you're using. The program highlights the best-looking sizes with outline-style numbers. All sizes of a TrueType font are highlighted. (If you have PostScript fonts and ATM installed, all the sizes are outlined.) Only the installed sizes of fixed-size fonts are highlighted, as shown in Figure 15-5.

Figure 15-5: Smooth sizes are outlined.

Font styles and families

Text varies by style as well as size. The Mac OS can display and print four basic styles — plain, bold, italic, and bold italic — and many others (as listed in your friendly Style menu in most text-oriented applications). The Mac OS can derive various styles by modifying the plain style, but you get better-looking results by installing separate styled versions of fonts. Many fixed-size, TrueType, and PostScript fonts come in the four basic styles. Some PostScript font families include 20 or more styled versions. The styled versions together with the plain version of a font are known as a *font family.*

Managing Fonts

A basic set of fonts comes with the Mac OS. You can add more fonts whenever you need to use them and you can remove fonts that you no longer need to use. In addition, you can display samples of your fonts.

Tip   A number of utility programs exist to help manage your fonts if you have a lot of fonts installed. These utilities generally enable you to store different sets of fonts and automatically move them in and out of the Fonts folder as needed. For example, you can create special sets of fonts for different projects and applications. Two such utilities are Suitcase from Extensis (800-796-9798; http://www.extensis.com) and MasterJuggler Pro from Alsoft (800-257-6381, http://www.alsoft.com).

Fonts and font suitcases

The fonts you see in Font menus are represented in the Finder by icons. Each type of font has a distinctive icon. The icon of a fixed-size font bears a single capital A. A TrueType font's icon has three capital As, each a different size to suggest the variable sizing of the font. The icons of PostScript fonts may look like a generic laser printer, or they may have custom graphics designed by the companies that make the fonts. Figure 15-6 shows examples of different font icons.

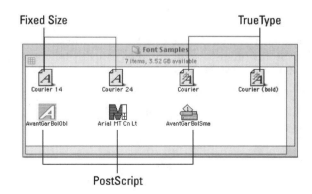

Figure 15-6: Each type of font file has a different icon in Finder.

For convenience, TrueType and fixed-size fonts are usually kept in *font suitcases*. You can think of font suitcases as special folders for holding fonts. Each font suitcase generally holds related fonts (although they don't have to), such as the different sizes in a set of fixed-size fonts or the different styles of a TrueType font family. Font suitcases can't contain PostScript fonts. Figure 15-7 is an example of a font suitcase.

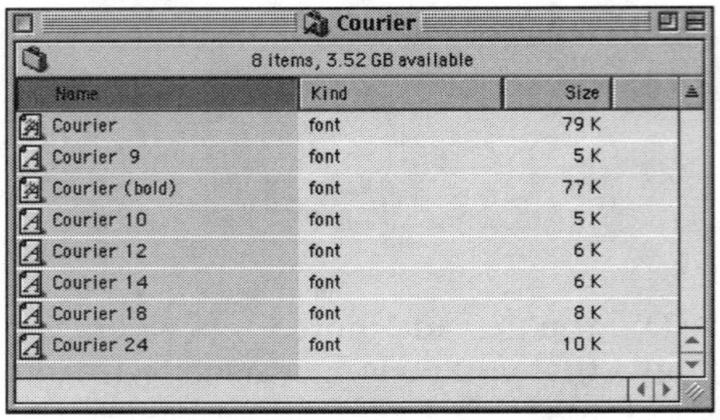

Figure 15-7: Font suitcases contain fixed-size and TrueType fonts.

You can create a new font suitcase by duplicating an existing font suitcase, opening the duplicate, and dragging the contents of the duplicate to the Trash. You can put any number of fonts in a suitcase as long as the total size doesn't exceed 16MB.

Adding fonts

To make a font available in your applications' Font menus, you add the font to the Fonts folder that is in your System Folder. The simplest way to add fonts is to drag their icons to the System Folder icon (not the System Folder window). You can drag font suitcases, folders containing fonts, or loose fonts to the System Folder icon. The Finder knows to put the fonts and font suitcases in the Fonts folder. However, the Finder does not distribute items for you if you drag them to the System Folder window instead of the System Folder icon. Figure 15-8 shows a font being dragged to the System Folder icon.

Before putting the fonts where they belong, the Finder displays an alert asking if that's what you want to do. This alert lets you know that the Finder has recognized the items you dragged to the System Folder icon, and it gets your OK before putting them in their places. Figure 15-9 is an example of the alert.

If you prefer, you can drag TrueType, PostScript, and fixed-size fonts directly to the Fonts folder icon. You also can open the Fonts folder and drag TrueType, PostScript, and fixed-size fonts to its window.

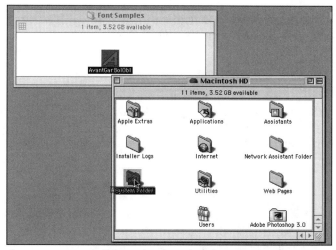

Figure 15-8: Install fonts by dragging them to the System Folder icon.

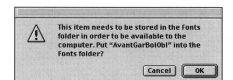

Figure 15-9: Finder knows where fonts go.

Newly added fonts become available in an application the next time you open it. If an application is open when you add fonts or font suitcases to your Fonts folder, you must quit the application and open it again to use the added fonts. The Finder displays an alert that notifies you when this condition exists.

Removing fonts

When you no longer want to use a font, you remove it or the suitcase that contains it from your Fonts folder. You can drag fonts and suitcases from the Fonts folder to another folder, the desktop, or the Trash. All applications except the Finder must be closed before you can remove any TrueType or fixed-size fonts from the Fonts folder. You can remove PostScript fonts any time. If you want to remove PostScript fonts but can't find them in the Fonts folder, look in the Extensions folder and the System folder. (PostScript fonts went in the Extensions folder or the System Folder prior to System 7.1.)

By removing unneeded font suitcases and loose fonts from your Fonts folder, you make your system perform better. Many applications start faster with fewer fonts, because it takes less time to initialize their Font menus. A shorter Font menu is easier to use as well.

Viewing font samples

You can see a sample of any TrueType or fixed-size font by opening the font. When you open a font suitcase, you see a window of fonts, not a font sample. Opening one of these fonts shows you a sample of it. Figure 15-10 shows examples of TrueType and fixed-size font samples.

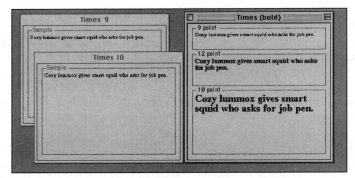

Figure 15-10: TrueType and fixed-size font samples

The Mac OS doesn't display samples of PostScript fonts. If you open a PostScript font, the Finder displays a message that describes the font and tells you to put it in your Fonts folder. Remember that each PostScript font in your Fonts folder should also have a corresponding fixed-size or TrueType font installed. If you want to see a sample of a PostScript font, open the corresponding fixed-size or TrueType font instead.

Setting Font Options

Although the Mac OS handles font display and printing automatically, you can set a few options that affect how fonts look. You can set a font-smoothing option in the Appearance manager, for example. If you use ATM with any Mac OS version, you can adjust how it scales PostScript fonts.

Font smoothing

Mac OS 9 can smooth fonts on screen by blending their jagged edges with the background color. This process is called *antialiasing*. You turn font smoothing on or off in the Font section of the Appearance control panel. When font smoothing is turned on, you can also specify the smallest font size that you want smoothed. The Mac OS will antialias all TrueType fonts this size or larger on monitors set to display at least 256 colors or grays (see Chapter 12). The Mac OS will not antialias any fixed size (bitmap) fonts. ATM, as described next, handles antialiasing of PostScript fonts. Figure 15-11 shows the font smoothing options in the Appearance control panel.

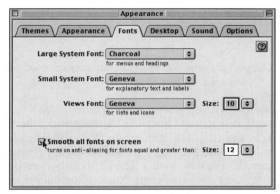

Figure 15-11: Setting font smoothing options in the Appearance control panel

Adobe Type Manager

You can set several options that affect how the optional Adobe Type Manager (ATM) software scales PostScript fonts onscreen and on printers that don't use PostScript. In addition, you can set options that affect ATM's performance. You make these settings in the ATM control panel. Figure 15-12 shows the ATM control panel.

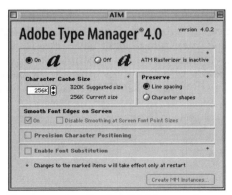

Figure 15-12: Setting ATM font options

Note   Abode Type Manager is only required if you're using PostScript fonts. If you don't find ATM in your Control Panels menu, you can install it by installing Adobe Acrobat, which may be included on the Mac OS 9 installation CD. If Acrobat isn't included on your Mac OS CD, you can download it from http://www.adobe. com/products/acrobat/. Note that ATM version 4.5.2 or higher is required with Mac OS 9 — other versions will crash and may keep your Mac from booting if installed. The ATM Deluxe control panel may also crash Mac OS 9 if it hasn't been updated to version 2.5.2 or higher.

ATM options

The Character Cache option affects performance. If applications seem to scroll more slowly with ATM turned on, try increasing this size.

The Preserve option determines whether ATM preserves line spacing or character shapes when it scales text. Preserving line spacing keeps line breaks and page breaks from changing with and without ATM, but this setting may clip the bottoms of some letters and vertically compress some accented capital letters. Preserving character shapes reduces the clipping but may change line breaks. The clipping occurs only onscreen and on output devices that don't use PostScript. No clipping occurs on a PostScript printer.

The Smooth Font Edges on Screen option smoothes font edges onscreen in the same way the Appearance control panel does, by blending their jagged edges with the background color. Whereas Appearance works with all TrueType fonts, ATM works on Type 1 PostScript fonts. ATM can antialias color text only when the monitor is set to display thousands or millions of colors. If the monitor is set to display 256 colors, ATM can antialias only black-and-white text.

The Precision Character Positioning option displays more accurate spacing, especially at small font sizes. Turning on this option causes ATM to calculate character positions on a fractional pixel basis, which may slow text display of some documents on slower computers.

The version of ATM included with Adobe Acrobat Reader does not have all the features of ATM Deluxe. ATM Deluxe can create substitute fonts dynamically when you open a document that contains fonts your system doesn't have. This font substitution feature preserves line breaks in documents but only approximates the look of missing fonts. Other ATM Deluxe features facilitate reviewing, organizing, adding, and removing large numbers of fonts. Adobe sells ATM Deluxe separately (408-536-6000, http://www.adobe.com).

Determining Font Priorities

If your Fonts folder contains fixed-size, TrueType, and PostScript versions of the same font, you may wonder how you specify the one you want to use. In fact, you don't specify. The Mac OS picks one for you according to its own priorities. These priorities are different for the display screen, a PostScript printer, and a printer that doesn't use PostScript.

Displaying fonts on screen

For screen display, the Mac OS first tries to find a fixed-size font in the exact size needed. If it can't find that, it looks for a TrueType version of the font that it can scale to the needed size. Lacking that, it tries to have ATM, if installed, scale a PostScript font to the needed size. ATM Deluxe can even use Adobe Multiple Master fonts to display temporary substitutes that closely match PostScript fonts not installed on your computer. If no other font is available, the Mac OS scales the best-available fixed-size font.

When both fixed-size and TrueType versions of the same font are present, the Mac OS always derives styled fonts from the fixed-size version, even if a styled TrueType version is installed. For example, if you have a fixed-size 12-point Times plain and a TrueType Times italic installed (but no fixed-size 12-point Times italic), the Mac OS derives a 12-point Times italic by slanting the fixed-size 12-point Times.

Individual programs can tell the Mac OS to ignore fixed-size fonts if a TrueType equivalent is available, and current versions of many popular programs now work this way. You may be able to turn this behavior on and off in some of your programs. Check each program's preference settings for one that tells the program that you prefer outline fonts. A decision to ignore fixed-size fonts in one program does not affect other programs — the Mac OS always prefers fixed-size fonts unless an application specifically overrides it.

Printing fonts on PostScript printers

When choosing among fixed-size, TrueType, or PostScript versions of the same font for printing on a PostScript printer, the Mac OS looks first for a PostScript font from the printer's ROM, RAM, or hard disk (if any). If the printer doesn't have the PostScript font, the Mac OS tries to download (copy) it from the computer's Fonts folder, Extensions folder, or System Folder. Failing that, the Mac OS tries to use a TrueType font; as a last resort, the Mac OS uses a fixed-size font.

If the Mac OS can find no PostScript equivalent for a TrueType font, it sends the TrueType font to the printer before sending the document to be printed. If the printer is one that can't handle TrueType fonts, the Mac OS converts the TrueType font to PostScript, with some loss of quality at small point sizes, and sends that. Either way, sending fonts causes a significant delay on many printers. If you use TrueType-only fonts with a PostScript printer that has its own hard disk or a large amount of memory, you may be able to reduce printing time by downloading (sending) the TrueType fonts to the printer in advance of printing documents. Fonts you download to a printer's hard disk remain there unless you remove them. Fonts you download to a printer's memory remain there until you turn off the printer, or (in some cases) until someone else prints on the printer with a different version of printer software than you use.

Printing fonts on a non-PostScript device

On a printer or other device that doesn't have PostScript, the Mac OS tries to use TrueType fonts. If your Mac doesn't have a needed TrueType font but does have ATM installed, the Mac OS looks for a PostScript version of the font. If neither type of outline font is available, the Mac OS uses a fixed-size font.

Tip   Look closely at some text in a TrueType font and at the same text in an equivalent fixed-size font. You'll see differences in letter shape, width, and height that may affect text spacing. The TrueType fonts match the PostScript fonts used in printers better than fixed-size fonts do. Fixed-size fonts display faster, however, and many of them look better onscreen in sizes smaller than 18 points.

If you print on a non-PostScript printer such as an Apple StyleWriter, Hewlett-Packard DeskJet, or Epson Stylus, and have both fixed-size and TrueType fonts installed, text may not look quite the same onscreen as it does on paper. Character shapes may be different. More importantly, the spacing of words in the line may not match. When this happens, the Mac OS has used a fixed-size font for display (at 72 dots-per-inch) and a TrueType font for printing (at a higher resolution). You can fix the problem by removing the fixed-size font from your System file. In some programs, you may also be able to set an option that tells the Mac OS to ignore fixed-size fonts.

FontSync

In Mac OS 9, Apple has included a new control panel, called FontSync, which helps manage the compatibility of fonts between two different Macs. Put simply, FontSync enables you to build a profile of the fonts installed on another Mac that has FontSync installed. You then bring that profile document to your Mac, and find out what fonts on your system don't match those on the other Mac. Now you know which fonts to use (or replace on your system) before you send your documents to that other Mac.

The power of FontSync is its capability to go beyond the basics of a font — its name and whether it's a TrueType or PostScript font — and look at other characteristics that govern fonts, such as the font's internal name, its visual characteristics, its internal kerning tables, and so on. By using FontSync, you can determine whether the fonts on your Mac are an *exact* match for the fonts on another system.

Note

It may not be obvious at first, but FontSync is best used in the order discussed in this section—you need to receive a FontSync profile from the Mac to which you intend to send your document and compare that profile to your Mac's fonts. The reason for this is simple: The Match FontSync Profile applet only tells you which fonts *are* installed on the current system that *aren't* on the profiled system. For example, if you have New Berolina MT on your Mac, but the profiled Mac doesn't have it, Match FontSync Profile will tell you that. Now you know you either need to install the missing font on the profiled Mac or avoid using the font on your Mac.

To use FontSync, its control panel needs to be installed. Drag its icon from the Font Extras folder (in the Apple Extras folder on your hard disk) to the System Folder icon so that it can be installed in the Control Panels folder. If FontSync isn't installed on your Mac, you can custom install it using the Mac OS 9 installation CD (as described in Chapter 31).

After installation, the FontSync control panel gives you control over which factors to use to determine font compatibility (see Figure 15-13).

Figure 15-13: The FontSync control panel gives you more control over font matching between two Macs.

With the FontSync control panel installed and the desired characteristics chosen, you can build a FontSync profile. In the Font Extras folder, Apple has created two AppleScript applets that enable you to create a font profile and compare font profiles.

To create a font profile for a given Mac, launch the Create FontSync Profile applet. The applet consults the FontSync control panel to find out what characteristics are set for the profile. After a dialog box appears to warn you that the process can take a while, you are given the opportunity to name and save your profile. The profile is then created.

After the process is complete, you'll have a new FontSync profile document. You can now take that document back to your Mac. There, you drag the profile to the Match FontSync Profiles applet. The AppleScript applet launches and again warns you that the matching process can take a while. Click OK. The next dialog box gives you an opportunity to save a log file of the Match FontSync Profile applet's findings — give it a name and save it.

After the Match FontSync Profile applet runs its course, you see either a dialog box telling you that your active fonts match those stored in the profile (hence, your two computer's fonts match up) or a dialog box reporting problems. If there are problems, consult the log file that the Match FontSync Profile applet created to find out what's different between the two machines.

Understanding Outline Fonts

To understand why TrueType fonts look different from equivalent fixed-size fonts, you need to know how outline-font technology works. Like PostScript fonts and other outline fonts, a TrueType font defines each character mathematically as a set of points that, when connected, outline the character's shape. The Mac OS can vary the font size by moving the points closer together or farther apart and then drawing the character again.

After scaling the outline to the size you want, the Mac OS fills the outline with the dots that make up the text you see onscreen and on paper. The dot size, which is determined by the resolution of the screen or other output device, governs the smoothness of the result at a given size. Devices with more dots-per-inch produce smoother results, particularly in smaller point sizes. Figure 15-14 shows how dot size affects smoothness.

At small sizes, however, simply scaling the font outlines results in text that has unpleasant problems, such as gaps in diagonal lines or unwanted dots on the edges of curves. These imperfections occur because the outline does not precisely fit the grid in small point sizes, especially if the dots are relatively large, as they are on the computer's 72-dots-per-inch screen. On the display screen, the Mac OS must draw a typical 11-point letter in a space 8 dots square. At small sizes and relatively low resolutions, deciding which dots to darken is difficult. The Mac OS reduces the character outline, lays it over the grid, and darkens the dots whose center points fall inside the outline, as shown in Figure 15-15.

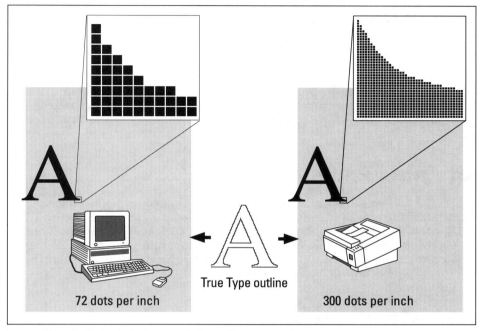

Figure 15-14: Output device resolution affects smoothness.

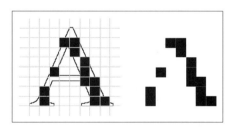

Figure 15-15: Scaling a font outline to a small size may leave gaps.

TrueType and PostScript fonts include a mechanism for adjusting the outline at small sizes on low-resolution devices. The font designer provides the font with instructions (also known as *hints*) that tell the Mac OS how to modify character outlines at small font sizes, as shown in Figure 15-16. This process is called *grid fitting*.

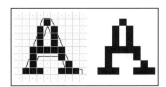

Figure 15-16: Hints modify outlines at small sizes.

High-resolution devices such as typesetters and film recorders usually don't need grid-fitting instructions — their grids are so fine that the character outlines don't need adjusting to get filled with dots. A 300-dots-per-inch grid is 4.17 times finer than a 72-dots-per-inch grid, and a 1270-dots-per-inch grid is more than 16 times finer.

Scaling and grid fitting occur so quickly that you usually don't notice a delay. TrueType and PostScript fonts are not as fast as fixed-size fonts, however, and occasionally the lag is perceptible onscreen.

Obtaining Fonts

The Mac OS comes with a standard set of TrueType fonts: Apple Chancery; Capitals; Charcoal; Chicago; Courier; Gadget; Geneva; Helvetica; Hoefler Text; Monaco; New York; Palatino; Sand; Skia; Symbol; Techno; Textile; and Times. Microsoft's Internet Explorer also installed some TrueType fonts, including Andale Mono; Arial; Arial Black; Comic Sans MS; Courier New; Georgia; Impact; Times New Roman; Trebuchet MS; Verdana; and WebDings.

Noncommercial fonts

You can get additional TrueType and PostScript fonts at nominal cost from sources of shareware and freeware (see Chapter 26). Figure 15-17 shows some examples of freeware and shareware TrueType fonts.

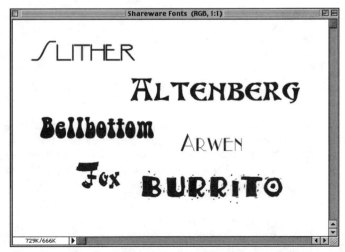

Figure 15-17: These are examples of freeware and shareware TrueType fonts.

Commercial fonts

Many type companies make TrueType and PostScript fonts, including:

Active Images
1-310-458-9094
http://www.comicbookfonts.com

Adobe Systems, Inc.
1-800-833-6687
http://www.adobe.com/type

Agfa Division, Bayer Corp.
1-978-508-5600; 1-800-424-8973
http://www.agfadirect.com

Bitstream, Inc.
1-617-497-6222; 1-800-522-3668
http://www.bitstream.com

Casady & Greene, Inc.
1-408-484-9228; 1-800-359-4920
http://www.casadyg.com

Castle Systems Design
1-415-459-6495
http://www.castletype.com

Deniart Systems
1-416-941-0919; 1-800-725-9974
http://www.deniart.com

dincTYPE
1-973-472-8765
http://www.girlswhowearglasses.com

Emigre
1-916-451-4344; 1-800-944-9021
http://www.emigre.com

The Font Bureau, Inc.
1-617-423-8770
http://www.fontbureau.com

FontShop International (FontFont)
http://www.fontfont.com

Font World, Inc.
1-716-686-1099
http://www.fontworld.com

Hoefler Type Foundry Inc.
1-212-777-6640
http://www.typography.com

International Typeface Corp.
1-212-949-8072
http://www.itcfonts.com

Letraset
1-201-845-6100
http://www.letraset.com/letraset

Linotype Library GmbH
49 (0) 06172 484 401
http://www.linotypelibrary.com

Monotype Typography Inc.
1-847-718-0400; 1-800-666-6897
http://www.monotype.com

P22 Type Foundry
1-716-885-4482; 1-800-722-5080
http://www.p22.com

T-26
1-773-862-1201; 1-888-T26-FONT
http://www.t26font.com

Tangram Studio
1-519-369-3898
http://www.bmts.com/~tangram/

Treacyfaces, Inc.
1-203-389-7037; 1-800-800-6805
http://www.treacyfaces.com

URW++ Design & Development GmbH
49 (40) 606050
http://www.urwpp.de

Summary

In this chapter, you learned that fixed-size (bitmap) fonts look good only at installed sizes, but that the Mac OS can smoothly scale TrueType fonts to any size for the display screen or any type of printer. PostScript fonts look good at any size on PostScript printers. With the addition of Adobe Type Manager (ATM) software, PostScript fonts also look good on the display screen and non-PostScript printers.

You also learned that all three types of fonts are kept in the Fonts folder, although PostScript fonts can also be kept in the Extensions folder or System Folder. For convenience, TrueType and fixed-size fonts are often kept in font suitcases. You can add and remove fonts by dragging their icons to and from the Fonts folder. The Mac OS handles font display and printing automatically, but you can configure font smoothing in the Appearance control panel. If you use ATM with any Mac OS version, you can adjust how it scales PostScript fonts.

In addition, this chapter explained how the Mac OS chooses between fixed-size, TrueType, and PostScript versions of the same font. The priorities are different for the display screen, PostScript printers, and non-PostScript printers.

This chapter also gave an overview of how outline fonts (TrueType and PostScript) work.

✦　　✦　　✦

Get Ready to Print

With the Mac OS, no matter what type of printer you have, you set up and control printing the same basic way in almost every application. The Mac OS enforces this consistency by providing complete printing services to applications. All applications use the same piece of software to prepare the page description for, and to communicate with, a particular type of printer. This software, called a printer driver, resides in the Extensions folder inside the System Folder.

You can choose a printer with the standard Chooser desk accessory, which comes with the Mac OS, and that choice persists among all applications and through restarts until you choose again. Apple's Desktop Printing software improves the administration of background printing and enables you to print documents by dragging their icons to a printer icon on the desktop. Desktop printing also enables you to choose a printer from a universal Desktop Printer menu or a Control Strip module, which bypasses the Chooser and gives you complete control of the printing process without leaving your application.

You control the rest of the printing process with your application's Page Setup and Print commands; the standard options for these commands are the same in all applications. Alternatively, you can select one document or a group of documents (created by one application or several) and then give the command to print the selected documents from the Finder.

You don't have to wait for documents to finish printing before continuing with other work. With many printer models, the Mac OS can manage printing in the background, so you can continue working on other tasks.

This chapter tells you how to set up for the specific printer or printers you use and how to manage background printing. You learn to use the desktop printer methods, and you also learn to use printers that don't show up as desktop printers. (For instructions on setting up and printing documents, see Chapter 17.)

Comparing Printer Driver Software

For each type of printer you use, your computer needs printing software in the Extensions folder. That software is called a *printer driver*. A printer driver prepares a complete description of each page to be printed in a format that the printer can interpret and then sends the page descriptions to the printer. Figure 16-1 displays the icons of the printer drivers that come with the Mac OS.

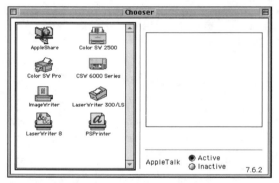

Figure 16-1: The Mac OS printer drivers

Your application prints by sending a description of your document to the printer driver software. The printer driver translates the description into data that the printer can use.

Many printers work with Macs, and each type of printer requires its own printer driver software. Printers made for the Macintosh market come with printer drivers. If you can't find the printer driver for your printer, contact its maker for replacement software.

In general, you should use the latest available version of a printer driver. For example, if you buy an Apple printer after upgrading to Mac OS 9 and the printer comes with older driver software than the driver that comes with Mac OS 9, use the driver that comes with Mac OS 9. The latest versions of printer drivers are usually available at low cost or for free from printer makers' Web sites. The latest drivers for Apple printers are available from Apple's Software Updates library (http://asu.info.apple.com/).

Tip If you're not sure which version of a printer driver you have, select its icon in the Extensions folder and choose Get Info from Finder's File menu. The driver's Info window reports the version number.

PostScript printer drivers

Printers that interpret PostScript commands to create printable images are called PostScript printers. Examples include most Apple LaserWriter models (but not the Personal LaserWriter LS, Personal LaserWriter 300, or LaserWriter Select 300), the Hewlett-Packard LaserJet series, Texas Instruments' MicroLaser series, GCC Technologies' Elite series, and NEC's SilentWriter and ColorMate series. Although some of these printers come with proprietary driver software, most of the printers also work with Apple's LaserWriter 8 drivers or Adobe's AdobePS drivers.

Apple's LaserWriter 8 drivers

The LaserWriter 8 version 8.7 driver that comes with Mac OS 9 has numerous improvements over earlier LaserWriter 8 driver versions, incorporating all changes made since the original LaserWriter 8 driver. Beginning back with LaserWriter 8 version 8.4.2 in Mac OS 7.6, if you have access to more than one PostScript printer, you can choose the one you want when you print a document. (With earlier Laser-Writer 8 drivers, you must choose the printer before printing.) When you print a document, you can also schedule when you want it to print, either relative to other documents waiting to be printed or at a specific time. Moreover, with LaserWriter 8 version 8.4 and later you don't have to worry about running out of disk space when printing a large document, as you do with earlier LaserWriter 8 drivers.

LaserWriter 8 version 8.7 also enables you to print multiple collated or uncollated copies of a document. You can "print to" Acrobat PDF files directly if Adobe Acrobat Distiller is installed on your Mac. You can define custom page sizes for printers that can accommodate them. You have more control over color matching with ColorSync. In addition, you can use the included Desktop Printing Utility to create more kinds of desktop printers than the Chooser can create.

LaserWriter 8 version 8.7 also includes a version of the desktop printing software that is open to most types of printers. Previously, only PostScript printers and Apple printers could show up as desktop printers. In addition, LaserWriter 8 version 8.7 supports the Unicode method of encoding text and the Euro currency symbol.

Finally, LaserWriter 8 version 8.7 now includes full AppleScript support, allowing most printing functions to be controlled via AppleScript (see Chapter 24 for more on AppleScript). And, the driver now offers software developers more choices, including the capability to add plug-ins to the driver that examine PostScript codes as they are processed and sent to the printer.

Adobe's AdobePS and PSPrinter drivers

Apple developed LaserWriter 8 in collaboration with Adobe Systems (creator of PostScript) to take advantage of PostScript Level 2. Adobe distributes a driver similar to LaserWriter 8 under the name AdobePS 8.6. If you buy a PostScript printer made by a company other than Apple, the printer may come with the AdobePS driver. Prior to AdobePS, Adobe made the PSPrinter 8.3.1 driver, which was similar to a version of LaserWriter 8 earlier than 8.4.

Most PostScript printers that work with PSPrinter 8.3.1 and AdobePS 8.6 also work with the LaserWriter 8 driver.

Caution
There's a known issue when you install AdobePS 8.5.1 on a computer that already has a current LaserWriter 8 driver, including version 8.7 that comes with Mac OS 9. Both drivers use a common file named PrintingLib (it's in the Extensions folder). When you install AdobePS, the Adobe PrintingLib file replaces the Apple PrintingLib file and LaserWriter 8 version 8.7 stops working. The solution is to reinstall the LaserWriter 8 driver or install AdobePS 8.6 or higher. To reinstall LaserWriter 8, do a custom installation of Mac OS 9. Click the Customize button in the last step of the Mac OS Install program, select the Mac OS 9 module, and choose Customized Installation from its pop-up menu. In the dialog box that appears, open the Printing component, select LaserWriter 8, and click OK. Then click Start. (For more information on custom installations, see Chapter 31.)

PostScript Printer Description files

The LaserWriter 8, AdobePS, and PSPrinter drivers let you configure specific features of a particular printer, such as its resolution (the number of dots it can print per inch) and the size and capacity of its paper trays. These PostScript drivers get a printer's optional features from a special file called a *PostScript Printer Description* (*PPD*) file. A set of PPD files comes with the LaserWriter 8 driver. The PPD files reside in a folder named Printer Descriptions inside the Extensions folder (which is in the System Folder). In addition, printer manufacturers include the appropriate PPD with each printer that has PostScript Level 2 or PostScript 3. If you don't go through the setup process with your printer, the LaserWriter 8, AdobePS, and PSPrinter drivers use generic settings based on the page sizes and features of the original Apple LaserWriter. (The setup process is described in "Choosing the Default Printer," later in this chapter.)

Non-PostScript printer drivers

Many printers do not use PostScript to create page images. Examples from Apple include all the various StyleWriter printers, the ImageWriter II, the Personal LaserWriter 300, and the Personal LaserWriter LS. Non-PostScript printers from other companies include Hewlett-Packard's DeskWriter and DeskJet series, the Epson Stylus models, and GCC Technologies' PLP II.

Each type of non-PostScript printer has its own printer driver software. With few exceptions, your Extensions folder must include a different driver for each non-PostScript printer that you use. Notable exceptions are:

✦ StyleWriter (original) can use the Color StyleWriter 1500 driver

✦ StyleWriter II can use the Color StyleWriter 1500 driver

✦ StyleWriter 1200 can use the Color StyleWriter 1500 driver

✦ Color StyleWriter 2400 can use Color StyleWriter 2500 driver

✦ Color StyleWriter 2200 can use Color StyleWriter 2500 driver

Other output device drivers

Other types of output devices, although not technically printers, also have printer driver software. These devices include fax/modems, plotters, and portable document makers such as Adobe Acrobat and Common Ground. If you have any of these devices, each must have a driver in your Extensions folder.

Choosing the Default Printer

The Mac OS can print to any printer, fax modem, or other output device for which you have a driver in your Extensions folder. Because you can use more than one printer or output device with your computer, you need to designate which one you want to make the default, or active, printer or device. Designating a default printer or device is a two-step process. First, you select the driver that the printer or device uses, and second, you select a specific printer that uses the driver. You can do both steps with the Chooser accessory program, as described in this section.

Selecting a printer driver

In the Chooser, you begin the process of designating the default printer or other device by selecting its driver. The left side of the Chooser displays an icon for each printer driver in your Extensions folder, each of which corresponds to the types of printers or other output devices you can use. To select a driver, click the appropriate icon or type the first part of that icon's name. Figure 16-2 is an example of the Chooser ready for selecting a printer driver.

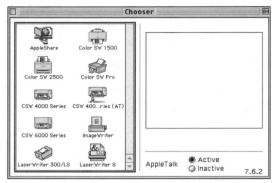

Figure 16-2: Select a printer driver on the left side of the Chooser.

Selecting a specific printer

After you select a printer driver to use on the left side, you select a specific printer on the right side of the Chooser window. The procedure is somewhat different for selecting a networked printer, a personal printer, or someone's shared printer.

Selecting a networked printer

If you select the driver for a networked printer, such as LaserWriter 8, the right side of the Chooser displays the names of all available printers that use the selected driver (assuming your Mac is correctly configured for network access). Select the default printer by clicking its name or by typing the first part of its name. (To select by typing, a heavy border must surround the list of printer names. If the border isn't there, press Tab until it is.) Close the Chooser after you select the name of the networked printer that you want to make the default printer. Figure 16-3 is an example list of printers that use the LaserWriter 8 driver.

If your network has zones, you see a list of network zones in the lower-left corner of the Chooser, and the right side of the Chooser displays printer names only for the currently selected zone. You can select a different zone to see the printers available in it. (If you don't see a list of zones, your network has no zones.)

If there are no names listed on the right side of the Chooser when a networked printer driver is selected on the left side of the window, then there are no printers of that type available on the network (in the currently selected zone, if your network has zones). If you want to begin using a printer that isn't available now, you may be able to create a desktop printer for it as described in "Using the Desktop Printer Utility," later in this chapter.

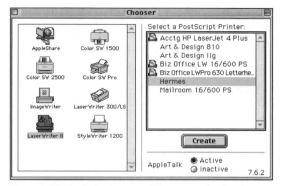

Figure 16-3: Select a specific networked printer on the right side of the Chooser.

Selecting a personal printer

If the printer driver you select on the left side of the Chooser is for a personal printer, such as LaserWriter 300/LS, the right side of the Chooser displays the ports to which it could be connected. A personal printer connects directly to your computer. Your computer may have a choice of ports or only one port. You select a port by clicking it in the Chooser. Figure 16-4 is an example list of ports for a personal printer.

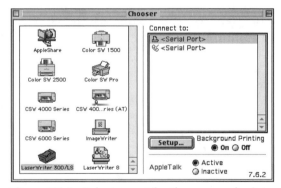

Figure 16-4: Select a port for the personal printer on the right side of the Chooser.

You may not be able to select a port for your personal printer unless you set the AppleTalk option to Inactive in the Chooser. If you don't want to make AppleTalk inactive, use the AppleTalk control panel to set the AppleTalk connection to something other than the port you want to use for your printer. For example, you can set the AppleTalk control panel's Connect Via option to Remote Only if it is installed on your computer.

Cross-Reference   For more information on the Remote Only option, see Chapter 20.

Turning off AppleTalk may not release the port you want to use for a personal printer. If you have trouble printing to a personal printer connected to a port that was used previously for an AppleTalk network, restart the computer after making AppleTalk inactive.

Tip   If you're having trouble turning off AppleTalk, you can also try setting AppleTalk to inactive using the AppleTalk control panel. Set the AppleTalk control panel to Advanced user mode (Edit ➪ User Mode), and then click the Options button to bring up the AppleTalk Options dialog box. Make AppleTalk inactive, and then click OK. Close the control panel and you may now be able to set up your printer's port in the Chooser.

Selecting a shared printer

If you select the driver for a personal printer on the left side of the Chooser, you may see more than ports on the right side. You may also see the names of shared printers listed there. Each shared printer is a personal printer connected to someone else's computer on your network. The names of shared printers appear only if other people on your network have made their personal printers available for sharing, as described later in this chapter. Additionally, you can only see the name of a shared printer when the computer to which it's connected is turned on. You select a shared printer by clicking or typing its name. Figure 16-5 shows a shared StyleWriter printer in the Chooser.

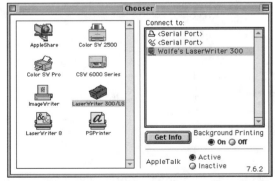

Figure 16-5: Select someone else's shared printer on the right side of the Chooser.

After selecting a shared printer, you can get information about it by clicking Get Info in the Chooser. The dialog box that appears reports the Mac OS version installed on the printer's computer, the name of that computer, and the fonts installed on your computer that are missing on the shared printer's computer. Documents containing fonts that are not installed on the shared printer's computer will print slowly or may print incorrectly.

Setting up the selected printer

After selecting a specific printer, it needs to be set up. For example, you definitely need to set up a printer that uses the LaserWriter 8 or PSPrinter driver. You may be able to set up a personal printer to let other people on your network share it and to keep a log of its usage.

To set up a printer selected in the Chooser, click either Create or Setup on the right side of the Chooser window. When you click Setup or Create, the printer driver either displays status messages describing its automatic setup process or a dialog box with setup options.

If no Setup or Create button appears on the right side of the Chooser, or if the button is dimmed (grayed out), then there is nothing to set up. This will be the case if you have not selected a specific printer on the right side of the Chooser.

LaserWriter 8, AdobePS, or PSPrinter setup

The first time you select a printer that uses the LaserWriter 8 driver, the AdobePS driver, or the PSPrinter driver, a Create button appears on the right side of the Chooser. When you click this button, the Mac OS determines the correct PPD file for the printer. If the printer can have optional equipment, such as extra paper trays or a RAM upgrade, the Mac OS determines the printer's configuration.

At the conclusion of this process, the Create button changes to a Setup button. If you click this button, a dialog box appears with additional buttons that you can click to change the printer's setup.

Personal printer setup

If your computer has a personal printer directly connected to one of its ports, you may be able to make the printer available for other people on your network to share. Your computer acts as a host for your personal printer on the network. This means that your hard disk must store all the print requests waiting to be printed by everyone who's using your printer, and that your computer must print those files in the background. If you continue working while your computer handles all that background printing, you may notice a performance slowdown.

You can share a personal printer that uses any Color StyleWriter driver, the Style-Writer 1200 driver, or the LaserWriter 300 driver. When you select a port for a personal printer that uses one of these drivers, a Setup button appears on the right side of the Chooser. Clicking this button displays the sharing setup dialog box for the printer. Figure 16-6 shows the sharing setup dialog for a personal printer that uses the LaserWriter 300/LS driver.

Figure 16-6: Setting up a personal printer for sharing

In the printer's sharing setup dialog box, turn on the Share this Printer option. Give the printer a distinctive name by which it will be known on the network. You also can specify a password that anyone who wants to use the printer will have to enter. You have the option of keeping a log of printer activity. Click OK to dismiss the dialog box.

Closing the Chooser

After selecting a driver, selecting a specific printer or device, and setting it up, you should close the Chooser. The printer or device you selected is now the default printer and you can print on it by using the Page Setup and Print commands in any application (as described in Chapter 17).

If a specific printer was selected for the first time, the Mac OS may create a *desktop printer* for it. When this happens, an icon representing the printer appears on the desktop. (You may have to wait several seconds before the desktop printer icon appears.) You can use desktop printers to change the default printer and to manage printing, as described in "Working with Desktop Printers" and "Managing Background Printing" later in this chapter.

What makes desktop printers appear?

Mac OS 9 normally creates a desktop printer after you select an eligible printer with the Chooser. Yet there may be a desktop printer icon on your desktop even if you have never used the Chooser. A desktop printer normally appears after you select an eligible printer with the Mac OS Setup program, which runs automatically when you first start your computer after installing the Mac OS. In addition, if you upgrade to Mac OS 9 from an earlier Mac OS version, a desktop printer may appear automatically for the printer you used most recently before upgrading.

If a desktop printer already exists for the printer you want to use, and its icon has a heavy black border, you don't have to select the same printer again with the Chooser. The heavy black border indicates the default printer. If the desktop printer doesn't have a heavy black border, then it isn't currently the default printer. You can select the printer again in the Chooser as described earlier. Alternatively, you can use Finder's Printing menu as described in "Working with Desktop Printers" later in this chapter.

Only some of the printers you select in the Chooser can become desktop printers. Any printer that uses one of the Apple LaserWriter, StyleWriter, or ImageWriter printer drivers will become a desktop printer. Don't expect to see desktop printers for printers, fax modems, or devices that use drivers released prior to Mac OS 8.5 (mid-1998). Companies that create printer drivers must enhance the drivers so that they create desktop printers, and this capability first became available for non-Apple printers with Mac OS 8.5.

Desktop printers require two extensions in your Extensions folder: Desktop Printer Spooler and Desktop PrintMonitor. If you remove these extensions or disable them with the Extensions Manager control panel, you won't be able to use desktop printers.

Using the Desktop Printer Utility

In addition to creating desktop printers with the Chooser, you can use the Desktop Printer Utility program. It can create regular desktop printers and three other kinds of desktop printers based on the LaserWriter 8 driver and on the AdobePS driver version 8.5.1 and later. If you want to create desktop printers that use other printer drivers, use the Chooser as described in the previous section, "Selecting a Printer Driver."

You'll find the Desktop Printer Utility in the Apple LaserWriter Software folder within the Apple Extras folder. The Desktop Printer Utility is part of a standard installation of Mac OS 9.

Types of desktop printers

You can create these five types of desktop printers with the Desktop Printer Utility:

✦ **Regular desktop printers**, which are the same as the desktop printers created by selecting the LaserWriter 8 driver and a particular networked printer in the Chooser (as described in the previous section, "Choosing the Default Printer)."

✦ **LPR (TCP/IP) desktop printers**, which use the cross-platform LPR (Line Printer Remote) protocol and connect via a TCP/IP network, such as an intranet or the Internet.

✦ **Hold desktop printers**, which keep print requests on hold until you connect your computer to a printer and can resume printing. You may find a hold desktop printer convenient when using a PowerBook away from your printer.

✦ **USB desktop printers**, for use with printers that connect to your Mac via a USB connection.

✦ **PostScript Translator desktop printers**, which are not actually connected to printers. Instead, they always create PostScript files that can be sent to a PostScript printer later.

In addition to these five types of desktop printers, the Desktop Printer Utility can be customized by software developers to create custom desktop printers that send PostScript files to a particular application for processing. For example, a custom desktop printer could be created to send PostScript files to a program that displays pages onscreen rather than printing them on paper, in essence providing a print preview.

Creating a new desktop printer

To create a desktop printer, open the Desktop Printer Utility. The program displays its New dialog box, in which you select the type of desktop printer to create. If the Desktop Printer Utility is already open, choose New from the File menu to display the New dialog box. Figure 16-7 shows the Desktop Printer Utility's New Desktop Printer dialog box.

Figure 16-7: Create several types of desktop printers with the Desktop Printer Utility.

Choosing a printer driver

At the top of the New Desktop Printer dialog box, choose the printer driver that you want the new desktop printer to use. The pop-up menu that lists your choices includes only Desktop Printer Utility–compatible PostScript drivers. The Laser-Writer 8 driver is the only compatible driver that comes with the Mac OS. In addition, the AdobePS driver that you can get from Adobe (see "Comparing Printer Driver Software" earlier in this chapter) is also compatible with the Desktop Printer Utility.

Selecting the kind of desktop printer

In the middle of the New Desktop Printer dialog box, select the kind of desktop printer you want to create and click OK. For the LaserWriter 8 driver, you can select any of these kinds of desktop printers:

✦ **Printer (AppleTalk)**, which creates a regular desktop printer.

✦ **Printer (LPR)**, which creates a desktop printer for a printer connected to your computer via a TCP/IP network such as the Internet or an intranet. When communicating with this printer, the Mac OS uses the standard LPR protocol. Several newer Apple LaserWriter models — 8500, 16/600PS, 12/640PS, 12/600PS, 12/660PS, and Pro 810 — can use LPR and a TCP/IP network as well as the traditional PAP protocol (Printer Access Protocol) and an AppleTalk network, which are common to all LaserWriter models.

✦ **Printer (no printer connection)**, which creates a desktop printer that you can use when your computer is not connected to an actual printer. Printed documents are held in the desktop printer for later printing, as discussed in "Managing Background Printing" later in this chapter.

✦ **Printer (USB)**, which enables you to create a desktop printer for a compatible printer that uses a USB connection instead of a typical networking connection.

✦ **Translator (PostScript)**, which creates a desktop printer that always saves printed pages as a PostScript file. (For more information on saving printed pages as PostScript files, see Chapter 17.)

Specifying a PPD file and printer

After you select the kind of desktop printer you want to create and click OK in the New dialog box, the Desktop Printer Utility program displays an untitled window. This window shows the PPD file selected for the desktop printer, as well as an additional setting for some kinds of desktop printers. You can change settings shown in a desktop printer window by clicking Change buttons in the window. Figure 16-8 is an example of an untitled desktop printer window.

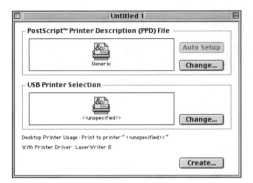

Figure 16-8: See and change the PPD file and other settings for a desktop printer.

To change a desktop printer's PPD file, click the Change button next to the PPD icon at the top of the Desktop Printer Utility window. This brings up a standard Open dialog box in which you can select a different PPD file from the Printer Descriptions folder in your Extensions folder.

To change a desktop printer's additional settings, click the Change button next to its icon in the Desktop Printer Utility window. This brings up a dialog box in which you can change the settings. For a regular desktop printer connected to an Apple-Talk network, you can choose a networked printer by zone and name, in much the same way as you can with the Chooser. For a desktop printer connected to a TCP/IP network such as the Internet, you can enter the printer's network address and queue. For a desktop printer that creates PostScript files, you can select a folder in which the files are saved. For a desktop printer with no connection to an actual printer, there are no additional settings besides the PPD file.

When you finish changing a desktop printer's settings, choose Save from the Desktop Printer Utility's File menu. In the standard Save dialog box that appears, name the desktop printer and select a folder location for it. Desktop printers do not have to live on the desktop.

Changing a desktop printer

You can use the Desktop Printer Utility to change the PPD file and other settings of any desktop printer based on the LaserWriter 8 driver. To change a desktop printer's settings, open the desktop printer with the Open command in the Desktop Printer Utility's File menu. The program displays the desktop printer's settings in a titled window similar to the untitled window of a new desktop printer (review Figure 16-8). Change the settings in this window by clicking Change, as previously described.

Working with Desktop Printers

You can handle desktop printers as you would a folder in the Finder. You can rename desktop printers, move them from the desktop to a folder, create aliases for them, and drag them to the Trash.

When you select a desktop printer in the Finder, a Printing menu appears in the menu bar between the Special menu and the Help menu. You can use Printing menu commands in the Finder to change the default printer, check printer status, and change printer setup. You may also be able to change the default printer using other techniques.

Changing the default printer

If you have more than one desktop printer, you choose one that represents the printer that you want to use by default. The Finder indicates which desktop printer is the default printer by drawing a heavy black border around its icon. You can choose the default printer by using the Printing menu in the Finder. You may be able to use a universal Desktop Printer menu or a Control Strip module. You can also use the Chooser to change the default printer.

Tip

Want more options? Select a desktop printer and press ⌘+L to make it the default printer or Control+click the desktop printer and choose Set as Default Printer from the contextual menu.

Printing menu

To set a default printer using the Finder's Printing menu, select the desktop printer that you want to become the default. When the Printing menu appears, choose Set Default Printer from it. The Printing menu is only available in the Finder. Figure 16-9 shows a couple of desktop printer icons and the Printing menu.

Figure 16-9: Setting a default printer with Finder's Printing menu

Desktop printer menu and Control Strip module

There are even more convenient methods than the Finder's Printing menu for changing the default printer. You can choose a desktop printer while using any application — no need to switch to the Finder to use the Printer menu. If the

Control Strip is installed, you can choose a printer from it. You can also choose a printer from a universal Desktop Printer menu. The Desktop Printer menu has a printer icon as its title and appears near the right end of the menu bar. Figure 16-10 is an example of the Printer Selector module in the Control Strip.

Figure 16-10: Choosing a default printer from the Control Strip

The Printer Selector control strip module and the Desktop Printer menu are not part of a standard installation on every Mac, but you can install them separately. The Printer Selector module is installed with the Control Strip.

 Cross-Reference   For instructions on installing the Control Strip, see Chapter 12.

To install the Desktop Printer menu, do a custom installation with the Mac OS Install program. In the last step of the program, click the Customize button, select the Mac OS 9 module, and choose Customized Installation from its pop-up menu. In the dialog box that appears, select Desktop Printing and click OK. Then click Start.

 Cross-Reference   Chapter 31 has detailed instructions for performing a custom installation.

Chooser

Although the Chooser is less convenient than the methods already described for designating the default printer, it works for all printers and output devices including those that can't have desktop printers. Just select the printer or other device in the Chooser as described in "Choosing the Default Printer" earlier in this chapter. If the printer that you select in the Chooser already has a desktop printer, the Chooser makes the selected printer the default printer without creating another desktop printer for it.

Checking a desktop printer's status

You can use menu commands in the Finder to check the current status, configuration, and installed font information for a desktop printer that is based on the LaserWriter 8 driver. This information appears in two views of a desktop printer's Info window. You can switch between viewing status and configuration information and viewing a list of installed fonts by choosing the view you want from the pop-up menu near the top of the desktop printer's Info window. Figure 16-11 shows examples of both views of a desktop printer Info window.

To display a desktop printer's Info window, select the desktop printer and choose Status & Configuration or Fonts from the Get Info submenu. This submenu appears in the Finder's File menu and in a desktop printer's contextual menu. If you have a non-PostScript printer, the command will simply get Get Info ➪ General Information.

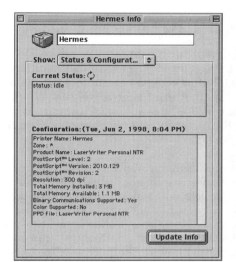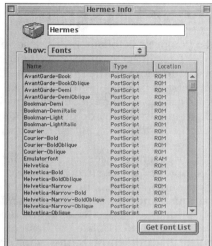

Figure 16-11: Viewing a desktop printer's current status, configuration, and fonts

Changing a desktop printer's setup

Change Setup, which is another command in the Finder's Printing menu, lets you change the PPD file and reconfigure any installed option of a desktop printer that is based on a LaserWriter 8 driver. Selecting a printer icon and choosing Change Setup brings up a dialog box that displays the current setup. The dialog box contains a button for changing the PPD file, other controls for changing the settings of options installed in the printer, and an Auto Setup button that has the printer driver inter-rogate the printer to configure those settings automatically. Figure 16-12 is an example of the LaserWriter setup dialog box.

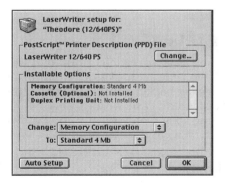

Figure 16-12: Changing a desktop printer's setup from the Finder

Managing Background Printing

When you print a document (as described in the next chapter), the printer driver creates page descriptions for each page to be printed. The driver may send the page descriptions to the printer immediately, forcing you to wait until the document finishes printing before you can do anything else. Alternatively, many printer drivers can save the page descriptions in a file for later automatic printing in the background, while you do other work in the foreground. A file of page descriptions is called a *print request*, a *print job*, or a *spool file*.

In the short time it takes to save a print request, the printer driver has control of the computer. You regain control as soon as a driver finishes saving. While you work (or not), the Desktop PrintMonitor application opens automatically in the background and handles the waiting print request by sending the saved page descriptions to the printer a bit at a time during the slices of time it gets to work in the background. (Unlike the Desktop PrintMonitor, the PrintMonitor application handles all waiting print requests for printers without desktop icons.) The background printing activity may make the computer feel less responsive, especially on a slow computer.

While a document is printing in the background, you can queue additional print requests by using the Print command in one or more applications. The Desktop PrintMonitor application (or PrintMonitor, for printers without desktop icons) normally handles the queued print requests in the order they were saved. You can override this sequence by setting a specific print time or a special priority, as described later in this section. You can also stop and start the print queue whenever you want.

The rest of this section tells you how to turn background printing on and off and then explains how to manage a queue of waiting print requests. There are separate explanations for managing a print queue with desktop printers and without them because the methods are different.

Turning background printing on and off

You can turn background printing on or off separately for each printer that can print in the background. With most printers, you can set background printing in the Chooser before you print documents. You can set background printing each time you print to a desktop printer that uses the standard LaserWriter 8 or AdobePS drivers. You can also turn background printing on and off for many non-PostScript printers, such as Apple's StyleWriter and Personal LaserWriter printers.

Setting background printing before printing

To use the Chooser to turn background printing on or off for a printer, you must first select the printer in the Chooser window (as detailed earlier in this chapter in "Choosing the Default Printer"). To recap, first select the printer driver on the left side of the Chooser. Next, on the right side of the Chooser window, select the specific printer by its name or by the port it connects to. Now you can set the Background Printing option in the lower right area of the Chooser. Figure 16-13 shows the Background Printing option in the Chooser.

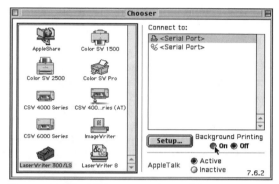

Figure 16-13: With some printer drivers, you turn background printing on or off in the Chooser.

Setting background printing when you print

You do not need to set background printing in the Chooser before printing to a desktop printer that uses LaserWriter 8 or AdobePS. Instead, you can turn background printing on or off whenever you use the Print command to print a document. In the Print command's dialog box, you choose the Background Printing group of options and set the "Print in" option for background or foreground printing. Figure 16-14 shows the Print command's "Print in" option for printers that use the LaserWriter 8 driver.

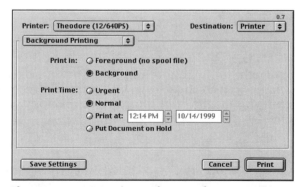

Figure 16-14: For printers that use the LaserWriter 8 driver, background printing is set in the Print dialog box.

Managing a desktop printer's queue

You can view and manage the queue of waiting print requests for each desktop printer individually. If your Mac doesn't create a desktop icon for a printer when you choose it with the Chooser, then you must use the methods described later for managing the print queue without desktop printers.

Viewing the print queue

At any time, you can see the queue of print requests waiting for a particular desktop printer by opening the desktop printer in the Finder. You open a desktop printer like a folder. Opening a desktop printer icon displays its window. At the top of the window are buttons for managing the queue of print requests and general information about the print queue. A box below the buttons identifies the print request now being printed (if any) and reports the status of that print job. Below that is a list of waiting print requests. You can sort the list of waiting print requests by name, number of pages, number of copies, or print time. Choose a sort order by clicking a column heading in the desktop printer's window. Figure 16-15 shows a desktop printer's window.

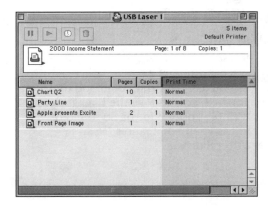

Figure 16-15: View queued print requests in a desktop printer's window.

Redirecting a print request

You can redirect a waiting print request by dragging it from its current desktop printer window to the icon or window of a compatible desktop printer. In general, desktop printers that use the same driver (they have the same icon selected on the left side of the Chooser) are compatible.

Changing the printing order

Print requests in a desktop printer's window print in the listed order when the list is sorted by print time. You can change the order of print requests by dragging them up and down in the window. A print request can be dragged by its icon, name, or any other text on the same line in the desktop printer's window. Figure 16-16 is an example of changing a print request's order in the queue.

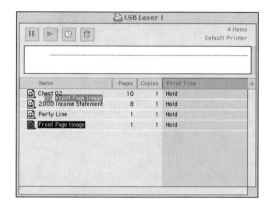

Figure 16-16: Change the order of print requests by dragging them in the desktop printer's queue.

Scheduling print requests

You can also change a print request's place in line by setting its priority to urgent, normal, or scheduled for a specific time and date. To set a print request's priority, select it and click the Set Print Time button (the one with the clock icon) in the desktop printer's window. Figure 16-17 shows the dialog box in which you set a print request's priority.

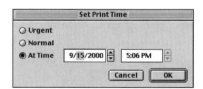

Figure 16-17: Schedule a priority or a specific time for a print request.

A print request's priority changes automatically if you drag it to a place among print requests of a different priority. For example, dragging a scheduled print request above an urgent print request makes the scheduled print request urgent.

Placing a print request on hold

You can postpone a print request indefinitely, even if the print request is currently being printed. Select a print request in the desktop printer's window and click Hold, which looks like a VCR's Pause button. To take a print request off hold, select it and then click Resume, which looks like a VCR's Play button. Clicking Resume displays the Resume Print Request dialog box, in which you can specify the page from which you want printing to resume.

Stopping or removing a print request

You can stop a print request by dragging it out of the desktop printer's window. To get rid of a print request altogether, either drag it to the Trash or select it and click Remove, which has a trash can icon.

Managing multiple print requests

You can schedule or resequence more than one print request at a time in a desktop printer's window. To select multiple print requests, press Shift while clicking them or drag across them.

Stopping and starting printing

To stop all printing on a particular desktop printer, select it and then choose Stop Print Queue from the Printing menu. A small stop sign appears on the desktop printer's icon.

To start printing again, select the desktop printer and then choose Start Print Queue from the Printing menu.

Manual paper feed notification

If you print a document using a printer's manual feed tray, you normally receive a notification alert when the printer is waiting for you to manually feed paper. The Printing menu makes it easy to turn off this notification. Just select the relevant desktop printer and choose Show Manual Feed Alert from the Printing menu so that there is no check mark next to it in the menu.

Instant reprints (well, almost)

It takes quite a while to save background print requests for some documents, and that's on top of the time it takes to open the application and the document before you can begin printing. For example, it may take several minutes to save a print request for a Photoshop image to be printed on a Color StyleWriter. You don't have to repeat that wait each time you reprint the image in the future if you can spare the disk space to store a copy of the print request. (Yes, you could print multiple copies of the image at one time and hand them out as needed — it doesn't take any longer to save a print request for multiple copies than for a single copy — but then you may end up with extra copies that you have to throw away, wasting ink and expensive special paper.)

Here is a procedure for reprinting without the delay of saving a new print request each time: Before printing a document for the first time, select the desktop printer and choose Stop Print Queue from the Finder's Printing menu. Then print the document, causing a print request to be created for the desktop printer. If you forget to stop the print queue before printing, immediately go to the Finder and stop the print queue or open the desktop printer and put the print request on hold. Next, open the desktop printer and drag the print request to any folder. When you're ready to make a print, hold down Option and drag the print request from that folder to the desktop printer. By holding down Option, you make a copy of the print request for the desktop printer and leave the original print request untouched for future reprints. If necessary, use the Finder's Start Print Queue command to start background printing. Et voilà! Reprints without saving new print requests or opening a document and its application!

Managing the print queue without desktop printers

You can use the PrintMonitor application to view and manage the queue of waiting print requests for some printers that don't have desktop icons. The PrintMonitor application handles printing of waiting print requests while you continue working with other applications. PrintMonitor opens in the background automatically whenever there are print requests in the PrintMonitor Documents folder (inside the System Folder), deletes each print request that it prints, and quits automatically when the PrintMonitor Documents folder is empty.

Some printers made by companies other than Apple come with their own applications for managing the queue of waiting print requests. For instructions on using one of these applications, check the documentation that came with your printer.

Viewing the print queue

While PrintMonitor is open in the background, you can make it the active application by choosing it from the Application menu. You also can open it at any time by double-clicking its icon, which is located in the Extensions folder. Making Print-Monitor active or opening it displays its window. The PrintMonitor window identifies the print request that is printing, lists the print requests waiting to be printed, and displays the status of the current print request. Figure 16-18 shows the PrintMonitor window.

PrintMonitor automatically hides its window when you switch to another application, but PrintMonitor remains open in the background as long as it has print requests to process.

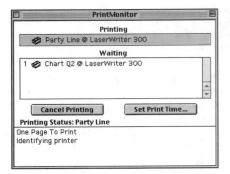

Figure 16-18: View queued print requests (without desktop printers) in the PrintMonitor window.

Changing the printing order

PrintMonitor ordinarily processes print requests in chronological order, oldest first. You can change the order by dragging print requests in the PrintMonitor window. You drag a print request by its icon, not by its name or sequence number. While dragging a print request, an outline of it follows the mouse pointer, as shown in Figure 16-19.

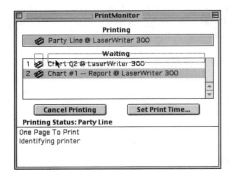

Figure 16-19: Change the order of print requests (without desktop printers) by dragging them in the PrintMonitor queue.

Scheduling printing requests

You can schedule when PrintMonitor will process a print request, or you can postpone a print request indefinitely. First, select the print request you want to schedule (by clicking it) in the PrintMonitor window. You can select the print request being printed or any print request waiting to be printed. Then click Set Print Time. Figure 16-20 shows the dialog box in which you set a time and date for processing a print request or postpone it indefinitely.

A print request scheduled for later printing appears in PrintMonitor's waiting list with an alarm-clock icon in place of a sequence number. A print request postponed indefinitely appears in the waiting list with a dash in place of a sequence number, and it will not be printed until you schedule a print time for it.

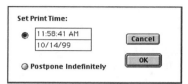

Figure 16-20: Scheduling a specific time for a print request (without desktop printers)

Stopping and starting printing

You can suspend all background printing by choosing Stop Printing from Print-Monitor's File menu. Before PrintMonitor stops printing, it finishes the print request that it is currently printing. To resume printing, choose Resume Printing from the File menu.

Setting PrintMonitor preferences

PrintMonitor can notify you when something happens that requires your attention during background printing. For example, PrintMonitor can notify you when you need to manually feed paper for background printing. An alert box, a blinking PrintMonitor icon in the menu bar, or both, can notify you. To specify how you want to be notified, you use the Preferences command in PrintMonitor's File menu. Note that if you turn off notification of manual paper feed and forget to feed paper when the printer needs it, the printer eventually cancels the print request automatically. Figure 16-21 shows the Preferences dialog box for PrintMonitor.

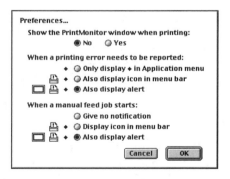

Figure 16-21: Setting PrintMonitor preferences

You can also use the Preferences command to specify how you want to be notified about printing errors, such as PrintMonitor not being able to locate a printer that is supposed to print a print request. PrintMonitor can just display a diamond symbol next to its name in the Application menu at the right end of the menu bar, or it can display the symbol and blink its icon in the menu bar, or it can do both of those things plus display an alert. You can turn off everything except the diamond in the Application menu.

Print later

If you want to print to a printer that doesn't have a desktop icon and that isn't connected to your Mac now, you can delay printing. Turn on background printing in the Chooser and print the desired documents. Then open PrintMonitor and use its Stop Printing command to suspend printing. Now any documents that you print wait in PrintMonitor's queue until you connect to a printer and begin printing with PrintMonitor's Resume Printing command. To avoid PrintMonitor's nagging alert messages and blinking icon in the menu bar, use PrintMonitor's Preferences to suppress notification of printing errors.

To shut down your Mac while it is not connected to a printer and background printing is turned on, you must respond correctly to two PrintMonitor alerts that appear during the shutdown process. The first alert tells you that something is being printed and asks whether you want to finish printing or print later; you must click Print Later. Then a second alert tells you that the printer can't be found. Click Cancel Printing to conclude the shutdown process without losing any queued print requests. (If you click Try Again instead, you abort the shutdown process, and PrintMonitor tries again to find the missing printer.) This process is somewhat confusing, because clicking Cancel Printing under other circumstances actually deletes the print request that is being printed.

Summary

In this chapter you saw that every printer you use must have a printer driver in your Extensions folder. A printer driver prepares a complete description of each page to be printed in a format that the printer can interpret and then sends the page descriptions to the printer. To begin using a printer, use the Chooser to select a driver and the specific printer. Selecting a printer in the Chooser normally creates a desktop printer. After the desktop printers are created, use the Finder's Printing menu, the optional universal Desktop Printer menu, or the optional Printer Selector module in the Control Strip to select the printer that you want to use. You don't have to use the Chooser again for desktop printers.

You can usually continue working while the Mac OS prints in the background. Queued print requests can be viewed by opening desktop printers. You can change the order of queued print requests, set their priorities or print times, put them on hold, or delete them. You can also stop and start any desktop printer's queue. Queued print requests of printers without desktop icons can be managed with the PrintMonitor program or another program supplied by the printer maker.

✦   ✦   ✦

Print Your Documents

You're ready to print. You've made the printer you want
to use the default printer, as described in Chapter 16.
Now it's time to set page-formatting options, specify how
many pages and copies to print, and actually start printing.
You can do all this from the Finder or from the applications
that created the documents that you want to print.

This chapter begins by introducing the Page Setup and Print
commands used to set page formatting and printing options.
Next, how to print from the Finder and other applications is
explained. The bulk of the chapter details the page-formatting
and printing options for printers that use Apple printer
driver software.

Print and Page Setup Commands

Almost every Mac OS application has the same commands
for printing documents — Page Setup and Print — and those
commands are usually in the File menu. Some applications
provide other methods of printing, such as a Print button in a
toolbar, but most alternate methods are based on the standard
Page Setup and Print commands. Learn how to use the standard
commands, and you will know how to print most documents. (A
few applications, such as FileMaker Pro, can be programmed to
bypass these commands completely. This chapter does not
cover printing from such programs.)

The Page Setup command is used to specify how the
document pages are to be formatted. You need to set the
paper size (such as letter or legal size), page orientation
(horizontal/landscape or vertical/portrait), a reduction or
enlargement factor, and other options that affect how the

document is to be arranged on the page. With some printers, you also can turn optional printer effects on and off.

The Print command is used to specify a range of pages, a number of copies, and a paper source. You may have additional options, depending on the type of printer driver you chose.

With both the Page Setup command and the Print command there may be additional options that are not described in this chapter because some applications and utility software add their own options to those commands. For example, the existence of a Page Setup option labeled ClickBook means that the ClickBook utility from Blue Squirrel (801-523-1063, `http://www.bluesquirrel.com`) is installed for printing double-sided pages or booklets on regular printers. For explanations of Print or Page Setup options not described in this chapter, check the documentation for the application you're using and for any printing utility software installed on your computer.

This chapter tells you how to set up and print pages on printers that use the following Apple printer driver software, which is included as part of a standard installation of Mac OS 9:

- ✦ LaserWriter 8
- ✦ Color StyleWriter 2500, Color StyleWriter 1500, and Color StyleWriter Pro (including older StyleWriter printer)
- ✦ Color StyleWriter 6000 series
- ✦ LaserWriter 300/LS
- ✦ ImageWriter

Your printer may use a different driver. In that case, the procedures for setting up and printing are similar to those described in this chapter, but the specific options are different. For details, refer to the documentation that came with the printer.

You use the Chooser or desktop printers to select a printer driver for your printer, as described in Chapter 16. That chapter also explains how to manage a queue of documents waiting to print in the background while you continue working on other tasks.

Printing from the Finder

If all you need to do is print a document — that is, you don't need to open it, review it on screen, or edit it first — you can print it directly from the Finder. You don't even have to open the application that created the document (although the Finder often opens it for you).

To print a document from the Finder, drag the document icon to a desktop printer icon. Some desktop printers send all documents to the applications that created them for printing, as described in the next paragraph. But desktop printers that use the LaserWriter 8 driver included with Mac OS 9 can print certain types of documents directly. These include PostScript, Encapsulated PostScript (EPS), PICT, and JPEG documents. The part of the LaserWriter 8 driver that sends documents directly to the printer is called the Download Manager. Programmers can extend it to handle more types of documents by creating plug-in software modules.

If a desktop printer can't print your document directly, it sends a request to the application that created the document, telling the application to print the document. The application opens, or becomes active if it's already open in the background, and displays the dialog box of its Print command so that you can set options. Some applications also display the Page Setup dialog box so that you can set page layout options. The specific options that you can set are somewhat different for each printer driver, as detailed later in this chapter. When you finish setting options, the application prints the document. If the application was not open when you started the printing process in the Finder, the application quits automatically. (Some applications stay open.)

If you don't want to use a desktop printer, select the document that you want to print and choose Print from the Finder's file menu. The Finder tells the application that created the document to print it, as described in the previous paragraph for desktop printers.

If you try to print a document but don't have the application that created it, a list of alternative applications is displayed in an alert box, the same as if you were trying to open the document. The File Exchange control panel displays this alert box. A different dialog box is shown if automatic document translation is turned off. For more information on these dialog boxes, see Chapter 7.

You can use the Finder to print several documents just as easily as to print one. You simply select the documents that you want to print and either drag them as a group to the desktop printer icon or choose Print from the Finder's file menu. The documents can be created by different applications, but they must all be in the same window or on the desktop. If the documents are in different folders, you can drag the documents to the desktop, select and print them, and then use the Finder's Put Away command to return them to the folders they came from. You can also print documents from different expanded folders that you can see in a list view of an enclosing folder or disk.

In addition to a Print command, the Finder's File menu also has a Page Setup command and a Print Window command (or a Print Desktop command if no folder or disk window is active). You do not use these commands to print documents from the Finder. These commands are for printing the Finder windows or the desktop. In fact, they have the same function in the Finder as the Page Setup and Print commands have in any other application.

Printing from Other Applications

In addition to printing from the Finder, you can print from within applications that can open the documents that you want to print. You have to open the document you want to print, and the document window must be in front of other document windows. Then you use the Page Setup and Print commands from the application's File menu to set options and actually start printing. The specific options that you can set are somewhat different for each printer driver, as detailed later in this chapter.

You don't have to set the Page Setup options each time you print a document. Just choose the Print command and your previous Page Setup settings are used again. If you use the Print command without ever setting Page Setup options for a particular document, the application supplies its standard Page Setup options.

In addition to a regular Print command, some applications also have a Print One Copy command. This alternative command streamlines printing by foregoing the usual Print dialog box. The application supplies its standard settings for the options in the Print dialog box.

In some applications, you can print the document in the front window by clicking a Print button in a toolbar. This action generally has the same effect as choosing Print from the File menu. In a few applications, the Print button displays the Page Setup dialog box before the Print dialog box.

A few applications can be set up to bypass the Print and Page Setup commands. For example, a FileMaker Pro database can be programmed to print a report using preset Page Setup and Print options. All you do is click a button in the database window or choose a command from the Script menu, and the report prints according to the preset options.

Setting LaserWriter 8 Options

This section describes how to set up and print documents on printers that can use Apple's LaserWriter 8 printer driver. All Apple LaserWriter printers with PostScript can use LaserWriter 8, as can most PostScript printers made by other companies.

Setting LaserWriter 8 Page Setup options

When you choose the Page Setup command for a printer that uses the LaserWriter 8 driver, you see a dialog box with settings for page attributes, including paper type, orientation, and scale. You can switch to settings for PostScript Options by choosing that category from the unlabeled pop-up menu at the top of the dialog box. With some PostScript printers, you can also switch to settings for Custom Page Size by choosing from this pop-up menu. Figure 17-1 shows the pop-up menu for switching among groups of options in the Page Setup dialog box for LaserWriter 8.

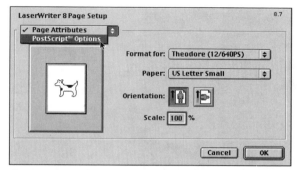

Figure 17-1: Choosing a group of options for LaserWriter 8 page setup

Tip Instead of choosing a group of options from the pop-up menu at the top of the Page Setup dialog box, you can move from group to group by pressing ⌘+down arrow (↓), ⌘+up arrow (↑), Page Up, or Page Down.

Page Attributes

When you choose Page Attributes from the unlabeled pop-up menu near the top of the Page Setup dialog box, these options display, as shown in Figure 17-2:

✦ **Format for** lets you choose which of your Mac OS desktop printers to format. The pop-up menu lists your desktop printers that use the LaserWriter 8 driver. The setup of the printer you choose here (in particular its PPD file) can affect the page format.

✦ **Paper** lets you choose a paper size such as US Letter (8½ by 11 inches), US Legal (8½ by 14 inches), and A5 and B5 (European standard sizes). There are two variations of some sizes, such as US Letter and US Letter Small. The Small variation has a larger unprintable area at the edges of the paper that matches the US Letter size of older LaserWriter drivers. The regular variation gives you the maximum printable area for your printer (as specified by the printer's PPD file). If you see the size Other listed for the Paper option, it means the document was previously printed using a paper size that is not available on the currently selected printer. If you choose another Paper setting, the Other choice will no longer be available.

✦ **Orientation** determines whether the top of the printed page will be on the short edge (portrait) or long edge (landscape) of the paper.

✦ **Scale** reduces or enlarges the printed image according to the percentage you enter. Full size is 100 percent, the minimum reduced size is 25 percent, and the maximum enlargement is 400 percent.

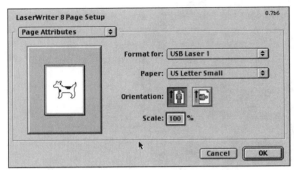

Figure 17-2: Setting Page Attributes options for LaserWriter 8 page setup

PostScript Options

When you choose PostScript Options from the unlabeled pop-up menu near the top of the Page Setup dialog box, these options display, as shown in Figure 17-3:

✦ **Flip Horizontal/Flip Vertical** create mirror images of your document. You can see the result in the illustration in the dialog box when you click the check box. Flip Horizontal flips the image right to left, which is useful if you are creating a film image on a Linotronic imagesetter for a transparency or if the pages have to be emulsion side down.

✦ **Invert Image** makes all the black parts of a page print white, and vice versa. You probably won't have much use for this parlor trick unless you create film negatives on a slide printer that has no method of its own for creating negative images.

✦ **Substitute Fonts** substitutes PostScript fonts for any fixed-sized screen fonts for which no PostScript or TrueType equivalent is available (as described in Chapter 15). For example, Geneva becomes Helvetica, Monaco becomes Courier, and New York becomes Times. The one drawback of font substitution is that although the variable-size font is substituted for its fixed-sized cousin, the spacing of letters and words on a line does not change, and the printed results often are remarkably ugly. For the best results, do not use fixed-size fonts that lack TrueType or PostScript equivalents, and leave the Substitute Fonts option off.

✦ **Smooth Text** smoothes the jagged edges of fixed sizes for which there are no matching PostScript fonts or TrueType fonts. For best results, avoid such fonts, and leave the Smooth Text option off.

✦ **Smooth Graphics** smoothes the jagged edges of bitmap graphic images created with painting programs. Smoothing improves some images but blurs the detail out of others. Try printing with Smooth Graphics set both ways, and go with the one that looks best to you. This option has no effect on graphics that are created with drawing programs such as FreeHand and Illustrator.

✦ **Precision Bitmap Alignment** reduces the entire printed image to avoid minor distortions in bitmap graphics. The distortions occur because of the nature of the dot density of bitmap graphics. For example, 72 dpi (dots-per-inch), which is the standard screen-image size, does not divide evenly into 300 dpi, 400 dpi, or 600 dpi (the dot density of many laser printers). When you are printing to a 300-dpi printer, for example, turning on this option reduces page images by 4 percent, effectively printing them at 288 dpi (an even multiple of 72 dpi). The reductions align the bitmaps properly to produce crisper output.

✦ **Unlimited Downloadable Fonts** allows you to use more fonts than your printer's memory can hold at one time by removing fonts from the printer's memory after they are used, making way for other fonts. Be aware that the constant downloading and flushing of font files takes time and thus slows printing. EPS (Encapsulated PostScript) graphics that use fonts that are not present elsewhere on the page will not print correctly because the printer will substitute Courier for those orphan fonts. If you see Courier in a graphic where you did not want it, make sure that this option is turned off.

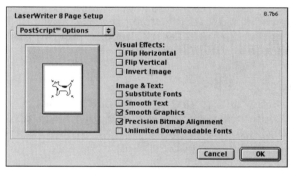

Figure 17-3: Setting PostScript Options for LaserWriter 8 page setup

Custom Page Sizes

You can define and use custom page sizes, if your printer allows them, by choosing Custom Page Sizes from the unlabeled pop-up menu near the top of the Page Setup dialog box. When you make this choice, you see a list of custom page sizes that are already defined. If you select a custom size, you see a preview of it in the dialog box. You can delete the selected size, edit it, or create a new custom size by clicking buttons in the dialog box. Figure 17-4 is an example of the Custom Page Sizes options in LaserWriter 8.

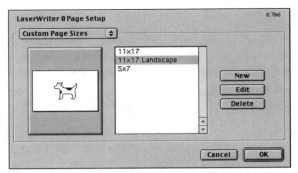

Figure 17-4: Setting Custom Page Sizes options for
LaserWriter 8 page setup

Click the New or Edit button to display a dialog box in which you enter or change
the paper size height and width. You can also specify the top, bottom, right, and
left margins. In addition, you may need to specify a width or height offset for the
custom page. For example, a printer that uses a roll of film or paper will print a
custom page that's smaller than the roll. The offsets tell the printer where to
position the page on the larger media. For cut sheets of paper or other media,
the page size is usually the same as the sheet size and there are no offsets.

All custom page sizes appear as choices for the Paper option in the Page Attributes
section of the Page Setup command. Every custom page size is available with every
printer that allows custom sizes and uses LaserWriter 8. In other words, none of the
custom page sizes is unique to a particular printer.

Saving custom Page Setup settings

If you don't like the Page Setup settings that LaserWriter 8 uses by default, have it
use your settings instead. After making your changes in the Page Setup dialog box,
press Option while clicking OK to dismiss the dialog box. An alert asks you to
confirm that you want to save the current Page Setup settings as the
default settings.

You have to perform this exercise separately in each application that has its own
Page Setup settings. You may be able to tell whether a particular application has its
own Page Setup settings by looking for the application's name in the pop-up menu
at the top left of the Page Setup dialog box. If that pop-up menu doesn't list the
current application's name, the application may use the generic Page Setup default
settings. Changing the generic Page Setup defaults in one application affects all
applications that use them (but doesn't affect applications with their own Page
Setup settings).

Setting LaserWriter 8 Print options

When you choose the Print command for a printer that uses the LaserWriter 8 driver, you see a dialog box with settings for the number of copies, page numbers to print, paper source, output destination, and more. You can switch among several groups of options by choosing a group from the unlabeled pop-up menu near the top of the dialog box. Figure 17-5 shows the pop-up menu for switching among groups of options in the Print dialog box for LaserWriter 8.

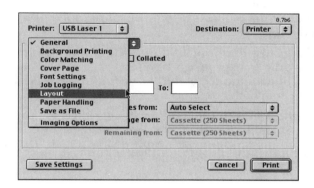

Figure 17-5: Choosing a group of options for LaserWriter 8 printing

Tip

Instead of choosing a group of options from the pop-up menu at the top of the Print dialog box, you can move from group to group by pressing ⌘+down arrow (↓), ⌘+up arrow (↑), Page Up, or Page Down.

The remainder of this section describes the Print command's options in more detail. The descriptions are organized according to the Print option groups used in LaserWriter 8 — General, Background Printing, Cover Page, Color Matching, Layout, Error Handling, Save as File, Imaging Options, and Printer Specific Options.

Universal options

No matter which group of options you choose in the Print dialog box for LaserWriter 8, these options are always available at the top and bottom of the dialog box (as was shown in Figure 17-5):

✦ **Printer** lets you choose which of your desktop printers is to print your document. The pop-up menu lists your desktop printers that use the LaserWriter 8 driver.

✦ **Destination** specifies whether the driver sends page descriptions to the chosen printer or to a file. The options for the latter setting are described later in this section under the heading "Save as File options."

✦ **Save Settings** makes the settings you have made in the Print dialog box the ones used by default for the currently chosen desktop printer.

General options

When you choose General from the unlabeled pop-up menu near the top of the Print dialog box for LaserWriter 8, these options display, as shown in Figure 17-6:

✦ **Copies** specifies the number of copies to print.

✦ **Collated**, when selected, specifies that multiple copies each print in correct page sequence. If unselected (or unavailable), all copies of one page print, then all copies of the next page, and so on. Collated printing may take longer than uncollated printing. Because each collated copy is sent to the printer as a separate print request, print requests from other computers may be interspersed between the collated copies.

✦ **Pages** specifies the range of pages to print. If you leave the first entry box blank, the document will print from page one. If you leave the second box blank, the document will print to the end of the document. To print a single page, enter its page number in both boxes.

✦ **Paper Source** specifies from where the chosen printer should get the paper to print your document — multipurpose tray, envelope feeder, paper cassette, manual feed, and so forth. You can choose one paper source for all pages or a separate source for the first page and for remaining pages.

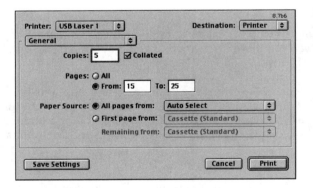

Figure 17-6: Setting General options for LaserWriter 8 printing

Background Printing options

When you choose Background Printing from the unlabeled pop-up menu near the top of the Print dialog box for LaserWriter 8, these options display, as shown in Figure 17-7:

✦ **Print in** specifies whether you want your document to print in the foreground or background. Foreground printing requires less disk space than background printing and your document may start printing faster, but it does not let you use the computer for anything else until printing stops. Background printing lets you work on other tasks while printing continues, but requires extra disk space for temporary spool (page description) files. Foreground printing is not available in some applications.

✦ **Print Time** specifies a priority for printing a document in the background —
urgent, normal, or hold — or a specific time and day when you want your
document printed. You can change this setting for a document waiting to be
printed in the background by opening the desktop printer icon (as described
in Chapter 16). The Print Time option is disabled if you set the Print in option
for foreground printing, which is always immediate.

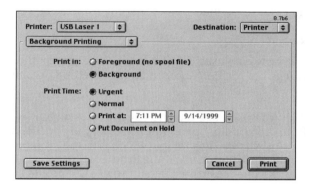

Figure 17-7: Setting
Background Printing
options for LaserWriter 8
printing

Color Matching options

When you choose Color Matching from the unlabeled pop-up menu near the top
of the Print dialog box for LaserWriter 8, these options display, as shown in
Figure 17-8:

✦ **Print Color** lets you choose to print your document in black and white, or in
color on a color printer, or in shades of gray on a monochrome printer. If your
computer has ColorSync installed and the folder contains printer profiles, you
can choose to have ColorSync or PostScript match the printed grays and colors
to the displayed colors as closely as possible. The PostScript setting for this
option requires a printer with at least PostScript Level 2 capability.

✦ **Intent** lets you choose a method of matching the gamut of colors in the document
to the gamut of colors that the printer can reproduce. The methods are:

• **Perceptual matching** scales all colors in the document to fit within the
printer's color gamut. This method gives good results for photographs
and other bitmap graphics. All colors in the document change, even
those that the printer can reproduce, but they all change by the same
amount so everything looks pretty good.

• **Relative colorimetric matching** doesn't change colors in the document
that the printer can reproduce. Colors that the printer can't reproduce
change to the closest reproducible color having the same lightness (but
different saturation). Colors that are different from each other in the
document may look the same as each other when printed.

- **Saturation matching** doesn't change colors in the document that the printer can reproduce. Colors that the printer can't reproduce change to the closest reproducible color having the same saturation (but different lightness). This is appropriate for charts and graphs, where you care more about keeping colors different than about preventing perceptible color shifts.

- **Absolute colorimetric matching** doesn't change colors in the document that the printer can reproduce. Colors that the printer can't reproduce are not printed. This may result in some loss of detail and sparseness in the printed document.

- **Auto selection matching** uses the Saturation matching method on text and line drawings but the Perceptual matching method on bitmap graphics.

✦ **Printer Profile** specifies the color profile to use for color matching. You choose a profile from the pop-up menu, which lists all the appropriate printer profile files in the ColorSync Profiles folder (which is in the Preferences folder inside the System Folder). Additionally, if the Print Color setting is PostScript Color Matching, you can choose Printer Default to use the profile currently stored in the printer. The Printer Profile setting is disabled if you set the Print Color option to Black & White or Color/Grayscale.

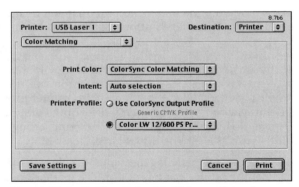

Figure 17-8: Setting Color Matching options for LaserWriter 8 printing

Cover Page options

When you choose Cover Page from the unlabeled pop-up menu near the top of the Print dialog box for LaserWriter 8, these options display, as shown in Figure 17-9:

✦ **Print Cover Page** specifies whether to print a cover page before printing your document, after printing your document, or not at all. A cover page reports the document's name, the owner's name of the computer that printed it, and when it was printed.

✦ **Cover Page Paper Source** specifies where the chosen printer should get paper to print a cover page. This option is disabled if you set the Print Cover Page option to None.

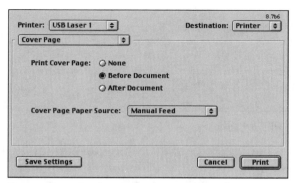

Figure 17-9: Setting Cover Page options for LaserWriter 8 printing

Font Settings

When you choose Font Settings from the unlabeled pop-up menu near the top of the Print dialog box for LaserWriter 8, one or both of these options display, as shown in Figure 17-10:

✦ **Annotate Font Keys** annotates font keys in the PostScript output. Font keys are comments added to the PostScript output to help troubleshoot font issues.

✦ **Font Downloading** offers a few different options for how fonts are sent to the printer:

- **Preferred Format**: Choose which type of font takes priority when downloading to the printer. If TrueType is selected, a matching TrueType font will be sent first if one is found. By default, the driver looks for Type 1 fonts first.

- **Always download needed fonts**: Downloads all fonts to the printer, regardless of whether the font is already stored on the printer.

- **Never generate Type 42 fonts**: Causes TrueType fonts to be sent as "unhinted" Type 1 fonts instead of translating them into PostScript fonts (also called Type 42 fonts) before sending them.

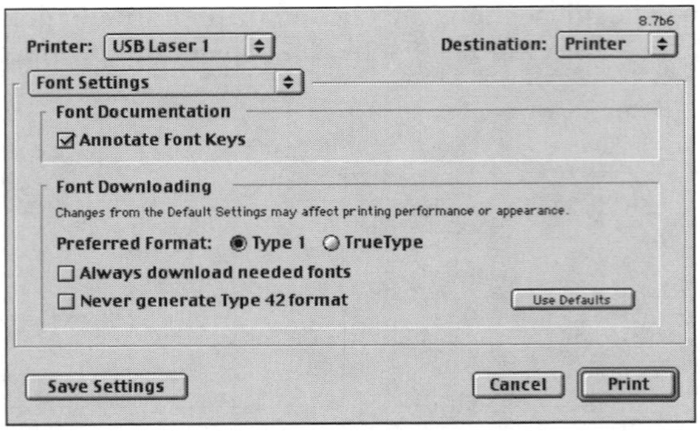

8.7b6
Printer: USB Laser 1
Destination: Printer
Font Settings
Font Documentation
Annotate Font Keys
Font Downloading
Changes from the Default Settings may affect printing performance or appearance.
Preferred Format: Type 1 TrueType
Always download needed fonts
Never generate Type 42 format
Use Defaults
Save Settings
Cancel
Print

Figure 17-10: Setting Font options for LaserWriter 8 printing

Job Logging options

When you choose Job Logging from the unlabeled pop-up menu near the top of the Print dialog box for LaserWriter 8, one or both of these options display, as shown in Figure 17-11:

✦ **If there is a PostScript error** specifies how the LaserWriter 8 driver handles PostScript errors: no special error reporting, display a summary of PostScript errors onscreen, or print detailed descriptions of PostScript errors.

✦ **Job Documentation** lets you decide if and how each print job will be logged — either with a full copy of the job or a log of jobs and their status.

✦ **Job Documentation Folder** shows the current selected folder for job documentation and enables you to change the folder by clicking Change and selecting a new folder.

8.7b6
Printer: USB Laser 1
Destination: Printer
Job Logging
If there is a PostScript™ error:
No special reporting
Summarize on screen
Print detailed report
Job Documentation
Generate Job Copy
Generate Job Log
Job Documentation Folder
Macintosh HD
Printing Logs Folder
Change...
Save Settings
Cancel
Print

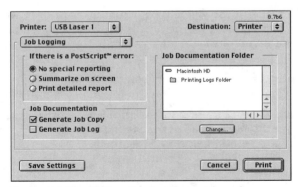

Figure 17-11: Setting Job Logging options for LaserWriter 8 printing

Layout options

When you choose Layout from the unlabeled pop-up menu near the top of the Print dialog box for LaserWriter 8, these options display, as shown in Figure 17-12:

✦ **Pages per sheet** lets you choose a number of minipages to print on each sheet of paper. Each minipage is a full-page image reduced in size so that two, four, or more minipages fit on a sheet of paper.

✦ **Layout Direction** specifies whether the minipages are arranged from left-to-right or right-to-left. This option is available if you set the "Pages per sheet" option to more than one minipage per sheet of paper.

✦ **Border** lets you choose the type of borderline to print around each reduced minipage. This option is available if you set the "Pages per sheet" option to more than one minipage per sheet of paper.

✦ **Print on Both Sides** lets you print on both sides of the page, in booklet format. Selecting this option enables you to determine which side of the page will be bound. (This option is only available with some printers.)

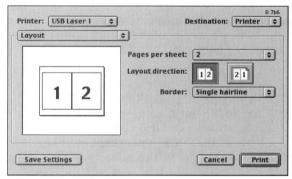

Figure 17-12: Setting Layout options for LaserWriter 8 printing

Save as File options

When you choose Save as File from the unlabeled pop-up menu near the top of the Print dialog box for LaserWriter 8, these options display, as shown in Figure 17-13:

✦ **Format** specifies the kind of file to save. Choose one of the following:

• **PostScript Job** creates a standard PostScript file for later printing.

- The three **EPS** (Encapsulated PostScript) formats create a one-page graphic for placement in another document. EPS Mac Standard Preview includes a black-and-white 72-dpi bitmap image for previewing onscreen. EPS Mac Enhanced Preview includes a color PICT preview image, which can be smoothly reduced or enlarged on the screen display. EPS Mac No Preview takes the least amount of disk space because it has no preview image. Without a preview image, you can't see the file onscreen, but this option prints just like the other EPS formats.

- **Acrobat PDF** creates a *PDF* (*Portable Document File*) that can be read by Acrobat Reader. This setting requires that Acrobat Distiller be installed on your Mac. Distiller is not included with the free Acrobat Reader — it's part of the full version of Acrobat, which you can buy through retailers. It's also bundled with recent versions of Adobe PageMaker and Adobe InDesign.

✦ **PostScript Level** specifies PostScript compatibility. Choose the Level 1 Compatible option for a file that can be used on printers with PostScript Level 1, 2, or 3. If you are using only PostScript Level 2 and 3 printers, choose the Level 2 and 3 option.

✦ **Data Format** specifies whether to use text characters or binary data in the PostScript file. Choosing the ASCII option creates a more widely compatible PostScript file than the Binary option, but the Binary option can speed printing on a printer that can handle it.

✦ **Font Inclusion** specifies how many fonts to embed in the PostScript file. The None setting, which does not embed any fonts, uses the least disk space but prints correctly only on a system that has all the needed fonts. The All option, which embeds every font used in the document, may use a great deal of disk space, but all the needed fonts will print from any system. The All But Standard 13 option embeds all the fonts used except the 13 fonts that commonly are factory-installed in PostScript printers.

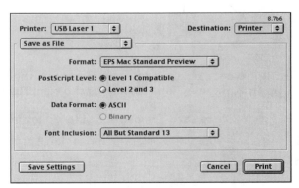

Figure 17-13: Setting options for saving PostScript files with LaserWriter 8

If you choose Acrobat PDF as the Format option, these options replace the PostScript Level, Data Format, and Font Inclusion options, as shown in Figure 17-14:

✦ **Compress Text and Line Art** specifies whether to compress text and graphics using the LZW method in the PDF file.

✦ **Embed All Fonts** specifies whether to embed all fonts used in the document as part of the PDF file.

✦ **Make Font Subsets** enables you to embed only the font information necessary to create the characters that appear in this document instead of embedding the entire font.

✦ **ASCII Format** specifies whether to use ASCII85 encoding for the document, which will result in a PDF file that is almost pure ASCII.

✦ **Compression** and **Downsample to** control the type of compression and the final resolution of bitmap graphics in the PDF file. These options are set separately for color, grayscale, and monochrome bitmap images.

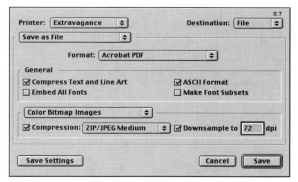

Figure 17-14: Setting options for saving Acrobat PDF files with LaserWriter 8

Imaging Options

When you choose Imaging Options from the unlabeled pop-up menu near the top of the Print dialog box for LaserWriter 8, one or more of these options display, as shown in Figure 17-15:

✦ **FinePrint**, if on, specifies that the printer should smooth jagged edges of text and graphic objects. Bitmapped images may print better with this option off. This option is only available with printers that have Apple's FinePrint technology.

✦ **PhotoGrade**, if on, specifies that the printer should enhance the shading and contrast of graphics. Text quality may be better with this option off. This option is only available with printers that have Apple's PhotoGrade technology.

✦ **Device Scaling Adjust** enables you to make fine adjustments in the size of the image to compensate for slight differences between different units of the same printer model.

The Imaging Options choice does not appear in the pop-up menu if none of these options apply to the current printer.

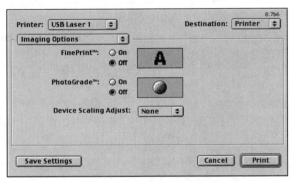

Figure 17-15: Setting Imaging options for LaserWriter 8 printing

Printer Specific Options

When you choose Printer Specific Options from the unlabeled pop-up menu near the top of the Print dialog box for LaserWriter 8, options that are specific to the current printer appear. For example, a LaserWriter Pro 630 printer has a Choose Resolution option in the Printer Specific Options group (rather than a Resolution option in the Imaging Options group). The Printer Specific Options choice does not appear in the pop-up menu if the current printer has no special options.

Setting Color StyleWriter Options

This section describes how to set up and print documents on printers that can use one of the three Color StyleWriter drivers. The included drivers are Color StyleWriter 2500, Color StyleWriter 1500, and Color StyleWriter Pro. All Apple Color StyleWriter printers except the 4100, 4500, and 6000 can use one of these drivers. If you have a Color StyleWriter 2200 or 2400, you can use the Color StyleWriter 2500 driver instead of the driver that came with the printer. If you have the Apple StyleWriter 1200, StyleWriter II, or original StyleWriter, you can use the StyleWriter 1500 driver.

Setting Color StyleWriter Page Setup options

When you choose the Page Setup command for a printer that uses a Color StyleWriter 1500, 2500, or Pro driver, you see a dialog box with settings for various page attributes. In addition, a Watermark button in the Color StyleWriter 1500 and 2500 dialog boxes lets you select a graphic to be printed lightly as a page background, like a watermark. Figure 17-16 shows the Page Setup dialog box and the Watermark dialog box for Color StyleWriter 2500.

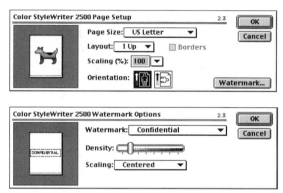

Figure 17-16: Setting page attributes (top) and watermark options (bottom) for Color StyleWriter page setup

Page attribute options

The Page Setup dialog box for the Color StyleWriter 1500, 2500, and Pro drivers has these page attribute options:

✦ **Page Size** lets you choose a paper size such as US Letter (8½ by 11 inches), US Legal (8½ by 14 inches), and #10 Envelope.

✦ **Layout** (not present with Color StyleWriter Pro) lets you choose a number of minipages to be printed per sheet of paper.

✦ **Borders** (not present with Color StyleWriter Pro) controls the printing of borders around minipages. This option becomes available if you set the Layout option to print more than one minipage per sheet of paper.

- **Scaling** reduces or enlarges the printed image according to the percentage you enter. You can either type a percentage or choose one from the pop-up menu. Full size is 100 percent, the minimum reduction is 5 percent, and the maximum enlargement is 999 percent.

- **Orientation** determines whether the top of the printed page will be on a short edge (portrait) or a long edge (landscape) of the paper.

Watermark options

The Watermark dialog box appears when you click the Watermark button in the Page Setup dialog box of the Color StyleWriter 1500, 2500, or Pro drivers. (A watermark is a faint image printed behind other text.) The Watermark dialog box has these options:

- **Watermark** specifies the graphic to be printed as a watermark. You choose one of the graphics listed in the Watermark pop-up menu, and a thumbnail preview of the watermark you chose appears in the dialog box. (You choose None if you no longer want a watermark.) The pop-up menu lists all graphics files of type PICT contained in the Printing Prefs folder, which is in the Preferences folder inside the System Folder. You can move files in and out of that folder with the Finder. In addition, you can create and edit watermark images with graphics programs such as ClarisWorks, Adobe Photoshop, and Macromedia FreeHand. If a watermark file contains text, make sure the fonts it uses are installed in your Fonts folder so that the text looks its best.

- **Density** adjusts the darkness of the watermark image. The thumbnail preview of the watermark image does not reflect changes to the Density setting.

- **Scaling** adjusts the size and placement of the watermark image on the page. You set this option by choosing from the Scaling pop-up menu. Your choices include:

  - **Centered** resizes the watermark to fill the center of the page without changing the watermark's original proportions.

  - **Align Top Left** places the watermark in its original size at the upper-left corner of the page.

  - **Stretch to Fit** resizes the watermark to fill the page from top-to-bottom and side-to-side, even if the watermark's proportions change.

Setting Color StyleWriter Print options

When you choose the Print command for a printer that uses a Color StyleWriter 1500, 2500, or Pro driver, you see a dialog box with settings for number of copies, page numbers to print, print quality, and more. The Color button lets you specify a color blending method and an optional color matching method. The Utilities button lets you specify that you want the printer to clean the ink cartridge or perform other available self-maintenance. Figure 17-17 shows the main and secondary Print dialog boxes for Color StyleWriter 2500.

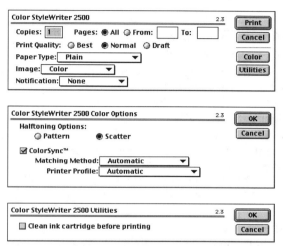

Figure 17-17: Setting options for Color StyleWriter printing (top), color printing (middle), and printer utilities (bottom)

Main Print options

The Print dialog box for the Color StyleWriter 1500, 2500, and Pro drivers has these main options:

✦ **Copies** specifies the number of copies to print.

✦ **Pages** specifies the range of pages to print.

✦ **Print Quality** offers a trade-off between appearance and speed, with Best quality the slowest and the best looking.

✦ **Paper Type** adjusts the printer for the selected type of paper.

✦ **Image** lets you choose the amount of color appropriate for your document. For color graphics or photos, choose Color or Grayscale. For text or line drawings without color or shades of gray, choose Black & White.

✦ **Notification** specifies a sound or message to use to notify you when your document finishes printing. You can choose any available system alert sound. (You can add or remove alert sounds with the SimpleSound program as described in Chapter 25.)

Color Options

The Color Options dialog box appears when you click the Color button in the Print dialog box for the Color StyleWriter 1500, 2500, and Pro drivers. The Color Options dialog box has these options:

✦ **Halftoning Options** specifies whether to blend colors and gray tones using a pattern of dots or a random scattering of dots.

✦ **ColorSync**, if turned on, specifies that Apple's ColorSync should match printed colors to displayed colors as closely as possible. This option is disabled unless the ColorSync software is installed and you set the Image option in the main Print dialog box to Color.

✦ **Matching Method** lets you choose the color matching method that's best for the content of your document. The Photographic method reduces color saturation, and the Business Graphics method increases color saturation. The Automatic method picks the Photographic method if the page contains mostly bitmap images or the Business Graphics method if the page contains mostly graphic objects.

✦ **Printer Profile** specifies the color profile to use for color matching. You choose a profile from the pop-up menu, which lists all the appropriate printer profile files in the ColorSync Profiles folder (which is in the Preferences folder inside the System Folder). This option is disabled unless the ColorSync option is turned on.

Utilities options

The Utilities dialog box appears when you click the Utilities button in the Print dialog box for the Color StyleWriter 1500, 2500, and Pro drivers. The Utilities dialog box has one or more options for cleaning the ink cartridge before printing. With the Color StyleWriter Pro driver, there are also options for preparing a new print head and for checking the printer alignment.

Setting Color StyleWriter 6000 Options

The last series of Color StyleWriter printer made by Apple — the Color StyleWriter 6000 series — offers a different driver and different controls from other StyleWriter printers.

Note   Apple warns that the Color StyleWriter 4000 series printer is not supported in Mac OS 9. A compatible driver for the printer is not included. As far as we know, no workaround is available; the solution is to use a different printer or an older version of the Mac OS.

Setting Color StyleWriter 6000 Page Setup options

When you choose the Page Setup command for a printer that uses the StyleWriter 6000 driver, you see a dialog box with settings for various page attributes. In addition, a Watermark button lets you select a graphic to be printed lightly as a page background, like a watermark. Figure 17-18 shows the Page Setup dialog box and the Watermark dialog box for StyleWriter 6000.

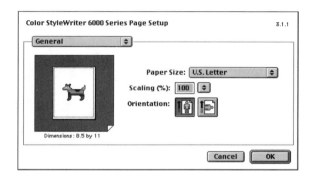

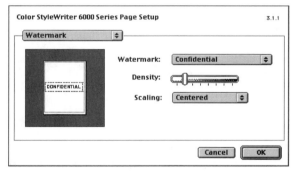

Figure 17-18: Setting page attributes (top) and watermark options (bottom) for StyleWriter page setup

All the Page Setup settings for the StyleWriter drivers are explained fully in the preceding section, "Setting Color StyleWriter Options."

Setting Color StyleWriter 6000 Print options

When you choose the Print command for a printer that uses the StyleWriter 6000 driver, a dialog box with an unlabeled pop-up menu, defaulting to General, displays. This menu gives you access to various Print options in a way similar to the LaserWriter 8 driver. All options are discussed here.

General options

When you choose General from the unlabeled pop-up menu near the top of the Print dialog box for the Color StyleWriter 6000, these options display, as shown in Figure 17-19:

✦ **Copies** specifies the number of copies to print.

✦ **Pages** specifies the range of pages to print.

✦ **Save Settings** makes the settings specified in the Print dialog box the ones used by default for this printer.

✦ **Revert to Defaults** changes the settings in the Print dialog box back to the factory defaults.

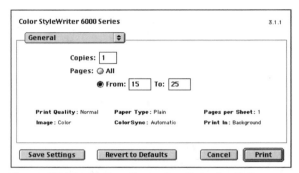

Figure 17-19: Setting General options for Color StyleWriter 6000 series printing

Paper Type/Quality options

When you choose Paper Type/Quality from the unlabeled pop-up menu near the top of the Print dialog box for the Color StyleWriter 6000, these options display, as shown in Figure 17-20:

✦ **Paper Type** specifies whether you'll be printing to plain paper or a special type of paper or output medium such as Premium Plus, Transparency, T-Shirt Transfer, or Glossy.

✦ **Print Quality** specifies Best, Normal, or Draft. Draft and Normal print more quickly and use less ink, but Best offers the highest resolution printing.

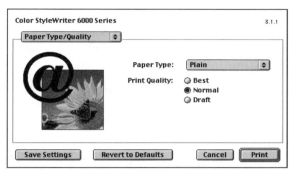

Figure 17-20: Setting Paper Type/Quality options for Color StyleWriter 6000 series printing

Layout options

When you choose Layout from the unlabeled pop-up menu near the top of the Print dialog box for the Color StyleWriter 6000 series, these options display, as shown in Figure 17-21:

✦ **Pages per sheet** lets you choose a number of minipages to print on each sheet of paper. Each minipage is a full-page image reduced in size so that two, four, or more minipages fit on a sheet of paper.

✦ **Print Borders** lets you choose whether a borderline will print around each reduced minipage. This option is available if you set the Pages per sheet option to more than one minipage per sheet of paper.

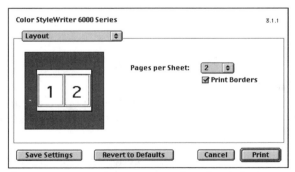

Figure 17-21: Setting Layout options for Color StyleWriter 6000 series printing

Color options

When you choose Color from the unlabeled pop-up menu near the top of the Print dialog box for the Color StyleWriter 6000 series, these options display, as shown in Figure 17-22:

✦ **Image** lets you choose whether to print the document in color, grayscale, or black and white.

✦ **Use ColorSync** improves the color matching between your monitor and printer when printing in color. This also opens up these options:

- **Matching Method**, which enables to you choose between Automatic, Photographic, and Business Graphics settings.

- **Printer Profile**, which enables you to choose a profile from the pop-up menu. The menu lists all the appropriate printer profile files in the ColorSync Profiles folder (which is in the Preferences folder inside the System Folder). You create these profiles in the ColorSync control panel.

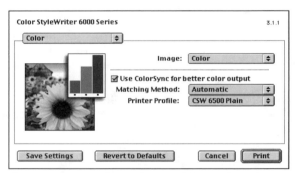

Figure 17-22: Setting Color Matching options for Color StyleWriter 6000 printing

Background Printing options

When you choose Background Printing from the unlabeled pop-up menu near the top of the Print dialog box for the Color StyleWriter 6000 series, these options display, as shown in Figure 17-23:

✦ **Print in** specifies whether you want your document to print in the foreground or background. Foreground printing requires less disk space than background printing and may cause your document to start printing faster, but it does not let you use the computer for anything else until printing stops. Background printing lets you work on other tasks while printing continues, but it requires extra disk space for temporary spool (page description) files. Foreground printing is not available in some applications.

✦ **Print Time** specifies a priority for printing a document in the background—urgent, normal, or hold—or a specific time and day when you want your document printed. You can change this setting for a document waiting to be printed in the background by opening the desktop printer icon (as described in Chapter 16). The Print Time option is disabled if you set the "Print in" option for foreground printing, which is always immediate.

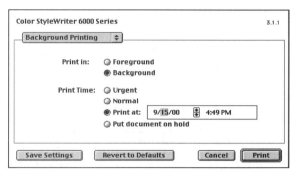

Figure 17-23: Setting Background Printing options for Color StyleWriter 6000 series printing

Services options

When you choose Services from the unlabeled pop-up menu near the top of the Print dialog box for the Color StyleWriter 6000 series, both of these options display, as shown in Figure 17-24:

✦ **Clean ink cartridges** before printing causes the Color StyleWriter to go through a cartridge-cleaning cycle before printing. The cleaning can be Simple, Clean, or Super Clean, each using more ink than the last. This option only needs to be selected when pages aren't printed crisply, output is smeared or blurry, or similar poor results are evident.

✦ **Align ink cartridges** before printing causes the printer to go through a cartridge alignment cycle before printing. This only needs to be selected if lines appear wavy or distorted in the printed output.

Note   Both of these options require that the printer be set to print in the foreground, as discussed previously in the "Background Printing options" section.

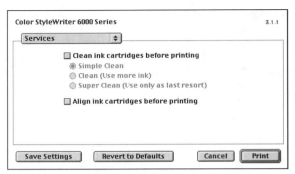

Figure 17-24: Setting Services options for Color
StyleWriter 6000 series printing

Setting LaserWriter 300/LS Options

This section describes how to set up and print documents on printers that use the
LaserWriter 300/LS driver. These drivers are for Apple laser printers that don't have
PostScript and that don't connect to a network, including the Personal LaserWriter
300, LaserWriter Select 300, and Personal LaserWriter LS.

Setting LaserWriter 300/LS Page Setup options

When you choose the Page Setup command for a printer that uses a LaserWriter
300/LS driver, a dialog box with settings for page size, scaling, and page orientation
displays. An Options button gives you access to printer effects. Figure 17-25 shows
the Page Setup dialog box and the Options dialog box for LaserWriter 300/LS.

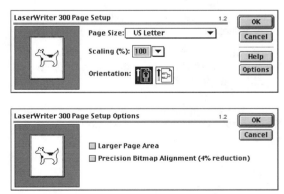

Figure 17-25: Setting page attributes (top) and
options (bottom) in LaserWriter 300/LS page setup

Page attribute options

The Page Setup dialog box for the LaserWriter 300/LS driver has these page attribute options:

✦ **Page Size** lets you choose a paper size such as US Letter (8½ by 11 inches), US Legal (8½ by 14 inches), and #10 Envelope.

✦ **Scaling** reduces or enlarges the printed image according to the percentage you enter. You can either type a percentage or choose one from the pop-up menu. Full size is 100 percent, the minimum reduction is 5 percent, and the maximum enlargement is 999 percent.

✦ **Orientation** determines whether the top of the printed page will be on a short edge or a long edge of the paper.

Page Setup Options

The Page Setup Options dialog box appears when you click Options in the Page Setup dialog box for the LaserWriter 300/LS driver. The Page Setup Options dialog box has these options:

✦ **Larger Page Area** lets you print closer to the edges of legal-size paper.

✦ **Precision Bitmap Alignment** reduces the entire printed image to avoid minor distortions in bitmap graphics. The distortions occur because of the nature of the dot density of bitmap graphics. For example, 72 dpi, which is the standard screen-image size, does not divide evenly into 300 dpi (the dot density of laser printers that use the LaserWriter 300/LS driver). Turning on this option reduces page images by 4 percent, effectively printing them at 288 dpi (an even multiple of 72 dpi). The reductions align the bitmaps properly to produce crisper output.

Setting LaserWriter 300/LS Print options

When you choose the Print command for a printer that uses the LaserWriter 300/LS driver, a dialog box with settings for number of copies, page numbers to print, paper source, and more displays. Clicking Options brings up a Print Options dialog box. Figure 17-26 shows the main Print and secondary Print Options dialog boxes for LaserWriter 300.

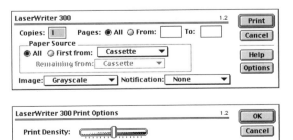

Figure 17-26: Setting options for LaserWriter 300 printing

In the main Print dialog box, you can set all pages to come from one paper source—paper cassette or manual-feed tray—or you can set the first page to come from one source and the remaining pages to come from another source. The LaserWriter 300/LS driver is not for PostScript printers and it cannot save page descriptions as a PostScript file.

The Image option lets you choose Grayscale for printing shades of gray, Black & White for fastest printing, or PhotoGrade (if the current printer is equipped with it) for enhanced grays. The Notification option specifies the sound or message to be used to notify you when your document finishes printing. You can choose any available system alert sound.

In the Print Options dialog box, you can set the print density by adjusting a slider. Moving the slider to the left makes printing lighter, thereby saving toner. Moving it to the right makes printing darker and uses more toner.

Setting ImageWriter Options

This section describes how to set up and print documents on printers that use the ImageWriter driver. The ImageWriter II and the original ImageWriter can use this driver.

Note   You may need to select a custom installation of Mac OS 9 to use the ImageWriter driver, which is not installed by default. After selecting a custom installation of the Mac OS, you can select the ImageWriter driver in the Printing module. (See Chapter 31 for more on custom installing the Mac OS.)

Setting ImageWriter Page Setup options

When you choose the Page Setup command for an ImageWriter II or original ImageWriter printer, you see a dialog box with settings for paper size, orientation, and special effects. Figure 17-27 shows the Page Setup dialog box for ImageWriter.

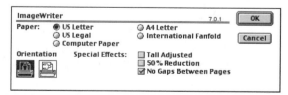

Figure 17-27: Setting page attributes and special effects for ImageWriter page setup

The Page Setup dialog box for the ImageWriter driver has these options:

✦ **Paper** lets you choose a paper size: single sheets of US Letter (8½ by 11 inches), US Legal (8½ by 14 inches), or A4 Letter (8½ by 11⅔ inches); Computer Paper (15 by 11 inches) or continuous, sprocket-fed International Fanfold (8¼ by 11 inches).

✦ **Orientation** determines whether the top of the printed page will be on a short edge (portrait) or a long edge (landscape) of the paper.

✦ **Tall Adjusted** correctly proportions graphics or text. Turning on this option prints graphics with correct proportions but widens individual text characters. Turning off this option prints text with correct proportions but elongates graphics.

✦ **50% Reduction** prints page images half their actual size.

✦ **No Gaps Between Pages** eliminates top and bottom margins, primarily for printing continuously on fanfold paper.

Hints for better ImageWriter printing

If pictures printed on an ImageWriter look vertically stretched, as though El Greco had drawn them, choose the Page Setup command's Tall Adjusted option. This option adjusts the computer output from 72 dpi to the 80-dpi vertical resolution of the printer, thus generating a proportional image.

To avoid the irregular word spacing that occurs in draft mode, change your document's font to a monospaced font, such as Monaco or Courier, for printing out a draft. The fixed-spaced font on the screen then will match the spacing of the printer's internal font, making the draft easier to read. Change your document to a more professional variable-sized font, such as Helvetica or Times, when you are ready to print your final copy. Be aware that if the position of line and page breaks is an issue, the font change does affect them.

Always install bitmap fonts in pairs—9-point with 18-point, 10-point with 20-point, and so on—so that the Font Manager portion of the Mac OS has the larger font available for scaling in Best mode. The best way to avoid spacing problems is to use TrueType fonts (or PostScript fonts and Adobe Type Manager software) and let the computer do the scaling for you.

A very clear font for use with the ImageWriter family is Boston II, a shareware font that is available from user groups and online information services.

Best quality looks clearest with a slightly used printer ribbon, not with a brand-new ribbon, because there is less smudging of characters from high levels of ink on the ribbon.

Do not stockpile ribbons for an ImageWriter; buy them one or two at a time. The ink in the ribbons dries out over time.

Setting ImageWriter Print options

When you choose the Print command for an ImageWriter II or an original ImageWriter printer, a dialog box with settings for print quality, page numbers to print, number of copies, and paper source displays. Figure 17-28 shows the Print dialog box for ImageWriter.

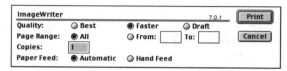

Figure 17-28: Setting options for ImageWriter printing

Choosing the Best quality option prints your document at 144 dpi, which is twice the screen resolution. Best quality is slower than Faster quality, which prints at 72 dpi. Draft quality prints text only (no pictures) with a font that is built in the printer. The built-in font's spacing matches the spacing of Monaco 10-point and other 10-point monospaced fonts. Printing proportionally spaced fonts in Draft quality results in poorly spaced letters and words that may be hard to read.

Summary

This chapter showed you how to print a document from the Finder using desktop printers or the Print command. You can also print a document from an application that can open it by using the application's Page Setup and Print commands. You use the same commands for all printers, but the options available in the Print and Page Setup dialog boxes depend on the printer driver for the printer. This chapter detailed the Page Setup and Print options for printers that use these drivers:

✦ LaserWriter 8

✦ Color StyleWriter 2500, Color StyleWriter 1500, and Color StyleWriter Pro (including older StyleWriter printers)

✦ Color StyleWriter 6000 series

✦ LaserWriter 300/LS

✦ ImageWriter

✦   ✦   ✦

Work with Sound, Video, and 3-D

T he Mac OS gives you many ways to enjoy audio and
video. Apple's QuickTime technology enables you to
watch digital movies, including MPEG video. You can also use
QuickTime to listen to digitized sound and synthesized music.
With QuickTime VR, you can view "virtual reality" panoramas
and objects interactively.

If your computer has a CD-ROM drive, you can use the
AppleCD Audio Player program to control playback of audio
CDs from your computer's CD-ROM drive, using simple push
buttons or sophisticated programming of tracks by name. If
your computer has a DVD-ROM drive, you can do all these
things plus play back DVD-encoded movies. If your computer
has video-input ports or a TV tuner expansion card, you can
use the Apple Video Player program to view videos from video
equipment such as a camcorder, VCR, or television, and to
capture that video input digitally on disk.

This chapter explains how to use all this audio and video
software.

Introducing QuickTime Movies

Apple's QuickTime software enables your computer to work
with data that changes over time, or *time-based data*, such as
motion pictures with sound. In other words, it lets you store
and watch movies on your computer. In fact, just about all
Macintosh computers can play QuickTime movies. QuickTime
doesn't require any special equipment, although faster
computers generally play movies more smoothly than slower
computers.

Apple's QuickTime software not only makes it possible to play movies on your computer, QuickTime makes movies ubiquitous! You don't need a special program to watch QuickTime movies. Most applications let you copy and paste movies as easily as you copy and paste graphics, and you can play a QuickTime movie wherever you encounter one. For starters, you can watch QuickTime movies from — and paste them in — SimpleText and the ScrapBook. Figure 18-1 is an example of a QuickTime movie in a SimpleText window.

Figure 18-1: Watching a QuickTime movie in SimpleText

There's more to QuickTime movies than a motion picture and a soundtrack. Recent versions of QuickTime expand the definition of movie considerably to include all kinds of interesting data that change or move over time. With the latest version of QuickTime, "movies" can include any combination of:

✦ **Motion pictures** — such as what you watch on TV or at the movies

✦ **Digitized sound recordings** — music and other sounds — that play in CD-quality sound (44.1kHz, 18-bit stereo)

✦ **Synthesized music** based on MIDI (Musical Instrument Digital Interface), which takes far less disk space to store than digitized sound, yet sounds realistic and plays in CD-quality

✦ **Text** for closed-caption viewing, karaoke sing-a-longs, or text-based searches of movie content

✦ **Three-dimensional graphics**, drawn live by QuickDraw 3D as they spin and move across the screen

✦ **Sprites**, which move independently, like actors moving on a stage with a motion-picture backdrop

✦ **MPEG** movies that use the common MPEG-1 video and audio standard

✦ **Panoramas and objects** that you can view in 360 degrees using QuickTime VR methods

✦ **Timecode information**, which displays elapsed hours, minutes, seconds, and frames at the bottom of a playing movie

✦ **Functional information**, such as information that tells QuickTime how other tracks interact

What's in a movie

The motion pictures, sound, and other types of time-based data in a QuickTime movie exist in separate tracks. A simple movie might consist of one video track and one sound track. A more complex movie may have several video tracks, several audio tracks, and closed-caption text tracks for text subtitles. Each video track could be designed specially for playback with a certain number of available colors (for example, 256 colors, thousands of colors, and millions of colors), each audio track could provide dialog in a different language (English, Spanish, Japanese, and so on), and each closed-caption text track could provide subtitles in a different language.

If a QuickTime movie contains MIDI-synthesized music, sprites, QuickDraw 3D graphics, or a QuickTime VR scene or object, then each is in a separate track. QuickTime takes care of synchronizing all of the tracks so that they play at the right time.

QuickTime magic

A computer shouldn't be capable of playing digital movies any more than a bumblebee should be able to fly. A single full-screen color picture on a 14-inch monitor takes a megabyte of disk space. To show 30 pictures, or frames, per second, which is what you see on TV, a computer has to store, retrieve, and display 30MB per second. Only the fastest computers and hard disk drives are that fast. Even if you have a fast computer, storage space is still a problem for movies. For example, a 1-minute video clip requires 1800MB of disk space.

QuickTime pulls every trick in the book to play movies. Most movies are smaller than the full 640 × 480 pixels available on a 14-inch color monitor. In QuickTime's early days, when PowerPC processors didn't exist and single-speed CD-ROM drives were state-of-the-art, QuickTime movies were the size of a large postage stamp (160 × 120 pixels). Today, quarter-screen movies (320 × 240 pixels) play back smoothly from a CD-ROM and fast Power Macintosh computers can play full-screen movies from a hard disk with relative ease.

QuickTime movies may play back fewer frames per second than TV or movies. You see 30 *fps* (frames per second) on TV or videotape in the United States and other countries that use the NTSC standard (25 fps in Europe and other places that use the PAL or SECAM standards). By comparison, many QuickTime movies are designed to play at 15 fps from a CD-ROM.

Compressed images

QuickTime not only handles time-based and interactive media, but it also extends the standard graphics format PICT to handle compressed still images and image previews. An application that recognizes QuickTime can compress a graphic image using any QuickTime-compatible software or hardware compressor that is available on your computer. All applications that can open uncompressed PICT images are also capable of opening compressed PICT images. QuickTime automatically decompresses a compressed PICT image without requiring changes to the application program.

Showing small pictures at slow frame rates reduces the amount of data to be stored, retrieved, and displayed, but not nearly enough. So QuickTime compresses movies, throwing out the redundant parts. Built-in and add-on *codecs*, or *compressor/ decompressor* software performs the compression. These special algorithms come in various formats, generally offering different trade-offs between picture quality and the amount of data required for a movie. A compressed movie contains less data to store on disk. Just as importantly, a compressed movie contains less data to be transferred each second from that hard disk, CD-ROM, or the Internet.

Getting QuickTime software

You get the QuickTime 4.0 software as a part of the standard installation of Mac OS 9. You can upgrade to QuickTime Pro for $29.95 by phone (1–888–295–0648) or from Apple's QuickTime site on the Web (http://www.apple.com/quicktime/). In some cases, you can get a free upgrade to QuickTime Pro when you purchase a retail version of the Mac OS.

Note   The standard QuickTime 4.0 installation upgrades QuickTime 3.0 Pro to QuickTime 4.0 Pro without the requirement of an additional payment. If you need to do a clean install of the Mac OS, you can enter your QuickTime 3.0 Pro registration information (if you've previously upgraded) in QuickTime 4.0's QuickTime control panel.

Some applications replace QuickTime with an earlier version than what was installed on your computer. All kinds of problems may ensue as a result of installing an earlier version of QuickTime, some of which seem unrelated to QuickTime. Not only may some QuickTime movies no longer play, but you may not be able to open as many different types of graphics and audio files as you could before the earlier version was installed. To fix these problems, install QuickTime 4.0 (actually, it's version 4.0.3 if you're keeping score) from the Mac OS 9 CD or from software you get from Apple's QuickTime Web site and do not allow installers to replace it with earlier versions.

What's in QuickTime 4.0 Pro?

What do you get when you plunk down $29.95 to upgrade from the basic edition of QuickTime 4 to QuickTime 4 Pro? The upgrade enables the PictureViewer Pro application to save still images (in BMP, JPEG, Photoshop, PICT, or QuickTime Image format). The upgrade similarly enables the QuickTime plug-in for Web browsers to save movies from the Web.

Moreover, the upgrade brings many improvements to the QuickTime Player application. Here's what QuickTime Player Pro can do that the basic QuickTime Player cannot:

✦ Create new movies

✦ Open a sequence of still images as a movie

✦ Import these media formats: 3DMF 3D image; regular and karaoke MIDI music; PICS animation; PICT image; System 7 Sound; and text

✦ Export movies to these media formats: BMP image, DV stream, PICT image, and QuickTime movie

✦ Export sound tracks to these sound formats: AIFF, System 7 Sound, Wave, and µLaw

✦ Apply video and audio compression

✦ Edit movies by drag-and-drop and with Cut, Copy, and Paste commands

✦ Extract individual tracks from a movie

✦ Show and set the movie poster frame

✦ Present a movie centered on a black screen

✦ Play a movie at half size and full-screen size

✦ Play a movie in a continuous loop

✦ Play only the selected part of a movie

✦ Adjust the size and orientation of each video track in the movie frame

✦ Show and set the following additional movie information: Colors, Controller, Files, General, and Preview

✦ Show and set the following additional video track information: Alternate Language; Format; Frame Rate; Gamma; General; Graphics Mode; High Quality; Layer; Mask; and Preload

✦ Show and set the following additional sound track information: Alternate Language, Files, General, High Quality, Preload, and Volume

Playing QuickTime Movies

QuickTime makes it possible to play movies in all kinds of applications and it establishes standard methods for controlling playback in all applications. There is a standard QuickTime movie controller, and there are standard methods for controlling play back when the controller is absent. The QuickTime Player application included with QuickTime has additional features that you can use to play movies. If you play movies that contain MIDI-synthesized music, you may be able to affect how they sound by setting some options in the QuickTime Settings control panel.

The QuickTime movie controller

You usually control playback of a QuickTime movie with a standard collection of buttons and sliders along the bottom edge of the movie. With this controller, you can play, stop, browse, or step through the movie. If the movie has a soundtrack, you can use the controller to adjust the sound level. The controller also gauges where the current scene is in relation to the beginning and end of the movie. By pressing certain keys while operating the controller, you can turn the sound on and off, copy and paste parts of the movie, play in reverse, change the playback rate, and more. Figure 18-2 summarizes the functions of a standard QuickTime movie controller. (Some applications have variants of the standard controller and may put the controller in a palette that floats above the document window.)

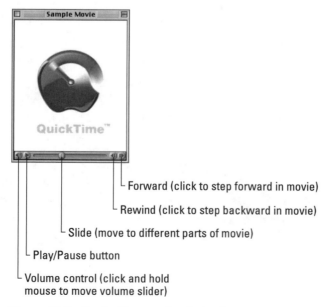

Figure 18-2: Controlling movie playback

Playing and pausing

To start a movie playing, click the play button. This button has a right-pointing triangle like the play button on a tape recorder or VCR. While a movie is playing, this button becomes a pause button.

Stepping forward and backward

The two step buttons at the right of the play bar step backward and forward at the rate of one frame per click. The step buttons have different effects on movies that don't have frames. For example, in a movie that has only sound or music tracks, each click of a step button skips ahead or back a quarter of a second.

Going to another part of the movie

The gray play bar in the middle of the movie controller shows the position of the currently playing frame relative to the beginning and end of the movie. To go to a different place in the movie, you can drag the frame marker in the play bar or simply click the play bar.

You can go immediately to the beginning or end of the movie. To go to the beginning, Option+click the forward-step button. To go to the end, Option+click the backward-step button.

Adjusting the sound

To adjust the sound level, use the button labeled with the speaker. Click and hold down this button to pop up a slider that you can use to raise or lower the sound level. You can turn the sound off and on by Option+clicking the speaker button. You can set the sound level to up to three times louder than its normal maximum by holding down Shift while adjusting the level with the slider. If the speaker button is absent, the movie has no sound.

Changing playback direction and speed

To play the movie backward, ⌘+click the reverse-step button. Control+click either step button to reveal a jog shuttle that controls the direction and playback rate. Dragging the jog shuttle to the right gradually increases the forward playback rate from below normal to twice normal speed. Dragging the jog shuttle to the left has the same effect on playback speed, but makes the movie play backward.

QuickTime controller shortcuts

The QuickTime movie controller responds to all kinds of keyboard shortcuts. Pressing Return or Spacebar alternately starts and pauses play forward. Pressing ⌘+period (.) also pauses playing. You can press ⌘+right arrow (→) to play forward and ⌘+left arrow (←) to play backward. Press the right arrow (→) to step forward and left arrow (←) to step backward. To raise or lower the sound level, press the up arrow (↑) or down arrow (↓). Shift+up arrow (↑) raises the sound level beyond its normal maximum.

Choosing a chapter

A text area appears to the left of the step buttons in the movie controller for some movies. This chapter-list button lets you go to predetermined points in the movie, much as index tabs let you turn to sections of a binder. Pressing the chapter-list button pops up a menu of chapter titles, and choosing a chapter title takes you quickly to the corresponding part of the movie. If the chapter-list button is absent, the movie has no chapters defined.

Playback without controllers

Applications may display movies without controllers. In this case, a badge in the lower-left corner of the movie distinguishes it from a still graphic. To play a movie that has a badge and no controller, double-click the movie. If you press Shift while double-clicking the movie, it plays backward. Clicking a playing movie stops it. You can also display a standard movie controller by clicking the badge. Figure 18-3 shows a QuickTime movie with a badge.

Figure 18-3: Identifying a movie without a controller

The QuickTime Player application

Although you don't need a special application to view QuickTime movies, QuickTime 4.0 includes one called QuickTime Player. With the QuickTime Player menu commands, you have more control over playing a movie. In some cases, however, you have less control over a movie. That's because the QuickTime Player application sports a new, sleeker interface that has traded some features with the desire to look more like a consumer device. So, although some of the controls are more like those found on a VCR, for instance, you don't always have access to the same controls that you have in the QuickTime controller, such as the one that appears in SimpleText when you view a movie through SimpleText.

First, let's look at the application's interface itself and how it differs from the standard QuickTime controls. Then, let's look at some of the additional features that the QuickTime Player Pro application offers. Some commands are not available in the basic edition of QuickTime Player, which comes with the free version of QuickTime 4.0. These commands become available when you upgrade to QuickTime 4.0 Pro. The following descriptions of QuickTime Player commands indicate the QuickTime Player versions in which the described command is available.

The QuickTime Player interface

When you launch a movie in the QuickTime Player application, you'll find a number of slight differences from the QuickTime controls found in other applications, as Figure 18-4 details.

Most of the differences are cosmetic, although some of them force you to click a few extra times to make things happen. A few features are missing — for instance, you can't use ⌘+click on the step buttons to bring up a shuttle jog control.

Also, some of these controls are hidden from view. To reveal the hidden controls, click the small button with four dots at the right side of the interface under the slider bar.

The Favorites is a "drawer," where you can store your favorite movies and/or Web sites of movies (these tend to be used more for streaming QuickTime, discussed later in this chapter). To open the Favorites drawer, grab the Favorite's handle and drag that part of the window down.(You can also choose Favorites ➪ Open Favorites Drawer.) You'll see the icons in the favorites drawer. To add the current movie as a Favorites, select Favorites ➪ Add Favorite from the menu; the current movie becomes a favorite.

Tip

You can change the volume quickly by dragging your mouse pointer across the volume level indicator (the lines, not the wheel) from left to right (or back again) while holding down the mouse button. Likewise, you can drag the mouse over the Balance, Bass, and Treble settings instead of clicking the plus and minus buttons.

Volume control

Forward and Backward

Play button   Info button

Pause button   Additional controls (hides and
                      reveals controls, shown revealed)

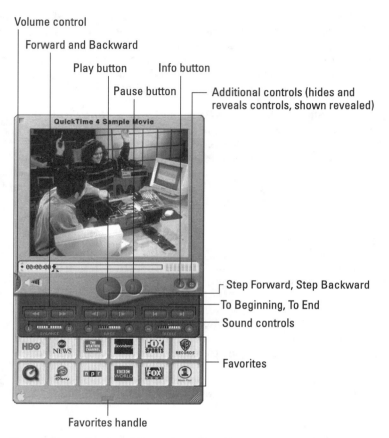

Step Forward, Step Backward

To Beginning, To End

Sound controls

Favorites

Favorites handle

Figure 18-4: The QuickTime Player interface

For the most part, you'll probably confine your mouse clicks to the controls in the QuickTime Player interface. Occasionally, however, you'll find it useful to actually click inside the movie window. QuickTime 4.0 supports the display of Macromedia Flash documents, which offer buttons and links that can be clicked in the movie window. If you're viewing an image (especially one that's available via a streaming QuickTime connection over the Internet), you may be able to click a button or link in the QuickTime Player's movie window.

Changing the window size

Unlike many other applications that can show QuickTime movies, the QuickTime Player application displays QuickTime movies in windows with size boxes. If you resize a movie window, QuickTime resizes the movie to fill the window. A resized movie generally plays less smoothly if you change its proportions. As a precautionary measure, QuickTime 4.0 normally forces movie windows to maintain their original proportions. To resize without this constraint, press Shift while dragging the size box.

A movie looks best at an even multiple of its original size, such as half-size or double size. QuickTime Player will constrain a movie to an optimal multiple of its original size if you press Option while dragging the movie window's size box. To quickly shrink a window to the nearest even multiple of its original size, Option+click its size box.

In addition to dragging a movie window's size box, you can use QuickTime Player menu commands to resize it. The basic edition of QuickTime Player has Full Screen, Double Size, and Normal Size commands.

Presenting a movie

Instead of displaying a movie in a window, you can present it centered on a completely black screen. In QuickTime Player Pro, choose Present Movie from the File menu. (The Present Movie command is not available in the basic edition of QuickTime Player.)

The Present Movie command displays a dialog box in which you can set the movie size and specify whether you want to play the movie normally or slide show fashion (i.e., one frame at a time). If your computer has more than one monitor, this dialog box lets you select the monitor on which you want the movie presented. Setting a movie's presentation size in this dialog box to Double or Full Screen usually produces better results than resizing the movie manually before presenting it.

If your monitor is capable of displaying several screen resolutions, such as 640 × 480 and 832 × 624, QuickTime Player may force it to switch temporarily before presenting a movie. QuickTime Player switches to the resolution that is closest to but not smaller than the movie's size before presenting a movie at normal size, double size, or half size. After presenting the movie, QuickTime Player switches back to the resolution you were using. As a side effect of this resolution switching, windows in other open programs and desktop icons may be repositioned. You may have to spend a little time moving icons and windows back to their former positions.

To stop a movie presentation, press Escape or ⌘+period (.). You can also stop the presentation of a normal movie by clicking the mouse button. With a slide show presentation, clicking the mouse button advances to the next movie frame; double-clicking goes back one frame.

Searching for a text track

While viewing a movie that contains a text track, you can search for specific text in the movie. In QuickTime Player Pro, choose Find from the Edit menu. (Text searching is not available in the basic edition of QuickTime Player.)

The Find command displays a dialog box in which you enter the text to find and specify whether to search forward or backward. If QuickTime Player finds the text you're looking for, it immediately shows the corresponding part of the movie and highlights the found text. You can search for another occurrence of the same text by choosing Find Again from the Edit menu. Figure 18-5 shows an example of a movie with found text highlighted.

Figure 18-5: Found text in a movie's text track

If the Find command is disabled (grayed out), the movie doesn't have a text track.

Choosing a language

QuickTime movies can have sound tracks in several languages. To select the language you want to hear, choose the Choose Language command from the Movie menu. QuickTime Player displays a dialog box that lists the available languages. If the Choose Language command is disabled (grayed out), the movie doesn't have sound tracks in multiple languages.

Playing continuously (looping)

You can set QuickTime Player Pro to play a QuickTime movie in a continuous loop, either always playing forward or playing alternately forward and backward. Choose Loop or Loop Back and Forth from the Movie menu. (These commands are not available in the basic edition of QuickTime Player.)

Playing part of a movie

In QuickTime Player Pro, you can select part of a movie and then play only the selected part. (You can't select part of a movie in the basic edition of QuickTime Player.)

To select part of a movie, first drag both of the selection triangles to the far left edge of the slider bar (see Figure 18-6). Now, move the slider to the place in the movie where you want to begin selecting. Then Shift+click the play button to start the movie and begin selecting. Release Shift to end the selection and stop playing. The selected part of the movie appears gray in the play bar. Figure 18-6 shows a movie that has been partly selected.

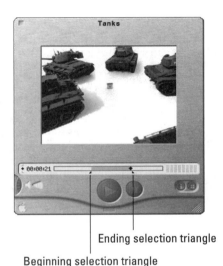

Figure 18-6: Selecting part of a movie with the Shift key or selection triangles makes part of the play bar turn gray.

Ending selection triangle

Beginning selection triangle

You can also use the small selection triangles just below the progress slider to select the first and last highlighted frames. Choose the beginning selection triangle and drag it to the first frame you'd like to select, then drag the ending selection triangle to the last frame you'd like to select. You can click a selection triangle, then use the left (←) and right (→) arrow keys to move frame by frame.

To play the selected part of a movie, choose Play Selection Only from the Movie menu and then click the play button. When there is a check mark next to Play Selection Only in the Movie menu, all the movie controls and QuickTime Player commands apply only to the selected part. For example, the Loop command causes only the selected part to play continuously. You can go immediately to the beginning or end of the selection by Option+clicking the appropriate step button.

You can extend or reduce a selection by moving the selection triangles to extend or reduce the selection. To adjust the end point of a selection precisely, click the selection triangle you want to affect and press the left (←) and right (→) arrow keys. To cancel a selection, drag both selection arrows to the far-left side of the play bar.

Playing every frame

In QuickTime Player Pro, you can prevent QuickTime from dropping any video frames to keep the video and audio tracks synchronized. If you want to see every frame even if it means playing the movie more slowly and without sound, choose Play All Frames from the Movie menu. (The Play All Frames command is not available in the basic edition of QuickTime Player.)

Playing all movies

You can have QuickTime Player Pro play all movies that are currently open by choosing Play All Movies from the Movie menu. (This command is not available in the basic edition of QuickTime Player.)

Streaming QuickTime

QuickTime 4.0 introduces a new technology to the world of QuickTime—*streaming media*. With streaming media, QuickTime movie files (whether they contain video, audio, text, or other elements) are sent over the Internet a piece at a time. Those pieces are reassembled in the QuickTime Player and played back almost as quickly as the data arrives over the Internet. In this way, movies can be viewed (or listened to) more quickly over the Internet. Likewise, live events can be displayed in "real-time" over the Web (see Figure 18-7).

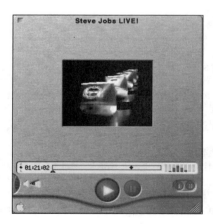

Figure 18-7: Apple often uses QuickTime to stream live keynotes and product announcements over the Web.

For the most part, this doesn't require much different interaction than regular movies. Most of the time, you view streaming QuickTime movies by clicking a hyperlink in your Web browser, which will launch the QuickTime Player and begin the movie. You can also access streaming media from the QuickTime Player itself, either by clicking a Favorite (in the Favorite's drawer) that leads to a streaming media site, or by choosing File ➪ Open URL and entering a streaming media URL.

Tip

For optimum streaming, QuickTime Player consults the settings for Internet connection in the QuickTime control panel. Make sure these settings are accurate (you tell the panel how fast your modem or network connection to the Internet is) and you'll get better playback from streaming movies.

With some streaming media movies, you can pause, play, and move back and forth within the movie file using the play bar or the forward and reverse controls. In others, especially live events, you won't have as much control — pausing and playing again will take you to the current moment in the live event instead of picking up where you left off.

Interacting with QuickTime VR Scenes

You can do more with QuickTime than play linear movies. Apple's QuickTime VR software lets you explore places as if you were really there and examine objects as if they were with you. When you view a QuickTime VR panorama of a place, you can look up, look down, turn around, zoom in to see detail, and zoom out for a broader view. When you view a QuickTime VR object, you can manipulate it to see a different view of it. As you explore a panorama, you can move from it into a neighboring panorama or to an object in it. For example, you could move from one room to another room and then examine an object there.

You can interact with a QuickTime VR panorama or object from any application in which you can view a linear QuickTime movie. You can use SimpleText, the ScrapBook, QuickTime Player, a Web browser, or any other application that can play QuickTime movies.

When you view a QuickTime VR panorama or object, a QuickTime VR controller sometimes appears at the bottom of the window. It's in the same place as the controller for a regular QuickTime movie (especially those viewed with the conventional controller in applications like SimpleText), but you don't use the QuickTime VR controller as the primary means of interacting with a QuickTime VR scene. You simply drag the mouse pointer to explore a QuickTime VR panorama or investigate a QuickTime VR object. The remainder of this section describes how to use the mouse pointer and the VR controller to interact with a QuickTime VR scene.

Exploring VR panoramas

To look around a QuickTime VR panorama, you click the picture and drag left, right, up, or down. The picture moves in the direction that you drag, and the pointer changes shape to indicate the direction of movement. Figure 18-8 shows a QuickTime VR panorama being moved to the right. The pointer in the center foreground indicates the direction of the pan.

Pan
Show hot spots
Zoom in
Zoom out
Go back
Show and set volume

Drag mouse pointer

Figure 18-8: Moving the picture in a QuickTime VR panorama to the right

The controllers often don't appear when you view a QuickTime VR image through the Web browser plug-in. If you have QuickTime Pro installed, however, you can save the panorama As Source (click and hold the mouse button on the QuickTime VR image), and then double-click it in the Finder to load it in a QuickTime VR window, complete with controls. Also, not all VR panoramas have sound tracks, but those that do include a volume slider at the left edge of the controls.

Investigating VR objects

To manipulate a QuickTime VR object, you click it and drag left, right, up, or down. As you drag, the object, or some part of it, moves. For example, it may turn around so that you can see all sides of it, or it may open and close. The author of the VR picture determines the effect.

When viewing a QuickTime VR object, you can also place the pointer near an inside edge of the VR window and press the mouse button to move the object continuously. Figure 18-9 shows several views of QuickTime VR object.

Figure 18-9: Manipulating a QuickTime VR object

Zooming in and out

While viewing a QuickTime VR panorama or object, you can zoom in or out. To zoom in, click the VR controller button that looks like a magnifying glass with a plus sign. To zoom out, click the button that looks like a magnifying glass with a minus sign. You can also press Shift to zoom in or press Control to zoom out.

As you zoom in on an object, it eventually becomes too large to see all at once in the QuickTime VR window. There are two ways to view another part of a zoomed-in object. You can click the controller button labeled with two crossed arrows and then drag the object or you can press Option while dragging the object. Either way, the object holds its pose as it moves around in the window. To resume normal operation, click the button again or release the Option key.

Interacting with hot spots

A QuickTime VR panorama or object can contain hot spots. These are areas of the picture that you click to cause some action to occur. Typically, the action involves going to another panorama or object. A hot spot can trigger another kind of action, such as displaying text in the empty area of the VR controller or taking you to a Web page.

Hot spots are normally unmarked. One way to find them is to move the pointer around the panorama or object. When the pointer is over a hot spot, its shape changes. A variety of different pointer shapes may indicate a hot spot. One common shape is a large white arrow pointing up.

You can also have QuickTime VR show the hot spots in the picture. To highlight the hot spots with translucent rectangles, click the VR controller button labeled with an up arrow and question mark. If you double-click this button, it stays down and you can see all hot spots as you drag the pointer to move the picture. Figure 18-10 is an example of an outlined hot spot in a QuickTime VR panorama.

Click to outline hot spots

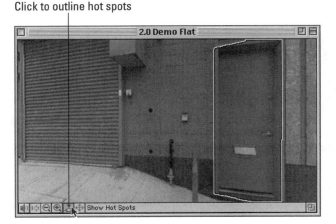

Figure 18-10: Hot spots revealed in a QuickTime VR panorama (the highlighted area around the door)

If clicking a hot spot takes you to another panorama or object, you can go back to your previous location by clicking the back button, which is labeled with a left arrow in the VR controller. If you've progressed through several hot spots, you can retrace your steps by clicking the back button repeatedly.

Viewing QuickDraw 3D Objects

There's more to QuickTime than interacting with VR panoramas and objects or playing regular movies. QuickTime incorporates Apple's QuickDraw 3D software, which renders three-dimensional images in real time. You don't need any special equipment, just a Mac with a PowerPC processor and at least 16MB of RAM. QuickDraw 3D works best on a monitor that is set to display thousands or millions of colors.

You can view and manipulate QuickDraw 3D graphics in any application designed to take advantage of it, such as the versions of SimpleText and Scrapbook that come with Mac OS 9. In participating applications such as these, QuickDraw 3D provides a viewer with buttons for changing the view of the image, as shown in Figure 18-11.

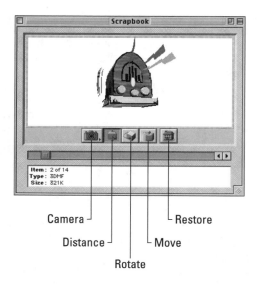

Figure 18-11: A QuickDraw 3D viewer has buttons for changing the view.

The QuickDraw 3D viewer's buttons let you move the image closer or farther away, rotate and tilt the image, move the image in the viewer frame, and restore the original view. In some applications, you get a five-button viewer, whereas other applications provide a four-button viewer. Here's how the buttons work:

✦ **Camera**. Choose a view from the menu that pops up when you click this button. Choices typically include Fit To View, Front View, Back View, Left View, Right View, Top View, and Bottom View.

✦ **Distance**. Click inside the frame and drag toward the bottom of the frame to move the image closer, or drag toward the top of the frame to move the image farther away.

✦ **Rotate**. Click the image and drag to rotate it, or click outside the image and drag to tilt it.

✦ **Move**. Drag the image to move it vertically or horizontally in the frame.

✦ **Restore**. Click the button to restore the initial viewing distance, rotation, and position in the frame. This button is not present in some applications.

QuickDraw 3D also establishes a common file format for 3D graphics, called 3DMF (for "3D metafile"). The 3DMF format for 3D graphics is analogous to the PICT format for 2D graphics.

You don't always interact with QuickDraw 3D graphics. QuickTime movies can show animated QuickDraw 3D graphics together with video and audio tracks.

Basic QuickTime Movie Editing

If you have QuickTime Player Pro, you're not limited to playing movies. You can also copy, paste, and otherwise edit movies. This section describes basic editing tasks that you can perform. (The free, basic edition of QuickTime Player doesn't include editing capabilities — you have to upgrade to QuickTime 4.0 Pro, as described in "Introducing QuickTime Movies" earlier in this chapter.)

Selecting and copying a movie clip

You can select all or part of a movie and copy it to the Clipboard so that you can put it in another movie. First you must select the part of the movie that you want to copy. Move the slider in the play bar until you see the beginning of the part that you want to select. Then hold down Shift and drag the slider until you see the end of the part that you want to select. As you drag, the play bar turns black to indicate the selected part. Alternatively, you can Shift+click near the end of the part that you want to select and then, while continuing to hold down Shift, drag the slider to the exact end of the selection. You can make a selection from right to left, as well as from left to right. Figure 18-6, shown previously, illustrates a movie that has been partly selected.

If you have trouble moving the slider to exactly the right place, try using the arrow keys in concert with the selection triangles. You can also make a selection by holding down Shift while playing a movie.

QuickTime Player includes the first frame of your selection in any operations, but not the last frame. If you'd like the last frame selected to be part of any commands (Copy, Paste, and so on) you need to move one frame *past* that frame, usually by clicking the end selection triangle and pressing the right arrow (→) key. To check the entire selection, choose Play Selection Only from the Movie menu and then play the movie. Only the selection plays when there is a check mark next to Play Selection Only.

To select a whole movie, choose Select All from the Edit menu. You can cancel a selection by choosing Select None from the Edit menu or dragging both selection triangles to the beginning of the movie.

To place the selected part of a movie on the Clipboard, choose Copy from the Edit menu. You can choose Cut instead, but this, of course, deletes the selected part of the movie in addition to placing it on the Clipboard.

Pasting a movie clip

After copying or cutting a movie clip to the Clipboard, you can paste it anywhere in the same movie or another movie. Simply move the slider to the place where you want to insert the movie clip, and choose Paste from the Edit menu. The QuickTime Player always inserts the pasted clip before the slider position.

If you want to review a clip after pasting it, use the Play Selection Only command.

Replacing part of a movie

You can replace part of a movie with a movie clip on the Clipboard. After copying the replacement clip, select the part of the movie you want to replace. Then hold down Shift and choose Replace from the Edit menu. While Shift is down, Replace appears in the Edit menu instead of Paste.

Deleting part of a movie

You can delete the selected part of a movie by choosing Clear from the Edit menu. Pressing Delete also deletes the selected part of a movie.

Instead of deleting the selected part of a movie, you can trim away everything that's not selected. Hold down Option and choose Trim from the Edit menu. While Option is down, Trim replaces Clear in the Edit menu.

You can use the Undo command in the Edit menu to restore a movie if you change your mind about clearing or trimming.

Deleting movie tracks

Rather than delete a selected part of a movie, you may want to delete an entire track. For example, you could delete the sound track to make a silent movie or you could delete the video track to make an audio-only movie. To delete tracks, choose Delete Tracks from the Edit menu. QuickTime Player displays a dialog box that lists the movie's tracks by name. You can select one or more tracks and click Delete to delete them. To select multiple tracks, ⌘+click each one. To select several adjacent tracks, click the first one and then Shift+click the last. Figure 18-12 is an example of the Delete Tracks dialog box.

Figure 18-12: Deleting tracks from a movie

Adding movie tracks

Instead of inserting a movie clip with the Paste command, you can add it to a movie as an overlaid track or tracks. The tracks you add play at the same time as the other tracks in the same part of the movie. For example, you can add a sound track to a silent movie, and both video and sound will play at the same time.

To add a track to a movie, you must copy it from another movie. However, the Copy command copies all the tracks from a movie. If you want to copy only one track from a movie, you must temporarily delete all the other tracks in the movie. Then, select and copy all or part of the movie. Immediately after copying you can restore the deleted tracks by choosing Undo Delete Tracks from the Edit menu. Next, switch to the movie in which you want to add the copied track, and move the slider on its play bar to the place where you want the new track to start playing. Now hold down Option and choose Add from the Edit menu. While Option is down, Add replaces Paste in the Edit menu.

If the track you add is longer than the existing tracks, QuickTime Player automatically makes the whole movie longer. You may want to delete the added length from the end of the movie, especially if the track you added was a sound track. When you add a long sound track, QuickTime Player pads the end of the video track with white.

Adding an echo effect

You can add a nifty echo effect to a QuickTime movie by adding a copy of its own sound track slightly offset in time. To do so, open the movie in QuickTime Player and follow these steps:

1. Use QuickTime Player's Delete Tracks command to delete all tracks except the sound track.

2. Use the Select All command (⌘+A) to select the entire movie, which is now just a sound track.

3. Use the Copy command (⌘+C) to copy the selection to the Clipboard.

4. Use the Undo Delete Tracks command (⌘+Z) to undo the track deletion.

5. Use the Select None command (⌘+B) to cancel the selection.

6. Move the slider to the beginning of the play bar.

7. Click the Step Forward button once to advance to the second frame of the movie.

8. Use the Add command (⌘+Option+V) to add the copied sound track.

Making a new movie

To make a new QuickTime movie with nothing in it, choose New from QuickTime Player's File menu. QuickTime Player displays an untitled movie window with a controller but no content. You can copy clips from other movies and paste or add them to your new movie.

You can also make a new QuickTime movie by importing another media file, such as a sound file or an animation file. Choose Import from the File menu and in the standard Open dialog box that appears, select the media file you want to import. QuickTime converts the media file to a movie and QuickTime Player opens the converted movie. You can now copy a clip from this movie and paste, replace, or add the clip to any other movie.

Setting a movie poster

You can designate a picture from a QuickTime movie to represent the movie in various circumstances, the most obvious of which is the Favorites drawer in the QuickTime Player. This picture is called the movie's poster.

Note

If you don't select a poster image, you'll often simply see a black icon in the QuickTime Favorites drawer, because many video clips begin with black screens and the Favorites drawer uses the first frame of a movie if a poster frame hasn't been specified.

For instance, you see a movie's poster when the movie is selected in an Open dialog box or another file-related dialog box that shows previews. QuickTime Player displays the poster in the Movie Information window that appears when you choose Show Copyright from the Movie menu. Figure 18-13 illustrates a poster in an Open dialog box.

Figure 18-13: Some applications display a movie's poster as a preview.

To set a movie's poster, go to the place in the movie that you want to use as the poster. Then choose Set Poster Frame from the Movie menu. This command works for QuickTime VR scenes and QuickDraw 3D objects, as well as linear QuickTime movies.

Saving a movie

After editing a movie, be sure to save it by choosing Save or Save As from the File menu. The size of a movie when you save it is the size it will be when it is opened subsequently. Also, the current states of the Loop, Loop Back and Forth, and Play All Frames commands are saved with the movie and will apply when the movie is opened again.

Dependent and self-contained movies

When you save a movie, you can make it a self-contained file or dependent on other files. A movie with file dependencies doesn't contain all the data for the movie. Instead, some of the movie data is saved in separate files that may be used by other movies. You conserve disk space by having several movies dependent on the same files. However, QuickTime can't play a movie if its dependent files are missing. For example, if you copy part of a movie from a CD-ROM and paste it into a new movie that you save on your hard disk with file dependencies, you won't be able to play the movie unless the CD-ROM is inserted. This situation doesn't exist with a self-contained movie—it has no file dependencies because it contains a copy of all its data.

Saving for the Web

When saving a QuickTime movie for playback in a Web browser, make the movie self-contained. In addition, you must end the movie file name with the suffix ".mov". Web browsers know that a file name with this suffix contains a QuickTime movie. If you omit the suffix, Web browsers won't play your movie.

Audio CDs

If your computer has a CD-ROM drive, you can listen to audio CDs with it. This section tells you how to play an audio CD automatically and how to control it with the Control Strip. This section also explains how to control the playing of audio CDs with the AppleCD Audio Player application, how to adjust the cable connections and control panel settings to hear audio CD sound on your computer, and how to have a CD play automatically when it is inserted or when your computer starts. This section also describes how to record passages from audio CDs as sound files.

Note   If you play an Enhanced CD from your CD-ROM drive and open a program, access a file, or use the Finder, the Enhanced CD may stop playing. Enhanced CDs contain audio and other types of media such as text, movies, or multimedia software. This problem does not occur when playing regular audio CDs, which contain only audio.

The AppleCD Audio Player

The AppleCD Audio Player application plays audio CDs from your CD-ROM drive. It has buttons that correspond to all the tangible push-button controls that you'd expect to find on a machine that plays CDs. Many of the Audio Player's onscreen buttons have keyboard equivalents. What sets the Audio Player apart from an ordinary CD player is its program mode. You can program a custom play list for every CD, and Audio Player remembers each play list you create. You can also enter CD and track titles, which Audio Player remembers as well. Figure 18-14 shows the AppleCD Audio Player and identifies its basic controls.

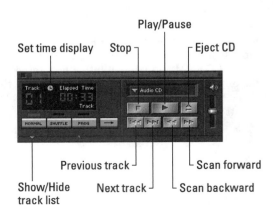

Play/Pause

Set time display   Stop   ⌐ Eject CD

Previous track ⌐   └ Scan forward

Show/Hide   Next track ⌐   └ Scan backward
track list

Figure 18-14: The AppleCD Audio Player program

The Audio Player program has an Options menu that you use to change the window color and the number-display color. You also can use this menu to play back the left channel or right channel only. In addition, if your computer has more than one CD-ROM drive, the Startup CD Drive submenu lets you choose the drive you want the Audio Player to control by selecting its SCSI ID number (or ATAPI number, if you have ATA drives in your computer). After changing the Startup CD Drive, you have to quit the Audio Player and open it again to enforce the change.

Using control panel buttons

You can play, pause, stop, skip backward, skip forward, scan backward, and scan forward by clicking the buttons on the right side of the control panel. Here's how the buttons work:

✦ Clicking Normal plays the CD tracks sequentially.

✦ Clicking Shuffle plays the tracks in random order. Each time you click Shuffle, the order changes.

✦ Clicking Prog plays the tracks in the order that you specify (as described in "Programming CD playback," later in this section).

✦ Clicking the arrow button next to Prog alternates between playing the CD one time or continuously in the mode that you've selected (normal, shuffle, or program).

✦ Clicking the small down arrow above the stop button displays a pop-up menu that lists the tracks on the CD. Use this menu to play a specific track.

✦ Clicking the clock icon near the time display also displays a pop-up menu. Use this menu to set the display to show elapsed or remaining time on the current track or on the entire disc.

Using keyboard controls

You can also operate many of Audio Player's controls from the keyboard. These keyboard shortcuts work when the Audio Player is the active application:

✦ Press the left-arrow (←) and right-arrow (→) keys to scan backward or scan forward track by track.

✦ Press Spacebar or Enter to alternately play and pause the CD.

✦ Press Delete or Clear to stop playing the CD.

✦ Press ⌘+E to eject the CD.

✦ Press the up-arrow (↑) and down-arrow (↓) keys to operate the volume control, if the Audio Player includes one. (The presence of a volume control depends on the capabilities of the CD-ROM drive.)

Naming CDs and tracks

When you insert an audio CD, the Audio Player pulls the track times off the CD, but not the track titles. It displays generic titles (Track 1, Track 2, and so forth), but you can replace them with the real track and CD titles. It takes only a couple of minutes to enter the titles for a typical CD, and you only have to do it once — the Audio Player remembers the titles by saving them to a file called CD Remote Programs in the Preferences folder. Once you enter the titles, they reappear every time you pop the CD back into the CD-ROM drive. Figure 18-15 is an example of track titles in the Audio Player.

Figure 18-15: The AppleCD Audio Player remembers the track titles that you enter for each CD.

Although it doesn't take long to enter titles for one CD, it takes hours to enter titles for 100 or more CDs. You can spare yourself this effort by using the TitleTrack CD Player from RiverSong Interactive (http://www.titletrack.com). This $15 shareware program downloads titles from a huge database on the Internet, and the titles appear in the AppleCD Audio Player as well as the TitleTrack CD Player.

If you want to enter titles, the Audio Player must be in Normal or Shuffle mode (not Prog mode). Click the tiny Edit List button (the small triangle located below the Normal button) to show the CD title and below it a track list. To enter track titles, press Tab to move through the track list, typing the titles as you go. To enter a CD title, click the CD title at the top of the play list and type the new title.

You can enter up to 62 characters for each track title. Although the track list itself can't display full titles that long, you can see full titles in a pop-up menu by clicking the CD title in the top right part of the Audio Player. To see more tracks, enlarge the window by dragging its size box.

The Audio Player stores the titles that you enter for each CD in the CD Remote Programs file in the Preferences folder (inside the System Folder).

Programming CD playback

To program the order in which the AppleCD Audio Player plays the tracks of a CD, click Prog. Then click the Edit List button (the small triangle below the Normal button) to display the track list and play list at the bottom of the Audio Player window. The track list appears on the left side of the window and lists all tracks sequentially. The play list appears on the right side of the window and you build it by dragging tracks from the track list to slots in the play list. The play list can include up to 99 tracks.

You can mix up the order of tracks on the play list any way you like, put the same track on the play list more than once, and leave tracks out of the play list altogether. You can rearrange tracks in the play list on the right by dragging them up or down. You can remove a track from the play list by dragging it back to the track list.

The Audio Player stores all your custom play lists in the CD Remote Programs file together with the CD and track titles that you entered. Figure 18-16 is an example of a custom play list being built.

Figure 18-16: Drag track titles to program a play list in the AppleCD Audio Player.

Hearing Audio CD sound

To hear audio CDs on your computer, you may need to set some sound input options in the Sound control panel. If you want to play audio CDs from an external CD-ROM drive, you first need to connect the drive's sound output either to the computer's input, to amplified speakers, or to a stereo system.

Playing CDs from an external CD-ROM drive

You may be able to play audio CDs from an external CD-ROM drive through your computer's low-fidelity internal speaker or through externally powered speakers that are connected to the computer's sound output port. Be sure to use magnetically shielded speakers near a monitor or disk. If you want to hear the computer's sounds and the audio CD sound through the same speakers, get a pair of powered speakers with mixed dual inputs (one input for the computer and the other for the CD-ROM drive).

External speakers are easy to hook up to an external CD-ROM drive, but you can't control their volume with the Audio Player or your computer's control panels. Furthermore, connecting external speakers to an external CD-ROM drive precludes recording CD sound from the drive (as described later in this section).

To control the volume of an external CD-ROM drive from your computer, or to record sound from the external drive, you need to connect the external drive's sound output jacks to your computer's sound input port with a stereo patch cord (available wherever stereo accessories are sold). Your patch cord must have a plug or plugs that fit the sound output jacks on your CD-ROM drive, as well as a plug or plugs that fit the microphone port on your computer. Most external CD-ROM drives have a headphone jack on the front, and many drives also have RCA-style jacks on the back. Your computer probably has a stereo minijack for its microphone input, like the kind used for cassette player headphones. Some computers also have RCA-style jacks for alternate sound input. By examining the output jacks on your CD-ROM drive and the input port on your computer, you should be able to figure out the kind of patch cord plugs that are required for your equipment.

With some Mac models, you must also move the External CD Sound file from the Apple Extras folder to the Extensions folder. According to Apple, the only Macs that require this are the Power Mac and Performa 5200 and 6200 series. If your Apple Extras folder doesn't contain the External CD Sound extension, you probably don't need it. Apple includes the extension with all computers that need it. Apple doesn't distribute the extension through its online Software Updates library or on Mac OS CDs. If you use powered speakers or a stereo system, you don't need the External CD Sound file.

Changing sound input options

To hear an audio CD, you may need to change a couple of sound input settings in the Sound control panel. You may have to make these changes whether you're using an internal CD-ROM drive or an external drive whose sound output is connected to your computer's microphone port (as described previously). You should make these changes only if you can't hear the audio CD—different Macintosh computers have different requirements and may work fine without these changes.

And, if you're playing audio CDs on an external CD-ROM drive that's connected to powered speakers or a stereo system, you can play and listen to audio CDs without making any of the control panel changes described here. In this case, you can even listen to an audio CD and use speech recognition at the same time, as long as the CD sound doesn't confuse the speech recognition software.

Although a Power Mac's microphone port is designed for the extra-long plug of Apple's PlainTalk speech recognition microphone, you can use an ordinary patch cord to connect an audio source to the microphone port. The PlainTalk microphone's plug reaches deep inside the Power Mac's microphone port to draw power for the microphone's internal preamplifier. A patch cord doesn't need electricity, so its regular ⅛-inch stereo miniplug need not reach the port's power lead.

Open the Sound control panel to see the sound options. Set the Sound Input option to Microphone for an external CD-ROM drive or to Internal CD for an internal drive, and turn on the Play sound through output device option. While looking at the Sound options, make sure the Computer System Volume option is not turned all the way down or muted. You should now hear the audio CD.

Recording Audio CD sound

You can record sound from an audio CD using the SimpleSound application or the Sound control panel. In both cases, you control the CD with the AppleCD Audio Player program. For more control over recording short segments from an audio CD, use the freeware utility program GrabAudio by Theo Vosse. You can record long segments of an audio CD as a sound-only movie by using QuickTime.

MP3s (MPEG3 audio files) are a popular mechanism for recording, playing back, and transporting electronic music files with CD quality. A number of MP3 recorders and players enable you to record tracks from your audio CDs and play them back on your computer. (This makes it possible, for instance, to compile a "favorite hits" playlist of music from different CDs, store the songs on your hard disk, and play them all back at once.) One popular program for encoding MP3 files is SoundJam MP (http://www.soundjam.com/).

Before you can record from an audio CD, you may have to set the computer's sound input source using the Sound control panel (as described previously).

Recording system alert sounds

If you're tired of the standard system alert sounds, you can record a new alert sound from your own audio CD using the AppleCD Audio Player program and the Sound control panel or the SimpleSound program.

The Sound control panel, and the SimpleSound program all display a standard dialog box for recording an alert sound. This dialog box contains buttons that resemble the controls on a conventional tape recorder. There are buttons to record, stop, pause, and play. In addition, there are buttons for canceling and saving a recording you have made. Figure 18-17 shows the standard dialog box for recording an alert sound.

Figure 18-17: The standard dialog box for recording a system alert sound

Before recording an alert sound from a CD, observe the Audio Player program while listening to the passage you want to record and note the track and time where the passage starts. Then use the Audio Player's controls to pause the CD a few seconds before the start of the passage. Make sure the Audio Player's volume control is all the way up.

To record using the Sound control panel, open the control panel and display its Alert Sounds settings. Switch back to the Audio Player, start the CD playing and, without hesitation, switch back to the control panel and click the Add button. You will see the standard dialog box for recording an alert sound (shown in Figure 18-17). Click Record a split second before the beginning of the passage that you want to record, and click Stop when you want it to finish (a second or two for an alert sound). Then click Save to save the alert sound with a name that you want.

To record an alert sound using the SimpleSound program, choose Alert Sound from SimpleSound's Sound menu. This displays the Alert Sounds window. Switch to the Audio Player and start the CD playing a few seconds before the start of the sound that you want to record. Immediately switch back to SimpleSound and click Add in the Alert Sounds window to display the standard dialog box for recording sound (shown in Figure 18-17). Click Record a split second before the beginning of the passage that you want to record, and click Stop when you want it to finish. Then click Save to save the new alert sound.

Recording AIFF sound files

In addition to recording alert sounds, the SimpleSound program can capture part of a CD as an AIFF digital sound file. First, use the AppleCD Audio Player program to start the CD playing about 15 seconds before the start of the section you want to capture. Without hesitation switch to SimpleSound and choose the New command (or press ⌘+N) to bring up the standard Mac OS sound recording controls. Click Record a split second before the beginning of the passage that you want to record, and click Stop when you want it to finish. Then click Save to save the digital sound file in the AIFF format.

Can you copy that?

Be careful what you copy. Sound and video recordings and broadcasts are protected by copyright, just like printed materials. Before capturing part of an audio CD, audiotape, phonograph record, radio broadcast, videotape, videodisc, television broadcast, or other recorded pictures and sound, you may need to get the copyright owner's permission. It's best to get permission in writing. You don't need permission to copy from works in the public domain, such as works created by United States government agencies. Works of state and local governments, as well as other national governments, may be protected by copyright. You also don't need permission if your copying comes under the doctrine of fair use as defined by the U.S. Copyright law. The law doesn't precisely define fair use, but does specify four criteria that must be considered:

1. The purpose and character of the use, including whether such use is of commercial nature or is for nonprofit educational purposes;

2. The nature of the copyrighted work;

3. The amount and substantiality of the portion used in relation to the copyrighted work as a whole; and

4. The effect of the use upon the potential market for or value of the copyrighted work.

Recording QuickTime sound movies

Any program that can open and save changes to QuickTime movies can record a passage from an audio CD as a QuickTime sound-only movie. SimpleSound, SimpleText, and QuickTime Player can do this. To begin, choose Open from the program's File menu. In the Open dialog box, open the audio CD, select the track that you want to record, and click the convert button. This displays a Save dialog box. Click Options in this Save dialog box to display the Audio CD Input Options dialog box. Adjust the slider controls in this dialog box to specify which part of the audio track to include. Set the sound quality here as well. Dismiss this dialog box and click Save in the previous dialog box. QuickTime copies the audio data from the CD to the movie file. Figure 18-18 is an example of the Audio CD Input Options dialog box.

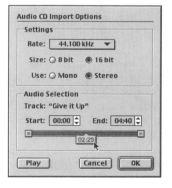

Figure 18-18: Selecting part of an audio CD track to save as a sound-only QuickTime movie

Playing audio CDs automatically

You can have your computer play an audio CD when the computer starts. Putting an alias of Track 1 from any audio CD into the Startup Items folder has the Finder automatically launch AppleCD Audio Player during startup and begin playing whatever CD is in the drive. The Track 1 alias works with any audio CD, not just the one used to make the alias. If there's no CD in the drive, the Mac OS requests one during startup. To make the alias, insert any audio CD, open its icon, select Track 1, and use the Make Alias command.

It's also possible to have your Mac automatically play an audio CD any time you insert one. Just turn on the Enable Audio CD AutoPlay option in the AutoPlay section of the QuickTime Settings control panel, as shown in Figure 18-19.

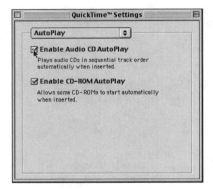

Figure 18-19: Setting the AutoPlay options in the QuickTime Settings control panel

The AutoPlay feature starts playing the CD earlier in the startup process than the Startup Items method and doesn't require the AppleCD Audio Player application. However, you do have to open AppleCD Audio Player (or its equivalent) if you want to control playback of an autoplaying CD while it's playing. (Of course, you can always just stop the autoplaying CD by ejecting it.) The AutoPlay feature does not work with some CD-ROM drives that are not sold by Apple.

Apple Video Player

If your computer has video inputs, chances are you can use the Apple Video Player application to play video and audio from a VCR, camcorder, or other video equipment on your computer screen. If your computer has a TV tuner installed, you can use the Video Player to tune in and watch TV shows. In addition, the Video Player can capture the video and audio and save it in a movie file on disk. You can use the Apple Video Player with the following Apple video input equipment:

✦ Apple Audio/Video card installed in a "beige" Power Mac G3 computer

AutoStart worms

There are two options in the AutoPlay section of the QuickTime Settings control panel, Enable Audio CD AutoPlay and Enable CD-ROM AutoPlay. Both seem harmless, but the second one opens the door for a malicious program called AutoStart 9805 Worm. If the Enable CD-ROM AutoPlay option is turned on, QuickTime looks for an AutoStart program on every disk you insert in your computer (not just on CD-ROMs), and automatically launches this program if it exists. The point of this mechanism is to enable programs on CD-ROMs to start themselves automatically. For example, a game CD-ROM could start itself as soon as you insert the CD-ROM.

The AutoStart 9805 Worm is the type of program that QuickTime will launch automatically, but this program makes an extension in your System Folder so that it can get control every time you start your computer. The program also reproduces itself on all your disks. (It can't spread to uninfected CD-ROMs because they are locked.) This program is a worm because it reproduces itself but does not infect other files. (A program that reproduces itself by infecting other files is a virus.) If a Zip disk or other removable disk becomes infected with the worm on your computer and you insert this disk in another computer that has the Enable CD-ROM AutoPlay option turned on, the worm spreads to that computer also.

You can significantly reduce the chance of your system being infected by the AutoStart 9805 Worm or similar programs by turning off the Enable CD-ROM AutoPlay option in the QuickTime Settings control panel. You do not need to turn off the Enable Audio CD AutoPlay option. If you're concerned that your computer may already be infected, you can detect and eradicate this worm by using the free EarlyBird program from Lineaux (`http://www.lineaux.com/index.html`) or any recent Macintosh virus-checking program.

✦ Built-in video ports on Power Mac 7500, 7600, 8500, and 8600 computers

✦ Apple Video System card or Apple TV/Video System card in the Power Mac and Performa 5200, 5300, 5400, 5500, 6300, 6400, and 6500

✦ Power Mac AV card in Power Mac 6100AV, 7100AV, and 8100AV computers

If your computer doesn't have video input capability, you may be able to add it by installing a video card made by Apple or another company such as ATI Technologies (905-882-2600, `http://www.atitech.com`) or IXmicro (408-369-8282, `http://www.ixmicro.com`). If you get a video card made by a company other than Apple, the card may use its own video player application instead of the Apple Video Player. For example, video cards from ATI Technologies use the Xclaim Video Player.

You can also buy more sophisticated video software that works with most major brands of video input equipment, including the Apple video input equipment listed previously and video cards from ATI Technologies, IXmicro, and Radius. Video editing and composing software such as Adobe Premiere and Avid Cinema can both capture movies like the Apple Video Player, and they can also slice, dice, chop, mix, combine, and bake new movies from pieces of captured movies.

This section explains how to connect your video source to your computer and watch and capture video input with the Apple Video Player.

Connecting a video source

Before you can watch or capture video from a VCR or other video equipment outside your computer, you need to connect the video equipment to your computer. This involves connecting a cable from the video output jack of the video source to the video input port on your computer, and connecting another cable from the audio output jack (or jacks, for stereo) of the video source to the computer's audio input port or microphone port.

The type of video cable you use depends on the type of output jack on the VCR or other video equipment. If the video equipment has an S-video output jack (which looks like a keyboard port or serial port on your computer), use an S-video cable. If the video equipment has a composite output jack (which looks like the RCA jacks on many stereo components), use a composite cable. Most consumer-grade camcorders, VCRs, and TVs have composite output jacks. High-end video equipment use S-video jacks. In some cases, you may be able to use standard coax cable (the type of cable you use for many cable TV connections) to connect a camcorder, VCR, or TV to your computer.

You can use an adapter to connect a composite cable to an S-video port on your computer. If your computer has only an S-video input port, it probably came with a composite cable adapter.

The video cable doesn't carry sound, so you have to connect a separate audio cable from the VCR or other video equipment to your computer. The plug at one end of the audio cable must fit the type of audio output jack on the video equipment, which is usually one or two RCA jacks. The plug at the other end of the audio cable must fit the computer's audio input port. Your computer may have a pair of RCA jacks for audio input or a stereo minijack (the microphone port).

Because the details of connecting video equipment to a computer vary according to the type of video input, you should consult the manual that came with your computer or video card for specific instructions.

Watching video

The Apple Video Player has a window for viewing video from an external video source or an internal TV tuner (if your computer has one). You select the video source and adjust the picture with controls in a separate Controls window. To see the controls for video source and picture, click the video screen icon on the left side of the Controls window. Figure 18-20 shows the main Video Player window and the Controls window.

Figure 18-20: Selecting a video source and adjusting the picture in the Apple Video Player

Capturing video

While watching video through the Apple Video Player, you can save a single frame as a picture file, copy a frame to the Clipboard, or save a video sequence as a QuickTime movie. You capture a single frame with the Copy Video Display command in the Edit menu, and you capture SimpleText picture files or QuickTime movie files with controls in the Controls window. To see the capture controls, you click the video camera icon on the left side of the Controls window. Figure 18-21 shows the capture controls.

Figure 18-21: Capturing single-frame or movie files with the Apple Video Player

To successfully capture a still picture or a movie, you may need to increase the memory size of the Apple Video Player using the Get Info command in the Finder. The memory requirements depend on the size of the Video window and on the complexity of the image. If the Video Player runs out of memory while attempting to capture an image, it displays a vaguely worded alert that an error occurred.

Capturing a still picture

When you see an image in the Video window that you want to save, click Freeze in the Controls window to capture it. The picture in the video window stops (although the video input continues unseen unless you pause or stop the VCR or other video source). If you like the still picture in the Video window, you can save it as a SimpleText picture file (a PICT file) by clicking Save in the Controls window. If you don't like the still picture, click Freeze again to resume viewing the video input.

The size of the Video window directly affects the size of the captured picture. Making the window smaller reduces the amount of disk space required to store the picture. To use the least amount of disk space, choose Smallest Size from the Video Player's Window menu.

Capturing a movie

To capture a video sequence as a movie, click Record in the Controls window as you see the sequence begin in the Video window. Recording begins, the Record button changes to a Stop button, and the Pause button becomes functional. Click Pause if you want to suspend the recording process while the incoming video continues playing. When you click Pause, it changes to a Resume button, and clicking Resume resumes recording with the sequence then playing in the Video window. To end the recording, click Stop. The Video Player then uses QuickTime to compress the movie so that it takes up less disk space (unless you turned off compression as described later), and displays a Save As dialog box so that you can name the movie file and select a folder for it.

While recording is in progress, the motion you see in the Video window may become more jerky than usual. This does not mean the recorded movie will be as jerky. The computer optimizes the number of video frames it can record per second by devoting less processing power to displaying the incoming video. You want the computer to record as many frames per second as it can, because a higher frame rate produces smoother motion. The computer can record video at a higher frame rate if you eliminate background-processing tasks that sap its performance. For example:

✦ Turn off the menu bar clock (see Chapter 12).

✦ Turn off virtual memory and restart the computer to make virtual memory changes take effect (see Chapter 19).

✦ If you use RAM Doubler instead of virtual memory, turn it off.

✦ Make sure file sharing is off and make AppleTalk and TCP/IP inactive (see Chapter 20).

✦ Insert a floppy disk, a CD-ROM, and any other type of removable disk you have so that the computer doesn't have to periodically check to see if you've inserted one.

Another factor that affects frame rate is the size of the Video window. The window size also affects the picture quality and file size of a captured movie. For the best quality movie in the least amount of disk space, choose Smallest Size from Video Player's Window menu. This sets the movie frame size to 160 × 120 pixels. Choosing Normal Size from the Windows menu sets the frame size to 320 × 240 pixels.

You can also increase a movie's frame rate and reduce its file size by having the movie compressed. Unfortunately video compression degrades picture quality. You can adjust the amount of compression or completely turn off compression by choosing Preferences from the Video Player's Setup menu and setting the Movie Compression option to None, Normal, or Most. The Normal setting reduces file size by 12 to 50 percent. The Most setting reduces file size up to 50 percent more than the Normal setting. The compression method that the Video Player uses, known as Apple Video, works best when the number of colors is set to thousands (not 256 or millions) in the Monitors & Sound control panel or the Monitors control panel (whichever your computer has).

Frame rate is also affected by the speed of the hard disk. You need a fast hard disk to record at high frame rates. To achieve the optimum frame rate of 30 fps (frames per second) with a normal frame size (320 × 240 pixels), your hard disk should be capable of sustained writes at 5MB per second or more. That rate is the maximum throughput of a regular external SCSI port, so you should connect your fast hard disk to a SCSI-2 port (10MB per second) or SCSI-3 port (20MB per second). Some Macs, such as the Power Mac 8500 and 8600, come with internal SCSI-2 ports. You can also install expansion cards with fast SCSI ports.

Frame rate and picture quality are irrelevant if your hard disk doesn't have enough space to record the movie. Capturing a normal frame size requires 2MB to 4MB per second, depending on the frame rate. That much disk space must be available to initially capture the movie; that is, when the Video Player automatically saves the uncompressed captured video in a temporary file. This temporary file is normally on the same disk as the Video Player program. If that disk becomes full and your computer has other hard disks, the Video Player looks for more temporary storage space on them. After recording the movie, the Video Player has QuickTime compress it and then releases the temporary storage space.

Apple DVD Player

Newer Macintosh models (including some Power Macintosh G3, Power Macintosh G4, PowerBook G3, and all iMac DV models) now sport a DVD-ROM drive as their main removable storage option. DVD-ROM is similar to CD-ROM, except that a DVD-ROM can store quite a bit more data than a CD. Other than that, the major difference is the DVD video standard, which makes it possible to store and playback commercial videos using a DVD player.

Macs equipped by Apple to display DVD movies include the appropriate hardware for DVD decoding, which makes it possible to view movies on screen. Along with DVD capability comes the Apple DVD Player, an application that enables you to view and control DVD movies on your DVD-equipped Macintosh.

The Apple DVD Player has two basic components: the playback screen and the Controller. The Controller is shown in Figure 18-22.

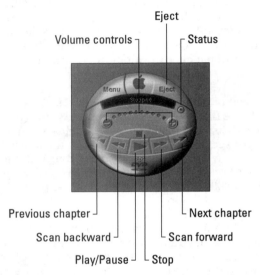

Figure 18-22: The Apple DVD Player interface

The playback controls are fairly familiar, offering the same controls you'd find on most VCRs or home electronics DVD players. One exception might be the Next and Previous Chapter buttons, which simply move you between video chapters — a standard element on many video discs (and somewhat akin to tracks on audio CDs).

Other controls include the Menu button, which returns you to the DVD video's menu screen, which most DVDs have. The Status button pops up a small menu that gives you statistics about the video that's playing.

For more specialized control, you use the area below the main controls — the part of the Controller with the DVD logo on it. Click that area to reveal the controls. That section is shown in Figure 18-23.

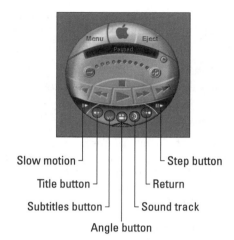

Figure 18-23: The Controller's additional controls

Slow motion ⌐ ⌐ Step button

Title button ⌐ ⌐ Return

Subtitles button ⌐ ⌐ Sound track

Angle button

The additional controls allow you to do the following:

✦ **Slow motion** — Watch the video in slower motion. Click the button to choose how slow the video should progress. To return to full speed, continue clicking until you cycle through.

✦ **Title button** — Go to the beginning of the current title.

✦ **Subtitles button** — Click to cycle through the available subtitle languages.

✦ **Angle button** — Some videos allow you to view a particular scene from different camera angles. To do so, click the Angle button to cycle through the available camera angles.

✦ **Soundtrack button** — On videos with more than one soundtrack, click this button to cycle through them.

✦ **Return button** — Click to return to the previous page of the disc's menu program, if relevant.

✦ **Step button** — Click to move through the video frame by frame.

Note that many of these options are also available in the menus provided by the disc itself, probably at the beginning of the disc before you begin viewing the feature. You can click the Menu button to return to those menus and select options in the movie window itself.

You have additional options in the menu items for the DVD Player. For instance, the Video menu enables you to change the size of the viewer window, with a few preset options (use ⌘+a number — 0,1,2,3 — to change the size of the viewer window from the keyboard). Also in the Video menu, you can choose Present Video on Screen to use the entire computer screen to display the video without the viewer window. With the viewer window gone, you can move your mouse back to the top of the screen to cause the menu bar to appear, then choose Video ➪ Present Video in Viewer to switch back to a window for viewing.

In the Window menu, you can choose to hide the Viewer or the Controller. To show the Viewer or Controller again, return to the Window menu and choose one of the Show options.

In the Edit menu, you can select Preferences to set various preferences for the DVD player, so that languages, subtitles (on the Language tab), and audio features (on the Audio tab) are set automatically when possible. On the Hot Keys tab, you can define the hot key combinations to use for hiding and showing the Controller or switching in and out of Presentation (full-screen) mode.

Finally, click the Parental Controls tab to turn on Parental Control for this DVD. You can set the lock level (the rating for a movie that requires a password) and enter a password. Now, if a movie is inserted that has a rating over the DVD parental lock rating, a password is required to view the movie.

Summary

In this chapter, you saw that QuickTime pulls every trick in the book to play digital movies on your computer. It plays movies at reduced frame sizes and at slower-than-normal frame rates, and that it works with compressed movies to reduce the amount of data it has to transfer from disk.

This chapter showed how to play a QuickTime movie with and without the VCR-like movie controller. With the controller, you can play and pause, step forward or backward, go to any part of the movie, adjust the sound level, change playback direction and speed, and more. This chapter also explained how to interact with QuickTime VR panoramas and objects. You can change your view of a VR panorama by panning, tilting, zooming, and clicking hot spots. You can manipulate a VR object to see a different view of it. You also learned how to manipulate 3D graphics displayed by the QuickDraw 3D system extension.

This chapter explained the basic ways that you can edit QuickTime movies with QuickTime Player Pro. You can select and copy a movie clip and paste it elsewhere in the same movie or another movie. You can delete or replace part of a movie. You can delete and add tracks in a movie. You can set a movie's poster. When you save your edits, you can make a movie self-contained or dependent on other files.

This chapter also explained how to play audio CDs with your computer's CD-ROM drive. You can use the AppleCD Audio Player application to control playing with all the push-button controls you'd expect to find on a CD player, and to program playback in ways few CD players can match. To hear audio CD sound on your computer, you may have to set some options in the Monitors & Sound control panel or the Sound control panel. To use an external CD-ROM drive, you have to connect it to your computer with an audio patch cord. You can also use the control panels or the SimpleSound application together with the Audio Player application to record parts of CDs as sound files.

This chapter described how to watch video on a computer with video-input equipment, and how to capture still pictures or QuickTime movies from incoming video. You have to connect cables from the video equipment to your computer's video and audio ports. Then you can use the Apple Video Player application (if your computer has Apple video input) to watch and capture incoming video.

Finally, this chapter described the Apple DVD Player application and how to use it to watch DVD videos on Macs that are equipped with a DVD-ROM drive.

✦   ✦   ✦

Beyond the Basics of the Mac OS

Manage Your Memory

In This Chapter

Gauging memory usage

Adjusting application memory usage

Adjusting system memory usage

Using a RAM disk

Increasing total memory

If you never open more than one program at a time and don't care about your computer's performance or effectiveness (not to mention your own), you can ignore the topic of memory management. But to get the most from your computer, you must pay attention to how you use its memory.

This chapter explains how to find out the amount of memory each open program is using. It tells you how to adjust the amount of memory your application programs use, and how to reduce the amount of memory the Mac OS uses. This chapter also describes several ways to increase the amount of memory available for opening programs.

Gauging Memory Use

Computers use memory like a large company might use office space (though on a very different time scale). Just as each department needs office space, each computer program needs a memory partition. Departments come in all sizes and so do computer programs. Over the years a company may eliminate some departments and use their space for new ones. Similar events take place on a computer but in a much shorter time. In a matter of hours, you may quit some programs and use their memory space to open others. Figure 19-1 shows the About this Computer dialog box, which offers a visual representation of the memory being used by applications on your Mac.

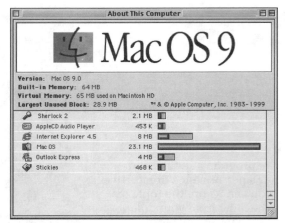

Figure 19-1: Gauging memory usage in the About This Computer window

To use your computer's memory most effectively, you need to know the total memory available, which programs are open, how much memory they use, and how much memory is currently unused. You also need to know roughly how much memory each program uses, because you may have to quit one or more open programs to make space for another one that you want to open.

Memory compared with hard disk space

For a program to be active so that you can work with it, the program needs to be loaded in system memory. When you open a program, the Mac OS allocates some memory space for the program, copies part of the program into that memory space from disk, and starts running the part copied into memory. The amount of space that an application takes up on the hard disk doesn't always have a direct relationship to the amount of memory it requires once loaded. For instance, a full installation of a program may take up 10MB of disk, but only require 5MB of memory because part of the application isn't loaded in memory when the program is launched. Conversely, many applications take only 2 to 5MB on disk, but require much more space in memory in order to load complex documents or other components. To find out how much memory an application is using, you need to consult the About This Computer dialog box or the Memory section of the Get Info dialog box, as described in this chapter.

About This Computer

For information on the condition of your Mac's memory, switch to the Finder and choose About This Computer from the Apple menu. The Finder displays a window that reports the total amount of memory installed in your computer and the largest amount available for opening another program. It also graphs the amount allocated to and currently used by the Mac OS and each open program. Figure 19-1 is an example of the About This Computer window.

To learn the exact amount the Mac OS or an open program is using at the moment, turn on Balloon Help and point at the item's memory-use bar in the About This Computer window.

The About This Computer window reports the size of the largest unused block of memory. There may be other unused blocks as well, each smaller than the largest block. This condition, known as fragmented memory, can make it difficult to open a large program. You'll find techniques for recognizing fragmented memory and dealing with it in "Adjusting Application Memory Use" later in this chapter.

What's more, the Mac OS may not report every bit of memory that's in use. For example, built-in video uses 40K to 600K on various computer models but some versions of the Finder do not include that amount in the Mac OS size. There may be an additional discrepancy of several K (kilobytes) due to rounding errors.

Memory-mapping utilities

For a more precise report of memory use than you get in the Finder's About This Computer window, use a utility such as Memory Mapper by R. Fronabarger. The software is available on popular Mac freeware Web sites and FTP archives, including CNet's `http://www.download.com/`. Memory Mapper shows not only how much memory each open application uses, but where the applications are in relation to each other and to blocks of unused memory. Figure 19-2 is an example of Memory Mapper's window, although the graph it displays is color-coded to the list of programs and is much easier to decipher on a color monitor than in this black-and-white reproduction.

You don't see one number for Mac OS size in the Memory Mapper window. Instead of reporting an aggregate amount as in the About This Computer window, Memory Mapper breaks out Mac OS memory use into several individual items, including:

✦ **High Memory**, which is used for video, sound, and disk cache
✦ **Finder**

✦ **Desktop PrintMonitor, File Sharing, QuickTime, Speech Recognition**, and other system extensions that are actually programs open in the background

✦ **System Heap**, which is used for fonts, icons, sounds, and other system resources

✦ **Low Memory Globals**, which is used for many system parameters

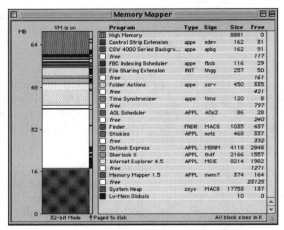

Figure 19-2: Checking memory use with Memory Mapper

Adjusting Application Memory Use

Each program that you open gets a piece of memory called a memory partition for its exclusive use. This section tells you how to change the size of an application's memory partition with the Finder's Get Info command, increasing the partition size to help the application perform better or decreasing the size so that you can open additional programs. This section also tells you how to avoid fragmenting unused memory as you quit some programs to free memory for opening others, and how to fix memory fragmentation if it does happen.

Application memory size

You can change how much memory an application program gets by setting the memory sizes in its Info window, which the Finder's Get Info command displays, or with the AppSizer utility program (described in Chapter 26). You must quit an open application before changing its memory-size setting. If an application is open, its Info window shows the memory-size settings but won't let you change them. You can't ever change the memory size of some kinds of programs such as desk accessories. If a program's size is permanently set, its Info window doesn't show any memory sizes. Figure 19-3 shows the Info window of an application that is not open.

Figure 19-3: Use the Get Info command to set memory sizes for an application.

Memory information is displayed in a separate section of a program's Info window. To see a program's memory information when its Info window is closed, select the program and choose Memory from the Get Info submenu of the File menu. The Get Info submenu also appears in a program's contextual menu. To see memory information in an open Info window, choose Memory from the pop-up menu near the top of the window.

Suggested, Minimum, and Preferred sizes

An application's Info window shows three memory sizes: Suggested, Minimum, and Preferred. The system won't open a program unless there is a block of available memory at least as large as the Minimum size. The system allocates more memory to the application's memory partition, if extra memory is available, but never more than the Preferred size. The Suggested size, which you can't change, is the amount of memory the program's developer recommends for acceptable program performance.

Setting the Preferred size higher than the Suggested size may improve performance or enable you to open more documents or larger documents. Setting the Preferred size below the suggested size usually has the opposite effect. For example, setting Netscape Communicator's or Internet Explorer's Preferred size below the Suggested size reduces the number of browser windows that you can have open simultaneously, limits your ability to view images or Java applets, or stops the application from working altogether.

Caution

Every application has a memory size that's not listed in its Info window. This fourth memory size, which is set by the program developer, specifies the least amount of memory in which a program will work without crashing. Most programs use this safe minimum size for the initial setting of the Minimum size in the Info window. Setting the Minimum size lower than the safe minimum may cause the program to crash. For example, Netscape Communicator 4.6 may crash if the memory size is set below 6144 (while virtual memory is turned on). One way to find out the safe memory setting is to attempt to enter a very low number in the Minimum size box. If the setting is too low, an alert box appears to tell you what the safe minimum size is.

Some programs require more memory with Mac OS 9 than they did with a previous version (especially versions before Mac OS 8.1). If a program refuses to open after you upgrade to Mac OS 9, try increasing its minimum memory size by 10 to 15 percent and opening it again.

Virtual memory's effect

A note at the bottom of some Info windows advises that turning on virtual memory changes the memory requirements. This note appears in the Info window of a program that is designed to enable the Mac OS to use part of the program's file on disk as if it were additional memory. All programs optimized for the PowerPC processor and some other programs are designed this way. This type of program requires less memory when virtual memory is turned on or the RAM Doubler utility software is installed and turned on (as described in the section "Increasing Total Memory" later in this chapter).

Memory fragmentation

As you open and quit a series of programs, the unused portion of your computer's memory tends to become fragmented into several noncontiguous blocks. You may find yourself unable to open a program because it needs a memory partition bigger than the biggest unused block (the Largest Unused Block amount displayed in the About This Computer window). The total of all unused blocks may be large enough to open the program, but the Mac OS can neither consolidate fragmented memory nor open a program in multiple blocks of memory. It's like looking for a parallel parking space on a street with several half spaces between parked cars. A small car wouldn't fit in any of the spaces, but if you could put the half spaces together you'd have enough room to park a truck. Figure 19-4 illustrates fragmented memory (compare the Largest Unused Block number in Figure 19-4 to Figure 19-1).

Is your memory fragmented?

To check for memory fragmentation, add up the memory sizes of all the open programs and the Mac OS as listed in the About This Computer window. Then subtract the total from the total memory reported in the About This Computer window. Also subtract 300K to 600K (depending on monitor resolution and number of colors) if your computer doesn't have dedicated video memory known as VRAM (Video Random Access Memory). In this case, your computer uses its main memory, sometimes called DRAM (Dynamic Random Access Memory), for the screen image. Examples of Macs that do this include the Power Mac 6100, 7100, and 8100 with a monitor connected to the system board video port.

If the number you come up with is substantially less than the largest unused block, your unused memory is probably fragmented into two or more blocks.

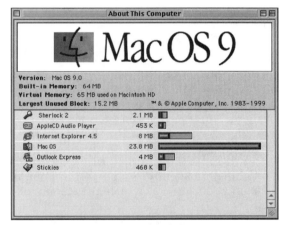

Figure 19-4: Opening and quitting programs repeatedly may fragment unused memory; this image shows only half the available Largest Unused Block than that of Figure 19-1.

Avoiding fragmented memory

You can avoid memory fragmentation by planning the order in which you open and quit programs. First, open the programs you're least likely to quit and then open the programs that are the most expendable in your work session, starting with the most important of them and finishing with the least important. When you need more memory to open another program, quit the most recently opened program. If that doesn't free enough memory, quit the next most recently opened program, and so on. This method frees up a contiguous block of memory. Quitting programs helter-skelter leads to memory fragmentation.

Tip

If you open several application programs during startup, you may have to quit some of them later to free memory for opening another. Naturally, you want to quit the applications least important to you. You free the most memory by quitting the applications opened last during startup. To make that easy, rename the items in your Startup Items folder so that the most important application comes first alphabetically, the next most important comes second, and so on. One way to do that is by putting a sequence number (01, 02, 03, and so on) at the beginning of the startup item name. This trick works only for ordering items of the same kind — aliases, application programs, control panels, documents, and so forth — because the Finder opens all of one kind of an item before opening any of another kind. (Startup Items are discussed in Chapter 11.)

The Finder sometimes hastens memory fragmentation in low-memory situations. If you try to open an application that needs more memory than is available, the Finder suggests quitting all programs with no open windows — or the largest open program, if all have open windows. Accepting the Finder's suggestion can fragment memory. To avoid memory fragmentation, you must quit programs in the reverse of the order in which they were opened.

Fixing fragmented memory

To consolidate fragmented memory, quit all open programs and then open them again. This method isn't completely foolproof. You may have a program that doesn't release all of its memory when you quit it. This error is called a *memory leak*. A program that makes use of shared library extensions may also leave memory fragmented after you quit it, in this case because the shared library continues to occupy memory after the program has quit.

So how do you fix memory fragmentation permanently? Simply restart your Mac. Restarting your computer fixes fragmentation and may reduce the amount of memory used by the Mac OS as well.

Tip

Some users make a point of restarting their Macs on a regular basis to guard against memory leaks and fragmentation, especially if they're likely to open and close many different applications during the course of a day. You might plan to restart your Mac each day at lunchtime, for example, if you've had an especially active Internet browsing session or if you've been opening and closing a lot of files. Although any application can add to memory fragmentation, some of the worst memory leak culprits are software programs written the fastest — usually Web browsers, e-mail programs, and other Internet-related tools that are developed quickly and brought to market every few months. If you have an application that seems particularly susceptible to memory leaks (most notable because when you quit that application — and others — the memory isn't returned to the system), you should see whether the software author is aware of the memory leak problem and whether the author has released an update.

If you don't want to restart or even quit all open applications, you can use the Memory Mapper utility to identify the applications that are open between blocks of unused memory and quit only those applications to consolidate memory. You can actually send a Quit message from Memory Mapper to any open program. To do that, select the program in Memory Mapper's window and choose Send Quit Event from the File menu.

Adjusting Mac OS Memory Usage

The Mac OS gives itself a big memory partition when you start your computer, shown by the length of the bar labeled Mac OS in the About This Computer window. This section explains how to reduce the size of the Mac OS by disabling marginally useful system extensions and control panels, turning off expendable system options, reducing the disk cache, and reducing or eliminating a RAM disk.

Minimum Mac OS size

Just how small can the Mac OS be? You can reduce its memory size to the minimum by pressing Shift while restarting your computer. Look for the message "Extensions Off" during startup. It confirms that you have suppressed loading of all items in the Extensions folder, Control Panels folder, and System Folder that would increase the Mac OS memory size. You have also bypassed opening items in the Startup Items folder, forced virtual memory off, and prevented file sharing from starting.

None of these changes persist when you restart without pressing Shift. To make changes stick, you must remove items from the special folders and change settings in the Memory and other control panels.

Startup items

Many of those lovely little icons that march across your screen during startup are chewing up memory as they go. They're not alone. Lots of other startup software that doesn't display icons also increases the Mac OS memory partition.

Many items identified as system extensions in a list view of the Extensions folder or System Folder increase the Mac OS memory size during startup. So do some other types of items besides extensions. But some items in the Extensions folder do not increase memory size. Chooser extensions for printers (LaserWriter, StyleWriter, ImageWriter, and so on), communications tools, MNPLinkTool documents, Finder Help, and the PrintMonitor application fall in this latter category.

Control panels that display an icon at the bottom of the screen during startup (or offer the option of doing so) have system extensions built in and most of them increase the Mac OS memory size. Control panels that don't display startup icons generally don't increase the Mac OS memory size, although there are exceptions, such as Easy Access.

The easiest way to manage extensions and control panels is with the Extensions Manager control panel (see Chapter 11). There are also commercial alternatives that provide more information and control than Extensions Manager. For example, Conflict Catcher from Casady & Greene, Inc. (408-484-9228, http://www.casadyg.com) tells you how much memory each startup item uses and when it was installed.

The key to adjusting memory size is to compare the Mac OS memory size before and after removing an item and weigh the potential memory savings against the benefit the item provides. It's a trial-and-error process unless you have Conflict Catcher or another utility that can determine the memory sizes of startup items.

To see the effect of removing startup items, you have to restart the computer.

Expendable options

You can reduce the Mac OS memory size by turning off a handful of system options that you might not be using. For example, if you're not using file sharing, you can recover 200K to 300K by turning it off in the File Sharing control panel. If you're not using speech recognition, turn it off in the Speech control panel. You can also save some memory by turning off AppleTalk in the Chooser.

Disk cache

A portion of the Mac OS memory partition always goes to the disk cache, which improves system performance by storing recently used information from the disk in memory. When the information is needed again, it can be copied from memory instead of from disk. Copying from memory is much faster than copying from disk.

You can use the Memory control panel to adjust the amount of memory allocated for the disk cache. Be aware that setting the disk cache very low degrades performance in many applications, particularly the Finder. The usual rule of thumb is to set the disk cache to 32K times the amount of your computer built-in memory in MB (megabytes). Virtual memory and RAM Doubler don't count in this calculation, but a RAM disk does.

For example, if your computer has 32MB of built-in memory, the standard disk cache size would be 1024K ($32 \times 32 = 1024$). If your computer has 48MB of built-in memory and a 16MB RAM disk, the standard disk cache size would also be 1024K ($32 \times (48 - 16) = 1024$). Figure 19-5 is an example of the disk cache setting in the Memory control panel.

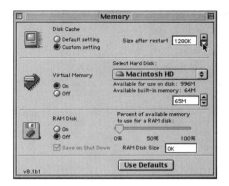

Figure 19-5: Setting the disk cache size

To change the disk cache size, select the Custom Setting option at the top of the Memory control panel. When you do this, an alert appears warning you not to change the cache size unless you know what you're doing. Click the Custom button in this alert box to proceed. You can now change the cache size by clicking up (↑) and down (↓) arrows at the top of the Memory control panel. The minimum disk cache size is 128K.

You can set the disk cache size according to the rule of thumb described previously by selecting the Default Setting option at the top of the Memory control panel.

RAM disk

While the disk cache is always on and the Mac OS manages it automatically, you can use another option in the Memory control panel to dedicate more memory to speeding up disk-related tasks. The RAM Disk option uses part of your computer's memory as if it were a hard disk. This disk is called a RAM disk because it exists in the computer's RAM (Random Access Memory), which is also known as built-in memory. You determine the size of the RAM disk by setting the amount of memory used by it using the slider bar in Memory control panel after turning the RAM Disk option on (click the radio button next to On). This amount is added to the Mac OS size in the About This Computer window. Figure 19-6 shows the RAM Disk option in the Memory control panel.

When you restart after turning on the RAM Disk option, the Mac OS creates a disk whose contents are stored in the computer's high-speed memory, not on a relatively slow, mechanical disk mechanism. A RAM disk has an icon that appears on the desktop, and you manipulate folders and files on a RAM disk the same as on any other disk. A RAM disk works much faster than a hard disk, but does not store items permanently.

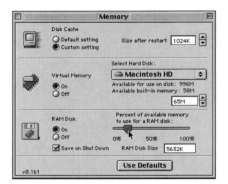

Figure 19-6: Setting up a RAM disk

The RAM Disk option is dimmed if your computer does not have enough unused memory for the minimum RAM disk size. The minimum size for the RAM Disk option is 480K.

Tip
What can you put on a RAM disk? Usually, temporary files that won't be missed much if you lose them due to a power outage or crash are put on a RAM disk, because data is in a precarious state when saved on a RAM disk. For instance, you could put the following on a RAM disk: game files, Web browser cache files (set through the Web browser's preferences), or scratch files that you're using to create images or animations. (Again, these should be backed up and any new files you create should be saved to the hard disk often.) Things not to put on a RAM disk include documents that you're making changes to, e-mail that you'd like stored permanently, or any applications or utilities that you haven't backed up to a physical disk. See Chapters 24 and 28 for more ideas on using a RAM disk.

RAM disk permanence

The contents of a RAM disk are preserved when you restart most Macs. This is true even if you use the emergency restart keys (⌘+Control+power button) or the Reset button that some Mac models have.

The original "beige" or "platinum" Power Macintosh G3 models, however, do not preserve a RAM disk across a restart. The Grackle memory controller chip in these models doesn't reliably maintain the contents of memory during a restart. The Grackle chip enables the G3 models to use SDRAM memory, which provides higher performance but which is more volatile than the fast-page mode memory used on older Mac models.

Mac OS 9 offers this option on Macintosh desktop machines that don't allow RAM disk contents to survive a restart. With Power Macintosh G3 and G4 machines, for instance, RAM disk contents are automatically saved when you restart — if it's possible. This is not as effective as earlier Macs because the RAM disk contents aren't saved if your startup disk is read-only (like a CD-ROM), too full to save the contents, or, in many cases, if there's corruption or a system freeze.

You can also choose to have RAM disk contents saved to disk when you shut down the Mac, a feature that wasn't present in earlier Mac OS versions. (Usually a shut down, as opposed to a restart, would destroy data on a RAM disk regardless of your settings or Macintosh model.) You can turn on the "Save contents to disk" option in the Memory control panel. In the past, only PowerBooks had this setting, but now it's available to many Mac models.

Resizing or removing a RAM disk

To resize or remove a RAM disk, first copy the files that you want to save from it to another disk. Then drag everything from the RAM disk to the Trash and empty the Trash. Finally, use the Memory control panel to turn the RAM disk off or change its size. Restart your computer to make the changes take effect.

RAM disk alternatives

Instead of creating a RAM disk with the Memory control panel, you can use a shareware application such as ramBunctious, which is described in Chapter 26.

The advantage to creating a RAM disk with an application is that you don't have to restart the computer to remove the RAM disk and recover the memory it used. The disadvantage to creating a RAM disk with an application is that you can't use it as a startup disk. (Many G3-and-higher Mac models can't use a RAM disk as a startup volume anyway.)

A RAM disk is not permanent

You can make a good effort to preserve a RAM disk, but its contents can easily be lost. If you use a RAM disk, observe these precautions:

✦ Don't store a file exclusively on a RAM disk. Copy documents from RAM disk to another disk frequently.

✦ Copy files from the RAM disk to another disk before shutting down.

✦ Don't use a program for the first time on a RAM disk. Test it on another disk first.

Increasing Total Memory

Enjoy whatever unused memory you have while it lasts. Software developers see unused memory as a vacuum to be filled with new programs and new features for old programs. Before long, you will want and then need more memory for new software and upgrades.

When you find yourself invariably quitting programs in order to open others, it's time to increase your computer's memory. As this section explains, you can increase memory by turning on or increasing virtual memory, by adding more memory modules, or by using a memory enhancement program such as RAM Doubler.

Virtual memory

You may be able to increase the total memory available for opening applications without upgrading your computer's built-in memory (RAM). The Mac OS can transparently use part of a hard disk as additional memory. This extra memory, called virtual memory, enables you to get by with less built-in memory. You buy and install only as much built-in memory as you need for average use, not for peak use.

Virtual memory has other benefits with many application programs. All programs that are optimized for the PowerPC processor (programs that use only native PowerPC instructions) require less physical memory when virtual memory is turned on. The same is true of some other programs. You can see the difference virtual memory makes for a program by using the Finder's Get Info command, as described in the previous section of this chapter.

In addition, the Mac OS may use less memory when virtual memory is turned on. This is particularly true on the iMac and other models that have a Mac OS ROM file in the System Folder. On these models, the Mac OS may use as much as 4MB less memory when virtual memory is turned on.

The downside to virtual memory is that it can slow the system, especially if it's not configured optimally.

Configuring virtual memory

The Memory control panel is used to turn virtual memory on and off. At the same time, you can set the size of total memory. If you have more than one disk volume with enough space to be used for virtual memory storage, you can choose one. The amount of disk space required equals the amount of built-in memory installed in your computer plus the amount of memory you want to add with virtual memory.

Removable disks can be used for virtual memory, although there are drawbacks to using most types of removable disks. You can also use a disk that is formatted in either the Mac OS Standard or Mac OS Extended format with Mac OS 9's virtual memory. After setting up virtual memory, you must restart your computer for any changes to take effect. Figure 19-7 shows the virtual memory options in the Memory control panel.

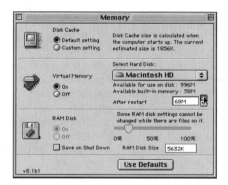

Figure 19-7: Setting up virtual memory

With virtual memory on, the About This Computer window normally reports the total amount of memory and the amount of built-in memory. It also tells you how much disk space is used for virtual memory storage. In Mac OS 9, application programs can suppress the display of virtual memory information in the About This Computer window.

After turning on virtual memory there is a noticeable reduction in the amount of space available on the disk volume used for virtual memory storage. (The amount of available space is displayed at the top of the disk window in the Finder.) An invisible file named VM Storage accounts for the reduction in disk space.

The higher you set virtual memory in the Memory control panel, the more it slows the system. If you use virtual memory mostly to reduce the memory requirements of PowerPC applications, set the virtual memory size to 1MB more than the amount of built-in memory. If you use virtual memory to make more memory available for opening programs, set it no higher than double the built-in memory. Use the additional memory for opening multiple small programs, not for opening one huge program.

The limit on total memory (virtual memory plus built-in memory) is 1GB (1024MB).

How virtual memory works

Virtual memory provides more memory for opening programs by keeping only the most active program segments in the computer's built-in memory. Less-used segments of open programs are kept in the invisible VM Storage file on the hard disk. When a program needs a segment not currently in built-in memory, the virtual memory system automatically swaps the least-used segment in built-in memory with the needed segment on disk. For example, a swap might occur when you switch programs. However, no swapping occurs unless you are trying to use more memory than your computer has built-in memory.

Virtual memory's capability of loading program pieces on demand is also respons-ible for reducing a PowerPC application's memory requirements. What makes PowerPC applications need more memory when virtual memory is off is how the Mac OS loads a PowerPC application into memory. Apple designed the Mac OS to load PowerPC applications in bigger pieces, called code fragments, than other applications' smaller pieces, called segments. Larger pieces should require more memory for the same reason that you need a bigger ferryboat to carry buses than cars. That's exactly the case with virtual memory turned off. A PowerPC application needs at least enough space for its largest code fragment, and usually more, when virtual memory is turned off.

In designing the system around large PowerPC code fragments, Apple planned to compensate by having the virtual memory system load and unload portions of code fragments on demand. With virtual memory turned on, code fragments don't have to be loaded whole and an application can get by with less memory.

How virtual memory affects performance

Because a hard disk is much slower than built-in memory, using virtual memory can degrade system performance. The performance penalty is barely noticeable if a swap between built-in memory and disk happens when you switch programs. The slowdown may be severe if you use virtual memory to open a program that's bigger than the amount of built-in memory left after Mac OS gets its share. The disk may thrash for several minutes as it tries to swap segments back and forth.

Tip   With virtual memory turned on, you can often improve system performance by using the Hide Others command in the Application menu. Hidden windows of background applications don't need updating, which may require disk access when virtual memory is on. However, some programs continue working in the background even with their windows hidden. For example, a database program might generate a report in the background. But the Hide Others command usually reduces the amount of background work going on.

The performance of code fragment management on PowerPC computers is actually better than the performance of virtual memory in general. That's because code fragments are never written to the VM Storage file. In fact, the VM Storage file is not involved at all in managing a PowerPC application's code fragments. The application file itself is the storage file. Using a technique called file mapping, the Mac OS loads code fragments directly from the application file into built-in memory. This technique eliminates the delay that sometimes occurs if a program's code is loaded in memory and then immediately written out to the VM Storage file. That thrashing never happens with file mapping.

File mapping benefits performance in another way. The Mac OS never writes code fragments back to the application file as it would if the code fragments went through the VM Storage file. The Mac OS assumes code fragments never change. So when part of a code fragment is no longer needed, a needed part can replace it right away. The Mac OS doesn't take the time to write the disused piece back to the disk because it can always read an identical copy that's still there in the application file.

Installing more memory

Virtual memory has its uses, but it can't take the place of built-in memory, which is also known as RAM. If you're not sure how much built-in memory your computer has, look in the About This Computer window. In that window, the Built-in Memory is the amount of memory installed in the form of RAM chips.

Do-it-yourself memory upgrade

If your computer needs more built-in memory, you may be able to upgrade it yourself. Upgrading involves opening the computer (tricky on some PowerBook models) and either installing or replacing some small, plug-in circuit board modules.

Each computer model has specific memory-configuration rules. Some Macs use *DIMMs* (dual in-line memory modules) and some use *SIMMs* (single in-line memory modules). Both DIMMs and SIMMs come in various capacities, measured in MB (megabytes), and speeds, measured in ns (nanoseconds). Most PowerBooks use special memory modules designed specifically for that model of PowerBook. (More recent PowerBooks use standard small-outline DIMMs that can be used in a number of different computer models.)

You can install memory modules only in certain combinations on each model. To find out which type of memory modules your computer uses, consult the latest free GURU (Guide to RAM Upgrades) application from the NewerRAM division of Peripheral Enhancements Corp. (316-943-0222, http://www.newerram.com). Another source of information is the electronic document Apple Memory Guide from Apple's Software Updates library (http://www.apple.com/swupdates/). You can also get advice from dealers and companies that sell memory.

Note Although you may be perfectly capable of installing SIMMs or DIMMs in your computer, Apple generally recommends that only an Apple-certified technician install them. Apple's warranty does not cover any damage that you or a noncertified technician cause when installing or removing SIMMs and DIMMs. Proceed with caution, but know that many computer owners install their own memory boards. The more paranoid owners may also remove what they install before taking their computers in for warranty service. Most technicians won't bother to ask unless they see damage or oddball parts, such as composite SIMMs or DIMMs.

Buying memory

You can order memory by mail from a plethora of companies that advertise in *Macworld* and other Macintosh magazines. Memory prices are highly competitive. When shopping for a memory upgrade, look for a lifetime warranty from a reputable company that as best as you can tell will be around to honor the warranty. RAM chips are very reliable, but they can fail.

Buy your memory from a company that includes illustrated installation instructions for your make and model. Pay a little extra to get the instructions if you have to.

Tip Most of the damage done to memory modules comes from static electricity. If you plan to install your own memory modules, it's a good idea to invest in a wrist strap that grounds you to your equipment (or some other grounding source) to avoid static electricity build-up. Grounding straps are available at electronics component stores such as Radio Shack (part no. 276-2397).

Steer clear of composite SIMMs and DIMMs. They may work on one computer, but on another they may cause sporadic startup failures, system errors, or mysterious crashes. You may have no trouble with one composite SIMM or DIMM, but install another and watch your computer have fits. You can spot a composite SIMM or DIMM by the large number of chips on it. For example, a regular 16MB SIMM uses 8 16-megabit chips, but a composite SIMM might use 32 4-megabit chips. The best way to avoid composite SIMMs and DIMMs is to buy from a reputable source.

Memory upgrade by a technician

If you don't want to upgrade the memory yourself, you can take your computer and your mail order SIMM or DIMM to an Apple dealer or other computer service center. An experienced technician should be able to install more memory in well under 30 minutes, so you shouldn't have to pay for more than a half-hour of labor. Some stores charge less to install memory they sell to you, so investigate that angle before bringing in your own memory.

RAM Doubler optimizing software

RAM Doubler from Connectix (800-950-5880, 650-571-5100, http://www.connectix.com) can actually triple the amount of total memory as reported in the About This Computer window. If you prefer, you can set RAM Doubler to extend memory by a lesser amount. You can even set RAM Doubler to not extend memory at all, but just to provide file mapping and code fragment management for PowerPC applications.

Compared with the Memory control panel's virtual memory, RAM Doubler is faster, more efficient, and uses very little hard disk space. It's great for older PowerBooks that can only have 8MB of RAM, because it doesn't use the power-draining hard disk like virtual memory does. Virtual memory's strengths are that it's free and is somewhat more reliable.

RAM Doubler accomplishes its magic by reallocating built-in memory automatically behind the scenes as you work. It takes over the memory reserved but not used by open applications (the lighter portion of the bars graphed in the About This Computer window) and temporarily reallocates the unused memory to applications that need it. RAM Doubler also compresses parts of programs in memory that probably won't be used again, such as parts that initialize a program when you open it. Also, RAM Doubler may store infrequently used areas of memory to disk, just like conventional virtual memory, especially if your computer has less than 8MB of built-in memory. RAM Doubler reduces overall system performance slightly, but you may not notice the difference in normal operations. However, it's not suitable for time-critical operations such as video digitizing.

You can't use RAM Doubler in combination with virtual memory. You can't set the memory size of any application higher than the amount of your computer's built-in memory; Connectix recommends leaving your programs set at their usual memory sizes.

RAM Doubler generally needs to be updated whenever you upgrade to a new version of the Mac OS. If you have RAM Doubler currently and you're installing Mac OS 9, you'll likely need to contact Connectix for an update or an upgrade. There are known issues with compatibility between RAM Doubler and Mac OS 9, which should be addressed by Connectix by the time you read this.

Summary

This chapter discussed the About This Computer window, which shows you the total memory available, which programs are open, how much memory each uses, and how much memory is currently unused. The Memory Mapper utility shows you a more detailed picture of this information.

This chapter also described how to set an application's minimum and preferred memory sizes with the Finder's Get Info command. The better your Get Info settings, the more reliably and efficiently your program will run. You can also manage your applications to avoid memory fragmentation, which can slow down your Mac and make it difficult to launch new applications.

If your Mac has a limited amount of built-in RAM, there are four ways to reduce the Mac OS size: disable nonessential startup items, turn off expendable options, reduce disk cache size, and reduce or eliminate a RAM disk. This can be helpful if you're willing to sacrifice some of the Mac OS's capabilities in order to run more (or larger) applications.

A RAM disk can store nonessential files (such as some preferences, Web browser cache, and game application files) to make your computer run a bit faster, because RAM is faster than a traditional disk. A RAM disk is more susceptible to losing data, though, so precautions need to be taken with any data stored on a RAM disk. The RAM disk also takes away from available system memory.

In this chapter, you learned how to increase the total memory available for opening programs. Options include turning on virtual memory, installing more RAM, and using RAM Doubler memory enhancement software.

✦   ✦   ✦

Set Up a Network

♦ ♦ ♦ ♦

In This Chapter

Hooking up a network

Configuring an AppleTalk network connection

Configuring a TCP/IP network connection

Connecting to a remote computer or AppleTalk network

Connecting to an ISP or TCP/IP network

Allowing remote access to your Mac or local network

♦ ♦ ♦ ♦

I f you have more than one computer in your office or home, you can benefit by connecting them in a network. The idea may seem intimidating, but a simple Mac OS network is easy to set up and doesn't cost much. Some of the things that you can do with a simple Mac OS network are:

♦ Share one Internet connection among several computers

♦ Share printers, including printers without network ports

♦ Share files from other computers in your company or home as if their files were on your desktop, and share files from your computer with other computers

♦ Access a central database while other computers do likewise

♦ Maintain a group schedule or calendar

♦ Back up hard disks of all networked computers on a central tape drive

♦ Access your hard disk from a remote location over a telephone line or Internet connection

♦ Allow access to your Mac from a remote computer

This chapter focuses on setting up a network so that you can use some of those services. The first section discusses hooking up a *local area network* (*LAN*) using either LocalTalk or Ethernet, the two most common types of network wiring for Mac OS computers. You can skip that section if your computer is already hooked to a network. The next two sections discuss configuring the Mac OS for AppleTalk and TCP/IP, the two most common kinds of Mac networks. The remainder of the chapter explains how to connect your computer to a remote computer or network by modem or over the Internet.

This chapter does not describe how to use network services after your network is set up. For information on printers and printing, see Chapters 16 and 17. For information on Internet services such as global e-mail and the World Wide Web, see Chapter 10. For information on accessing shared files and network equipment, see Chapter 21. For information on sharing your files with other computers, see Chapter 22.

Hooking Up a Network

The first step in setting up a local network is to hook up lines of communication between the computers and printers that you want on the network. Basically that involves running a cable to each computer and printer. You may also need a cable connector box for each computer and a central junction box. If your computer is already connected to a network, you can skip this section.

This section describes how to hook up a LocalTalk network using inexpensive LocalTalk connector boxes and either Apple's LocalTalk cables or an ordinary telephone cord. This section also describes how to hook up an Ethernet network using 10Base-T parts, which are the lowest in cost of the many Ethernet cabling alternatives. In addition, this section discusses how to bridge a LocalTalk network and an Ethernet network.

This section also covers a technology available in the latest Power Macintosh, iMac, and iBook models — AirPort wireless networking. These connections actually don't require special wiring because they use radio signals to transmit data between machines equipped for wireless network. (You can also transmit data between wireless machines and an Ethernet network with the addition of a special device called an AirPort hub.) Although it may sound like amazing new technology that is difficult to set up, wireless networking is actually fairly simple to set up in Macs that support AirPort.

Besides Ethernet and LocalTalk, Macs can be connected using other types of network wiring such as Token Ring. Because Mac OS computers don't come with token ring network ports, one must be added in the form of a network interface card. If your organization has a Token Ring network, you undoubtedly have a network administrator or other expert who has already connected your computer to it or will do so for you. Setting up a Token Ring network or any network other than Ethernet or LocalTalk is not something that you want to attempt on your own. At any rate, it's outside the scope of this book.

Wiring a LocalTalk network

The simplest and cheapest type of Mac OS network wiring is LocalTalk. Many Mac OS computers have a LocalTalk network port, as do most printers that can be connected to a Mac OS network. It costs less than $20 per computer and printer (for a network cable and connector box) to set up a small LocalTalk network. All the software you need is built into all versions of the Mac OS. LocalTalk performance is generally suitable for networks of a couple dozen or fewer computers and printers, although performance depends greatly on how much the computers use the network. LocalTalk wiring is primarily for Mac OS-only networks, although it is possible to buy LocalTalk expansion cards to hook up Windows and DOS PCs.

To hook up a LocalTalk network, plug a small network connector box into the printer port of each computer and into the LocalTalk port of each network printer or other network device (such as a network modem) and run wires between the connectors. There are two types of LocalTalk connectors. In some cases, you can network two devices without connectors.

Note LocalTalk networking requires a LocalTalk port, which is usually the Printer port on many Power Macintosh models. Models like the "blue and white" Power Macintosh G3, the iMac, and the Power Macintosh G4 no longer include a LocalTalk port for this sort of network, although add-on cards and devices exist for some models. If you're planning to network the latest Mac models, it's best to choose Ethernet networking, because Ethernet is higher speed and Ethernet ports are built into the latest Power Macintosh, iMac, iBook, and PowerBook models.

PhoneNet-style LocalTalk

The most common type of LocalTalk connector box has a modular phone jack. You link the connector boxes with an ordinary telephone cord, the kind used to connect a telephone to a modular wall socket. Be sure to use a four-wire cord, not two-wire (look for four colored wires showing through the clear RJ-11 modular plugs). In many homes and small businesses, you can use the existing telephone wiring and jacks in the walls to extend your network from room to room. With the four-wire cables common in homes, for example, the telephone uses the red and green wires and the network can use the yellow and black wires.

This type of connector was pioneered and patented under the PhoneNet brand name by Farallon Communications (510-814-5000, http://www.farallon.com). Many other companies now license the technology from Farallon and sell compatible connectors at lower cost. Some of the cheaper connectors use less durable parts.

For networking only two devices — for example, two computers or one computer and one printer — you can save money by using Farallon's one-jack PhoneNet pocket connectors. Later you can add to this minimal network with dual-jack connector boxes.

Apple-style LocalTalk

Instead of phone cords and PhoneNet connector boxes, you can use Apple's proprietary LocalTalk connector boxes and cables. However, this type of wiring and connector costs more and generally doesn't offer any advantage over PhoneNet. If you already have some Apple LocalTalk supplies, you can get adapters from Farallon to mix them with phone wiring.

Serial-cable LocalTalk

If your network has only two computers or one computer and a printer, you don't have to use LocalTalk connectors. You can connect the two devices with a serial printer cable, such as the one you would use to connect a StyleWriter to a computer. This is the cheapest way to network two devices, but they must be near each other because the cable is not very long.

Wiring an Ethernet network

An Ethernet network is significantly faster than a LocalTalk network, but Ethernet costs somewhat more. The cost to set up a small Ethernet network starts at $20, $50, or $120 per computer or printer, depending on the type of built-in port (if any). The cost and performance of Ethernet scales up to accommodate networks of all sizes. The software for accessing an Ethernet network is included with the Mac OS, although you may have to perform a custom installation to get it installed. An Ethernet network can include computers using Mac OS, Windows, Unix, and other operating systems. They can use commonplace application software — for example, Internet applications — to communicate and share services.

See Chapter 10 for more information on Internet applications.

Ethernet cables

Ethernet networks may be wired with several types of cable. The most popular is 10Base-T or 100Base-T cable, also known as *unshielded twisted-pair (UTP)* cable. It looks like telephone cable and uses RJ-45 connectors that look like big modular phone connectors. Other kinds include thinnet, thick coax, and fiber-optic Ethernet cables.

UTP cable is graded according to how well it protects against electrical interference. Category 3 cable is adequate for 10Base-T networks. Category 5 offers more protection, but costs more. The additional cost for Category 5 is insignificant when compared to the cost of installation. Properly installed Category 5 cable can also be used for a 100Base-T Ethernet network, which is ten times faster than a 10Base-T network. This means that you could upgrade a 10Base-T network to a 100Base-T network without any rewiring. The only caveat is that 100Base-T has more stringent rules about cable installation than 10Base-T. For example, sharp bends are not allowed in 100Base-T cables.

Ethernet ports

Even if you use UTP cable, hooking up an Ethernet network is more complicated than hooking up a LocalTalk network. For starters, you can't count on every computer having a built-in Ethernet port.

Some computers have a built-in RJ-45 port for 10Base-T Ethernet. In some cases, such as the iMac, iBook, "blue" Power Macintosh G3, and the Power Macintosh G4, this port can also be used for 100Base-T Ethernet. Other Mac OS computers have an AAUI (Apple attachment unit interface) port to accommodate any kind of Ethernet cable. An AAUI port requires a connector box, called a *transceiver*, designed for the particular type of Ethernet cable in your network.

A few Mac models have both 10Base-T and AAUI ports; you plug in a 10Base-T cable directly or use a transceiver for another kind of Ethernet cable.

Computers without built-in Ethernet need an Ethernet adapter to connect to an Ethernet network. Most Power Macintosh models compatible with Mac OS 9 also include Ethernet connections. The exceptions are Performa models and some "consumer" Power Macintosh models, such as the Power Macintosh 6500 series. You can add Ethernet cards to these computers fairly easily, using either a PCI-based Ethernet card (in some models that support PCI expansion cards) or Communications Slot Ethernet cards designed specifically for the Performa line.

For computers without internal expansion slots, there are external Ethernet adapters. A PowerBook that accepts PC cards (also known as PCMCIA cards) can use an Ethernet adapter on a PC card. Printers that have only a LocalTalk port can use a LocalTalk-to-10Base-T adapter. All these Ethernet adapters are available from many manufacturers, including Farallon, Asanté, and Dayna.

Ethernet connections

Ethernet networks that use 10Base-T or 100Base-T cable usually have junction boxes called hubs. You connect each computer, Ethernet-capable printer, or other Ethernet device to a hub with a length of UTP cable. Each computer or other device plugs into a different port on the hub. Hubs come in many different sizes, although 5-port, 8-port, and 16-port hubs are the most common. Prices start at about $50 for a generic 5-port 10Base-T hub and go up for more ports and a name brand. 100Base-T hubs cost more than 10Base-T hubs.

If you use up all the ports on one hub, you can connect another hub to it. This is called *daisy chaining*. Up to three hubs can be daisy chained with UTP cable. This limit does not apply to daisy chaining with thinnet cable, and many 10Base-T and 100Base-T hubs have thinnet ports for this purpose.

It's actually possible to construct a small 10Base-T Ethernet network without a hub. You can use Farallon's EtherWave family of transceivers and adapter cards to daisy chain up to eight computers and printers with 10Base-T cable. EtherWave transceivers cost more than ordinary transceivers, but wiring costs are usually lower and you don't have to buy a hub.

You can also directly connect two computers equipped with 10Base-T Ethernet ports by using an Ethernet crossover cable—you don't need a hub or special transceivers. Global Computer Supplies (http://www.globalcomputer.com/; 800-845-6225) carries these cables in 3-foot, 12-foot, and custom lengths for less than $10.

Bridging Ethernet and LocalTalk

Sometimes a hybrid network, part Ethernet and part LocalTalk, makes sense. For example, you might have a printer with a LocalTalk port (and no Ethernet port) that you want to use with an iMac, which has no LocalTalk port, or with several computers that have Ethernet ports. Or you might have some older computers connected in a LocalTalk network that you'd like to connect to an iMac or to several computers on an Ethernet network. Fortunately you can interconnect the dissimilar networks with a *bridge*.

LocalTalk Bridge

Apple's free LocalTalk Bridge 2.1 software creates a two-way connection between a LocalTalk network and an Ethernet network. The LocalTalk computers can use printers, shared files, and other network services on the Ethernet network. Computers on the Ethernet network can use printers, shared files, and other network services on the LocalTalk network. You install LocalTalk Bridge 2.1 on the computer that is connected to both the Ethernet network and the LocalTalk network. If you prefer, you can make the connection private, so that only the computer with the LocalTalk Bridge can use network services on both networks. LaserWriter Bridge is available from Apple's Software Updates library (http://www.apple.com/swupdates/). It is unsupported software, and Apple no longer tests it for compatibility with new OS versions such as Mac OS 9. You may have better luck if you run LaserWriter Bridge on a Mac that has an early Mac OS version (ideally Mac OS 8.1) installed.

The LocalTalk Bridge software tends to sap the performance of the computer it's installed on. Moreover, this product has become hard to find and expensive compared to other products, which may indicate that Apple intends to discontinue it.

Farallon EtherMac iPrint Adapter LT

You can avoid all the shortcomings of bridge software with a separate device such as the $99 EtherMac iPrint Adapter LT from Farallon Communications (510-814-5000, http://www.farallon.com). Although this device is marketed specifically as a means of connecting an iMac or a Power Macintosh G3 or G4 to a LocalTalk printer, such as a LaserWriter, it has broader applications. You can use the iPrint to connect a single newer Mac or an entire Ethernet network to up to eight LocalTalk printers and computers. After you connect a LocalTalk network and an Ethernet network to the iPrint, the computers on either network can use printers, file servers, and other services on the other network.

There are a couple of network connection options if you want to use an iPrint to connect an iMac or a Power Macintosh G3 or G4 to an older Mac and a LocalTalk printer. One option is to leave the old Mac on a LocalTalk network with the laser printer, connect them to the iPrint with a LocalTalk cable, and connect the newer Mac to the iPrint with an Ethernet cable. This way you save the cost of an Ethernet hub and an Ethernet transceiver or adapter card for your old Mac. The other option is to connect the computers to an Ethernet hub, connect the hub to the iPrint with an Ethernet cable, and connect the iPrint to the laser printer with a LocalTalk cable. This costs more money, but your computers share files over Ethernet, which is much faster than LocalTalk.

Setting Up AirPort Connections

If your newer Macintosh, iMac, or iBook model supports AirPort connections, then you can create a wireless network between your Macs. There are a few different ways to do this, depending on which of your machines supports wireless connections and how you'd like to connect them.

New Feature *AirPort* is Apple's name for a technology referred to as the IEEE 802.11 standard. It should be compatible with most IEEE 802.11 devices, including those not sold by Apple. AirPort should also be compatible with upgrade cards for devices that don't support Apple's AirPort technology, such as PowerBooks.

AirPort supports a peer-to-peer connection, where two Macs equipped with special AirPort cards (a required upgrade for an AirPort-capable Mac) can simply switch their AppleTalk setting to AirPort and begin sharing files, assuming they're within 150 feet or so of each other. This is the easiest way to share files wirelessly, although it offers limited connections otherwise.

You can also use one AirPort-capable Macintosh as a *wireless hub*, enabling other AirPort-capable Macs to not only connect to that computer, but also to connect to other computers connected to the hub machine. If you have an AirPort-capable Power Macintosh G4, for instance, with an AirPort card installed, you can also connect that machine to a cable-based Ethernet network. Now, another AirPort-capable Mac, such as an iBook, can share files with the Power Macintosh G4, as well as with other computers connected to the Power Macintosh G4 via an Ethernet network.

Another option is the *AirPort Base Station*, a small device that receives and transmits wireless data, while also being connected to either a modem connection or an Ethernet connection. This enables your wireless-capable computers, such as an iBook, access to other non-AirPort equipped computers on a network. It also enables you to offer a wireless Internet connection to your iBook or similar machine without requiring a cable to the iBook's modem or Ethernet port.

Once you have the AirPort card installed in an AirPort-capable Mac, all you need to do is access the AirPort Setup Assistant or AirPort application to set up the card and use it. You can also activate and configure AirPort using its control strip module. Then, set your TCP/IP control panel to use the AirPort for receiving and sending network data, as described in the section, "Configuring a TCP/IP connection."

Configuring an AppleTalk Connection

To use network services on your computer, the Mac OS must be configured to get network services from the port that is physically connected to the network. You can configure the Mac OS for more than one kind of network, with each kind of network providing a specific set of services. The most common kinds of Mac OS networks are AppleTalk and TCP/IP. Apple Talk and TCP/IP are *protocols*, which are "languages" that computers speak to each other over a network. All the computers on a network that use the same protocol (that is, speak the same language) can exchange information over the network. On an AppleTalk network, computers speak the AppleTalk protocol. On a TCP/IP network, they speak the TCP/IP protocol.

An AppleTalk network provides Mac-oriented services such as printer sharing, file sharing, data sharing, and program sharing. Apple designed AppleTalk to be easy to use and reliable. AppleTalk has been built in every version of the Mac OS. Until the advent of Open Transport networking software in 1995, AppleTalk was the primary kind of Mac OS network and all other kinds of networks were subordinate.

Note that connecting to a network does not necessarily make specific network services available. For example, connecting to an AppleTalk network makes it possible to use a network printer, but you can't actually print to a network printer unless one is connected to the network and set up as described in Chapter 16. Likewise, connecting to an AppleTalk network makes it possible to share files with other computers on the network, but to actually share files the computers must have file sharing set up as described in Chapter 22.

This section describes how to configure an AppleTalk network connection with the AppleTalk control panel and how to turn an AppleTalk connection on and off.

To use TCP/IP network services such as the Internet, the Mac OS on your computer must be configured for a TCP/IP network as described in "Configuring a TCP/IP Connection" later in this chapter.

Specifying an AppleTalk connection

By default, the Mac OS connects to an AppleTalk network at the printer port. (If your Mac doesn't have a printer port, like USB-based iMacs and Power Macintosh G3 and G4 machines, your connection probably defaults to the Ethernet port.) If your AppleTalk network is connected to a different port, you need to make that setting in the AppleTalk control panel. Figure 20-1 shows an AppleTalk control panel with several port choices.

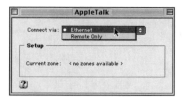

Figure 20-1: Choose a connection port for an AppleTalk network in the AppleTalk control panel.

AppleTalk ports and zones

The AppleTalk control panel lists the available network ports in a pop-up menu. You choose the one through which your computer connects to an AppleTalk network. If your computer is connected to an AppleTalk network that's divided into multiple zones, the AppleTalk control panel also specifies the zone in which your computer resides. Depending on the characteristics of your computer and network, you may be able to change the network connection port, the zone, or both. If your computer has only one network connection port, you can't change the port. If your computer is connected to a network with only one zone, there won't be any zones to choose from. If someone else sets up your computer's AppleTalk network connection, the port and zone settings may be locked so that you can't change them.

If you change the connection port in the AppleTalk control panel, a message warns that you'll lose any network services that you're using with your current AppleTalk connection. This is because you can maintain a connection to only one AppleTalk network at a time. When you switch to a different network port, you can no longer access any printers, shared files, file servers, or other AppleTalk network services on the former AppleTalk connection port. Changing the AppleTalk connection port does not affect network services on other kinds of networks, such as Internet services on a TCP/IP network.

AppleTalk user modes

You can see more settings or fewer settings in the AppleTalk control panel by changing the user mode. There are three modes: Basic, Advanced, and Administration. To change the user mode, choose User Mode from the Edit menu, and select the mode in the dialog box that appears. If you select Administration mode, you can set a password that protects Administration mode settings. Figure 20-2 shows the User Mode dialog box.

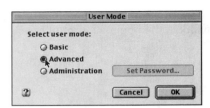

Figure 20-2: Select a user mode for the AppleTalk control panel.

The Advanced mode displays the network address that was dynamically assigned to your computer when it connected to the network. Selecting the User defined check box lets you assign a fixed address to your computer. If you assign a fixed address, you must be sure that no other computer on the network has the same address. Clicking Options brings up a dialog box in which you can turn AppleTalk on and off. Figure 20-3 shows the AppleTalk control panel's Advanced mode.

Figure 20-3: The AppleTalk control panel's Advanced mode

The Administration mode lets you assign a fixed network address as in the Advanced mode. In addition, you can lock each of the three AppleTalk settings independently — port, zone, and AppleTalk network address. Locked settings can't be changed in Basic or Advanced modes. Figure 20-4 shows the control panel's Administration mode.

Figure 20-4: The AppleTalk control panel's Administration mode

Tip If you're planning to control local settings in the Administration mode, then assign a password so users can't easily access the Administration mode. To do that, click Set Password in the User Mode dialog box. Enter the password twice (to verify that it's the same both times) and click OK.

AppleTalk configurations

Sometimes you'll find that you need to change AppleTalk settings on a regular basis, but it's not always easy or convenient to remember the changes you need to make for a given circumstance. Rather than setting options in the AppleTalk control panel directly, you can create saved configurations, which enable you to name a set of settings, and then create and name another set. After your configurations are created, you can easily move back and forth between them.

Cross-Reference Creating configurations is especially useful if you're using the Location Manager, discussed in Chapter 12.

You do this with the Configurations command in the File menu. This command displays a dialog box that lists groups of AppleTalk settings by name and has buttons for acting on the group that's selected in the list. First, select the Default configuration and click Rename. Next, give your current AppleTalk settings a name that will help you remember how the settings are configured.

To create a new configuration, select one of the existing configurations and click Duplicate. Give the configuration a new name and click OK. Now, back in the Configurations window, select the new configuration and click Make Active, as shown in Figure 20-5. You are switched back to the AppleTalk dialog box, where you can change the settings to reflect the new configuration. When you click the AppleTalk control panel's close box, you'll be asked to save any changes for this new configuration. Now, you can switch easily between two or more configurations using the File ➪ Configurations command.

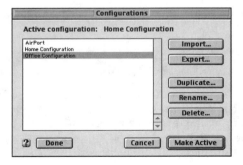

Figure 20-5: The Configurations dialog box enables you to work with named groups of settings for different networks or locations.

Turning AppleTalk off and on

If you're not using an AppleTalk network, you can turn it off altogether with the Chooser accessory program, the AppleTalk control panel, or the Control Strip. Turning off AppleTalk saves power on a PowerBook. If AppleTalk is set to connect via the printer port or another serial port, turning off AppleTalk also frees this port for another purpose such as connecting a serial printer. However, it's not necessary to turn off AppleTalk just to free the printer port, as detailed in the sidebar "AppleTalk Without a Serial Port."

Turning AppleTalk off and on with the Chooser

To turn off AppleTalk, open the Chooser (under the Apple menu) and in the lower-right corner of its window set the AppleTalk option to Inactive. If you turn off AppleTalk, it remains off until you turn it on again by selecting the Activate option in the Chooser. Figure 20-6 shows the AppleTalk option in the Chooser.

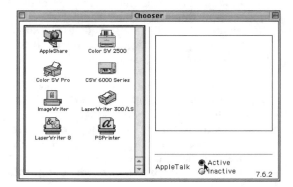

Figure 20-6: Turn AppleTalk on or off with the Chooser.

If you attempt to turn off AppleTalk while you are using a network service such as file sharing, you get a warning message that current services will be disconnected.

AppleTalk without a serial port

You may need to turn off AppleTalk so that you can print to a StyleWriter or other serial printer through the printer port while using the modem port for a modem. If your computer has only one serial port, you may need to turn off AppleTalk so that you can use the port with an external modem. The trouble is, however, that if you turn off AppleTalk, you won't be able to use applications such as NetPresenz that require AppleTalk.

You can keep AppleTalk turned on and still use a serial printer and a modem by selecting Remote Only in the AppleTalk control panel. Remote Only is also part of the Remote Access software, which is described later in this chapter.

Turning AppleTalk off and on with the AppleTalk control panel

You can also use the AppleTalk control panel to turn AppleTalk off and on. With the AppleTalk control panel set to Advanced or Administration mode, click the Options button to bring up the AppleTalk Options dialog box. There you can select Inactive to turn off AppleTalk or select Active to turn on AppleTalk. Figure 20-7 shows the AppleTalk control panel's Options dialog box.

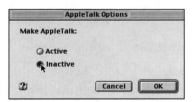

Figure 20-7: Turn AppleTalk on or off via the AppleTalk control panel's Options dialog box.

Turning AppleTalk off and on with the Control Strip

If the Control Strip is available on your computer, you can use it to turn AppleTalk off and on. Turn off AppleTalk by choosing AppleTalk Inactive from the pop-up menu of the AppleTalk Switch control strip module. Turn AppleTalk on by choosing AppleTalk Active from this menu. Figure 20-8 shows the AppleTalk Switch control strip module.

Figure 20-8: Turn AppleTalk off and on with the Control Strip.

Configuring a TCP/IP Connection

To use TCP/IP network services such as the Internet, the Mac OS must be configured to connect to a TCP/IP network through one of your computer's ports. Your computer may connect to a TCP/IP network in a number of different ways, including Ethernet, PPP (Point-to-Point Protocol via a modem), AirPort, and others.

This section describes how to configure a TCP/IP network connection with the TCP/IP control panel. If you want to set up a TCP/IP network just to access the Internet, consider using the Internet Setup Assistant program instead of the control panels described here.

 The Internet Setup Assistant is described in Chapter 10.

In Mac OS 9, you can also configure a TCP/IP connection and then use that connection for file sharing or program linking. In the past, these services were only available over AppleTalk connections. Now, however, it's possible to simply set up your TCP/IP connection and use File Sharing and Program Linking over the TCP/IP connection. This is accomplished by setting up a TCP/IP connection, and then using File Sharing's TCP/IP options, as discussed in Chapter 22.

Preparing for a TCP/IP connection

Before setting up a TCP/IP connection, you need to know some facts about the network. You may have to get the facts from an expert such as your local network administrator or your Internet service provider (ISP). Here is what you need to know:

✦ Type of network connection: is it PPP, Ethernet, MacIP, or some other

✦ Your TCP/IP configuration method, such as manual, PPP Server, BootP Server, DHCP Server, RARP Server, or MacIP Server

✦ Domain name server (DNS) address or addresses, each being a set of four numbers separated by periods similar to 192.14.59.10 (provided automatically by some configuration methods)

✦ IP address of your computer, which is a set of four numbers separated by periods similar to 192.14.59.35 (provided automatically by most configuration methods)

✦ Subnet mask (provided automatically by most configuration methods)

✦ Router address (provided automatically by most configuration methods and not applicable for some networks)

✦ Phone number your computer calls to connect to the Internet (needed only for PPP or other dial-up connection)

Specifying a TCP/IP connection

A TCP/IP network connection is specified by entering the information obtained from your Internet service provider or network administrator in the TCP/IP control panel. If someone else sets up your computer's TCP/IP network connection, the connection and configuration settings may be locked so that you can't change them. Figure 20-9 shows a TCP/IP control panel configured for a typical dial-up (telephone) connection.

TCP/IP user modes

You can see more settings or fewer settings in the TCP/IP control panel by changing the user mode. There are three modes: Basic, Advanced, and Administration. To change the user mode, choose User Mode from the Edit menu and select the mode in the dialog box that appears. Figure 20-10 shows this dialog box.

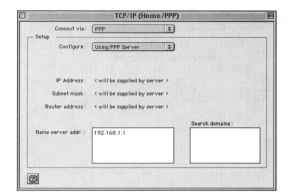

Figure 20-9: Specify a TCP/IP network connection in the TCP/IP control panel.

Figure 20-10: Select a user mode for the TCP/IP control panel.

The Basic user mode shows the settings that most people need. The Advanced mode shows additional settings for special situations. The Administration mode provides control over which settings can be changed. Administration mode lets you set a password that protects Administration mode settings. In the Administration mode, you can lock several TCP/IP settings independently. Locked settings can't be changed in Basic or Advanced modes.

TCP/IP configurations

If you need to change TCP/IP settings on a fairly regular basis, you can create saved configurations, which allow you to simply name a set of settings, and then create and name another set. After your configurations are created, you can easily move back and forth between them.

Cross-Reference

You may also want to create different TCP/IP configurations if you're using the Location Manager, as described in Chapter 12.

You create a new configuration with the Configurations command in the File menu. This command displays a dialog box that lists groups of TCP/IP settings by name and has buttons for acting on the group that's selected in the list (see Figure 20-11). First, select the Default configuration and click Rename. Next, give your current TCP/IP settings a name that will help you remember how the settings are configured.

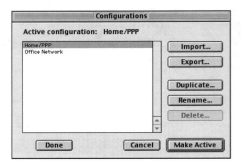

Figure 20-11: The Configurations dialog box lets you work with named groups of settings for different networks or locations.

To create a new configuration, select one of the existing configurations and click Duplicate. Give the configuration a new name and click OK. Now, back in the Configurations window, select the new configuration and click Make Active. You are switched back to the TCP/IP dialog box, where you can change the settings to reflect the new configuration. When you click the TCP/IP control panel's close box, you'll be asked to save any changes for this new configuration. Now, you can switch easily between two or more configurations using the File ➪ Configurations command.

Introducing Remote Network Connections

Your computer can connect remotely to another computer, an AppleTalk or TCP/IP network, or an ISP. Your computer makes remote connections through its modem and a telephone line. The remote computer, network, or ISP must have a compatible modem.

When connected to a remote computer, you can access its shared files. You can also access shared files, file servers, network printers, and other network services on the network that the remote computer is connected to. You access all the remote services exactly as though you were connected locally to the computer or network (as described in Chapter 21). Their owners or network administrators may restrict your access to shared files, file servers, and so forth. Conversely, no one using a remote computer or network can take advantage of your remote connection to access files you are sharing on your local network (as described in Chapter 22). You must run a file server program on your computer to make your files available to remote network users.

Note   With Mac OS 9, it's no longer necessary to create a remote network connection to use File Sharing and Program Linking with remote computers. Instead, you can use an active TCP/IP network, such as a connection to an ISP (an Internet connection). Then, you can use the new settings in the File Sharing control panel to access other File Sharing servers over TCP/IP, instead of over an AppleTalk network. File Sharing is discussed in Chapter 22.

Remote network only

When you set up your computer for a remote connection, you can disconnect your local AppleTalk network. There are two reasons you may need to do this. For one, you may be unable to see remote printers or file servers that have the same names as printers or file servers on your local network unless you disconnect the local network. (Local services have priority over remote services.) You may also want to disconnect your local AppleTalk network so that you can use your serial ports for other purposes. For example, you may want to use the printer port for a StyleWriter printer and use the modem port for a modem that connects you to a remote AppleTalk network.

To disconnect your local AppleTalk network, set the AppleTalk connection to Remote Only in the AppleTalk control panel.

Remote access speed

Several factors affect the speed of a remote connection, including the software, the computer's serial port, and the modem or other connection equipment. The Remote Access control panel can connect at speeds up to 230 Kbps (230,400 bits per second). No modem can transfer data over a regular phone line at these speeds, but a two-channel ISDN terminal adapter can connect at 112 Kbps or 128 Kbps over an ISDN phone line. This is half the speed of a LocalTalk network, but only a small fraction of a 10Base-T Ethernet network's speed.

If you have a modem with built-in data compression hardware, you may still be able to benefit from speeds up to 230 Kbps. In this case, your modem transfers data to and from your computer several times faster than it transfers data over the phone line. Your modem makes up the speed differential by reducing the amount of data it transfers over the phone line by compressing data before sending it and decompressing it after receiving it.

Not all the built-in serial ports on Mac OS computers are capable of 230 Kbps. While most Power Macintosh models have high-speed serial ports, some don't. The Power Mac 5200, 5300, 6200, 6300 series do not have high-speed serial ports. Neither do the PowerBook 1400, 2300, and 5300 models. Maximum serial-port speed on these computers is 57.6 Kbps (57,600 bits per second or bps).

If your Macintosh does not have serial ports, then you're likely connecting using an internal modem. All internal modems on the latest Macintosh models (iMac, Power Macintosh G3 and G4, iBook, and PowerBook G3) offer high-speed connections.

Making a Remote Network Connection

Connecting to a remote network involves several different pieces of software. This section describes how to set up and establish a remote connection using the following software:

✦ **Modem** control panel, which you use to set up your computer's modem for remote access

✦ **DialAssist** control panel, which you can use to simplify remote access calls that involve long distance, credit card, international, or private PBX phone numbers

✦ **Remote Access** control panel, which you use to configure all remote connections and that you can use to start, stop, and monitor a connection

✦ **Control Strip**, which you can use to start, stop, and monitor a connection

Using the Modem control panel

You use the Modem control panel to specify the port to which the modem is connected and to identify the type of modem that you have. You can also set several dialing options. Figure 20-12 is an example of the Modem control panel.

Figure 20-12: The Modem control panel sets up your modem to make a remote connection.

Modem user modes

You can see more settings or fewer settings in the Modem control panel by changing the user mode. The two modes are Basic and Administration. To change the user mode, choose User Mode from the Edit menu and select the mode in the dialog box that appears. Figure 20-13 shows this dialog box.

The Basic user mode shows the settings that most people need. The Administration mode provides control over which settings can be changed. Administration mode lets you set a password that protects the Administration mode settings. In the Administration mode, you can lock several Modem settings independently. Locked settings can't be changed in Basic mode.

Figure 20-13: Select a user mode for the Modem control panel.

Modem configurations

If you use more than one modem with your Macintosh (or if you'd like to save different configurations for the same modem, such as sound or dialing options), you can create saved configurations, which allow you to name a set of settings, and then create and name another set. After your configurations are created, you can easily move back and forth between them.

You may also want to create different modem configurations if you're using the Location Manager, as described in Chapter 12.

You do create a new configuration with the Configurations command in the File menu. This command displays a dialog box that lists groups of Modem settings by name and has buttons for acting on the group that's selected in the list (see Figure 20-14). First, select the Default configuration and then click Rename. Next, give your current Modem settings a name that will help you remember how the settings are configured.

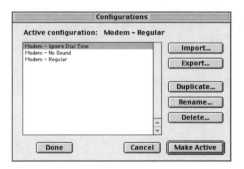

Figure 20-14: The Configurations dialog box enables you to work with named groups of settings for different networks or locations.

To create a new configuration, select one of the existing configurations and click Duplicate. Give the configuration a new name and click OK. Now, back in the Configurations window, select the new configuration and click Make Active. You are switched back to the Modem dialog box, where you can change the settings to reflect the new configuration. When you click the Modem control panel's close box, you'll be asked to save any changes for this new configuration. Now, you can switch easily between two or more configurations using the File ⇨ Configurations command.

Modem scripts

You identify the type of modem you have by choosing a modem script for it from the Modem pop-up menu in the Modem control panel. A *modem script* contains the sequence of modem commands needed to start and stop remote connections with a particular type of modem. In some cases, the Modem pop-up menu lists more than one modem script for a modem. Each of the alternatives makes a different kind of connection, typically a connection at a different speed.

The remote access software included with Mac OS 9 comes with over 60 modem scripts. In addition, modems usually come with modem scripts that need to be installed on the computer. If your modem is not listed in the Modem pop-up menu, make sure your modem software is installed properly. Modem scripts go in the Modem Script folder in your Extensions folder. You can also check with the modem manufacturer to see whether a modem script is available for use with Apple Remote Access.

Using the DialAssist control panel

The DialAssist control panel simplifies making long distance, credit card, international, and private PBX phone calls for a remote network connection. You enter the area or city code you're calling from and choose other dialing codes from four pop-up menus — DialAssist modifies the phone number accordingly. The results of the DialAssist control panel are shown in the Remote Access control panel. Figure 20-15 shows the DialAssist control panel.

Figure 20-15: The DialAssist control panel simplifies complicated phone numbers for remote access.

The DialAssist control panel comes preconfigured with some common dialing codes. You can add, change, or remove codes by clicking these buttons at the bottom of the control panel:

✦ **Country** to change codes for incoming and outgoing calls for any country

✦ **Prefix** to change codes for getting an outside line from a PBX

✦ **Long Distance** to change access codes for long distance service providers

✦ **Suffix** to change credit card, calling card, or other suffix codes

Using the Remote Access control panel

The Remote Access control panel is used to configure a remote connection to a computer, network, or ISP. Once you have entered the necessary connection information, you connect by clicking the control panel's Connect button. You can also connect automatically by using an application that accesses the Internet or a remote TCP/IP network. You can change this behavior and set a variety of other options that affect the connection by clicking the Options button in the control panel. Figure 20-16 shows the Remote Access control panel.

Figure 20-16: The Remote Access control panel configures all remote connections in Mac OS 9.

Remote Access configuration

To configure the Remote Access control panel, you specify whether to connect as a registered user or as an anonymous guest. To connect as a registered user, you must provide a username or account ID, a password, and the phone number to call to make a connection. As a guest, all you need to provide is the phone number.

If there is a Use DialAssist option visible above the phone number in the Remote Access control panel, you can turn it on to have the DialAssist control panel help you dial complicated phone numbers. The DialAssist option appears only if the user mode is set to Advanced or Administration, as described later in this section under the heading "Remote Access User Modes." The DialAssist control panel is described earlier in this section under the heading "Using the DialAssist Control Panel." Figure 20-17 shows the Remote Access control panel with the DialAssist option in use.

Figure 20-17: The DialAssist option, if present and selected, provides a separate space for entering an area code or city code and a pop-up menu for choosing a country to call.

If you turn on the Use DialAssist option, the Remote Access control panel provides two spaces for the phone number you are calling, one labeled Number and the other labeled Area Code, and a pop-up menu labeled Country. Do not include an area code or city code in the space labeled Number. Enter the area code or city code for the number you are calling in the space labeled Area Code. In addition, you need to indicate the country you are calling by choosing it from the Country pop-up menu. When you enter the Area Code and Country, the Remote Access control panel has the DialAssist control panel use this information to construct the number that will be dialed. The full number that will be dialed appears in the Remote Access control panel next to the Preview label.

If you do not turn on the Use DialAssist option or it is not present, then you need to enter the full phone number in the entry box labeled Number. For a long distance number, you must include the long-distance access code and area code prefixes, such as 1-800-. For an international call, you must include the international access code and the country code prefixes. For a credit card or calling card call, you must include the card number as a suffix.

When you enter a phone number, you can include hyphens, spaces, parentheses, and slashes for readability. The Remote Access control panel ignores them in the phone number. Commas in the phone number instruct the modem to pause during dialing. Most modems pause two seconds for each comma.

Tip   Again, assuming you're not using Dial Assist, you can set up Remote Access to use your phone company's special codes for a variety of services. For instance, you can add ***70,** to the beginning of the phone number in the Number entry box to turn off call waiting with many phone systems. If you have a special prefix for long-distance dialing (like **1010321,**) you can enter that before the number. Use commas to create a short pause that is sometimes required by the phone company before you dial the main number.

Need to store more than one set of Remote Access settings? You do that with the Configurations command in the File menu. This command displays a dialog box that lists groups of settings by name and has buttons for acting on the group that's selected in the list. There are buttons for making the selected group active, creating a new group by duplicating the selected group, renaming the selected group, and deleting the selected group. Other buttons let you export the selected group as a file and import a group that someone else has exported. Figure 20-18 is an example of the Configurations dialog box.

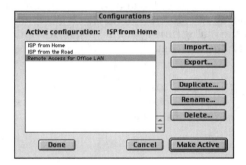

Figure 20-18: The Configurations dialog box lets you work with named groups of settings for different networks or locations.

Remote Access connection status

At the bottom of the Remote Access control panel status information is displayed during a connection. You can reduce the size of the control panel to show only the status information by clicking the disclosure triangle in the top-left corner of the control panel. Figure 20-19 shows the reduced view of the Remote Access control panel.

Figure 20-19: The Remote Access control panel displays the connection status.

While connected, the Remote Access control panel has a Disconnect button. You can terminate the connection by clicking this button.

Remote Access manual dialing

If you're calling from a place where you must dial the number yourself (such as when making an operator-assisted call), don't click the Connect button in the Remote Access control panel. Instead, choose Dial Manually from the Remote Access menu and follow the instructions on the screen.

Remote Access options

Clicking Options in the Remote Access control panel brings up a dialog box in which you can set options that affect the connection. The options are organized into three groups: Redialing, Connection, and Protocol. You display a group of options by clicking its tab at the top of the dialog box. Figure 20-20 shows the Redialing options of the Remote Access control panel.

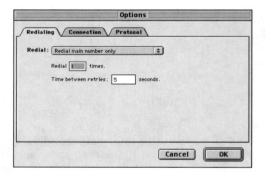

Figure 20-20: Set redialing and other options in the Remote Access Options dialog box.

The Redialing options determine whether the Remote Access control panel redials when the phone number is busy and whether it dials an alternate number if there is no answer on the main number. You can specify the number of times to redial before giving up and how long to wait between attempts. This interval should be at least five seconds so that your modem has time to reset itself between dialing attempts. If you specify an alternate phone number, the Remote Access control panel tries it once if the main number doesn't answer.

The options on the Connection tab control the amount of detail in the connection log and the behavior of connection reminders. Figure 20-21 shows the Connection options of the Remote Access control panel. You should leave verbose (detailed) logging turned off unless you need details to troubleshoot connection problems. A detailed log uses up more disk space.

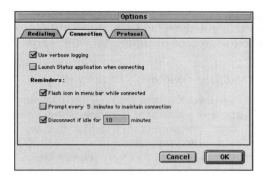

Figure 20-21: Set connection options in the Remote Access Options dialog box.

The Reminders options, which are under the Connections tab, determine how Remote Access reminds you of a connection and whether it automatically terminates the connection under certain circumstances. These options are useful if you pay for the amount of time you are connected:

✦ Turn on the **Flash icon in menu bar while connected** option to have the Remote Access icon flash above the Apple menu icon while you're online.

✦ Turn on the **Prompt every *x* minutes to maintain connection** option and a dialog box will appear periodically and automatically stop the connection if no one responds to it. Activating this option displays an entry box that enables you to change how frequently the idle message appears (default is five minutes).

✦ Turn on the **Disconnect if idle for *x* minutes** option to instruct Remote Access to disconnect if no remote activity takes place over a set amount of time. Activating this option displays an entry box that enables you to alter the amount of time before Remote Access disconnects (the default is ten minutes).

Note If you turn on the Disconnect if idle option but Remote Access never disconnects automatically, then some application is continuing to use the connection. You may be able to set application preferences to prevent continuous or periodic use of the connection. For example, set your e-mail program so that it does not check for mail every five minutes. Also, some Web pages contain items that continuously access the Internet. If you suspect this is happening, go to another Web page, close the Web browser window, or quit the Web browser application.

The options on the Protocol tab let you choose a network protocol for the connection. Because Remote Access can be used to connect to either an ISP or an Apple Remote Access Protocol server, it's important to pick the appropriate protocol for a successful connection. The protocol options in the Use protocol pop-up menu include:

✦ Choose **Automatic** to let Remote Access pick an appropriate protocol, depending on the type of connection you're trying to establish. (This is a good option only if you don't know what type of connection you're trying to establish.)

✦ Choose **PPP** for a connection to an ISP or remote TCP/IP network.

✦ Choose **ARAP** for a connection to a network server that uses the Apple Remote Access Protocol (ARAP), such as a Mac that is running Remote Access Personal Server 1.0 to 2.1. If you're connecting to a Mac that is running Remote Access Personal Server 3.0 or later, you can choose PPP or ARAP. PPP gives you faster access, but is more complicated to set up. Figure 20-22 shows the Protocol options with PPP chosen.

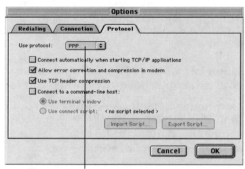

Choose the protocol

Figure 20-22: Set protocol options in the Remote Access Options dialog box.

If you choose the PPP protocol, you can set several additional options. One PPP option controls whether you can make an automatic connection. If you turn on automatic connection, the Mac OS makes a connection whenever an application accesses the Internet or remote TCP/IP network. The wording of this option ("Connect automatically when starting TCP/IP applications") suggests that the automatic connection happens the moment you open the application. In fact, the automatic connection may happen some time later when you do something in the application that causes it to access the Internet or remote network. For example, you can set a Web browser's preferences so that it will not access the Internet until you choose a bookmark, click a link, or otherwise specify a Web location that you want to see.

The Allow error correction and compression in modem option determines whether to allow your modem's hardware to compress data that is sent using the modem and check for errors in data transmission. If your modem has these capabilities, turning on this option may improve the performance of the connection.

The Use TCP header compression option determines whether the Mac OS will try to compress TCP headers for efficiency. You should leave this option turned on because the ISP or remote network server can refuse header compression without causing a problem.

If you need to connect to an ISP or remote network that requires you to enter specific information, such as your account name and password, you can enable that by selecting Connect to a command-line host. If you turn on this option, you can then select a method for entering the information. One method is to type the information in a terminal window. (As you're connecting with Remote Access, a terminal window appears enabling you to type commands to the remote computer.) The other method is to specify a connection script that enters the necessary information for you. You can create a connection script by clicking the Settings button in the terminal window to record your typing while you make a connection.

Remote Access user modes

The Remote Access control panel has three modes: Basic, Advanced, and Administration. The Basic mode shows the settings most people need. The Advanced mode includes an additional option that determines whether the DialAssist control panel automatically modifies the phone number for long distance, credit card, international, or PBX dialing. Administration mode lets you lock several settings independently. Locked settings can't be changed in Basic or Advanced modes. You can also set a password that protects Administration mode settings.

To change the user mode, choose User Mode from the Edit menu and select the mode in the dialog box that appears. Figure 20-23 shows this dialog box.

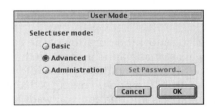

Figure 20-23: Select a user mode for the Remote Access control panel.

Using the Remote Access control strip module

If your computer has the Control Strip active, you can use it to start, stop, and monitor a remote connection. You can also use the Control Strip to choose a different named configuration of the Remote Access control panel and to open this control panel. Figure 20-24 is an example of the Remote Access control strip module.

Figure 20-24: Use the Control Strip to control and monitor a remote connection.

Remote Access configuration

The Remote Access pop-up in the Control Strip lists names of all configurations saved in the Remote Access control panel. The configuration marked with a bullet in the pop-up is the active configuration that is used the next time you make a connection. To make a different configuration active, press the Remote Access icon in the Control Strip and choose the configuration from the pop-up menu. To open the Remote Access control panel so that you can change configuration settings, choose Open Remote Access from the pop-up menu.

Remote Access connect and disconnect

You can start a remote connection by choosing Connect from the bottom of the Remote Access pop-up menu in the Control Strip. During a connection, Connect changes to Disconnect in the pop-up menu. Choosing Disconnect stops the connection.

Remote Access connection status

You can see the connection status by looking at the Remote Access icon or at the top of the Remote Access pop-up menu. During a connection, a line representing a network wire displays at the bottom of the icon. This line flashes while a connection is starting up or stopping. When the connection is idle, this line is not displayed.

The Remote Access control strip module can also report the duration of the current connection or the amount of time remaining. This statistic appears next to the Remote Access icon in the Control Strip. To specify which statistic you would like to see, press the icon and choose Status Display from the pop-up menu. A dialog box appears in which you can select the type of status information you want to see in the Control Strip. Figure 20-25 shows this dialog box.

Figure 20-25: Select the type of connection information to display in the Remote Access control strip module.

Using Remote Access Personal Server

Prior to Mac OS 9, the Remote Access Personal Server was add-on software that you had to buy from Apple. Now it's included with the standard Mac OS 9 installation.

The Remote Access Personal Server enables you to set up your Macintosh computer so that other computers (called "client" computers) can dial your modem and connect using their Remote Access control panel. You can elect, using Personal Server, to enable that user to access either the Personal Server machine that's being dialed in to or any machine that's connected to the Personal Server Mac. If you work while traveling or from home, this software makes it possible to dial in to another Mac and exchange files as if you were on an AppleTalk or TCP/IP network.

Caution   You need to think carefully before enabling the Personal Server options on your Macintosh. While it may be a good idea to enable access for yourself to the Personal Server machine (perhaps while working from home or traveling), it also introduces a potential security risk to your network. For example, enabling access to your entire network via a modem connection could enable an unauthorized user access to your company or organization network without your knowledge. If your computer is part of a larger network, you should probably ask the system administrator's advice in setting up Remote Access Personal Server.

To activate the server, open the Remote Access control panel and choose Answering from the Remote Access menu. The Answering dialog box appears (shown in Figure 20-26), allowing you to select options that allow others to dial into your Macintosh:

✦ **Answer calls** — Select this option to allow the Remote Access Personal Server to answer incoming calls and enable remote users to attempt to connect to this machine.

✦ **Maximum connection time** — Select this option and enter an amount of time in the entry box that appears (the default is 60 minutes). You don't have to limit connections if you leave this option off.

✦ **Allow access** — Choose whether the remote user should have access to only the Remote Server computer or to any computer that the Remote Server is connected to. If the "entire network" option is chosen, the remote user will have access to any computer connected via a network to the Personal Server computer.

✦ **PPP Server setup** — Choose this option and users can dial in to the Personal Server machine using PPP instead of the Apple Remote Access Protocol. This makes it possible for the remote computer to share files with the Personal Server machine, as well as to gain Internet access via the Personal Server (assuming the Personal Server machine has an active Internet connection).

Figure 20-26: Setting Answering options for Remote Access Personal Server

If you choose to enable incoming PPP access, you'll need to assign a default client IP address for the machine that's connecting to yours. In most cases, this number should be an available IP address on your local TCP/IP network—ask your system administrator for details. You can also select the Allow client to use own IP address setting if the client has manually configured TCP/IP for connecting to your network.

Summary

This chapter showed you how to hook up a simple local area network (LAN). You can create a LocalTalk network with inexpensive connector boxes and either Apple's LocalTalk cables or ordinary telephone cords. For a better performing (although more expensive) LAN, you can create an Ethernet network using 10Base-T, which is the lowest in cost of the many Ethernet cabling alternatives. You can also create both LocalTalk and Ethernet networks and bridge them with Apple's LaserWriter Bridge 2.1 or LocalTalk Bridge 2.1 software. With the latest Mac models you can create a wireless network (or a combination of wired and wireless networks) using the AirPort technologies that Apple has introduced for newer Macs.

Configuring the Mac OS for network connections is the next step after your wiring is in place. You use the AppleTalk control panel to configure an AppleTalk network connection or the TCP/IP control panel to configure a TCP/IP network connection.

In addition, this chapter explained how to connect to a remote computer, remote network, or an Internet service provider (ISP) by modem. To connect to a remote computer or AppleTalk network, use the Modem and Remote Access control panels or the Remote Access Client program. To connect to an ISP or remote TCP/IP network, use the Modem control panel and either the Remote Access control panel or the PPP control panel.

Finally, this chapter discussed how to set up Remote Access Personal Server to enable other computers to access your Mac or your local network using either Remote Access or PPP protocols.

✦   ✦   ✦

Access Shared Files and Network Services

Just as you may have books of your own but expand your reading by going to the community library, you can work with more files than you have on your local hard disk by working with shared folders and disks from your local network. What's more, you can go beyond the limits of your local network and use the Internet to obtain files from all over the world.

This chapter explains how to gain access to files from your local network, a remote computer, a remote network, or the Internet. If your computer is not already on a network, Chapter 20 explains how to hook it up to a local network, a remote computer, or a remote network. If your computer is not set up to use the Internet, Chapter 10 tells you how to set it up. The same chapter describes a way to make a folder from your computer available as a Web site on the Internet. Chapter 22 explains how to share your folders and disks with other people whose computers are connected to your network.

Using Shared Folders and Disks

If your computer is on a local network, you can connect to shared folders and disks on the network and work with files from them. In addition, you can connect to shared folders and disks on a remote computer or network by modem and phone line.

Mac and Windows file sharing

If you use a Mac and a Windows PC, you probably need to transfer files back and forth. For small files, you can use floppy disks (if both computers have floppy disk drives) or other removable disks. For large files or frequent file transfers, it may make sense to share files over a network.

To use Mac file servers from a Windows PC, you need software that adds AppleTalk protocols to Windows. PC MacLAN for Windows lets a PC use shared Mac folders, disks, and printers as if they were on a Windows network. Conversely, a PC can share selected folders with Macs on the network. The Windows user simply clicks a folder with the right mouse button, selects AppleTalk Sharing from the pop-up menu that appears, and enters the name to use for the shared folder and who has permission to use it. Up to ten Macs can connect to a PC's shared folders at the same time. PC MacLAN is from Miramar Systems (805-966-2432, http://www.miramarsys.com).

If Macs are in the minority on your network, you may need to install software that enables your Mac to use Windows networking protocols. Dave, from Thursby Systems (817-478-5070, http://www.thursby.com), enables you to use shared folders from Windows PCs and to share your folders and disks with PC users. You can connect to shared Windows folders using the Chooser by clicking the Dave Client icon instead of the AppleShare icon. Alternatively, you can connect using Dave Access. Once you have connected to a shared Windows folder, you can make an alias of it to simplify future connections. To share your folders with Windows PCs, you use the Dave Sharing control panel. Your shared folders show up on Windows PCs in their Network Neighborhood.

For a network between Macs and Windows PCs, Ethernet works great. Many Macs have built-in Ethernet capability and need only a transceiver for a particular type of Ethernet cable, with 10Base-T cable, the most popular by far. Some Macs even have a built-in 10Base-T port and don't require a transceiver. Macs without any kind of built-in Ethernet need an Ethernet adapter, and a variety of adapters are available from many manufacturers. Most PCs need an Ethernet network interface card (NIC). There are several options for connecting computers with Ethernet (as discussed in Chapter 20).

This section explains how to connect to shared folders and disks and how to work with them on your computer. In Mac OS 9, you can connect to shared folders and disks using the Chooser, the Network Browser, a Navigation Services dialog box, or aliases. When you work with a shared folder or disk, the person who owns it may restrict your access to its contents. Subject to these restrictions, you can transfer items between your local disks and the shared folder or disk. You may also be able to open documents and applications directly from the shared folder or disk.

Identifying yourself to a file server

Shared folders and disks are located on computers that are connected to the network. Computers that share folders and disks are known as file servers. A file server can be a computer whose principal job is sharing disks for the network at-large. In addition, people can make their personal computers into part-time file servers by using Mac OS file sharing (as described in Chapter 22). The same procedure is followed to connect to shared folders and disks on either kind of file server.

Before you can connect to shared folders and disks on a file server, you need to know the name of the file server. If your network has zones, you also need to find out the name of the zone in which the file server is located. This information is all you need to know to connect to shared folders and disks that allow guest access. Some shared folders and disks may require that you to connect as a registered user to work with their files. In this case, you must know your registered name and password on the file server where the shared folders or disks are located. You may have a different registered name and password on each file server. The owner of each file server assigns you a registered name and password, and may allow you to change your password.

Connecting with the Chooser

To make a connection to a shared folder or disk, open the Chooser (under the Apple menu). Look at the bottom-right corner of the Chooser and make sure that AppleTalk is active (so that you can use your local network). Next, select the AppleShare icon on the left side of the Chooser to display a list of file servers on the right side of the Chooser. If you see a list of zones on the left side of the Chooser, your network contains zones; you may need to select a different zone to see the file server you want listed on the right side of the Chooser. (If you don't see a list of zones in the Chooser, your network has only one zone.) From the list of file servers, select the one that has the shared folder or disk you want to use. Figure 21-1 shows the Chooser with a file server selected in a network without zones.

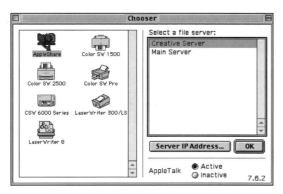

Figure 21-1: In the Chooser, you can select the file server that has a shared folder or disk that you want to use.

File servers that use the TCP/IP network protocol instead of AppleTalk are not listed in the Chooser when you click the AppleShare icon. To connect to shared folders and disks on one of these servers, click the Server IP Address button in the Chooser. In the dialog box that appears, enter the file server's IP address (a four-part number such as 198.162.2.100) or its URL (such as afp://server-name/volume-name/folder-path). You can get a server's IP address or URL from the server's owner.

afp:// is the URL protocol for the Apple File Protocol, which allows you to connect over a TCP/IP network to an AppleShare or Apple File Services server. For more on URLs, see Chapter 10.

Identifying yourself

When you have selected the file server that has the shared folder or disk that you want to use, click the OK button in the Chooser. A dialog box appears, enabling you to identify yourself as a registered user or guest of the file server. Figure 21-2 is an example of this dialog box.

Figure 21-2: Identify yourself as a guest or registered user of a file server.

To connect as a registered user, select the Registered User option and enter your registered name and password in the spaces provided. The owner of the file server that you want to access must have assigned this name and password. If your own computer is set up as a file server (using Mac OS file sharing) and you're connecting to it from another computer, enter the owner name and password. When you enter your password, you must type it exactly right, including uppercase and lowercase letters (it's case sensitive). Then click OK.

If you're not a registered user and the Guest option isn't dimmed, you can connect to shared folders and disks on a file server that allows guest access. If the Guest option is dimmed, guests are not permitted to access any shared folders or disks on the selected file server. Ask the owner of the file server to give you a registered name and password.

Before connecting to a file server, you may be able to change your password on it. Click Change Password and a series of dialog boxes leads you through the process of changing your password. If you get a message saying that your password couldn't be changed, you probably don't have permission to change your password on the file server you're about to connect to. Contact the owner of that file server to find out.

Keychain access

You have another option before you connect to the server. If you check the Add to Keychain check box, both the username and password are stored in your personal keychain, which enables you to access this particular server in the future without entering a login name and password (as long as your keychain is unlocked). Check the check box, and then click Connect.

After you've selected a network volume, if your keychain is locked, you'll see a dialog box asking you to which keychain you want the item added to and what your keychain password is. This unlocks the keychain and adds the password to it. If the keychain isn't locked, your name and password are added directly to the open keychain. Then, in both cases, you'll be connected to the server volume.

Note
Even though you choose a specific volume before you see any messages from the keychain (if you do see a message) your username and password are stored for the entire server. In the future, you can access any volume from that server using your keychain.

The next time you go to access a server that has been saved on your keychain, you'll see a different message. This message asks you if you want to enable the Chooser to access your keychain. If you do, simply click Allow to access the server volume. You can also select one of two options. If you choose Allow access without warning when using keychain *Keychain Name*, then you won't see this message again as long as you have the keychain named *Keychain Name* open (this will change for the active keychain name). If you'd prefer that the Chooser be enabled to access whatever keychain is open, select the option Allow "Chooser" to access items without warning while running.

The third time you access a network volume, the volume will open immediately if the keychain is unlocked. If the keychain is locked, you'll see the standard Keychain dialog box. You can choose the keychain you want to unlock from the Unlock Keychain dialog box, then enter that keychain's password. After the keychain is open, the network volume is accessed.

Selecting network volumes

After connecting you as a registered user or guest of a file server, the Chooser displays a dialog box that displays the name of the file server and lists its shared folders and disks. Select the names of folders or disk that you want to access. If you like, you can also click the check boxes next to items that you want to use each time you start your computer. Once you've made your selections, click OK.

To select more than one item name, Shift+click each name. You can scroll through the list or type the first few letters of a shared item's name to find it. If a listed item is dimmed, either you're already using that folder or disk or the owner of that folder or disk hasn't granted you access privileges to see it. Figure 21-3 is an example of the Chooser's dialog box that lists a file server's shared items.

Click checkbox to log into this server every time your Mac starts up

Figure 21-3:
Select shared folders and disks from a file server.

Note

If you mark a check box and are a registered user, two options appear in the dialog box below the list of items. Select the option Save My Name Only if you want the system to ask for your password before opening the shared folder or disk during startup. Use this option to prevent unauthorized people from accessing the shared folder or disk from your computer by restarting it. If you select the option Save My Name and Password in the Keychain, your computer automatically accesses your keychain when it opens the checked items during startup.

An icon appears on your desktop for each shared folder or disk you connect to. The icon for a shared folder looks the same as the icon for a shared disk. The Mac OS considers all shared folders and shared disks to be a kind of disk.

Connecting with the Network Browser

Instead of connecting to shared folders and disks using the Chooser, you can use the Network Browser (under the Apple menu). When you open the Network Browser, it displays a list of *network neighborhoods*, which, by default, represent the different networking protocols that you can access to reach file servers.

The Network Browser uses network neighborhoods to divide servers according to the protocol they're using. If you have AppleTalk servers on your network, they appear under the AppleTalk entry. If you have TCP/IP-based servers (for File Sharing over TCP/IP or AppleShare IP servers using the TCP/IP protocol), then you either see those in the Local Services neighborhood or in a neighborhood named for your local domain name, such as "wahoo.com" or "mac-upgrade.com."

Note

If you have Web-sharing active on Macs connected to your network, you may also see those Web servers active in the Local Services neighborhood listed in the Network Browser. That the same computer can be both a file server and a Web server explains why you sometimes see the same computer name twice. (Web servers, however, have a slightly different icon than do file servers.) Likewise, if a server has a registered domain name, that domain name may appear in the Network Browser as a neighborhood, and the server's icon may appear in multiple neighborhoods.

To connect to a shared folder or disk on a file server, you must open the file server in the Network Browser. Figure 21-4 is an example of the Network Browser.

Figure 21-4: In the Network Browser, you can connect to shared folders and disks from any file server on your network.

To open a file server in the Network Browser, do one of the following (you may be asked to enter a password or access your keychain, described in the next two sections, before you see the available shared folders and disks):

✦ Double-click the file server's name or icon. A list of shared folders and disks from the file server replaces the list of file servers in the Network Browser.

✦ Click the disclosure triangle to the left of the file server's icon so that it points down. The shared disks and folders from the file server are listed below it in the Network Browser.

✦ Select the file server (by clicking it once) and choose Open in Place or Open in New Window from the File menu. The Open in Place command replaces the list of file servers with a list of shared folders and disks from the file server you open. The Open in New Window displays the list of shared folders and disks in a new window, leaving the list of file servers displayed in a background window.

✦ Choose a file server or a shared disk from the pop-up menu of the Favorites button or the Recent button. These pop-up menus are described in more detail later in this section.

✦ For a file server that uses the TCP/IP network protocol, choose Connect to Server from the pop-up menu of the Shortcuts button. In the dialog box that appears, enter the file server's IP network address (a four-part number such as 198.162.2.100) or its URL (such as afp://server-name/volume-name/folder-path).

✦ For a Web server listed in the Network Browser, double-click its icon. You'll be switched to your default Web browser to access the server. If the server requires a password, you'll be asked to enter your username and password. If it doesn't require a password, the Web server's index page or directory will display in the browser window.

✦ For an FTP server listed in the Network Browser (or if you access it using the Connect to Server option from the Shortcuts pop-up menu), you may be asked to enter a name and password. You'll then see a directory listing for the FTP server in the Network Browser window.

Identifying yourself

When you open a file server or shared disk in the Network Browser, a dialog box appears asking you to identify yourself as a registered user or guest of the file server. Figure 21-5 is an example of this dialog box.

Note   If you don't see this dialog box, your keychain may already have your username and password stored for this server. See the next section for more on how the keychain works.

Figure 21-5: Identify yourself as a guest or registered user of a file server.

To connect as a registered user, select the Registered User option, and enter your registered name and password in the spaces provided. The owner of the file server that you want to access must have assigned this name and password. If your own computer is set up as a file server (using Mac OS file sharing) and you're connecting to it from another computer, enter the owner name and password. When you enter your password, you must type it exactly right, including uppercase and lowercase letters (it's case sensitive). Then click OK.

If you're not a registered user and the Guest option isn't dimmed, you can connect to shared folders and disks on a file server that allows guest access. If the Guest option is dimmed, guests are not permitted access to any shared folders or disks on the file server. Ask the owner of the file server to give you a registered name and password.

Before connecting to a file server, you may be able to change your password on it. Click Change Password, and a series of dialog boxes leads you through the process of changing your password. If you get a message saying your password couldn't be changed, you probably don't have permission to change your password on the file server you're about to connect to. Contact the owner of that file server to find out.

Keychain access

You have another option before you connect to the server. If you check the Add to Keychain check box, both the username and password are stored in your personal keychain, which enables you to access this particular server in the future without entering a login name and password, as long as your keychain is unlocked. Check the check box, and then click Connect.

After you've selected a network volume, if your keychain is locked, you'll see a dialog box asking you to which keychain you want the item added to and what your keychain password is. This unlocks the keychain and adds the password to it. If the keychain isn't locked, your name and password is added directly to the open keychain. Then, in both cases, you are connected to the server volume.

Note   Even though you choose a specific volume before you see any messages from the keychain (if you do see a message) your username and password are stored for the entire server. In the future, you can access any volume from that server using your keychain.

The next time you go to access a server that has been saved on your keychain, you'll see a different message. This message asks you if you want to enable the Network Browser to access your keychain. If you do, simply click Allow to access the server volume. You can also select one of two options. If you choose Allow access without warning when using keychain *Keychain Name*, then you won't see this message again as long as you have the keychain named *Keychain Name* open (this will change for the active keychain name). If you'd prefer that the Network Browser be enabled to access whatever keychain is open, select the option Allow "Network Browser" to access items without warning while running.

The third time you access a network volume, the volume will open immediately if the keychain is unlocked. If the keychain isn't unlocked, you'll see the standard Keychain dialog box. You can choose the keychain that you want to unlock from the Unlock Keychain dialog box, and then enter that keychain's password. After the keychain is open, the network volume is accessed.

Opening shared folders and disks

After connecting you as a registered user or guest of a file server, the Network Browser displays a list of the shared folders and disks that the file server allows you to see. In this list, the icon for a shared folder looks the same as the icon for a shared disk because the Mac OS considers all shared folders and shared disks to be a kind of disk. You can open the shared folders and disks using any of these methods:

✦ Double-click a shared folder or disk. Its icon appears on the desktop and opens in the Finder.

✦ Select a shared folder or disk and choose Open in New Window from the File menu. An icon for the shared folder or disk appears on the desktop and opens in the Finder.

✦ Choose a shared folder or disk from the pop-up menu of the Favorites button or the Recent button. These pop-up menus are described in more detail under the next four headings.

You can open only one folder or disk at time with the Network Browser. In contrast, the Chooser lets you select multiple shared items on the same file server and connect to them all at once.

Using the Shortcuts button

The Network Browser's Shortcuts button (the pointing-finger icon) provides quick access to the file servers on your AppleTalk network, as well as a means of connecting to file servers on a TCP/IP network. Clicking this button displays a pop-up menu, as shown in Figure 21-6.

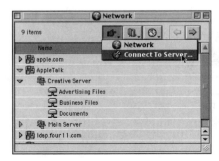

Figure 21-6: The Shortcuts menu provides quick access to file servers on your AppleTalk network and lets you connect to a file server on a TCP/IP network.

Choosing Network from the Shortcuts pop-up menu takes the Network Browser back to a list of file servers (and zones, if your network has them).

Choosing Connect to Server from the Shortcuts pop-up menu enables you to connect to a file server by entering an IP network address (such as 192.168.1.254) or a URL (such as afp://server-name/volume-name/folder-path). The file server must be one that uses the TCP/IP network protocol instead of the AppleTalk network protocol. You can get a server's IP address or URL from the server's owner.

New Feature   You can enter an FTP URL (such as `ftp://mirrors.apple.com/`) to access the FTP server from within the Network Browser. In Mac OS 9, the Network Browser is actually a full-featured FTP client, capable of uploading and downloading files from FTP servers. FTP is discussed in more detail later in this chapter in the section "Obtaining Files from the Internet."

Using the Favorites button

The Network Browser's Favorites button (the bookmarked-folder icon) lists your favorite shared folders, shared disks, file servers, and zones in a pop-up menu when you click it. Figure 21-7 is an example of this pop-up menu.

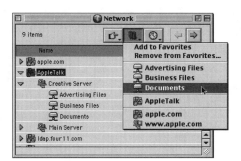

Figure 21-7: The Favorites menu lists your favorite shared folders, disks, file servers, and zones.

When you choose an item from the Favorites pop-up menu, the Network Browser displays it. If you're not already connected to a shared folder or disk from the same file server, the Network Browser asks you to identify yourself as a registered user or guest (as described previously).

You can add items displayed in the Network Browser to the Favorites pop-up menu. To add an item, select it and choose Add to Favorites from the Favorites pop-up menu. Alternatively, you can drag the item to the Favorites button. In the Network Browser, only your favorite shared folders, shared disks, and file servers appear in the Favorites pop-up menu. Other kinds of favorites, such as regular folders and files that are in shared folders and disks, appear in the Apple menu's Favorites menu and in the Favorites pop-up menus that are found in many Open and Save dialog boxes.

All your favorite items have aliases in the Favorites folder inside the System Folder. This folder is normally listed in the Apple menu.

You can remove items from the Favorites pop-up menu using the Remove Favorites command. This command displays a dialog box that lists all items in the Favorites folder, including items that don't appear in the Network Browser's Favorites pop-up menu. To delete a favorite, select it in the Remove Favorites dialog box and click Remove. You can select multiple favorites to remove by Shift+clicking and Command+clicking them.

To rename a favorite, change the name of its alias in the Favorites folder. You can also add and remove favorites by adding and removing aliases in the Favorites folder.

Using the Recent button

The Network Browser's Recent button (the clockface icon) lists your most recently used shared folders and disks in a pop-up menu when you click it. Figure 21-8 is an example of this pop-up menu.

Figure 21-8: The Recent menu lists your most recently used shared folders and disks.

When you choose an item from this menu, the Network Browser displays it. If you're not already connected to a shared folder or disk from the same file server, the Network Browser asks you to identify yourself as a registered user or guest (as described previously).

The number of items listed in the Recent pop-up menu is controlled by options in the Apple Menu Options control panel. To change the number of items, enter a different number for the Servers option. If you enter zero for the Servers option or turn off the Remember recently used items option, the Recent pop-up menu will be inactive the next time you open the Network Browser.

Some items listed in the Recent pop-up menu have aliases in the Recent Servers folder inside the Apple Menu folder. Other items listed in the Recent pop-up menu have aliases in the Recent folder that is in the Network Browser folder inside the Preferences folder in the System Folder. You can edit the Recent pop-up menu by renaming, adding, and removing items in these two folders. The Recent Servers folder gets moved to the Trash if you turn off the Remember recently used items option in the Apple Menu Options control panel.

Using the Back and Forward buttons

You can go back to see the last item you opened in the Network Browser window by clicking the Back button (the left-arrow icon). After going back, you can go forward by clicking the Forward button (the right-arrow icon).

Connecting with Navigation Services

You can connect to shared folders and disks directly from the Navigation Services dialog box that some applications use for opening and saving files. To have the Navigation Services dialog box display a list of the file servers on your network, press the Shortcuts button (with the pointing-hand icon) and choose Network from its pop-up menu. If your network has multiple zones, they appear in the Navigation Services dialog box as well. Figure 21-9 is an example list of file servers in a Navigation Services dialog box.

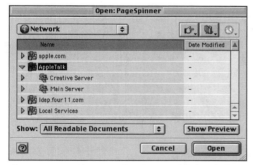

Figure 21-9: In a Navigation Services dialog box, you can connect to shared folders or disks from any file server on your network.

Once you see the list of file servers in a Navigation Services dialog box, follow the same procedure as previously described for the Network Browser to connect to a shared folder or disk. After connecting to a shared folder or disk, browse it in the Navigation Services dialog box as if it were a local hard disk.

Cross-Reference

For more information, see Chapter 7.

Connecting with aliases and network locations

You don't have to go through the Chooser or the Network Browser to use a shared folder or disk again. Connect once as described previously and while the shared item's icon is on your desktop, make an alias of it. You can also make an alias of a file or folder contained in the shared folder or disk. If you open the alias of something located on a file server, the Mac OS connects to the file server and opens the alias's original item for you. You have to enter your password again unless you were connected as a guest when you made the alias.

You can use the Network Browser to make an alias of any item you can see in it. One method is to select the shared item and choose Make Alias from the Network Browser's File menu. An alert message advises you that the alias must be created on the desktop; click OK to do this or Cancel to call it off. You can also make an alias by dragging an item from the Network Browser to the desktop.

When you make an alias of a file server, the file that is created is not actually an alias. It is a network location. Opening a network location (for example, by double-clicking its icon) opens the Network Browser and displays a list of the file server's shared folders and disks that you are allowed to see. (When you make an alias of a shared folder, shared disk, folder, or file, you get an alias.)

Recognizing your access privileges

Connecting to a shared folder or disk doesn't necessarily give you unlimited access to its contents. Access to the contents can be restricted on a folder-by-folder basis. What you can do with a folder depends on the access privileges that its owner granted you. You may be allowed to open a folder, or confined to putting things into it, or forbidden from using it at all. If you can open a folder, you may be allowed to see only files, only folders, or both files and folders inside it. The Finder indicates your access privileges to folders inside a shared folder or disk with special folder icons and small icons in folder and disk windows. You can also determine your privileges by displaying a folder's Info window.

Ascertaining privileges from folder icons

Often you can ascertain your privileges for a folder by looking at the folder's icon. A folder icon with a belt around it indicates that you don't have any access privileges. A belt-strapped folder icon with an accompanying down arrow is a drop box; you can drop items into the folder but cannot open it or use anything inside it. A small padlock appears on the icon of a folder that is locked. A locked folder can't be renamed, moved to a different folder, or put in the Trash. Usually, however, you can copy files to and from it. Figure 21-10 shows examples of the special folder icons.

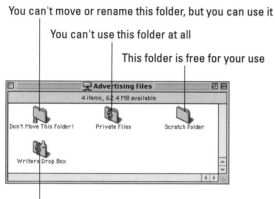

You can't move or rename this folder, but you can use it

You can't use this folder at all

This folder is free for your use

Figure 21-10: Special folder icons indicate access privileges.

You can only drop things on (or in) this folder

Privileges in an Info window or sharing window

In addition to interpreting access privileges from icons, you can look at the Info window of a shared folder or disk that you're using. For an item shared from another computer, the Info window or sharing window tells where the item is, the name under which you're connected, and your access privileges for that item. Table 21-1 shows the access privileges that you need to perform common tasks with a shared folder or disk. Figure 21-11 shows examples of the Info window and the sharing window.

Table 21-1 Access Privileges for Common Tasks	
To Do This with a Shared Folder or Disk:	*You Need These Privileges:*
Copy a file from it	Read Only or Read & Write
Copy a folder from it	Read Only or Read & Write
Create a file in it	Read & Write
Create a folder in it	Read & Write
Discard a file from it	Read & Write
Discard a folder from it	Read & Write
Drag something to it	Write Only or Read & Write
Open a file from it	Read Only or Read & Write
Save changes to a file in it	Read & Write

To view sharing information, select the shared folder or disk and choose Sharing from the Get Info submenu of the File menu. You can also choose this command from the folder or disk's contextual menu. If an item's Info window is open but is not displaying its sharing information, choose Sharing from the Show pop-up menu near the top of the Info window.

Figure 21-11: See access privileges using the Get Info ⇨ Sharing command.

Unless you're the owner of the item, you can only view the privileges. Only the item's owner can change its privileges (as described in Chapter 22).

An owner's special privileges

If you connect to a file server as its owner, you can see and use everything on that file server's disks. In other words, you have full access privileges to all items, whether or not they have been designated for sharing. This feature is handy if you need copies of files from your computer while you're not at your desk. If you leave file sharing turned on (as described in Chapter 22), you can connect to your computer from another computer on your network. Then you can copy your files to the computer you're using. From there you can read, change, or print the files you copied. However, other people can also access all your files if they learn your owner name and password. You can reduce this risk at the expense of convenience, as discussed in Chapter 22.

Transferring network files

The most common use of shared folders and disks is to transfer files or folders between your computer and a shared folder or disk. For the most part, you transfer files and folders to and from a shared folder or disk just as you would copy files to and from a floppy disk.

Opening network files

When you open a shared document, the Finder searches your local disks for the application needed to open the document. If you don't have the necessary application, the Finder opens the application across the network. Running applications over a network is usually slower than running an application on your computer. To give you an estimate of network activity, the Mac OS displays a small double-arrow in the upper-left corner of the menu bar while it is sending or receiving anything over the network.

Disconnecting from shared folders and disks

In general, you remain connected to a shared folder or disk until you deliberately disconnect from it. You disconnect from a shared folder or disk by removing its icon from your desktop. You can drag the desktop icon to the Trash, or you can select it and use the Finder's Put Away command.

Restarting or shutting down your computer also disconnects you from all shared folders and disks, although you may be reconnected to individual shared folders or disks automatically on startup if you selected this option in the Chooser (see "Connecting with the Chooser" in the previous section). Putting a PowerBook to sleep disconnects all shared folders and disks. Putting a desktop Mac to sleep does not disconnect shared folders and disks.

There are a couple of ways that you can be disconnected involuntarily from a shared disk. For one, the owner of a shared folder or disk can summarily disconnect you. If you are connected to a shared folder or disk on a remote computer or network, the duration of your connection may be limited. When your time runs out, you are automatically disconnected. You can usually reconnect if a timed connection expires or a file server's owner disconnects you.

Of course, you will be disconnected without warning if the file server shuts down or if some problem arises with the network equipment. In addition, you will be disconnected from shared folders and disks on a PowerBook if that PowerBook goes to sleep. In contrast, you generally will not be disconnected from shared folders and disks on a desktop computer that goes to sleep.

Disconnecting a shared folder or disk may not disconnect your computer from its file server. Your computer remains connected to a file server as long as any of its shared folders or disks are on your desktop. While your computer is connected to a file server, you don't have to enter your user name or password to connect to any shared folders or disks that the owner has given you access privileges to see. In other words, you can reconnect to a shared folder or disk without entering your password if you are still connected to another of the file server's shared folders or disks. The file server's security can be breeched by this convenience if you're not careful.

To keep file servers secure, disconnect from all shared folders and disks before leaving your computer unattended. If you leave shared folders and disks on your desktop when you step away, anyone who can use your computer can connect to other shared items that you have access privileges to see on the same file server. Removing all shared folder and disk icons from your desktop means that you must enter your name and password again to reconnect, but so must anyone else.

Obtaining Files from the Internet

In addition to using files from shared folders and disks on your network, you can obtain useful (and sometimes, absolutely frivolous) files on the Internet from other computers all over the world. The process of copying files from the Internet to your computer is called *downloading*. Similarly, if you send a file from your computer, you are *uploading* the file.

On the Internet, files are sent using a protocol (network language) called *FTP* (File Transfer Protocol). A computer can make files available using this protocol by running a type of program called an *FTP server*. This term also refers to the combination of the server program and the computer that's running it. You may sometimes hear people refer to an *FTP site*, which is a collection of files on an FTP server that are available for downloading. An FTP site has the same function on the Internet as a shared disk on your network.

To receive or send files using this protocol, you use a program called an *FTP client* on your computer. The FTP client connects your computer to an FTP server and handles downloading and uploading (receiving and sending) the files. An FTP client has the same function on the Internet as the Chooser or Network Browser and Finder on a local network.

There are FTP clients built into Internet Explorer and Netscape Navigator. There's also a basic FTP client built into the Network Browser. In addition, there are independent FTP client programs, such as the low-cost shareware Fetch and Anarchie Pro (more about these later). They are available from FTP sites on the Internet.

Getting ready to download

Before downloading any files, you should specify where to put them. The best place to do this is the Internet control panel, as follows:

1. If necessary, click the Edit Sets disclosure triangle to expand the control panel and see its individual preference settings.

2. From the Edit Set pop-up menu, choose the set of preferences that you want to edit.

3. Next, click the Web tab to see Web and FTP options.

4. In the area labeled Download, click the Select button. This brings up a Navigation Services dialog box, in which you select the folder that you want to use for downloaded files. Figure 21-12 shows the Web and FTP preferences in the Internet control panel.

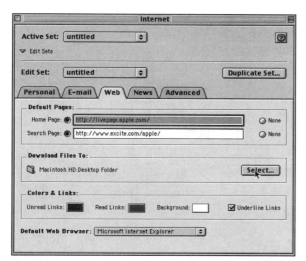

Figure 21-12: Set the folder for downloaded files with the Internet control panel.

If you don't use the Internet control panel, you should set the destination folder in your Web browser or FTP client. Most modern FTP clients use the Internet control panel's settings, so only use the application's download preference (in the application's Options or Preferences menu) as a last resort.

Downloading files

Here's how most FTP file transfers work: While browsing a Web page, you come across a description of a file that interests you, with a link to download the file. You click the link, and the browser opens a file-transfer progress window and downloads the file to your hard disk. Pretty easy, right? That's because browsers understand how to handle URLs that begin with ftp:// — they route them to their built-in FTP client programs. Figure 21-13 shows how this works in Internet Explorer.

Downloading with FTP client programs

Sometimes you want to download a file from an FTP site but you don't want or need to fire up a Web browser. Or perhaps you want to upload a file, which most Web browsers can't do. Instead, you can use one of the independent FTP client programs that are available for the Mac OS. Of these, the two most popular are Anarchie Pro and Fetch. Both are shareware, but ask your Internet service provider if they have a license to distribute Fetch free.

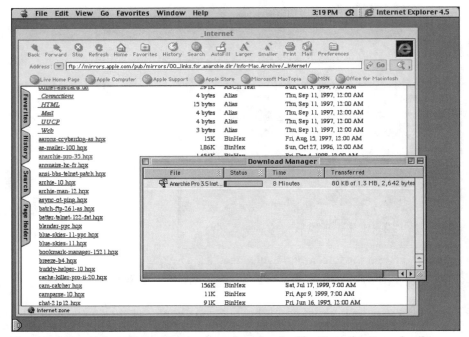

Figure 21-13: Using Internet Explorer to download a file. Note the Download Manager window that displays downloading progress.

Cross-Reference   For information on obtaining shareware, see Chapter 26.

Anarchie Pro

Anarchie Pro is a terrific FTP program written by Peter N. Lewis. Anarchie Pro lets you work with files on FTP servers in much the same way that you work with files in Finder. Some other FTP programs make you deal with files in directory dialog boxes (similar to the Open and Save dialog boxes).

With Anarchie Pro, if you want to download a file from an FTP server, you go to that server (usually in the Bookmarks window) and double-click a folder icon that represents one of the file directories on the FTP server. You can also open an individual server by choosing Get via FTP from the File menu and entering the FTP server address, your username, and your password.) A window opens with the contents of the directory (as it might if you had a Finder window open to a list view). To download a file or group of files from the open directory, select them and drag them to your Mac OS desktop. Uploading is as simple as dragging files from your desktop to a directory window. Anarchie Pro also keeps a handy set of bookmarks with pointers to useful FTP sites of interest to Mac OS users. Figure 21-14 shows the Mac OS desktop with an FTP server's Internet folder open to display the Anarchie Pro files.

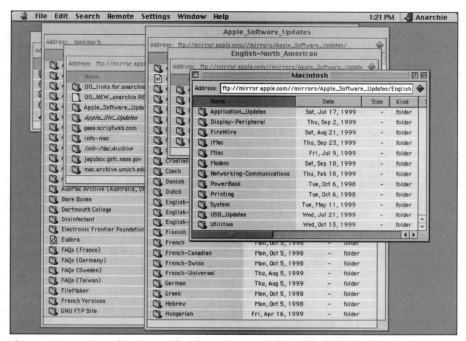

Figure 21-14: Anarchie Pro makes browsing and downloading files from FTP servers easy.

Anarchie Pro also has the distinction of being one of the first Internet applications to support Mac OS 9's new Keychain feature, enabling you to store passwords for FTP sites using keychains. To add a particular Web site to your keychain, use the File ➪ Get Via FTP command to open a new connection. In the Get Via FTP window, enter the FTP server, path (if appropriate), your username, and your password. Make sure the Add to Keychain check box is selected, and then click List. The site is added to your keychain. Now, you can choose File ➪ Save Bookmark to save this location in your Anarchie Bookmarks list. In the future, you can simply double-click the bookmark to open the FTP site without entering your username and password again (assuming that your Keychain is unlocked).

Tip

Anarchie Pro version 3.5 or higher is required for keychain access. It also includes a command on the Edit menu that enables you to quickly lock and unlock your keychain from within the program.

Fetch

Fetch was developed by Dartmouth University and was one of the earliest FTP programs available for the Mac OS. Working with files in Fetch 3.0.3 isn't quite like working with files in the Finder. After connecting to a server, you can double-click a folder to see its contents, but the folder's contents don't appear in a new window. Instead, the folder opens in the same window. So, you can only see one folder at a time. To see a previous folder, choose it from a pop-up menu at the top of the Fetch window. You download files by dragging them to your desktop and upload files by dragging from your desktop to the Fetch window. Fetch also lets you keep a list of shortcuts for fast access to favorite FTP sites.

FTP, the Keychain, and Network Browser

Chapter 10 discussed adding secure Web sites to your keychain, making it easy to access sites that require a username and password. The same is possible with FTP sites, especially if you have a keychain-enabled application like Anarchie 3.5 Pro.

But even if you don't have such an application, it's still possible to store usernames and passwords for FTP sites in the keychain. First, create an Internet Location File, which you should be able to do by dragging a URL from your FTP application to the desktop. If not, look for an option in the File menu of your FTP program that enables you to save an Internet Location File.

Next, drag the Internet Location File to the keychain. Enter a username and password. After they're entered, the location is now stored on the keychain. You can visit the FTP site in a keychain-enabled application and the username and password are automatically sent.

You can also, if you like, browse FTP sites using the Network Browser. To do this, double-click the site in the keychain. In the Get Info box for this keychain item, click Go There. The FTP site is logged in to and opened in your Network Browser. You can double-click folders to dig into them, or double-click a file to download it to your Mac. You can also drag-and-drop icons from the Network Browser to the desktop.

Note   As noted elsewhere in this chapter, you can also access FTP sites directly in the Network Browser. Use the Connect to Server command in the Shortcuts pop-up menu, then enter an FTP URL. A dialog box that enables you to enter a username and password (or that lets you select Anonymous) displays. Click Connect to connect to the server, whose directories will appear in the Network Browser window.

Decoding and decompressing files

Files that you download from the Internet must be converted to a form that your Mac can use. The reason that this is necessary has to do partly with the Internet and partly with the Mac OS. First, most Internet protocols know how to deal with plain text files fairly simply — e-mail documents, Web pages, and other types of Internet transmissions all send plain text from server to client. But pictures, formatted text, sounds, application programs, and most other kinds of Mac files aren't plain-text files; they're a kind of file called a *binary file*. In some cases, binary files must be converted to text files to be sent over the Internet. In other cases, you need to convert a file to a special format in order to retain the special data and resource forks of a Macintosh file.

Note   This binary vs. text discussion is something of an oversimplification, but a common one. ASCII text files are files that store codes for individual characters, allowing the file to be read by nearly any text editor on any computer platform. (SimpleText and the freeware application BBEdit Lite create ASCII text files.) Binary files contain binary data that is not human-readable in an editor; instead, the file contains data that describe a formatted document, an image, or a program. To store a Macintosh-specific binary file on distant FTP servers (which may be using an OS different than the Mac OS) it's best to encode the file for FTP transmission. Usually, you encode it as a MacBinary or BinHex file, as described in this section. Both of these file formats maintain the special data and resource forks that make a Mac binary file unique.

There are several standards for encoding binary files. The two most commonly used for Mac files are called *BinHex* and *MacBinary*. In general, MacBinary produces smaller encoded files, which take less time to download. However, BinHex-encoded files download somewhat more reliably than MacBinary-encoded files.

Besides being encoded, files that you download from the Internet are usually compressed. This is a scheme in which a binary file is run through a compression program before it is encoded with BinHex or MacBinary. The resulting compressed binary file is considerably smaller in size than the uncompressed file and, as a result, it takes less time to upload and download. And you can use a compression program to create an *archive*, which is a single compressed file that contains one or more files or folders of files. This makes multiple files easier to transmit over the Internet and store on server computers.

There are many methods for compressing files. With Mac files, the most common compression method is the one used by the StuffIt family of programs from Aladdin Systems (408-761-6200, http://www.aladdinsys.com). *Stuffed* files are compressed with this method. With Windows and DOS files, the most common compression method is called *ZIP*, after the PKZip DOS program that originated it. *Zipped* files are compressed with this method.

You can usually tell what type of file you're downloading by looking at the series of letters after the period at the end of the file's name. This part of the name is called the *extension*. Table 21-2 deciphers the extensions of encoded and compressed files that you're likely to encounter while cruising the Internet.

Table 21-2
File Name Extensions for Encoded and Compressed Files

File Name Extension	What It Means
.bin	Encoded in MacBinary format (also known as BinHex5)
.gz	Compressed with Unix *GNU Zip* program
.hqx	Encoded in BinHex4 format
.img	Encoded as a disk image
.sea	Self-Extracting Archive — compressed with StuffIt or another program, but no separate decompression utility is needed
.sit	Compressed with StuffIt
.smi	Encoded as a self-mounting disk image
.tar	Multiple files combined into one with the Unix tar program
.uu or .uue	Encoded in UUencode format
.z or .Z	Compressed with Unix *compress* program
.zip	Compressed with the DOS or Windows PKZip or WinZip program

Using file converter software

When you receive a file that has been encoded and possibly compressed as well, software on your computer must decode and decompress the file before you can use it. First, the software decodes the BinHex or MacBinary file and saves a decoded version of the file. Then the software decompresses this file and saves yet another file. The last file is the one you can actually use. You end up with two or three files: the encoded version (typically with an extension of .hqx or .bin), the compressed version (usually with the extension .sit or .sea), and the binary file. You'll probably want to throw away the encoded and compressed versions after you have the decoded binary file.

The application programs that handle decoding and decompressing are sometimes called *helper* applications because they work in conjunction with FTP clients, Web browsers, and other Internet programs that receive and send files on the Internet. The Web browser or FTP client inspects a downloaded file's extension and tells the appropriate helper application to decode or decompress a file. The helper opens (usually into the background), does its job, and quits. Often, you won't even be aware that the process has taken place.

StuffIt Expander

A pair of helper applications that come with Mac OS 9 will handle virtually all of your decoding and decompressing needs. The first member of this matched pair is called StuffIt Expander, and it's free from Aladdin Systems. StuffIt Expander can decode and decompress most Mac files you find on the Internet. It can decode BinHex (.hqx, .hcx, or .hex) or MacBinary (.bin) files, and it can decompress StuffIt (.sit), Compact Pro (.cpt), and ZIP (.zip) files. StuffIt Expander is incredibly easy to use; if your Internet applications don't open it automatically as needed, you can simply drag-and-drop files on the StuffIt Expander icon. You can also set StuffIt Expander preferences to automatically decode and decompress all files that show up in a particular folder that you choose.

StuffIt Expander can handle many more encoding and compression methods if you install the $30 shareware package called DropStuff with Expander Enhancer, also from Aladdin Systems. The Expander Enhancer part of this package enables StuffIt Expander to expand files compressed with virtually every compression format found on Mac OS, Unix, Windows, and DOS computers. These include ARC (.arc), gzip (.gz), Unix Compress (.Z), UUencode (.uu), and StuffIt SpaceSaver files. It will also join files that were segmented with another StuffIt product. With DropStuff with Expander Enhancer installed, StuffIt Expander is also accelerated on PowerPC computers.

The DropStuff part of the shareware package enables you to compress and encode files that you want to send on the Internet. You can have your Internet applications open it automatically, and you can compress and encode files by dragging them to the DropStuff icon.

The really great thing about the StuffIt Expander package is that it operates transparently. When you click an FTP link in your Web browser, the browser downloads the file from the FTP server and then hands off the file to StuffIt Expander, which decodes the file (converting it back into a binary file), decompresses the file further if necessary, and automatically quits. StuffIt Expander can also handle batches of files to be decoded and decompressed at the same time, and (if you prefer) it's smart enough to automatically delete the BinHex-encoded files after it finishes decoding them.

ZipIt

If you need to compress files that you want to send to a Windows PC on the Internet, there are two choices. If you want to compress files using the ZIP method, which is the standard method on PCs, you can run the ZipIt program on your Mac. This program can also decompress ZIP files on your Mac. ZipIt is $15 shareware. (There are others available as well, including PKZip Mac, MacZip, and UnZip for Mac, all available from popular download servers such as `http://www.download.com/` on the Web. See Chapter 26 for more on finding shareware.)

Instead of using the ZIP format, you can compress using the StuffIt format that's commonly used on Macs. You can compress files in this format with the DropStuff program that's part of the DropStuff with Expander Enhancer shareware just described. PC users who want to expand your compressed files will need the free Aladdin Expander for Windows program from Aladdin Systems.

Summary

This chapter showed you how to connect to and work with shared folders and disks from file servers on your local network. The file servers can be computers that specialize in sharing folders and disks, or they can be personal computers using Mac OS file sharing. The basic means of connecting to shared folders and disks is the Chooser. You can also connect using the Network Browser and Navigation Services dialog boxes. You can add your network connections to your keychain, freeing you from remembering your usernames and passwords for servers. And, you can streamline subsequent connections to a shared folder or disk by opening an alias of it or of any item in it.

This chapter also explained that the owner of a shared folder or disk can restrict your access to it. To determine your access privileges to a folder, you can look at its icon, open it, and look for small icons in the header of its window, or inspect the Sharing section of its Info window. This chapter also discussed transferring and opening files on the network. In addition, you learned how to disconnect from shared folders and disks.

Besides sharing folders and disks on your local network, you can download and upload files on the Internet. This chapter told you about downloading with a Web browser or an FTP client. After the files are downloaded, they will probably need to be decoded and decompressed so that you can use them.

✦　　✦　　✦

Share Your Files

Just as you can share books with people who live and work near you, the Mac OS enables you to share disks, folders, and the files in them with people whose computers are on the same network as your computer. You control who can connect to your shared folders and disks, and you determine what other people can do with the contents of your shared folders and disks.

This chapter explains how to share some of your folders or disks with other people on your network. First, you plan for file sharing and identify your computer on the network. Next, you start the Mac OS file-sharing feature on your computer and designate which disks or folders contain files that you want to share. Then you can identify who you want to let access your shared items. For each of your shared folders you can restrict the type of access some people have. At any time you can monitor file-sharing activity to see who is connected to your computer and how much of its processing power is consumed by file sharing.

Other people connect to and work with your shared folders and disks using the same procedures that you use with theirs. Chapter 21 describes how to gain access to other peoples' shared files on your local network, a remote computer, a remote network connect, or the Internet. If your computer is not already on a network, Chapter 20 explains how to hook it up to one.

Planning for File Sharing

The personal file-sharing capabilities of the Mac OS make sharing items across a network surprisingly easy, but not without some cost. This section discusses the capabilities and limitations of Mac OS file sharing so that you can decide in advance whether it meets your needs. The alternative to file sharing is a dedicated, centralized file server.

Distributed or centralized file sharing

Your network can implement file sharing in a distributed or centralized fashion. With distributed file sharing, which is also known as *peer-to-peer file sharing*, each computer makes files, folders, and disks available to other computers on the network. While your computer shares your files with other computers, you are free to use your computer for other tasks. Reduced performance of your computer while other computers are accessing it is the price you pay for making files from your computer available for people using other computers to share. In addition, the Mac OS file sharing limits the number of people that can share the same folder or disk at the same time, which makes file sharing unsuitable for serving files to large numbers of computers on a network.

By contrast, a network with centralized file sharing dedicates one computer (or more) to providing file-sharing services. That computer runs file server software, such as Apple's AppleShare IP software or Mac OS X Server, which enables the computer to serve files to a large number of other computers. Other computers on the network get shared files from the dedicated file server (or file servers) rather than from each other. Usually, a computer that acts as a dedicated file server needs to be fast and to have one or more large hard disks. The Mac OS does not include file server software; you must purchase it separately.

Although the Mac OS file-sharing capabilities are designed for distributed file sharing, you can use file sharing on a dedicated computer to create a file server for a small network. Folders or entire hard disks on that file-server computer can be made available to other computers on the network as described in the remainder of this chapter.

The problem with such a file server is its performance. The Mac OS assumes somebody is using the dedicated computer for more than sharing files and reserves about 50 percent of the dedicated computer's processing power for nonfile-sharing tasks. Apple's AppleShare IP 6.2 provides even faster file service, and other services to boot, but it costs $999. Apple's Mac OS X Server costs $499 for unlimited Apple File Services serving.

Limitations on file sharing

With personal file sharing you can designate up to ten disks or folders whose contents you want to share (as described later in this chapter). Only the disks and folders you designate count toward the limit of ten shared items; folders inside the designated disks and folders don't count toward the limit.

Up to ten other computers can be connected to your shared folders and disks at one time, but only five can access files simultaneously. This limit applies only to file sharing, not necessarily to other network activity such as using a multiuser database file located on your computer.

You can identify registered users and groups of users and specify which of them can connect to your shared folders and disks. In addition, you can restrict who can access each folder and what kind of access is allowed: reading, writing, both, or neither. You'll find more on identifying who can access your shared items and on controlling access to your shared items later in this chapter.

If you need to exceed the limitations described here, your network needs a dedicated file server such as AppleShare IP 6.2 or Mac OS X Server.

AppleShare IP and Mac OS X Server

A network with more than ten people actively sharing files needs a dedicated file server administered by software such as Apple's AppleShare IP 6.2 software. The AppleShare IP software extends network file-sharing and background-printing services beyond what the Mac OS provides. Installing AppleShare IP turns a computer into an efficient centralized file server capable of sharing the files and folders on its hard disk (or disks) among up to 500 simultaneous users (10,000 registered users) of Mac OS, Windows 95/98, and Windows NT computers. In addition to being a Mac OS file and printer server, AppleShare IP provides Internet services such as e-mail, Web, and FTP.

Apple also has another solution for centralized serving — Mac OS X Server. This server package, built on the UNIX-like and Mach (a UNIX variant) underpinnings of Mac OS X, offers Apple File Services support as well as sharing of many Ethernet-capable PostScript printers. Designed as a full-service Web and Internet server, as well as an Apple File Services server, Mac OS X Server offers impressive performance and capabilities. One of those capabilities — NetBoot — actually allows some newer Mac OS machines to boot from the remote server, making it possible for a room full of iMacs, for instance, to all receive their System Folders and applications from a centralized server.

Centralized disk storage reduces the amount of local disk storage required by each networked computer while providing a way for people who work together to share information. People can store files on the server's disks where other people can open or copy them. Many people can access the server's disks and folders simultaneously, and new files become available to everyone instantly. Unlike the file sharing provided by the Mac OS, no one uses the server's computer to do personal work because it is dedicated to providing network services. Conversely, your computer is not burdened when someone else on the network accesses one of your shared items on the AppleShare server's disks.

A centralized file server is set up and maintained by a trained person called a *network administrator*. Both AppleShare IP and Mac OS X include organizational, administrative, and security features to manage file access on the network. The network administrator does not control access to folders and files on the server's disks; that is the responsibility of each person who puts items on the disks.

Continued

(continued)

AppleShare IP's file server is compatible with the Mac OS file sharing. You use the methods described in this chapter to make your files available for sharing, whether those files are on your computer's hard disk or the file server's hard disks. Files on the file server's hard disks are accessed using the methods described in Chapter 21.

The AppleShare IP print server supports up to 30 AppleTalk PostScript printers, 10 queues, and 32 simultaneous print sessions, so users don't have to wait for print jobs to finish or have their computers bogged down by background printing. It can balance the total printing load among all available printers, so that faster printers do more of the work. The printer server is available to Mac OS and Windows computers on the network.

AppleShare IP 6.0 software runs on a Mac computer with a PowerPC G3, 604e, 604, or 601 processor; it also runs on a Power Mac 6500 (which has a PowerPC 603e processor). AppleShare IP 6.0 requires 48MB of RAM (64MB with virtual memory turned off). Mac OS X Server requires a G3 processor and 64MB of RAM (with 128MB or more recommended in certain situations).

Guidelines for file sharing

These guidelines and tips for sharing folders and disks help optimize file sharing and help prevent problems:

✦ Share from the highest level of your disk and folder structure. For example, a disk can't be shared if it contains an already-shared folder (no matter how deeply nested in the unshared disk). If you attempt to share a disk or folder that contains an already-shared folder, you get a message that the disk or folder cannot be shared because it contains a shared folder. To work around this situation, identify the shared items (as explained in "Monitoring File Sharing Activity" later in this chapter), unshare it, and then share the enclosing disk or folder.

✦ Share as few folders as possible. The more shared folders that are being accessed, the greater the memory and processing demands on your computer. Sharing too many folders can slow your system to a crawl.

✦ Check any applicable licensing agreements before sharing folders that contain programs, artwork, or sounds. Often, licensing agreements or copyright laws restrict use of these items to a single computer.

✦ Select a single computer and dedicate it to the task of acting as a file server for the shared information. This method is often the most efficient way to share numerous files or to share folders with several users simultaneously.

Identifying Your Computer

Before you can begin sharing files, you must give your computer a network identity. Identifying your computer involves entering the name of its owner, a password to prevent other people from connecting to your computer as its owner, and a name for your computer. With Mac OS 9, those items are specified through the Mac OS Setup Assistant program. The Assistant comes up automatically the first time you restart the computer after installing OS 9. You can run it again at any time; it's located in the Assistants folder on the startup disk.

You can also specify your computer's network identity with the File Sharing control panel (Figure 22-1), on the Start/Stop tab.

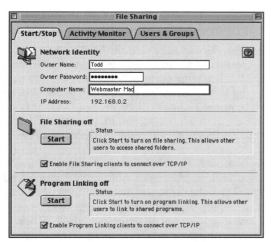

Figure 22-1: Specify a Mac's network identity in the File Sharing control panel.

The Owner Password can be up to eight characters long. A password is case sensitive, meaning that if you create a password that includes uppercase and lowercase letters, you must always type that password with the same uppercase and lowercase letters to gain access. Select a password that is easy for you to remember but difficult for others to guess. Mix letters with numbers; try replacing the letters *I* and *O* with the numbers 1 and 0 (for example, "brownie" becomes "br0wn1e"). You must know the Owner Password to access your own computer from another computer on the network as the owner. For privacy, the system displays bullets in place of the actual password characters in the File Sharing control panel.

The computer name that you enter should be one that other people will easily recognize when they see it in the Chooser among the list of AppleShare file servers. The name must be unique on your network. If you enter a name that another computer is already using, the system displays an alert telling you to use a different name.

Turning File Sharing Off and On

After your computer's network identity is set in the File Sharing or Sharing Setup control panel, you can use the same control panel to turn file sharing on and off at any time. You must turn on file sharing when you want to make your shared folders and disks available to people using other computers on the network. You do not need to turn on file sharing to connect to shared folders and disks from file servers on the network.

Turning on file sharing increases the Mac OS memory size by 200K to 300K. File sharing also slows your computer — noticeably, if you have an older Power Macintosh that you've upgraded to Mac OS 9. And, your computer is theoretically more vulnerable to invasion while file sharing is on, although you can institute effective security measures (lock the door, so to speak) as described in "Controlling Access to Your Shared Items" later in this chapter. All in all, it's a good idea to leave file sharing turned off unless other people need to access your shared files over the network.

When you turn off file sharing, other computers on the network cannot connect to your shared folders or disks. Turning off file sharing does not change which folders and disks are designated for sharing (as described in the next section) or the access privileges set for your shared items (as described in the subsequent section, "Controlling Access to Your Shared Items"). With file sharing turned off, other computers simply can't connect to your computer for file sharing. They may still be able to connect to your computer if it provides other network services, such as access to a multiuser database file.

Turning on file sharing

To turn on file sharing, click Start in the File Sharing section of the File Sharing control panel or the Sharing Setup control panel, whichever your computer has. The Start button's label changes to Cancel, and the status message next to the button describes what is happening while file sharing is starting up. It may take from several seconds to several minutes for file sharing to start up, depending on the number of disk volumes and shared items on your computer. You can close the control panel anytime after clicking Start, but you won't know precisely when file sharing is enabled if you do. Your computer is ready to share its files when the button's label changes to Stop and the File Sharing control panel reports "File

Sharing on" or the Sharing Setup control panel's status message reads "File sharing is now on." Figure 22-2 shows how the File Sharing control panel looks when file sharing is turned on.

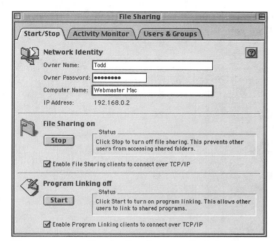

Figure 22-2: File sharing is turned on in the File Sharing control panel.

There are other ways to turn on file sharing. You can use the Control Strip if it's installed on your computer. Or you can speak the command "Start file sharing" if Speakable Items speech recognition is installed and active on your computer. Figure 22-3 shows the File Sharing control strip module in Mac OS 9.

Cross-Reference

For more information on the Control Strip, see Chapter 12. For more information on speech recognition, see Chapter 23.

Figure 22-3: Turn on file sharing in the File Sharing control strip module.

If you shut down or restart your computer after turning on file sharing, the Mac OS automatically starts file sharing the next time the computer starts up.

File Sharing over IP

To turn on File Sharing over IP (allowing File Sharing clients to share files over the Internet or over another IP-based network) you need to take another step. In the File Sharing control panel, select the check box next to Enable File Sharing clients to connect over TCP/IP (see Figure 22-4). Now, when you click Start, File Sharing is started for IP-based clients as well as regular AppleTalk-based clients.

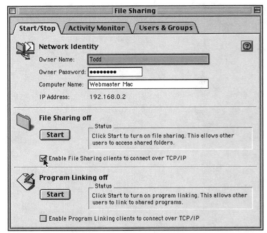

Figure 22-4: Turn on file sharing over IP networks (including the Internet) if you want remote computers to be capable of signing in.

Caution

Turning on File Sharing over IP creates another level of security problems on your Mac. Not only can remote clients log in to your Mac, but now they can do so over the Internet (if your Mac is connected to the Internet). That could mean trouble, especially if you don't take close stock of your security precautions. See "Controlling Access to Your Shared Items" later in this chapter. And before turning on the IP sharing option, think carefully about whether you really need to turn on File Sharing over IP networks. If you don't, leave the option turned off, even if you are using File Sharing over your local network.

Turning off File Sharing

To turn off file sharing, click Stop in the File Sharing section of the File Sharing control panel or the Sharing Setup control panel. A dialog box appears asking you to specify the number of minutes' warning to be given to anyone who is sharing items from your computer. (Allow enough time for people sharing items from your computer to close any shared items.) Every computer that's connected to yours displays a message indicating that access to your computer is going to be disconnected at the end of the time you specified. (The same events happen when you shut down or restart your computer with file sharing on.) Figure 22-5 shows the dialog box in which you specify how much time remains until file sharing stops; Figure 22-6 shows the message box that appears on other computers that are connected to your computer for file sharing.

Figure 22-5: Determine how long before File Sharing shuts down.

Figure 22-6: What users see when a shut down is imminent

If you've designated a time frame for shut down, you can cancel the shut down and leave the server running, if desired. To do that, click Cancel in the File Sharing window (on the Start/Stop tab) or select Cancel File Sharing Shutdown from the File Sharing item on the control strip.

Designating Your Shared Items

After identifying your computer and turning on file sharing, you can designate the folders and disks that contain files that you want to share. You can share up to ten folders and disks (including CDs and removable hard disks) at a time. To share just one file, you must drag it into a folder and share the folder. You can't share volumes under 2MB in size, which includes floppy disks.

When you share a folder or disk, every item it contains is shared, including enclosed folders. You can't share a document by itself (outside a folder). After you share a folder or disk, you can drag items to the shared folder or disk to share them as well.

Aliases in shared folders or disks are shared, but their original items are shared only if they are in shared folders or disks. If network users try to use a shared alias whose original item is not in a shared folder or disk, the Mac OS tells them the original item can't be found.

Making an item shared

You make a folder or disk a shared item and see its sharing information by using the Sharing command. The Sharing command is in the Get Info submenu, which is in the File menu, and in the contextual menu of folders and disks that can be shared. Figure 22-7 shows a shared folder's sharing information.

Figure 22-7: The Sharing command displays sharing information for the selected folder or disk.

To share one of your folders or disks, select it and use the Sharing command. This displays the item's sharing information in its Info window. In this window, turn on the option Share this item and its contents. The other sharing options in this window establish which users can access the shared item and what privileges they have (as explained in "Controlling Access to Your Shared Items" later in this chapter). A folder's initial settings enable only the item's owner to access the folder; the owner can add items, delete items, and save changes to files in the folder.

The settings made in an item's sharing information persist until the Sharing command is used again to change them. Shutting down or restarting your computer does not affect sharing settings; neither does turning off file sharing.

Network Trash

If someone drags a file or folder from your computer to the Trash on his or her desktop, the Finder creates an invisible folder on your computer with the name Network Trash Folder. As long as the user doesn't empty the Trash, the items thrown away appear inside the Network Trash Folder in folders labeled Trash Can #1, Trash Can #2, and so on—one for each computer with something of yours in its Trash. To restore an item that someone else has trashed, use a utility program such as ResEdit (described in Chapter 26) to make the Network Trash Folder visible. Then find the item that you want to rescue and drag it out of the Trash Can folder it's in. You can set access privileges to prevent others from trashing your shared items (as described in "Controlling Access to Your Shared Items" later in this chapter).

Recognizing your shared items by their icons

The icon of a shared folder on your computer appears with network cables, which indicate its shared status. When someone is using your shared folder, the folder icon has faces on it. Unlike folder icons, disk icons don't change when you share them. Figure 22-8 shows how shared folders look.

Figure 22-8: Shared folders have distinctive icons.

You can't rename a folder or disk that you have shared nor can you drag it to the Trash. Also, you can't eject and put away a removable disk or CD that contains shared folders. To do any of these things, you first must turn off file sharing or turn off the option Share this item and its contents in the item's Info window.

Identifying Who Can Access Your Shared Items

You could let everyone access your shared folders and disks, or you could let no one but yourself (the owner) access your shared items. But you don't have to take an all-or-nothing approach. This section explains how to use the Users & Groups tab in the File Sharing control panel to identify individuals and groups of people who you want to grant or deny access to your shared items. The next section, "Controlling Access to Your Shared Items," tells you how to specify which of those people or groups has privileged access to a shared folder or disk and its contents.

Users & Groups

The Users & Groups tab of the File Sharing control panel displays named icons for people and groups who can access your shared items. There's always an icon for the computer's owner. The owner icon is marked with a clipboard. There's also always an icon for guests — that is, any unidentified person using a computer on your network. The guest icon is marked with a suitcase. You create additional icons for registered network users to whom you want to grant greater access privileges than guests have. You can also create groups of registered users. You can create any number of registered users and groups in Users & Groups. Figure 22-9 is an example of Users & Groups.

 As you read this section you'll note options that you can set to allow users to link to programs on your computer. This is a technology in the Mac OS called Program Linking that enables one computer to share a program on another computer using Apple Events. This is discussed in more detail in Chapter 24.

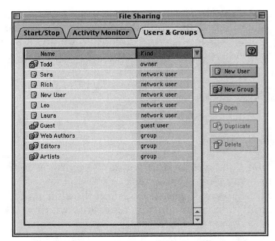

Figure 22-9: Users & Groups determines who can connect to your shared folders and disks.

Sorting users and groups

When working in Users & Groups, it can be helpful to sort the Users & Groups list by kind so that all groups are listed together alphabetically and all network users are listed together alphabetically. Click the column heading to sort the list by that heading. You can also use the sort direction button (the up- or down-pointing lines) to change the sort direction.

Selecting multiple users or groups

You can perform some operations in Users & Groups on more than one user or group at the same time. Hold down ⌘ and click to select multiple icons one by one, or Shift+click to select a range of icons.

The owner

The owner icon controls your ability to access your computer when you connect as its owner from another computer. The owner can have the unique ability to access all disks whether they're designated for sharing or not. The owner icon bears the name of the computer's owner and looks different from other icons in Users & Groups — it looks like a face with a clipboard.

The owner's access privileges are changed in the owner's window, which you display by double-clicking the owner icon and selecting Sharing from the pop-up menu. You can also change the owner's name and password in the owner window by selecting Identity from the pop-up menu; the Mac OS automatically updates the Owner information on the Start/Stop tab. Figure 22-10 shows the Identity, Sharing and Remote Access options for the owner.

Figure 22-10: The three faces of the Owner window

Here's a quick look at the various options:

✦ Turning on the Allow user to change password option enables you to change the owner password remotely.

✦ Turning on the Allow user to connect to this computer option gives you access to your computer from another computer connected to the network.

✦ The Allow user to see all disks option enables you to see and use any items on any disk attached to your computer. This setting gives you access to all disks and folders on your computer (while you are connected to your computer from another computer), whether they are shared or not. When you connect as the computer owner you have unlimited access whether or not you're named the owner of a shared folder and regardless of the privileges assigned to shared disks and folders.

✦ Turning on Allow user to dial in to this computer makes it possible for the owner to access this machine via Remote Access. If Remote Access answering is turned on, then you can use Mac to call this computer by modem and sign in to access file sharing. (See Chapter 20 for more on Remote Access answering.)

✦ The Call back at # option enables the Remote Access server to call this user back at a particular phone number to verify that the user is in the correct location and to save on toll charges for the user (for example, if you're calling in to work from home and it's long distance, your company will foot the bill).

Guests

The Guest icon controls the ability of any unidentified network user to connect to your shared folders and disks. You can deny guests any access, or you can allow guests to connect to your shared folders and disks and restrict guest access to shared folders and disks individually (as described in the "Controlling Access to Your Shared Items" section later in this chapter).

Caution   Enabling guest access for File Sharing over IP is not recommended, especially if your Mac is connected to the Internet. If you have Guest access enabled and File Sharing over IP enabled, anyone who has a File Sharing client (Mac or third-party Windows clients) and your IP address will be able to access your shared files.

To disable all guest access, open the Guest icon in Users & Groups, select Sharing from the pop-up menu, and turn off the Allow guests to connect option. Now, only registered users are enabled to connect to your shared items. Figure 22-11 shows the three views of the Guest window.

Figure 22-11: The Guest account offers fewer options.

Registered network users

Registering network users helps secure your shared items from unauthorized access. You can specify whether each registered user can connect to your shared folders and disks, as described in this section. You can also give a registered user special access privileges to shared folders as described in "Controlling Access to Your Shared Items" later in this chapter.

Creating a new network user

To register a network user, first open Users & Groups. Next, click New User or choose New User from the File menu to create a new user icon in Users & Groups. An icon named New User appears in Users & Groups, and the icon opens to display the user window for that new network user.

Rather than create a new user, you can duplicate one or more existing users in Users & Groups by selecting one or more user icons and clicking Duplicate or choosing Duplicate from the File menu.

Identifying a network user

When you create a new user, the new username is selected and you can replace it by typing the name of the network user who you want to register. After duplicating a selection of multiple users, you have to select and rename the duplicates one by one.

You should ask a network user what name he or she would like to use when connecting to your computer to share your files, and suggest that he or she use the owner name in his or her File Sharing control panel. If you devise the name yourself, you must tell the network user his or her registered name because the user must type the exact name to connect to your shared folders and disks. Network usernames are not case sensitive, so a user doesn't have to match your use of uppercase and lowercase letters when connecting to your computer. As soon as you give a network user a name, he or she is registered on your computer.

You can add another level of security by assigning to a registered user a password that he or she needs to type to access your shared items. You assign a password in the user window, which you display by opening the user icon. Enter a password up to eight characters long. Remember that the user must type the password exactly as you type it here, including uppercase and lowercase letters. Figure 22-12 shows the Identity and Sharing views of a user window.

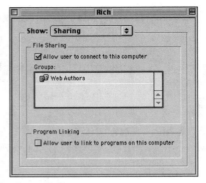

Figure 22-12: A registered user's file sharing privileges

Setting a network user's privileges

These are some of the privilege options for a user:

✦ If the Allow user to connect option is turned on, the network username can be used to connect to your shared folders and disks. Turn off that option to deny access to anyone using that registered name.

✦ If you want to let this user change the password at will, turn on the Allow user to change password option. When you finish setting the registered user's access privileges, close the user window to make your changes take effect.

✦ The Allow user to dial in to this computer option lets you determine whether this user is given access via Remote Access answering.

✦ If you do allow the user to connect, you can specify a callback phone number using the Call back at # option. When Apple Remote Access Personal Server gets a call from a user who has a callback number, the program hangs up and calls the user back at the specified number. This procedure prevents an unauthorized person from gaining access to your shared folders and disks by learning a registered user's password and trying to call from an unauthorized location. When you specify a callback number, you have to pay the cost of the phone call for the connection, but you know that the person connecting to your shared folders and disks has the correct password and is calling from the registered user's computer.

Remember that access privileges are associated with a registered username, not with a particular person. Any person who connects to your computer with a valid username (and password, if any) has the privileges you set for that registered user-name. If you're concerned about the security of your shared items, you can tell your registered users not to divulge their passwords and periodically ask them to change their passwords.

Changing a network user's privileges

You can modify a registered user's name, password, and access privileges, or remove the user from your set of registered users at any time. To modify a user, double-click the user's entry in Users & Groups, or select the username, and click Open.

To remove a registered user, drag its icon from Users & Groups to the Trash. Alternatively, you can select one or more user icons and click Delete or choose Delete from the File menu.

Groups of users

Office or work environments usually consist of groups of people, such as departments or project teams, who need to share certain items. Mac OS file sharing enables you to specify special access privileges for groups as well as for individual users. *Groups* are simply collections of individual registered users, and you can grant specific access privileges for a shared folder or disk to a group instead of to a single user. (The procedures for setting access privileges of shared folders and disks are covered later in "Controlling Access to Your Shared Items.")

Creating a group

To establish a group of users, open Users & Groups and click New Group or choose New Group from the File menu. An icon named New Group appears in Users & Groups, and the icon opens to display the group window for that new group. The group icon looks different than a single-user icon.

Rather than create new groups, you can duplicate one or more existing groups in Users & Groups by selecting one or more group icons and clicking Duplicate or choosing Duplicate from the File menu.

Right after you create a new group, the new group name is selected. You can replace it by typing a name of your own choosing. If you duplicate a selection of multiple groups, you have to select and rename them one by one.

Note   Don't invent group names that might offend someone who uses your shared files. Your group names are not private if you use them to set specific access privileges to shared items. At least some people who connect to your computer will be able to see some of your group names.

Adding users to a group

To add registered users to a group, drag their user icons to the group icon or group window. You can also add a user to a group by dragging the group icon to the user icon. To speed the process of adding users to groups, select multiple users and drag them to the group icon together. You don't need to include the owner icon in groups because the owner always has full access to everything on all disks.

To see the members of the group, open the group icon. The group window shows a user icon for every user in the group. If you want to see or change information for a registered user, you can open the user icon wherever you see it — in a group window or in the User & Groups window. You cannot create a new user directly in a group window, however. Figure 22-13 is an example of a group window.

Figure 22-13: See the members of a group.

Removing users from a group

To remove users from a group, open the group icon to display its window, and drag the user icons that you want to remove from the group window to the Trash. You can also remove users from a group by selecting the user icons in the group window and choosing Remove from the File menu. Users are removed right away; they don't wait in the Trash until you empty it.

Seeing the groups a user belongs to

To see all the groups to which a registered user belongs, open the user icon and choose Sharing from the pop-up menu at the top of the user window. The user window displays a list of groups to which the registered user belongs, as shown in Figure 22-14.

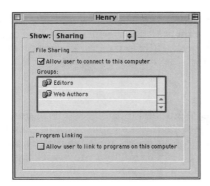

Figure 22-14: See the groups to which a registered user belongs.

Controlling Access to Your Shared Items

Even if you enable guests and registered users to connect to your shared folders and disk, by default Mac OS 9 doesn't permit them to see or change the contents of any shared items. Besides that extreme, you can grant full or partial access to each shared folder independently. Moreover, each shared folder can have different access privileges for three categories of users: the owner, one user or group, and everyone. For example, you might want to ensure that a user or group of users has access to a folder of templates on your computer but cannot modify the templates. Access privileges also enable you to selectively share a folder of confidential documents, such as new product plans.

This section explains how to use the Finder's Sharing command to set separate access privileges for the owner, one registered network user or one group, and everyone else. (The previous section, "Identifying Who Can Access Your Shared Items," tells you how to identify network users and groups of users to whom you want to grant or deny access to your shared folders.)

Setting specific access privileges

You set the access privileges of a folder or disk in its Info window. This window appears when you select the folder or disk and choose the Sharing command from the Get Info submenu of the File menu or the contextual menu of the folder or disk.

The Info window (with Sharing selected from the pop-up menu) displays icons to indicate the access privileges of each user category. You set access privileges by choosing from pop-up menus. Figure 22-15 shows a pop-up menu for setting access privileges.

You can set one of these four privilege levels for each user category in the access privileges pop-up menus:

✦ **Read & Write** lets users open the folder and see enclosed folders; see, open, and copy enclosed files; and create, delete, move, and change enclosed files and folders.

✦ **Read** only lets users open the folder and see enclosed folders, and see, open, and copy enclosed files.

✦ **Write** only lets users drag files and folders to the folder, but does not allow users to open the folder. This privilege makes sense only for folders enclosed by a shared folder or disk. Users can't access any write-only disk or a write-only folder that's not enclosed in a shared folder.

✦ **None** denies users access to the folder.

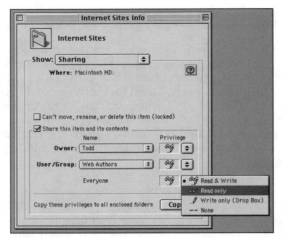

Figure 22-15: Set access privileges with pop-up menus.

Selecting specific or adopted access privileges

By default, folders inside a shared disk or shared folder adopt the access privileges of the enclosing folder or disk. Instead, you can set specific access privileges for any enclosed folder. The Use enclosing folder's privileges option in an enclosed folder's Info window or sharing window controls whether the folder has specific access privileges or adopts the privileges of its enclosing folder. This option appears only for folders that are inside a shared folder or shared disk.

A folder with adopted privileges that is moved to a new folder takes on the privileges of its new enclosing folder. In contrast, a folder with specific access privileges keeps its specific privileges when moved to a different enclosing folder.

Setting specific privileges for an enclosed folder

To set specific access privileges for an enclosed folder, display the enclosed folder's Info window or sharing window, turn off the option labeled Use enclosing folder's privileges or Same as enclosing folder, and set the specific access privileges that you want the enclosed folder to have. Figure 22-16 is an example of an enclosed folder's Info window or sharing window with specific, not adopted, privileges set.

Adopting the enclosing folder's privileges

To make an enclosed folder adopt the access privileges of its enclosing folder, bring up the enclosed folder's Info window or sharing window and turn on the Use enclosing folder's privileges option. When you turn on that option, the Mac OS dims the controls for setting access privileges. Figure 22-17 is an example of an enclosed folder's Info window or sharing window with adopted privileges set.

Figure 22-16: Set specific access privileges for an enclosed folder.

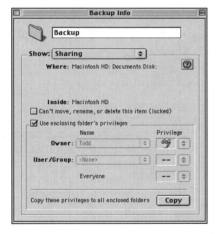

Figure 22-17: An enclosed folder with adopted access privileges

Changing all enclosed folders' privileges

If you change a folder's privileges and want to force all enclosed folders to have the same privileges, click Copy in the enclosing folder's Info window.

Think twice before clicking a Copy button. Forcing enclosed folders to use the privileges of their enclosing folder turns off the Use enclosing folder's privileges or Same as enclosing folder option in all enclosed folders. Henceforth none of the enclosed folders are updated automatically when you change the enclosing folder's privileges. You'll have to click Copy every time you change the enclosing folder's privileges.

You don't need to (and generally shouldn't) click Copy when you first make a disk or folder available for sharing. At that time all the enclosed folders automatically adopt the privileges of the enclosing folder or disk. Any new enclosed folders that you create also automatically adopt the privileges of the enclosing folder.

Specifying who has access privileges

The Info window or sharing window displays three categories of users for whom you can set access privileges:

✦ **Owner** names the owner of the computer from which the folder was created (not necessarily your computer) or a registered user or group to whom the current owner assigns ownership.

✦ **User/Group** names one registered user or one group of users with special access privileges to the shared folder or disk.

✦ **Everyone** refers to anyone who connects to the computer as a guest or as a registered user.

The three categories of users are dimmed if the Share this item and its contents option is off, or for enclosed folders if the Use enclosing folder's privileges option is on.

Owner privileges

Ownership of a folder or disk gives you the right to modify its access privileges. You can transfer ownership of a folder or disk to a registered user, to a group, or to all network users that you enable to connect to your computer. If the folder or disk is on your computer, you choose a new owner from the Owner pop-up menu in the folder or disk's Info window or sharing window. If the folder or disk you own is on someone else's computer, you type the name of the new owner in the space provided. Figure 22-18 shows both procedures.

The Owner pop-up menu lists the registered users and groups to whom you can transfer the ownership of the folder. If you have added a new user or group that doesn't appear in the pop-up menu, close the Info window or sharing window and then reopen it to make the new name appear.

No pop-up menu appears for a shared folder or disk that you own on someone else's computer, so you must type the new owner's name. The name you type must match the name of a registered user or a group in Users & Groups of the computer where the folder or disk is located. Leave the Owner name blank if you want to transfer ownership to everyone.

Figure 22-18: Change the owner of a shared folder or disk.

Note

If you're accessing a volume or folder on a remote machine, and you want to change the Owner of that item, the item must have Share this item and its contents checked. Remember that if you access a machine remotely as the owner, you can access all files on that volume, even if they aren't currently being shared. If they aren't being shared, however, you can't change Sharing privileges for the item.

After you transfer ownership of a folder or disk, the new owner can restrict your access to that item and its contents — but only when you try to access the folder from another computer on the network. Giving away ownership of a folder or disk on your computer doesn't take away your ability to open, use, or modify it from your own computer. In effect, an item can have dual ownership, giving two users ownership privileges. If you make another user the owner of an item on your computer, both you and that other user have ownership privileges. You can reclaim sole ownership at any time by making yourself the owner in the item's Info window or sharing window.

User/Group privileges

You can give one registered user or a group of registered users greater access privileges than other network users to a shared folder or disk. If the folder or disk is on your computer, you choose a registered user or group from the User/Group pop-up menu in the folder or disk's Info window or sharing window. If the folder or disk you own is on someone else's computer, you type the name in the space provided. Figure 22-19 shows both procedures.

Note   That you can only set privileges for one group may seem confusing at first. Actually, it simply means that, in some cases, you might need to create "supergroups" or additional groups that include all the users you want to give access to a particular folder. For instance, if you want to give access to a particular folder to both the "writers" group and the "designers" group, create a new group and put all the users from both of those groups in it. (You can do this by dragging group icons to the new group's window in Users & Groups.) Then assign the new group privileges to the folder that you want all those users to access. Users can belong to many different groups.

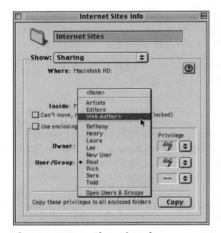

Figure 22-19: Changing the user or group that has special access privileges to a shared folder or disk

The User/Group pop-up menu lists all the registered users and groups in Users & Groups. If you have added a new user or group that doesn't appear in the pop-up menu, close the Info window or sharing window and then reopen it to make the new name appear.

The pop-up menu doesn't appear for a shared folder or disk that you own on someone else's computer, so you must type the name of a registered user or group in the space provided. The name you type must match the name of a registered user or group in Users & Groups of the computer where the folder or disk is located. If you want to change the User/Group to none, delete the User/Group name and leave it blank.

The Everyone category

The Everyone category includes all registered users that you let connect to your computer. This category also includes guests (unregistered users), if you allow guests to connect. If you want registered users but no one else to have access to the shared folders on your computer, disable Guest access in Users & Groups (as described in "Identifying Who Can Access Your Shared Items" earlier in this chapter). Then set the Everyone category to the privileges you want all registered users to have.

A registered user or group of users that is specified for the User/Group or Owner category can have greater privileges than those that are granted by the Everyone category.

Common access-privilege scenarios

Controlling who can do what with files in shared areas opens new possibilities for working in groups. Using access-privilege settings, you can keep folders private between two users, make the folders accessible to everyone on the network, or assign combinations between these extremes. The remainder of this section describes setting access privileges for five interesting file-sharing scenarios.

Universal access

Enabling access to everyone on the network to a shared item and its contents is easy: just set the Everyone category to Read & Write. You don't actually have to set the User/Group and Owner categories. Figure 22-20 shows the access privileges for universal access.

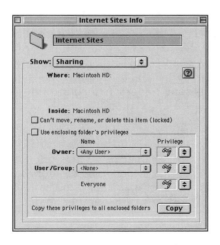

Figure 22-20: Access privileges for universal access

Restricted access

If you want to give one registered user or one group access to a shared item but deny access to guests, name that user or group in the User/Group category and set the User/Group privileges as you like. Be sure the Everyone category has no privileges. Figure 22-21 shows the access privileges for restricted access.

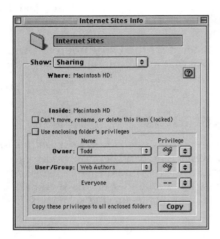

Figure 22-21: Access privileges for restricted access

Private access

If you own a folder on someone else's computer, you can keep that folder private by setting the User/Group and Everyone categories to have no privileges. Only you and the user of that computer can access your folder. Figure 22-22 shows the necessary settings.

To keep a folder or disk on your own computer private, make sure that its Share this item and its contents option is off; use Finder's Sharing command to verify its status. You'll still be able to access that folder when you use another computer to connect to your computer as its owner. Remember that a computer's owner normally has full access privileges to every disk and folder when connecting over the network.

A private in-box folder

Setting up a folder to act as an in-box (or in-basket) enables other network users to deposit documents, folders, and other items in that folder. In-box folders sometimes are referred to as drop boxes, meaning that other users can drop in items, but only you can take those items out. A drop box must be inside another shared folder to enable network users to access it.

Figure 22-22: Access privileges for private access

You prevent all other people from seeing, removing, or changing your folder's contents by setting the User/Group and Everyone categories to Write Only. Figure 22-23 shows the privilege settings for a private in-box folder.

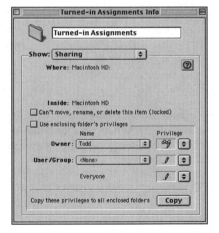

Figure 22-23: Access privileges for an in-box folder

A bulletin board

Another useful configuration of access privileges is to set up a folder to act as a bulletin board, enabling other users to open and read documents, but preventing them from adding or changing documents. They could submit items for posting to the bulletin board by dropping them in an in-box folder (as described previously).

To establish a bulletin-board folder, set the Everyone category to Read Only. If you don't want to share your bulletin-board folder with everyone, set the Everyone category to have no privileges. Then specify a user or group for the User/Group category and set the User/Group access privileges to Read Only. You might want to name a small group as the owner of the folder so that members of the owner group could help with bulletin-board administration. Figure 22-24 shows the settings for a bulletin board folder.

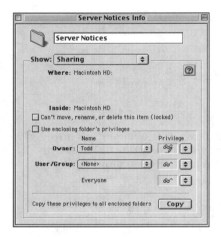

Figure 22-24: Access privileges for a bulletin-board folder

Controlling Security Risks

File sharing poses a security risk, especially if you make an entire hard disk available for sharing and if you enable guests to connect to it. When you make an entire hard disk available for sharing, you either have to trust everyone you let access it or you have to go to a lot of trouble to set specific access privileges for various folders that you want to keep network users out of. There's always the risk of forgetting to deny access to a folder that you don't want network users to share.

Guests pose a particular security risk because they can connect without a password. By disabling guest access in Users & Groups, you can require everyone who connects to your computer to enter a password. Although passwords can be divulged, stolen, or guessed, requiring passwords is still more secure than not requiring passwords.

The computer owner's special ability to connect to all disks and work without restrictions also threatens the computer's security. Anyone who can learn or guess your owner name and password can crack your computer from another computer on your network.

And, with the addition of the File Sharing over IP option and the Remote Access Personal Server in Mac OS 9, all of these security risks are amplified by the fact that your potential "hacker" doesn't have to be physically near your Macs — the hacker could enter by modem or Internet connection.

Controlling access to disks, folders, and files

Here are some ways in which you can improve file-sharing security:

✦ Share folders, not entire disks.

✦ Register all your users and give them passwords. If possible, avoid guest access altogether.

✦ Organize registered users in groups. Make a folder for each group and put in it files and folders for group members to share. You can make a registered user a member of more than one group.

✦ For each group folder you create, set its User/Group to be the group for which you created the folder. Also set the User/Group privilege level that you want group members to have. If possible, set the Everyone privileges for all of your shared folders to none. If you want group members to have less access to some items, put those items in a folder inside the group's folder and set specific lesser privileges for that enclosed folder.

✦ If you decide to enable guests, let them connect to one shared folder and put files and folders you want them to share in this folder. If you want to let guests use additional folders, put them inside this one shared folder. Your registered users will also have access to this folder. Of course, you can also let registered users connect to additional shared folders.

✦ Set a privilege level for your guest folder's Everyone category. If you want guests to have less access to some items, create a folder inside your main guest folder and set specific access privileges for the enclosed folder. For all shared folders outside your guest folder, make sure that the Everyone category has no privileges.

✦ Do not overvalue the security of registered users and passwords. An authorized person may connect to one of your shared folders from any computer on the network and then leave this computer without disconnecting. Someone else can then come along and use this computer to access all your shared files (subject to the access privileges you set). Remind people who connect to your shared folders that they must put away all your shared folders (by dragging them to the Trash) when they finish using them. Also, remind them to lock their keychains and/or log out of the Mac if it is set up for Multiple Users. If they don't, unauthorized users may be able to access shared folders using their account, even if they don't know the password.

✦ Consider removing the owner's special access to all folders and disks, essentially treating the owner like an ordinary registered user. This makes your computer more secure. This also makes file sharing less convenient because you have to assign access privileges to the owner for every disk or folder that you want to access (as owner) over the network. To remove the owner's special access privileges, open the owner in Users & Groups. In the owner window, turn off the Allow user to see all disks option.

✦ If you enable File Sharing over IP or Remote Access answering, consider disallowing any Guest access and make sure your Everyone privileges are always set to None on shared folders. Be especially vigilant in these cases, because any savvy Mac user who knows your IP address could gain access to your shared files.

Coping with network insecurity

Can crackers (another epithet for hackers) invade your network? Mac OS file sharing puts your disks at risk if your computer is connected to a network or the Internet. The risk of invasion exists even if you normally have file sharing turned off. Someone who spends 40 seconds at your keyboard can open your File Sharing control panel or Sharing Setup control panel, change your owner password (without knowing your current password), start file sharing, and close the control panel, leaving no sign of these activities. Then, at his or her leisure, the cracker can use another computer on the network to connect to your computer as its owner and snoop through everything on your disks without leaving any electronic footprints.

You eventually would notice if someone changed your files, of course, and you would discover that your password had been changed if you tried to connect to your computer from another computer. But a less easily detectable invasion involves altering access privileges with Users & Groups and the Finder's Sharing command; this procedure could take less than 10 minutes.

Apple could make your system more secure by adding password access to the File Sharing control panel and Users & Groups. In the meantime, you can password-protect your owner account using Multiple Users (described in Chapter 13) and your documents and applications using Apple File Security encryption (described in Chapter 7). If you want to go to greater lengths, you can encrypt your entire disk with PGPdisk from Network Associates (408-988-3832, http://www.nai.com/default_pgp.asp) or the CryptDisk shareware by Will Price. Otherwise, you must either remove the File Sharing extension from your Extensions folder or trust everyone who has access to a Mac on your network.

Finally, don't forget that the best server protection can be had by switching to AppleShare IP or Mac OS X Server, both of which go to great lengths to secure your server volumes and user settings from tampering.

Locking folders

To prevent anyone from renaming a folder, deleting it, or moving it to another folder, bring up the folder's sharing window and turn on the Can't move, rename, or delete this item option. This option works like the Locked option in the Info windows of files. It affects you or anyone else using your computer, as well as network users who access the folder from another computer. This option affects a folder even if you don't make the folder available for sharing. This option is not available for disks, although they are always locked when they are shared.

Monitoring File-Sharing Activity

When Mac OS file sharing is on, you can see who is connected to your computer and list your shared folders and disks. To monitor file-sharing activity, open the File Sharing control panel and select the Activity Monitor tab. A list of your shared folders and disks (enclosed folders are not listed) displays. You also see a list of the network users currently connected to your computer. An activity indicator shows how much of your computer's total processing time is being spent handling file sharing. Figure 22-25 shows how all this looks.

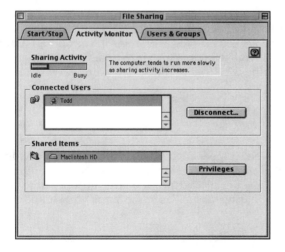

Figure 22-25: See who is connected and what you are sharing.

Any guest currently connected to your computer is listed as <Guest>. Because guests are anonymous, there's no way to tell which guest is who.

Send secret messages

You can send a message to anyone connected to your shared folders or disks. Open the File Sharing control panel and click the Activity Monitor tab. Then Option+double-click the name of any user (even <Guest>) displayed in the Connected Users list. This displays a dialog box in which you type your message. When you click OK, the message appears on the other user's screen in a small dialog box. If you want to send the same message to more than one user, Shift+click or ⌘+click to select their names before you Option+double-click one of them and type the message.

You can disconnect one or more users by selecting them in the list of connected users and clicking Disconnect. Shift+clicking or ⌘+clicking selects multiple users. When you click Disconnect, the system asks you to specify the number of minutes you want to elapse before the disconnection occurs. It's good networking etiquette to give people enough time to save any changes they have made to the files before you disconnect them. To disconnect a user immediately, specify 0 minutes. This disconnection doesn't turn off file sharing.

Remember that this procedure disconnects a user only temporarily. The same user can connect again and access your shared folders. To keep a user from connecting again, use Users & Groups to deny that user access to your computer.

You can also review and change the access privileges of items in the shared items list of the File Sharing control panel. You select one or more items in the list and click Privileges to bring up the sharing windows of the selected items.

Summary

This chapter showed you that the peer-to-peer (distributed) file sharing provided by the Mac OS is great for a small group, but that a dedicated file server, such as AppleShare IP or Mac OS X Server, is generally better for a large group. There are some basic guidelines for good file sharing, as well as some steps you should take to plan your file sharing.

The File Sharing control panel is used to identify your computer with a name, an owner, and an owner password, and to turn file sharing on and off. The Finder's Sharing command is used to designate which folders and disks are available for sharing. This chapter also told you how to use Users & Groups to register network users with names and passwords; how to create groups of registered users; and how to set general access privileges for each registered user, the owner, and guests.

After you've created groups and users, you set privileges for individual folders and disks. You can set each folder and disk's privileges separately for three categories of network users: all network users (everyone), one registered user or group of your choosing, and the owner. The owner can be any registered user or group you choose. You can set specific privileges for an enclosed folder, or a folder can adopt the privileges of the folder that encloses it.

Although file sharing poses risks to your computer's security, there are some strategies for controlling the risks. Plus, using the File Sharing control panel, you can monitor and manage your users and even send them messages.

✦   ✦   ✦

Master Speech

Keyboarding and mousing are not particularly natural
ways to communicate. For years, computer designers
have looked for a more natural way to operate computers. One
of the most compelling ways to work with a computer is simply
to talk to it. Present-day Mac OS computers have taken the first
steps toward achieving the science fiction of *Star Trek*, when
people of the future speak naturally and conversationally with
their computers. When the crew of the spaceship *Enterprise*
traveled back in time to a mid-1980s San Francisco in the movie
Star Trek IV, chief engineer Scotty tried to use a Mac SE by
speaking into the mouse. Of course it was a big joke. Macs
have been capable of speaking text aloud since 1984, but it
wasn't until 1993 that Apple introduced speech recognition.

Apple calls its speech technology PlainTalk. That name isn't
always seen in Apple's documentation or product descriptions
because the company now distributes the text-to-speech and
speech recognition parts of PlainTalk separately. Apple generally
identifies the separate parts of PlainTalk as English Text-to-
Speech and English Speech Recognition.

As mentioned in Chapter 1, PlainTalk is updated for Mac
OS 9 and now features additional recognized words as well as
better integration with AppleScript and Mac applications. This
chapter describes how to use the speech software that may be
installed on your computer, beginning with a discussion of
speech software versions and requirements. After that, the
chapter tells you how to use text-to-speech capabilities and
speech recognition capabilities.

Speech Requirements and Sources

PlainTalk in Mac OS 9 is comprised of two different
technologies — Text-to-Speech and Speech Recognition. Any
Macintosh capable of running Mac OS 9 is compatible with both
Text-to-Speech and Speech Recognition. For the most part,
Speech Recognition also requires either a built-in microphone

(like those built into PowerBooks and iMacs) or a special PlainTalk microphone, which is generally included with most Power Macintosh models. The microphone is specially designed to enable the computer to understand your speech more easily.

By default, Apple includes Text-to-Speech software as part of the standard installation of Mac OS 9. In fact, it's generally turned on so that Talking Alerts is active. With Talking Alerts, alert boxes are read aloud by the computer after they've appeared on the screen for ten seconds. The idea behind this feature is to let you know that the Mac has displayed an alert box even if you aren't looking at the screen.

The other technology, English Speech Recognition, comes with Mac OS 9, but it is not part of a standard installation. You must do a custom installation of Mac OS 9 (as described in Chapter 31) and select the English Speech Recognition module.

Additional information about PlainTalk — as well as updates for the software, when they're announced — is found at Apple's Speech Web site: `http://www.apple.com/macos/speech/`.

Text-to-Speech

There are several ways to get a Mac OS computer to speak. You can use an application that has commands for speaking the text in a document. You can program the computer to speak. And you can have the computer automatically read out the text of alert messages. Regardless of what your computer speaks, it can speak in different voices, and later versions of speech software let you choose the voice. This section tells you how to choose a voice and make your computer speak. There's also a discussion of speech quality at the end of the section.

Choosing a voice

The PlainTalk Text-to-Speech software can talk in different voices. You choose a voice for the system as a whole. Each application can use the system voice, pick its own voice, or let you choose a voice for that application's speech. However, not all applications give you a voice choice.

Choosing a system voice

You can choose your computer's voice and set a speaking rate with the Speech control panel. In the Options menu, select Voice. Now the control panel will change to reveal a pop-up menu that lists the available voices, a slider that adjusts the speaking rate, and a button that lets you hear a sample using the current settings. Figure 23-1 shows the Speech control panel's Voice settings.

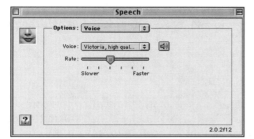

Figure 23-1: Set the computer's speaking voice and speaking rate.

Choosing an application voice

The method for choosing an application's speaking voice varies among applications. For instance, in SimpleText you choose a voice from the Voices submenu of the Sound menu. Figure 23-2 is an example of SimpleText's Voices submenu.

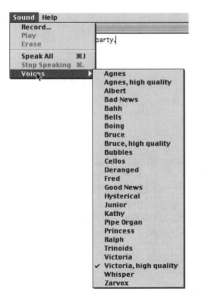

Figure 23-2: Choosing a speaking voice for SimpleText

Where voices are installed

For each speaking voice available on your computer there is a voice file in the Voices folder, which is in the System Folder. You get several male, female, and robotic voices when you install English Text-to-Speech. The exact assortment depends on the capabilities of your computer model, as explained in detail at the end of this section.

You can remove voices by dragging their files out of the Voices folder. If you obtain additional voices from another source, you can make them available by dragging them to the Voices folder.

Talking Alerts

You can use the Speech control panel to set up the manner in which the computer announces its alert messages. In the Speech control panel, choose Talking Alerts from the Options pop-up menu. There you'll find an option for having the computer read the text of alert messages aloud, a slider for adjusting how long the computer waits after it displays an alert message before it speaks, and an option for having the computer speak a phrase such as "Excuse me!" when it displays an alert. There's also a button that lets you hear a sample alert using the current settings. Figure 23-3 shows the Speech control panel's Talking Alert settings.

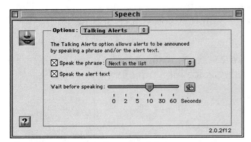

Figure 23-3: Set the computer to announce alert messages.

If you choose to have the computer speak a phrase when it displays an alert, you can also choose the phrase that you want to hear from a pop-up menu. The pop-up menu includes a choice that tells the computer to use the next phrase listed in the menu each time it speaks an alert. The pop-up also includes a choice that tells the computer to pick a phrase at random from the list each time it speaks an alert. If you'd like to add your own phrase, choose Edit Phrase List from the pop-up menu. In the dialog box that appears, you can add, remove, or edit phrases.

If you set the time the computer waits before speaking an alert to more than two seconds, the computer plays the alert sound (a beep or similar sound that was chosen in the Sound control panel) as soon as it displays an alert and then waits to speak. If you set the time to wait before speaking to less than two seconds, the computer does not play the alert sound when it displays an alert message.

Reading documents aloud

To have your computer speak the text in a document, you need one of the many applications that include commands for speaking. SimpleText is one, and AppleWorks, FileMaker Pro, and WordPerfect are others. Various applications have different methods for initiating speech. For example, SimpleText has a Speak command in its Sound menu, whereas AppleWorks has a Shortcut button. Most applications that can speak text will speak the currently selected text (highlight the text with your mouse) or all text in the active document if no text is selected.

Text-to-speech also augments other types of software, such as:

✦ outSPOKEN from ALVA Access (510-923-6280, `http://www.aagi.com`), which uses text-to-speech software to read out the text and the graphics of standard Mac OS applications such as word processors, spreadsheets, communications programs, and more.

✦ Write: Outloud by Don Johnston Inc. (847-526-2682, `http://www.donjohnston.com`), which is a talking word processor that helps students with disabilities

✦ eText by META Innovation (61 3 9439 6639, `http://www.meta-inn.com`), which uses text-to-speech to teach typing for computers

✦ Storybook Weaver Deluxe from The Learning Company (617-494-5700, `http://www.learningco.com`), which can read aloud storybooks that children write in English or Spanish

* MacYack Pro from Scantron Quality Computers (800-966-1508, `http://www.lowtek.com/macyack/`), which lets you add speech to any word processor; hear dialog boxes; see and hear customized messages at startup and shutdown; hear calculations instantly; correct pronunciation errors; create double-clickable speech files; have speaking alert sounds; add speech to HyperCard stacks; and use AppleScript to add speech to other programs

Speaking on command

In addition to having documents and alerts read to you, you can program your computer to speak on command. This can be done with AppleScript (which is described in Chapter 23) or with a macro utility, such as QuicKeys from CE Software (515-223-1801, `http://www.cesoft.com`). The QuicKeys Speak Ease shortcut speaks text you enter in its text window or text you copy from a document (up to 32K) to the Clipboard. Whenever you type the shortcut's keystroke, the computer speaks the text that you entered or copied. You also can set up a timer so that the computer speaks the text at specified intervals. Figure 23-4 shows the QuicKeys dialog box in which you specify your text-to-speech source.

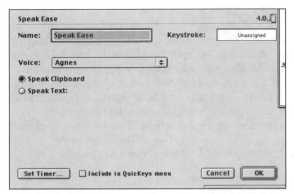

Figure 23-4: Choose the source for the text that you want spoken in the QuicKeys Speak Ease shortcut dialog box.

Speech quality

Several factors affect the quality of computer-generated speech. Clarity of intonation obviously affects how easily you can understand your computer's speech. Less obvious factors include handling contractions, sequencing words idiomatically, avoiding robotic cadence, and generating the sounds of speech.

For natural-sounding speech, the text-to-speech system needs to compensate for idiomatic differences between written and spoken text. This includes expanding contractions, changing word order, and making substitutions. For example, when the system sees "$40 billion" it should not say "dollars forty billion." The system also has to deal with ambiguous abbreviations such as "St. Mary's Church is on St. Mary's St."

Besides saying the right words in the right order, the text-to-speech system has to pronounce them correctly. Consider the different ways "ough" is pronounced in the words enough, ought, slough, dough, through, and drought. Pronunciation also depends on sentence structure, as in "A strong wind can wind a kite string around a tree." Moreover, the system has to avoid putting the emPHASis on the wrong sylLAble. Names pose a special problem because their spelling is even less reliable a guide to pronunciation than ordinary English words.

Getting the words and pronunciation right isn't enough. Without the right cadence, spoken words may sound robotic. Beyond just sounding unnatural, the wrong phrasing may convey the wrong meaning. Compare the meaning of "Atlas already ate, Venus" to "Atlas already ate Venus."

The most computationally intensive part of speech synthesis is producing the sound of a human voice speaking the text. Each moment of speech requires many mathematical calculations and ample memory. The higher the quality of speech, the greater the computational and memory demands. In other words, a higher-performance computer is capable of higher-quality speech.

Apple's text-to-speech software has two levels of speech quality, each demanding a different level of computer performance. The levels in Mac OS 9 are called MacinTalk 3 and MacinTalk Pro. Each consists of a system extension and a set of voices. When you install text-to-speech software, the Installer program gives you the parts that are appropriate for your computer.

Note   Earlier versions of the Mac OS included MacinTalk 2, which was capable of generating text-to-speech on pre-Power Macintosh machines. Because Mac OS 9 only supports Power Macintosh machines or higher, only the higher-quality MacinTalk versions are included.

Making speech sound more natural

The Mac does a pretty good job of speaking text, but you can adjust the cadence and pronunciation of the speech to make it sound more natural. You make these adjustments by adding punctuation and emphasis codes.

When the Mac reads text, it tends to pause less often than a person would. You can make the Mac pause more often by inserting extra commas where you want pauses. For example:

```
"You have a lunch date, at 12:30, on Tuesday, at the Sam & Ella
Cafe."
```

To insert a brief pause, put single quotation marks around a phrase. For example:

```
"Exclusive to the 'Coast Starlight' is the 'Pacific Parlour Car.'"
```

Also, the Mac tends to emphasize too many words, making it hard to tell which are important. You can insert the *[[emph -]]* code before a word you want to have less emphasis. This code must have exactly one space before the hyphen, and none anywhere else. Here is an example:

```
"The shuttle bus runs every half [[emph -]] hour, on the half
[[emph -]] hour."
```

If you need to add emphasis, insert the *[[emph +]]* code. This code also has exactly one space in it. Here is an example:

```
"Food and drink are [[emph +]] not allowed in the museum."
```

MacinTalk 3

MacinTalk 3, the midlevel speech synthesizer, sounds less robotic than earlier MacinTalk versions because it's based on an acoustic model of the human vocal tract. MacinTalk 3 has 19 voices, including several novelty voices (robots, talking bubbles, whispering, and singing).

MacinTalk Pro

MacinTalk Pro, which is the best synthesizer, bases its audio signal on samples of real human speech. It sounds more like a human voice than the other synthesizers, especially when synthesizing a female voice. To assist with pronunciations, MacinTalk Pro has a dictionary of 65,000 words plus 5000 common U.S. names. To generate cadence, it uses a sophisticated model of the acoustic structure of human speech that resulted from many years of research. MacinTalk Pro has three English voices — Agnes, Bruce, and Victoria. Each is available at two different quality levels — Regular and High Quality. You can select these voices in the Speech control panel by selecting Voice from the Options pop-up menu, and then viewing the Voice pop-up menu.

Speech Recognition

Apple made headlines in 1993 when it introduced its speech recognition technology, which was then called Casper. Now called English Speech Recognition, the technology enables many Mac models to take spoken commands from anyone who speaks North American English. You don't have to train the computer to recognize your voice. You just speak normally, without intense pauses, unnatural diction, or special intonation.

English Speech Recognition is designed to understand a few dozen commands for controlling your computer. You can add to and remove some of the commands that the speech recognition system understands, but you can't turn it into a general dictation system.

This section explains how to configure speech recognition and how to speak commands. It tells you what commands the speech recognition system understands and how you can add your own speakable commands. The section concludes by describing some applications that make special use of speech recognition.

Note

In Apple's implementation, speech recognition is used for speaking commands to your Mac, not for dictating text within documents. IBM has recently announced Via Voice for Macintosh (http://www.ibm.com/software/speech/), an application that enables you to "type" by speaking. Dragon Systems (http://www.dragonsys.com/) has announced a similar product.

Configuring speech recognition

You configure speech recognition with the Speech control panel, which enables you to turn speech recognition on and off, make limited adjustments to what is recognized, and specify the kind of feedback you get when you speak commands.

On and off

Speech recognition is turned on or off by choosing Speakable Items from the Options menu in the Speech control panel. After the control panel changes, you can turn Speakable Items on or off. You can also specify whether the computer should listen for the names of buttons such as OK and Cancel when speech recognition is on. Figure 23-5 shows the Speakable Items section of the Speech control panel.

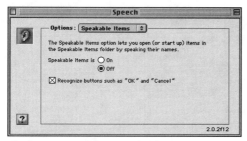

Figure 23-5: Turn speech recognition on and off and set it to listen for button names.

Feedback

Turning on speech recognition brings up a feedback window, which floats above all other windows. At the left side of the feedback window, an animated cartoon character indicates whether the computer is standing by, is listening for a command, is hearing sounds, recognizes your spoken words as a command, or doesn't recognize your spoken words. Beneath the character, some italicized text reminds you what you must do to make the computer listen for a command: press the named key or speak the indicated code name (as described later in this section). The feedback window can also display your voice commands in writing along with a written response. You can hide and show the text of your voice commands by clicking the feedback window's zoom box. Figure 23-6 is an example of the speech recognition feedback window.

Figure 23-6: Getting feedback on your spoken commands

You determine how the computer lets you know whether it heard and recognized your spoken commands by setting options in the Feedback section of the Speech control panel (choose Feedback from the Options pop-up menu).

Once in the Feedback section, you can choose the feedback window's cartoon character from the Character pop-up menu. You can turn the Speak text feedback option on or off to control whether the computer speaks its response to your commands in addition to displaying them in writing in the feedback window. You can also choose a sound from a pop-up menu that lists the sounds in the System file; the computer will play that sound when it recognizes what you said. Figure 23-7 shows the Feedback section of the Speech control panel.

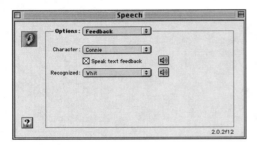

Figure 23-7: Specify how you want the computer to respond to your spoken commands.

A new feature in Mac OS 9 is the presence of the Speakable Commands list using an Apple Guide menu. You can scroll through the list to see all of the available commands. The context for commands switches when you switch applications. The Finder offers different commands from Outlook Express, for example. In general, any command that appears in the list should be a command that can be issued for the current application. Go ahead and try it out if you're interested in seeing what the command does.

Tip   The Commands window has its own speakable commands. Say "Close commands window" to get it off the screen or "Open commands window" to see it again. You can also click its close box, if you feel a bit more adept with the mouse than with your voice.

Speaking commands

You don't want the computer listening to every word you say, or it might try to interpret conversational remarks as commands. There are basically two methods for controlling when the computer listens for commands: the push-to-talk method and the code name method. The push-to-talk method is the most reliable method because the computer listens for commands only while you are pressing a key that you designate. With the code name method, the computer listens for its code name and tries to interpret the words that follow it as a command.

Push-to-Talk method

To use the push-to-talk method of signaling the computer that you are speaking a command, choose Listening from the Options menu of the Speech control panel. Set the Method option to Listen only while key(s) are pressed. The Key(s) option specifies the key or keys that you must hold down to make the computer listen for a spoken command. You can change the setting of the Key(s) option by pressing a different key or combination of keys. Generally, you must use Escape, Delete, or any key on the numeric keypad either alone or together with any one or more of the Shift, Option, or Control keys. You can't use letter keys or number keys on the main part of the keyboard. Figure 23-8 shows the Speech control panel set for the push-to-talk method with the Escape key, which is the initial setting.

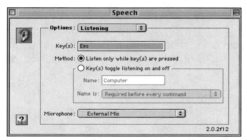

Figure 23-8: Setting speech recognition for push-to-talk listening

Code Name method

If you prefer to have the computer listen for a code name that you say before speaking a command, bring up the Listening section of the Speech control panel and set the Method option to Key(s) toggle listening on and off. Then you can type a name for the computer in the space provided. You can use the nearby pop-up menu to specify when you must speak the name. You can make the code name optional, but not without risk: The computer could interpret something you say in conversation as a voice command. Figure 23-9 shows the Speech control panel set for the code name method.

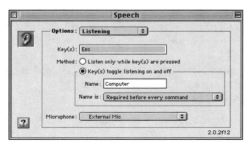

Figure 23-9: Setting speech recognition for code name listening

You can configure speech recognition so that you don't have to speak the code name if you spoke the last command less than 15 seconds ago (or another interval that you specify). The idea is that when you have the computer's attention, you shouldn't have to get its attention immediately following the previous command. You can tell whether you need to speak the code name by looking at the speech recognition feedback window. If you see the code name beneath the feedback character, you have to speak the name before the next command.

Attention key

When you set speech recognition to listen for its code name, you can press a key or a combination of keys to turn listening on and off. Turning listening off puts speech recognition on standby, which may improve the performance of the computer. You specify the key or keys at the top of the Listening section of the Speech control panel.

Tip You can tell when speech recognition is in standby mode, because the feedback character closes its eyes, reads the paper, or otherwise indicates that you don't have its undivided attention.

Speakable commands

After setting up and turning on speech recognition, you are ready to speak commands (such as "Make this speakable"), with the expectation that the computer will carry out your order. But what commands will the computer obey? The answer is pretty simple: items in the Speakable Items folder and some buttons in dialog boxes.

Speakable Items folder

Speech recognition recognizes the names of items in the Speakable Items folder (which you can access from the Apple menu) as commands. Saying the word "open" before the name of an item in the Speakable Items folder is generally optional unless the item name begins with the word "open." For example, if you have a speakable item named "AppleWorks," you could open it by saying either "open AppleWorks" or "AppleWorks." In essence, the speech recognition software acts as if you'd double-clicked the item in the Speakable Items folder.

Apple offers a little help when it comes to naming items that you add to the Speakable Items folder. Some of Apple's suggestions:

✦ Try to name items so that they don't sound too much alike ("Navigator" and "Communicator" are probably better than "Netscape Navigator" and "Netscape Communicator," at least in our experience).

✦ Use long command names — they are more easily recognized.

How to speak

Speech recognition is liberal about the use of *a*, *an*, *the*, *and*, and *or* in spoken commands. For instance, you can say either "close window" or "close the window." Moreover, you can often substitute *these* for *this*, as in "Make this speakable" and "Make these speakable." The computer is somewhat more likely to recognize a phrase that exactly matches a speakable item. If the computer has trouble recognizing a spoken command, try saying the exact name of the speakable item.

When speaking a command, do not pause between words, but pause slightly when saying a command with initials or an acronym, as if you were spelling it out for someone. For example, if you had a speakable item named "open PPP control panel," you should say "open P P P control panel."

If a name includes an ampersand, a slash, or another symbol, speech recognition ignores it. For example, if you had a speakable item named "open Monitors & Sound" you could say either "open Monitors Sound" or "open Monitors and Sound."

✦ If you need acronyms or a series of letters in a name, put spaces in between. "Connect using P P P" is better than "Connect using PPP."

✦ Avoid using numerals in your file names. For instance, PlainTalk doesn't notice the difference between "Outlook Express 4.5" and "Outlook Express 5." If you need to add items like these, it's best to spell out the number, such as "Outlook Express Five."

Application speakable items

PlainTalk 2.0 now differentiates between commands that are generally available throughout the Mac OS and those that are specific to a particular application. In the Speakable Items folder, you'll find that commands in the root level of the Speakable Items folder are for global use. Each "speakable" application will also have a subfolder that is used to store its specific commands.

To create the subfolder for a new application, all you need to do is switch to the application in the Finder and speak the command "Make this Application Speakable." A new subfolder is created in the Speakable Items folder, where you can easily add new commands, as discussed later in this chapter.

Note   If you're creating your own commands, you should avoid naming application-specific commands the same as global commands because the application-specific command will override the global command.

Menu items

To enable Speech Recognition to recognize menu commands, create an AppleScript application for each menu command. This works only for scriptable applications. Some applications are already supported by Speakable Items, with commands such as "Get My Mail" (for Outlook Express) and "Go Home" (for Internet Explorer or Netscape Communicator).

Cross-Reference   For more information on AppleScript, see Chapter 24.

More speakable commands

You make the computer understand more spoken commands by adding items to the Speakable Items folder. Anything that you can open in the Finder becomes a speakable command when you add it to the Speakable Items folder.

Aliases

If there are documents, applications, folders, control panels, or any other items that you want to open by spoken command, simply put aliases of them in the Speakable Items folder. You can do this very easily by selecting the items in the Finder and speaking the command "Make this speakable." The result is an alias in the Speakable Items folder for every item you originally selected, and the aliases have exactly the same names as the original items. If the computer doesn't recognize the name of an item you add to the Speakable Items folder, try restarting the computer.

You can change the speakable command that opens an alias by editing the name of the alias. You should remove the word *alias* from any alias names that include it, although speech recognition usually ignores *alias* at the end of a speakable item's name. If the computer doesn't respond when you say "open" followed by the name of a speakable item, change the item's name so that it begins with "open."

If speakable items have names that sound similar, the computer may have trouble distinguishing them. If the computer frequently mistakes one speakable item for another, try changing the name of one or both so that they don't sound alike. Also, the computer has more trouble identifying short names than it does identifying long names. To prevent these problems, make the names of your speakable items as long and unique sounding as possible.

AppleScript and the Script Editor

To make a multistep speakable command, use the Script Editor program to create an AppleScript application that you put in the Speakable Items folder. Remember that anything in the Speakable Items folder acts as if it was double-clicked, including AppleScript applets.

With some applications you can record an AppleScript application of a procedure while you carry it out. Using the Script Editor, you simply set it to record an action, which makes the resulting script an applet. Drop it in the Speakable Items folder and give it a good, speakable name. Now, when you speak the name of the AppleScript as a command (for example, "Print this document"), the AppleScript executes and the command takes place.

Cross-Reference For more information on AppleScript and Apple events, see Chapter 24.

Speech recognition applications

It would be very difficult, if not impossible, to add enough items to the Speakable Items folder to gain anything approaching complete control of an application. Yet applications have access to the speech-recognition infrastructure behind the Speakable Items folder, and an application developer can use that infrastructure to give you extensive spoken control of an application. These applications offer enhanced control through speech recognition:

✦ Speech Typer by Michael F. Kamprath (`http://www.kamprath.net/claireware/`) takes speech recognition beyond speakable commands into the realm of data entry. It lets you type any predefined phrase in any application you may be using. Because you must predefine spoken phrases, Speech Typer doesn't turn speech recognition into a full-fledged dictation system, but it does enable you to dictate commonly used words and phrases.

✦ MT-NewsWatcher by Simon Fraser (`http://www.best.com/~smfr/mtnw/`) is a speech-controlled Internet newsreader.

✦ Dynamic English by DynEd International (650-578-8067, `http://www.dyned.com`) teaches English as a second language by using speech recognition to improve articulation and fluency and to reinforce language structure and vocabulary.

✦ Hearts Deluxe (and other games) by Free Verse Software (212-929-3549, `http://www.freeverse.com`) lets you play the classic card game of hearts against a cast of characters using only your voice.

Summary

This chapter covered the requirements and sources for Apple's PlainTalk Text-to-Speech and Speech Recognition software. There are several ways to get a Mac OS computer to speak. You can use an application that has commands for speaking the text in a document. You can program the computer to speak. And you can have the computer automatically read out the text of alert messages. Regardless of what your computer speaks, it can speak in different voices, and with later versions of speech software you can choose the voice. The quality of the speech depends on which speech synthesizer your computer uses and the voices you choose.

You also saw how to use speech recognition software. You use the Speech control panel to turn recognition on and off and to specify how you want the system to respond when it recognizes a spoken command. You saw the push-to-talk method of speaking commands and the code name method. Finally, you learned which spoken commands the computer understands and how you can add more with aliases and AppleScript.

✦　　✦　　✦

Automate with Scripts

Although computers have been touted for years as the ultimate tool for "automating" our lives, too often there's nothing particularly automatic about the process at all. So far you've seen technologies in Mac OS 9 that help you launch documents, edit text, create multimedia, print, and perform hundreds of other tasks. And while there are certainly impressive components in all of those technologies, none of them is doing much by itself — they tend to require user input.

AppleScript can change some of that. AppleScript provides the freedom to create slightly more automated tasks, thanks to its scripting language — a miniprogramming language of sorts — that enables you to tell your applications to perform certain tasks automatically. AppleScripts can be simple or highly complex, depending on your skill at programming and your knowledge of all AppleScript's nuances. This chapter can't show it all to you, but you'll learn a good deal of it. And even programming novices can get AppleScripts up and running thanks to tools, such as the Script Editor, which are included with Mac OS 9.

A discussion of AppleScript needs to begin, however, with the underlying technologies that make AppleScript possible. First is a discussion of Apple Events, which are the means by which applications can communicate with one another. After you understand Apple Events, it's on to an introduction of AppleScript and a look at the tools that enable you to run, modify, and create scripts of your own.

Apple Events

Programs can share services behind the scenes by sending and receiving messages called *Apple events*. When an application receives Apple event messages sent by another program, the receiving application, also known as the *server application*, does something. The action that the server application takes depends on the contents of the Apple event messages. This action can be anything from executing a particular command to taking some data, working with it, and then returning a result to the program that sent the Apple events, also known as the *client application*.

When you choose Shut Down or Restart from the Special menu, for example, the Finder sends the Apple event Quit to every open program. That's why those programs seem to quit automatically when the Shut Down or Restart command is invoked. When you drag and drop icons in an application, the Finder sends the Apple event Open Documents, which includes a list of all the items represented by the icons that you dragged and dropped. Programs that make aliases automatically or that shut down your Mac for you accomplish these tasks by sending Apple events to the Finder.

A program, however, does not automatically send or receive Apple events; the developer must build in the capability to receive and act on Apple events. More and more developers are putting Apple-event capability in their applications. Most applications introduced or revised since the middle of 1991 can receive and act on at least the four basic Apple events: Open Application, Open Documents, Print Documents, and Quit Application, each of which is defined in Table 24-1.

Table 24-1	
Basic Apple Events Messages	
Message Sent to Application	*What Happens*
Open Application	The application opens
Open Documents	The application opens the specified documents
Print Documents	The application prints the specified documents
Quit Application	The application quits

The Finder uses these basic Apple-events messages to open programs, open documents, print documents, and quit programs. When you double-click a program icon, the Finder sends the program an Open Application message. When you double-click a document, the Finder sends the program that created the document an Open Application message and an Open Documents message with the name of the document you double-clicked. When you select one or more documents and choose Print from the Finder's menu, the Finder sends the application an Open Application message, a Print Documents message with the identity of the documents you selected, and a Quit Application message. When you choose the Shut Down or Restart command, the Finder sends a Quit Application message to each open program. For programs that don't understand the basic Apple events, the Finder uses its traditional means of opening, printing, and quitting.

Programs that go beyond the four basic Apple-events messages understand another two dozen core Apple-events messages. These messages encompass actions and objects that almost all programs have in common, such as the Close, Save, Undo, Redo, Cut, Copy, and Paste commands. Programs with related capabilities recognize still more sets of Apple-events messages. Word-processing programs understand messages about text manipulation, for example, and drawing programs understand messages about graphics manipulation. Program developers can even define private Apple-event messages that only their programs know.

The Mac OS provides the means of communicating Apple-events messages between programs. The programs can be on the same computer or on different computers connected to the same network. A program doesn't have to be open or even accessible to receive messages; the Mac OS stores messages and forwards them when the program becomes available. Only application programs can send and receive Apple events; "true" control panels and desk accessories cannot, although these items are becoming rarer. Control panels that are actually applications (they are listed in the Applications menu when open) are not subject to this limitation. And a desk accessory can work around this limitation by sending and receiving through a small surrogate application program that is always open in the background. This background application does not have to appear in the Application menu, and the computer user does not have to know that the application is open.

To understand how Apple events work, think of them as a telephone system. The Mac OS furnishes a "telephone" and "voicemail" for each program, as well as the wires that connect them. For messages sent across a network, the Mac OS uses the built-in AppleTalk networking software and LocalTalk, Ethernet, or other networking connectors and cables (described in Chapter 20). Application programs talk on the telephone and leave Apple-events messages for each other. Desk accessories aren't capable of talking on the phone, but some of them have agents that forward incoming and outgoing messages.

Apple events offer many intriguing possibilities for the world of personal computing. No longer does one application need to handle every possible function; instead, it can send messages to helper applications. For example, Sherlock handles some commands from their File menus, such as Get Info and Open Enclosing Folder, by sending Apple-events messages to the Finder, which actually carries out the commands.

Introducing AppleScript

Apple events aren't just for professional software engineers. Mac enthusiasts who have little technical training can use Apple events to control applications by writing commands in the *AppleScript* language. For example, suppose you want to quit all open applications so that you can open one really big application. The Mac OS doesn't have a Quit All command, but you can create one with an AppleScript command. You can use AppleScript commands to automate simple tasks such as this one, as well as to automate more complex tasks, as the following sections explain.

AppleScript language

AppleScript is a user-oriented programming language that enables you to send Apple events to programs. With AppleScript, you write your own programs, called *scripts*, to perform complex tasks easily. You can use AppleScript to move data between applications. You can develop your own tools to accomplish exactly what you need.

Because AppleScript is aimed at users, Apple has made the scripting language as easy as possible to understand and use. The language flows fairly naturally and has an English-like syntax. You can look at scripts and know right away what they're supposed to do. Also, AppleScript removes the need for you to decipher the codes that make up Apple events. Instead, you get information from the application itself about what words to use to represent the Apple events that the program understands. Inside an application, a Get Data event is represented by codes such as "core" and "getd," but with AppleScript you may see only "get." This way, even novice users can understand AppleScript.

As an added bonus, AppleScript can actually watch you as you work with an application and write a script for you behind the scenes. This process is called *script recording*.

Although AppleScript is designed for end users, it offers all the capabilities of a traditional programming language and won't frustrate programmers and more advanced users. You can store information in variables for later use; write if-then statements to execute different commands, depending on some condition that you specify; or repeat a set of commands as many times as you want. AppleScript also offers error checking and object-oriented programming.

AppleScript pieces

There are several AppleScript items in the System Folder or the Extensions folder. Chief among these is the AppleScript extension, which contains the actual AppleScript language. Another important AppleScript item is a folder named Scripting Additions. This folder contains special files, called *scripting additions*, which add commands to the AppleScript language, much as plug-in files add capabilities to Adobe Photoshop or a Web browser. In Mac OS 9, there can be two Scripting Additions folders: one in the System Folder and another in the Extensions folder. (By default, Mac OS 9 creates the Scripting Additions folder found in the System Folder, but applications sometimes require one in the Extensions folder.) However, if there are any duplicate items in the two Scripting Additions folders, the one in the System Folder takes precedence.

AppleScript also includes a simple application, Script Editor, for creating and editing scripts. You can use the Script Editor to record, write, and edit scripts for any application that is compatible with AppleScript. A prime example of a scriptable application (an application that you can control with AppleScript) is the Finder.

Note

Looking for some sample scripts? If you have upgraded to Mac OS 9 from a previous edition of the Mac OS, you'll likely find a folder called Automated Tasks in the Apple Menu Items folder in your System Folder. Likewise, you may find a folder called More Automated Tasks in the AppleScript folder within the Apple Extras folder. You may also find additional sample scripts in the CD Extras folder on your Mac OS 9 CD-ROM.

If you do a lot of scripting, you may want to replace the Script Editor with a more capable application such as Scripter from Main Event Software (202-298-9595, http://www.mainevent.com) or Script Debugger from Late Night Software (604-929-5578, http://www.latenightsw.com).

Introducing Script Editor

Script Editor is the program that you use the most when you use AppleScript. This simple program enables you to write and run scripts. Find the Script Editor icon on your hard drive and open it.

When you open Script Editor, an empty window appears. This *script window* can contain one script. The bottom pane of the script window is the script editing area, where you type and edit the text of the script. The top pane of the window is the *script description area*. You use this area to type a description of what the script does. Figure 24-1 shows an empty script window.

Figure 24-1: The new script window that appears when Script Editor opens

The middle area of the window has four buttons. The first button puts you in Record mode. When you click this button, AppleScript begins watching as you work with applications. If you are working in an application that accepts recording, AppleScript writes out the script commands that correlate to the things that you do with the application. Pressing ⌘+D also starts recording.

Clicking Stop takes you out of recording mode or stops a script that is running, depending on which action is relevant at the time. Pressing ⌘+period (.) is the same as clicking Stop.

Run starts running the script in the script editing area. You also can press ⌘+R to run the script.

Finally, clicking Check Syntax compiles the script. *Compiling* a script means putting it in a format that AppleScript recognizes as a script. While AppleScript compiles your script, it checks your script for things that it doesn't understand. For example, if you forget a parenthesis where AppleScript expects to find one, it lets you know. After you fix any syntax errors, AppleScript compiles the script.

Recording a Script

One of the easiest ways to see how AppleScript looks is to record your actions and let AppleScript write a script for you. You cannot record scripts for every scriptable program because software developers must do more work to make an application recordable than to make it scriptable.

One recordable application is the Finder. Experiment with it to see how script recording works by opening the Script Editor and clicking Record in a new script window. A tape cassette icon flashes over the Apple menu while you are recording a script to remind you that AppleScript is recording your actions. Now switch to the Finder, make a new folder, set its label, open it, move its window, and set its view options. When you finish, switch back to Script Editor and click Stop. AppleScript displays a script that when run will mimic all your actions. Figure 24-2 is an example of a script you might record in Finder.

To test the script, return to the Finder and delete the new folder you created. (This ensures that the Finder starts out the same way as when you recorded your script.) Now switch back to Script Editor and click Run in your recorded script's window. AppleScript plays back everything you did. When the script finishes running, there should be a new folder set up exactly as when you finished recording your script. Now switch to Script Editor again and examine the script. You'll find the script to be fairly understandable — it may not be fluent English, but many of the commands make sense as you read them.

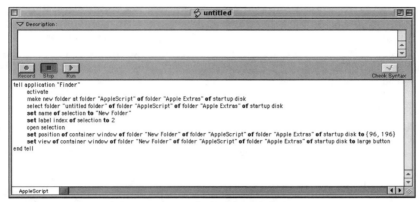

Figure 24-2: A sample script recorded in the Finder

Analyzing a Script

Having looked through the script that AppleScript wrote in the previous Finder example, you may be surprised to learn that AppleScript doesn't know anything about the Finder operations. AppleScript doesn't know how to set an icon's label, how to move windows, or how to do any of the things that your script did in Finder. In fact, AppleScript knows how to perform only five commands: Get, Set, Count, Copy, and Run. AppleScript learns how to perform other commands in a script from the application controlled by the script. Each scriptable application contains a dictionary that defines the AppleScript commands that work with the application.

Note

In technical discussions of AppleScript, you may hear a scriptable application's dictionary of AppleScript commands referred to as the application's "aete" resource. "Aete" is the name assigned to the resource where AppleScript dictionary items are stored in an application file's resource fork.

Look at the sample script you recorded. The first line says "tell application 'Finder'." To AppleScript, this means "start working with the application named Finder." When a script is compiled, AppleScript looks at the application you specified. By looking at the program's dictionary, AppleScript figures out what Apple events the program understands. AppleScript learns, for example, that the Finder understands the "make" Apple event. The dictionary also tells AppleScript what kind of information, or *objects*, the application knows how to work with, such as files, folders, and disks. Finally, the dictionary tells AppleScript what words to use as AppleScript commands instead of the codes that the application understands.

When you run your sample script and AppleScript reaches the "tell application 'Finder'" line, AppleScript starts sending Apple events to the application program named in that line. AppleScript translates every command it encounters in your script into an Apple event code based on the program's dictionary, and it sends that code to the application. The application receives the Apple event and takes the appropriate action.

When AppleScript reaches the End Tell command that appears at the bottom of the script you recorded, it stops sending messages to the Finder. If you are working with several applications, you may have another Tell command that names a different application, in which case AppleScript starts talking to this application, sending it Apple event codes.

You can look at the dictionary of an application to see what commands the application understands. In Script Editor, choose Open Dictionary from the File menu. A standard Open dialog box appears. Select the Finder's icon in the System Folder and click Open. The Script Editor displays a dictionary window for the Finder, as shown in Figure 24-3.

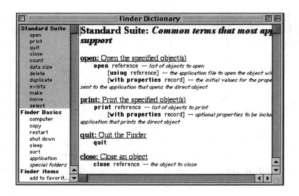

Figure 24-3: A scriptable application's AppleScript dictionary defines the commands that the application understands.

The left side of the dictionary window displays a list of commands, classes of objects, and suites that the application recognizes. A *suite* is a group of commands and other items for a related activity, but you don't have to worry about suites when you're scripting.

You can select one or more terms listed on the left side of a dictionary window to see detailed descriptions of the terms on the right. Just as you can get more information about a command from a program's dictionary, so can AppleScript.

Because AppleScript gets all the relevant information from the application itself, you never have to worry about controlling a new application. As long as the application has a dictionary, AppleScript can work with it.

Scripting additions also have dictionaries, which you can open the same way as you open applications' dictionaries. In fact, in the Open Dictionary dialog box, Script Editor provides a button that takes you directly to the Scripting Additions folder.

Saving Your Script

The Script Editor enables you to save your scripts in four distinct forms. You choose the form from a pop-up menu in the Script Editor's Save dialog box, as shown in Figure 24-4.

 New Feature   In Mac OS 9, the Script Editor has the newfound capability to save files as a Mac OS X Applet. In certain cases, you can run such an applet in Apple's advanced Mac OS X operating system. If you have experience with AppleScript you may have noticed that Apple has also changed the terminology for scripts a bit — what were once called AppleScript *applications* are now called *applets*.

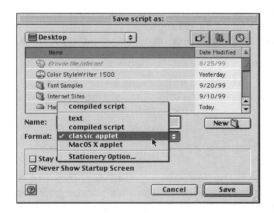

Figure 24-4: There are four options for saving an AppleScript script.

The pop-up menu contains four options:

✦ **Compiled Script** saves the script in a compiled form that you can open with the Script Editor and run or change from there. You should also save scripts as compiled scripts if you intend to run them from within applications (for example, Outlook Express, which enables you to access scripts from a special menu) or if the script will be a folder action.

✦ **Text** saves the script as a plain text document, which you can open in Script Editor, in any word processing program, and in many other applications.

✦ **Classic Applet** saves the script as an application, complete with an icon. Opening the icon (by double-clicking it, for example) runs the script. You must have AppleScript installed to open a script application.

✦ **Mac OS X Applet** saves the script as an application suitable for Mac OS X.

If you choose Classic Applet from the pop-up menu in the Save dialog box, two check boxes appear in the dialog box. The Stay Open check box, if checked, causes the script application to stay open after its script finishes running. If the Stay Open check box is not checked, the script application quits automatically after running its script. Checking the Never Show Startup Screen check box suppresses the display of an identifying "about" window when the script application is opened.

Creating a Script from Scratch

You now know how to use Script Editor to record your actions and write an AppleScript script. This type of script, however, has limited value. A recorded script is not much more intelligent than a simple macro because the script doesn't take advantage of AppleScript's full programming language. Furthermore, not all applications that work with AppleScript permit recording, so you can't always rely on being able to record.

More frequently, you'll use AppleScript to create more complex scripts from scratch. This section shows that you can create a full-blown script quickly and use the resulting custom utility to augment a program's capabilities.

Making a Finder utility

One of the nice features of the Mac OS is that it enables you to drag files to the System Folder and have the Finder figure out where those files should go. Control panels are stored in the Control Panels folder, Fonts go in the Fonts folder, Desk Accessories are placed in the Apple Menu Items folder, and so on.

This capability, however, is limited to whatever the programmers at Apple provide. For example, if you drag an After Dark module to the System Folder, the Finder won't put the module in the After Dark Files folder. You must dig your way through the System Folder hierarchy to get to the relevant folder.

You can, however, write a simple script that uses the Finder and mimics the System Folder's behavior, but moves files to the folders in which you want those files to go. The script is more powerful than the System Folder because the target folder can be anywhere. For example, you can make your QuickTime movies find their way to a folder that's nowhere near your System Folder.

Beginning the script

Open Script Editor or create a new window if Script Editor is already open. This blank window is where you'll write your script.

You can change the default size of a new script window. First, make the script window the size you want, and then choose Set Default Window Size from the File menu in Script Editor.

The first thing this script must do is provide a way to select the file to move. One of the scripting additions that comes with AppleScript, Choose File, enables you to bring up a dialog box for selecting a file from within the script.

In the script editing area of the window, type

```
choose file
```

and then click Check Syntax. The Script Editor formats your script, changing the text fonts as it compiles the script, using different type styles to show different kinds of words. Geneva 10-point Bold, for example, represents words that are native to AppleScript, whereas Plain Geneva 9-point represents words that come from another application. (If you don't like these typestyles, you can change them via the AppleScript Formatting command in Script Editor's Edit menu.)

Click Run to run the script you wrote, selecting any type of file and clicking Open. AppleScript shows you the result of the script in a window named, appropriately enough, "the result." (If this window isn't open, choose Show Result from the Controls menu.) The window contains the word "alias" and the path through your folders to the file you selected. This word does not mean that the file is an alias — in the context of a script, alias means the same thing as file path. Figure 24-5 is an example of the result window.

Figure 24-5: Checking a file specification in Script Editor's "the result" window

The result of the Choose File command is called a *file specification* or *file spec*. A file spec tells the Mac OS exactly where to find a file or folder. You will need the file spec later in the script, so you must put it in a *variable*, which is a container for information. You can place data in a variable and then retrieve it whenever you want before the script finishes running. You can also place new data in a variable during the course of the script.

On the next line of the script, type

```
copy the result to filePath
```

This line places the result of the Choose File command in a variable named filePath. To access the information, type the name of the variable in your script; AppleScript understands this name as a representation of the file spec you got from the first command.

You may notice the capital P in the filePath and wonder whether capitalization is important when entering AppleScript commands. In general, you can capitalize any way that makes commands easier to read. Many AppleScripts authors adopt the convention of capitalizing each word except the first word in a variable name, hence filePath. That just makes it easier to see which words represent variables.

When you run the script, you'll see that the Copy command doesn't change the result of the script. Because the result is just being copied to a variable, the result itself doesn't change.

Working with the Finder

Ultimately, the script you are creating decides where to move a selected file based on the file's four-letter file type. That means that you have to get the file type of the selected file. You can use the Finder to get this information. Enter these commands in the script, starting on the third line of the script:

```
tell application "Finder"
copy the file type of file filePath to fileType
end tell
```

The first of these lines tells AppleScript to start using the Finder. Remember that after encountering this Tell command, AppleScript knows all the commands and objects from the Finder's AppleScript dictionary.

The second line asks the Finder for the file type of the selected file and then copies that information to the variable named fileType. Even though the word "Finder" doesn't appear in this line, the Tell command in the preceding line tells AppleScript to direct these requests to the Finder.

Finally, the End Tell command tells AppleScript to stop working with the Finder for now.

Run the script, select a file, and look at the result. The result window contains the four-letter file type of the file you selected, displayed as a piece of text.

Executing script commands conditionally

For the next part of the script, you have to provide the information—you can't get it from the Finder. You need to write the commands that will move the file to the folder you want, based on the file type of the file (stored in the variable fileType).

To accomplish this task, you write a series of conditional statements, or *conditionals* for short. A conditional is a command or set of commands that AppleScript runs only when a certain condition is met. AppleScript evaluates the condition you set forth; if the condition is true, AppleScript runs the specified commands.

The condition you will set up for each conditional is whether the information in the variable fileType is equal to a four-letter string that you will provide. You attach to the conditional a command that moves the file to a designated folder. In other words, if the information in the variable fileType is equal to a particular four-letter string, AppleScript moves the file to a certain folder. In AppleScript, the conditional looks like this:

```
if fileType is "TEXT" then move file filePath to folder "Text
Files" of startup disk
```

In this example, the condition is whether the information in fileType is "TEXT," which is the four-letter type of plain-text files like those created in SimpleText. If it is, AppleScript moves the file specified by the variable filePath to the folder named Text Files on the startup disk.

Include as many of these conditionals as you want. In each conditional, use a different four-character file type for the type of file to move, and specify the path of the folder to which you want AppleScript to move files of that type. A quick way to enter several conditionals is to select one conditional, copy it, paste it in the script, and change the relevant pieces of information. You can repeat this for each conditional you want to include.

Finding a folder path

If you don't know the full path of a folder, you can use a script to get this information. Open a new window in Script Editor and type the following script in the script editing area:

```
choose folder
```

Run the script and select a folder. The result is a file spec for the folder you selected. You can copy only the text and paste it in any script.

When you type a long command, the Script Editor never breaks it automatically (as a word processor would). You can break a long line manually by pressing Option+Return. (Do not break a line in the middle of a quoted text string, however.) AppleScript displays a special symbol (¬) to indicate a manual line break. Here's an example:

```
if fileType is "Moov" then move file filePath ¬
to folder "Movies" of startup disk
```

Figure 24-6 shows an example of a script with three conditional statements that move a selected file depending on its file type.

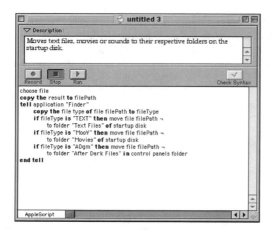

Figure 24-6: A sample script with conditional statements

Trying out your script

After creating a new script, you must run it and test it thoroughly. To test the script that moves files according to their type, run the script. When the dialog box appears, select a file that is of a type your script should recognize but that is not in the destination folder, and click Open. Switch to the Finder, and make sure that the file you selected moved from the source folder to the destination folder. Then repeat the test, selecting a different file type that your script should recognize.

Creating a drag-and-drop script application

Although the sample script you created is useful, it would be more useful as an icon on your desktop to which you could drag-and-drop files and have them move to their appropriate spots, just as you can with the System Folder. You wouldn't have to run Script Editor every time you want to move files, and you could move more than one file at a time. AppleScript gives you this capability.

Finding a file's type

You may not know the file type of the files that you want to move. For example, you may know that you want to put After Dark modules in the After Dark Files folder, but you may not know that the four-letter file type of After Dark modules is ADgm. To make a script that reports the file type, copy the following five-line script to a new Script Editor window:

```
choose file
copy the result to filePath
tell application "Finder"
copy the file type of file filePath to fileType
end tell
```

Run this five-line script and select a file whose four-character file type you need to learn. If the result window is not visible, choose Show Result from the Controls menu. The result of the script is the file type of the selected file. You can copy and paste the result from the result window into a conditional statement in any script window.

It's even easier to determine a file's type using Sherlock 2. In Sherlock, make sure the Files channel is selected, and then click Edit. Now drag any file from the Finder to the middle of the More Search Options window. The file's type is displayed toward the bottom-right corner.

You already know that AppleScript can make standalone applications from your scripts. With a little extra work, you can make an application with drag-and-drop capability so that you can simply drag files to it.

Remember that when you drag and drop a set of icons to an application on the desktop, the Finder sends that application an Open Documents message that includes a list of the files you dragged to the icon. This message is sent to all applications, even to applets that you create yourself with AppleScript.

You need to tell your script to intercept that Apple event and run the appropriate commands. Place the following line at the beginning of your script:

```
on open (itemList)
```

Now enter the following line at the end of your script:

```
end open
```

Note   Click Check Syntax after you've entered these lines in your script and you can check the syntax and see the Script Editor neatly indent certain lines in the window.

The first line tells the script to intercept the Open Documents message and to put the list of files in a variable named itemList. The End Open command helps AppleScript know which commands to run when the open message is received.

Any lines between the first and second lines are run when the script receives an Apple-event Open Documents.

Save this script by choosing the Save As command from the File menu. From the pop-up menu in the Save As dialog box, choose the Application option. If you switch to the Finder and look at the icon of the application you just created, you'll see that the icon contains an arrow that indicates that this application is a drag-and-drop application. Script Editor knows how to use this kind of icon because it sees that the application's script intercepts the Apple event Open Documents.

The script won't be fully operational until you make a few more changes. As the script stands, it places the list of files in a variable, but it doesn't do anything with that information. If you dragged several files to the application now, the script would merely bring up a dialog box asking you to pick a file and then quit, having accomplished nothing.

First, delete what now are the second and third lines of the script (the ones beginning with the words "choose" and "copy"), and replace them with the following:

```
repeat with x from 1 to the number of items in itemList
copy item x of itemList to filePath
```

Between the End Tell and End Open commands, enter the following:

```
end repeat
```

Figure 24-7 shows the complete sample script modified for drag-and-drop operation.

Figure 24-7: A sample script ready to be saved as a drag-and-drop script application

In the modified script, AppleScript repeatedly executes the commands between the Repeat and End Repeat commands for the number of times specified in the Repeat command. This arrangement is called a *repeat loop*. The first time AppleScript executes the Repeat command, it sets variable x to 1, as specified by "from 1." When AppleScript encounters the End Repeat command, it loops back to the Repeat command, adds 1 to the variable x, and compares the new value of x with the number of items that were dragged to the icon ("the number of items in itemList"). If the two values are not equal, AppleScript sequentially executes the command following the Repeat command. If the two values are equal, the copy command is performed for the last time and AppleScript goes to the command immediately following End Repeat. The End Open command ends the script.

The first command in the repeat loop that you just created takes item x of the variable itemList (where, once again, x is a number ranging from 1 to the number of items in itemList) and then copies that information to the filePath variable.

Save the script as a classic applet and switch back to the Finder. (You might want to save it to the Desktop, at least for experimental purposes.) You now have a drag-and-drop application that you can use to move certain types of files to specific folders. Anytime you want to add a file type, use Script Editor to open the script, add a conditional that covers that file type, and save the script. You can have the script move several different types of files to a single folder, if you want, but you can't have the script move different files of the same type to different folders.

To edit a script application, drag its icon to the Script Editor icon, and Script Editor will open the script for you. (Remember that double-clicking a script application runs it.) You can also launch the Script Editor and choose Open Script from the File menu.

AppleScript and the Mac OS

In Mac OS 8.5, Apple made major improvements and changes to the AppleScript commands for the Finder and the standard scripting additions files. In addition, many more control panels, extensions, and applications are scriptable. The following became scriptable in Mac OS 8.5: Appearance; Apple Help Viewer; Apple Menu Options; Apple System Profiler; Application Switcher; ColorSync Extension; Desktop Printer Manager; File Exchange; Location Manager; Network Setup Scripting; and Sherlock.

In addition, Mac OS 9 adds script capability to ColorSync 3.0 and its control panel settings, the Memory control panel, and the LaserWriter 8 driver. AppleTalk is also now better integrated with PlainTalk, the speech recognition technology discussed in Chapter 23.

All of these Mac OS components, like the Finder, have their own AppleScript dictionaries. To learn more about the commands that can be processed by these components, drag and drop their icons to the Script Editor icon (which opens their respective dictionaries) or use the Open Dictionary command in the Script Editor's File menu to hunt down the components and create scripts that affect them.

The changes to the Finder are not supposed to affect the operation of existing scripts. Nevertheless, you should carefully test any existing scripts that contain Finder-related commands. If you open scripts in the Script Editor that were created in Mac OS versions before 8.5, you may see some changes in wording.

Some terms may have the word "deprecated" or the word "obsolete" added. For example, the term "file type" may be changed to "file type obsolete." You can usually update obsolete and deprecated terms by deleting the words "obsolete" and "deprecated," and then compiling the script again. If this method isn't successful, check the Finder's dictionary to learn whether the spelling of the term has changed slightly. There are many other ways to control the Finder in Mac OS 8.5 and 9 than in previous Mac OS versions. Investigate them in the Finder's AppleScript dictionary.

For more information on these and other AppleScript changes, check the AppleScript Web site (http://applescript.apple.com).

Working with Folder Actions

In Mac OS 8.5, Apple introduced the capability to specify actions to take place automatically whenever you interact with particular folders or disks. For example, you could specify that every time a file is added to a certain folder, a copy of the file is to be placed in another folder. Folder actions can take place in response to opening or closing a folder, adding items to or removing them from an open folder, or changing the size or location of a folder window. The Folder actions can also take place in response to the same kinds of interactions with disks and disk windows. These scripts run only if the folder is open (its window is displayed) or the folder is expanded in the list view of a folder that encloses it.

You determine the actions that apply to a folder or disk by attaching AppleScript scripts to it. This section takes a look at attaching folder actions to folders and how you can create folder actions for yourself.

Security with folder actions

You must be careful with folder actions because they can do almost anything you can do to your computer. Folder actions can automatically do all of the following and more:

✦ Create, move, duplicate, and delete files and folders

✦ Unmount disks (except the startup disk) and mount unmounted disks

✦ Set control panel options

✦ Connect to other computers on your local network or to the Internet

✦ Connect to Web sites on the Internet

✦ Transfer files to or from other computers on your local network or the Internet

   ✦ Send and receive e-mail

   ✦ Start other programs and use them to make changes to documents on
     your disk

To guard against your computer being controlled by another computer on your
network, folder-action scripts must be located on a disk connected directly to your
computer. The Folder Actions extension will not run a folder-action script unless it
is located on your startup disk or a hard disk connected to your computer. Neither
will it run scripts located on disks that can be removed (this excludes the startup
disk, because it cannot be ejected until you shut down). Even folders on removable
disks and network volumes must use folder actions from your startup disk or local
hard disks. In other words, a folder on a removable disk can't use folder actions
located on it.

Caution   To keep your computer secure and the information in it private, do not use any
folder-action scripts from unfamiliar sources. The danger in folder-action scripts is
that they are fairly easy to create, and an unscrupulous person could conceal side
effects ranging from mischievous to destructive. This doesn't mean that you
should fear all folder actions or not use scripts from people you don't know personally. After all, you would probably consider using other kinds of software created by reputable strangers. You wouldn't use system extensions or utility applications from sources you weren't sure of, and you should treat folder-action scripts
with the same caution.

Attaching folder actions

To attach a folder-action script to a folder or disk, choose Attach a Folder
Action from its contextual menu (Control+click the folder or disk icon to display
its contextual menu). A dialog box appears in which you select an AppleScript
script file to use as a folder action. A folder with an attached folder action has a
distinctive script badge on its icon. Figure 24-8 is an example of attaching a folder-
action script.

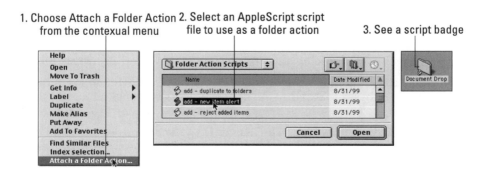

Figure 24-8: Attach an AppleScript script as a folder action.

What makes folder actions happen?

Folder actions can happen only under very particular circumstances. To trigger a folder action, a visible change must occur to a folder or disk's window or contents. For example, moving a file to a folder window would create a visible change, and could trigger a folder action. In contrast, moving a file to a closed folder would not create a visible change and would not trigger a folder action. You may not see a visible change happening in a folder window that is covered by an overlapping window. Likewise, you may not see a visible change taking place in a part of a folder window that is currently scrolled out of view.

At first glance, it may seem that a folder must simply be open—its window must be displayed—to trigger a folder action. This is not true. A folder can trigger folder actions if its contents are visible in another folder window being viewed as a list. In other words, folders that are expanded in a list view—that have their disclosure triangles pointing down—can trigger folder actions. Folders that are collapsed in a list view—that have their disclosure triangles pointing to the right—can't trigger folder actions.

A special application named Folder Actions is responsible for running all folder-action scripts. If Folder Actions is not in the Extensions folder during startup, no folder actions occur.

Scripts for folder actions can be located anywhere on your startup disk or other hard disk connected to your computer. The standard location is the Folder Action Scripts folder inside the Scripts folder in the System Folder.

Sample folder actions

Ten folder-action scripts come with Mac OS 9:

✦ **add - duplicate to folders** tries to copy added items to other folders. The other folders must have aliases whose names begin "~!" in the attached folder. The script labels items that were successfully copied by assigning them the penultimate label (initially named Project 1), and labels items that were not copied by assigning them the last label (initially named Project 2). Adding items to the attached folder triggers this script.

✦ **add - new item alert** advises that items have been added to the attached folder and offers to bring the folder window to the front so that you can see what was added. Adding items to the attached folder triggers this script.

✦ **add - reject added items** places added items in a Rejected Items folder on the desktop, advises that this happened, and offers to bring the Rejected Items folder to the front. Adding items to the attached folder triggers this script.

✦ **add - set view prefs to match** changes the view options of added folders to match the attached folder. Adding items to the attached folder triggers this script.

✦ **close - close sub-folders** closes the windows of open folders contained in the attached folder. Closing the attached folder's window triggers this script.

✦ **mount/unmount server aliases** has two actions. On opening the attached folder, the script asks whether you want to connect to each shared folder or disk that has an alias in the attached folder. On closing the attached folder, the script tries to unmount (put away) all shared folders and disks. Opening the attached folder or closing its window triggers this script.

✦ **move - align open sub-folders** staggers all open subfolder windows of the attached folder and resizes them to match it, so you can see all their title bars. Moving or resizing the attached folder triggers this script.

✦ **open - open items labeled 1** opens items in the attached folder that have the first label (initially named Essential). Opening the attached folder triggers this script.

✦ **open - show comments in dialog** displays a dialog box containing the comments for the attached folder and offers to clear the comments or open the folder's Info window. Opening the attached folder triggers this script.

✦ **remove - retrieve items** tries to return items that are moved out of the attached folder, and explains that items can't be removed from the folder. This script may fail to return items moved to closed folders. Removing items from the attached folder triggers this script.

You can use the scripts as-is or you can modify them to suit your needs. For example, most of the folder-action scripts that display advisory messages can be modified by changing one line of each script to not display messages. You modify the scripts using the Script Editor application. Modifying and creating folder actions are discussed later in this section.

Removing folder actions

You can remove folder-action scripts from a folder or disk using the folder or disk's contextual menu. Control+click the folder or disk to display its contextual menu and choose the script you want to remove from the Remove a Folder Action submenu.

Creating a folder action script

You can easily modify the drag-and-drop script application you created in the section "Creating a Drag-and-Drop Script Application" so that it becomes a folder-action script. Once you attach the script to a specific folder, you can simply drag items to the open folder (or the folder expanded in a list view), and the items are routed automatically to the appropriate locations.

Instead of beginning the script with an On Open command, use an On Adding Folder Items To command, as follows:

```
on adding folder items to this_folder after receiving
added_items
```

In this line, the variable this_folder will contain the path of the folder that is associated with the script. The variable added_items serves the same function as itemList in the drag-and-drop application script—it will contain the list of items that were dragged to the folder.

You need to balance the new first line of the script by replacing the End Open command at the end of the script with this line:

```
end adding folder items to
```

After the On Adding Folder Items To command, the script needs to tell the Finder to determine how many items were dragged to the folder. The script must activate the Finder to get this information from it. Place these two lines after the On Adding Folder Items To command:

```
tell application "Finder"
activate
```

Next add the following line, which saves the number of items that were dragged to the folder in the variable item_count:

```
set the itemCount to the number of items in the added_items
```

You can now start a repeat loop as before, but you must modify it to read as follows:

```
repeat with x from 1 to itemCount
copy item x of added_items to filePath
```

Now delete the Tell Application "Finder" command that follows the Repeat command and move the End Tell command after the End Repeat command. The final script is shown in Figure 24-9.

Figure 24-9: A folder-action script to route files of particular types to specific folders

Save the script as a compiled script (not as a script applet). To attach your script to a specific folder, simply Control+click the folder to display its contextual menu, and choose Attach a Folder Action from it. In the standard Open dialog box that appears, select the script you saved. After you have attached the folder action script to a folder, a distinctive badge appears on the folder's icon. Remember that the folder must be open (or expanded in a list view of an enclosing folder) for the attached folder action script to run.

To learn more about creating folder action scripts, study the sample folder-action scripts supplied with Mac OS 9. They are located in the Folder Action Scripts folder within the Scripts folder in the System Folder. Also check out the AppleScript Help that comes with Mac OS 9 by choosing Help Center from the Help menu and clicking AppleScript Help in the Help Center window.

Using AppleScript with Applications

The Finder is only one application that you can use with AppleScript; more and more vendors are including AppleScript capability in their applications. This section provides several examples of scripts that use some popular scriptable programs. These scripts are reasonably small, so you can type them quickly. The scripts also provide an idea of other things that AppleScript can do.

Disk Copy and a Web browser

Many people find that a Web browser performs better if its cache is on a RAM disk. But if you use the Memory control panel to create the RAM disk, it's always there using up memory even if you're not browsing the Web. One solution is to use the Disk Copy utility to create a RAM disk.

Disk Copy can create a file that contains an image of the browser's cache disk. You can mount the disk image file with *RAM caching* activated, which places its entire contents in RAM, just like a RAM disk. Later, you can put away the disk image whenever you want (once you've closed the Web browser), freeing the memory it used.

You can create a small script to mount the RAM disk and launch your Web browser application. You would open this script application in lieu of opening the browser directly. For quick access to this script application, you could name it "Browse the Internet RDC" (where RDC stands for "RAM disk cache") and put it or an alias of it on the desktop or in your Apple menu. Figure 24-10 shows the script.

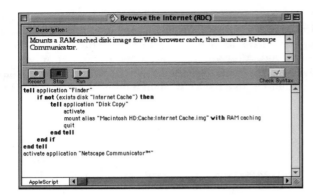

Figure 24-10: A script application that mounts a RAM-cached disk image that is used for a browser cache and then activates the browser

Before creating the script application, you must open Disk Copy and create the Internet Cache disk image file, or you won't be able to save the script application successfully. Before running the script application for the first time, you must mount the disk image, open your Web browser, and change the location of its cache to the mounted disk image. If you open the Web browser directly without first mounting the disk image, the browser resets the cache to its default location, and you have to set it back to the mounted disk image again.

Note   This script seems to work better with Netscape's browsers than with Microsoft Internet Explorer 4.5. You can experiment with Internet Explorer, but don't be surprised if it doesn't move cache files to the disk image, even if you've set its preferences to do just that.

When you type the script from Figure 24-10 in a Script Editor window, be sure you replace "Internet Cache" with the actual name of your RAM disk, and replace "Macintosh HD:Cache::Internet Cache.img" with the path to your Disk Copy disk image file. Also, put the exact name of your browser in the last statement of the script.

Another short script application can automate the process of quitting the Web browser and putting away the mounted cache disk. The same script can also disconnect a dial-up Internet connection. For easy access to this script application, you could name it "Quit Browsing the Internet RDC" and put it, or an alias of it, in the Apple menu. Figure 24-11 shows this script.

When you type the script from Figure 24-11 in a Script Editor window, be sure you replace "Internet Cache" with the actual name of your mounted cache disk. Also, put the exact name of your browser in the first line of the script.

So far these scripts are pretty good, but they don't account for the possibility of quitting the Web browser without using the Quit Browsing the Internet RDC script. If you simply select the Quit command in the browser, the RAM disk will stay mounted, taking up valuable RAM.

Figure 24-11: A script application that quits a Web browser, puts away the RAM-cached disk image that is used for its cache, and disconnects the dial-up Internet connection

There is a way to write the original Browse the Internet RDC script so that it automatically puts away the RAM disk when you quit the browser. What you do is add some script commands that periodically check to see whether the browser is still open and put away the RAM disk if it's not. To make the AppleScript application stay open in the background so that it can monitor the browser's status, you must turn on the Stay Open option when you save it. Figure 24-12 is an example of this script with Netscape Communicator as the browser.

 Tip   Note the use of comment in the script example in Figure 24-12. You can add comments at the end of a statement by placing two dashes (--) before the comment. The Script Editor will then format the comment in italics when you check the script's syntax. These comments are for your use only—they are ignored by AppleScript.

Figure 24-12: The last 11 lines of this stay-open script application put away the RAM disk that is used for a Web browser's cache after you quit the browser.

This script could also include a command that disconnects your PPP connection after you quit the browser. For example, inserting the PPP Disconnect command before the Put Away command would disconnect an Open Transport PPP connection before putting away the RAM disk.

Note If you've already checked the syntax of the original script, you can copy and paste the exact name of your Web browser from the "activate application" command to the "if" statement in the second part of the script so that the proper application name is found in the processes list.

Outlook Express

With AppleScript, you can add to the capabilities of Microsoft Outlook Express. Outlook Express 4.5 is installed by default by the Mac OS 9 installer. It's also available for free from Microsoft's Web site and may have been updated by the time you read this (http://www.microsoft.com/ie/mac/oe/).

Outlook Express 4.5 (and higher) is both scriptable and attachable. This means that you can execute AppleScript scripts directly from the application itself—you don't have to switch to Script Editor or choose script applications from your Apple menu. Outlook Express has an AppleScript menu that lists compiled scripts (not script applications) that you can add to the Script Menu Items folder in the Outlook Express folder. The AppleScript menu in Outlook Express is very handy for small utility scripts that augment the e-mail application's capabilities.

Although Outlook Express comes with scripts for tasks such as changing the color of message headings in mailboxes, inserting text files in messages, and saving selected text of a message, there are also many other freely available scripts that you can get from the Internet. For example, there are scripts to have Outlook Express read your e-mail messages aloud to you using the Mac OS text-to-speech software (see Chapter 23), forward messages as attachments, count words in messages, and delete old sent messages. The AppleScript Archive on the "Unofficial" Microsoft Outlook Express Web site (http://www.macemail.com/oe/pages/applescript.shtml) is an excellent source for scripts for Outlook Express.

For example, one script that you can download augments Outlook Express' capability to check e-mail. While the command to send and receive e-mail is built into Outlook Express, it relies on other software, such as Open Transport PPP (via the Remote Access control panel), to open and close dial-up Internet connections. You can automate your Internet e-mail with a script. First, the script dials through Open Transport PPP. Then the script accesses your mail through Outlook Express. Finally, the script hangs up through Open Transport PPP.

Linking Programs

You have seen how AppleScript can automate tasks on your own machine. You can also send Apple events to open applications on other machines in a network. As a result, you can use AppleScript to control applications on other people's machines. Sharing programs by sending and receiving Apple events across a network is called *program linking*.

Program linking adds tremendous potential to AppleScript. If you are in charge of a network, you can use AppleScript to perform network installations or backups. If you have a script that uses many applications, you can speed up the script by sending a command to a remote application and retrieving the data later. You send only a blip across the network; the remote application does the work while other parts of your script are running, and you get the results later. In addition, this capability can help you get around memory problems that might otherwise arise from opening several applications using a script.

Setting up program linking

Program linking can be controlled much like file sharing. You can turn program linking on and off, can control who on the network is allowed access to your programs, and can deny access to specific programs.

Starting and stopping program linking

If you want to allow other network users to link to programs on your computer, you must activate program linking. To do this, click the Start button in the Program Linking section of the File Sharing control panel. Your computer is ready for program linking when the button's label changes to Stop and the File Sharing control panel reports "Program Linking on." Figure 24-13 shows how the File Sharing control panel looks when program linking is turned on.

> **Note**
>
> Program Linking also has an option in Mac OS 9 that enables program linking to work over a TCP/IP network, including the Internet. Turn on the option Enable Program Linking clients to connect over TCP/IP to enable program linking, including AppleScript access, over a TCP/IP network.

To turn off program linking, click Stop in the Program Linking section of the File Sharing control panel. Clicking Stop prevents all programs on the computer from receiving Apple events from any other computer on the network.

> **Note**
>
> It's possible to use program linking between different Mac OS versions (with varying degrees of success). If you plan to enable program linking on a Mac running Mac OS 7.6-7.6.1, you'll find the command in the Sharing Setup control panel. In Mac OS 8-9, it's in the File Sharing control panel.

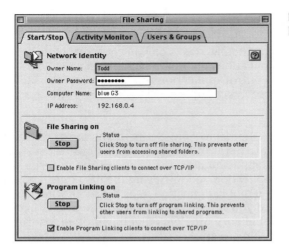

Figure 24-13: Program linking is turned on.

Authorizing access to shared programs

You control which network users can link to programs on your computer with the Users & Groups tab in the File Sharing control panel. To enable everyone on the network to link to your programs, open the Guest icon in Users & Groups, choose Sharing from the Show pop-up menu, and turn on the Allow guests to link to programs on this computer option. To prevent unidentified network users from linking to your programs, turn off this option. Figure 24-14 shows the guest window.

Figure 24-14: Setting guests' program-linking privileges

If you don't give guests program-linking privileges, you need to designate which registered users in your Users & Groups can link to your programs. To enable a registered user to link to your programs, open that user's icon on the Users & Groups tab of the File Sharing control panel. In the user's window, turn on the Allow user to link to programs on this computer option. (For information on registering users, see "Identifying Who Can Access Your Shared Items" in Chapter 22.) Figure 24-15 shows a user window.

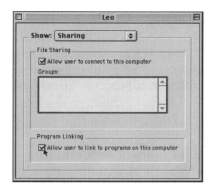

Figure 24-15: Setting a registered user's program-linking privilege

You can block any registered user from linking to your programs by turning off that user's Allow user to link to programs on this computer option.

Denying access to specific programs

Even though you may enable certain network users to link to your programs, you may want to specifically deny access to a particular application. You control program linking for each application in its sharing window, which appears when you select the program in Finder and choose Sharing from the Get Info submenu of the File menu. Figure 24-16 is an example of a program's sharing window.

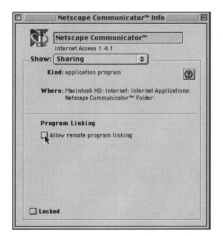

Figure 24-16: Preventing other users from sharing a specific program

To prevent an application from receiving Apple events sent by another computer, turn off the "Allow remote program linking option" in its sharing window and then close the window. If the option is dimmed, the program is open; you must quit a program before changing its program-linking option.

Scripting across a network

Using AppleScript to run a program across the network doesn't take much more work than writing a script to use a program on the same computer. Start program linking on a networked computer. Now go to another computer on the network. Open the Script Editor and type this command:

```
choose application
```

This command brings up a dialog box in which you select an application on your computer or on the network. On the left side of this dialog box, select the computer you set up (you may need to select a zone if your network has zones and the computer is in a different zone). The applications that are running on the selected computer are displayed on the right side of the dialog box. One application is the Finder. Select it and click OK. Figure 24-17 shows the dialog box with a computer and its Finder application selected.

Note

If you need to access the remote computer over TCP/IP (for instance, over the Internet), turn on the small IP option next to the Cancel button. This changes the dialog box so that you can enter an IP address and click the Get Applications button to list applications on that remote computer. The remote computer must be running Mac OS 9 and have the "Enable Program Linking clients to connect over TCP/IP option" turned on in its File Sharing control panel.

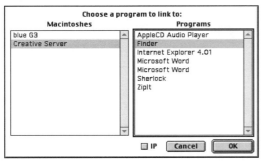

Figure 24-17: Choosing a program to link to

Open the result window in Script Editor, if it's not open already. You see that the result of this short script is the network path of the application you selected: the name of the application, the name of the computer, and the name of the zone (if your network has more than one zone).

Enter the following line below the first one and then run the script, selecting the same application on the same computer:

```
copy the result to netpath
```

This script places the path to the application in a variable named netpath. To send Apple events to this application, enter the next two lines in the script:

```
tell netpath
end tell
```

This Tell command specifies the name of the application using the netpath variable instead of using the word "application" and the literal name of the application. The effect is the same: AppleScript starts sending Apple events to the application, which in this case happens to be on a different computer.

Enter these command lines between the Tell and the End Tell command lines:

```
activate
beep
say "Your computer is under my control. Resistance is futile."
set windowList to windows whose closeable is true
set nbrWindows to count of windowList
if nbrWindows > 0 then
set openItemsList to item of every window whose closeable is
true
say "I will now close all your windows."
repeat with aWindow in windowList
close aWindow
end repeat
say "I will now open them again."
if nbrWindows > 1 then open reverse of openItemsList
if nbrWindows = 1 then open openItemsList
end if
get count of every item of font
set fontCount to count of items in font
set half to round (fontCount / 2)
open font
say "You have " & fontCount & ù
" fonts. That is too many. Get rid of " & half & ù
", or I will call the font [[emph -]] police."
say "I now return control to [[emph +]] you. Have a nice day!"
```

The Say command causes an error if the target computer does not have a scripting addition to handle it. If the target computer has Mac OS 8.5–9, the Standard Additions file handles the Say command. If the target computer has Mac OS 7.6–8.1, it must have the Say scripting additions file in its Scripting Additions folder (either the one in the System Folder or the one in the Extensions folder). The Say scripting addition is available free from Apple's Speech Technology site on the Web at http://www.apple.com/macos/speech.

To make matters worse, the scripting addition for the Say command that comes with Mac OS 8.5–9 is not compatible with the Say scripting addition that you get separately for Mac OS 7.6–8.1. If the target computer does not have the same scripting addition for the Say command as your computer — because your computer has Mac OS 9 and the other computer has an earlier Mac OS version — then the Say command will not work. If the Say command does not work for any reason, the script abruptly stops working with an error alert on your computer.

There is a way to work around the incompatibility between the two versions of the scripting addition for the Say command. If you know the target computer has Mac OS 7.6–8.1 and your computer has Mac OS 9, you can replace the Say command with «event aevtSay» (you type the symbols surrounding this text by pressing Option+\ and Option+Shift+\). This is the Apple-event code for the Say command as implemented by the Say scripting addition. These shenanigans with the Say command illustrate how knotty AppleScript problems can get. As your scripts get more complex, you can expect to spend more time carefully testing them and fixing bugs. Scripts take time to develop, but if you use them frequently, the effort pays off.

If you can't install the Say scripting additions file or Mac OS 8.5 (or higher) on the target computer, you can make the script work by removing the Say commands from it. (It just won't be as much fun.) You cannot replace the Say commands with Display Dialog commands because AppleScript does not allow Display Dialog commands to be sent to a linked computer.

When you run the script, it displays a dialog box in which you select the Finder that is running on another computer. Before the script can send Apple events to that Finder, however, the script must connect your computer to the other computer. To do this, the script displays a connection dialog box like the ones you use to connect to other computers for file sharing, as shown in Figure 24-18.

Figure 24-18: Linking to another machine as a registered user

In the connection dialog box, you specify whether you want to connect as a guest (if the other computer allows guests) or as a registered user. To connect as a registered user, enter your name and password as they were set up in the other computer's Users & Groups screen or control panel. If you connect successfully, the script runs.

Before going over to the other computer to check the results, try running the script again. This time, you don't have to go through the logon process. Once you connect to another application, you don't have to go through the connection dialog each time you want to send an Apple event. You have to reenter your password if someone quits the application you're linked to or turns off program linking on the target computer.

Now go to the other computer and look at the Finder. You should see the Fonts folder opened, as your script directed.

That's all the work you have to do if you want to script a remote application. You don't have to use the Choose Application command, either. You can simply write the network path of the application, as in this example:

```
tell application "Finder" of machine "Creative Server"
...
end tell
```

For a TCP/IP connection, you can substitute an IP address for the machine name, as in

```
tell application "Finder" of machine "eppc://192.168.0.3"
```

or you can use a domain name, as in

```
tell application "Finder" of machine "eppc://mac1.mac-
upgrade.com/"
```

Note

The eppc:// represents Apple's protocol for program-to-program communications over the Internet.

Program linking offers many possibilities for scripters. For example, you could use a script to create a large catalog by farming out different sections of that catalog to several networked computers. Each machine could work on its section and the script could pick up the resulting file via file sharing from the computers as they finish their individual sections. As another example, a network administrator could backup crucial documents from computers across the network to a central tape drive and then shutdown the individual computers.

Working around program-linking barriers

One of the biggest problems with using Apple events over a network is that some applications do not accept Apple events that come from a remote computer. There is a way around this problem, however. Script applications — that is, scripts that you save as applications from the Script Editor — accept Apple events from across a network. When a script application runs a script, the application acts as if the script is on the local computer. If you're trying to control a remote application that does not allow networked Apple events, you can send a message to a script application on the remote computer. The script application, in turn, executes a script to control other applications on the same computer.

To see how this process works, create this simple script application on a networked computer:

```
on netMessage()
tell application "Finder"
open about this computer
end tell
end netMessage
```

This script has a handler for netMessage, just as the earlier drag-and-drop script had a handler for open. This netMessage handler tells the Finder to display the About this Computer window. This script has no problem sending Apple events to the Finder on the same computer because no network is involved.

When you save this script as a script application, be sure to turn on the Stay Open option in the Save dialog box. With this option checked, the script stays open once you open it, rather than quitting after the script runs.

Open the script application and go to another networked computer that has AppleScript installed. On that computer, write this script:

```
choose application
copy the result to netPath
tell netPath to netMessage()
```

Run the script, and use the dialog box to select the name of the script application that you left open on the other computer. The script gets the result and tells the script application to "netMessage." The script application on the other computer receives this message and runs the commands in the netMessage handler, showing the About this Computer window on that computer.

Summary

In this chapter, you learned how applications can communicate by sending each other messages called Apple events. When an application receives an Apple event, it performs a task specified by the event. You can use the Apple-event mechanism to automate tasks involving one or more applications. You do this with AppleScript scripts. AppleScript is a programming language designed with everyday users in mind, but with enough power for advanced users and programmers.

You learned how to create scripts with the Script Editor application. An easy way to create scripts for some applications is to have AppleScript record your actions as a script. You then save the recorded script and run it again to repeat the same actions.

You also learned that a recorded script has limited value. To take full advantage of AppleScript, use the Script Editor or another script-editing program to create scripts from scratch. You type AppleScript statements into a new Script Editor window, check the syntax for errors, and run the script to test it. Your script might use conditional statements to perform some operations only when the specified conditions are met. Repeat loops execute a group of statements over and over. When you're done, you can save the script as a script application and you can attach it to a folder to define a folder action.

This chapter described several examples of how to use scripts to control applications other than the Finder. A script can mount a disk image in RAM and then open the Web browser that uses the disk image for its cache. Another script can dial-up a PPP connection to the Internet and then send and receive e-mail with Outlook Express.

Finally, this chapter showed how AppleScript can control applications over a network or the Internet on computers that have program linking set up and turned on. You turn on program linking with a computer's File Sharing or Sharing Setup control panel. You use Users & Groups to designate which users can link to programs on your computer. And you use Finder's Sharing command to designate which programs other computers can link to. Once your computer is connected to another computer for program linking, you can use AppleScript to control applications on the other computer.

✦   ✦   ✦

Making the Most of the Mac OS

Put Accessory Programs to Work

Apple has always included accessory programs with the Mac OS. Accessory programs enhance the features and capabilities of the Mac OS. Each accessory is a small, focused program that provides a narrowly defined set of features and capabilities. Some are indispensable, such as the Chooser, which you use to set up or select a printer and to access files over a network. Others are more diversionary, such as the Apple DVD Player or the AppleCD Audio Player, which plays music CDs. Some you will use all the time, such as Sherlock 2, which quickly search your disks for items that you can't find by browsing. Others you hardly ever use, but will be mighty glad to have when you need them, such as Disk First Aid.

Introducing Accessory Programs

In the old days, accessory programs were all desk accessories and you could open them only from the Apple menu. These days some accessories are application programs and others are desk accessories, and very little differentiates them. You can put both kinds of programs in folders, on the desktop, or in the Apple menu. Each desk accessory can have its own unique icon, although some use the generic desk accessory icon, which looks like a backward generic application icon.

You move and copy desk accessories by dragging their icons in the Finder, just as you would with an application. If you want to install a desk accessory in the Apple menu, simply drag it to the System Folder icon. The Finder recognizes desk accessories and puts them in the Apple Menu Items folder. For historical reasons, desk accessories can also exist in suitcase files, like fonts.

You can open a desk accessory in much the same way that you can open an application program. For example, you can open a desk accessory by double-clicking it or by choosing it from the Apple menu. But unlike an application program, you can't open a desk accessory by opening one of its documents because desk accessories don't create documents in the traditional way. (Some of them, like Note Pad and Stickies, have a single document that's stored in the System Folder. The typical desk accessory doesn't have an Open or Save command, however.) Thus, you can't open a desk accessory by double-clicking a document or by dragging a document to the desk accessory icon.

Another difference between most desk accessories and applications is the way you quit them. Like application programs, desk accessories have a Quit command in the File menu. In addition, most desk accessories quit automatically when you close their windows.

Accessory Program Encyclopedia

Each accessory program has a unique set of features and capabilities that enhance the Mac OS. This section describes the features and capabilities of the accessory programs that come with the Mac OS. The accessory programs are discussed here in alphabetical order.

As you go through this section, note that most accessory programs have detailed descriptions but a few have only brief descriptions. Accessory programs that are covered in depth elsewhere in this book have brief descriptions here that refer you to another chapter for details. The detailed descriptions here, which tell how to use the programs, are for accessory programs that are not covered elsewhere in this book.

Apple Applet Runner

Java is a programming language that has received a lot of attention because Java makes it easy to create small applications, called applets, that can be automatically received by your browser from a Web page, and that extend the functionality of the page. For example, if you have a Java-enabled browser (such as Netscape Navigator, Netscape Communicator, and Microsoft Internet Explorer) you could go to a stock page and have continually updated stock quotes scroll in ticker-tape fashion across your screen. Netscape provides its own implementation of Java along with its browsers. Microsoft Internet Explorer uses Apple's Macintosh Runtime for Java (MRJ) instead of its own version of Java.

Okay, so being able to run applets inside Web pages is a nice feature, but other than that, how important is Java? For the near term, not very. Yes, there are some applications that are available for Java, and those applications often can run on the Macintosh. So far, few of them are full-featured enough to be worth switching to. A move toward more applications on the Web is also promising — one day we may access applications (word processing, spreadsheets) over the Web in much the same way that you can access a calendar, Web e-mail, and other features through popular "portal" Web pages. For now, though, Java is still a developing technology.

Sun Microsystems, the company that invented Java, is still inventing it, and as the language changes, it is moving away from its original selling point to software developers, which was that it was completely cross-platform. Cross-platform meant that a programmer using Java theoretically could write a program once, then run it on Macs, Windows machines, or UNIX systems. But as Sun has released new versions of Java that are incompatible with previous versions, and Microsoft has created other incompatible Java versions, that dream seems to be fading. In the meantime, Apple has committed to supporting Java in its system software, both on Mac OS 9 and in Mac OS X.

Different versions of MRJ support different aspects of Sun's Java language. MRJ 2.1.4 supports all of the features of Sun's Java 1.1.7, which enables developers to create applets that look very much like Macintosh applications. The supported features of Java 1.1.7 include security and signed applets, JavaBeans component software, the JAR file format, Math Package, Remote Method Invocation, and other Java specifications. (For a complete list, consult http://www.apple.com/java/ on the Web.) MRJ greatly increases the speed of Java applets on the Mac OS, as well as being certified by Oracle Corporation to run its Oracle Developer 1.6.1 tools. The latest Java releases support AppleScript and QuickTime for Java, as well.

If you want to try some Java applets, you can do it with the Apple Applet Runner, a program that lets you run Java applets outside of a browser. You'll find the Apple Applet Runner and a folder of sample applets inside the Mac OS Runtime for Java folder. If you don't find the Applet Runner, you may need to perform a custom installation of Mac OS Runtime for Java from your Mac OS 9 CD-ROM.

Note   At the time of writing it wasn't clear whether the Applet Runner would be included on the Mac OS CD-ROM. If the Applet Runner isn't installed when you install the Mac OS or custom install Macintosh Runtime for Java, you can get it by downloading the latest full release of Macintosh Runtime for Java from Apple's Web site at http://www.apple.com/java/.

Once you've found the Applet Runner, just double-click its icon to open it, and then choose one or more of the sample applets from the Applets menu. Figure 25-1 shows some sample Java applets in the Apple Applet Runner.

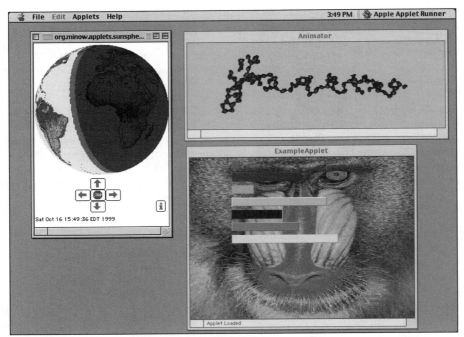

Figure 25-1: Run Java applets with the Apple Applet Runner.

Note

Despite the similar names and the fact that they're both associated with Web browsers, Java and JavaScript are almost completely unrelated. JavaScript is a scripting language developed by Netscape to help Web page developers automate the Netscape Navigator browser. JavaScript was originally called LiveScript, but when Java became "The Next Big Thing," Netscape changed LiveScript's name to try to ride Java's marketing coattails.

AppleCD Audio Player

The AppleCD Audio Player application plays audio CDs in your CD-ROM drive. You can play, pause, stop, skip back, skip forward, scan back, and scan forward by clicking the buttons on the right side of the control panel. What's more, you can program a custom play list for every CD, and Audio Player remembers each play list you create. You can also enter CD and track titles, which Audio Player remembers as well. Figure 25-2 shows the AppleCD Audio Player program.

Cross-
Reference

See Chapter 18 for more details on using this accessory.

Figure 25-2: The AppleCD Audio Player program plays audio CDs in your CD-ROM drive.

Apple DVD Player

The Apple DVD player applications enable you to play DVD movies on Macintosh models equipped with a DVD-ROM drive and the proper decoding hardware. (This includes all Power Macintosh, iMac DV, and PowerBook models that have shipped with DVD-ROM drives. The program will also work with some third-party DVD-ROM drives that include decoding hardware.) Using the DVD Player's Controller, you can access most of the features of modern DVD movie discs, including subtitles, additional languages, alternative camera angles, and more. Figure 25-3 shows the Apple DVD Player Controller.

Cross-Reference   See Chapter 18 for more details.

Figure 25-3: The Apple DVD Player plays DVD movies on many Mac models.

Apple File Security

Located in the Applications menu in the Security folder, Apple File Security enables you to encrypt and decrypt files as a way to password protect them and compress their contents at the same time. You can drag-and-drop files on the Apple File Security icon to encrypt or decrypt them (according to their current state), or you can double-click Apple File Security to locate files to encrypt or decrypt using the Open dialog box. Once encrypted, a file can't be read without a password or passphrase.

Apple System Profiler

If you ever need to call Apple for technical support for your computer, you may be asked all kinds of questions you don't know the answer to. What's your processor type? Exactly which version of the system are you running? Which SCSI bus is your startup drive on? And so on.

The Apple System Profiler answers these questions and more. Just by running this program, you can discover the details of your computer's setup in several categories. Version 2.4.2 comes with Mac OS 9. Figure 25-4 shows some of the System Profile category.

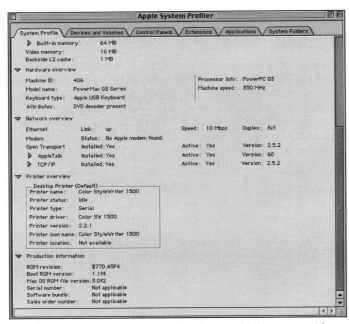

Figure 25-4: Apple System Profiler 2.4.2, which comes with Mac OS 9, tells you more than you ever wanted to know about your hardware and software.

To see another category of system information, click its tab in the application window or choose the category from the Commands menu. Note that subcategories have disclosure triangles next to them that enable you to hide or show their information.

You can choose from among these categories:

✦ The **System Profile** category provides details about your system's software, memory, hardware, network, printer, and production information. This category has six subcategories, which you can show or hide by clicking the disclosure triangle next to the subcategory name in the application window. The six subcategories are:

- The **Software overview** subcategory provides information about the Mac OS running on your computer: the version of the Finder and System, whether an enabler is active, whether Multiple Users is installed, which version of QuickTime is installed, and whether file sharing is on or off. The software overview also profiles your startup device, listing name, type of device, device (ATA or SCSI) ID number, and the type of bus (ATA or SCSI) and SCSI bus number, if applicable.

- The **Memory overview** subcategory provides details about disk cache, virtual memory, built-in memory, and external caches.

- The **Hardware overview** subcategory identifies the machine ID, model name, keyboard type, processor type, machine speed, and FPU type, if applicable.

- The **Network overview** subcategory displays details about networking options that are installed and active, the modem's status, and what versions of Open Transport, AppleTalk, and TCP/IP are in use. Under AppleTalk you can find out about file sharing, AppleTalk zones, active network ports, what network this computer is part of, what its node number and hardware address are, and what router it uses. For TCP/IP, you can determine whether personal Web sharing and multihoming are on or off and get information about the broadcast, netmask, IP address, default gateway address, domain, and name server address.

- The **Printer overview** subcategory displays information about each desktop printer's name, driver, version, icon name, and location.

- The **Production information** subcategory tells you which ROM revision the computer is using.

✦ The **Devices and Volumes** category provides a hierarchical chart of information about all the devices connected to your computer. The highest level of the hierarchy is the type of device: SCSI bus, PCI slot, floppy drive, network, USB, Firewire, ATA bus, and so on. As you read across you see more detailed information about each type of device. For example, for SCSI devices, a list of all devices attached to the SCSI bus in order by SCSI ID number displays. For each device, you can see what type of device it is, what driver it's using and the vendor, revision number, product ID, and serial number. For a removable-media drive, you can see whether a disk is currently inserted. For a storage device, you can see information about all the volumes on it; for each volume, you can check the format, size, space available, percent full, and whether the volume is write protected or file sharing is on. You determine the level of detail displayed by clicking disclosure triangles that hide or reveal more details about each device.

✦ The **Control Panels** category lists all of the control panels currently in the System Folders of your choice, displaying the name, version, and file size of each control panel. This feature also tells you whether a control panel is from Apple and whether it's enabled. Selecting a control panel brings up more information, such as where the control panel is located and its creation and modification dates. Some control panels also display a brief description of their functions when selected.

✦ The **Extensions** category lists all of the extensions currently in the System Folders of your choice, displaying the name, version, and file size of each extension. This feature also tells you whether an extension is from Apple and whether it's enabled. Selecting an extension from the list brings up more information, such as where the extension is located and its creation and modification dates. Some extensions also display a brief description of their functions when selected.

✦ The **Applications** category lists all of the application programs on your disks. This feature displays the name, version number, memory size, file size, and whether it's an Apple application. Selecting an application from the list brings up information about where the application is located and its creation and modification dates. Some applications also display a brief description of their functions when selected.

✦ The **System Folders** category displays a list of system folders on the startup disk (and any other selected volume) on your computer.

Each time you open System Profiler, it gathers information for the System Profile category. You can also set up System Profiler to gather information for any other category at the same time. To do this, choose Preferences from the Edit menu and then select the categories you want.

You can also create reports of System Profiler information by choosing New Report from the File menu. A dialog box in which you select the categories of information you want in the report appears. Reports can be in Apple System Profiler format or in text format. You select the report format at the top of the report window. In addition, you can set a standard report format with the Preferences command.

The Commands menu enables you to update a system profile at any time. For the Control Panels, Extensions, Applications, and System Folders sections of the Apple System Profiler, you determine which volumes the Apple System Profiler searches by choosing Search Options in the Commands menu and then selecting the volumes you want in the dialog box that appears.

Apple Verifier

The Apple Verifier is a drag-and-drop program in the Security folder (inside the Applications folder) that enables verification of the digital signature attached to applications and other files. If you have a digitally signed file, drag it to the Apple Verifier to test its authenticity.

Apple Video Player

The Apple Video Player application plays video and audio from a VCR, camcorder, or other video equipment on a computer with video inputs. The application can also display TV shows on a computer with a TV tuner installed. In addition, the Video Player can capture the video and save it in a movie file on disk. Figure 25-5 shows the Apple Video Player's main window and its Controls window.

 Cross-Reference For detailed information, see Chapter 18.

Figure 25-5: The Apple Video Player plays and captures TV and video on a computer with video inputs.

Calculator

The Calculator desk accessory adds, subtracts, multiplies, and divides numbers that you enter. You can type numbers and operation symbols, or click the keys in the desk accessory. In addition, you can copy the text of a calculation — for example, 69.95+26.98+14.99*.0725 — and paste it in the Calculator. Figure 25-6 shows the Calculator desk accessory.

 **Figure 25-6:** The Calculator desk accessory does simple arithmetic.

The Chooser

The Chooser desk accessory enables you to select a printer or other output device and to create desktop printer icons, as described in Chapter 16. You also use the Chooser to connect to shared folders and disks from other computers on the same network as your computer. Figure 25-7 shows the Chooser desk accessory.

Cross-Reference For more information, see Chapter 16.

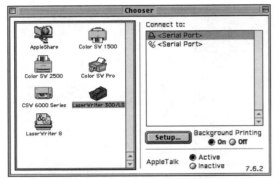

Figure 25-7: The Chooser desk accessory lets you select a printer and connect to shared folders and disks.

Desktop Printer Utility

Desktop printing enables you to print a file by dragging its icon directly to the desktop printer icon on your desktop. With this method of printing, you don't need to open the document or the application that created it, and you don't need to go through the Chooser to select a new printer if its icon is already on your desktop.

The Desktop Printer Utility, which is part of the standard installation of Mac OS 9, is an application for making desktop printer icons for PostScript printers. You'll find it in the Apple LaserWriter Software folder inside the Apple Extras Folder. The Desktop Printer Utility works with printers using the LaserWriter 8 driver, as well as AdobePS driver version 8.5.1 or higher. The Desktop Printer Utility creates desktop icons that let you choose a connected printer and print to it immediately. In addition, this utility creates desktop icons for printing to PostScript files, for holding files to print at a later time, for sending files over the Internet for printing, and for translating files into PostScript for printing by specific applications. Figure 25-8 shows the Desktop Printer Utility.

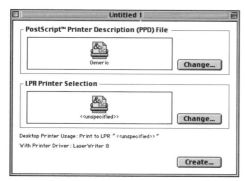

Figure 25-8: The Desktop Printer Utility
creates desktop printers for PostScript printers.

Cross-
Reference

For a full description of the Desktop Printer Utility, see Chapter 16.

DigitalColor Meter

If you work with color images, you may need to know precisely what color is
displayed at a point on the monitor. The DigitalColor Meter application measures and
records the RGB values of colors on your monitor. If you have an Apple ColorSync or
AppleVision monitor, DigitalColor Meter translates displayed colors to an industry-
standard color standard such as Pantone and CIE. DigitalColor Meter may be in your
Apple menu. If not, look for it in the Monitors Extras Folder, which is inside the Apple
Extras folder.

Opening DigitalColor Meter brings up a window that displays a magnified view of
the area around the mouse pointer, together with information about the color value
at or near the mouse pointer. Figure 25-9 is an example of DigitalColor Meter
displaying RGB values.

Figure 25-9: DigitalColor Meter measures
the color at or near the mouse pointer.

The Aperture Size slider lets you adjust the size of the area under scrutiny. At the smallest aperture setting, DigitalColor Meter measures the single pixel lying directly beneath the pointer. At larger aperture settings, DigitalColor Meter determines the average color of the pixels inside the aperture.

You can hold a sample of the color you're pointing to — so that you don't lose the color as you move the pointer — by pressing ⌘+H. While a color is on hold, you can see its value in any of the available color standards by selecting the color standard in the DigitalColor Meter window. If you select the RGB standard, the Meter menu lets you choose whether DigitalColor Meter displays the color measurement as percentages of red, green, and blue; as values between 0 and 65535 for red, green, and blue; or as Hex values between 00 and FF for red, green, and blue. The Hex measurement is useful for specifying a color in the HTML code of a Web page. The other values are useful for specifying a color in a graphics or publishing application. If your graphics program expects RGB values between 0 and 255, convert DigitalColor Meter's higher values by dividing each value by 256 and rounding up to the nearest whole number.

An easy way to enter the DigitalColor Meter's measurement into another program is with the Copy and Paste commands. While pointing at a color in DigitalColor Meter, press ⌘+C to copy the color measurement to the Clipboard. (You can't use the Copy command in the Edit menu since you'd have to move the mouse pointer to the menu!) Then switch to your other program and enter the color values there by choosing Paste from the Edit menu or pressing ⌘+V.

Disk Copy

Disk Copy is a program that enables you to create and mount *disk images* on your Mac's desktop. A disk image is simply a file that, when mounted, acts as if it were a floppy disk (or a similar removable disk). There are two different kinds of floppy disk images — self-mounting images (.smi) and regular disk images (.img). A self-mounting image mounts on any Macintosh when double-clicked. With regular image files, the Disk Copy software needs to be on your Mac, then you can double-click a disk image to mount it. Both types of images are stored as compressed archives, which makes them smaller for transport over the Internet or other networks. Figure 25-10 shows a mounted disk image.

Figure 25-10: A disk image, once double-clicked, becomes a mounted disk.

You can create your own image files with Disk Copy. Launch Disk Copy and drag a folder or disk icon to the Disk Copy window. (You can make disk images of entire disks that include CDs, Zip disks, and others.) The Save Disk Image As dialog box appears. Give the disk image a name and choose the folder where you'd like it saved. (You may want it saved on the desktop.)

You can also choose from a number of options in the dialog box, including whether the image will be Read Only or Read and Write and whether the image should be mounted once it's created. You can also choose the size of the image from a fixed size, such as 1.4MB or 500MB, or you can choose the Data Size option, where the size varies with the data you're creating an image of. (Images can be larger than the files you're originally placing on them.) After you've made your selections, click Save.

Tip   Disk images aren't a bad way to archive files that you'd like to store for accessing later, because the image itself (if it's saved as Read Only Compressed) is a compressed file, but it can be mounted and accessed as if it were a removable disk.

Disk First Aid

The Disk First Aid program checks the condition of a disk's directory, which keeps track of where files are stored on the disk, and can often repair any problem it finds. A directory can become damaged when the computer crashes or freezes. To use Disk First Aid, select one or more disks in its window and click Verify or Repair. Figure 25-11 shows the Disk First Aid window.

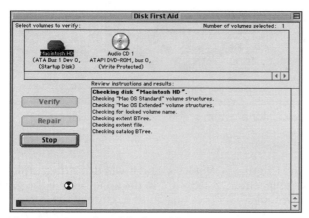

Figure 25-11: The Disk First Aid program

Disk First Aid is in the Utilities folder on the startup disk.

Cross-Reference   For more information on Disk First Aid, see Chapters 29 and 30.

Graphing Calculator

The Graphing Calculator is a special calculator program originally designed to show off PowerPC's processing power. It can graph an equation in the same time that it takes the ordinary Calculator to perform arithmetic on a lesser Mac. Figure 25-12 shows the Graphing Calculator and its full keypad.

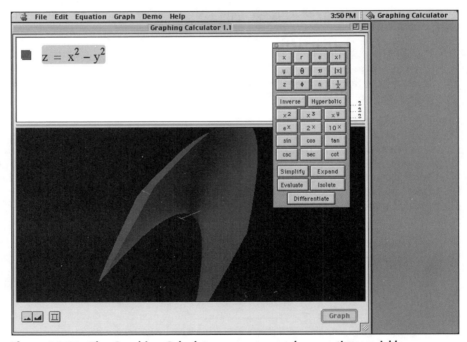

Figure 25-12: The Graphing Calculator program graphs equations quickly on PowerPC computers.

You can enter equations in the Graphing Calculator and it will draw the graph the equation represents. For example, enter "$z = x^2 + y^2$" in the space above the graph. For exponents, type a caret symbol ($\wedge$) by pressing Shift+6 to move the cursor up above the line; when you're done entering an exponent, press the right arrow ($\rightarrow$) key to return to normal.

You will see the graph of this equation—a three-dimensional parabola—drawn. Using the mouse, you can spin the graph about an axis and see it from another angle. Hold down the mouse button over the image and move the mouse left or right. The graph will spin in the direction you move the mouse.

The Graphing Calculator knows how to draw in two or three dimensions and knows about the variables x, y, and z. You can use these variables in your equations. You can also use constants such as pi, infinity, and e.

Unlike many calculators, the Graphing Calculator understands equations as you learned them in math class. If you need help entering parts of your equation, use the Show Keypad command from the Equation menu. That provides a floating window with buttons for sine, cosine, exponents, and other commonly used functions. Other useful functions, such as Square Root and Derivative, are also available in the Equation menu.

The Edit menu lets you invoke the Copy Graph command to copy the graph to the Clipboard so that it can be pasted in other documents—very handy for school reports. You can also use standard Cut, Copy, and Paste commands to bring equations into word processors. And you can use the Preferences menu item to change the size of the graph grid, or the font and size of the typefaces used.

The Demo menu steps through the graphing of a set of equations. It's useful when trying to learn all that the Graphing Calculator can do, but it's probably best used to impress folks with the power and speed of your computer.

 Tip
The Graphing Calculator has a number of features that are not documented in its help system. Pacific Tech, which created the code behind the Graphing Calculator, has posted information about some of Graphic Calculator's hidden commands on a Web site at `http:// www.pacifict.com/Secrets.html`. Some of these are general tips, such as dragging and dropping equations and graphs from the Graphing Calculator to the desktop to make clipping files, then restoring them by dragging and dropping them back on the Graphing Calculator. But there is also an extensive list of keyboard shortcuts for working with mathematical expressions and typesetting features, and for entering Greek letters and special mathematical symbols.

Key Caps

The Key Caps program shows all the characters that you can type in any font installed in your system. You choose the font from Key Cap's Font menu, which appears to the right of the Edit menu when the Key Caps desk accessory is active. Key Caps changes to show the effect of pressing Shift, Option, or Control separately or in combination. Figure 25-13 is an example of the Key Caps program.

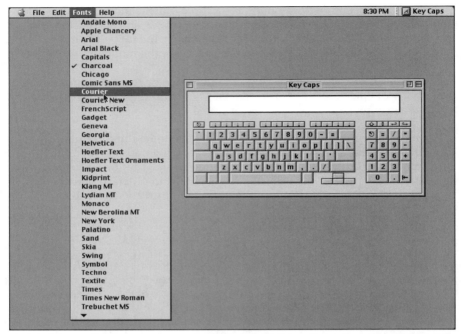

Figure 25-13: The Key Caps program shows the effect of pressing any combination of keys in any font you have.

In Key Caps, pressing Option outlines the keys that, when pressed along with Option, don't directly produce a character. Each of those Option+*key* combinations, which are called *dead keys*, adds an accent or other diacritic to certain subsequently typed keys. Pressing a dead key—for example, Option+E for an accent—outlines the keys that can have that diacritic added. Figure 25-14 shows how dead keys appear in Key Caps.

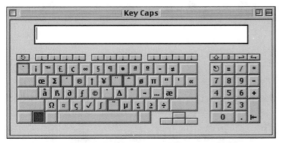

Figure 25-14: Reviewing dead keys and their effects

Printing Key Caps

You may want to print Key Caps as a handy reference, but it has no Print command. To work around this situation, follow these steps to take a picture of the screen and print that picture:

1. Open Key Caps, choose the font that you want it to show, and press any modifier keys (Shift, Option, Control, or ⌘) that you want to be in effect. Move the mouse pointer to an empty area of the menu bar; hold down the mouse button; temporarily release the modifier keys; press Caps Lock+⌘+Shift+4; again press the modifier keys that you released temporarily; and, finally, release the mouse button. Your gyrations should be rewarded by the sound of a camera shutter as the system snaps a picture of the Key Caps window.

2. Now open your startup disk and look for a document named Picture 1. (If you take additional snapshots, those snapshots are numbered sequentially.)

3. Print this document using SimpleText or any graphics program.

Note Pad

The Note Pad saves brief messages that you type or paste in it. You can print notes, go to any note by number, and find text in one note or all notes. Each note can contain up to about 32,000 characters. You can drag text between the Note Pad and another application that has adopted Mac OS drag-and-drop editing, such as AppleWorks, the Scrapbook, and SimpleText (see Chapter 7). You can scroll and resize the Note Pad window. In addition, you can set the font and size of the text in the notes by choosing Preferences from the Edit menu. Figure 25-15 shows the Note Pad.

Figure 25-15: Keep brief notes in the Note Pad program.

To create a new page for notes, use the New command from the File menu, or press ⌘+N. Click the dog-ear in the lower-left corner to flip forward or backward through the notes.

Note   The Note Pad is now found in the Apple Extras folder instead of its traditional location on the Apple Menu. If you'd like to place it back on the Apple menu, drag its icon to the Apple Menu Items folder in your System Folder.

PictureViewer and PictureViewer Pro

PictureViewer is a simple application for viewing and making minor changes to still images; it comes as part of QuickTime 4.0. PictureViewer Pro is an enhanced version that you get if you upgrade to QuickTime 4.0 Pro. PictureViewer is found in the QuickTime folder inside the Applications folder on your startup disk.

Cross-Reference   QuickTime is discussed in more detail in Chapter 18.

PictureViewer lets you open and view images in several image formats, among them BMP, GIF, JPEG, MacPaint, PICT, PNG, Photoshop, QuickTime Image, SGI, Targa, TIFF, and QuickDraw GX Picture. You can also use PictureViewer to view other image formats for which you have installed graphics importers.

To open an image file in PictureViewer, you can drag the file's icon to the PictureViewer icon. Alternatively, you can choose Open from PictureViewer's File menu. The Open dialog box lets you see a preview of the image if one already exists, or create a preview if none exists. To create the preview, click Create in the Open dialog box, as shown in Figure 25-16.

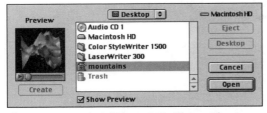

Figure 25-16: QuickTime 4.0's PictureViewer application previews images in its Open dialog box.

You can resize an image in PictureViewer window by choosing Half Size, Normal Size, Double Size, or Fill Screen from the Image menu. Although the image window has no grow box, you can, nevertheless, drag the bottom-right corner of its window to resize it. PictureViewer normally constrains the window to an optimal size. To resize freely, you must Shift+drag. Option+dragging resizes the image in preset percentages (100%, 75%, 50%, 25%, and 10%).

To change an image's orientation in the window, choose Rotate Right, Rotate Left, Flip Horizontal, or Flip Vertical from the Image menu. After you've made changes, you can print it or copy it to the Clipboard. If you have PictureViewer Pro, you can save your changes to the image by choosing Export from the File menu.

QuickTime Player

QuickTime Player specializes in QuickTime movies. While you may be able to play movies in SimpleText and other ordinary applications, QuickTime Player provides greater control over the movie. For example, you can change the size of a movie window and you can view detailed information about a movie in a separate window. You can even edit movies with some versions of QuickTime Player. Figure 25-17 shows the QuickTime Player interface.

Figure 25-17: QuickTime Player features a new interface with plenty of bells and whistles.

Apple offers two editions of QuickTime 4.0 — regular and Pro — and each has its own version of QuickTime Player. The Pro edition enables you to cut, copy, and paste parts of movies, create new movies, and import and export individual movie tracks. QuickTime Player Pro also enables you to apply filters and special effects.

New in QuickTime 4.0 is support for streaming video and for Macromedia Flash content, both of which the QuickTime Player supports. Using the Favorites Drawer in the QuickTime Player, you can access your favorite movie files as well as streaming content sent from name-brand news and entertainment sources on the Web.

You'll find QuickTime Player inside the QuickTime folder on your startup disk.

Cross-Reference

QuickTime Player is discussed in more detail in Chapter 18.

Scrapbook

The Scrapbook stores and retrieves text, pictures, sounds, movies, and other types of information that you paste into it, one item at a time. You can copy an item to or from the Scrapbook by dragging from or to another application that has adopted Mac OS drag-and-drop editing, such as AppleWorks, SimpleText, or the Finder. Figure 25-18 shows an image pasted in the Scrapbook.

Cross-Reference

See Chapter 7 for details on drag-and-drop editing.

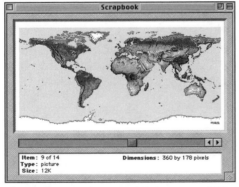

Figure 25-18: The Scrapbook stores all kinds of clippings pasted in it.

As you scroll through items, the Scrapbook reports the number of the item, the type of the item, and its size. For picture items, the Scrapbook also reports the item's dimensions and the amount (if any) by which the item is reduced for display in the Scrapbook. The Scrapbook also reports the duration of sounds and movies.

Relieving Scrapbook clutter

After extensive use, your Scrapbook may become cluttered with old clippings. If you can't bear to throw them out, make a copy of the Scrapbook file in your System Folder (use the Finder's Duplicate command and store the copy in some other folder) before you start weeding. Later, you can use the old copy that you made by double-clicking it.

A factory-fresh copy does not replace your Scrapbook when you upgrade the Mac OS. The Mac OS installer program notices the old Scrapbook file and leaves it alone. To get the standard Scrapbook when you upgrade the Mac OS, move the Scrapbook file out of the System Folder before you start the installer program.

Script Editor

The Script Editor is used to write, record, and edit AppleScript scripts. You'll find it in the AppleScript folder inside the Apple Extras folder on the startup disk. Figure 25-19 is an example script in a Script Editor window.

 Cross-Reference For more information on AppleScript and Script Editor, see Chapter 24.

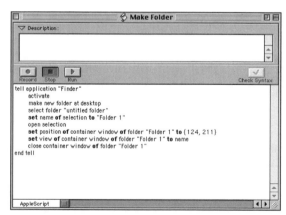

Figure 25-19: Write and edit AppleScript scripts in the Script Editor program.

Sherlock 2

Sherlock 2 is an update of the popular Sherlock application in Mac OS 8.5 for searching hard disk, document content, and the Internet. Sherlock's new brushed-metal look (like the QuickTime Viewer's new look) gives it an interesting interface, while new features make it possible to search Internet e-commerce sites, locate people via the Internet, and generally use Sherlock 2 for all of your searching, whether you do it on the Internet, on your local disks, or on your organization's network. Figure 25-20 shows the Sherlock 2 window.

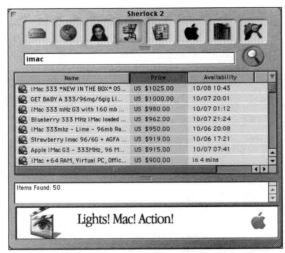

Figure 25-20: The Sherlock 2 program finds files, document content, and Internet content.

You switch between Sherlock's capabilities by clicking the Channel icons at the top of the Sherlock window. The disk icon, for instance, represents local and network disks; the world icon searches the World Wide Web's popular search engines; the woman icon represents people searches in popular "white pages" search engines.

As you move between different channels, the interface changes along with the channel, to represent the type of data that you're searching for and the optimum way for results to be displayed. For instance, when you click the Files channel icon, you can search by file name, content keyword, or other search criteria. Results are listed by Name, Kind, Date Modified, and so on. On the Shopping channel, you search by keyword and results are listed by price and availability.

One of Sherlock's most impressive features is the capability to search within textual documents (including PDF and HTML files) on your hard disk. To do this, you need to schedule indexing time, so that Sherlock can take time to create an index of your disks. Complete and up-to-date indexes make finding things within your documents easier.

Cross-Reference Searching with Sherlock 2 is covered extensively in Chapter 6.

SimpleSound

SimpleSound is a small application that you can use to record sound. You can record sound files and new system alert sounds. The Alert Sounds window shows a list of all alert sounds currently in your System file. You can also open sound files, each in its own window. Figure 25-21 shows the Alert Sounds window and the windows of two sound files.

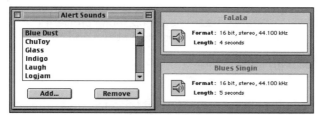

Figure 25-21: Record system alert sounds and individual sound files in the SimpleSound program.

Playing sounds

You can play an alert sound by clicking its name in the Alert Sounds window. Selecting an alert sound in the Alert Sounds window also makes it the system alert sound, just like selecting it in the Sound control panel (see Chapter 12).

To play an open sound file, make its window active and use the Play command in the Sound menu, or double-click the icon in the sound's window. You can stop a playing sound with the Stop command in the Sound menu, by clicking the icon in the sound's window once or by pressing ⌘+period (.).

Making sounds

Before making a new sound, set the sound quality by choosing a quality level from the Sound menu. Higher quality sound requires more storage space on disk. There are four sound-quality level choices:

✦ **CD Quality** records in stereo with 16-bit samples and a 44.1kHz sampling rate.

✦ **Music Quality** records in mono with 8-bit samples and a 22kHz sampling rate.

✦ **Speech Quality** records in mono with 3-to-1 compression and a 22kHz sampling rate.

✦ **Phone Quality** records in mono with 6-to-1 compression and a 22kHz sampling rate.

To make a new alert sound, click Add in the Alert Sounds window. To make a new sound file, use the New command in the File menu. Either action brings up a dialog box with buttons that work like a traditional tape recorder. The dialog box also shows the elapsed recording time and the remaining time available. Click Record to record or rerecord sound from the computer's microphone or from another audio source. (You set the sound input source in the Sound In section of the Sound control panel, as described in Chapter 12.) Then click Play to hear your recording. When you're satisfied with your recording, click Save and type a name for the new sound when asked. Figure 25-22 shows the dialog box in which you record a sound.

Figure 25-22: The SimpleSound program's dialog box for recording a new sound

New alert sounds are saved in the Finder sound format (also known as the snd format) and are put in the System file. You can open the System file and drag sounds to the desktop.

New sound files are saved in the audio interchange file format (AIFF), and each sound goes in the folder that you select when you save the sound.

SimpleText

SimpleText is often thought of as just a tool for opening Read Me files, but it can do quite a bit more. SimpleText can read text aloud as well as open graphics files and copy selected portions of an image to the Clipboard. Furthermore, unless you have removed QuickTime, you can use SimpleText to play QuickTime movies and open and manipulate QuickDraw 3D graphics.

Text editing

The text-editing features of SimpleText are not fancy. You have no control over paragraph formatting. The paragraph width changes as you resize the SimpleText document's window. Line spacing and tab stops are fixed.

In plain-text documents, you can make selections and cut, copy, and paste text. You can change the font, font size, and font style, but you must apply each attribute separately. (You cannot create styles that assign font, font size, and font style all in one operation.) Moreover, the text-editing capabilities described in this paragraph do not work in read-only SimpleText documents — the kind with an icon that looks like a newspaper.

Speech and sound

To make SimpleText read aloud, select some text in a SimpleText document and then choose Speak Selection (⌘+J) from SimpleText's Sound menu. If you make no selection, the Sound menu offers the command Speak All. Choose a voice from the Voices menu. Some voices simulate realistic humanlike speech, whereas others are mechanistic, humorous, or musical.

You can also record a voice annotation or other sound and attach it to a plain-text document for later playback. Choosing Record from the Sound menu brings up a dialog box for recording up to 25 seconds of sound. Clicking Save in this dialog box saves the sound in the current SimpleText document. To play a saved sound, choose Play from the Sound menu.

Graphics and other media

SimpleText can also open graphics files, 3D objects, and QuickTime movies. You can drag a multimedia file to the SimpleText icon to open it, or use the Open command in SimpleText's File menu. SimpleText can open PICT files directly. If you have QuickTime installed, SimpleText uses it to convert other graphics files to PICT. Depending on the version of QuickTime, you may be able to open and convert BMP, GIF, JPEG, MacPaint, PICT, PNG, Photoshop, QuickTime Image, SGI, Targa, TIFF, and QuickDraw GX Picture files.

After SimpleText opens a graphics file, the mouse pointer appears as a crosshairs pointer, which you can use to select a portion of the image and copy it to the Clipboard. Opening a QuickDraw 3D graphic with SimpleText lets you manipulate the 3D graphic using the standard QuickDraw 3D controller. When you use SimpleText to open QuickTime movies, the movie appears in a window with a standard QuickTime movie controller at the bottom.

 For more information on these multimedia controllers, see Chapter 18.

Stickies

The Stickies application displays notes similar to Post-it Notes on your screen. You can set the color and the text font, font size, and font style for each note. You can drag selected text to move it within a note, copy it between notes, or copy it between a note and another application that has adopted Mac OS drag-and-drop editing, such as SimpleText and the Note Pad. Stickies windows have no scroll bars, but you can scroll by pressing the arrow keys or by dragging inside the note. Figure 25-23 displays several examples of Stickies notes.

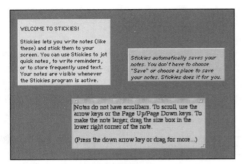

Figure 25-23: The Stickies application displays notes similar to Post-it Notes.

Summary

This chapter gave a brief look at a number of the accessory programs that are included with Mac OS 9. These include multimedia programs such as the Audio CD Player and DVD Player, traditional desk accessories like Key Caps and the Scrapbook, and newer accessories such as the Apple File Security and Apple Verifier programs that access Apple's latest technologies. Other accessories include the new Sherlock 2 program and the QuickTime Player, both with impressive-looking interfaces and new features in their latest versions. In addition, there are utilities such as Disk First Aid, Disk Copy, and the Desktop Printer Utility that are often overlooked by Mac OS 9 users even though they offer interesting and useful capabilities.

✦   ✦   ✦

Enhance with Utility Software

Every system software upgrade, including Mac OS 9, offers significant enhancements in performance and ease of use over older Mac system software. However, even Mac OS 9 can stand some assistance in performing its disk and file management, alias management, networking, and other duties. Software that enhances the Mac OS to even further increase your productivity is the subject of this chapter.

Many programmers have developed small accessory applications, control panels, and system extensions that enhance the performance of the Finder and other system software. Mac OS users are an idiosyncratic lot and like to personalize their systems. These shareware, freeware, and commercial software utilities personalize the activities of the Finder and other system software so that the computer does exactly what you need it to do, when you need it to do it. With these programs, you can open specific files directly without having to know where they are located. You can also throw away files while using an application without going to the Finder, create aliases in new ways, and make using your Mac much more fun.

The software items described in this chapter are listed alphabetically, with a short description of each of their features, and with the names of their authors, their system requirements, and prices. Software is updated often, especially noncommercial software, and you may find that newer versions of programs have features not described here.

Where to Get Utility Software

There are several avenues to acquire the software listed in this chapter. All the software is available from some software library on the Internet or from a commercial online information service. Much of the software is available on CD-ROM from user groups. And some of the software is available from Apple. Start with these sources:

✦ **Macworld's Macdownload** software library (`http://www.macdownload.com`) has much of the software listed in this chapter, plus many more shareware, freeware, and Apple utilities. All are available for the cost of downloading.

✦ **C-Net's Download.com** software library (`http://www.download.com`) offers extensive shareware, demo software, and freeware. And if you can't find it there, you may find a shareware or freeware title you're seeking at its sister site, Shareware.com (`http://www.shareware.com`). All software is available for the cost of downloading.

✦ **America Online** (800-827-6364) has a large collection of shareware, freeware, and Apple utility software, all available for the cost of downloading.

✦ **Info-Mac Archive** is a major storehouse of shareware, freeware, and demo versions of retail software. All software is submitted to a central location and redistributed to mirror sites throughout the world, such as AOL's FTP mirror site (`ftp://mirrors.aol.com/pub/info-mac/`) and Apple's FTP mirror site (`ftp:// mirror.apple.com/mirrors/Info-Mac.Archive/`). At most mirror sites, you browse for files by category. MIT's HyperArchive mirror has an Info-Mac search facility (`http://hyperarchive.lcs.mit.edu/ HyperArchive.html`), as does the University of Illinois (`http://uiarchive. cso.uiuc.edu/pubindex/info-mac/wgindex.html`).

✦ **Umich mac.archive** is another major storehouse of shareware, freeware, and demo versions of retail software. Like Info-Mac, Umich has mirror sites throughout the world, such as AOL's FTP mirror site (`ftp://mirrors.aol. com/pub/mac/`) and Apple's FTP mirror site (`ftp://mirror.apple.com/ mirrors/mac. archive.umich.edu/`). There's a list of mirror sites at the main Umich mac. archive site (`http://www-personal.umich.edu/ ~sdamask/umich-mirrors/`).

✦ **Filez** (`http://www.filez.com/zhub.shtml`) and **Shareware.com** (`http://www.shareware.com`) have extensive, searchable directories of shareware and freeware.

✦ **VersionTracker Online** (`http://www.versiontracker.com/`) is a great way to keep up with the latest new Macintosh shareware, freeware, demos, and free updates to commercial software.

✦ **Berkeley Macintosh Users Group** (BMUG) (510-549-2684, `http://www.bmug. org`), **Arizona Macintosh Users Group** (AMUG) (602-553-8966, `http://www. amug.org`), and other user groups sell collections of shareware and freeware on CD-ROM. Apple will refer you to the user group nearest you (800-538-9696).

✦ **Apple's Software Updates library** (http://www.apple.com/swupdates/) has all Apple utility software and much of, but not all of, Mac system software. Everything in the library is available for the cost of downloading.

How to use utility software

This chapter describes utility software but does not include detailed operating instructions. Because noncommercial software is usually distributed online or on disk, it doesn't come with printed manuals. Instead, noncommercial software usually comes with a documentation file, frequently called "Read Me." You should also check for onscreen help in the Help menu or at the top of the Apple menu.

About shareware and freeware

The software described in this chapter is not available in any store. This software is distributed on the Internet, through online information services, by user groups, and person-to-person. Whatever you pay for an online connection or a user group's CD-ROM goes strictly to the online service or user group; none of that money goes to the authors of the software. That's fine with some authors, who distribute their products as *freeware* and don't expect to be paid.

Authors of *shareware* encourage you to try their software and to share copies with friends and coworkers. Each person who decides to keep a shareware product sends payment directly to the author. Many shareware authors also accept payment through Kagi Software (http://www.kagi.com), which is a clearinghouse on the Internet.

It's important to understand that freeware and shareware are not in the public domain. Most freeware authors and all shareware authors retain the copyrights to their work. You can use it and you can generally pass it around, but you can't sell it.

Shareware and freeware programs typically are written by enthusiasts who can't afford to provide technical support by telephone, as the developers of commercial programs can. Moreover, shareware and freeware authors can't afford to thoroughly test their software with many combinations of computer models, Mac OS versions, and other software.

Shareware and freeware programs aren't always as stable as commercial software. Be sure to follow the instructions and discussions provided by the authors in their Read Me or Help files before using any of these programs. Be forewarned: Use shareware and freeware at your own risk.

Support shareware authors

Shareware depends on the honor and honesty of the people who use it. If you decide to keep shareware installed on your disk, the Honorable Society of Civilized People politely insists that you immediately send payment to the author. The fees that you pay for the shareware you use today (generally $5 to $50) help fund development of more great shareware. For detailed information about the amount of payment requested for a particular shareware product and where to send payment, check the product's Read Me file, About command (in the Apple menu), or onscreen help.

System Utilities Listing

Apple, commercial developers, and shareware and freeware authors offer thousands of utility programs. Many new programs become available each day. The software listed in this chapter has been culled from the pack based on its usefulness, ease of use, completeness, and reliability. This list is not meant to be all-inclusive, but rather to be an example of the types of software that are available to enhance the performance of your computer with the Mac OS. The great variation in computer models and configurations makes it impossible to predict accurately whether a utility will work on your system. Some Read Me files and documentation mention the systems and configurations required and known conflicts, but others do not. Many will probably work with Mac OS 9 as well, but at the time this book went to press compatibility with Mac OS 9 was unknown for many of these utilities.

Authors of noncommercial software don't typically have the facilities to test their programs with a variety of software combinations and computer models. Instead, they fix problems reported by people who try out the utility programs. If you decide to try a program, check the Read Me file or other included documentation for compatibility information of the version you get. If the compatibility information doesn't assure you that the utility program you want to try is compatible with your computer model and Mac OS version, you should take the precaution of making a backup of your hard disk before trying the utility program.

The Web has additional information about some shareware and freeware programs. The program descriptions in this chapter include URLs of Web pages wherever possible. When you use these URLs, remember that Web pages come and go. If you try a URL cited here and it doesn't work, look for the program in the Info-Mac Archive and other places mentioned in the previous section.

Agent Audio

Agent Audio lets you replace the snd resources (sounds) of any file or application that already contains them. Select the program you wish to customize and Agent Audio enables you to view and edit the available sounds or extract and archive the sounds into playable snd files. This application by Clixsounds (http://www. clixsounds.com) requires a color monitor and 2MB of RAM and costs $12.

Alias Crony

Alias Crony can scan all of your online volumes to create lists of attached and unattached aliases; retrieve aliases and originals; and link, update, delete, and move aliases. It also creates "SuperAliases" of applications that can reside on separate volumes and still possess drag-capability, enabling you to drag items onto the alias to launch the application. This application by Rocco Moliterno of Yellowsoft (http://www.geocities.com/yellowsoft/) costs $10.

Alias Menu

Add drop-down menus to your menu bar that you can access from any application. Place folders with aliases in the folder and the folders become menu items. When you choose the menu item, every alias in the folder is launched, enabling you to quickly launch related applications, documents, and utilities. This application by Benoit Wildemann (http://www.integra.fr/bw/aliasmenu-us.html) costs $25.

AliasZoo

AliasZoo is a quick and easy way to get control over the mountain of alias files living on your hard drive. It searches a hard drive or folder and displays a report listing details on the aliases it finds, deletes orphaned aliases quickly and easily, and includes Apple Guide support. This application by Cliff McCollum (http://www. islandnet.com/~cliffmcc/) of Blue Globe Software costs $15.

AMICO (Apple Menu Items Custom Order)

AMICO lets you change the order of items in the Apple menu without renaming them. You can also add gray divider lines and divider titles between groups of items. This extension by Dennis Chronopoulos costs $10.

AppSizer

AppSizer enables you to change the amount of memory allocated to applications (the suggested size in the Info window) as you launch them. This control panel from Peirce Software (http://www.peircesw.com) costs $19.95.

BatteryAmnesia

BatteryAmnesia provides a safe, fast, and automatic way to deep discharge a PowerBook's (NiCad) or nickel-hydride (NiMH) battery, bypassing the low-battery warning messages, and preventing the sleep state normally brought on by those messages. It runs your PowerBook's battery down until a hardware shutdown occurs, which is at a lower voltage, providing the best discharge possible without an expensive external battery conditioner. This application by Jeremy Kezer (http://www.kezer.net/shareware.html) requires a PowerBook and costs $10.

Blitz

The Blitz file management utility can catalogue hard disks and large removable drives such as CD-ROMs when volumes are dragged and dropped onto its application. Blitz records large catalogues using very little disk space, while providing extremely fast search functionality. This application by Matthew Bickham requires a computer with a color monitor (256 colors or better) and costs $10.

BunchOApps

BunchOApps lists your most recently run applications and installed applications and launches them when selected. You can specify how many applications to remember (up to 25). This Control Strip module by Patrick McClaughry requires Apple's Control Strip or Men & Mice's Desktop Strip and is free.

Carpetbag

Carpetbag enables various system resources, such as fonts, sounds, and FKeys, to be kept outside your System file. Place PostScript fonts in one specified folder outside the System Folder and Adobe Type Manager (ATM) and the LaserWriter driver will see them. This control panel by James W. Walker (http://www.jwwalker.com/) costs $5.

ClickTyper

ClickTyper offers key-free typing to people with limited ability to use their hands. ClickTyper creates a virtual onscreen keyboard where you enter text, navigate a document, and perform other operations, such as printing and shutting down. The application's two modes — Mouse Mode and Click Mode — allow you to choose the amount of movement you must make. In Click Mode, ClickTyper highlights areas of the keyboard; clicking anywhere confirms that the desired "key" is in the highlighted area. ClickTyper highlights smaller and smaller areas until you identify the precise key. This application by Ivan Gobbo (http://www.kagi.com/inai/ct/) costs $20.

Clock Synch

Clock Synch synchronizes the clocks between two or more computers on an AppleTalk network, by setting the clocks of the servant computers to that of a master computer. This application by Jeremy Kezer (http://www.kezer.net/shareware.html) requires an AppleTalk network and costs $15.

CMScript

CMScript enables you to run AppleScripts related to the "context" — the application that you are currently in — from Contextual Menus. CMScript comes with Context Grabber, a plug-in that aids in script creation by determining the current context, copying the appropriate Apple event for the current context to the clipboard (for pasting into a script), and/or creating template scripts that are preconfigured for the current context. This extension by Michael Schürig (http://www.schuerig.de/michael/) is free.

CoolViews

CoolViews lets you set preferences for the list views of all folders on your system and lets you modify other aspects of the Finder windows such as background color and date formats. This control panel by Graham Herrick, Quadratic Software (http://www.quadratic.com) requires a monitor with 256 colors or grays. CoolViews costs $20.

CopyPaste

CopyPaste enhances the Mac OS clipboard functionality by remembering the last ten items copied and keeping them accessible via menu or key commands and includes hot keys for switching between applications you're copying and pasting between. It can also append the Clip Sets to text files or save the clipboards on shutdown or restart. This extension from ScriptSoftware (http://www.scriptsoftware.com) costs $20.

Default Folder

Default Folder enhances Open and Save dialog boxes, making file management easier by letting you specify where files should always be saved by certain applications, providing a pop-up menu of recently used folders, moving items to the Trash from within dialog boxes, and adjusting multiple save options. This control panel by St. Clair Software (http://www.stclairsoft.com) costs $25.

Desktop Resetter

Desktop Resetter lets you define preferred locations for desktop icons and restore icons to these positions easily when other users rearrange them or when you change monitor resolutions. Desktop Resetter can remember different icon setups for different monitor resolutions. This application by Nick D'Amato (`http://members.home.net/goddfadda/resetter.html`) costs $10.

Dialog View

Dialog View lets you enlarge Open and Save dialog boxes so that you can see more files and folders with less scrolling. It also lets you choose a font for the file list in these dialog boxes (a condensed font will show longer file names). This control panel from James W. Walker (`http://www.jwwalker.com/`) costs $10.

Disk Rejuvenator

Disk Rejuvenator addresses problems of hard disks becoming inaccessible from the standard Open dialog boxes and of custom icons disappearing (which can be caused by the Finder information for the root of the disk becoming corrupted). It corrects the problems by examining your disk's attributes and correcting those that are in need of correction. This application by Aladdin Systems (`http://www.aladdinsys.com`) is free.

DiskSurveyor

DiskSurveyor provides a graphical display of the files and folders that reside on your hard drive and shows the amount of space these individual items are taking up. You can open and manage folders from within the display and create disk summary files that list all the files found on CD-ROMs or any other volume. This application by Tom Luhrs, Twilight Software, requires a monitor set to display at least 256 colors or grays and costs $10.

DoDelete

A drag-and-drop utility for securely deleting files. DoDelete uses Department of Defense recommendations for permanently removing data from your hard disk. Deleting with this program makes it virtually impossible to recover files using utility programs or other methods. DoDelete from Claireware (`http://www.kamprath.net/claireware/dodelete.html`) is shareware and costs $5.

Download Deputy

Download Deputy lets you queue a number of remote files for batch downloading. You create lists of URLs by typing them in a URL window, by dragging them to the window from your browser, or by activating the URL Grabber, which keeps track of every FTP address you click on as you browse. You can start a batch download manually or schedule downloads for a later time. Download Deputy can perform a number of actions once download is complete: It can close your PPP connection, expand files with StuffIt Expander, quit, and shut down. The URL Grabber feature requires Netscape Navigator 3.0 or later. The Download Deputy application, from ilesa Software (`http://www.ilesa.com`), costs $21.

DragThing

DragThing is an application dock designed to tidy up the icons littering your desktop. Simply drag an application from the Finder to an empty square in a dock and then drag documents to the application to open them. Double-click a docked application to launch it or bring it to the front. In addition, the docks can contain files, folders, disks, and servers. There is also an option to display the name of the active application in a special dock. This program by James Thomson (`http://www.dragthing.com`) costs $15.

Drop Slot

Drag and drop unsorted files onto the Drop Slot application icon, and they are automatically stored in folders on your hard drive in the same way the System Folder automatically moves its items to the correct folder. Drop Slot stores files by type, prompting you for destinations and storing types it recognizes in folders you designate. This application by Rick Christianson costs $10.

Drop*PS

Drop*PS sends text files containing PostScript code to any PostScript printer, independently of installed printer drivers. This application by Bare Bones Software (`http://www.barebones.com`) is free.

Drop-Rename

Drop-Rename enables you to search for and rename files or folders with a variety of options, such as changing name cases and file extensions, changing specified search strings under certain conditions, and more. Multithreading lets it run easily in the background. You can also create "Renamelets," which are customized self-running applications for operations you perform regularly. This application by Chaotic Software (`http://www.chaoticsoftware.com`) costs $10.

DropStuff with Expander Enhancer

DropStuff with Expander Enhancer creates compressed StuffIt archives when you drag your files and folders onto the DropStuff icon. With Expander Enhancer installed, the StuffIt Expander program is capable of decompressing archived files in a wide variety of formats. DropStuff with Expander Enhancer by Aladdin Systems (http://www.aladdinsys.com) is included with Mac OS 9 in the Internet Utilities folder (inside the Internet folder on the startup disk) and has a shareware fee of $30.

EMMpathy

EMMpathy fixes PowerBook 520 and 540 Smart Battery memory-related errors and includes VST's Smart Battery Probe, an advanced smart-battery diagnostic. This application by Bill Steinberg and VST Technologies (http://www.vsttech.com/) is free.

Fat Cursors

Fat Cursors installs slightly larger arrow and I-beam pointers and features a "find pointer" function. This is particularly handy for PowerBook users. This control panel by Robert Abatecola costs $10.

File Buddy

File Buddy enhances file management. You can obtain a wide set of file and folder information using extensive search criteria; find files containing specified resources and delete or modify these resources; modify batches of file names and extensions; create aliases; find and delete duplicates, unattached aliases, and old preferences files; rebuild the desktop; and more. This application by Laurence Harris costs $25.

File eXpress

Drop files on the File eXpress FXPackager's mailbox icon, and you can send them to any other machine running File eXpress on your AppleTalk or TCP/IP network. The program places a FXInBox folder on your desktop for your incoming files. This application by Ruskin Group is free for noncommercial use.

FileLock

Big Al FileLock is a simple password-protection program that lets you place a password on any file. Users are forced to enter the correct password to open the file. This application by Al Staffieri, Jr. costs $10.

FileTyper

Drop files on FileTyper's icon to quickly change types, creators, attribute flags, and date stamps on files. It also supports processing batches of files, filtering, and directory searches. This application by Daniel Azuma (`http://www.ugcs.caltech.edu/~dazuma/`) costs $10.

FinderNote

FinderNote is a simple text editor whose documents are saved as clippings and can be read in the Finder (on the desktop) without needing to run any application. This application by Jae Ho Chang (`http://www.xs4all.nl/~jaeho`) is free.

FinderPop

FinderPop extends the capabilities of contextual menus. You can access contextual menus simply by clicking and holding down the mouse button. FinderPop submenus let you peek into closed folders and disks, view all open the Finder windows or everything that's located on the desktop, and switch between currently running programs. You can also add aliases to a special FinderPop folder; these items then appear in the contextual menu (or in a submenu) for easy access. For example, you can select several files, Control+click one of the selected icons, and then choose an application from the FinderPop menu to open the files with that application. This control panel by Turlough O'Connor is free.

Folder Icon Maker

Folder Icon Maker creates folders with custom icons when you drag an application or document to the FIM application. A new folder is created in the directory containing the file. FIM also supports PICT data as a source for custom folders and works with folder resource files. This application by Gregory Robbins is free.

Font Book

Font Book creates overviews of a font that can be printed and used as quick reference materials. There are a dozen ways to set up the sample pages, including an ASCII reference sheet, a layout that uses the font in standard type styles, several layouts showing the font in various sizes, one layout showing the font in a long piece of text, and several design layouts. This application by Matthias Kahlert (`http://www.kagi.com/mkahlert/fb/default.html`) costs $10.

!ForceQuit

!ForceQuit enhances the conventional Force Quit (Option+⌘+Escape) feature of the Mac OS. You can either totally enable or disable forced quits or disable forced quits only for selected applications. This extension by Daffy Software is free.

GifConverter

GifConverter does more than its name implies. It handles a variety of file formats, including TIFF, RIFF, PICT, JPEG, PNG, MacPaint, and Thunderscan. It reads and writes all those formats plus it can create startup screens and black-and-white EPS files. GifConverter provides image-editing tools that let you scale and rotate an image, change its resolution, change color palettes, and dither colors. GifConverter is AppleScript-compatible and comes with several batch-conversion scripts. This application by Kevin A. Mitchell (http://www.kamit.com/gifconverter/) costs $30.

GoMac

GoMac behaves like the Windows 95/98 task bar and includes a Program Bar that displays open applications and a Start menu that lists all installed applications, recently accessed servers, files and folders, other easy navigation tools, and a small pop-up calendar. This control panel from PowerOn Software (http://www. poweronsoftware) costs $29.95.

GrabAudio

GrabAudio lets you record any part of an audio CD quickly and easily using simple digital-audio marking features. This application by Theo Vosse requires an Apple CD300 CD player or better and the Apple CD software (which is included with the Mac OS). GrabAudio is free.

GraphicConverter

GraphicConverter converts an amazing number of graphics file formats found on Mac, Windows, UNIX, Amiga, and Atari computers. GraphicConverter imports 100 different file formats and exports more than 40 different file formats. In addition, the program has tools and filters for editing pictures. This application by Thorsten Lemke (http://www.lemkesoft.com) costs $35.

Greg's Browser

Greg's Browser gives Mac OS 9 a Browser window similar to the browser interface in NeXTStep and OpenStep (and the main Finder interface in Mac OS X Server and

Mac OS X). Some say this interface is more convenient than the Finder, especially if you're connected to many network volumes. This application by Greg Landweber costs $20.

GURU

GURU provides information concerning memory upgrades for every model of Mac OS computer ever made by Apple and other companies. GURU is updated regularly. It also includes memory information on all Apple LaserWriter printers. Memory information includes RAM, DRAM, VRAM, EDO, SDRAM, PSDRAM, Static RAM, and FRAM. This application from the NewerRAM division of Peripheral Enhancements Corp. (http://www.newerram.com) is free.

Helium

Helium enhances the Mac OS balloon-help feature, by enabling you to use key commands to make help balloons appear and disappear automatically or to toggle balloon help on and off, as well as setting a more legible font size for the help text. This control panel by Tiger Technologies (http://www.tigertech.com) costs $7.

HourWorld

HourWorld Lite displays a map of the world that indicates where the sun is currently shining and where it has set. It allows you to display five clocks set to the local time of cities around the world. The full version offers more clocks, the capability to print almanacs of sunrise and sunset times, phone call coordination, and global positioning features, plus an editable database. The lite version of this application by Paul Software Engineering (http://www.hourworld.com/prod01.htm) costs $15, and the full version costs $29.95.

Icon Archiver

The Icon Archiver is a database utility that can quickly scan whole disks or folders for icons and icon archives and can create archives of compressed icons. It filters icons by size and color depth, provides a wide variety of icon views, removes duplicate icons, and sorts icons using multiple criteria. This application by Alessandro Levi Montalcini (http://www.montalcini.com) costs $25.

I Love Native!

I Love Native! enables you to check whether an application, control panel, system extension, shared library, or code resource file is written in PowerPC, 68K, or fat (both PowerPC and 68K) code. It enables you to create either a PowerPC-only or a

68K-only application from a fat application to reduce the application's file size. It also enables you to combine a PowerPC-only and a 68K-only application into a fat application (both 68K and PowerPC applications must be the same program). This application by Jerry Du is free.

The InformINIT

The InformINIT is a regularly updated guide for information on extensions and control panels, listing almost every system extension Apple has ever produced with information on what they do, who needs them, version numbers, RAM consumption, and tips and tricks. This application by Dan Frakes (http://mc04.equinox.net/informinit/) costs $15.

IPNetRouter

IPNetRouter lets you share one dial-up Internet account among any number of computers on a local network (Ethernet, LocalTalk, or both). In addition to this feature, which is known as IP masquerading, IPNetRouter offers IP multihoming (using multiple IP interfaces simultaneously) and IP forwarding (routing IP traffic between network interfaces). This application from Sustainable Softworks (http://www.sustworks.com) costs $89.

John's RAM Disk Backup

John's RAM Disk Backup is a pair of utilities that enable you to save the contents of any disk named RAM Disk when you shut down the Mac and restore them when you restart. You place the Backup RAM Disk utility in the Shutdown Items folder. It copies the RAM Disk contents to a folder in the System Folder on shutdown. Restore RAM Disk goes in the Startup Items folder and copies items from the System Folder copy to your RAM disk. This application duo (search for it as RAM Disk Backup) by John C. Rethorst is free.

Jon's Commands

Jon's Commands is an AppleScript addition that provides a number of useful AppleScript commands. There are commands for deleting, renaming, or moving a file or folder; retrieving data from and posting data to the Clipboard; getting a list of keys that are currently being pressed; getting information about an alias; and more. This extension from Jon Pugh (http://www.seanet.com/~jonpugh/#Software/) is free.

Kaleidoscope

Kaleidoscope completely overhauls the Mac OS interface using plug-in Color Scheme files that are fairly simple to create using another program called Kaleidoscope for Laymen. It includes an Aaron plug-in (described earlier in this chapter), a WindowShade widget, dynamic draggable windows, customizable Finder window backgrounds, and much more. This control panel by Greg Landweber (http://www.kaleidoscope.net/) costs $20.

KeyQuencer Lite

KeyQuencer Lite is a powerful keyboard-shortcut utility with several dozen ready-to-play macros. One keystroke flips your monitor to a different color setting. Another lets you take a screen shot (a captured PICT file) of anything you rope off with the selection rectangle. Other KeyQuencer Lite macros do things such as type the date, move a window, adjust the speaker volume, or switch to the next open program. You must build every KeyQuencer Lite macro manually; however, the task is made simpler with built-in menu commands. This control panel from Binary Software (http://www.binarysoft.com/kqmac/kqmac.html) costs $30.

MacErrors

MacErrors helps you decipher those mysterious Macintosh system errors. You can enter the error ID and press Return to display the error's result code and description, or move through the list of errors using the arrow keys. This application by Marty Wachter costs $10.

Mac Identifier

When the Mac OS is unable to provide model or icon information about the computer that it is running on, Mac Identifier provides the information from a special database of stored model names. This is useful for network administrators and users who need to share other's disks. This control panel by Maurice Volaski (http://www.fluxsoft.com) costs $5.

Mac OS Purge

Mac OS Purge optimizes the Mac OS memory very quickly. It's especially useful under tight memory conditions, such as when running with small amounts of RAM or when run between launching memory-intensive applications. It runs, purges, and returns to the Finder. This application by E. Kenji Takeuchi is free.

MacSlack

MacSlack lets you determine how much space is wasted on your hard drive due to "slack space" (the space left over when a file doesn't completely fill a cluster on the hard drive). It calculates how much of that space is reclaimable if you partition the drive, thereby reducing cluster size. MacSlack also calculates how much space is reclaimable if you reformat the entire drive using the Mac OSExtended format (also known as HFS+). This drag-and-drop application by Eric Bennett (`http://www.pobox.com/~ericb/eric/aboutme.html`) is free.

Memory Mapper

Memory Mapper creates a precise report of current memory use on your computer. It graphically displays how much memory each open application uses and where the applications are in relation to each other and to blocks of unused memory. Memory Mapper provides detailed information about the Mac OS memory use, breaking it into several items, including High Memory (video, sound, and disk cache), the Finder, system extensions that are actually programs open in the background, System Heap (fonts, icons, sounds, and other system resources), and Low Memory Globals (system parameters). This application from Jintek and R. Fronabarger (`http://www.jintek.com/freeware.html`) is free.

Memory Minder

Memory Minder's interface lets you examine how much memory your open applications are actually using and lets you adjust the preferred memory size while an application is open (changes take effect the next time you launch the application). This type of management should enable you to keep more applications open simultaneously. This application by Andrew S. Downs costs $10.

Mt. Everything

The Mt. Everything enhanced hard-disk management application is most beneficial for users with multiple drives. It displays the types, manufacturers, and partition maps of devices connected to your SCSI bus; mounts partitions and drives without the necessity of restarting; supplies its own driver software; and supports removable media. This control panel by Horst H. Pralow is yours to use for the cost of a postcard sent to the author as specified in the program's documentation.

MultiTimer Pro

MultiTimer Pro compiles autosaved data logs of the time you spend on your computer, including time spent in specific applications, online time, and other tasks. MultiTimer Pro lets you create special modules to represent each project, which ensures accurate records of your sessions. You can record multiple projects simultaneously using MultiTimer Pro, and you can paste log files with MultiTimer Pro module data into spreadsheets. This application by Karl Bunker (`http://www.ironsoftware.com/`) costs $15.

MyBattery

MyBattery shows the voltage levels for three different PowerBook batteries. The program also lets you enable and disable AppleTalk and turn your modem on and off. This application by Jeremy Kezer costs $10.

MyEyes

MyEyes draws a pair of eyes on the menu bar that constantly follows the pointer's movement. MyEyes helps PowerBook users who have trouble seeing the pointer find it more quickly. This extension by Federico Filipponi costs $10.

NetCD

NetCD creates a controller window for playing audio CDs on the Mac. In addition, the program can download the title and track list for each of your audio CDs from the CDDB database on the Internet to your computer. Whenever you insert the same CD again, its track and title information appears in NetCD or in the AppleCD Audio Player or the audio CD control strip module that come with Mac OS 9. This application by Toby Rush (`http://macinsearch.com/users/tobyrush/software.html`) is free.

Net-Print

Net-Print prints or saves text from the Internet or any application. You can combine text selections from multiple sources on a single page or in a single file. In addition, you can include source information such as URL, title, and date. This control panel by John Moe (`http://www93.pair.com/johnmoe/`) costs $10.

NetStickies

NetStickies adds AppleTalk network functionality to the Stickies application that comes with Mac OS 9. You can send and receive sticky notes from other users who have NetStickies installed, send text clippings from a text drag-and-drop, and send clipboard text. The target user receives the text as a sticky note that is immediately visible onscreen. This extension by Ron Duritsch is free.

Newer Technology Gauge Series

The Gauge Series profiles and measures the performance of various hardware components in your computer, including Level-2 cache, CPU, RAM, SCSI devices, and PCI Slots. This set of applications from Newer Technologies, Inc. (http://www.newertech.com/software/newertools.html) is free.

OneApp Secret Folder

Secret Folder lets you conceal a folder and its contents. It protects documents and avoids their being seen, modified, or erased by other users. The program can be protected with a password for extra security. This shareware utility from OneApp Software (http://www.oneappsoftware.com/) costs $20.

Open with Process

Open with Process adds a command to the Finder's contextual menus in Mac OS 9. This command enables you to open a file in an application other than the one that created it. In the Finder, select the items you want to open, Control+click to display the contextual menu, and choose Open with Process. This command sends an Open Document event to any currently running application you choose. This contextual menu plug-in by George Temple (http://www.monmouth.com/~ttempel) costs $1.

OSA Menu

OSA Menu adds an icon to the menu bar that gives you access from within applications to scripts written with an OSA-compliant script editor. You can start and stop recording a script directly from the OSA Menu, run scripts, and access the script folders for the current application as well as for universal scripts. This extension by Leonard Rosenthol (http://www.lazerware.com/) is free.

Path

Path adds a command to the Finder's contextual menus in Mac OS 9. This command enables you to copy the full path names of selected files and folders to the Clipboard. You choose whether to include the AppleTalk zone and server in the path name. This contextual menu plug-in by George Tempel (http://www.monmouth.com/~ttempel) costs $1.

PlugAlert

PlugAlert detects when the power adapter has become unplugged from the wall or your PowerBook and also indicates when the wall outlet isn't supplying electricity. This extension by Sean Hummel is free.

PopChar Pro

PopChar Pro simplifies "typing" of unusual characters. Pull down the PopChar menu and select the character you want; PopChar Pro automatically inserts it in the current document as if you had typed the proper key combination on the keyboard. This control panel from Uni Software Plus (`http://www.unisoft.co.at/products/popchar.html`) costs $39.

PopupCD

PopupCD provides a pop-up remote control for quick and easy access to your audio CDs through your CD-ROM drive. The remote control has all the functions normally used with conventional CD players, as well as a playing time indicator and a pop-up track menu. You can access all functions with configurable keyboard hot keys as well through the onscreen remote. If you're tired of launching or switching applications just to control your CDs, PopupCD can be an elegant and unobtrusive alternative. PopupCD can also record audio clips directly from CD to hard drive. This control panel by John Brochu (`http://www.tiac.net/users/jbrochu/`) requires the Apple CD-ROM software, which is included with the Mac OS. It costs $15.

PowerBar Pro

PowerBar Pro is an application launcher that features handy Finder-action tiles, such as Move to Trash, Empty Trash, and Restart. Tiles can launch QuicKeys macros, Control Strip modules, or other PowerBar palettes. When you hold the mouse down on a folder tile, a pop-up menu shows everything inside. This application by Scott Johnson, Trilobyte Software, costs $25.

PowerMenu

PowerMenu extends the capabilities of Mac OS 9's contextual menus. These menus make it easy to launch applications, open documents, and open files in programs other than the creating program. You can manipulate the Finder files from the contextual menu; for example, copying and moving files between folders without dragging and dropping, or copying multiple files from various locations and then pasting them all in one location with a single command. This control panel, extension, and CMM plug-in by Mark Aiken (`http://www.kagi.com/authors/marka/pm.html`) costs $15.

PowerSaver Tweak

PowerSaver Tweak provides more control over power-conservation settings than the standard Energy Saver and PowerBook control panels. It lets you configure the conservation settings for specific applications, screen dimming, drive spindown, system sleep, and CPU cycling for up to 50 applications (unregistered copies allow for up to 4 applications). For example, you can prevent your PowerBook from cycling while you are playing a particular game. Or use PowerSaver Tweak so that your hard drive never spins down while using Microsoft Word. This control panel by Jeremy Kezer (http://www.kezer.net/shareware.html) requires a PowerBook or a computer with PCI expansion slots and costs $10.

Power Speed Mouse

Power Speed Mouse enables you to speed up your mouse. It's particularly beneficial if you're using a large monitor, because the mouse speeds up over long distances but otherwise moves normally. The application has options for speeding up the mouse and returning the mouse to normal. Speeds must be reset across restarts. This application by Alamo Computer is free.

Power Windows

This program by Greg Landweber enables you to drag solid or translucent windows in Mac OS 9 instead of simply dragging the outline of a window. This shareware extension from http://www.kaleidoscope.net/greg/ costs $10.

Program Switcher

Program Switcher enables you to assign keystrokes to the Finder-related functions for rapid desktop shortcuts, such as showing and hiding applications. This control panel by Michael F. Kamprath (http://www.lkamprathnet/claireware/) costs $10.

QuickNailer

QuickNailer displays thumbnail previews of your graphics and movie files, and saves the previews in a catalog or in Web pages (HTML files). This utility can also display full-size images, present slide shows, and show file information. It uses QuickTime for file-format translation. This application by Stephen Baber (http://www.amug.org/~sbaber/) costs $18.

RamBunctious

RamBunctious creates RAM disks with a variety of user-configurable options. You can create RAM-only or disk-based volumes. For disk-based volumes, a write-through option saves data to a disk image file for added security. RamBunctious carries out the write-through operations at user-specified intervals or when the disk is put away; you can initiate a write-through at any time by clicking a button in the control window. This window also enables you to change a disk's settings at any time. RamBunctious can be controlled with AppleScript and comes with several example scripts. This application by Elden Wood and Bob Clark (http://www. kagi.com/authors/rambunctious/) **costs $12.**

ReminderPro

ReminderPro lets you schedule one-time or repeating reminders as you work on your computer. The package includes a Control Strip module for scheduling reminders instantly, and the ReminderPro system extension, which works continuously in the background to display reminders at the appropriate times as well as automating tasks like scheduled launching of applications, opening of documents, and automatically running AppleScripts at designated times. This extension by Manoj Patwardhan of Crystal Software, Inc. costs $18.

ResEdit

Apple's ResEdit enables you to edit system and application resources, such as icons, menus, and the text of alert messages. You can do many fun things with ResEdit but beware—only work on *copies* of the files that you are editing. If you make a mistake, you could ruin the file. This application by Apple Computer (http://swupdates.info.apple.com/) **is free.**

SCSI Probe

SCSI Probe identifies and mounts SCSI devices connected to your Mac. SCSI Probe displays device type, vendor, product, and version information for any device connected to the SCSI bus. An included startup extension lets you mount volumes without going through the control panel. This control panel by Robert Polic is free.

ShrinkWrap

ShrinkWrap creates disk image files similar to Disk Copy (which was described earlier in this chapter) when you drag-and-drop floppy drive icons onto the ShrinkWrap icon. It also opens Disk Copy disk images and automatically compresses and decompresses archived image files on the fly with Aladdin's StuffIt Expander. ShrinkWrap, distributed by Aladdin Systems (831-761-6200, http://www.aladdinsys.com), **costs $30.**

Shutdown Delay

Shutdown Delay displays a dialog box at restart or shutdown time that allows you to complete the original command, return to the desktop, restart, shut down, or force quit and return to the Finder. This control panel by Alessandro Levi Montalcini (http://www.montalcini.com) costs $10.

Sloop

Sloop adds pointer focusing to the Mac OS: Whatever window the pointer is over automatically moves to the front (acquires focus) — which is a navigational strategy that is popular in X Windows, which provides windows for the UNIX OS. You can configure Sloop to operate exclusively in specific applications or as a general desktop feature. This extension from Quadratic Software (http://www.quadratic.com) costs $20.

Snapz Pro

Capture any part of your screen (windows, menus, sections) using many popular file formats and even assign them associations with popular applications. Snapz Pro lets you take screenshots while menus are open, the mouse is active, screens are being dragged across the screen, and more. A new feature is the capability to have Snapz Pro make a QuickTime movie of your moves on the desktop — perfect for creating onscreen demos and tutorials. This shareware control panel from Ambrosia Software (http://www.ambrosiasw.com/) is $20.

Snitch

Snitch extends the capabilities of the Finder's Get Info window through a set of plug-ins, enabling you to see and change a variety of information about files and folders. Plug-in capabilities include letting you see and change creator and type codes, see preview information, preview the first 100 bytes of a file's data and resource forks, and update aliases. A batch info window enables you to edit several items at once. This control panel from Nifty Neato Software (http://www.niftyneato.com) costs $20.

SoundApp

SoundApp is a sound playback and conversion utility for the Mac OS. Use it as a sound-playing helper application with Web browsers. In addition to managing a collection of play lists, SoundApp can play or convert files dropped on it in a variety of formats and sample rates. This application by Norman Franke III is free.

SoundMaster

SoundMaster makes your computer play sounds when you perform various tasks on your system such as inserting a disk, emptying the trash, shutting down, or performing keyboard functions such as tabbing, deleting, and scrolling. This control panel by Bruce Tomlin costs $15.

SpeechTyper

Using Apple's PlainTalk technology, SpeechTyper recognizes predefined phrases that you speak aloud. In response, it types commonly used words or phrases in the active document. You can program SpeechTyper with many different phrases, and then speak the whole phrase or part of it (or a "shortcut" word) to type it in your documents. This shareware control panel from Claireware Software (`http://www.kamprath.net/claireware/`) costs $10.

SpeedShare and SpeedShare Pro

SpeedShare and SpeedShare Pro enable you to share files on a remote Mac over the Internet even without a permanent Internet address. When you run the SpeedShare server software, you make all or some of the items on your Mac available by setting up a server name and password and connecting to the Internet. Users who have installed the SpeedShare Client software can now access the SpeedShare Server via QDEA's Rendezvous or through a direct TCP/IP address. (Rendezvous keeps track of the dynamic addresses of the Macs currently using SpeedShare on the Internet so that they can connect to each other.) Clients can browse, move, and copy files on connected SpeedShare servers. The Pro version is enhanced for professional environments and offers features such as very fast transfer of files over LANs and multiple simultaneous connections from many users. Both client applications from Qdea (`http://www.qdea.com`) are free; SpeedShare Server costs $49.95 and SpeedShare Pro Server costs $129.95.

Super Comments

Super Comments permits comments to be viewed in Open dialog boxes and edited in Save dialog boxes. This control panel by Maurice Volaski (`http://www.fluxsoft.com`) costs $10.

Super Save

Have your keystrokes captured and backed up to text files stored in the System Folder. This way, every keystroke you make up to a crash or freeze is saved, so you can recover all of your work. Super Save can also send events to selected applications telling them to autosave the current document. This shareware control panel by Claireware (http://www.kamprath.net/claireware/) costs $10.

SuperTools

SuperTools is three applications that speed the launching, printing, and erasing of documents. SuperPrint is a drop box desktop printer that prints a document on a currently selected printer when you drag-and-drop the document's icon on SuperPrint. SuperLaunch lets you bundle a series of documents to create workbooks by dragging the collection on top of the SuperLaunch icon. SuperTrash permanently erases a document by writing zeroes on top of its data before deletion. This application by Pascal Pochet costs $25.

SwitchBack

SwitchBack synchronizes two folders on the same volume, on two different volumes, or on two different computers connected by a network so that copies of the most recent versions of files are found in both places. It works with all Mac OS computers and also backs up DOS disks. This application by Glendower Software Ltd. costs $30.

System Picker

System Picker lets you keep more than one valid System Folder on a single disk volume and choose the folder that will be the active System Folder on restart. It scans all volumes to create a list of usable System Folders that are accessible via a pop-up menu. This application by Kevin Aitken is free. Apple distributes System Picker as unsupported software on its FTP site at ftp://ftp.apple.com/devworld/utilites/.

TechTool Freeware

TechTool Freeware performs various simple diagnostic and repair operations, such as analyzing your system file for damage, cleaning the floppy drive, deleting and rebuilding the desktop, resetting PRAM, and displaying the date the computer was manufactured and the number of hours it has been used. This application from Micromat Computer Systems (http://www.micromat.com/micromat/software.html) is free.

Tex-Edit Plus

Tex-Edit Plus is a small, fast text editor that offers a number of word-processing features, including find and replace, change case, block formatting, customizable tabs, and line spacing. Tex-Edit is scriptable. You can access scripts from the menu bar. Scripts included with the program offer quick document modifications; for example, changing text to HTML, switching between smart and dumb quotes, and formatting for Mac e-mail messages that were created in Windows and vice versa. This application from Tom Bender, Trans-Tex Software (`http://members.aol.com/tombb/`), costs $10.

TitlePop

The TitlePop extension turns a document window's title into a pop-up menu that lists items for windows that belong to the current program and an item for background programs, which are shown in hierarchical menus below their respective program items. You can bring any window to the front by selecting it from the TitlePop menu. This extension by Jouko Pakkanen is free.

Trash It!

The Trash It! Control Strip module can empty the Trash without warnings about locked or busy files. It accepts drag-and-drop multiple-file and -folder deletions, and can delete the desktop on mounted volumes and floppies. This control strip module by Ammon Skidmore, Skidperfect Software, requires the Extensions Strip, Control Strip, or Desktop Strip software. It is free.

TypeIt4Me

TypeIt4Me works inside any application that allows text-entry, letting you type small abbreviations for predefined strings like names, addresses, and difficult-to-type phrases. It's similar to the commercial program QuicKeys; however, instead of assigning key commands, you assign your own special abbreviations. This control panel by Ricardo Ettore costs $30.

UltraFind

UltraFind quickly searches any mounted media on your desktop or network, including remote volumes via modem using ARA, provides detailed information about items, copies or moves them across the network, performs backups, or deletes selected items. It can also extract information from damaged files. This application by UltraDesign Technology (`http://www.ultradesign.com`) costs $39.

USB Overdrive

USB Overdrive enables you to install nearly any USB keyboard, mouse, or joystick and get full functionality in Macintosh applications and games. The software enables you to configure the controller with custom setup functions, including mapping controls to keys, mouse strokes, or macros. This shareware control panel by Alessandro Levi Montalcini (`http://www.usboverdrive.com/`) costs $20.

Virtual

Virtual, an adaptation of Sun Microsystems' window manager, "olvwm," enables you to simulate more than one monitor on your desktop, drawing as many virtual screens as you like, as well as the windows of open applications inside them. You can create windows' representations in Virtual, place them in different virtual screens to organize them in workgroups, make some windows sticky, or assign whole applications to a particular virtual screen. This application by Pierre-Luc Paour (`http://www.kagi.com/paour`) costs $10.

Window Picker

Window Picker lets you find any open window in the Finder and bring it to the front using Mac OS 9's contextual menus. This contextual menu plug-in from Hi Resolution is free.

WrapScreen

WrapScreen implements a wraparound mouse pointer: instead of stopping at the right edge of the screen, for example, the pointer appears at the left edge. This control panel by Eric Arbourg is yours to use for the cost of a donation.

Summary

In this chapter, you saw that shareware and freeware are available from many Internet sites, America Online, user groups, and Apple Computer. You can distribute copies of most shareware and freeware, but authors generally retain copyrights to their software. Shareware authors ask that you send payment for products that you decide to keep, but freeware authors don't ask for payment. The utilities listed in this chapter are a sample of the utility shareware and freeware that's available to enhance the Mac OS.

✦ ✦ ✦

Discover Tips and Secrets

Scattered throughout the previous chapters of this book are scores of tips and secrets for getting more out of Mac OS 9. For your convenience, this chapter and the next chapter contain a digest of the most useful tips and secrets plus some tips that don't appear elsewhere in this book. This chapter has tips for the desktop: icons, folders and windows, the Trash, the Apple Menu, and fonts. Chapter 28 concentrates on system-related tips: dialog boxes, file sharing, system utilities, control panels and extensions, applications, and memory and system performance.

To use some of these tips, you need a copy of ResEdit, Apple's no-cost resource editor. You can get ResEdit from Apple's Software Updates library (http://www.apple.com/swupdates/), online services such as America Online (keyword: filesearch), and Macintosh user groups. You can also get a copy of ResEdit from Macworld's Macdownload software library (http://macdownload.com). For more sources of shareware and freeware, see Chapter 26.

Icons

This section contains tips for saving time and effort when editing icon names, for making and using aliases on the desktop, and for getting icons to look the way you want.

Spotting a name selected for editing

For a visual cue that you have selected the name of an icon on a color or grayscale monitor, use the Appearance control panel to set the text-highlight color to something other than black and white. Then you'll know that a name highlighted in color (or gray) is ready for editing, whereas a name highlighted in black and white is not. Figure 27-1 is an example of a file name highlighted and ready for editing and a file that has been merely selected and is therefore not editable.

Figure 27-1: A distinctive highlight color makes it easy to spot an icon whose name is ready for editing (right).

Edit, don't open

If you have trouble editing icon names without opening the item, remember to click the item name, not the icon. Keep the pointer over the item name and wait for the name to highlight automatically. (The lag time between your click and the name highlighting depends on the double-click speed set in the Mouse control panel: a slower double-click speed means a longer wait for the name to highlight.)

And then there's the really easy way. Select the icon and press Return. You're immediately in editing mode.

Undoing an accidental name change

If you rename an icon by mistake, choose Undo from the Edit menu (or press ⌘+Z) to restore the original name. Another way to restore the icon's original name is to press Backspace or Delete until the name is empty and then press Return or click outside the icon. (You cannot undo your changes to a name after you finish editing it, only while it is still selected for editing.)

Copy/paste icon names

While editing a name, you can use the Undo, Cut, Copy, Paste, and Select All commands in the Edit menu. You can also copy the entire name of any item by selecting its icon (or its whole name) and then choosing the Copy command from the Edit menu. This capability is handy when you're copying a disk and want to give the copy the same name as the original.

You can copy the name of a locked item — select the item and use the Copy command — but you can't change the name of a locked item. (Unlock a file by using the Get Info command (⌘+I), a folder by using the Sharing command, or a floppy disk by sliding its locking tab.)

The Mac OS doesn't limit you to copying one icon name at a time. If you select several items and then use the Copy command, the names of all the items are put on the Clipboard, one name per line. The total you can copy is about 32MB, or more than 1000 items.

Removing the "alias" from alias names

When you use the Finder's Make Alias command, the resulting alias has the word alias at the end of its name. To remove the word alias from the end of an icon name, select the name for editing, press the right-arrow (→) or down-arrow (↓) key to move the insertion point to the end of the name, and press Delete five or six times. Pressing Delete five times leaves a blank space at the end of the alias name to distinguish it from the original name; pressing Delete six times removes this space.

Aliases where you want them

Making an alias of an item that's not on the same disk as the alias is a three-step process if you use Finder's Make Alias command. First, make the alias on the same disk as its original item; second, copy the alias to the destination disk; and third, delete the first alias. A better way is to make an alias exactly where you want it in the first place. In Mac OS 9, simply hold down ⌘+Option while dragging the original item to the disk where you want an alias.

Desktop aliases

Rather than drag frequently used programs, control panels, documents, and folders themselves to the desktop, make aliases of those items and place the aliases on the desktop. You get quick access to the original items through their desktop aliases. Also, you can open several related items at the same time by opening aliases on the desktop, even if the original items happen to be in different folders or on different disks.

If your desktop becomes too cluttered with aliases, you can store related aliases together in a desktop folder and tuck the folder conveniently out of the way at the bottom of your screen as a pop-up window. Figure 27-2 shows aliases on the desktop and in a pop-up window.

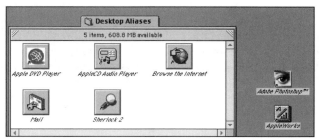

Figure 27-2: Keep frequently used items handy with aliases of them on the desktop or in pop-up windows.

Viewing aliases as buttons makes them even easier targets for drag-and-drop (if they're applications), plus you can single-click them to launch the aliases.

Permanently removing *alias*

If you always remove the word *alias* from the end of new alias names, you may prefer never to have the word appended to file names at all. You can make a change with ResEdit so that Finder never appends alias to the names of new aliases. Follow these steps:

1. Make an alias of ResEdit and place it on the desktop.

2. Open the system folder and Option+drag Finder to the desktop, which creates a duplicate Finder. Drag this duplicate Finder to the ResEdit icon to open it.* You see a window full of icons, with each icon representing a different type of resource in the Finder.

3. Double-click the STR# resource type, opening a window that lists all the Finder's string-list resources by number.

4. Locate STR# resource number 8200 and double-click it to open it. The alias suffix is in string #1. This is the text that the Finder appends to the original file name to make up the alias name.

5. Change the string to one blank space rather than making it completely empty, so that the names of original files and their aliases will be different.

6. To finish, close all the ResEdit windows or simply quit ResEdit. Answer Yes when you are asked if you want to save your changes.

7. To see the results of your work, drag the original Finder to a folder outside the system folder, and then drag the altered Finder to the System Folder and restart your computer.

*Always work on a copy of the original file when using ResEdit. You might think ResEdit keeps your changes only in the computer's memory until you save them to disk because the program asks whether you want to save changes before closing a file or quitting the program. But that alert is a cruel joke. As you make changes to a file, ResEdit actually updates the file on disk. If you get the alert and answer No, ResEdit reverses the changes and your file is safe. But if your computer crashes (does anyone have a computer that does not crash?), or if ResEdit quits unexpectedly before you have the opportunity to reverse your ResEdit changes, you'll find the changes in place when you restart your computer and reopen the file with ResEdit. Be aware, and may the power of ResEdit be with you.

Express access to CD-ROMs

Cut through the drudgery of wading through folders on a CD-ROM by making aliases of items inside the CD-ROM folders. Because CD-ROMs are permanently locked, you must put the aliases on your hard disk (or a floppy disk). Opening an alias makes a beeline to the original item on the CD-ROM. If the CD-ROM isn't in your drive, the Finder asks you to insert it. Figure 27-3 is an example of a disk insert message. When you need the item again, the Mac OS tells you the name of the disk to insert so that it can open the alias's original item. If you change your mind or can't find the needed disk, click Cancel.

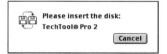

Figure 27-3: If you open an alias whose original item is on a disk that's not inserted, the Mac OS prompts you to insert the specific disk.

Cataloging items on removable disks

You can use aliases to keep track of, and quickly open, items on removable disks — even floppies and others that aren't inserted in your computer. Make aliases of the items on a removable disk by selecting them and ⌘+Option+dragging them to your startup disk. (If you use the Make Alias command to make the aliases, you have to copy the aliases to the startup disk and then delete the aliases from the floppy disk.) When you need the item again, the Mac OS tells you the name of the disk to insert so that it can open the alias's original item. If you change your mind or can't find the needed disk, click Cancel.

Keychain alias

Create an alias to your keychain file (located in the System Folder in the Preferences folder in the Keychains folder) and put it on the desktop or in the Apple Menu, or add it as a Favorite. Then, whenever you double-click the file (or launch it from a menu), one of two things happens. If your keychain is locked, you can unlock it. If it's unlocked, the Keychain Access control panel displays.

Making many aliases

You can make aliases for several items in the same window at the same time. First, select all the items. Then ⌘+Option+drag the items in the same window, to a different window or to the desktop. Alternatively, you can use the Make Alias command (⌘+M). An alias appears for each item that you selected. All the new aliases are selected automatically so that you can drag them to another place without having to manually select them as a group. If you accidentally deselect the items, you can easily group them together for reselecting by arranging or sorting the window by kind or date created.

Reverting to standard icons

You can revert to an item's standard icon after replacing the icon with custom graphics. Just select the item and use the Finder's Get Info command (⌘+I) to display the item's Info window. Select the icon in the Info window and a box appears around the icon to indicate that you have selected the icon. Choose Clear or Cut from the Edit menu or press Delete or Clear.

Fixing blank icons

Sometimes a file that you copy to your disk ends up with a generic (blank) icon. You really don't want to rebuild your desktop files just to fix one icon (especially if you have a large disk). Instead, open the icon's Info window (⌘+I) and select the icon in the Info window. Now copy, paste, and cut the icon—in that order. If you are lucky, the correct icon shows its face.

Here's how it works: Copying the icon makes it possible to paste; pasting the icon causes the Finder to internally mark the file as one that has a custom icon; and cutting the icon causes the Finder to unmark the file and restore its standard icon. You can't do the cutting step unless you have done the pasting step, and you can't do the pasting step unless you have done the copying step.

Customizing folder icons

If you think you have too many boring, look-alike folders cluttering your desktop, you can enliven those folders by superimposing relevant application icons. Follow these steps:

1. Copy a folder icon from its Info window (which you display by choosing the Finder's Get Info command) and paste the icon in a color paint program.

2. Open the folder that contains the application whose icon you want to use, and make sure you've got View by Icon chosen in the View menu. Next, open the View Options control panel (View ➪ View Options) and select the small icon size. Now, take a screen snapshot of the application icon. (To take the screen shot, press ⌘+Shift+4 and drag a selection rectangle around the icon.) Hold down Control while releasing the mouse button to copy the screen shot to the Clipboard.

3. In the color paint program, paste the icon on top of the pasted folder icon.

4. Copy the composite icon from the paint program, paste it in the folder's Info window, and close the Info window.

When you select the custom icon in the paint program, you must take care to select a rectangular area no larger than 32 × 32 pixels (the maximum size of an icon). If you select a larger area, including lots of white space around your custom icon, the Finder shrinks the selection to 32 × 32 when you paste it in the folder's Info window, and your custom icon ends up shrunken and difficult to see. If you select an area smaller than 32 × 32, the Finder centers the selection in the folder's icon space, and the custom icon does not align horizontally with a plain folder icon (which is flush with the bottom of its icon space).

You can avoid this rigmarole by using the freeware utility Folder Icon Maker by Gregory Robbins. Just drag a great-looking application or document icon to Folder Icon Maker and presto — Folder Icon Maker creates a new folder with a small version of that icon superimposed on it.

The custom icon obscures any subsequent changes that you make to the folder's color (by changing its label) or to the folder's file-sharing status (with the Finder's Sharing command).

Distinctive volumes

It's not unusual to have more than one hard disk icon on the desktop. This happens when you have more than one disk drive or when you have partitioned a large hard drive into multiple volumes (see Chapter 28). Although it's not hard to identify each disk volume by name, it is easier to tell them apart if their icons look different. You can certainly make disk volumes distinctive by giving each a different custom icon. A subtler alternative that you may find every bit as effective is to make each volume icon a different color. To colorize a volume icon, select it and choose a colored label from the Label submenu of the File menu.

Bad disk icon

If you have problems with a custom disk icon — for instance, if your hard disk icon appears as a generic document icon — try the freeware utility Disk Rejuvenator (see Chapter 26). This utility is also handy if you have a problem accessing your hard disk from standard Open dialog boxes. If you have problems with a custom folder icon, drag the folder's contents to a new folder and then drag the troublesome, now-empty folder to the Trash.

Desktop and Startup

This section covers tips for customizing your desktop, as well as the sights and sounds that you see and hear during and after startup.

Rebuilding the desktop

To rebuild the desktop of any disk whose icon normally appears on the desktop after startup, press ⌘+Option while starting your computer. For each disk in turn, the Finder asks whether you want the disk's desktop to be rebuilt. To rebuild the desktop of a floppy disk or another removable disk whose icon is not on the desktop, press ⌘+Option while inserting the disk. Figure 27-4 is an example of a rebuild confirmation dialog box.

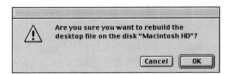

Figure 27-4: You must confirm rebuilding each disk's desktop individually.

Custom startup screen

Instead of the plain old "Welcome to Mac OS" startup screen, your computer can display a special picture. If your system folder contains a file named StartupScreen that contains a PICT resource with ID 0, the graphic image in that resource replaces the standard startup screen. You can use any of several programs to create such a startup screen for your computer, or you can create one using just ResEdit and the Scrapbook (see the sidebar "Creating your own startup screen").

If you use a graphics program to create your custom startup screen, save the file as Startup Screen or StartupScreen as the file type (generally by choosing it from a pop-up menu in the Save As dialog box). In some graphics programs, you choose Resource File as the type of file to save and then specify a resource ID of 0 instead.

Creating your own startup screen

If you don't have a graphics program that can save a startup screen but you do have ResEdit, you can use it and the ScrapBook to create your own startup screen file. Follow these steps:

1. Paste the image that you want to use as a startup screen into the ScrapBook.

2. Close the ScrapBook and use ResEdit to open a copy of the ScrapBook file (located in the System Folder).

ResEdit displays a window containing icons that represent different types of resources in the ScrapBook file.

3. Open the ScrapBook file's PICT-resources icon and scroll through the images until you see the one that you want for your startup screen. (If you don't see the image, you may need to increase ResEdit's memory partition.)

4. Copy the PICT resource that you want to use.

5. Create a new document in ResEdit, call it StartupScreen, and save it in the System Folder. Paste the PICT resource that you just copied.

6. Open the PICT-resource icon in the new document, select the image that you just pasted, and choose Get Resource Info (⌘+I) from the Resource menu. In the Resource Info window that appears, change the ID number to 0.

7. Quit ResEdit and click Yes when asked whether you want to save the changes that you made.

8. Restart your computer to see the custom startup screen.

Startup movie

If you have QuickTime installed, you can have a movie play during startup by naming it Startup Movie and placing it in the System Folder. (To halt the startup movie, press ⌘+period (.) or any other key.)

Startup sounds

You can put a sound file in the Startup Items folder (inside the System Folder) and that file will play after your extensions load when you start your computer. (If you have Multiple Users active, the sound file will not play until after you've logged in to your account.)

If your computer has a microphone, you can use the SimpleSound program or the Sound control panel to record a message for the next person who uses the computer, or just for fun. To halt startup sounds, press ⌘+period (.).

Squelching the startup chime

Have you ever wanted to silence the computer's startup chime? On some Mac models, you can't quiet the startup chime by turning down the volume level in the Sound control panel. If you want to eliminate the computer's startup chime, try one of these methods:

✦ Plug an earphone or headphones into the sound output port — you don't have to wear them.

✦ On a desktop computer with speakers in the monitor, turn on the monitor a few seconds after starting the computer. (This happens automatically with some Apple monitors because the monitor and its speakers don't turn on until the computer's ADB port comes to life, which happens after the startup chime.)

If your Mac does silence its startup chime when you turn down the sound volume all the way, you may wish to have the sound volume automatically turned up again after startup. You can accomplish this with the two very simple AppleScript applications shown in Figure 27-5.

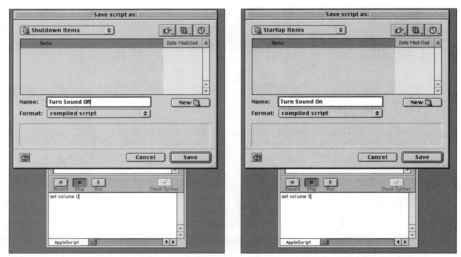

Figure 27-5: Two one-line AppleScript applications that turn system sound off (left) and on (right)

To create AppleScript applications that turn off the system sound during shutdown and turn it on during startup, follow these steps:

1. Open the Script Editor program (in the AppleScript folder inside the Apple Extras folder). In the script-editing window that appears, type the following one-line AppleScript statement:

```
set volume 0
```

2. Choose Save As from the File menu. In the Save As dialog box, open the Startup Items folder so that the script is saved there. In addition, choose Application from the pop-up menu so that the script is saved as an application. Also turn on the Never Show Startup Screen option to prevent a dialog box from appearing every time the script application runs.

3. Change the AppleScript line to the following, replacing *x* with a number from 1 (lowest volume) to 7 (highest volume):

```
set volume x
```

4. Repeat Step 2 to save this script as an application, except this time save it in the Shutdown Items folder.

5. Quit Script Editor.

Bigger pointers

If your computer's pointer is just too small for you to comfortably keep track of in its travels around your desktop, try Robert Abatecola's shareware Fat Cursors. Fat Cursors enlarges both the arrow pointer and the I-beam-shaped text pointer.

Several utilities just make it easier to locate a normal-sized pointer. Eyeballs installs a pair of eyes that watch your pointer from the menu bar. FindCursor, ZoomToCursor, and CursorBeacon each create a different type of visual commotion around the pointer when you press a specified key combination.

Custom system beeps

You can create your own custom system alert sounds on your computer from any audio CD. Follow these steps:

1. Using the AppleCD Audio Player, play the audio CD from which you want to make the alert sound and note the track and time where the passage you want to record starts. Pause the CD a few seconds before the start of the passage.

2. Open the Sound control panel and click the Sound button. Set the volume control to a comfortable level. In your Sound control panel's Sound Input option, set it to Internal CD or DVD. Turn on Play sound through output device. Then switch to the Alert view by clicking Alert Sounds.

3. Switch to the Audio Player and click or press Play (or the Spacebar). Immediately switch to the Monitors & Sound control panel and click Add and then Record (the timing can be tricky). Click Stop to finish your new alert sound — a second or two at most is plenty.

4. Name and save your new alert sound.

Startup booby trap

Don't hold down the Power-on key on the keyboard for more than a second or two when starting a Power Mac. Doing so sets the stage for the unexpected appearance of the mysterious programmer's window (a dialog box — containing only a greater-than symbol — that provides access to a limited set of program debugging tools known as the Mini Debugger). This baffling window appears sometime later, seemingly unbidden and definitely unwanted, when you press the ⌘ key. (You can make the programmer's window appear at will by holding down ⌘ and pressing Power-on.)

If the programmer's window appears on your screen, you can usually resume work without restarting by typing the letter G (short for Go) and pressing Return. If you type anything else and press Return, you may have to restart, losing all unsaved work.

If you hold down the Power-on key too long when starting up and later press Control+⌘, the computer restarts as if you switched the power off and on. In this case, you have inadvertently invoked the emergency restart sequence, which normally involves holding down Control+⌘ and pressing Power-on.

Caution   Don't use this technique as a shortcut for the Restart command, which causes the Mac OS to go through a proper shutdown sequence. Use it only in lieu of restart-ing with the power switch — for example, if your computer crashes.

Better file-sharing startup

Although you can have the Mac OS automatically connect to shared folders and disks at startup, doing so can really slow network performance (especially if everyone on the network does it). To reduce network traffic while keeping shared folders and disks conveniently accessible, use aliases to connect to them whenever you need them. To set up the aliases, use the Network Browser or the Chooser to connect to the shared folders and disks. Then select the shared folders and disks and make aliases. Put copies of the aliases on the desktop, in the Apple Menu Items folder, and anywhere else you want quick access to the shared items.

When you open the alias of a shared folder or disk, or drag something to the alias, your computer automatically asks you for a password and then connects to the shared folder or disk. (If you have Keychain access setup for this server and your keychain is unlocked, you don't even need to enter a password.) Similarly, you can make aliases of items inside the shared folders and disks and use those aliases to simplify accessing the original items over the network.

Unfortunately, aliases of shared items do not always work correctly when the original items are on file servers that use the Windows NT Services for Macintosh.

Thawing a frozen program

Applications sometimes freeze and don't respond to ordinary controls such as Cancel buttons or pressing ⌘+period (.). When this happens use the Force Quit command: press ⌘+Option+Escape. This combination brings up a dialog box with a Force Quit button and a Cancel button. Clicking Cancel (not Force Quit) sometimes seems to act like a whiff of ammonia for a program that has passed out. It doesn't often work, but when it does, it beats the alternatives. Be sure to save your work and restart the computer right away after reviving a frozen program.

If this step freezes your computer even more (and you can't bring back the Force Quit alert box), and you've waited for a while to make sure things don't right themselves, you can attempt to recover to the Finder. Press ⌘+Power-on. This brings up the programmer's window. Enter **G F** (which may or may not stand for "Go Finder" depending on whom you ask) and press Return. If you're lucky, you'll recover to the Finder. Save other documents (your system is likely very unstable) and restart.

First or last in a hurry

In most folder and disk windows, you can highlight the item that comes first alphabetically by pressing any number key or the Spacebar. In most cases, you can highlight the item that comes last alphabetically by pressing the Option key along with any number key.

These tricks (which stem from the capability to select an item by typing the first part of its name) work fine unless you have many item names that come after a bullet (•), including names beginning with most accented capital letters, most symbols you type with the Option and Shift keys, and some symbols that you type with the Option key alone.

If nothing is selected in the active Finder window (or on the desktop, if no window has racing stripes to indicate it is the active one), you can highlight the first or last item by pressing Tab or Shift+Tab. With an item highlighted, pressing Tab or Shift+Tab highlights the item that follows or precedes it alphabetically, and pressing an arrow key highlights the closest item on the desktop in the direction of the arrow.

Startup messages

Do you like to have reminders at startup, but don't want to use Stickies? Create a clipping file of your notes and place an alias of it in the Startup Items folder. Rename it to be alphabetically last, so it opens after other startup items. At startup, the Finder does not have to launch an application to display the note, which you can easily dismiss with ⌘+W. If you keep the clipping on your desktop, you can view it anytime you want within seconds.

To edit a clipping file directly (without dragging it to the Note Pad or some other application), get the freeware FinderNote by Jae Ho Chang, eMusicas Software (described in Chapter 26).

Futuristic Finder

Want to glimpse the future, when Web browsers may usurp the Finder's role? If you drag a folder to a browser window of Netscape Navigator or Netscape Communicator, it lists the folder contents. In Microsoft Internet Explorer, type **file://localhost/** to see a list of disks on your desktop, and click a disk name to see its contents. Files and nested folders become clickable links, and if you click an HTML file (a Web page), a text file, a JPEG graphic file, or another file format that the browser can handle, it displays the file's contents. You can even save the listing in the browser window as a file. Figure 27-6 is an example of a futuristic Finder.

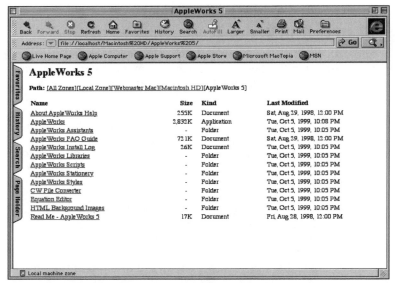

Figure 27-6: Use a Web browser to peruse the contents of your folders and disks.

You can also view files for which you have configured the browser to use a plug-in or a helper application. For instance, you can view a QuickTime movie by clicking its file name in the browser window if you have configured the browser application to use the QuickTime plug-in or the QuickTime Player application. It's a perfect way to catalog and browse clip art.

Quit the Finder

There are two good reasons to quit the Finder. First, you may have a Finder-replacement application that you'd like to use for your only interface to your Mac. Or, you may have a single application — usually a game — that needs as much RAM as you can possibly give it for best performance.

The Finder doesn't have a Quit command, but it will accept an Apple Event that tells it to quit. So, open the AppleScript Editor and create this script:

```
tell application "Finder"
quit
end tell
tell application "AppleWorks"
launch
end tell
```

You can substitute whatever application you'd like for AppleWorks. Or, you can enter the name of the game or multimedia application that needs access to as much RAM as possible. Click Check Syntax in the Script Editor and you'll be asked to locate AppleWorks or whatever application you've entered. Now, save the script as an applet. Whenever you launch it, the Finder will quit and the chosen application will launch.

How do you get the Finder back? Quit all open applications, including the application you've chosen to replace the Finder. When you quit the last application, the Finder starts automatically. Or, you can create another AppleScript that tells the Finder to launch, then activate it from whatever application you have launched.

Folders and Windows

The tips in this section involve customizing and the manipulating the Finder windows and folders.

Locking folders

Everyone knows how to lock a file with the Finder's Get Info command, but how do you lock a folder? You can do it with one of the options normally used for setting access privileges of a shared folder. Just select the folder that you want to lock and choose Sharing from the Get Info submenu of the File menu to bring up the folder's file-sharing privileges window. In this window, check the box labeled Can't move, rename, or delete this item. For this trick to work, file sharing must be turned on in the File Sharing or Sharing Setup control panel, whichever your computer has. (You don't have to actually share the folder or change any other sharing options.)

Note File Sharing can slow down your Mac and open it up to potential security risks, especially if you have File Sharing over IP turned on, you have shared folders you've forgotten about, or you allow guest access. Weigh this against the advantages of locking folders — remember that you can use Multiple Users (see Chapter 13) to secure your desktop, preferences, and documents from others who use your Mac.

Special folder replacement

Should you happen to discard one of the special folders inside the System Folder, you can make a replacement by using the Finder's New Folder command (File menu). After creating a new folder, change its name to that of the special folder you want: Apple Menu Items, Control Panels, Extensions, Fonts, Preferences, Startup Items, and so forth. Close the System Folder, wait a few seconds and reopen it, and its icon gets the distinctive appearance of the special folder that you're creating.

Closing all but one window

Here's a quick way to close all the Finder windows except one. Drag the window you want kept open to the bottom of the screen to make it a pop-up window. Next, close all remaining open windows by Option+clicking the close box of any open window or by pressing ⌘+Option+W. Finally, drag the pop-up window back to the middle of the screen to make it a regular window once more.

Special folder mistakes

The Finder sometimes makes mistakes when it puts items in the System Folder's special folder for you. The Finder may put some items in the correct places and incorrectly leave others in the System Folder itself. For example, it may put font files and font suitcases in the Fonts folder but leave a folder containing fonts in the System Folder. To correct this problem, you must open the folder containing fonts and drag the fonts to the System Folder icon or to the Fonts folder.

Abridged System Folder

Does finding the Apple Menu Items folder, Startup Items folder, or some other item in your System Folder take too long? Make aliases for the System Folder items that you access often — including an alias of the System Folder itself — and consolidate the aliases in a new folder. You can open and find an item in that folder faster than you can in the System Folder.

To make the new folder look like a System Folder, copy the icon from the System Folder's Info window and paste it into the new folder's Info window.

Labeling system clutter

Installer programs simplify the process of updating or installing software, but too many of these programs rudely scatter files all over the System Folder without so much as a by-your-leave. Some installers even commit the unforgivable offense of overwriting your existing control panels and extensions with older versions. Although you may be able to limit this subterranean mischief by doing a custom installation, there's an easy method for keeping tabs on the changes. Follow these steps:

1. Before running an installer program, label every item that you want to keep track of in the System Folder. Use the Label command in the Finder's File menu. Labeling the contents of your System Folder after a clean installation of the Mac OS starts you on the right foot when it comes to resolving conflicts and crashes. Use the Preferences command in the Finder to rename one of the labels as "Mac OS."

2. Back up your hard disk and run the installer. If the installer forces you to restart the computer but you don't want new extensions loaded until you see what they are, disable extensions (by holding down Shift during the restart).

3. To locate the new items, open Sherlock 2 and make sure the Files channel is selected.

4. Now, drag the System Folder icon to the Search Items window in Sherlock (the top pane.) This adds the System Folder as one of the items you can search.

5. Make sure there's a check mark next to the System Folder and deselect other volumes or folders.

6. Select the Edit button next to Custom. In the More Search Items window, set the search criteria to find any item in the Finder selection whose label is *none*. Click OK.

7. Now, click the Search button in Sherlock 2. When the list of found items appears, you can select all and then copy and paste the list into the Scrapbook or any text document for later reference. You can also select any number of found items quickly and change the label using the Open Enclosing Folder command (⌘+E).

At best, labeling system files can help reduce System Folder clutter and save RAM and hard disk space. At the very least, you know exactly which files the installer added. All else being equal, knowledge is always better than ignorance. (Unless you eat hot dogs.)

Removing items from the System Folder

Be sure to put items that you drag from the System Folder's special folders in the Trash, on the desktop, or in an ordinary folder. If you merely drag items from the Control Panels folder or Extensions folder to the main level of the System Folder, those items may still be active.

Easy startup items

If you want an item to open at startup time, put an alias of it in the Startup Items folder. Don't put original items there because returning them to their original locations when you no longer want them opened at startup time can be a drag. (Get it?!)

When you finish using an alias, drag it to the Trash or use the Finder's Move to Trash File command (⌘+Delete).

Seeing desktop items

If the windows of open programs obscure desktop icons, hide those windows by choosing Hide Others from the Application menu while the Finder is active. If the Finder windows cover desktop icons, close all the windows at the same time by pressing Option while clicking the close box of any Finder window. You can collapse all of the active application's windows by Option+clicking the active window's collapse box.

Shrunken tabs

Is the bottom of your screen becoming crowded with pop-up window tabs? Shrink the size of the tabs. Grab a tab you'd like to shrink and drag it up until its pop-up window becomes a regular window. Position some of the remaining tabs about ½ to ¾ inches apart. Now drag the window back down to the bottom of your screen, between the two close-set tabs, until you see it change back to a tab. The tab will keep its new smaller size even if you later drag it to a new position.

Drag to scroll

You can scroll a folder or disk window without using the scroll bars. Press the ⌘ key and start dragging inside a folder or disk window. The pointer changes to look like a gloved hand and the window contents scroll as you ⌘+drag.

Alternatively, place the mouse pointer in the window and drag toward the area that you want to view. When you drag the pointer up, down, left, or right past the window's active area scrolling begins. Dragging past a window corner scrolls diagonally. To scroll slowly, drag just to the window's edge (and continue holding down the mouse button). Increase scrolling speed by dragging beyond the window's edge.

Manipulating background windows

Sometimes you need to get at something in a background window that's covered by a window in front, but you don't want to bring the background window forward. For instance, you might want to drag some carefully selected icons from the frontmost Finder window to a folder in a background window. If you can see any part of the background window, you can move it without bringing it to the front by ⌘+dragging the background title bar or window frame.

Also, you can collapse a window in the background without bringing it to the front by ⌘+double-clicking it. (These tricks only work with background windows that belong to the active application and you must have the Double-click title bar to collapse window option selected on the Options tab of the Appearance control panel.)

When windows open unbidden

Many CD-ROMs are set up to open windows automatically when you insert them. Some of these windows are full of custom icons and can take an inordinately long time to display. To keep windows from opening, simply hold down Option while inserting the CD. The same trick works for other types of removable disks.

Expanding multiple folders

You can use keyboard commands to see the contents of multiple folders in a window that's set to list view. Select the folders (press ⌘+A to select all) and press ⌘+right arrow (→) to expand the selected folders and see their contents. To also expand all folders contained in the selected folders, press ⌘+Option+right arrow (→). Pressing ⌘+left arrow (←) collapses all selected folders, and pressing ⌘+Option+left arrow (←) collapses all selected folders and all folders in them.

Viewing empty folders

You can force empty folders to the bottom of a window. Just turn on the Calculate Folder Sizes options with the View Options command in the View menu, and then choose the by Size item from the Sort List or Arrange submenu of the View menu.

Finding empty, locked, or shared folders

If you want to find all the empty, locked, or shared folders on your disk, use the Sherlock 2 program. Set it to find items whose folder attribute is empty (or locked or shared). This capability to search for folders that are or are not empty, locked, or shared is not very well known but can be extremely useful. After finding all shared folders, for example, you can select some or all of the found folders and use the Sharing command (in the File menu, select Get Info, then Sharing) in Sherlock to change the access privileges of all the selected folders at once. Likewise, you could find all empty folders and move them to the Trash. Figure 27-7 shows the More Search Options window of the Sherlock 2 program set to find empty folders.

Figure 27-7: To find empty folders, set up a Sherlock 2 search as shown here.

Copy fitting

When you copy batches of files from your hard disk to floppies or other removable disks, you must do some arithmetic beforehand so that the Finder won't tell you that there's not enough room on the disk. To have the Finder help you figure out how many files will fit on a floppy or a removable disk, follow these steps:

1. Create a new folder on the hard disk. The new folder must be in a window, not directly on the desktop.

2. Use the Finder's Get Info command (⌘+I) to bring up the folder's Info window.

3. Begin dragging files to be copied into the folder. As you drag, the Finder updates the folder's size in its Info window.

4. When the size approaches 1.4MB for a high-density floppy, 800K for a double-sided floppy, or 94MB for a Zip disk, stop dragging files into the folder; the disk will be nearly full.

If the Trash is empty, you can collect items in it instead of in a specially created folder. This method has two advantages: You can quickly return all items to their original places by choosing the Put Away command from the File menu (⌘+Y), and you don't have to wait for the Finder to make copies of items that come from several disks. (The Finder doesn't copy items to the Trash, but it must copy items that you drag from one disk to a folder on another disk.) The Get Info command reports the size of the Trash only to the nearest K; however, it gives you the exact number of bytes in a folder.

If you have a large hard disk, you may notice that there is some space left over on the floppy disk after you copy the files there. This is because the smallest possible file takes less space on a floppy disk than on a hard disk unless the disk was initialized with the Mac OS Extended format. With the Mac OS standard format, the difference between a file's size on a floppy and a hard disk increases as the capacity of the hard disk increases. For example, on a 2GB hard disk each file uses a minimum of 32K, and your average error per file copied will be 16K. This can add up pretty quickly. An alternative method that avoids this problem is to use the Disk Copy program to create a Read and Write 1.4MB floppy disk image, mount that on the desktop, and then copy files to it. When it's full, you can copy from it to a floppy. The extra copying to and from the disk image doesn't take very long because Disk Copy keeps the disk image contents on the hard disk (or in RAM, which is even faster).

The Trash

This section's tips are all about throwing files away and retrieving them from the Trash if you change your mind.

Stop all Trash warnings

The next time you empty the Trash you can skip the standard Trash warning (for example, "The Trash contains 104 items, which use 3.9MB of disk space. Are you sure you want to remove these items permanently?"). First, select the Trash icon, and then choose the Get Info command (⌘+I). In the Trash Info dialog box that appears, turn off the Warn before emptying option—you'll never see the Trash warning again. Figure 27-8 shows the Trash Info dialog box with the warning option turned off.

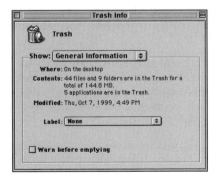

Figure 27-8: Use the Get Info command to disable the warning that appears when you empty the Trash.

Discarding locked items

When you use the Empty Trash command, the Finder normally doesn't discard locked items that you dragged to the Trash. Instead of unlocking each locked item with the Finder's Get Info command (⌘+I), you can simply press Option while choosing Empty Trash from the Special menu.

Retrieving trash

To put items that are currently in the Trash back where they came from, open the Trash, select the items, and choose Put Away (⌘+Y) from the Finder's File menu. The Finder returns each selected item to its previous folder, although not necessarily to the same place in the folder window.

Rescuing items

Sometimes, the Trash contains a folder named Rescued Items. This folder usually contains formerly invisible temporary files that were found when you started your computer. The Rescued Items folder may appear after a system crash, and you may be able to recreate your work up to the time of the system crash from the contents of the Rescued Items folder.

Apple Menu

Use the tips in this section to get more organized with the Apple menu.

Apple-menu organization

After you add more than a few items to the Apple menu, it becomes a mess. You can group different types of items by prefixing different numbers of blank spaces to their names — the more blank spaces, the higher on the Apple menu.

Prefixing a name with a hyphen or exclamation point makes the name appear below names that are prefixed with spaces and above names that have no prefixes. To make items appear at the bottom of the Apple menu, prefix them with a ◊ (Option+Shift+V) or • (Option+8). Figure 27-9 shows how these prefixes affect the order of items.

If you have a hard time remembering what all the special symbol keyboard commands are, use the Key Caps utility located under the Apple menu. Or, try Günther Blaschek's excellent program PopChar Pro (http://www.unisoft.co. at/products/popchar.html), which automatically pops up a list of all letters, numbers, and symbols available in the current font when you move the pointer to a predesignated hot spot.

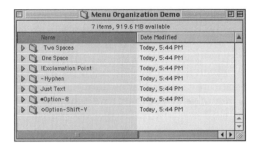

Figure 27-9: Use special keyboard characters and extra spaces to arrange items in a list to your liking.

Fast Apple-menu changes

To add or remove Apple-menu items quickly, list the Apple Menu Items folder in the Apple menu. How? Make an alias of the Apple Menu Items folder and put the alias in that folder.

Too-full Apple menu

If your Apple menu contains so many items that you must scroll to see them all, consider organizing them in folders within the Apple Menu Items folder. The contents of each folder appear in hierarchical submenus if the Submenus option is turned on in the Apple Menu Options control panel. Figure 27-10 is an example of Apple-menu subfolders.

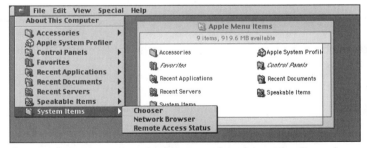

Figure 27-10: Keep your Apple menu short by putting items in folders inside the Apple Menu Items folder.

Universal Show Clipboard

Some application programs lack a Show Clipboard command; others that do have such a command use a private Clipboard whose contents may look different when pasted into another program. Put a Show Clipboard command in your Apple menu and then use the command to review the standard Clipboard contents from any application program.

First, make an alias of the Clipboard file, which is in the System Folder. Then place the alias in the Apple Menu Items folder and rename the alias Show Clipboard. Now choose Show Clipboard from the Apple menu; your computer switches to the Finder and opens the Clipboard.

Invisible file aliases

Do you crave the convenience of accessing items stored in the invisible Desktop Folder from the Apple Menu? Because the Desktop Folder is invisible, alias-creating utilities are of no help.

The trick is to access your computer via file sharing. When you access your computer from another machine via file sharing, the Desktop Folder becomes visible at the root level of your hard disk. Create an alias of the Desktop Folder (be sure to lock that Desktop Folder alias in its Info window to prevent it from becoming invisible) and transfer the alias to your computer.

Alternatively, you can use a disk utility such as File Buddy (described in Chapter 26) to make an alias of the invisible Desktop Folder.

The non-ABCs approach to arranging menu items

Forcibly reordering items in the Apple menu by placing spaces or special symbols at the beginning of the items' names has side effects that you may not like. The spaces or symbols visibly alter the names and conspicuously shift the names to the right. To invisibly force the order you want, follow these steps:

1. Open the Note Pad or a new document in SimpleText or a word processor.

2. Press Return to create a blank line, select the blank line, and copy it to the Clipboard.

3. Switch to the Finder.

4. In the Apple Menu Items folder, select the name of the item that you want to appear at the top of the Apple menu.

5. Press the up-arrow (↑) key to move the insertion point to the beginning of the selected name and then paste.

6. The entire name goes blank, but don't fret—just press Return or click outside the name, and the name springs back into view. The renamed item jumps to the top of the window if you're viewing by list. To increase an item's alphabetic buoyancy, paste the blank line two or more times at the beginning of the item's name.

Some programs don't work properly with documents or folders whose names contain blank lines. In particular, you may be unable to print PageMaker or QuarkXPress documents in which you have placed a PostScript graphics file whose name begins with a blank line. If you have trouble after pasting a blank line in the name of a file or folder, remove the item from the Apple Menu Items folder, replace it with an alias, and then try this naming trick on the alias.

Hierarchical information manager

You can turn your Apple menu into a contact database. By treating folder names as single-line entries in a database, you can easily create an elegant hierarchical database of often-used addresses, phone numbers, client contacts, and other information that you are tired of fumbling for on your crowded desktop or hard disk.

You can access the data instantly from the Apple menu and its submenus, and view the data by traversing the menu structure without actually choosing any menu item. (When you finish viewing the data, just drag the mouse pointer away from the menus and release the mouse.) For a persistent display, choose the menu item whose submenu contains the data that you want to see; the Finder opens the folder that contains the data.

Adding, deleting, and modifying data is a snap. Follow these steps:

1. Choose the menu item whose submenu you want to change and open the folder in which you need to make changes.

2. To add a line of data, use the Finder's New Folder command (⌘+N) and type the data as the new folder's name (up to 31 characters).

3. To change data, edit the corresponding folder names.

4. To remove a line of data, drag corresponding folders to the Trash.

5. To add a submenu, open a folder and add folders to it.

Continued

(continued)

Because items appear alphabetically by name in the submenus, you may have to put extra spaces or other special characters at the beginning of folder names to arrange the names in the order you want. (You usually have to do this with a multiple-line address, for example.)

Another neat trick: Use aliases to duplicate data that you want to appear in several places in the database. After making an alias of the folder that you want to clone, simply drag the alias to the folder that represents the other location in the database where you want the information to appear. Cloned parts of your hierarchical database stay up-to-date because aliases don't contain any duplicate data that can get out of sync; the aliases simply point to the folders that contain the actual data.

No matter how large your database of folders becomes, the Finder always calculates its size on disk as zero! Yes, this is too good to be true. In fact, your data, consisting only of nested named folders, is kept in the startup disk's invisible directory file, which contains information about the hierarchical organization of fields and folders on that disk. The Finder reports only the sizes of aliases and other actual files that you may have in your hierarchical folders.

Keeping contact information in a hierarchical Apple menu has two advantages over using contact-database software such as Now Contact: You can always locate your contacts without opening (or keeping open) another program, and you can find any contact quickly without typing or even remembering a name. Managing hundreds of contacts is easier with contact-database software, though.

Apple menu options

If you use the Apple Menu Options control panel to list recently used documents, applications, and servers but don't necessarily want all three submenus active, set the number to zero in the Apple Menu Options control panel for those submenus that you don't want to activate. The items with a zero value disappear from the Apple menu.

Fonts

This section has tips for working with and modifying the System Folder's Fonts folder. When making changes to the Fonts folder, remember that any fonts that you add generally aren't available to open programs until you have quit the open programs and reopened them. Moreover, you must quit all open programs before removing fonts from the Fonts folder.

Duplicating fonts

Because you can't rename individual fixed-size or TrueType fonts with the Finder, you can't duplicate them in the same folder (you can't have two items with the same name in the same folder). However, you can rename or duplicate PostScript fonts and font suitcases.

To duplicate a fixed-size or TrueType font, press Option and drag the font to another folder or to the desktop. (Dragging to another disk automatically makes a copy of the font on the target disk.)

You can create a new, empty font suitcase file by duplicating an existing font suitcase file, opening the duplicate, and dragging its contents to the Trash.

Deleting a damaged font

If you somehow manage to damage a font suitcase, you may not be able to delete it simply by opening the Fonts folder and dragging the suitcase to the Trash. Try dragging the Fonts folder from the System Folder to the desktop first. Then open the Fonts folder and drag the damaged suitcase to the Trash. Empty the Trash and put the Fonts folder back in your System Folder. If you can't drag the damaged suitcase to the Trash, try this: With your original Fonts folder still sitting on the desktop, create a new folder named Fonts inside the System Folder. Drag everything except the damaged suitcase from the old Fonts folder (on the desktop) to the new Fonts folder. Restart the computer and then drag the old Fonts folder (which still contains the damaged suitcase) to the Trash.

Personalized sample text

You don't have to read about "cozy lummoxes" and "smart squids" when you open a TrueType or fixed-size font file in the Finder. Use ResEdit to change the sample text as follows:

1. Open your System Folder and press Option as you drag a copy of the Finder to the desktop.

2. Open this duplicate Finder with ResEdit.

3. Open the duplicate Finder's STR# resource icon, and then open the STR# resource whose ID is 5816.

   A window appears that displays the sample text.

4. Edit the text to your liking.

5. Quit ResEdit, answering Yes when you are asked whether you want to save your changes.

6. Drag the original Finder from your System Folder to a folder outside the System Folder, and drag the modified Finder from the desktop to the System Folder.

7. Restart your computer and test the results of your modifications.

Summary

This chapter gave you some tips for the desktop and on organizing the Mac OS virtual desktop for better efficiency. You also saw that you don't have to use the same, boring (even if they are 3D) icons everybody else uses. Customizing icons, either by altering the default icon, using a custom icon, or removing the icon completely, is easy.

You also picked up some tips on enlivening the startup process. You can change the look of your startup screen. You can have your computer play a QuickTime movie, display a message, or a play a sound during startup. You can also replace the Finder with a Web browser or quit the Finder completely.

This chapter offered several ideas for working with folders and windows. You can lock folders with the Sharing command. You can also scroll windows without using the scroll bars and move background windows without making them active. You can manage your pop-up window tabs if they get out of hand. You can set the view options for your folders. In addition, you can use the Sherlock program or Find File program to spot empty folders.

You also got some tips on working with the Trash. You can stop Trash warnings with the Get Info command, and you can remove locked items by pressing Option. The Put Away command makes it easy to retrieve items from the Trash.

This chapter gave you some tips for organizing your Apple menu and some ideas for adding items to it. You can change the order of items by prefixing their names with blank spaces and other special characters. You can add a universal Show Clipboard command to the Apple menu, and you can access the entire contents of your desktop from the Apple menu.

Finally, this chapter told you how to create new font suitcases and how to delete damaged font suitcases.

✦   ✦   ✦

Discover More Tips and Secrets

This second chapter of tips and tricks covers shortcuts and productivity boosters for your system in general: Open and Save dialog boxes, file sharing, Mac OS extensions and control panels, using the Mac OS with your applications, and memory and performance issues. Finally, the tips section ends with a few Mac OS "Easter eggs."

To use some of the tips in this chapter, you need a copy of ResEdit, Apple's no-cost resource editor. You can get ResEdit from Apple's Software Updates library (http://www.apple.com/swupdates/), online services such as America Online (keyword: filesearch), and Macintosh user groups. You can also get a copy of ResEdit from Macworld's Macdownload software library (http://macdownload.com). For more sources of shareware and freeware, see Chapter 26.

Open, Save, and Navigation Services

The tips in this section will help you zoom through the dialog boxes that appear when you choose Open, Save, Save As, and other disk-related commands. All of these tips apply to the classic Open and Save type of dialog box. As noted in the descriptions of individual tips, some tips also apply to the Open and Save dialog boxes' heir apparent, the Navigation Services dialog boxes.

Find an alias's original item

You can go quickly to an alias's original item in an Open, Save, and Navigation Services dialog box by pressing Option while opening the alias (by double-clicking it, for example). Alias names appear in italics in these dialog boxes, just as they do in the Finder windows.

Folder switching

If you find that you frequently go back and forth between two folders, put an alias of each folder in the other. Whichever folder you are in, you can go to the other in one step by opening its alias. Also, you can bookmark your frequently visited folders using the Favorites pop-up in the Navigation Services dialog box.

Aliases for favorite folders

Putting aliases of your often-used folders on the desktop or inside disk windows enables you to open a folder quickly from an Open or Save dialog box. Instead of working your way down through one branch of your folder structure and then working your way up another branch to the folder that you want, you zip to the desktop level or the disk level and then open the alias of the folder that you want. This process is like jumping from one branch of a tree to the root level and then jumping to a spot on another branch without crawling up the trunk and along the other branch.

Note   Navigation Services' Open and Save dialog boxes make this even easier with their access to Favorites. Simply add your often-used folders as Favorites in the Finder and you can quickly access them without even returning to the desktop. Adding Favorites is discussed in Chapter 7.

You can get to aliases of often-used folders on the desktop quickly by pressing ⌘+D. Get to aliases at the disk-window level by choosing the disk from the pop-up menu in an Open or Save dialog box.

Sidestepping a double-click

As usual, you can open an item in an Open dialog box by double-clicking the item. If, before you release the mouse button, you realize that you double-clicked the wrong item, continue holding down the mouse button and drag the pointer to the item that you want to open. When you release the mouse button, the currently selected item opens.

This trick also works when you are opening a folder in a Save dialog box, but does not work in a Navigation Services dialog box (but see the next tip).

Canceling a double-click

To cancel a double-click in an Open, Save, or Navigation Services dialog box, hold down the mouse button on the second click and drag the pointer outside the dialog box before releasing the mouse button.

Shared folder access from the Save dialog box

Don't you hate it when you get to a Save dialog box only to learn that you aren't connected to the shared folder that you want to save in? Just make an alias of the Recent Servers folder and put it on the desktop. Now you can quickly open the Recent Servers folder from any Save dialog box and then open and connect to any shared folder or disk in the Recent Servers folder. Beats a trip to the Chooser any day. (If you don't have an alias of the Recent Servers folder on the desktop, you can open the folder from the Apple Menu Items folder. Still beats a trip to the Chooser.) Figure 28-1 is an example of getting to a shared folder via an alias in the Save dialog box.

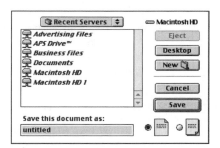

Figure 28-1: Place an alias of the Recent Servers folder on the desktop and you can quickly open recent servers in a Save dialog box

File Sharing and Networking

This section describes tips for easier networking, plus the ins and outs of file sharing.

Picking a secure password

Pick a password that is easy for you to remember but difficult for other people to guess. For better security, mix letters with numbers; try replacing the letters I and O with the numbers 1 and 0. Another trick is to use the initial letters of an easy-to-remember phrase. For example, "The White House is at 1600 Pennsylvania Avenue" becomes TWHia1600PA. Don't use birthdays, anniversaries, or family members' names.

Want to make sure you haven't chosen a too obvious password? Ask a good friend, relative, or coworker to play hacker: have them try to guess your password, writing down their guesses on a piece of paper. If your password is on the list, or is very similar to one on the list, choose a less obvious password.

Sharing disks or enclosing folders

When you share a folder, the Mac OS won't let you share the enclosing folder or the disk that contains it. You have to drag the shared folder to another place or unshare it before you can share the enclosing folder or disk. To avoid this situation, share from the highest level of your disk and folder structure.

Improved file-sharing performance

For best performance of your computer, share as few of your folders as possible. The more items that others can access on your computer, the greater the demands on your computer's performance. Sharing too many folders can slow your system to a crawl. When you need to share numerous files or to share a folder simultaneously with several users, consider setting up a dedicated computer to act as a centralized file server for the shared information (a great way to recycle older computers).

Faster file sharing

If you've ever shared files from your computer, you know how bogged down your Mac can get, especially if the file sharing is done remotely. Combat slow system performance by creating a RAM disk (it must be larger than 2MB, the limit for file sharing) and placing all the items that you wish to share on it. Then share the RAM disk by selecting the RAM disk and choosing Sharing from the Get Info submenu of the File menu.

Drag to share

Here's a slick way to share your disks and folders: Forget the Finder's Sharing command. Instead, open the File Sharing control panel and click the Activity Monitor tab. Now simply drag a folder or disk that you want to share into the Shared Items area of the control panel. The item's info window pops up and displays Sharing settings. Turn on the Share this item and its contents option and set the access privileges.

Trouble renaming hard disks

Are you stymied because you're unable to change the name of your computer's hard disk? Make sure file sharing is turned off in the File Sharing control panel, whichever you have. While file sharing is on, you can't change the name or icon of an item that's available for network access.

Cut file-sharing red tape

Getting access to shared items involves wading through a fair amount of bureaucracy, whether you use the Chooser or the Network Browser. Aliases cut through the red tape.

First, access a shared disk or folder one time, using the Chooser or the Network Browser. Next, select the shared item or any folder or file in it, and then choose Make Alias from the File menu (⌘+M). Finally, copy the alias to your desktop or hard disk. An alias keeps track of its original item even if the original item is on another networked computer.

After you make an alias of a shared item, you can access it by opening the alias either from the Finder or from an Open command's dialog box. Dragging something to the alias of a shared disk or folder also accesses that shared item automatically. You still must enter a password unless you initially accessed the original item as a guest or you've added this login to your keychain. If the shared item is not available (when, for example, the computer where the item resides is turned off), a message tells you so.

Aliases of shared items don't always work if the shared items are located on servers that use Windows NT Services for Macintosh.

Office on a removable disk

Because aliases can give you nearly automatic access to items on a networked computer via file sharing, take the previous tip a step further: Put an alias of your hard disk on a floppy or removable disk for quick access to your files from any computer on your network.

For this trick to work, your computer must have file sharing turned on. You can check the status of file sharing and turn it on if it is off by using the File Sharing control panel. You can also use the Control Strip if it is installed on your computer.

With file sharing turned on, insert a removable disk and make an alias on it for each of the other disks on your computer's desktop. Eject and lock the removable.

As long as file sharing is active on your computer, you can use this removable disk to access your hard disk from any other computer on your network. Simply insert the disk, open the alias for the disk that you want to use, and enter your password when asked. Correctly entering your password gives you access to all applications, folders, and documents on your disk from any remote Mac OS computer. You don't have to bother with opening the Chooser, selecting AppleShare, selecting your computer, and typing your name as the registered user.

An alias on your removable disk may not work as expected if the alias's original item has the same name as a disk on the computer you're using. For example, if your hard disk is named Macintosh HD and the hard disk on the computer you're using to access it also has a hard disk by that name, opening the alias on your removable may open the local hard disk instead of your hard disk over the network. You can work around this problem by temporarily renaming the hard disk on the computer you're using or by giving your hard disk a unique name before creating the aliases. Remember that if the computer you're using has file sharing turned on, you must turn it off before you can rename any of the computer's disks. If you make any of these changes to a borrowed computer, be sure to change them back when you finish.

What people have trashed

Items from your shared disk or folder that someone has dragged to the Trash — but not yet permanently removed — on another computer do not appear in your Trash. The Mac OS puts those items in folders whose names begin Trash Can #. You cannot see these folders with the Finder because they are in an invisible folder inside the shared folder or disk. To see the Trash Can # folders, use a utility program such as Norton Utilities for Macintosh from Symantec (408-253-9600, http://www.symantec. com) or File Buddy (described in Chapter 26).

Log-in shortcuts

When connecting to a shared folder or disk, you may have a choice of connecting as a guest or a registered user. In the dialog box that gives you this choice, you can press ⌘+R for Registered User or ⌘+G for Guest, eliminating an extra trip to the mouse. This shortcut is especially nice for keyboard-oriented folks.

Control Panels and Extensions

This section includes the what, where, and why of control panels and extensions, along with tips on how to get the most out of them.

Take a picture

You can take a picture of your desktop with a built-in feature of the Mac OS. Pressing ⌘+Shift+3 takes a picture of your whole screen; ⌘+Shift+4 lets you drag out a rectangular picture selection. Use Caps Lock and ⌘+Shift+4 to take a picture of a window in the active application by clicking the window. To place the picture on the Clipboard instead of in a SimpleText picture file on your startup disk, add the Control key to either of those key combinations.

You can even capture the screen while a menu or pop-up menu is open. Click the menu title to open the menu and then press a key combination to capture all or part of the screen. To capture more sophisticated shots (such as an icon in mid-drag), you need a screen-capture utility such as the shareware Screen Catcher from St. Clair Software (http://www.stclairsw.com) or the shareware Snapz Pro from Ambrosia Software (http://www .ambrosiasw.com).

Easy Access shortcuts

Instead of using the Easy Access control panel to turn Mouse Keys, Slow Keys, or Sticky Keys on and off, you can use the keyboard. (To get Easy Access, you must do a custom installation of the Mac OS, as described in Chapter 31.)

The Mouse Keys feature of Easy Access enables control of the pointer from the keyboard. To turn Mouse Keys on or off, press ⌘+Shift+Clear. Mouse Keys requires a numeric keypad to work.

The Slow Keys feature of Easy Access guards against accidental keystrokes by requiring that a key be held down for one or two seconds before the keystroke is entered. To turn Slow Keys on or off, hold down Return for about ten seconds. After five seconds you'll hear a beep; five seconds after that you'll hear an ascending tone (on) or a descending tone (off).

The Sticky Keys feature of Easy Access lets you type keyboard combinations such as ⌘+S one key at a time. To turn Sticky Keys on or off, press Shift five times in a row without moving the pointer.

Use the Map control panel

The Map control panel can be a fun little resource for time zone information, but, in Mac OS 9, it interferes with the Date & Time control panel, so it isn't installed by default. Instead, it's placed in the Apple Extras folder in the Map Control Panel folder. To activate it, drag its icon to the System Folder.

To set your location using the Map control panel, follow these steps:

1. Open the Date & Time control panel.

2. Deselect Set Daylight-Saving Time Automatically and deselect Daylight-Saving Time is in effect (if appropriate).

3. Open the Map control panel and set your location, then close the control panel.

4. Reselect Set Daylight-Saving Time Automatically and close the Date & Time control panel.

Now you can use the Map for other purposes and avoid having it interfere with your time stamps and Internet e-mail, among other things. (You'll need to repeat this step whenever you change locations if you continue to use the Map control panel.)

Big map

You can enlarge the world map in the Map control panel by pressing Option while opening the control panel. To magnify more, press Shift+Option while opening the map. Figure 28-2 shows the world map magnified.

Figure 28-2: You can zoom in on the Map control panel to get more detail (sort of).

Time-zone tracking

If you regularly contact people in multiple time zones, you can use the Map control panel to keep track of local times for those people. With the Map control panel open, type the name of the city and click the Find button. Then type the person's name over the city name and click Add City. Now you need only type a person's name in Map and click Find to find his or her time zone.

If you want Map to remember a person whose city isn't on the map, you can substitute a known city in the same time zone or add the unknown city. Whenever you add a new place or person to Map, verify the time zone and correct it, if necessary.

Virtual memory turn-off

Instead of opening the Memory control panel on those occasions when you need to turn virtual memory on or off, restart your computer while holding down the ⌘ key. Holding down the ⌘ key at startup automatically disables virtual memory; restarting without pressing ⌘ restores virtual memory to its previous settings. Holding down Shift during startup also disables virtual memory along with all extensions, whereas ⌘ does not disable all extensions. However, some third-party extensions or control panels may be disabled individually by a ⌘ key restart. If you have a startup file that's sensitive to the ⌘ key, check its documentation or Read Me files to see if you can change the key that acts as a disabler during startup.

Note In our testing with Mac OS 9, turning virtual memory off with ⌘ worked erratically at best. (On many systems it didn't work at all.) Try it out on your Mac to see if this trick works on your machine.

Stuck in the past

If your Time and Date control panel insists that it's really 1956, you aren't stuck in a time warp—you just need to replace the lithium battery on the system board. When the computer is off, the battery keeps the clock ticking and powers the parameter RAM (PRAM), which stores settings for many control panels, including Mouse, Keyboard, and Startup Disk. You'll find Apple part numbers for batteries for all but the latest Macs, which shouldn't need batteries yet, in Apple's Technical Information Library article 11751, which is available on the Web (http://til.info. apple.com/techinfo.nsf/artnum/n11751).

Apple considers the clock battery user-replaceable on some desktop Macs and includes instructions in the owner's manuals for these models. You can remove the Mac's cover (as described in the computer's manual), eyeball the battery, and decide for yourself whether you want to try replacing it. You'll find pictures of the battery location in many models on The Macintosh Battery Web site (http://www.academ.com/info/macintosh/).

The specific procedure for replacing a clock battery varies because the clock battery location depends on the computer model. The following description gives an idea of the work involved.

Remember that while the cover is off the computer you could accidentally damage something inside that would be expensive to repair. Proceed with caution; if you're the least bit squeamish, let a technician do the work.

Before replacing the battery it's a good idea to use the free TechTool program (described in Chapter 26) to save the settings stored in the computer's parameter RAM (PRAM). The PRAM stores a number of control panel settings as well as secret settings (such as the number of hours the computer has been used); removing the battery may reset these settings to factory defaults.

To replace a Mac's clock battery, remove the computer's cover and touch the metal power supply housing to drain off any static charge you may be carrying. Next, pry off the plastic cage that covers the battery. (Not all batteries have a protective cage.) Carefully note the orientation of the old battery's positive and negative ends. Then pop out the old battery and snap in a new one with the same orientation as the old one. Replace the battery cage and the Mac cover, and restart the computer. If you saved PRAM settings with TechTool, use it now to restore the settings. Otherwise, check your control panel settings and change them as needed.

Password-protecting a hard disk

If you have a PowerBook that you use in locations where you worry about people snooping through your files, you can block their access to the hard disk by protecting it with a password. With this protection in place, people must know the password to start up the PowerBook and optionally to wake it from sleep. You configure this protection in the Password Security control panel. Click the Setup button in this control panel to display a dialog box in which you can set or change the password, optionally specify a hint for remembering it, and specify whether you want sleep protected as well as startup. Before this dialog box appears, you must enter your password (if you have one).

If you have partitioned your PowerBook's hard disk into multiple volumes (as described at the end of this chapter), Password Security protects only one volume. If more than one volume has a System Folder, the computer may start up from a volume that is not protected.

Whatever you do, don't forget your password. You can't bypass the security dialog by starting up with the Shift key pressed, or by starting up from a Mac OS CD, because the password control is handled at the disk-driver level. If you forget your password, you have to take your PowerBook with proof of purchase to an authorized service center, where a technician can bypass the security dialog.

Note   You can't set up password security on an external hard disk that's connected to your PowerBook—it only works for the internal disk.

PowerBook airport security

When you take a PowerBook through airport security and are asked to turn it on, the last thing you want to do is wait through a lengthy startup. Waking a sleeping PowerBook is fast enough, but who wants to waste battery power while the PowerBook sleeps through check-in? Instead, use the Password Security control panel. The Password Security dialog box comes up quickly on startup and proves that you have a computer, not a bomb. Then press Cancel to shut down quickly so you can make your plane.

Whatever you do, don't forget your password, because you can't bypass the Password Security dialog box by starting up with the Shift key pressed or by starting up from a CD or a floppy disk—the password control is handled at the disk-driver level. If you forget your password, you have to take your PowerBook with proof of purchase to an authorized service center, where a technician can bypass the security dialog box.

If you have an older-model PowerBook, you can't use the Password Security control panel. In this case, either hold down Shift for a fast startup at the airport or download one of the many quick-start extensions available online. John Bullock's Scout's Honour, John Bascombe's Airport Quickstart, and Jon Wind's Zorba are all freeware extensions designed to provide quick startup and shutdown for airport security agents. And they work on any model PowerBook.

Applications and Accessories

This section has tips for using Mac OS features while working with your applications and accessory programs.

QuickTime controls

The standard controller for a QuickTime movie (the one found in SimpleText and other programs that play QuickTime movies with controls) is full of hidden controls, including:

✦ Make the sound level louder than its normal maximum by holding down Shift while clicking the speaker icon and adjusting the sound level with the volume slider.

✦ Adjust the sound level by pressing the up–arrow (↑) and down–arrow (↓) keys. (This also works in QuickTime Player.)

✦ Turn the sound on or off by Option+clicking the speaker icon. (You can turn the sound all the way off by simply clicking the speaker icon in QuickTime Player.)

✦ Alternately start and pause playback by pressing either Return or the Spacebar. (This also works in QuickTime Player.)

✦ Step forward or backward by pressing the right-arrow (→) or left-arrow (←) key. (This also works in QuickTime Player.)

✦ Play the movie forward by pressing ⌘+right arrow (→). (This also works in QuickTime Player.)

✦ Play the movie backward by ⌘+clicking the reverse-step button or pressing ⌘+left arrow (←). (⌘+clicking doesn't work in QuickTime Player, but ⌘+left arrow (←) does.)

✦ Control the playback direction and speed by Control-clicking either step button to reveal a jog shuttle.

✦ Jump to the beginning or end of the movie by Option+clicking a step button, as indicated by the direction of the step button. (QuickTime Player has its own buttons for this function.)

Audio CD AutoPlay

You can have your computer automatically play an audio CD during startup or any time that you insert an audio CD into the CD-ROM drive. Turn on the Enable Audio CD AutoPlay option in the AutoPlay section of the QuickTime Settings control panel. If the CD starts playing automatically but you don't hear anything, you probably need to change the sound input settings in your Sound control panel so that the sound source is the CD drive. Figure 28-3 shows the QuickTime Settings for AutoPlay.

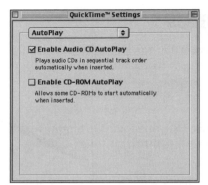

Figure 28-3:
Set your computer to automatically play an audio CD inserted in the CD-ROM drive.

The other option in the AutoPlay section of the QuickTime Settings control panel, Enable CD-ROM AutoPlay, can cause problems. When this option is turned on, your computer can become infected with the AutoStart 9805 Worm (as described in Chapter 18).

Audio-only QuickTime movies

It's easy to record a passage from an audio CD as a sound file—the QuickTime system extension makes it possible. (Remember that many uses of sounds copied from a CD constitute a violation of copyright law unless you first obtain permission from the copyright holder.) You just need SimpleText and an audio CD. Then follow these steps to record the CD passage:

1. Insert the audio CD that you want to use for your clip.

2. Open SimpleText and choose Open from SimpleText's File menu.

3. In the Open dialog box that appears, open the audio CD, select the track that you want to record, and click the Convert button to bring up a Save dialog box.

4. In the Save dialog box, name the sound-only movie and select a folder location for it.

5. Still in the Save dialog box, click the Options button to bring up QuickTime's Audio CD Import Options dialog box. Adjust the slider controls to specify which part of the audio track to include, set the sound-quality options, and close the Audio CD Import Options dialog box.

6. Back in the Save dialog box, click Save.

   QuickTime copies the audio data from the CD to the movie file. You now have an audio-only movie file that plays in QuickTime Player or in SimpleText.

Scripted calculator

You can copy the text of a calculation—for example, 69.65+26.98+14.99*.0725—and paste it in the standard Calculator control panel. Be sure to use the asterisk symbol (*) for multiplication and the slash (/) symbol for division, and don't include any blank spaces in the text you copy.

Scrapbook renewal

If you tossed one of the items that was preinstalled in the Scrapbook, you can get it again by reinstalling the Scrapbook from the Mac OS installation CD or disks. Temporarily move your current Scrapbook File from your System Folder to the desktop. Next, do a custom installation of the Mac OS, selecting Scrapbook in the Apple Menu section of the Install Mac OS window. (See Chapter 31 for detailed instructions on doing a custom installation.) This should install a new Scrapbook File.

Open the new Scrapbook File. Drag the missing item to the desktop to create a clipping file that contains it. Select the Scrapbook File that you previously dragged to the desktop, choose Put Away from the Finder's file menu, and click OK when the Finder asks whether it's OK to replace the Scrapbook File in the System Folder with the one that you're moving (putting away) from the desktop. Open the Scrapbook again, and drag the clipping file from the desktop to the Scrapbook window.

Put Note Pad back

The Note Pad isn't installed on the Apple Menu by default in Mac OS 9, as it was in previous Mac OS versions. But it's still installed—it's just stored in the Apple Extras folder. You can drag the Note Pad application back to the Apple Menu Items folder in the System Folder, you can add an alias of it to the System Folder, or you can make it a Favorite.

Multiple Note Pads

If you'd like different Note Pads for different reasons, you can do that easily. Open the System Folder, drag the Note Pad File out to another location. Rename it to reflect its contents. Now, relaunch the Note Pad application. It creates a new, blank Note Pad in the System Folder.

To see the contents of your previous Note Pad, double-click the renamed file. It opens in Note Pad instead of the default. This way you can archive old Note Pads that aren't much use anymore, or you can create as many individual Note Pad documents as you like and place them on the Apple menu (perhaps in a subfolder) or in a pop-up window. Then, double-click the Note Pad you need to reference.

Note   You can also back up the Note Pad file in this way.

Note Pad notetaker

The next time you need to look through a plain-text document — especially if you want to find specific text in it — try the Note Pad. Although the Note Pad has no Open command in its File menu, it can display the contents of a plain-text document, including SimpleText documents and text-clipping files. To view a text file, you simply drag its icon to the open Note Pad. Even better reasons for using the Note Pad are that it opens instantly and ordinarily uses less than half the memory of SimpleText and other text editors such as BBEdit Lite and Tex-Edit Plus. Moreover, the Note Pad can search read-only SimpleText documents (the kind with a "newspaper" icon), which SimpleText itself can't do.

Take a clipping

Instead of saving text or pictures in files created in an application (such as SimpleText or a word processor), you can make a clipping file. Select part of a document that you want to make into a clipping file and try to drag it to the desktop or to the icon or window of a folder or disk. If the application you're dragging from supports drag-and-drop editing between applications, the Finder creates a clipping file containing what you dragged. If nothing happens, or if the selection changes when you try to drag to the desktop, the application you're dragging from doesn't work with drag-and-drop editing. In that case, you can make a clipping file by selecting, copying, and pasting in a document of an application that does work with drag-and-drop editing, and drag the selection to the desktop from there. Applications that work include SimpleText, Note Pad, Stickies, and the Scrapbook. Once you've created your clipping file, rename it so that you can tell at a glance what's in it. If you forget, just double-click the clipping file; the file opens without launching an application.

While a clipping file is open, you can copy its entire contents and paste the copied contents in a document. Another way to put the contents of a clipping file in a document is to drag the clipping file to the document window. The document window you drag to must belong to an application that supports drag-and-drop editing between applications.

Close a Stickies note without warning

When you click a Stickies note close box, a dialog box pops up asking you to confirm that you want the note deleted. To skip the warning, Control+click the note's close box.

Placing graphics in SimpleText

How are graphics put in a Read Me file or other SimpleText document, and how does it get the special newspaper-style icon that designates a read-only SimpleText document? As you may know, the obvious methods — pasting graphics in the text and locking the file with the Finder's Get Info command — don't work. You need a secret keystroke and a resource editor such as Apple's ResEdit. Here is the procedure:

1. Open the SimpleText document that you want to enrich with graphics. Place the insertion point wherever you want to insert a graphic and press Option+Spacebar followed by several blank lines to leave space for the graphic. (The number of lines isn't critical; you can adjust it later.)

2. Paste the graphics into the Scrapbook.

3. Use ResEdit to open a copy of the SimpleText document. If ResEdit tells you that opening the document will add a resource fork (where SimpleText stores graphics) and asks if you want to do that, answer OK. If ResEdit doesn't ask about adding a resource fork, then the document already has one.

4. One by one, in the order of their intended appearance, copy each graphic from the Scrapbook and paste it in the SimpleText document's ResEdit window. When you paste the first graphic, a PICT resources icon appears in the window.

5. Open the PICT resources to see the individual pasted PICT graphics. Select each graphic and choose Get Resource Info from ResEdit's Resource menu (or press ⌘+I). In the Resource Info window that appears, change the ID number. Make the ID number 1000 for the graphic you want placed first, 1001 for the graphic to be placed second, and so on.

6. Close all the ResEdit windows, saving changes when asked.

7. Open the edited document file using SimpleText. You should see a graphic in each place you inserted an Option+space. The graphics are always centered in the document window. If a graphic overlaps text, simply add blank lines for additional space. Sometimes graphics seem to vanish after you add or remove a line. To display the images, scroll the document or collapse and expand the window to refresh it.

8. To prevent other people from changing the document and to give it the newspaper-style icon, close it and use ResEdit's Get File/Folder Info command to change the document type to ttro.

Batch copy or delete

Have you ever heard this jibe from a Windows user? "At least in Windows you can delete or copy a batch of files by typing a command such as Copy C:\draw*.eps D:." Mac OS users have the same functionality using Sherlock 2. Use Sherlock to find a batch of files from multiple folders on one disk or on multiple disks. Then select all or part of the found items and drag the batch from the Items Found window to the Trash or to any disk or folder.

Hide windows while switching

To hide the active program's windows as you switch to a particular program, press Option while choosing the other program from the Application menu, or press Option while clicking another program's window. You hide windows and switch to the Finder by pressing Option while clicking the desktop or an icon in the Finder.

If you have displayed the Application Switcher window (by tearing off the Application menu), Option+clicking an item hides the current application's windows as you switch to another application.

Hide windows to boost performance

When you have several programs open, you can spend a great deal of time waiting while inactive programs redraw portions of their windows as dialog boxes come and go. This delay is particularly protracted when you're using virtual memory, because the window redrawing may require disk access. Eliminate the delay by choosing Hide Others from the Application menu. Hidden windows don't require updating.

About This Computer contextual menu

If you choose About This Computer from the Apple menu, you can do more than review a list of open programs and the memory they use. Control+click any listed program to pop up a contextual menu from which you can bring up Mac OS Help or switch to the program. Double-click any item in the window to switch to it.

Memory and Performance

The tips in this section help you make the most of your computer's memory and increase its performance.

Quitting startup programs

If you have several programs open during startup, you may have to quit some of them later to free memory to open another program. Naturally, you want to quit the programs that are the least important to you. You get the maximum benefit from quitting those programs if they are the last items opened during startup. To make that happen, rename the items in your Startup Items folder so that the most important item comes first alphabetically, the next most important comes second, and so on. Better yet, you can avoid renaming original items by placing aliases in the Startup Items folder.

Reducing system memory size

You can reduce the Mac OS memory size (as reported by the About This Computer menu item in the Apple menu) to its minimum by pressing Shift while restarting your computer. Look for the message "Extensions Off" during startup. This message confirms that you have suppressed loading of all items in the Extensions folder, the Control Panels folder, and the System Folder that would increase the Mac OS memory size. You have also bypassed opening items in the Startup Items folder, reduced the disk cache to its minimum size, forced virtual memory off, and prevented file sharing from starting.

None of these changes persists when you restart without pressing Shift. To make persistent changes, you must disable items with the Extensions Manager control panel (or drag items out of the special folders) and then change settings in the Memory and File Sharing control panels.

You can also save memory by turning off file sharing if you're not using it. Reducing the disk cache size reduces the Mac OS memory size K for K — but slows system performance.

You can also use Shift to bypass just the items in your Startup Items. Instead of holding down Shift as your Mac starts up, begin holding down Shift just as the screen changes from listing extensions icons to displaying the blank desktop.

Note

When starting up with extensions disabled while using Multiple Users, you'll be required to enter a password for the system. It must be the owner's password. You'll then be shown the desktop, and Startup Items (or all extensions and control panels plus Startup Items, depending on when you press Shift) will be disabled.

Fragmented memory

To check for fragmented memory, add up the memory sizes of all the open programs and the Mac OS as listed in the About This Computer window. Then subtract this sum from the total memory reported there. Also subtract 300K to 600K (depending on monitor resolution and number of colors) if your computer doesn't have dedicated video memory known as VRAM (video RAM). In this case, your computer uses its main memory, sometimes called DRAM (dynamic random access memory), for the screen image. Examples of Macs in that category include a Power Mac 6100, 7100, or 8100 with a monitor connected to the system board video port. If the number you come up with is substantially less than the largest unused block, your unused memory is probably fragmented into two or more blocks.

An extra maintenance disk

If you want to fix or optimize your only hard disk with a utility program that can't be run from the disk it's fixing (and the program won't fit on a floppy and you don't have a high-capacity removable disk such as a Zip disk), use a RAM disk as follows:

1. Use the Memory control panel to create a RAM disk just the size of the application you need to use. After you restart the computer, the RAM disk will use part of the computer's RAM as if it were a disk.

2. Restart, copy the utility program you need from the hard disk to the RAM disk, and open the program from the RAM disk.

3. If you can't work on your hard disk because it's the startup disk, restart from a Mac OS installation CD.

To consolidate fragmented memory, quit all open programs and then open them again. Restarting your computer also fixes fragmentation and may reduce the amount of memory used by the Mac OS as well.

You can avoid memory fragmentation by planning the order in which you open and quit programs (see "Quitting Startup Programs" earlier in this section). Open the programs that you're least likely to quit first; open the programs that you're most likely to quit last. When you need more memory to open another program, quit the most-recently opened program. If that doesn't free enough memory, quit the next most-recently opened program, and so on. This method frees a contiguous chunk of memory. Quitting programs helter-skelter leads to memory fragmentation.

Partitioning a hard disk

If you work with many small files on a large hard disk that doesn't use the Mac OS Extended format, you can save a significant amount of disk space by partitioning the disk into several smaller volumes. This is because the Mac OS file system allocates a minimum amount of disk space for each file, regardless of its actual contents. The minimum file size for a particular disk is set when it is initialized and is incrementally larger for larger disks (or volumes). For example, a short memo that takes up 16.5K on a 1GB hard disk would take only 4K on a 230MB volume, saving 12K per small file.

Most formatting programs set a minimum file size of 4K on volumes with capacities between 224MB and 255MB, 8K on volumes with capacities between 480MB and 511MB, 16K on volumes between 992MB and 1023MB, and so on.

If you work mostly with large files, large volumes are more efficient. The Mac OS Extended format nearly eliminates the file size advantage of partitioning a hard disk into smaller volumes.

Each partitioned volume looks and acts exactly like a hard disk. Every volume has its own disk icon on the desktop, and all volumes appear at the desktop level of the dialog boxes you use for opening and saving files in an application. Think of volumes as individual disks that happen to be stored on the same mechanism.

Partitioning has other advantages besides using disk space more efficiently. For one, items are easier to find on smaller volumes. You can secure an individual volume's contents with a password or lock it against overwriting. Accidental corruption of one volume is unlikely to affect other volumes.

On the downside, partitioning reduces storage flexibility. Each volume has a separate amount of available space. If you fill one volume, you can't store any more on it even though other volumes on the same drive have plenty of space available. Also, making multiple volumes increases the clutter of icons on the desktop. What's more, partitioning generally requires formatting a disk, which erases its contents. Backing up before and restoring after takes a lot of time and exposes your files to greater risk than doing nothing. For example, aliases may become unlinked from their original items when restored to a partitioned volume, which is essentially a new disk.

The disadvantages of partitioning are minor compared to the space savings you can obtain if you have a large hard disk. Unless you work mostly with files larger than 8K, you should consider partitioning a hard disk whose capacity is larger than 500MB. Either that, or convert the disk to the Mac OS Extended format (see Chapter 5 for more on converting to Mac OS Extended format).

Caution

Before partitioning a hard disk you *must* back it up. Partitioning your disk requires a reformat, which destroys all the data on that disk! That includes any additional volumes that have already been created as partitions on that same drive. You won't be able to access any of your existing files after partitioning until you have restored them from a backup. Make sure your backup program enables you to restore folders individually, because after partitioning you will have smaller disk volumes and all your folders may not fit on one volume. Restored aliases are more likely to work if you restore them to a volume whose name is identical to the disk they came from.

You partition a disk with a disk setup program. You can probably use the disk setup program that came with your computer, or with your hard disk if you have added another hard disk or replaced your original hard disk. For example, the Drive Setup program that comes with Mac OS 9 can partition a number of disks, including all IDE/ATA drives and any drive that came preinstalled in a Mac (see Figure 28-4). You can also buy a disk setup utility, such as Hard Disk ToolKit from FWB (415-482-4800, http://www.fwb.com).

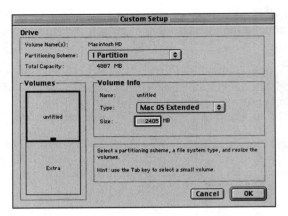

Figure 28-4: After choosing a volume and clicking Initialize in Drive Setup, you can click Custom Setup to change your drive's partitions.

If you want to use a partitioned disk to start up your computer, you must install the Mac OS on one of the volumes. In some cases, your computer may not start up or may delay starting up unless you install the Mac OS on the preferred startup volume. The preferred startup volume is usually the first volume to appear on your desktop when you start up from another disk, such as a Mac OS installation CD or floppy disk. The preferred startup volume is also usually the first volume you create when you partition a disk. Some disk setup programs let you designate the preferred startup volume; Apple's Drive Setup does not.

You can install the Mac OS on more than one volume, but there is generally no reason to use up disk space this way. (The exception is if you needed to dual-boot into two or more Mac OSs, especially if you're a developer or a system administrator who needs to test or support more than one Mac OS version.) You can change which volume you start up from using the Startup Disk control panel, which is discussed in Chapter 12.

Optimum volume size

The most difficult decision to make when partitioning a hard disk is to decide how many volumes to create and what size to make each one. Generally, you want to make a volume large enough to hold all related items and leave room to add items in the future. For example, you can create one volume to hold all your software—application programs and system software—and another volume to hold all your documents. Unless you create very large documents (in which case you may be better off not partitioning), the volume for applications and the System Folder probably needs to be bigger than the volume for documents.

The size of a volume determines the minimum size of a file on that volume. The smallest amount of space that can be allocated to a file on a volume is called the *allocation block size*. Larger volumes have larger allocation block sizes. For example, a 100-word memo needs only about 600 bytes of storage space, but it uses up to 16.5K (16,896 bytes) on a 1GB volume or 8K (8192 bytes) on a 500MB volume. Finder rounds file sizes up to the nearest whole number, so a list view would report the size of a 16.5K file as 17K.

Some documents and all programs get a minimum of two blocks. One block is for the file's data and the other block is for the file's resources. For example, a SimpleText document always occupies at least 33K on a 1GB hard disk.

Minimum allocation block size grows by 0.5K for every 32MB in volume capacity, as tabulated in Table 28-1.

Table 28-1
Smallest File Sizes for Various Volume Sizes Using Mac OS Standard Format

Volume Size	Smallest File	Volume Size	Smallest File	Volume Size	Smallest File
0 to 31MB	0.5K	832 to 863MB	13.5K	1664 to 1695MB	26.5K
32 to 63MB	1K	864 to 895MB	14K	1696 to 1727MB	27K
64 to 95MB	1.5K	896 to 927MB	14.5K	1728 to 1759MB	27.5K
96 to 127MB	2K	928 to 959MB	15K	1760 to 1791MB	28K
128 to 159MB	2.5K	960 to 991MB	15.5K	1792 to 1823MB	28.5K
160 to 191MB	3K	992 to 1023MB	16K	1824 to 1855MB	29K
192 to 223MB	3.5K	1024 to 1055MB	16.5K	1856 to 1887MB	29.5K
224 to 255MB	4K	1056 to 1087MB	17K	1888 to 1919MB	30K
256 to 287MB	4.5K	1088 to 1119MB	17.5K	1920 to 1951MB	30.5K
288 to 319MB	5K	1120 to 1151MB	18K	1952 to 1983MB	31K
320 to 351MB	5.5K	1152 to 1183MB	18.5K	1984 to 2015MB	31.5K
352 to 383MB	6K	1184 to 1215MB	19K	2016 to 2047MB	32K
384 to 415MB	6.5K	1216 to 1247MB	19.5K	2048 to 2079MB	32.5K
416 to 447MB	7K	1248 to 1279MB	20K	2080 to 2111MB	33K
448 to 479MB	7.5K	1280 to 1311MB	20.5K	2112 to 2143MB	33.5K
480 to 511MB	8K	1312 to 1343MB	21K	2144 to 2175MB	34K

Continued

Table 28-1 (continued)

Volume Size	Smallest File	Volume Size	Smallest File	Volume Size	Smallest File
512 to 543MB	8.5K	1344 to 1375MB	21.5K	2176 to 2207MB	34.5K
544 to 575MB	9K	1376 to 1407MB	22K	2208 to 2239MB	35K
576 to 607MB	9.5K	1408 to 1439MB	22.5K	2240 to 2271MB	35.5K
608 to 639MB	10K	1440 to 1471MB	23K	2272 to 2303MB	36K
640 to 671MB	10.5K	1472 to 1503MB	23.5K	2304 to 2335MB	36.5K
672 to 703MB	11K	1504 to 1535MB	24K	2336 to 2367MB	37K
704 to 735MB	11.5K	1536 to 1567MB	24.5K	2368 to 2399MB	37.5K
736 to 767MB	12K	1568 to 1599MB	25K	2400 to 2431MB	38K
768 to 799MB	12.5K	1600 to 1631MB	25.5K	2432 to 2463MB	38.5K
800 to 831MB	13K	1632 to 1663MB	26K	2464 to 2495MB	39K

Shortcuts to sleep

A computer that's capable of sleep will go to sleep if you use these shortcuts rather than the Sleep command in the Finder's Special menu or the Control Strip:

✦ Press Power to bring up the Restart-Sleep-Shut Down alert box and click Sleep.

✦ Press ⌘+Shift+0 (zero) if you're more of a keyboard person and are using a PowerBook (and some newer Mac models).

* Press ⌘+Option+Power if you're a keyboard aficionado using a desktop Mac that's capable of sleep. Be sure you press this key combination precisely. Other key combinations very similar to this one will shut down or restart the computer unceremoniously and may result in data loss and disk corruption. Don't use this shortcut unless you have an excellent memory for key combinations and careful fingers.

Sleeping desktop computers

Some desktop Macs can't be put to sleep with the Energy Saver control panel. If you have one of these Macs, you can use the shareware control panel Sleeper from St. Clair Software to make some parts of your system sleep. Sleeper spins down hard disks and dims the display after periods of inactivity. You can use Sleeper's screen dimming in conjunction with another control panel that reduces power on an Energy Star monitor, such as Apple's Energy Saver control panel, and you can have Sleeper bring up a screen saver, such as After Dark, instead of dimming the display. Sleeper does not affect CD-ROM drives, tape drives, or the processor and other system-board circuitry, all of which remain fully active.

RAM disks

You can speed up surfing the Internet's World Wide Web by putting your Web browser program's disk cache on a relatively small RAM disk. With its cache on a RAM disk, the Web browser reloads pages it has saved to the cache more quickly, accesses the hard disk less frequently, and cleans up its cache almost instantaneously. To get set up, use the Memory control panel to create a 1MB to 5MB RAM disk. After restarting to mount the RAM disk, set the Web browser to use the RAM disk for its cache. For example, in Microsoft Internet Explorer you make this setting in the Advanced section of the Preferences dialog box. Note that the memory you allocate to a RAM disk is reported as part of the Mac OS by the Finder's About This Computer command.

To reclaim the memory used by a RAM disk, you must turn off the RAM disk feature and restart your computer. You can avoid this hassle by creating a RAM disk with the RamBunctious program (described in Chapter 26). It creates a RAM disk as an application (sounds weird, but it's true), and you get your memory back as soon as you quit or drag the RAM disk icon to the Trash. You can even automate mounting the RAM disk before opening the Web browser by using the Disk Copy to create the RAM disk (see Chapter 24).

Download to RAM disk

When using an online service such as America Online or CompuServe, download files to a RAM disk rather than to your hard disk to save on download time. Just make sure that you don't forget to save your RAM disk contents before shutdown.

Eggs and Hacks

Apple's software engineers, true to their kind, have sprinkled "Easter eggs" — cute or funny animations or other surprising actions — in their work. To finish things off, here's a list of some of the treasures you can find hidden in the Mac OS.

About the Finder

In the Finder, pressing Option changes the first command in the Apple menu to About The Finder. Choose this command, and instead of the usual memory usage chart, you see a color picture of the Apple campus. Wait about 10 seconds, and credits start scrolling up the screen. Figure 28-5 shows the About The Finder window.

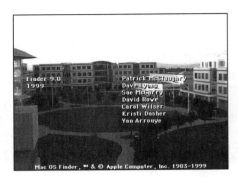

Figure 28-5: The credits are rolling for the Mac OS.

Sing it to me

If your computer has text-to-speech software installed, four of the supplied voices sing rather than speak text. The Bad News voice sings to the tune of a Chopin Prelude. The Good News voice sings to the tune of "Pomp and Circumstance." The Pipe Organ voice sings to the tune of the theme music for the "Alfred Hitchcock Presents" television show. The Cellos voice sings to the tune of Edvard Grieg's "In the Hall of the Mountain King" from *Peer Gynt*. To hear the tunes clearly, you need to have these voices sing (speak) a selection of text without punctuation marks. When these voices encounter punctuation, they start their tunes over.

Try this: In a new SimpleText document, type **la la la** several times in succession. Select what you have typed, copy it, click at the end of the document, and keep pasting it until you have a dozen lines of "la la la" in the document. Choose one of the singing voices from the Voices submenu of the Sound menu and use the Speak All command to hear the voice sing. Bonus: Some of the novelty voices, such as Boing, Bubbles, and Hysterical, also sound pretty weird when you have them speak this text.

Tell me a joke

If you have Speech Recognition installed and turned on, you can get your computer to tell you knock-knock jokes. You say, "Tell me a joke." The computer responds, "Knock, knock." You reply, "Who's there?" The computer answers with a name or some word, such as "orange." You repeat the word and then say "who?" Figure 28-6 shows a transcript of one of these jokes in the speech feedback window.

Figure 28-6: Get Speech Recognition to tell you a joke.

Finder hacks

If you have itchy fingers and an idle copy of ResEdit, you can put a personal stamp on your Mac's Finder. This sidebar lists some interesting changes, or *hacks*, that you can make to the Finder. The basic procedure is the same for all the hacks listed below. As a rule, always use ResEdit on a copy of the original file instead of the original file itself. (For the reasons why, see Chapter 27.)

✦ Change the suffix for an alias as follows:

1. Open STR# resource.

2. Open resource 8200.

3. Change the alias suffix in string #1 to something else (up to 31 characters).

✦ Change the initial name of a new folder as follows:

1. Open STR# resource.

2. Open resource 4500.

3. Alter string #3 to change *untitled folder* to something else (up to 31 characters).

✦ Change the sample text displayed when you open a TrueType or fixed-size font as follows:

1. Open STR# resource.

2. Double-click resource 5816.

3. Edit the phrase in string #1.

Successfully performing any of these hacks gains you membership in the Loyal Order of the DogCow ("All hail Clarus — aya, aya, moof!"), which entitles you to wear an extra-large T-shirt and shorts to work and to litter your workspace with candy-bar wrappers and empty cola cans!

Summary

In this chapter of system-related tips and tricks, you learned to navigate through Open, Save, and Navigation Services dialog boxes more efficiently. You can use the keyboard instead of the mouse. You can use folder aliases to jump from one folder directly to another. And you can side step or cancel a misplaced double-click.

File sharing is very handy, especially when you know a few tricks. You can improve performance by sharing fewer folders and by putting shared files on a RAM disk. Cut file-sharing red tape with aliases. Carry around replicas of all your hard disks on a single floppy disk; they're fully functional as long as you're near your network.

There are a number of useful, hidden shortcuts for your control panels and system extensions. You can activate Easy Access features with the keyboard. Add a hidden alert sound to the Sound control panel. Temporarily turn off virtual memory when you start up your Mac. If you're tired of waiting for your PowerBook to start up when you take it through airport security, use a utility to avoid the wait.

This chapter also gave you some tips for getting the most from applications and accessories. You can operate the QuickTime movie controller from your keyboard; set your computer to automatically play any audio CD that you insert in the CD-ROM drive; make an audio-only QuickTime movie; magnify the Map control panel; copy or delete a batch of items all at once (without typing a DOS-style command); hide a program's windows while switching to another program. In addition, you can boost performance by hiding windows.

If your memory isn't what it should be, use the tips in this chapter to reduce system memory size and relieve fragmented memory. If you have a lot of memory, use part of it for a RAM disk. If you're not using your disk efficiently, you can back it up and partition it in order to get more than one volume from a single hard drive. With a RAM disk, you can accelerate your Web browser's handling of its cache, speed up downloading of files, or even run a utility program to perform maintenance on your hard disk. Sleep won't help your computer's memory, but tips in this chapter tell you several ways to put your computer to sleep quickly.

Finally, this chapter revealed a couple of Easter eggs and disclosed a list of Finder hacks that work in Mac OS 9.

✦   ✦   ✦

Troubleshoot Problems and Maintain the Mac OS

CHAPTER

29

No computer, not even a Macintosh, is trouble-free. Inevitably, your computer will experience some mishap or other — a freeze, crash, startup problem, or strange behavior of some type. These problems can have a range of causes, from conflicts caused by various system extensions or old applications to misconfigured hardware devices, corrupted system software, or faulty hardware. It is impossible to discuss all the problems that you might encounter, but there are general principles applicable to a variety of problems.

This chapter discusses the sorts of problems that all Macs are likely to experience at some time or other. In addition, you look at steps to reduce the likelihood of problems occurring and to minimize the consequences that result when problems do occur. You also learn about specific tools that can make troubleshooting more painless.

Although it's possible to solve some problems by trial and error, you can avoid much of the headache by taking steps to understand what is actually happening and applying techniques sensibly.

Preventive Measures

The best way to deal with a problem is to prevent it from happening in the first place. Of course, some problems will occur regardless of anything you do in advance. Nevertheless, a bit of prevention can go a long way.

Backups

A computer user who does not make backups is like a sky diver who fails to check his or her parachute before jumping. You may be lucky for a while, but it simply is not worth the risk to your life or your data, as the case may be. The question is not whether you will accidentally delete an important file or whether your hard disk or other storage device will fail; the only question is when it will happen. There are times when it pays to be a pessimist, and at no time is the payoff greater than when you are able to recover gracefully from what could otherwise be disaster for you and your data.

Software and media

At one time, Mac users could back up all their files conveniently on diskettes. In this era of multigigabyte hard drives, that is no longer practical. For many Mac users, a backup device such as a tape drive or removable disk (Zip, Jaz, SyQuest, or magneto-optical drive) is a necessity, along with appropriate backup software. A discussion of backup hardware and software is beyond the scope of our discussion, but reviews of these devices and software programs do appear periodically in publications such as *Macworld*. Useful backup programs include Retrospect and Retrospect Express from Dantz Development (510-253-3000, `http://www.dantz.com/`) and Personal Backup from ASD Software (909-624 2594, `http://www.asdsoft.com/`).

Whichever backup hardware and software you choose, it is important to perform backups regularly. A six-month-old backup may not be much help if disaster strikes. Don't forget to make backups of files that are on diskettes or other removable media but that are not on your hard disk.

Backup rotation

In putting together a backup strategy, it's important to plan to rotate your media and archive your backups periodically. While it's a good strategy to back up every few days or once a week, writing to the same removable media over and over again can sometimes be little or no protection at all. If a virus or data corruption is introduced to your files, you may inadvertently overwrite good backups with bad data. Likewise, if the backup media goes bad, you could end up with no advantage to your backup sessions.

If you're backing up for a business or organization or in situations where your data is very important, you want a bulletproof rotation scheme with your media. In this scenario, you need quite a few backup disks or tapes. Here's the plan:

1. Every other day, back up to a new disk or tape. This could be, for instance, Monday, Wednesday and Friday. For the first week, each will require a full backup, because you'll be using a new disk or tape. Subsequently, you can use your backup software's incremental backup feature to backup *some* of the disks more quickly.

2. After the first week, drop the Friday disk or tape out of the rotation and save it in a secure location (off-site, in a safety deposit box, in secure storage). This is your archive disk or tape for the week.

3. On the following Monday and Wednesday, you can perform an incremental update to the backups. On the following Friday, create a new, full backup that will again be archived.

In this scheme you're able to keep your backup data relatively fresh while guarding against catastrophe and data corruption. At the most, you've lost two days (often one business day) of data in the event of hard disk failure. (If your disk fails on Thursday, you have Wednesday's backup. If it fails on Sunday, you have Friday's backup.) If you contract a virus or notice disk corruption at some point, you have a number of backups to choose from, including backups that are one day old, three days old, a week old, two weeks old, and so on. (If you find corruption on Thursday, you have Wednesday's backup, Monday's backup, and the previous Friday's archive. Then you have previous week's archives as well.) Hopefully, there is a recent version that lacks the corruption. If your data is even more mission-critical, you should back up every day and/or avoid incremental backups of any kind, instead archiving each backup on a fresh tape or disk.

For personal backup, the scheme can be a little less arduous. We recommend backing up once or twice a week, rotating between at least two different disks, and then archiving your data every two weeks or once a month, depending on the sensitivity of the data. It can be a pain to enter two weeks worth of Quicken checkbook data or lose changes in files over the past few weeks, but at least you'll probably have a good backup to work with. Although you probably don't need to back up applications and system software, because you can reinstall them if necessary, you should back up your documents this frequently. (You can also back up your Preferences folder in the System Folder often so you can restore changes to application preferences in the case of a hard disk crash.) You may also want an archive of application updates and software downloaded from the Internet, just so you can get to those patches and updates quickly if you need to reinstall. It's best to archive data periodically and keep at least two different backup tapes or disks active at once for some measure of redundancy.

Periodic maintenance

You can use many of the tools available for troubleshooting before problems become evident. In some cases, your Mac may already be experiencing problems that you are unaware of. By catching problems in the early stages, you can save yourself (and your Mac) a lot of grief.

Disk diagnostics

If the directory structure of a Mac disk—whether a hard disk, floppy disk, Zip, or other removable disk—becomes damaged, you may experience a variety of problems, including inability to access one or more of your files. In severe cases, the entire contents of a disk may become inaccessible.

Apple's Disk First Aid (which was introduced in Chapter 25 and is described in more detail in the "Troubleshooting Tools" section of this chapter) can detect and repair problems with the directory structure of a Mac disk. It's a good idea to run Disk First Aid periodically on your disks, even if you aren't experiencing any problems. Apple recommends running Disk First Aid monthly as a precautionary measure; if you use your Mac intensively on a regular basis, you may wish to run Disk First Aid more often than that.

Other utilities, notably commercial products such as TechTool Pro from Micromat Computer Systems (800-829-6227, http://www.micromat.com/) and Norton Utilities for Macintosh from Symantec (408-253-9600, http://www.symantec.com/), can perform a check similar to Disk First Aid's, sometimes fixing problems that Disk First Aid can't. Before running a commercial disk utility, make sure that it is fully compatible with your Mac model and the version of the Mac OS you are running.

Rebuilding the desktop

If the desktop database on your hard disk becomes damaged, you may see generic (blank) icons instead of the distinctive icons that tell you what kind of file you're looking at. Another symptom of desktop database trouble is being unable to open documents by double-clicking their icons or by dragging compatible documents to them, even if the icons are not generic. Also, problems with the desktop database can cause folder and disk icons to display slowly, although the type of view and the view options you have selected also have an effect on performance.

Apple recommends rebuilding the desktop monthly. You probably won't hurt anything by rebuilding frequently but it may be a waste of your time, because rebuilding can take several minutes per disk depending on the number of applications and files you have. You can try rebuilding once a month, and keep up with that schedule if you feel it improves the performance of the Finder. In any case, it is a good idea to rebuild the desktop at least once a month if you install software frequently.

You can rebuild the desktop by restarting your computer with the Ô and Option keys held down. At the end of the startup cycle, the Finder displays an alert asking you to confirm that you want to rebuild your disk. Figure 29-1 is an example of this alert.

Note If you have Multiple Users active, you should hold down ⌘ and Option immediately after logging in to your account and before the desktop appears. Users with Panels access cannot rebuild the desktop.

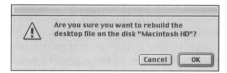

Figure 29-1: Rebuild the desktop by restarting your Mac while pressing ⌘+Option.

If more than one disk is connected to your computer when you rebuild the desktop, the Finder displays a separate alert box for each disk in turn. The same is true if you have partitioned your hard disk into multiple volumes (each with its own desktop icon).

Rebuilding without restarting—A dubious practice

It's possible to rebuild the desktop on your startup disk without restarting the computer, although there is some risk involved. What you do is close all folder and disk windows, close all control panels, put away any open dialog boxes, and then force the Finder to quit by pressing ⌘+Option+Escape. That brings up an alert box in which you click the Force Quit button if you're sure you want to go through with this. Then all the desktop icons, the folder and disk windows, and the Finder menus go away as the Finder quits.

Now hold down the ⌘ and Option keys until the Finder displays its alert asking you to confirm rebuilding the desktop. The risk in forcing the Finder to quit is that you're not giving it a chance to clean up after itself by, for example, closing the desktop database in an orderly fashion. That's right—forcing the Finder to quit could induce problems with the desktop database! You face even more weirdness if you leave control panels or dialog boxes open when you force the Finder to quit, because the Finder can't save any changes made to settings in those windows.

You can also write an AppleScript that can send a Quit Apple Event to the Finder. This enables the Finder to quit more gracefully. If you don't specify another application to launch, you can quickly hold down ⌘ and Option after the Finder has quit and before it restarts. This enables you to rebuild the desktop. (Quitting the Finder with an AppleScript script is discussed in Chapter 27.)

You can rebuild the desktop database on floppy disks and other removable disks by pressing ⌘+Option while inserting the disk. The Finder displays its confirmation alert before rebuilding. There's no need to rebuild the desktop database on CD-ROMs and DVD-ROMs because these discs are read-only.

If you are experiencing problems that appear to be the result of a corrupted desktop database and rebuilding the desktop does not solve the problem, use the Extensions Manager control panel (described in "Troubleshooting Tools" later in this chapter) to choose just the base extensions before restarting. In the case of severe corruption of the desktop, you may wish to use a utility such as the freeware utility TechTool or its commercial sibling TechTool Pro from Micromat to remove the desktop database completely, forcing a new one to be built from scratch.

Note   If you remove the desktop database in this way, you will lose any comments that you entered in the Info window of files and folders in the Finder.

Disk defragmentation

Just as the Mac's RAM can become fragmented (as described in Chapter 19), disk space can also become fragmented. In addition, unlike applications that each must reside in a single contiguous block of RAM, files themselves (including applications) can become fragmented on a disk. A single file may be split into several pieces spread around in different locations physically on a disk. Fragmentation degrades disk performance because the disk drive must take extra time to move from one piece of a file to the next.

A fragmented file is analogous to a single track on an audio CD being split into multiple segments, so that the beginning of the track might be at the beginning of the CD, the middle at the end, and the end of the track some place in the middle. If audio CDs were mastered in that fashion (which, fortunately, they are not), you would likely notice a delay as the CD player's laser moves to play the next segment.

In a disk with no fragmentation, each file physically resides in a single contiguous block. As a disk begins to fill up and new files are created and deleted with increasing frequency, files and the free space start to become fragmented. Disk performance can suffer, often severely, if the fragmentation becomes heavy. In addition, a heavily fragmented disk is more likely to experience a variety of problems, including corrupted directory structures and damaged files.

Without any special software, you can eliminate fragmentation by copying the entire contents of a disk to another disk, erasing the disk, and copying everything back. An easier solution is to use a commercial disk defragmentation utility, such as the SpeedDisk component of the Norton Utilities from Symantec (408-253-9600, http://www.symantec.com/), or DiskExpress Pro or PlusOptimizer from Alsoft (800-257-6381, http://www.alsoft.com/). Note, however, that older disk optimization utilities are not compatible with the Mac OS Extended format (HFS Plus); you should check for compatibility before attempting to run a disk optimizer on a Mac OS Extended volume.

Before optimizing any disk, it is especially important to make a full backup, because virtually every byte on the disk may be erased and moved to a different location.

Protection from computer viruses

Although computer viruses are not nearly as prevalent on Macs as on Microsoft Windows PCs, Mac viruses do exist, and many of the so-called "macro viruses" developed on PCs (generally infecting Microsoft Office documents) can infect Macs. Viruses can invade your computer through documents or applications that you have downloaded from the Internet, through electronic mail attachments, or through any type of removable disk (including floppy disks) you may use with your computer. Although some viruses may be relatively innocuous, doing little more than taking up space on disk and slowing down your computer a bit, others can be highly destructive, causing crashes and erasing files.

The only way to protect your Mac from computer viruses is to install an antivirus utility on your computer. Antivirus software warns you if a virus attempts to infect your system, scans your disks for viruses that may be lurking (or may already have caused some damage), and eradicates almost any virus that it finds. The most popular free antivirus software program, John Norstad's Disinfectant, alas, is no longer being updated, but several commercial antivirus utilities are available. These include Dr. Solomon's Virex (781-273-7400, http://www.drsolomons.com/) and Norton AntiVirus for Macintosh from Symantec (408-253-9600, http://www.symantec.com/).

Whichever antivirus software package you choose, it is essential to keep it up-to-date; each time a new virus appears, the antivirus packages must generally be updated to recognize it. Most of the time, you receive updates by downloading them from the software publisher's Web site or accessing them in public download Web sites or FTP sites. In some cases, you may have a limited "subscription" to updates to the virus software itself. With Virex, you can pay an additional fee to have updates e-mailed directly to you. Norton AntiVirus includes a LiveUpdate feature that can automatically download the latest virus definitions for you. Norton AntiVirus also offers a free trial version that you can download directly from the company's Web site.

Computer viruses, worms, and Trojan horses

A *computer virus* is a piece of software designed to spread itself by illicitly attaching copies of itself to legitimate software. Although not all viruses perform malicious actions (such as erasing your hard disk), any virus can interfere with the normal functioning of your computer.

A *macro virus* is a virus written in the *macro language* of an application (a programming language that enables you to automate multiple-step operations in an application). By far, most macro viruses infect Microsoft Word (version 6.0 and later) and Excel (version 5.0 and later) documents. Like other viruses, macro viruses can be very destructive.

Viruses, alas, are not the only potentially destructive software that you may encounter. *Worms* are similar to viruses in that they replicate, but they do not attach themselves to files. A *Trojan horse* is an intentionally destructive program masquerading as something useful such as a utility, software updater, or game. Although worms and Trojan horses are not viruses, most commercial antivirus programs can detect and remove them.

Keeping software up-to-date

Believe it or not, a good portion of the software on your computer may be infested with bugs. (*Bugs* in this case refers to programming errors or other flaws in software, not garden-variety insects.) Some of these bugs may be features that do not work as documented, and others may be more serious, causing crashes or data loss. Even the Mac OS is not immune to bugs.

Usually, once a software publisher becomes aware of a problem, it takes action to correct it right away, often by providing free updaters, which update the software to a newer version, or by documenting workarounds. In some cases, a bug may be an incompatibility with some other software or hardware product. You can keep informed of bugs and bug fixes by registering your products, often by sending in a postcard that came packaged with the product or registering over the Internet, and by checking the publisher's Web site frequently.

Late-breaking news regarding the Mac OS, including announcements of updates and compatibility information, is found at Apple's Mac OS Web site (http://macos. apple.com/macos/) and Apple's Software Updates library (http://www.apple. com/swupdates/). You can also use the Software Update feature to automatically update Apple's Mac OS and other software over the Internet (see Chapter 12 for details).

Remember that older software may not be compatible with the most recent Mac OS from Apple, despite extensive compatibility testing by Apple and software publishers. For this reason, it is often a good idea to keep all your software current — applications, your Mac OS, and any third-party operating system extension you have installed.

Good (and bad) housekeeping practices

In the course of using your computer, some activities help minimize problems, while others are all but guaranteed to create them.

Shutting down

You can create problems through seemingly innocent actions such as shutting down your computer. The proper way to shut down your computer is to press Power and click Shut Down in the alert box that appears. As a shortcut, you can press ⌘+Shift+Option+Power. You can also shut down by choosing Shut Down from the Finder's Special menu.

If you shut down your computer by switching off the power, you may damage the disk directory. The Disk First Aid program (discussed in "Troubleshooting Tools" later in this chapter) can usually repair this type of damage. However, you're better off not causing the damage in the first place. Left uncorrected, disk directory damage leads to more directory damage and may eventually result in lost data.

When to wait before you update

Every piece of software — including software updates — may have bugs. Unless you are experiencing a severe problem that an update is designed to correct, it often makes sense to wait at least a few days (or weeks) before installing a just-released update. Over the years, there have been many cases of a software publisher (including Apple) pulling an update from distribution because of serious bugs that were not foreseen by the programmers. In many cases, bugs in an update are documented in the accompanying Read Me file. Although Read Me files rarely make stimulating reading material, reading them before installing can save you much grief.

If you must run older software on your computer (for example, if a product you need is no longer being updated), it is especially important to exercise caution before updating the Mac OS. Although incompatibilities are often documented in the Mac OS Read Me files, some incompatibilities may not yet be discovered. These surprises are another reason why backups are so important.

Installing software

Before installing any software, there are a few precautions you should take. First, peruse the Read Me files and the installation instructions. You may discover that the program is not compatible with your particular Mac model or the Mac OS version you are using. Be suspicious of any software more than a year or so old.

Older software, especially utilities, system extensions, and games, can be a hazard. Before installing older software, check whether an update or a more recent version is available. Be particularly cautious of third-party extensions and control panels from companies other than Apple.

If you have enough disk space, it's usually best to install software using the easy, standard, typical, or default installation for the type of computer you have (desktop or portable). If you perform a custom installation, you can too easily omit a component that may be essential for the software to run. If the default installation will not install all the components you need or want, you can usually install those items separately by running the installer a second time.

Finally, before installing any software, it is a good idea to restart your computer. Depending on the software, you may want to disable some or all of your system extensions before beginning installation. You can do this by using the Extensions Manager control panel to choose base extensions only or by restarting with Shift held down.

Experimenting

Although experimenting with your Mac is an excellent way to learn, it is important to take care in what you do. In particular, avoid removing items from the System Folder or files from the folders in which your applications reside unless you are certain the items are not needed. These files may be essential to the operation of your Mac or your applications, and they may not function unless they are in a specific location.

Protecting your Mac from unauthorized experimentation

If other people use your Mac, there are a couple of precautions you can take to reduce the damage they might cause. These steps aren't effective against people with malicious intent, more advanced users, or even particularly inquisitive children, but they are helpful if you allow friends, relatives, or colleagues to use your computer occasionally.

✦ To reduce the risk of accidentally removing items from the System Folder and the Applications folder, you can use the General Controls control panel to turn on the options Protect System Folder and Protect Applications folder. Turning on these options prevents items at the top level of the System Folder and Applications folder from being moved, removed, or renamed. Items in folders in the System Folder and Applications folder, however, can still be moved, removed, or renamed.

✦ To hide some of the more advanced features of the Finder from casual users, you can turn on the Simple Finder option in the Finder's Preferences dialog box, which you display by choosing Preferences from the Finder's Edit menu. After turning on the Simple Finder option, only the most basic commands appear in the Finder's menus, eliminating items such as Move to Trash, Make Alias, and Sharing.

✦ Use Multiple Users to create accounts for other users. You can assign privileges to any user regarding their access to the Control Panels, extensions, and various applications or utilities on the Mac. You can even create a guest account for occasional users who don't merit their own personal account on your Mac. See Chapter 13 for details.

✦ Use Apple's File Security application to encrypt and archive files on your Mac.

✦ Lock your keychain! The Keychain Access control panel offers several ways to automatically lock your keychain when your Mac is not in use. See Chapter 12 for more on the keychain control panel.

Although these precautions can help thwart a casual user from messing up your machine, you will need to use a special utility to provide any real protection. While Multiple Users can help a lot, devious users can defeat it. You may want to look at more robust security programs such as FileGuard or DiskGuard from ASD Software (909-624-2594, http://www.asdsoft.com/) or DiskLock from PowerOn Software (800-344- 9160, http://www.poweronsw.com/).

Cleaning up and reducing clutter

Just as furniture accumulates dust and desks accumulate papers, your Mac can accumulate a significant amount of clutter. The clutter can manifest itself in unneeded items on your desktop, duplicate files on your hard disk, old applications that you no longer run, and documents that you just don't need any more.

Although there's not necessarily any harm in being a packrat, unneeded clutter can slow you down, slow your computer, and increase the likelihood of running into problems. In particular, having different versions of the same application can result in unpredictable behavior, and older applications may not be fully compatible with your other, more recent software. In addition, clutter can make it hard to find the files or applications you need. Having a large number of files in a single folder can reduce performance, and keeping your system clean will lessen the likelihood of running out of disk space.

Periodically, you might want to take some time to clear up the clutter taking over your hard disk, deleting old applications, aliases you no longer use, and files whose purpose ceased to be relevant. A utility such as Apple System Profiler or Spring Cleaning from Aladdin Systems (408-761-6200, http://www.aladdinsys.com/) can help simplify the cleanup process.

Maintenance schedule

Taken together, all of the maintenance tasks discussed in the preceding sections — backing up, rebuilding the desktop, defragmenting, virus checking, securing your system and periodic cleaning up — can help ensure that your Mac experience is relatively error and hassle free. Here, then, is a quick summary of the steps to take to maintain your Mac and the recommended frequency:

✦ **Daily**. For the most part, you should turn on and shut down your Mac only once per day (at the beginning and end of your work day or Mac session), if you elect to do so at all. You can put your Mac to sleep, spin down the hard disk, and make other energy-saving settings in the Energy Saver control panel (see Chapter 12). Otherwise, more harm than good comes from restarting more than once per day. However, you may find it useful to *restart* the Mac (using the Restart command in the Finder) more than once per day if, for instance, you find RAM becoming fragmented thanks to opening and closing files and applications over and over again. You should also check your disk space levels — open the Macintosh HD icon and look at the status section of the window at the top to make sure you have disk space available. Less than 50MB or so of disk space could begin to create problems, so you should backup and archive unnecessary documents or applications. In a business setting you may also want to backup on a daily basis or every other day, according to a well-planned rotation schedule.

✦ **Weekly**. On a weekly basis you should run your virus-checking software if it's not already designed to run in the background. If your machine is for personal use, you might want to backup on weekly basis, again according to a media rotation schedule. You may also want to run Disk Tools on a weekly basis.

✦ **Monthly**. On a monthly basis, you should rebuild the desktop database, as described in the section "Rebuilding the Desktop" earlier in this chapter. You should also run Disk Tools, if you don't already run it more frequently, update your virus definitions if your virus software doesn't do this for you automatically, and every one to three months, defragment your hard disk.

✦ **Every three to six months**. Every three to six months perform a more serious tune-up session. Update parts of the Mac OS with incremental updates that have appeared on Apple's Web site. (You can accomplish this in Mac OS 9 with the Software Update control panel.) Boot from a Mac OS CD or utility CD and run a disk doctor session from Norton Utilities or Micromat's TechTool Pro. You should also perform a disk housecleaning session, removing applications, Preferences file, unused third-party extensions, and other software that your Mac no longer needs. A tool such as Aladdin's Spring Cleaning can help with this.

Troubleshooting Tools

The proper tools are just as important to a Mac user as they are to a carpenter or mechanic. Of course, the tools are generally software, not hammers and screwdrivers. The Mac OS comes with a number of utilities that can make troubleshooting much less of a chore, and there are third-party utilities that pick up where Apple's utilities leave off or fall short. Many Mac problems cannot be solved without using these tools.

Apple System Profiler

The Apple System Profiler (described in Chapter 25), normally the first item under the Apple menu, makes it easy to get detailed information about your Mac's hardware and software configuration.

This utility aids in troubleshooting in several ways. If you call Apple's or another company's technical support number, the technician is likely to ask you specific questions about your Mac's configuration. Chances are that the answers to those questions are in one of Apple System Profiler's reports. In addition, having a printed report from Apple System Profiler handy while reading Read Me files or news of software updates can alert you to potential incompatibilities.

Moreover, the information that this utility provides can help you troubleshoot problems more easily. You can use the device and network information to troubleshoot certain hardware configuration problems. You can create reports about extensions and control panels that separate items that are part of the Mac OS from items from other sources. These reports, used in conjunction with the Extensions Manager (described later in this section), can aid in resolving extension conflicts. The System Folder Information report can tell you whether you have multiple System Folders on your startup disk (generally not a good practice). The Application Information report makes it easy to see which versions of applications you have installed and whether you have multiple copies of your applications. Figure 29-2 shows the version of Apple System Profiler that comes with Mac OS 9.

If you have never run Apple System Profiler before, it is a good idea to create and print a detailed report of your Mac's configuration. If at some point you begin to experience problems, you can print another report and see what has changed. Figure 29-3 is an example of the report created by the Apple System Profiler.

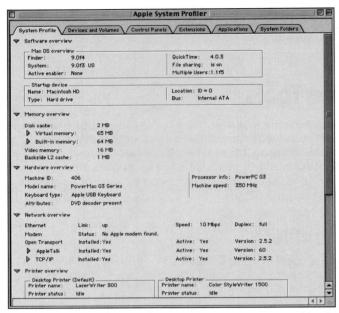

Figure 29-2: The Apple System Profiler provides a wealth of information about your Mac's configuration.

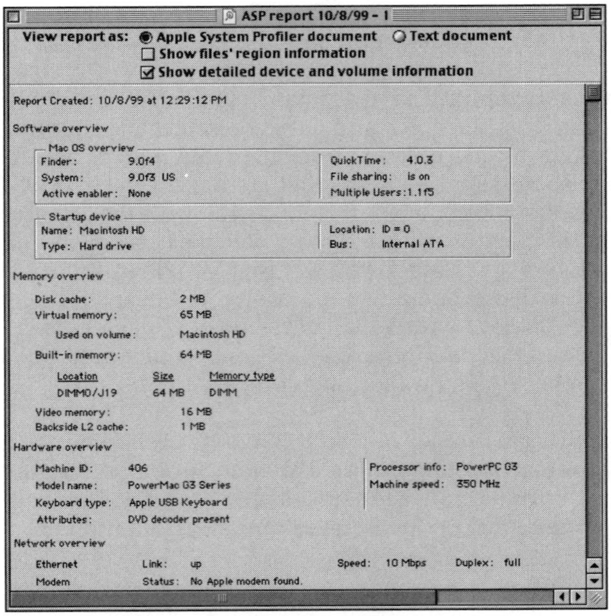

Figure 29-3: Use Apple System Profiler to generate detailed reports such as this one.

Disk First Aid

Disk First Aid (introduced in Chapter 25) is Apple's tool for detecting and correcting problems with the directory structure on a Mac hard disk. Disk First Aid is found on a Mac OS installation CD-ROM. With Mac OS 9, you also have a copy of Disk First Aid in the Utilities folder on your startup disk.

The version of Disk First Aid included with Mac OS 9 can repair damage to the startup disk. If you're currently running an earlier version of the Mac OS, you should start up from the Mac OS 9 CD to run Disk First Aid. Also, file sharing should be turned off for Disk First Aid to check for or repair damage, and First Aid will not work correctly if you attempt to use other programs while it's running.

To use Disk First Aid, simply open it and select the disks you wish to check. Each disk has an icon in the Disk First Aid window. You can select multiple disks by Shift+clicking each one or by holding down Shift while dragging across them. Then click Verify to check the selected disks or click Repair to check and correct any problems found on the selected disks. It is a good idea to Verify or Repair at least twice, because Disk First Aid may be able to find or correct different problems on different passes. Figure 29-4 is an example of the Disk First Aid window.

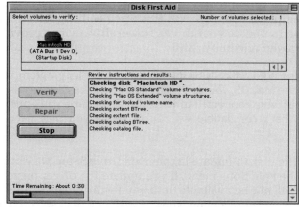

Figure 29-4: Disk First Aid can correct problems with the directory structure on a Mac disk.

If Disk First Aid finds problems that it cannot fix, you may need to use another utility to correct the problem or, as a last result resort, back up and reinitialize your hard disk.

Drive Setup

The Drive Setup utility enables you to test, initialize, and partition Apple hard disk drives, many third-party disks that have been initialized with Drive Setup, and some other kinds of storage media (such as some removable cartridge disks and magneto-optical disks). Drive Setup performs the same functions (and more) as Apple HD SC Setup and Internal HD Format, which are completely superseded by Drive Setup in Mac OS 9. You can usually find Drive Setup on a Mac OS startup CD-ROM and in the Utilities folder on your startup disk.

If you have a non-Apple hard disk (or an Apple hard disk that's been formatted with a third-party disk utility), you need to use the disk utility program that came with your hard disk or that you purchased separately, such as Hard Disk Toolkit from FWB Software (650-482-4800, http://www.fwb.com/) or LaCie Storage Utilities from LaCie (503-844-4500, http://www.lacie.com/).

This section discusses Drive Setup's capabilities and how to use them.

Updating the driver

The driver on a hard disk (or removable disk) is the software that tells the Mac how to access the information on the disk. Updating the driver can sometimes correct certain disk-related problems. In addition, if your hard disk does not have the latest version of the driver (for example, if your disk was formatted with an older version of Drive Setup), you may wish to update your driver. Newer drivers may provide better performance and improved reliability.

Note   Updating the driver is done automatically by the Mac OS 9 Installer program, so if you've recently installed the Mac OS, you don't have to update the driver again on any compatible drives that were connected to your Mac at the time you updated. If you add a new disk that's compatible with Drive Setup, you may need to update its driver.

To update the driver, select the disk to update in the main Drive Setup window and choose Update Driver from the Functions menu. If you update the driver on your startup disk, the new driver will not be available until you restart your computer. Figure 29-5 is an example of Drive Setup's main window with one disk selected and ready to have its driver updated.

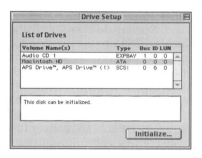

Figure 29-5: Drive Setup enables you to initialize, test, and update the drivers on Apple hard disk drives and some removable media.

Testing a disk

Drive Setup can perform a comprehensive test of a disk by copying and saving a block of data from the disk, writing and verifying a test pattern to the disk, restoring the original data, and checking that there is no discrepancy. This test is different from the one that Disk First Aid performs. Disk First Aid just checks the validity of the disk directory structure for consistency with the files written on the disk; Drive Setup actually tests every sector of the disk surface to ensure that it can be both read and written in a consistent and predictable manner. Drive Setup can mark any unreliable blocks that it finds so that no data is stored there. Drive Setup displays a message describing any problems that it finds.

Caution While Apple says this test is harmless to the data on the drive, it's always a good idea to have a fresh backup before performing any disk testing.

To perform the comprehensive read/write test on your startup disk, you need to start up from another disk, such as a Mac OS startup CD-ROM. Otherwise, Drive Setup will perform a less comprehensive read-only test. Also, if your computer is capable of sleep, be sure it is set to never sleep using the Energy Saver control panel. To test a disk with Drive Setup, select the disk to test in the main Drive Setup window and choose Test Disk from the Functions menu. The comprehensive disk test can take several hours to complete on a large hard disk, although you can stop the test at any time without the risk of damaging anything.

Initializing a disk

Initializing a disk prepares it for storing Mac files. It also erases all the files and folders on the disk. Before initializing a disk that has any files or folders on it, you must first make backup copies of the files and folder you want to keep.

When Drive Setup initializes a disk, it erases the disk by creating a new disk directory just like the Finder's Erase Disk command. Erasing does not actually clear out what was stored in old files, but it enables the Mac OS to reuse the disk for new files by writing over the old content (just as you can record over a used videotape or audiotape). In addition, you can set an option to have Drive Setup format the disk surface during initialization. Formatting a disk records new timing marks on the disk surface and checks for bad spots on the disk. You can also set an option to have Drive Setup write zeros over the entire surface of a disk while initializing it, completely and irretrievably replacing all data. You may be able to recover files after erasing a disk, but you can seldom recover file contents after formatting. You can never recover file contents after zeroing-out the disk surface.

Normally, Drive Setup does not format a disk or write zeros across it during initialization. You set these options by choosing Initialization Options from the Functions menu. This displays a dialog box in which you can select either or both of two options: Low level format and/or Zero all data. Selecting either of these options significantly increases the time that it takes to initialize a disk. If you select either of these options, you should make sure your computer will not enter sleep mode. Use the Energy Saver control panel to adjust sleep settings.

Cross-Reference   For more on the Energy Saver control panel, see Chapter 12.

To initialize a disk, select it in the main Drive Setup window and click the Initialize button. Drive Setup displays the Initialize dialog box, in which you confirm that you want to proceed with initialization even though this will erase all data on the disk. Figure 29-6 is an example of Drive Setup's Initialize dialog box.

Figure 29-6: Initializing a disk erases all files and folders on it.

The Initialize dialog box contains a Custom Setup button, which you can click to divide the disk into several volumes or choose the type of disk format. Clicking this button displays the Custom Setup dialog box shown in Figure 29-7.

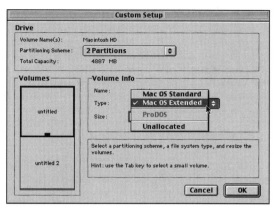

Figure 29-7: You can partition a disk into multiple volumes and choose the type of disk format using Drive Setup.

If you divide the disk into multiple volumes, each volume will have a separate disk icon on the desktop after initialization. You work with each volume as a separate disk. There are a few advantages to partitioning a large disk. First, you may be able to store and access information more quickly with a smaller partition. Second, if you are using a Mac OS Standard partition (as opposed to a Mac OS Extended partition), you will effectively increase your overall storage capacity, because smaller files will take up less space. Finally, if you wish to install multiple operating systems on this disk in addition to the Mac OS, you will need to create partitions for the other operating systems. Note that partitioning an already initialized disk erases any data that may be present. (For more information, see Chapter 28.)

If you click Custom Setup while running Mac OS 9 (as well as with Mac OS 8.1–8.6), you can choose the type of disk format for each disk volume. You can have a volume initialized using the Mac OS Standard format (also known as HFS) or the Mac OS Extended format (also known as HFS Plus). The Mac OS Extended format has a number of advantages over Mac OS Standard format, but there are also some potentially serious drawbacks. (For more information on the Mac OS Extended format, see Chapters 5 and 28.)

Mounting and write-protecting disks

If a disk attached to your system does not appear on the desktop, you can use Drive Setup to mount it. Simply select the disk you wish to mount in the main Drive Setup window and choose Mount Volumes from the Functions menu. You can use this command to mount a disk that you have removed by dragging its icon to the Trash.

Disks generally mount automatically on the desktop during startup, but you can change this behavior if the disk is one that Drive Setup supports. You can also write-protect (lock) a disk so that data can be read from it, but not written to it. After selecting the disk in the main Drive Setup window, choose Customize Volumes from the Functions menu. This displays a dialog box in which you can select "Automount on startup" to make sure that the disk mounts automatically on startup. (For internal hard disks, this option is normally selected.) In the Customize Volumes dialog box, you can also select Write protected to lock the disk. Figure 29-8 is an example of this dialog box.

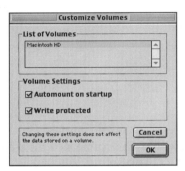

Figure 29-8: Set a disk to mount automatically on startup or write-protect a disk using Drive Setup.

Don't let the Mac OS extended format jeopardize your data!

Before converting a disk to the Mac OS Extended format, make certain that all your disk utility software is compatible. Ask each software publisher whether its utility will work with the Mac OS Extended format. Then search your disks for incompatible versions of disk utilities and isolate them in a special folder or remove them. Inadvertently using an incompatible utility may damage a disk that uses the Mac OS Extended format. For example, Norton Disk Doctor versions 3.5.1 and earlier can render Mac OS Extended disks unusable. Norton Disk Doctor 3.5.2, 4.0, 5.0, and later safely recognize Mac OS Extended disks. The latest version of Disk First Aid, included in Mac OS 9, can repair some of the damage caused by disk utilities that are incompatible with the Mac OS Extended format, but it is best not to take any chances.

Furthermore, you must use Mac OS 8.1–9 to see the contents of a disk in Mac OS Extended format. If you open a Mac OS Extended disk with an earlier version of the Mac OS, all you see is a document that explains why you can't see the disk's contents.

Extensions Manager

Many Mac problems can be traced to extensions — those operating system additions whose icons you see marching across the bottom of the screen when your Mac starts up. Third-party (non-Apple) extensions and older extensions tend to be the most problematic. The Extensions Manager control panel (described in Chapter 11) greatly simplifies troubleshooting extension problems.

The Extensions Manager actually controls all kinds of startup items, including extensions, some control panels, shared program libraries, communications tools, and more. For brevity, all startup items are commonly referred to as *extensions*.

Configuring for troubleshooting

To use Extensions Manager effectively for troubleshooting, it's usually a good idea to start by making a copy of the set of extensions that you are currently using. To do this, click Duplicate Set and pick a name for the copy. You can then make changes to the duplicate set and compare it with your original configuration. You can also save the set as a text file (by choosing Save Set as Text from the File menu) and print it out. If you want a report that lists only Apple extensions or only non-Apple extensions, use the Apple System Profiler instead of Extensions Manager.

It is often best to view the list of extensions by package, so that you can easily enable or disable groups of related items all at once. To set this grouping, choose As Packages from the View menu. In addition, you can more easily see which items are disabled if you sort the list of extensions by the On/Off column in the Extensions Manager. To sort this way, click the On/Off column heading. The disabled items can be made to appear at the top of the list by clicking the triangular sort direction indicator at the right end of the column headings. Figure 29-9 is an example of the Extensions Manager set to view by package and sorted by On/Off status with the disabled items listed first.

If you're not sure whether you need a particular extension, click its icon in the Extensions Manager. Then look at the bottom of the Extensions Manager window to see information about the item. If you don't see the item information section of the window, click the disclosure triangle labeled Show Item Information.

It is a good idea to disable any extensions that you are quite sure you don't need, because many extensions take up memory and may conflict with other extensions, the Mac OS, or particular applications. (If you are unsure whether you need a particular extension made by Apple, it's best to leave it enabled.) If you do decide to disable any extensions, you should make a note of which ones you disable. Then restart your Mac and test your system by trying a variety of your usual daily activities to make sure you haven't inadvertently disabled features you need.

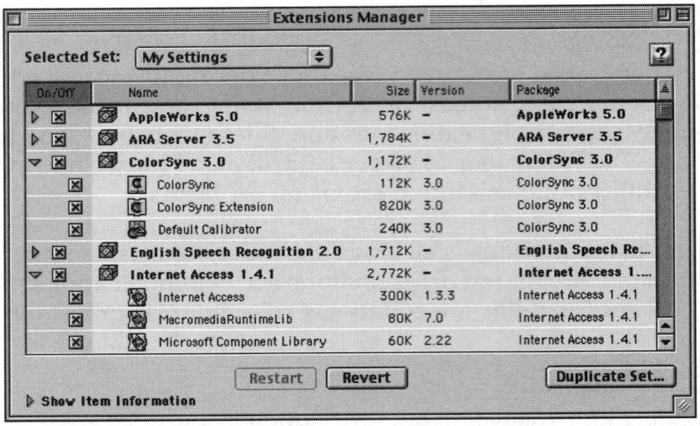

Figure 29-9: Use Extensions Manager to enable or disable extensions. For convenience, view by package and sort by On/Off status.

Troubleshooting extensions systematically

Taking a systematic approach is the most efficient way to troubleshoot extension problems. First, disable all extensions by restarting your Mac with Shift held down. (Alternatively, you can choose All Off from the Edit menu in Extensions Manager and then restart your computer; holding down Shift has the advantage of not changing the settings in Extensions Manager.) If the problem persists after disabling all extensions, then the problem is not the result of an extension conflict. Because some extensions are necessary for the normal operation of your Mac or its applications, your Mac behaves differently when you restart with all extensions disabled; some features are not available, including the capability to access a CD-ROM drive or a network.

Note   If you have Multiple Users enabled and you start with extensions off, you need to enter the owner's password to gain access to the Finder.

The next step is to choose the Mac OS base set from the pop-up menu at the top of the Extensions Manager and restart again. If you are able to duplicate the problem, then one or more of the items enabled in the base extension set may be damaged or not compatible with your computer. In either case, you will likely need to reinstall the Mac OS.

Not all the base extensions are essential for the normal operations of all Macs. For example, you don't need the network-related extensions if you are not on a network. Similarly, you might not need the text-to-speech extensions if you don't want your Mac to talk to you.

Changing the order in which extensions load

In some cases, you may be able to resolve an extension problem by changing the order in which the Mac OS loads extensions when your Mac starts up. The Mac OS extensions load in this order: first, items in the Extensions folder load alphabetically; then items in the Control Panels folder load alphabetically; and finally, any startup items in the System Folder itself load alphabetically.

To change the order in which extensions load, change their names. For example, if you place a space character before the name of an extension, that extension will load before extensions that start with a letter of the alphabet. In addition, a tilde (type Shift+` for ~) or a degree symbol (type Option+0 for °) at the beginning of an extension's name causes the extension to load after extensions whose names start with a letter. To force a control panel to load before all other control panels regardless of their names, move it to the Extensions folder. Then put an alias of this control panel in the Control Panels folder.

If you don't run into any problems with just the base extensions enabled, the next step is to choose the Mac OS All set and see whether the problem occurs again. Even if the problem does not occur, you might want to go through the additional items in the Mac OS All set and disable those items that you are sure you don't need. Again, if you make changes, you should note them, restart your Mac, and test your system.

Tip   Some extensions provide little useful information at the bottom of the Extensions Manager window. In these cases, you may wish to choose Get Info from the Extensions Manager's File menu. This displays the selected item's Info window (in the Finder), where you will probably find the publisher's name and the copyright date. The publisher's name may give you a clue as to the extension's purpose.

The next step is to start enabling extensions made by companies other than Apple. It is best to do this individually or by package, restarting and testing after each change. Troubleshooting extension problems can be time-consuming, but sometimes there is no other way to solve a particular problem.

Other utilities

Although you can correct many types of Mac problems using only the software that Apple provides, there is still a need for utility programs from other companies. These utilities have some capabilities that Apple's software lacks and can aid in troubleshooting problems when Apple's utilities fall short.

No Mac user should be without these types of utilities:

✦ **Backup software.** Having good backup software and using it regularly allows you to recover from serious crashes and other problems without having to worry about losing your data.

✦ **Antivirus software.** Although viruses are the cause of only a small proportion of Mac problems, viruses can be extremely destructive and cause serious problems. No matter how careful you are, the only way to protect yourself from viruses is with a good antivirus program.

✦ **Diagnostic utilities.** Commercial utility packages such as the Norton Utilities and TechTool Pro duplicate some of the functionality of Apple's utilities, but also can do a lot more. These programs can sometimes correct disk problems that Disk First Aid misses and often offer additional features, such as the capability to optimize a disk.

Before installing utility software, it is important to make sure that it will be compatible with your Mac model, Mac OS version, and disk format (Mac OS Standard or Extended).

Recovering from Freezes and Crashes

The steps you take right after a problem occurs can determine how quickly a problem can be resolved. Some actions can make the problem worse or even create new problems. This section describes the steps to take, in order, if your Mac or an application should freeze or crash.

Document the problem

In many cases, simply restarting your computer can solve the problem. However, if you do not document exactly what happened and ignore the problem, chances are excellent that the problem will occur again, possibly with more serious consequences.

Right after the problem occurs, you should make a note of the following:

✦ What you did immediately prior to the problem

✦ Other applications that were running at the same time

✦ Whether you had recently installed any other software

✦ What exactly happened, including the precise wording of any error messages

This information can often enable you to figure out the cause of the problem fairly quickly, or at least narrow the causes.

Wait

If your Mac appears to be frozen, wait at least a minute or so before taking action, particularly if the pointer has become the wristwatch icon. Even if the pointer has not changed to a different icon, it is still possible that your Mac is performing some time-consuming operation. If the problem occurs during startup, it is best to wait at least several minutes, because at startup the Mac OS performs some diagnostics and may be repairing itself.

Use the keyboard to recover

If nothing happens when you click the mouse, or if the mouse pointer is frozen, try using the keyboard to recover. Possible steps for recovering from a freeze are described in this section.

While taking these steps, take careful note of what works and what doesn't, especially if your Mac uses a USB mouse and keyboard (the iMac, "blue" Power Macintosh G3, and all Power Macintosh G4 models use USB keyboards). Occasionally an apparent freeze is actually a problem with the USB keyboard or mouse disconnecting or an error with the USB Manager. If your mouse pointer and/or keyboard stop reacting, but you still notice screen activity (the clock is updating, e-mail is checked in the background, and so on), you should disconnect and reconnect the mouse and/or keyboard to see if they are re-recognized by the system.

Likewise, if you have an ADB keyboard and mouse, make sure they haven't been accidentally unplugged, resulting in a mouse pointer that won't respond. You might assume your Mac is frozen when that's not really the case.

Canceling an interminable operation

Sometimes an application takes so long to complete an operation that you wonder if it is stuck and will ever finish. In fact, you may occasionally encounter a programming error that does make an application get stuck. One of these key combinations may unstick the application and give you full control of your system:

- ✦ ⌘+period (.) cancels the operation in progress.
- ✦ ⌘+S saves the current open document.
- ✦ ⌘+Q quits the application running in the foreground.

If you are able to recover from a frozen mouse using these key combinations, it is a good idea to restart your Mac. Before you cut power or push your Mac's restart button, try restarting from the Finder. To do that, you'll have to force a frozen application to quit.

Forcing an application to quit

If ordinary keyboard shortcuts do not allow you to save your work and quit an application gracefully, the next step is to attempt to force the application to quit. After forcing an application to quit, you can save your work in other open applications and restart your computer.

To force an application to quit, press ⌘+Option+Escape. If this key combination is successful, an alert box appears that gives you the option to Force Quit the application or cancel. This alert box warns that all changes that you have made to documents since you last saved them will be lost. If you're using Mac OS 9, this alert box also advises you to restart the computer after the forced quit. Figure 29-10 shows the Force Quit dialog box in Mac OS 9.

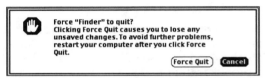

Figure 29-10: Force an application to quit by pressing ⌘+Option+Escape when more graceful methods fail.

If an application gets in so much trouble that you must force it to quit, it may have corrupted other open applications or even the Mac OS. This corruption may not surface immediately, but some time later you may encounter another freeze or crash with more devastating results. Guard against additional problems by restarting your computer after forcing an application to quit. Yes, restarting is an ordeal. Do it anyway.

In some cases, after clicking Force Quit, nothing happens or your Mac becomes completely frozen. In this case, you may be able to recover to the Finder. Otherwise, you have to force your Mac to restart.

Recover to the Finder

If Force Quit doesn't work, you may have another recourse. Press ⌘+Power to bring up the programmer's dialog box. Now, at the prompt, type **G F** (include a space between the two letters) and press Return. This may quit the application and return you to the Finder. Your Mac is likely very unstable. You should save data in other applications and Restart as soon as possible.

Note   Depending on whom you ask, "G F" may or may not stand for "Go Finder." It doesn't really matter, but if you'd like to associate it with something, "Go Finder" is usually the result of the command, when it's successful.

Restart your computer

The proper way to restart your computer is, of course, to press Power or choose Restart from the Special menu in the Finder. If you press Power, an alert box appears, asking whether you want to cancel, shut down, restart, or sleep (if your computer is capable of sleep). You can bypass this alert box and restart by pressing ⌘+Option+Power or shut down by pressing ⌘+Option+Shift+Power. If there are any open applications when you use these restart methods, the Mac OS tells them to quit in an orderly fashion. You get a chance to save any unsaved changes before the computer restarts.

Sometimes the orderly methods for restarting don't work and you have to force your Mac to restart. You can usually force a restart by pressing ⌘+Control+Power to restart your computer. When you force a restart, any work you have not saved is lost.

Some Mac models have a reset button on the computer itself (not on the keyboard). This reset button is marked with a triangle. Pressing this button restarts the machine. If you press the reset button, any changes that you have not saved are lost. Most PowerBook models have a reset switch on the back panel of the Power-Book (consult your documentation). Early iMacs have a recessed reset switch on the side panel (also marked with a small triangle) that requires an unbent paperclip to push it. The slot-loading iMac (and iMac DV models) have a reset button on the side of the machine.

If ⌘+Control+Power does not work, then press your Mac's restart switch. If you don't have a reset switch, switch off the power to your Mac. If your Mac does not have a power switch, then unplug the computer from the wall or switch its surge protector off. If you need to shut down your Mac, wait at least 30 seconds before turning it on again. If you switch off the power to your Mac, any changes that you have not saved are lost.

Run Disk First Aid

After forcing your Mac to restart, it is a good idea to run Disk First Aid or a similar utility. In Mac OS 9, you may not have to do anything. After an improper shutdown or restart, Mac OS 9 automatically performs the same check that Disk First Aid performs unless you have turned off the option Warn me if computer was shut down improperly in the General Controls control panel. When Mac OS 9 performs its automatic disk check and repair, an alert box advises you that an improper shutdown occurred. This alert box also contains a gauge that measures the progress of the automatic disk check and repair.

System Error Messages

Unlike a crash or a freeze that prevents your Mac from functioning without any warning or explanation, the Mac OS is capable of recognizing some types of serious error conditions and reporting them to you. These errors can be problems specific to a single application or to the Mac OS.

System errors can often be traced to an incompatibility, such as between an application and the Mac OS, the Mac OS and an extension you added, or an application and an extension. Other system errors can be traced to a single application, damaged system software, or the settings of a particular control panel.

Applications that quit unexpectedly

If an application encounters a serious problem, it may quit unexpectedly without crashing or freezing the entire system. The Mac OS displays an alert box that tells you a particular application has quit unexpectedly due to an error. The alert box may identify the type of error with an error code number. Figure 29-11 is an example of this alert box. In Mac OS 9, this alert can appear as a nonblocking alert.

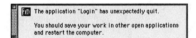

Figure 29-11: The Mac OS alerts you when an application quits unexpectedly without crashing the entire system.

When an application quits unexpectedly, make a note of the error code (if there is one included in the alert); save your work in open applications and quit them; and restart your computer. Then see whether you can duplicate the problem. For help troubleshooting applications, see "Application Problems" later in this chapter.

General system errors

Sometimes a serious error occurs that prevents you from using any open application (including the Finder). In this case, the Mac OS displays a system error alert. System errors are also known as bombs because the alert box that reports one has a bomb icon in it.

If a system error occurs, you must restart your computer. You may be able to do this by clicking the Restart button in the system error alert box. Often this button does not work, and you have to force the computer to restart as described in the previous section. Be sure to use Disk First Aid to check and repair the hard disk after a system error.

System error messages and codes

System error messages and error code numbers are frequently either vague or so technical as to make sense only to Mac programmers. Nevertheless, by looking up the error message or code number reported in an alert box, you may discover clues leading to a solution to the problem. A list of system error messages and codes is available on the Internet in Apple's Tech Info Library (http://til.info.apple. com/techinfo.nsf/artnum/N1749). (This list isn't always relevant for Mac OS 9, because many errors discuss non-Power Macintosh computers. However, the article includes links to related articles that also include error-message explanations.) Regardless of whether the error message makes sense to you, it is important to write it down, because it may help a technical support person narrow the cause of the problem.

Startup Problems

Some Mac problems can prevent your Mac from starting. Instead of a smiling Mac icon that normally appears at the beginning of the startup process, you may see a flashing disk icon or a flashing System Folder icon with a question mark in its center. Alternatively, you may see a sad Mac icon. It's also possible that your computer may freeze during the startup process. Startup problems can result from an extension conflict, improperly connected hardware devices, or corrupted, missing, or damaged system software.

It is normal for a Mac to start much more slowly after a crash. However, if a sad Mac icon or the flashing question mark icon appears on startup, it is likely that the Mac OS is corrupted or that there is a hardware problem.

If you are experiencing startup problems, the first thing to do is to make sure that all your hardware devices are connected properly. In particular, make sure that you have turned on all your SCSI devices (such as external disk drives and scanners) before you turn on your Mac. It is also important to make sure that the SCSI chain is terminated properly. (If one or more devices on the SCSI chain are turned off, there is a good chance the SCSI chain is not terminated properly.) You also should make sure that each SCSI device has a unique SCSI ID number. Apple System Profiler can help resolve SCSI conflicts.

Note   For more information about SCSI issues, choose Mac Help from the Help menu in the Finder, and search for the term SCSI.

Assuming that you find no hardware configuration problems, try restarting with Shift held down to disable extensions. (Use the ⌘+Control+Power key combination to restart if your Mac has frozen during startup.) If you are able to restart successfully, you can assume that the problem is the result of an extension conflict.

(See the discussion of Extensions Manager in the earlier section "Troubleshooting Tools.") If the problem is not an extension conflict, you might want to try resetting the PRAM (parameter RAM), as described in "Systematic Troubleshooting Steps" later in this chapter.

If you are still unable to start successfully, try starting from another disk such as a Mac OS CD-ROM. On many Mac models, you can force the machine to start up from a CD-ROM by holding down the C key when restarting. You can only start your computer from a CD-ROM that contains a System Folder for a Mac OS version that's compatible with your computer. If necessary, you can force the computer to eject the CD-ROM currently in the drive by holding down the CD-ROM eject button when you restart the computer; you will then have the opportunity insert a startup CD-ROM.

If your Mac doesn't start from the CD-ROM while you are holding down the C key and you're sure the CD-ROM has a System Folder, try restarting your computer while holding down ⌘+Option+Shift+ Delete. This key combination causes the Mac to ignore the internal hard disk when looking for a startup disk. If this trick works, you can then use Drive Setup or another utility to mount the hard disk, and run a diagnostic program such as Disk First Aid. In any case, after successfully starting from another disk, run diagnostics or reinstall the Mac OS, if needed.

Tip

If your Mac has SCSI devices connected, you can choose a particular SCSI device from which the Mac OS should attempt to start up. Hold down ⌘+Option+Shift+ Delete+ the number key that corresponds to the SCSI ID number of the device you'd like to use for startup.

You can troubleshoot many types of problems that interfere with the normal startup of a Mac by following the procedures described in the "Systematic Troubleshooting Steps" section later in this chapter.

Application Problems

Applications may crash or fail to open for a number of different reasons. There may not be enough free memory; the application's memory partition may be too small; there may be a conflict between the application and the Mac OS or an extension; the preference file (or files) may be corrupted; or the application itself may be damaged.

Memory problems

An application that doesn't have enough memory may crash. When this happens, you typically see an alert box naming an application that unexpectedly quit because of an error of type 1, 2, or 3. In some cases, the alert message may not name a specific application; instead it says that application "unknown" has unexpectedly quit. (If you keep track of which applications you are running, you should be able to determine what the unknown application was.)

If your applications crash in this unceremonious manner, check your computer's memory usage by choosing About This Computer from the Apple menu, as described in Chapter 19. If the largest available block of memory is small, or if memory is sufficiently fragmented, there may not be enough available memory to give the next application you open its preferred amount. You may still be able to open the application, but it will get less than its preferred amount of memory. The application may get as little as the minimum amount of memory set for it in its Info window.

You can check and adjust an application's memory requirements in its Info window. First, select the application in the Finder. Then, choose Memory from the Get Info submenu. This submenu is in the Finder's File menu and in the application's contextual menu.

An application's Info window lists three memory sizes: Suggested, Minimum, and Preferred. Very often applications are less reliable when they get less than the Suggested size. If an application seems to crash when its current memory size (as reported in the About This Computer window) is less than its Suggested size (as reported in its Info window), try changing its Minimum size so that it is at least as much as its Suggested size. Some applications are more reliable when they have more memory than the Suggested size. Try setting the Preferred size higher than the Suggested size. You must quit an open application before you can change its Minimum or Preferred memory sizes.

If your computer never seems to have enough memory available to give applications their preferred memory sizes, you need to increase the total amount of memory available. You can increase (or turn on) virtual memory in the Memory control panel, install more memory, or use memory-optimizing software. Turning on virtual memory actually reduces the memory requirements of most applications on a PowerPC Mac and a few applications on other Macs.

 Cross-Reference All these techniques are detailed in Chapter 19.

Corrupted preferences

Applications store settings and status information in preference files and folders located in the Preferences folder within the System Folder. If a preference file becomes damaged, an application may crash, exhibit unusual behavior, or refuse to run at all.

If you experience problems with a specific application, locate the preference file or folder for the application in the Preferences folder and drag it to another folder or to the desktop. The next time you open the application, it creates a new preference file (or folder) automatically. Although you will probably lose all your personal preference settings for the application, you may find that the application behaves properly with its new preferences file. If removing a preferences file does not resolve the problem, you can restore your personal preference settings by dragging the old preferences file back to the Preferences folder.

Some applications place several items in the Preferences folder, sometimes in a single folder. It is possible that the application will not run at all once you have removed a particular item from the Preferences folder. In this case, it may take some experimentation to determine which files can safely be removed.

Incompatible program

Mac OS 9 features a new error code (internally called Type 119) that tells you specifically when you've attempted to launch a software application that is incompatible with the Mac OS 9. These are applications that generally will crash if launched because of a fundamental incompatibility. Instead of a crash, you are shown an error message and told to update the software (see Figure 29-12).

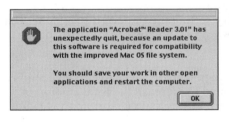

Figure 29-12: Mac OS 9 catches this new error and advises you to upgrade the offending software application.

When to reinstall

If you have ruled out insufficient memory and corrupted preference files as the cause of a problem with a specific application, it may be that the application file or a file associated with it has become damaged or corrupted.

Sometimes an application will not run or be incapable of carrying out certain operations if it cannot find particular files. This situation can arise if an application was installed using a custom installation that omitted necessary files. An application may also be unable to find files it needs if you change System Folders after installing it. You change System Folders when you start up from a different disk and when you do a clean installation of the Mac OS.

You can usually restore missing application files by installing the application again from the original disks or CD-ROM. Be sure to use the easy installation or standard installation, not the custom installation unless you know specifically which files are missing. You may also be able to restore missing files from a backup, but figuring out which files are required can be difficult.

Patches and updaters

A solution to a problem you are experiencing with an application may be available as a patch or updater from the publisher. See the discussion on keeping your software up-to-date in the section "Preventive Measures" earlier in this chapter.

Technical support and other resources

Generally, no one knows an application better than the people who created it. Many software publishers have Web pages with detailed discussions of problems and solutions. In addition, some publishers provide excellent support by telephone. Taking advantage of the support resources provided by the publisher can often lead to a quick and relatively painless solution.

In addition, there are numerous other resources that you can make use of, such as user groups, Internet discussion groups, and Web sites. These sources are detailed in the section "Troubleshooting Resources" at the end of this chapter.

Systematic Troubleshooting Steps

Many Mac problems can be solved through the series of systematic trouble-shooting steps presented in this section. Not all of these steps are relevant for all problems; tailor the steps you take to the specific problem. However, it's best not to skip a step unless you are sure it will have no bearing on the problem. (Most of these steps are described in more detail elsewhere in this chapter.)

Back up

At the first sign of trouble, make sure you have recent copies of your important files. The problems you are experiencing could damage files, or the problems could lead to other problems that damage your files. If at all possible, retain old backup files that you made before your trouble began. Avoid deleting or replacing old backup files while you're having trouble. Your trouble may have already damaged some files, and backup copies of damaged files will also be damaged. Old but healthy backup files are better than new but damaged backup files. See the discus-sion of backups in the section "Preventive Measures" earlier in this chapter.

Document the problem

Take detailed notes about the problem, about what you were doing immediately before the problem occurred, and about any software that you may have installed recently. (Be sure to keep the notes on paper rather than on your computer because a crash can make the notes inaccessible.)

Run diagnostics

After any sort of crash, it is a good idea to run a diagnostic utility such as Disk First Aid. If Disk First Aid tells you that it cannot fix a problem, try a commercial diagnostic program such as the Norton Utilities or TechTool Pro. Running a commercial diagnostic program in addition to Disk First Aid is a good idea in any case, because these utilities can catch and fix problems that Disk First Aid might miss. (See the discussion of Disk First aid and other utilities in the section "Troubleshooting Tools" earlier in this chapter.)

Before running a diagnostic utility, it is best to restart your computer from another disk. Many diagnostic utilities cannot fix some types of problems if they are run from the startup disk that you wish to check. (Only the most recent versions of Disk First Aid can correct problems on the startup disk.)

In addition, if you are experiencing a systemwide problem and the problem goes away when you start from another disk, there is very likely a problem with the Mac OS or some item in the System Folder of your normal startup disk. The remainder of this section discusses several possible causes and cures for Mac OS problems.

Check for viruses

Although the vast majority of Mac problems are not the result of viruses, it is still important to rule out viruses as a cause. Any current commercial antivirus utility does a good job of finding and eliminating viruses that have infected your disks. See the description of viruses and related phenomena in the section "Preventive Measures" earlier in this chapter.

Resolve extension problems

Extension conflicts are among the most common problems that Mac users experience. See the discussion of Extensions Manager in the section "Troubleshooting Tools" earlier in this chapter.

Rebuild the desktop

When the desktop database becomes badly corrupted, a variety of different problems can result. Rebuilding the desktop can correct a number of otherwise mysterious Mac ailments. See the discussion of desktop rebuilding in the section "Preventive Measures" earlier in this chapter.

Zap the PRAM

The Mac stores certain systemwide preferences in an area of nonvolatile memory called *PRAM* (parameter RAM). On Macs with PCI expansion slots, additional system settings are stored in another area of persistent memory called NVRAM (nonvolatile RAM). Restoring the PRAM and NVRAM to the factory presets can solve a number of different problems. When the PRAM or NVRAM becomes corrupted, your Mac may not be able to start at all.

The settings for a number of control panels, including Memory, Monitors, Sound, Monitors & Sound, Keyboard, Mouse, Trackpad, AppleTalk, Date & Time, and Map reside in PRAM or NVRAM. Before resetting the PRAM and NVRAM, you should take note of the settings of those control panels.

To reset (or "zap") the PRAM, restart your Mac and immediately press ⌘+Option+ P+R. You will most likely need to use both hands to do this (unless you have very large hands). Press those keys until you hear the startup chime twice in succession.

On a PowerBook 5300 or 1400, you must shut down the computer to reset its PRAM. Then turn on the PowerBook and immediately press ⌘+Option+P+R. A single chime will be heard, the screen will go dark, and the green sleep light will go on and stay on. Press the Reset button (on the back of the PowerBook) once or twice and the PowerBook will start after a brief pause. If the Reset button doesn't work, press Power on the keyboard.

To reset the NVRAM on a Mac with PCI slots, you must first shut down your computer. You can't reset the NVRAM when you restart, only after a full shutdown. Press Power to turn on the computer and immediately press ⌘+Option+P+R. You must press these keys before you see the gray screen on your monitor. After the gray screen appears, you can continue pressing ⌘+Option+P+R to reset the PRAM.

After resetting the PRAM or NVRAM, you may need to go back and make some changes to your control panels. In particular, you may need to adjust your video and sound settings; your network, printer, and modem connections; and your memory settings.

Note   On the iBook, NVRAM is reset when you press the Reset button (which is recessed and requires an unbent paperclip to access it).

Perform a clean installation of the Mac OS

A clean installation of the Mac OS, as described in Chapters 30 and 31, creates a brand-new System Folder. Although a clean installation is one of the most laborious troubleshooting options available, in some cases, it may be the only solution.

The real work of performing a clean installation is not in running the installer program. The hard part of a clean installation is in getting the new System Folder to behave like the old one, but without the problems. The new System Folder will not contain any extensions, control panels, fonts, preference files, or application support folders that you added over time to the old System Folder.

After performing a clean installation, do not immediately move items from your old System Folder to your new one if at all possible. Instead, install extensions, control panels, fonts, and application support folders from the original installation disks. In any case, proceed with caution when adding items to the new System Folder because it is entirely possible that in doing so you may reinstate the problem. (However, you significantly reduce the likelihood of that happening if you perform all the steps mentioned in this section.) Add a few items at a time and test your system for a while before adding more.

Back up and initialize your startup disk

Initializing your hard disk is the most drastic step you can take to resolve a thorny problem. If you take this step, you start on a clean state—an empty hard disk. You initialize most Apple hard disks and some other brands as well with Drive Setup.

If you have a hard disk that was formatted using a third-party utility, use the disk utility program that came with the hard disk or that was purchased separately. (See the discussion of initializing a disk with Drive Setup in "Troubleshooting Tools" earlier in this chapter.) In some cases, especially with third-party IDE/ATA drives, you may be able to reformat with Drive Setup. This is recommended, because Drive Setup is updated along with the Mac OS and managed carefully by Apple.

Before taking this step, you should first exhaust all other options. But if diagnostic programs such as Disk First or Norton Utilities detect problems that they cannot fix, initializing may be the only option.

Before initializing your hard disk, it is essential to have a complete backup of your hard disk. Initializing completely erases your hard disk. It is a good idea to have at least two complete backups just in case one is damaged.

When you restore data to a freshly initialized disk, it is best to install the Mac OS and your applications from the original disks rather than rely on the copies from the backup. When possible, restore only your data files from the backup. It is a good idea to restore items gradually, rather than all at once.

What to do when nothing works

If none of the steps described previously leads to a solution to the problems you are experiencing, it is entirely possible that you have a hardware problem. Before taking your Mac to the shop, you might want to take advantage of the other troubleshooting resources described at the end of this chapter.

Performance Problems

Some Mac problems manifest themselves in slow performance rather than in crashes or system errors. The causes of performance problems are often the same as the causes of other problems, and the general troubleshooting techniques presented in this chapter can often solve performance problems as well.

If your Mac has been performing more slowly than usual, here are a few possible causes and solutions.

Memory problems

Check the settings in the Memory control panel. If virtual memory is turned on (as it normally is), you may run into performance problems. The higher you set the amount of virtual memory, the more likely you are to encounter performance problems. You will probably first notice sluggishness when you switch between different applications. To avoid severe slowdowns, do not set the total amount of memory to more than about two times the actual built-in memory. In addition, applications run more slowly if there is not enough free RAM for them to occupy their "preferred" memory partition size.

It is also possible that your disk cache size is too small. If you click Use Defaults in the Memory control panel, the Mac OS sets a recommended disk cache size based on the amount of built-in memory in your computer.

 For more information on virtual memory and the disk cache, see Chapter 19.

Disk fragmentation

When the files on a disk become fragmented, disk performance can suffer considerably. See the discussion of disk optimization in "Preventive Measures" earlier in this chapter.

Viruses

Some viruses may have no noticeable effect on your computer other than to slow it down. A virus-checking program can detect and eliminate most of the viruses that have infected your computer. See the description of viruses and related phenomena in "Preventive Measures" earlier in this chapter.

Video performance

If you have a video card that offers graphics acceleration, be sure to install any software that came with it.

In addition, you can improve the video performance considerably on some Mac models by reducing the number of colors displayed on the screen using the Monitors control panel or the Control Strip. For most applications, 256 colors are adequate, although thousands of colors are better for graphics-intensive activities, including surfing the Web. Also, some QuickTime movies are optimized for playback with thousands of colors. Millions of colors look great, but are required primarily for graphics professionals and people who edit high-resolution photographic images.

Speed up your Mac

By changing the settings in a few control panel panels, you can make your Mac faster (or at least make it seem faster):

✦ In the General Controls control panel, reduce the number of times a menu item "blinks" (flashes on and off) when you select it. By default, it blinks three times; turning menu blinking off (or reducing the number of blinks) can make your Mac's response time noticeably faster. In General Controls, you can also increase the speed at which the insertion point blinks, which can make your Mac seem faster.

✦ In the Mouse or Trackpad control panels, increase the pointer-tracking speed. This is particularly useful if you have a large screen. You can also adjust the double-click speed.

✦ In the Keyboard control panel, increase the speed at which a key being held down begins to repeat. You can also increase the rate at which it repeats.

Mouse and keyboard settings are discussed in detail in Chapter 12.

Troubleshooting Resources

Resolving Mac problems is simpler and more pleasant if you take advantage of available resources.

Macintosh Help and other onscreen documentation

Believe it or not, your Mac may already know the answer to a pesky problem that has been plaguing you — all you have to do to find the answer is ask. You can search for and browse detailed information about how to use your Mac, including troubleshooting information, right on your computer screen. You can get this onscreen help in the Finder by choosing Mac OS Help from the Help menu. In addition, choosing Show Balloons from these menus display useful information in cartoon-style balloons when you point at things on the screen.

 Cross-Reference   For more information on built-in help, see Chapter 9.

Also, numerous Read Me files are installed with the Mac OS and the applications that you install. These onscreen documents often provide helpful troubleshooting information. Look for them in the main level of the startup disk, in the Mac OS Read Me Files folder on the startup disk, and in the folders of individual application programs.

Documentation, manuals, and books

Many computer users treat manuals as a last resort. Although manuals can indeed be useful when all else fails, it's better to consult them when you first get started with a product, not when problems start arising. In addition, there are several books devoted exclusively to Mac troubleshooting, including Ted Landau's comprehensive *Sad Macs, Bombs, and Other Disasters and What to Do About Them* (3rd edition, 1997, Peachpit Press, ISBN: 0201688107) and Todd Stauffer's *Macworld Mac Upgrade and Repair Bible* (1998, IDG Books Worldwide, ISBN: 0764532170).

Internet resources

If you have access to the Internet, a wealth of excellent troubleshooting resources is available to you. A few places to start are:

✦ **Apple Tech Info Library** (http://til.info.apple.com/). The Tech Info Library is Apple's technical support database. You can use it to search for information on literally thousands of Mac problems. In Mac OS 9, you can easily access the Tech Info Library using Sherlock's Apple channel. (Click the Apple logo in the channels section at the top of the Sherlock window.) For more on Sherlock see Chapter 6.

Tip

When searching the Tech Info Library, broaden your search by separating individual terms with the word **and** or with commas. Otherwise, you'll limit the search to the entire phrase you type. For instance, **powerbook shutdown** searches for only that phrase while **powerbook and shutdown** or **powerbook, shutdown** searches for articles that include both terms, whether or not they're next to one another in the articles' text.

✦ **Apple's Support Site** (http://www.apple.com/support/). Here you'll find various support resources, including specific articles in the Tech Info Library, access to online documentation, and the Tech Exchange, a Web-based bulletin board where Mac users and Apple employees ask and answer technical questions. You may be surprised how often your question has already been asked and answered in the Tech Exchange.

✦ **MacFixIt** (http://www.macfixit.com/). An excellent independent source of information on troubleshooting Mac problems, MacFixIt often documents software incompatibilities before Apple does.

✦ **Macintosh Crash/Freeze Tips** (http://www.zplace.com/crashtips/). This site has detailed information on resolving many specific problems that can cause your Mac to crash.

✦ **Macintosh Guide: Troubleshooting** (http://www.cis.yale.edu/ macguide/Trouble/Trouble.html). This page provides a detailed troubleshooting flowchart and links to other Mac troubleshooting sites.

✦ **Usenet newsgroups.** Usenet newsgroups are online discussion forums (or bulletin boards) where participants can post questions and read responses from other participants. Useful newsgroups for troubleshooting Mac problems include comp.sys.mac.system, comp.sys.mac.apps, comp.sys.mac.comm, and comp.sys.mac.hardware.misc. (See Chapter 10 for more information about newsgroups.)

User groups

One of the best ways to take advantage of the skills and experience of knowledgeable Mac users is to join a user group. To find a user group near you, see Apple's User Groups page at http://www.apple.com/usergroups/ or call Apple at 800-538-9696.

If there is no Mac user group located near you, consider joining one of the larger Mac user groups, such as the Berkeley Macintosh Users Group (BMUG) (510-549-2684, http://www.bmug.org/) or the Arizona Macintosh Users Group (AMUG) (602-553-8966, http://www.amug.org/). You can take advantage of membership benefits such as newsletters, various discounts, and access to extensive libraries of freeware and shareware, even if you cannot attend local meetings.

Technical support from Apple and other companies

In addition to having extensive technical support resources on the Web (see Apple's Technical Support page at http://www.apple.com/support/), Apple also offers technical support by telephone. For the first 90 days after purchasing a Mac, you can get free "up-and-running" support by calling 800-500-7078. Apple also provides free general information and answers to frequently asked questions through an automated service at 800-SOS-APPL. In addition, Apple offers technical support for a fee at 888-APL-VALU.

If you are having a problem with a hardware or software product from a company other than Apple, the best way to resolve the problem is to take advantage of that company's technical support services. Many companies offer technical support through their Web sites and technical support hotlines.

Summary

This chapter showed you a variety of Mac problems and possible solutions, beginning with preventive measures, including making backups, protecting yourself from computer viruses, and performing periodic maintenance, such as running disk diagnostics, rebuilding the desktop database, and optimizing your disks. These preventive measures can help reduce the occurrence and severity of problems.

Next, you saw how to use specific utilities, including Apple System Profiler, Disk First Aid, Drive Setup, and Extensions Manager to make troubleshooting easier. You learned what to do when faced with freezes and crashes, system errors, startup problems, and application problems. You also learned to take a systematic approach to solving a variety of problems. Then you were given a few suggestions for dealing with performance problems.

Finally, you took a brief peek at the resources available in books, on the Internet, and by telephone for troubleshooting Mac problems.

✦   ✦   ✦

Installing the Mac OS

Get Ready to Install

◆ ◆ ◆ ◆

In This Chapter

Comparing Mac OS versions from 7.5 to 9

Obtaining installation software

Preparing for installation

Doing a clean installation

Switching between two Mac OS versions

◆ ◆ ◆ ◆

Installing a newer Mac OS version on your computer is not something you can do casually. This chapter describes what you need to do to prepare for installation. First, you need to assess the equipment requirements and compare the features of newer Mac OS versions to determine whether the upgrade to Mac OS 9 is best for your computer. Second, you need to obtain the installation software. Third, you need to prepare for installation by making a backup copy of your disk, checking its condition, and more. Fourth, you need to decide whether to install a brand-new copy of the Mac OS or upgrade your existing System folder with the new Mac OS. In case you need to have two versions of the Mac OS installed on the same disk, this chapter concludes by telling you how to switch from one to the other.

You will find the actual installation instructions for Mac OS 9 in Chapter 31.

Comparing Mac OS Versions

If you use an older version of the Mac OS, you may be wondering whether your Mac can be upgraded to a newer Mac OS version and which version is best for you. To help answer these questions this section lists the equipment requirements for the Mac OS 9. This section also summarizes the features of Mac OS versions back to System 7.5. (Prior to Mac OS 7.6, the versions were named "System" instead of "Mac OS.") You can use this information to determine which versions your Mac can use now, how much more memory and disk space you might need to add to use Mac OS 9, and whether the features of a Mac OS 9 are worth the upgrade.

Check your computer's vital statistics

You can easily find out how much memory or disk space your computer has or which version of the Mac OS it uses. If the Apple System Profiler program is listed in your Apple menu, choose it. Check the System Overview section or the System Profile section of this program for the system version and the amount of built-in memory on your computer. Then check the Volumes section or the Devices and Volumes section to learn the amount of disk space available.

If the Apple System Profiler isn't available on your computer, you can use other methods to get your computer's vital statistics. To learn the Mac OS version and the amount of memory that are installed on your Mac, make the Finder the active application (choose it from the Application menu at the right end of the menu bar) and choose About This Computer or About This Macintosh from the Apple menu. The About This Computer window or the About This Macintosh window reports the Mac OS version number in the upper-right corner. If this window displays an amount labeled Built-in Memory, that's how much memory is installed in your computer. If you don't see an amount labeled Built-in Memory, then the amount labeled Total Memory tells how much memory your computer has installed. (In System 7–7.5.5, the Built-in Memory amount isn't reported if it's the same as Total Memory, which happens when virtual memory is turned off in the Memory control panel.)

To check the amount of hard disk space available, open the icon of the hard disk where you want to install the Mac OS. The available space is reported at the top of the disk's window.

If the amount of memory or hard disk space is reported in K (kilobytes), you can convert the reported amount from K to MB (megabytes) by dividing the number of K by 1024 (for example, 2048K ÷ 1024 = 2MB).

Equipment requirements

The more recent the Mac OS version, the greater its equipment requirements. The newer versions require more powerful processors, more built-in memory, and more hard disk space. The disk space requirements vary quite a bit, depending on several factors. One factor is the selection of Mac OS modules you install. Another factor in Mac OS 8.1–9 is the format of the hard disk; less space is required on a disk that uses Mac OS Extended format than on a disk using Mac OS Standard format. If the disk uses the Mac OS Standard format, then the disk capacity also affects the amount of space used by the Mac OS. On smaller Mac OS Standard format disks, the Mac OS uses less disk space.

Table 30-1 compares the processor, memory, and disk requirements for Mac OS 7.6–7.6.1, Mac OS 8–8.1, Mac OS 8.5–8.6, and Mac OS 9.

Table 30-1 Mac OS Equipment Requirements				
	Mac OS 9	Mac OS 8.5–8.6	Mac OS 8–8.1	Mac OS 7.6–7.6.1
Processor	PowerPC	PowerPC	PowerPC or 68040[1]	PowerPC, 68040, 68030[2]
Memory (minimum)	32MB of RAM (virtual memory set to at least 40MB)	16MB (virtual memory set to 24MB)	12MB (virtual memory set to 20MB)	8MB
	64MB of RAM recommended	24MB recommended	20MB recommended	16MB recommended
Disk space	95–280MB	95–210MB	50–140MB	40–120MB

1 The QuickDraw 3D option included with Mac OS 7.6–8.5 requires a PowerPC processor.

2 Mac OS 7.6–7.6.1 doesn't work on a Mac SE/30, IIx, or IIcx even though these models were factory-equipped with 68030 processors.

Feature summary

Table 30-2 lists the major features and capabilities added to or removed from the Mac OS beginning with System 7.5.

Table 30-2 Mac OS Features at a Glance						
Feature	9	8.5–8.6	8–8.1	7.6–7.6.1	7.5.3–7.5.5	7.5–7.5.1
Appearance themes	•	•	○	○	○	○
Apple File Security	•	○	○	○	○	○
Apple Guide	•	•	•	•	•	•
Apple Location Manager	•	•	•[1]	○	○	○
Apple Remote Access	•	•	•	•	○	○
Apple Verifier	•	○	○	○	○	○
Apple-menu submenus	•	•	•	•	•	•
AppleScript and scriptable Finder	•	•	•	•	•	•
AppleScript over IP	•	○	○	○	○	○

Continued

Table 30-2 (continued)

Feature	9	8.5–8.6	8–8.1	7.6–7.6.1	7.5.3–7.5.5	7.5–7.5.1
Application Switcher window	•	•	°	°	°	°
Big desktop patterns	•	•	•	•	•	•
Button views	•	•	•[1]	°	°	°
Charcoal system font	•	•	•[1]	°	°	°
Classic networking	°	°	°	°	•	•
Collapsible windows	•	•	•	•	•	•
ColorSync	•	•	•	•	°	°
Contextual menus	•	•	•[1]	°	°	°
Control Strip	•	•	•	•	•	•
Cyberdog[4]	°	°	•	•	°	°
Desktop pictures	•	•	•[1]	°	°	°
Desktop printing	•	•	•	•	•	°
Drag-and-drop editing	•	•	•	•	•	•
Draggable window frame	•	•	•[1]	°	°	°
Easy Open	•	•	•	•	•	•
Euro currency symbol	•	•	°	°	°	°
Faster AppleScript	•	•	°	°	°	°
Faster network copies	•	•	°	°	°	°
Favorites folder	•	•	°	°	°	°
File Exchange control panel	•	•	°	°	°	°
File Sharing over IP	•	°	°	°	°	°
Find by Content (Sherlock)	•	•	°	°	°	°
Find File program(5)	°	°	•	•	•	•
Folder actions	•	•	°	°	°	°
FontSync	•	°	°	°	°	°
Help Viewer	•	•	°	°	°	°
Hide desktop in background	•	•	•	•	•	•
Icon badges	•	•	°	°	°	°
Icons in window title bars	•	•	°	°	°	°

Feature	9	8.5–8.6	8–8.1	7.6–7.6.1	7.5.3–7.5.5	7.5–7.5.1
Improved Note Pad	•	•	•	•	•	•
Improved Scrapbook	•	•	•	•	•	•
Improved Sharing window	•	•	•[1]	°	°	°
Improved View menu	•	•	•[1]	°	°	°
Internet applications	•	•	•[1]	°	°	°
Internet control panel	•	•	°	°	°	°
Internet location files	•	•	°	°	°	°
Internet Setup Assistant	•	•	•[1]	°	°	°
Keychain Access	•	°	°	°	°	°
Language Kits[1]	•	°	°	°	°	°
Launcher	•	•	•	•	•	•
Mac OS Extended format[3]	•	•	•[1]	°	°	°
Mac OS Runtime for Java	•	•	•[1]	°	°	°
MacLinkPlus	°	°	•	•	°	°
Menu bar clock	•	•	•	•	•	•
Move To Trash command	•	•	•[1]	°	°	°
Multilingual Web browsing	•	•	°	°	°	°
Multiple system fonts	•	•	°	°	°	°
Multiple Users	•	°	°	°	°	°
Multiprocessor support	•	•	•	•	°	°
Multithreaded Finder	•	•	•[1]	°	°	°
Navigation Services	•	•	°	°	°	°
Network Browser	•	•	°	°	°	°
Network time servers	•	•	°	°	°	°
Open Transport networking	•	•	•	•	•	°
OpenDoc	°	•	•	•	°	°
Personal Web Sharing	•	•	•[1]	°	°	°
Platinum appearance	•	•	•[1]	°	°	°
Pop-up windows	•	•	•[1]	°	°	°

Continued

Table 30-2 *(continued)*

Feature	9	8.5–8.6	8–8.1	7.6–7.6.1	7.5.3–7.5.5	7.5–7.5.1
Power key turns off	•	•	•	•	•	°
PowerTalk	°	°	°	°	•	•
QuickDraw 3D	•	•	•	•	°	°
QuickDraw GX printing	°	°	°	°	•	•
QuickDraw GX typography	°	•	•	•	•	•
QuickTime Pro²	•	•	°	°	°	°
Remote Access Server¹	•	°	°	°	°	°
Resize list view columns	•	•	°	°	°	°
Search Internet (Sherlock)	•	•	°	°	°	°
Show Original (of alias)	•	•	•[1]	°	°	°
Simple Finder	•	•	•[1]	°	°	°
Smart scroll bars	•	•	°	°	°	°
Smarter file sharing for removable disks	•	•	•	•	•	°
Software Update	•	°	°	°	°	°
Sound tracks	•	•	°	°	°	°
Special Documents folder	•	•	•	•	•	•
Spring-loaded folders	•	•	•[1]	°	°	°
Standard view options	•	•	°	°	°	°
Stickies	•	•	•	•	•	•
Sticky menus	•	•	•[1]	°	°	°
Text smoothing	•	•	°	°	°	°
Text-to-speech	•	•	•	•	•	•
Translucent icon drag	•	•	•	•	•	°
View options for each folder	•	•	•[1]	°	°	°
Window collapse box	•	•	•[1]	°	°	°

•Included with this version of the Mac OS.

° Not included with this version of the Mac OS.

¹Items previously sold separately

²QuickTime Pro is version 4 in Mac OS 9 and 8.6, version 3 in Mac OS 8.5

³Mac OS Extended format is available in Mac OS 8.1 but not Mac OS 8.

⁴Cyberdog is included with Mac OS 8 but not Mac OS 8.1.

⁵Sherlock replaces the Find File program in Mac OS 8.5–9, but includes the same functionality

Obtaining Installation Software

These days, Apple distributes the Mac OS only on CD-ROM—it's grown way too large for floppy disks—and all supported Macs ship with CD-ROMs built in. (Not all Macs, by contrast, have floppy drives anymore.)

Note

If your Mac doesn't have a CD-ROM drive, your alternative is to share the installation CD over a network. You can simply mount the shared CD on the desktop of the Mac where you'd like the installation to take place, then double-click the Installer program. This should work fine, but you should avoid pronounced network activity during the installation in order to assure that data is transferred as quickly as possible to the installation computer. You can also use Disk Copy to create a disk image of the Mac OS 9 Installation CD that you can place on a network drive or on the local computer's drive and mount the disk image to installed the Mac OS. (You should make sure this doesn't violate your license to use the software.) Note that a network-based installation will not work on the Power Macintosh 6100, 7100, and 8100 series, because those Macs must be started up from the Mac OS 9 CD-ROM in order to install the OS.

Major releases of the Mac OS, such as Mac OS 9, are sold by the Apple Store (http://store.apple.com/) in retail stores and through catalogs. Mac OS 9 features a rebate for owners of Mac OS 8.5 or 8.6. Also, if you bought a new Macintosh on or after the Mac OS 9 introduction date (or if you are the owner of an iBook or Power Macintosh G4, regardless of when you bought it), you're probably eligible for the Mac-Up-to-Date program, which allows you to upgrade to Mac OS 9 for $19.95. See http://www.apple.com/macos/uptodate/ or call 800-335-9258.

Interim versions of the Mac OS—along with many other sorts of updaters released by Apple—tend to be distributed over the Internet or via an online service using disk image files rather than CD-ROMs. This keeps costs down for Apple and makes it possible for you to download the updates as soon as they're made available. Generally, these disk image files can be mounted directly on your desktop by double-clicking the file. A disk icon appears on the desktop that works like a typical removable disk.

And, in Mac OS 9, the new Software Update feature allows you to download and automatically install updates offered by Apple as soon as they're made available online. See Chapter 12 for more on Software Update.

Preparing for Installation

Before installing Mac OS 9 or another new Apple technology, you need to determine whether the new software will work with the software you already have. Ideally, you would make a list of every piece of software that's not part of the Mac OS and then check with the software publishers or distributors to make sure the versions you have are compatible with what you're about to install. If you have the time and patience to do that, great; if not, at least do the following to minimize the risk of incompatibilities:

✦ Make a backup of your hard disk and of any RAM disk you have.

✦ Verify the directories of all your hard disk volumes.

✦ Update hard disk driver software.

✦ Turn off any security, virus protection, and screen-saver software.

✦ Turn on standard extensions.

✦ Read the text files on the installation disk—in Mac OS 9, there's a file named "Before You Install." This document is also shown to you by the Install Mac OS 9 application.

✦ Optionally, label all items in your System Folder with the Label submenu of Finder's File menu (Mac OS 8–8.6) or the Labels menu (Mac OS 7.6–7.6.1 and System 7–7.5.5). After installation, the new items will be the unlabeled ones.

✦ If you are installing on a PowerBook, make sure it's plugged in.

✦ If you're installing on a computer that can go to sleep, make sure it won't go to sleep during installation.

The remainder of this section discusses these tasks in more detail.

Backing up disks

If you use more than one hard disk, or if your hard disk is partitioned into multiple volumes, make backups of all of them. Making backups is like buying car insurance— it's a terrific imposition and you hope it's a total waste of effort. Do it anyway.

If you have a RAM disk, copy its contents to another disk before upgrading or installing any Mac OS version. Alternatively, you can save the RAM disk as a disk image file using Apple's free Disk Copy program or Aladdin Systems' ShrinkWrap shareware. The RAM disk may be turned off and its contents lost during the installation process.

To back up today's large hard disks, you need some type of high-capacity backup storage device, either another hard disk of equal or greater capacity, a tape drive, an Iomega Zip drive, an Imation SuperDisk, or a hard disk with removable cartridges. If you have a second hard disk, you can back up your main hard disk by simply dragging its icon to the backup disk's icon. That method isn't very efficient if you want to keep your backup up-to-date on a regular basis, but it's adequate for preinstallation purposes.

Online installation software

Apple maintains a software library on America Online and the Internet, and you can copy software from those sources to your hard disk. New versions of individual Mac OS pieces show up in Apple's online software library before they're available on CD-ROM. The library also contains older versions of many Mac OS pieces, including System 7.0.1 complete (other Mac OS versions are not available from the library). Here's how to access Apple's software:

✦ On the Internet, point your Web browser to `http://asu.info.apple.com/` and follow the links to the to featured download item.

✦ On America Online, use the keyword **applecomputer** to go directly to the Apple Computer window. All software is located in the software area of that window.

Major upgrades to the operating system, such as Mac OS 8, Mac OS 8.5, and Mac OS 9, are not available for free downloading online. These must be purchased from a software retailer. However, incremental updates (such as the updater to change Mac OS 7.6 to 7.6.1 or 8.5 to 8.6) are available for free downloading.

Note

At a typical capacity of 100 to 250MB, it can take a lot of removable disks to completely back up your hard disk. (Some removable drives can store gigabytes of data on one disk, which is ideal for this sort of backup.) Even just backing up your System Folder can easily take more than one typical removable disk. It may be cheaper to simply buy a second hard disk than to buy enough backup disks to mirror your entire hard disk. And an external hard disk—whether SCSI, USB, or FireWire-based—can be handy for other troubleshooting tasks, too.

You could back up to removable disks by dragging folder icons, but it's simpler to use a special backup utility such as Retrospect Express from Dantz Development (925-253-3000, `http://www.dantz.com`). These utilities automate the process of backing up a large hard disk to several smaller removable disks. Retrospect Express also makes it easy to keep your backup files current. Each time you back up, they copy only the files and folders that have changed since the last backup. That minimizes the amount of time and number of removable disks needed for backup.

If you're up to the investment, a CD-R (CD-Recordable), CD-RW (CD-Rewriteable), or DVD-RAM (DVD-Random Access Memory) drive is another option for backup. With these drives, you can generally write about 700MB to a CD or 2.6GB (or more) to a DVD. This gives you an easy-to-store archive of your files that can often be read in any CD-ROM drive (or DVD-ROM drive, if you're creating a DVD-RAM disc). The downside is that creating a CD or DVD tends to be slow, and you'll have to use special software—in most cases, you can't just drag-and-drop to a writeable CD or DVD.

If you have a tape drive, you must use backup software such as Dantz's Retrospect. You can't back up folders to a tape by dragging icons in the Finder.

Verifying disk directories

It's important to check the condition of a disk before installing the Mac OS on it. The installation software automatically checks the disk as part of a normal installation of Mac OS 9.

You can check disks any time with Apple's Disk First Aid utility, which comes with the Mac OS. Disk First Aid checks the condition of a disk's directory, which keeps track of where files are stored on the disk, and can often repair any problem it finds. The Mac OS maintains each disk directory automatically, updating it every time you save changes to a file or create a new file. The directory can become damaged when the computer freezes or crashes, when an application quits unexpectedly, and so on. The damage may be so slight that you don't notice a problem, but over time the damage can grow and become irreparable. Disk First Aid is easy to use — you simply select one or more disks in its window and click Verify or Repair. Figure 30-1 is an example of the Disk First Aid window.

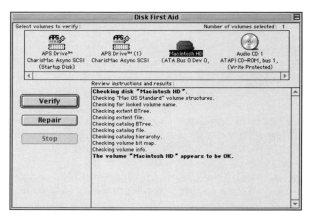

Figure 30-1: Disk First Aid verifies and repairs disk directories.

Your best bet is to start up from the Mac OS 9 CD and run its version of Disk First Aid (version 8.5.4). Disk First Aid versions 8.1 and earlier have a limitation that you can avoid by starting your computer from a Disk Tools floppy disk or a Mac OS CD-ROM and opening the copy of Disk First Aid from there. Versions of Disk First Aid earlier than 8.2 can't repair problems it finds on the current startup disk or on the disk that contains the running Disk First Aid program. This limitation doesn't get in your way if you start from a Mac OS 9 installation CD-ROM and run Disk First Aid from it.

Norton Utilities and Mac OS Extended format

Do not use Norton Utilities version 3.5.1 or earlier with a hard disk that has been initialized (erased) in the Mac OS Extended format. This format, which is also known as HFS Plus, is optional with Mac OS 8.1–9. You can damage a Mac OS Extended hard disk with Norton Utilities 3.5.1 and earlier. If you suspect you have damaged a Mac OS Extended disk by using Norton Utilities 3.5.1 or earlier on it, avoid making further changes to it and contact Symantec Technical Support immediately (541-465-8440). Symantec has a repair procedure that can be done over the phone and is free to registered owners of Norton Utilities.

Some disk problems are beyond Disk First Aid's restorative powers. If Disk First Aid says it can't fix a problem, put the problematic disk through the repair process several more times anyway. The problem may be one that Disk First Aid can fix bit by bit. If after several repair attempts Disk First Aid doesn't tell you that the disk appears to be okay, you need to bring in a high-priced disk mechanic — TechTool Pro from Micromat Computer Systems (800-829-6227, http://www.micromat.com/) or Norton Utilities from Symantec (408-253-9600, http://www.symantec.com). TechTool Pro and Norton Utilities can detect and fix significantly more problems than Disk First Aid. If they can't repair the disk, they may be able to recover individual files that the Finder can no longer access. After recovering lost files and copying them to another disk together with other files that haven't been backed up, you can resurrect the disk by reformatting it.

Updating hard disk driver software

The driver software that resides on every hard disk and removable hard disk cartridge must be compatible with the Mac OS version in use or problems can result. For example, old driver software made by Transoft causes a problem with the Mac OS. The old Transoft driver considers the startup disk to be ejectable, which causes the Mac OS to display a message asking you to insert the startup disk when you shut down the computer, even though the startup disk was never ejected. To check whether your startup disk has a Transoft driver, select the disk's desktop icon and choose Get Info from the Finder's File menu. If the Info window's "Where" information contains "NS-SCSI" or "NS-ACAM" then the disk contains a Transoft driver. Transoft drivers were distributed with various brands of hard disks, notably APS Technologies, as well as with Transoft's SCSI Director formatting utility. The problem does not affect APS hard disks with Power Tools software versions 3.0 and later, nor does it affect Transoft SCSI Director version 3.0.9 and later.

Updating disk driver software takes just a minute and generally doesn't affect disk contents in any way. (To update the driver on an old hard disk formatted with Apple's HD SC Setup version 2.0, you must reformat the hard disk, erasing the disk contents in the process.)

Turn off At Ease security before updating driver

If your computer has Apple's At Ease software installed, you should turn off its disk security feature before updating your hard disk's driver with Drive Setup 1.3.1 or later. Otherwise you may be greeted by a flashing question mark when you next start up the computer. To turn off At Ease disk security, follow these steps:

1. Start the At Ease Administration program.

2. Choose System Settings from the Security menu.

3. Make sure the option Prevent users from bypassing security by starting up from a floppy disk is not selected.

If you neglect to follow this procedure before updating the hard disk driver, you can work around the problem by following these steps:

1. Restart from the Mac OS installation CD-ROM. (With the flashing question mark displayed, insert the CD-ROM and hold down the C key until you see the Welcome message.)

2. Use the Drive Setup program from the CD-ROM to update the driver again. The hard disk icon should appear on the desktop.

3. Restart the computer and turn off At Ease's disk security option (follow the three steps above). Restart again and use Drive Setup 1.3.1 or later to update the driver one more time. Then restart and turn on At Ease's disk security.

If you're installing Mac OS 9 on an Apple hard disk, the installer program updates the driver for you—there's no need to run a separate program. If you're not installing on an Apple hard disk, you need to use the most recent version of the formatting utility program last used on the disk.

Caution

The hard disk driver software installed with Mac OS 9 is not compatible with computers that have 68000 processors. If a hard disk that uses Apple driver software is connected when you install Mac OS 9, you won't be able to use that hard disk subsequently with a Mac Plus, SE, original Classic, Portable, or PowerBook 100 computer.

Other hard disk utilities

You generally need a disk-formatting utility program other than Drive Setup to update the driver software on a brand of hard disk other than Apple. Likewise, you need a different formatting utility to update the driver on an Apple hard disk whose driver someone once updated using a non-Apple formatting utility.

If you have an internal or external hard disk from a company other than Apple, contact the company for the latest version of its hard disk formatting utility. If that version is more recent than the one you have, use the more recent version to update your non-Apple hard disk's driver.

You can also switch to a different brand of driver software, such as Hard Disk Toolkit from FWB Software (415-463-3500, http://www.fwb.com). However, once you switch from an Apple driver to another brand, you generally can't switch back without initializing the drive.

Before switching to another brand of driver software, consider that Apple always updates its hard disk driver software to be compatible with the latest Mac OS. Other companies sometimes take longer than Apple to update their hard disk drivers for the latest Mac OS. The startup disk is particularly susceptible to incompatibilities between disk driver software and the Mac OS, so don't switch the startup disk from an Apple driver to another brand without good reason.

Configuring extensions

Some system extensions and control panels can interfere with installing or upgrading Mac OS 9. You can get around this problem by simply booting from the Mac OS 9 CD. If you can, disable any special security software, plug in your PowerBook (if you're installing to a PowerBook), and startup from the CD. To boot from the CD, place the CD in the CD-ROM (or DVD-ROM) drive and restart the computer. As it starts up, hold down the C key. If this doesn't work, boot into the Mac OS from your hard disk and use the Startup Disk control panel to select the CD, then restart.

If you can't boot from the CD for some reason, you can still forge ahead and install the Mac OS. (Make sure you've backed up and done any troubleshooting to determine why you couldn't startup from the CD.) In this case, to avoid problems caused by antivirus, security, screen-saver, or energy-saver software, be sure to do the following before you begin the installation process:

✦ Disable At Ease or other security software that locks or restricts access to files, folders, or disks.

✦ Disable software that protects against viruses.

✦ Turn off screen-saver software.

✦ Deactivate all but the standard set of extensions and control panels for your version of the Mac OS, plus any other extensions and control panels required for installation, as follows:

   • If you are upgrading from System 7–7.1.4, turn off all extensions by holding down Shift while restarting your computer.

• If you're upgrading from Mac OS 7.6–8.6 or System 7.5–7.5.5, open the Extensions Manager control panel and from its pop-up menu choose the extensions set that activates all the standard extensions for your Mac OS version. This extension set's name begins with your Mac OS version and may include the word only or all, as follows: System 7.5 Only, Mac OS 7.6 all, Mac OS 8 all, Mac OS 8.1 all, or Mac OS 8.5 All, or Mac OS 9 All. Figure 30-2 shows this setting in Mac OS 8.5.

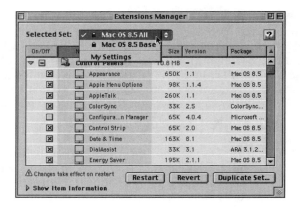

Figure 30-2: Activate only the standard extensions and control panels (plus any that are required for special equipment).

• If you have special equipment that requires extensions or control panels to start up, turn them back on in the Extensions Manager.

✦ Make sure the computer is not set to go to sleep or shut down automatically.

Tracking installer program actions

When you update the Mac OS or reinstall it, the installer program does more than add entirely new items. It also removes existing items from the startup disk (for which the installation software includes replacements), and then copies the replacements into the correct places on the startup disk. But the installer program gives you no record of what it has done. You can use the Label submenu of the Finder's File menu (Mac OS 8–9) or the Labels menu (Mac OS 7.6–7.6.1 and System 7–7.5.5) to keep tabs on the changes by following these steps:

1. Print a report of the System Folder contents before using the installation software. To do that, open the System Folder, use the View menu to view the window contents as a list, choose Select All from the Edit menu, and press ⌘+Option+right arrow (→) to expand all folders within the System Folder. Then choose Print Window from the File menu to print the hierarchical list of System Folder contents.

Alternatively, you can make a document containing an alphabetical list of everything in the System Folder. This is easy to do with the Finder's Find command. Start by opening the startup disk icon and selecting the System Folder icon. Next choose Find from the Finder's File menu, and set the search criteria to find items in the current Finder selection whose name is not "????" (or any other name you know doesn't exist). When the list of found items appears, you can select all, copy the items, and paste them into the Scrapbook, the Note Pad, or any text document for later reference. Figure 30-3 shows an alphabetical list of System Folder items that has been pasted into the Note Pad.

Note

In Mac OS 9's Sherlock 2, you'll need to drag the System Folder icon to the Search Items window to add it as a "volume" to search.

Figure 30-3: Use Find File (System 7.5–7.5.5 and Mac OS 7.6–8.1) or the Sherlock program (Mac OS 8.5–9) to make a list of all System folder items in the Note Pad.

Note Pad contents:
```
Apple DVD Player Help
EM Extension
Protection Extension
16 Hues
240 Grays & 16 Colors
256 Grays
3.0 Preferences
3Com Impact Analog 14.4
3Com Impact ISDN 56K
3Com Impact ISDN 56K MLPPP
3Com Impact ISDN 64K
3Com Impact ISDN 64K MLPPP
3D Graphics
98293
aa
aa idx
aa.htm
aaFmSet.htm
aaRTOC.htm
About Apple Guide
About Your Macintosh
About Your Macintosh
About Your Macintosh idx
Acrobat™ Reader Prefs
Acrobat™ Weblink Prefs
ActiveX Controls
add - duplicate to folders
```
1

2. Label every item that you want to keep track of in the System Folder. The simplest method is this: After expanding all folders as described in step 1, choose Select All from the Edit menu and choose one of the labels from the Label submenu of the File menu (Mac OS 8–9) or the Label menu (Mac OS 7.6–7.6.1 and System 7–7.5.5).

Alternatively, you can use multiple labels to categorize items. For example, you could label all items that are part of the Mac OS with one label and all items you have added with a different label. Use the Finder's Preferences command (Mac OS 8–9) or the Labels control panel (Mac OS 7.6–7.6.1 and System 7–7.5.5) if you want to change label names or colors (see Chapter 5).

3. Install the Mac OS as described in Chapter 31. The installation process removes some of the items you labeled and adds other items, which are all unlabeled.

4. To see which items are new or replacements look in the System Folder for unlabeled items. You can search for unlabeled items in the System Folder using the Find File section of the Sherlock program (Mac OS 8.5–9) or the Find File program (Mac OS 7.6–7.6.1 and System 7.5–7.5.5). Start by selecting the System Folder icon or folders inside it if you want to look for new items only in them. (In Sherlock 2, drag the System Folder icon to the Search Items window to add it as a searchable volume, and then select it.) Next, set the Find File criteria to search for items in the Finder selection whose label is None (or is not the label you applied in step 2).

   To determine which items are completely new and which were deleted, print another report or make another alphabetical list of the System Folder contents following the procedures described in Step 1. Compare the newer and older reports or the newer and older alphabetical lists. Brand-new items appear in the newer list but not in the older list. Deleted items appear in the older list but not in the newer list.

5. The one thing this procedure does not tell you is which unlabeled replacement items are newer versions of the items they replaced and which replacements are the same versions as the items that they replaced. However, there's a rough correlation between an item's version and its modification date. So you can get a rough idea of which items are new versions by using Sherlock or the Find File program to find the unlabeled items and then viewing the found items by date. Items at the top of the list are more likely to be new versions than are items at the bottom of the list.

Installing on a PowerBook

Although you can install or upgrade the Mac OS on a PowerBook under battery power, it's better to have the PowerBook plugged in. If you are called away during installation, the PowerBook could go to sleep if it's operating on batteries.

You cannot install or upgrade the Mac OS correctly on a PowerBook's hard disk when it is in SCSI disk mode. A PowerBook is in SCSI disk mode when it is connected with a SCSI adapter cable to another computer and that computer is using the PowerBook as an external hard disk. In this scenario, you would be running the installer program on the other computer, not on the PowerBook, and the installer program would not install the pieces of the Mac OS specifically designed for PowerBooks.

To install or update the Mac OS correctly on a PowerBook, you must run the installer program on the PowerBook. You can use a CD-ROM in a drive connected to the PowerBook or in a shared drive that you access over a network.

Performing a Clean Installation

Ordinarily, Apple's installation software upgrades the Mac OS that already exists on a computer, merging the new with the old. You get some entirely new items and some replacements for existing items that haven't changed, but preference files and files that contain your data are not replaced. For example, installing Mac OS 9 replaces the Internet control panel but not the preferences file where the Internet control panel stores settings. Upgrading the existing Mac OS is the right thing to do unless your system has become unreliable and you can't seem to resolve its problems.

You can usually eliminate nagging system problems by installing a pristine copy of the Mac OS. This is known as a clean installation, and it's a favorite tonic of telephone technical support personnel because it's so effective. The trouble is, a clean installation of the Mac OS forces you to laboriously reinstall all of the control panels, extensions, fonts, Apple menu items, Startup items, and anything else that you have added to your System Folder since you started using your computer. You also have to reconfigure your control panels and reset options in most of your application programs because all of their settings are kept in preference files in the System Folder. And that's not all. You also need to reinstall application programs that keep auxiliary files and folders in the System Folder, such as most Claris and Adobe applications. Sure, you could copy files from the old System Folder to the new one, but that defeats the purpose of a clean installation, which is to stop using old, possibly damaged files. Performing a clean installation of the Mac OS is like moving to a new apartment because your old one smells bad. It might be easier to figure out what's causing the stink and fix it.

 Cross-Reference   For troubleshooting guidance, see Chapter 29.

Before going to the trouble of a clean installation, you should try replacing the Mac OS files in the System folder without touching the other files you have added there. To do this, you must be able to start your computer from the Mac OS installation CD (as described in Chapter 29). Then you can drag the System file, Finder file, and System Resources file (Mac OS 8.5–9 only) out of the System Folder on your normal startup disk. Finally, do a standard installation — not a clean installation — of the Mac OS, as described in Chapter 31.

There are times when a clean slate is the simplest cure, or at any rate a useful diagnostic tool, because a computer clearly doesn't have a hardware malfunction if it works reliably with a cleanly installed System Folder. Apple's installation software makes it easy to do a clean installation of Mac OS 9, as discussed in Chapter 31.

After doing a clean installation, you may find that your printer's icon is missing from the left side of the Chooser. This means that the printer driver software for your printer is not included with the Mac OS. In this case, you must reinstall the software that came with your printer. Better yet, check with the printer's manufacturer to see whether updated software is available. Most older Apple StyleWriter and Color StyleWriter printers can use the latest StyleWriter and Color StyleWriter drivers installed with the Mac OS (see Chapter 16).

Using Multiple Systems

You can switch between two versions of the Mac OS, if necessary, even if you have only one hard disk. To install a second System Folder on a disk, perform a clean installation as described in the previous section. As part of a clean installation, your old System Folder is renamed Previous System Folder. Change its name and then name the new System Folder something more descriptive, such as System Folder 8.5 and System Folder 8.1. The System Folder can have any name and still function properly.

Apple ordinarily advises against installing two System Folders on the same disk, claiming you can't be sure which System Folder will be used during startup and become the active (or *blessed*) System Folder. Although multiple System Folders can lead to confusion, they don't have to lead to disaster. You can designate which System Folder will be the blessed one during the next startup or restart by using the System Picker utility (described in Chapter 26). Mac OS 8–9 requires System Picker 1.5 or later.

If you can't get System Picker, you can switch to a System Folder by deblessing all the others. To debless a System Folder, open it and drag the System file into the Startup Items folder. If you want to switch System Folders, first debless the current System Folder (the one with a small Mac OS badge). Then bless another System Folder by opening it, opening its Startup Items folder, and dragging the System file from the Startup Items folder to the System Folder. Close the System Folder window and make sure the System Folder icon now has a badge, which indicates that it's currently blessed, and then restart the Mac.

Summary

In this chapter, you saw which features and capabilities were added to, and which were removed from, successive Mac OS versions. From reading this chapter you also know what kind of processor, how much RAM, and how much hard disk space the various Mac OS versions require.

You read that major releases of the Mac OS are sold on CD-ROMs. You can get software updates from the Apple Software Updates library on the Internet and America Online.

It was recommended that before installing a new version of the Mac OS, you back up your disks, verify disk directories, update hard disk driver software, and turn off all but the standard Apple extensions and control panels plus any that are required for any special equipment on your computer. This chapter also explained how you to track installation activity with the Labels menu. In addition, this chapter made suggestions for trouble-free installation on PowerBooks.

Also covered in the chapter were the pros and cons of a clean installation. Although a clean installation prevents the carrying over of damaged files from the previous Mac OS, a normal installation is usually quite effective and not nearly as much work.

This chapter concluded by telling you how to switch systems when more than one is installed on your hard disk.

✦   ✦   ✦

Install Mac OS 9

Since the earliest days of the Macintosh, installing system software has been easy. Mac OS 9 makes it even easier with the Mac OS Install program. This program coordinates the installation of the basic system software as well as a host of supplemental modules such as Internet Access, ColorSync, QuickTime, Text-to-Speech, and more.

You set up the installation by selecting a destination disk and by optionally selecting a clean installation. Then you can do any of these types of installations:

+ **Standard installation** includes the basic system software modules and the most common supplemental modules. All installed modules are automatically tailored for the type of Mac that's running Mac OS Install. To select additional modules for Mac OS 9, you must do a custom installation.

+ **Custom installation** includes only the modules you select, and gives you the opportunity to selectively install portions of each module.

+ **Universal installation** allows you to install a Mac OS version that will work with any supported Power Macintosh machine.

+ **Minimal installation** includes only the most basic Mac OS files necessary to get your Mac started up and running. The minimal installation can vary according to how much space you have available on the disk to which you're installing.

Before starting installation, you must make sure your computer can use the Mac OS version you want to install.

Compatibility

Unfortunately, Mac OS 9 isn't for everybody. Some Macs can't use Mac OS 9 at all. On other Macs, you can install Mac OS 9 only after fixing problems. This section details these restrictions. (For a comparison of equipment requirements for different Mac OS versions, see Chapter 30.)

Processor requirements

Mac OS 9 requires a computer with a PowerPC processor. You can generally tell by a Mac's model name whether it can use Mac OS 9 or not. Any model with G3 or G4 in its name can use Mac OS 9, and so can the iMac and iBook. In addition, older models whose names contain four digits — for example, PowerBook Duo 2300, Power Mac 6100, and Performa 5200 — can use Mac OS 9. If a model's name has only three digits, it must use Mac OS 8.1 or earlier.

A Mac that has been upgraded with the logic board of a four-digit model can also use Mac OS 9. For example, a PowerBook Duo 230 that has been upgraded with a 2300 logic board can use Mac OS 9. A Mac that has a PowerPC upgrade card added to its logic board can't use Mac OS 9. For instance, a PowerBook 540c or a Quadra 650 with a PowerPC upgrade card must use Mac OS 8.1 or earlier.

A Mac with a 68030, 68020, or 68000 processor can't use Mac OS 9, even if the Mac has an accelerator card with a 68040 or PowerPC processor. These systems must use Mac OS 7.6.1 or earlier, although some upgrade card manufacturers have created workarounds to allow you to run Mac OS 8.1 or higher on some upgraded systems. (All Macs with 68000 or 68020 processors, and some with 68030 processors, must use System 7.5.5 or earlier.)

iMac and iBook computers

iMac and iBook computers can use Mac OS 9, although some iBook and iMac DV models shipped with a special version of Mac OS 8.6. The iMac DV uses a special version of the Apple DVD Player that is incompatible with other DVD-equipped Macs. Note that attempting to reinstall (or "downgrade" to) the regular version of Mac OS 8.6 (from a Mac OS 8.6 CD instead of the System CD bundled with the computer) on an iBook or iMac DV may not enable all of its features and could cause problems.

Mac 5200, 5300, 6200, and 6300 computers

Some Performa and Power Macintosh computers in the 5200, 5300, 6200, and 6300 series can't use Mac OS 9 until a hardware problem is fixed. The problem does not affect the 5260, 6320, or 6360 models. You can test for the problem by using the

5xxx/6xxx Tester utility in the Utilities folder on the Mac OS CD-ROM. In addition, the installation software for Mac OS 9 checks for the problem and alerts you if repairs are needed. The repairs are covered under an Apple warranty extension program that's in effect until 2003.

Accelerated 6100, 7100, 8100, and 9150 computers

The Mac OS Install program may not recognize a Power Mac or Performa 6100, 7100, 8100, or 9150 computer whose clock speed has been boosted with an accelerator. If this happens to you, remove the accelerator while installing Mac OS 9.

If you have an accelerator card (for instance, a G3 accelerator card) installed in your 6100, 7100, 8100, or 9150 computer, the installer may not be capable of installing Mac OS 9. You should contact the card manufacturer for updated drivers and/or remove the card to install Mac OS 9.

To install on a Power Macintosh 6100, 7100, or 8100, you must start up from the Mac OS 9 CD.

Installation on removable disks

If you wish to install Mac OS 9 on an Iomega Zip or Jaz disk, you must reconfigure the virtual memory settings or install Iomega driver version 6.0.2 or later. To reconfigure the virtual memory settings, restart with the ⌘ key held down, open the Memory control panel, turn on the Virtual Memory option, select a disk other than a Zip or Jaz disk, and restart. Otherwise, you can use a Zip or Jaz disk for Virtual Memory if you install version 6.0.2 or later of the Iomega driver. A more recent version of the Iomega driver is included on the Mac OS 9 CD-ROM.

You can't start up from a USB drive (and, at the time of writing, the same was true for Firewire drives), so installing the Mac OS on a removable disk in a USB or Firewire removable drive is of little value unless you're performing a universal installation to be used on a Mac with a SCSI or IDE-based removable drive of the same type.

400K floppy disks

Mac OS 9 can't use 400K floppy disks. If you have information on 400K floppies, copy it to another disk before installing Mac OS 9.

Program memory requirements

Some programs need more memory with Mac OS 9 than with Mac OS 7.6.1 and earlier. If a program refuses to open with Mac OS 9, try increasing its minimum memory size by 200K or 300K in its Info window. You can display this window by selecting the program's icon and choosing Get Info from the Finder's File menu (for more information, see Chapter 19).

DOS Compatibility cards

If you're upgrading from Mac OS 8.1 or earlier and you have an Apple DOS Compatibility card, you'll find that the card no longer works with Mac OS 9. There's no fix — you need to stick with an older version of the Mac OS to use the DOS card.

Ultra-Wide SCSI cards

Apple warns that older Ultra-Wide SCSI cards require a firmware update before they'll function correctly with Mac OS 9. (If you're running Mac OS 8.5 or higher already, this probably won't affect you.) Check the card manufacturer's Web site or support personnel for a firmware upgrade or details.

Third-party Finder and utility software

Apple also warns that third-party Finder and utility software — especially software that alters the Finder in some way, changing the way menus appear or how files are stored — may not work with Mac OS 9. (This is especially true if you're upgrading from Mac OS 8.1 or earlier.) Be particularly vigilant about utilities that automatically compress, decompress, or alter files, because you may not be able to access them after the upgrade to Mac OS 9.

Standard Installation of Mac OS 9

A standard installation of Mac OS 9 includes the basic system software and several supplemental system software modules. If you want to pick and choose the modules to be installed, you must do a custom installation. For an explanation of the custom installation procedure, including a list of the system software modules, see "Custom Installation of Mac OS 9" later in this chapter.

Note   Apple recommends that you start up from the Mac OS 9 Installation CD to install the Mac OS. To do this, place the CD in your CD-ROM or DVD-ROM drive, restart your Mac and hold down the C key after the startup chime. Continue holding it down until you see the Mac OS 9 splash screen.

The Mac OS Install program leads you through the four steps necessary to install Mac OS 9. In the first three steps, you select a destination disk, read a document about installing Mac OS 9, and agree to a software license. In the fourth step, you set a couple of options before installation starts. When you finish these four steps, the Mac OS Install program checks the condition of your hard disk's directory, updates your hard disk driver software (if you have an Apple hard disk), and then installs the basic system software and some common supplemental system software modules.

Starting the Mac OS Install program

To start the Mac OS Install program, insert the Mac OS 9 CD-ROM disc, find the Mac OS Install program, and double-click its icon. After a few seconds, the Install Mac OS 9 window appears, displaying some introductory information. Click Continue to begin installation. Figure 31-1 shows the introductory information in the Install Mac OS 9 window.

Figure 31-1: Read the introductory information in the Install Mac OS 9 window.

Selecting a destination

The first step to installing the Mac OS is to choose a disk for it. A pop-up menu lists the available disks. When you choose a disk from the pop-up menu, the Mac OS Install program reports the disk's system software version and the amount of free space available. This step also gives you the option of selecting a clean installation. Figure 31-2 shows this first step in the Install Mac OS 9 window.

Cross-
Reference

For general advice on performing a clean installation, see Chapter 30.

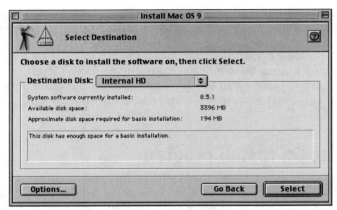

Figure 31-2: Choose a hard disk and optionally select a clean installation.

A standard installation of Mac OS 9 requires around 150MB to 200 MB of free space (more or less, depending on your computer model). If you want to make more space available on the hard disk you've chosen, you can switch to the Finder, delete some files from that disk, and then switch back to the Mac OS Install program. (Use the Application menu at the right end of the menu bar to switch to and from the Finder.)

If you want to do a clean installation, click Options at the bottom of the Install Mac OS 9 window. In the dialog box that appears, turn on the option Perform Clean Installation and click OK.

After choosing a destination disk and deciding whether to perform a clean installation, click Select at the bottom of the Install Mac OS 9 window to go to the second step. You can also go back to the introduction by clicking Go Back.

If you chose a destination disk that already has Mac OS 9 installed, the Mac OS Install program displays an alert box explaining the situation and giving you three choices: Cancel, Reinstall, or Add/Remove. If you want to choose a different destination disk, click Cancel. If you want to replace the system software with a clean copy, click Reinstall. If you want to add or remove portions of the system software, click Add/Remove. If you click Add/Remove, the Mac OS Install program skips the second and third installation steps and switches from a standard installation to a custom installation. In this case, you should continue reading at "Custom Installation for Mac OS 9."

Reading installation information

In the second installation step, the Install Mac OS 9 window displays a document containing last-minute installation information for Mac OS 9. It's tempting to skip this document, but the information provided is important, so you should at least skim it for the mention of your computer model, printers you use, and software you use. You can print the document by clicking Print at the bottom of the window. You can also save the document on disk, but there's no need to because it's already available on the installation CD-ROM.

Note

The CD-ROM contains other text documents with additional information about Mac OS 9. You would be wise to read these documents as well. You don't have to quit the Mac OS Install program to read these documents. You can switch to the Finder (by choosing it from the Application menu) and double-click the documents whose names begin with About in the CD-ROM window.

After reading the installation and compatibility document, click Continue at the bottom of the window to go to the third step. You can also return to the previous step by clicking Go Back.

Agreeing to the software license

In the third installation step, the Install Mac OS 9 window displays a license agreement. The license agreement is filled with lawyerspeak, but you should look through it so you know what you're agreeing to. For example, one provision states that you may only install the software on one computer at a time. You can print the license agreement or save a copy on disk by clicking Print or Save at the bottom of the window.

Tip

The Software License Agreement screen offers a small pop-up menu where you can choose a different language if you'd prefer to read the agreement in something other than English.

Click Continue when you're ready to go to the last step. A small dialog box appears, asking if you agree or disagree with the terms of the license. You cannot continue with the installation unless you click Agree.

Selecting options

In the last installation step, you set some options, as detailed in the following paragraphs, before starting installation. In addition, you can initiate a custom installation instead of a standard installation (see "Custom Installation of Mac OS 9" later in this chapter). Figure 31-3 shows the last step of the Mac OS Install program for Mac OS 9.

Figure 31-3: Set options and start installing Mac OS 9.

The hard disk driver update option

The Mac OS Install program normally updates the driver software on Apple hard disks. If you don't want this to happen, click Options at the bottom of the Install Mac OS 9 window and in the dialog box that appears, turn off the Update Apple Hard Disk Drivers option.

For more information on updating hard disk drivers, see Chapter 30.

The installation report option

The Mac OS Install program normally creates a report that details which files were installed and where. You can suppress this report by clicking Options at the bottom of the Install Mac OS window and turning off the Create option in the dialog box that appears.

Installation starts

To begin the installation, click Start in the Install Mac OS window. The Mac OS Install program checks the destination disk's directory to ensure that files can be written to the disk properly. Next, the Mac OS Install program updates the drivers of Apple hard disks unless you have turned off the Update Apple Hard Disk Drivers option, as described previously. These procedures in no way affect the contents of your disk.

After checking the disk directory and updating Apple hard disk drivers, the Mac OS Install program begins installing system software modules. A standard installation proceeds automatically unless a problem occurs. Otherwise, a standard installation doesn't require more of your attention until it finishes.

You can always cancel an installation that's under way by clicking Cancel. If you cancel an installation in progress, the Mac OS Install program displays an alert asking how you want to proceed. You can stop installation, skip installation of the module currently being installed, or try installing again.

When you restart the computer after a successful installation, Mac OS Setup program opens automatically and asks you for information to configure the computer. (For details, see "Mac OS Setup Assistant" at the end of this chapter.) In addition, after the first restart, the Finder may automatically rebuild the desktop database of all disks (see Chapter 29).

Custom Installation of Mac OS 9

A custom installation of Mac OS 9 provides the opportunity to select individual system software modules and to select individual components of modules. For example, you must do a custom installation to install the Easy Access and CloseView control panels, which are part of the Mac OS 9 module. A custom installation also provides the opportunity to remove all or part of a module.

To do a custom installation of Mac OS 9, follow the first three steps of the four-step procedure that you use for a standard installation as described in "Standard Installation of Mac OS 9" earlier in this chapter. In the fourth step, click Customize in the Install Mac OS 9 window. Clicking Customize reveals a checklist of available system software modules. Each module can be included or excluded individually. You can also include or exclude portions of some modules. Figure 31-4 shows the last step of the Mac OS Install program configured for a custom installation.

Figure 31-4: Select modules for a custom installation of Mac OS 9.

Selecting modules

There are ten modules in the checklist for a custom installation of Mac OS 9. The first eight modules are initially selected because they are part of a standard installation. You can easily change the selection by clicking a module's checkbox. To display information about a module, click its information button at the right side of the checklist.

Note   Selecting the information button will also tell you how much disk space is required by that module to install the items that are currently selected.

You can choose from these modules:

✦ **Mac OS 9**, which includes the core system software.

✦ **Internet Access**, which includes Microsoft Internet Explorer or Netscape Communicator, Microsoft Outlook Express, Internet Setup Assistant, Internet control panel, StuffIt Expander, and Installer for DropStuff with Expander Enhancer (all described in detail in Chapter 10).

✦ **Apple Remote Access**, which lets your computer connect to the Internet, a remote TCP/IP network, or a remote AppleTalk network by modem. It also includes the Apple Remote Access Personal Server software for allowing other Remote Access clients to access your computer (see Chapter 20 for details).

✦ **Personal Web Sharing**, which lets your computer host a Web site (see Chapter 10 for details).

✦ **Text-To-Speech**, which lets your computer speak text aloud (see Chapter 23 for details).

✦ **Mac OS Runtime for Java**, which lets you run Java applets and applications on your computer (see Chapter 25 for details).

✦ **ColorSync**, which manages color to improve consistency from scanner to monitor to printed page (see Chapter 12 for details).

✦ **English Speech Recognition**, which enables your computer to recognize North American English speech (see Chapter 23 for details).

✦ **Language Kits**, which enables you to display and edit in languages other than English on your Mac (see Chapter 12 for details).

✦ **Network Assistant Client**, which is used in conjunction with the Network Assistant Administrator software (Apple software available for purchase) by system administrators.

Selecting portions of modules

You can selectively install portions of a module by choosing Customized Installation from the pop-up menu next to the module's name. This brings up a dialog box that contains a checklist of components and, in some cases, groups of components that you can install. To expand a component group, click the disclosure triangle next to it. You can get information about a component by clicking its information button at the right side of the checklist. Select the components to install by clicking the appropriate checkboxes. You can select all or none of the components by choosing from the pop-up menu at the top of the dialog box. Figure 31-5 shows the checklist of components for the Mac OS 9 module.

Note   A check mark in a component's box means that it will be fully installed. A minus sign ("–") means that only some of the items in that component have been selected. If the checkbox is empty, then none of its items are slated for installation.

Figure 31-5: Select components to be installed from one Mac OS 9 module.

Universal Installation of Mac OS 9

When you perform a standard installation, the Mac OS Install program installs the correct files and resources for the computer model you're using. This is very handy as it keeps your System Folder from becoming bloated with unnecessary files. However, it makes life difficult if you're installing Mac OS 9 on a different computer than it will be used on.

To get around this problem, you need to perform a universal installation. This places all of the files for all Mac models on the selected hard disk. The resultant System Folder is much larger, but it will be able to start any kind of computer that can use the Mac OS version you install. If you're creating an emergency startup removable disk, for instance, do a universal installation so that it can be used on any computer.

To create a universal installation of Mac OS 9, you must do a custom installation as described previously in "Custom Installation of Mac OS 9." In the last step of the Mac OS Install program, be sure to select the Mac OS 9 module. You don't have to select the other modules (Internet Access, Text-To-Speech, and so on) if you know you're not going to need them with this disk. Now choose Customized Installation from the pop-up menu next to Mac OS 9 to bring up the checklist of components for the Mac OS module. In the Selection menu, choose Universal Installation. Click OK in the checklist window (see Figure 31-6). When you're ready to proceed with installation, click Install. You should be able to use the resulting disk to start any computer that can use the Mac OS version you installed.

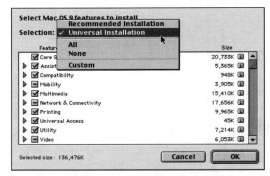

Figure 31-6: Choose Universal Installation from the Selection menu.

New Feature

Aside from Universal installations, you can also perform what Apple calls a Feature Set installation, which is new to Mac OS 9. (So new, in fact, that we couldn't preview the feature at the time of writing.) If these Feature Set installations are available in your Mac OS 9 Installer, you'll see different Feature Set installations in the Selection menu. These may include Education, Business, and Gaming, among others, that install Mac OS features that are useful for those types of environments. Select one of these Feature Set installations instead of Universal Installation if you'd like to install Mac OS 9 components that are best suited for a particular environment.

Minimal Installation of Mac OS 9

While it's no longer possible to fit even a minimal installation of Mac OS 9 on a floppy disk, it is possible to squeeze a minimal installation of Mac OS 9 on a 94MB Zip disk or an 88MB SyQuest cartridge. Mac OS 9 seems to fit on these disks even though Apple suggests you have a minimum of 95MB of hard disk space.

To fit Mac OS 9 on a Zip disk, you must do a custom installation. In the last step of the Mac OS Install program, select only the Mac OS 9 module. Then choose Customize Installation from the pop-up menu for the Mac OS 9 module to bring up the checklist of components, and select the component Core System Software. You can also select other components as long as the selected size reported in the bottom left corner of the dialog box does not exceed about 96,000K (assuming you're using a Zip disk).

The smallest System Folder you can install with the Mac OS 9 Install program takes about 20MB. To get a minimal System Folder, you must do a custom installation as described previously in "Custom Installation of Mac OS 9." In the last step of the Mac OS Install program, select only the Mac OS module. The resulting svelte System Folder starts fast and uses substantially fewer megabytes of RAM than a standard System Folder because it includes only a few control panels and extensions.

Mac OS Setup Assistant

The first time you start the computer after installing Mac OS 9, the Mac OS Setup Assistant program opens automatically. It asks for some basic information about yourself and how you will use your computer. It requests the information in several sections, which it displays one at a time. After entering information in one section, you go to the next section by clicking the right-arrow button. You can also go back to the previous section by clicking the left-arrow button. You enter information in these sections:

✦ **Regional preferences**, which sets the keyboard layout and the formats for time, date, text, and numbers based on the region or language you select.

✦ **Name and organization**, which identify you when your computer is connected to a local network. In addition, some application programs pick up this information automatically to save you typing.

✦ **Time and date**, which set your computer's clock and calendar. They establish the creation date and modification date for each of your files, set the date on e-mail you send, and so forth.

✦ **Geographic location**, which is used to adjust for time-zone differences.

✦ **Finder preferences**, which lets you set the Simple Finder option in Mac OS 9 (see Chapter 5).

✦ **Computer name and password**, which identifies your computer when it is connected to a local area network and which prevents other network users from accessing your computer as its owner.

✦ **Shared folder**, which lets you create and name a folder whose contents can be accessed by everyone connected to your local network.

✦ **Printer connection**, which specifies whether your printer and computer have a direct connection or a network connection. If your printer has a network connection and is turned off, the Setup Assistant will not notice it and you will have to use the Chooser to select it later (see Chapter 16).

✦ **Printer type**, which appears if you specified a direct printer connection. It also specifies which driver software and port the printer uses.

✦ **Printing connection**, which appears if you specified a network printer connection. It lets you specify your favorite network printer. If your favorite printer isn't listed or no printers are listed, don't worry. You can use the Chooser later to designate your favorite printer (see Chapter 16).

When you finish entering the printer type or printer connection, the Mac OS Setup Assistant displays a Conclusion section. This section contains three buttons: Show Details, Cancel, and Go Ahead. To recap the information you entered, click Show Details. To quit the Mac OS Setup Assistant without having it save any of your information, click Cancel. To have the Mac OS Setup Assistant create settings based on the information you entered, click Go Ahead.

If you click Go Ahead, the Mac OS Setup Assistant configures your system with the information you entered. When it finishes, it gives you two choices: Quit or Continue. If you want to begin working immediately, click Quit. If you want to set up an Internet connection now, click Continue. Clicking Continue opens the Internet Setup Assistant program, which is described in detail in Chapter 10.

Summary

This chapter showed you how to install Mac OS 9. It told you which computer models are compatible with Mac OS 9 and which compatible models have known issues with Mac OS 9 that need to be fixed or worked around. You learned to perform a standard installation and to customize that installation to suit your needs. In addition, this chapter told you how to create a startup disk with either a universal Mac OS 9 installation for use with any compatible Mac, or with a minimal Mac OS 9 System Folder. Finally, this chapter described how to use the Mac OS Setup Assistant when you restart after installing Mac OS 9.

✦   ✦   ✦

Glossary

68K applications Programs written for Macs with 68000, 68020, 68030, and 68040 processors. Most of these programs also work on Macs with PowerPC processors, but more slowly than programs written expressly for PowerPC processors.

active program The program whose menus are currently displayed in the menu bar.

adorn The process of changing the formatting of a *subscriber*.

AirPort Apple's name for its implementation of the IEEE 802.11 standard for wireless networking.

AirPort Base Station A device, sold by Apple, that allows wireless-enabled computers to connect to an Ethernet-based network and/or a modem connection.

alert box A window in which the Mac OS or an application program notifies you of a hazardous situation, a limitation in your proposed course of action, or an error condition.

alias A stand-in or agent for a real program, document, folder, or disk. The alias does not duplicate the item it represents; instead, the alias points to the item it represents.

allocation block size The smallest amount of space that can be allocated to a file on a volume. Larger volumes, when formatted with the Mac OS Standard format, have a larger allocation block size.

antialias The process of smoothing text by blending its jagged edges with the color of the background. Text smoothing is an option of the Appearance control panel and of the ATM control panel.

Apple events The Mac OS language for *interapplication communication (IAC)*. Applications can send Apple events messages to one another. When an application receives an Apple event, it takes an action according to the content of the Apple event. This action can be anything from executing a particular command to taking some data, working with it, and then returning a result to the program that sent the Apple event.

Apple Guide A help system that provides step-by-step interactive instructions for completing certain tasks.

AppleScript An English-like programming language that you can use to send *Apple events* to programs. With AppleScript you can write your own programs, called *scripts*, to perform complex tasks easily. For example, you can use an AppleScript to move data between many applications.

AppleTalk The networking protocol built into all Mac OS computers and most LaserWriter printers for passing messages and information to each other. The content that is passed back and forth could be *Apple events*, page images to be printed, e-mail, file contents, or any other kind of information. The content and the protocol can be transmitted through *LocalTalk* cabling, *Ethernet* cabling, or other media.

applets Small Java-language programs that are commonly embedded in Web pages to make them more interesting or useful. This term is also used to describe AppleScript scripts that have been saved as small applications.

application program Software that enables a computer to perform a set of related tasks for a specific purpose, such as word processing, working with spreadsheets or graphics, or Web browsing. See *program* and *software*.

application programming interfaces (API) Commands written by operating system programmers to enable application programmers to access the operating system's features.

Application Switcher The floating window that appears when you "tear-off" the Application menu (select the menu and drag straight down with the mouse).

authentication The process of identifying a user's ID and password in order to make a network connection.

autoscrolling The process of scrolling through a window or a list without using the scroll bars by placing the pointer in the window or the list, pressing the mouse button, and dragging toward the area you want to view.

background program A program that runs during the intervals, typically less than one-eighth of a second long, when the active program isn't using the computer. It usually works while the active program waits for you to do something.

balloon help A help system that makes a cartoonlike balloon appear when you drag the mouse slowly over a standard object in the Mac OS interface. The balloon may tell you what the object is, what it does, or what happens when you click it.

binary file A file of formatted text, pictures, sound, movies, other data, or program code.

BinHex A file transmission program that converts a *binary file* into a plain text file so it can be sent over a network. A BinHexed file must be decoded back into a binary file before it can be used on the receiving computer.

bit A single binary digit.

bitmap font Same as *fixed-size font*.

blessed A term used for the active System Folder.

bookmark A way to store *Web page* locations (*URLs*) that you want to remember and go to frequently.

bridge Software or hardware used to connect two different types of networking hardware. For instance, a bridge is used to connect LocalTalk and Ethernet networks so that they can exchange data.

bug A programming error or other flaw in software. A minor bug may affect what you see or how a program works in a noncritical way. A serious bug may cause crashes or data loss. Not the same as a *virus*.

built-in memory Apple's term for physical *RAM*, that is, the memory chips that are actually installed in the Mac.

button icons *Icons* in the Finder that can be clicked once to open the associated item.

case sensitive Describes a password in which capitalization matters; for example, capital *A* is not the same as lowercase *a*.

character A written representation of a letter, digit, or symbol; a basic element of a written language.

Clarus See *DogCow*.

click-and-a-half A gesture used to make a disk or folder spring open that is performed by beginning to double-click the disk or folder but not releasing the mouse button after the second click.

clean installation This type of installation deactivates your old System Folder and installs a new one with new copies of Mac OS software. You must then reconfigure control panels, reinstall application programs, and reset preferences in them.

client A program that requests and receives information or services from a server.

clipping file A file created by Finder to hold material that has been dragged from a document to the desktop or a folder window.

codec Compressor-decompressor software or hardware. (See *compressor*.)

color depth The number of bits of information that are required to represent the number of colors available on the screen. For instance, a screen that can display 256 colors is set at a color depth of 8 bits.

color picker The dialog box in which you specify a custom color either by clicking a color wheel or by entering color values.

compile To put a *script* in an internal format that *AppleScript* can run. Before compiling a script, AppleScript checks it for things that AppleScript doesn't understand. For example, if you forget a parenthesis where AppleScript expects to find one, it lets you know.

compression algorithm A method for compressing and decompressing data. Each compression algorithm generally works best with one type of data, such as sound, photographs, video or motion pictures, and computer-generated animation. Three characteristics of a compression algorithm determine how effectively it compresses: compression ratio, image fidelity, and speed.

compression ratio Indicates the amount of compression and is calculated by dividing the size of the original image by the size of the compressed image. Larger compression ratios mean greater compression and generally (although not always) poorer image quality.

compressor Something that compresses data so that it takes less space to store, and decompresses compressed data back to its original form for playing or changing. A compressor may consist of software, hardware, or both. Sometimes also called *codec*, a shortened form of "compressor-decompressor."

conditional A programming command that evaluates a condition (stated as part of the conditional) to determine whether another command or set of commands should be performed. (Also referred to as a *conditional statement*.)

contextual menu A menu that lists commands relevant to an item that you Control+click.

control panel A small program that you use to set the way some part of the system looks and behaves.

cooperative multitasking A scheme of *multitasking* where the applications determine how much processor time they use.

custom installation You can selectively install portions of the Mac OS modules. Do this only if you are sure that you know which individual items must be present for the software to work properly.

daisy chaining The process of connecting one peripheral or network device to another device, linking them so that they can share data. This is often done with Ethernet networking hubs to extend the size of an Ethernet network. It's also how multiple Firewire and SCSI devices are connected to a single Macintosh computer so that they can all be accessed by that computer.

dead keys The keys that generate accented characters when typed in combination with the Option key and in proper sequence. For example, typing Option+E followed by O generates ó. The Key Caps desk accessory outlines the dead keys when you press Option.

default button The button in a dialog box or alert box that has a heavy border. It represents the action you'll most often want to take. If the most common action is dangerous, a button representing a safer action may be the default button.

default browser The Web browser application that launches when you open the Browse the Internet program, use the Connect To program, open an Internet *location file,* or otherwise don't specify a particular browser application.

desk accessory A type of program that doesn't have documents and can't receive Apple events.

desktop database Invisible files used by Finder to keep track of the location, icon, and Info window comments for every file, folder, and disk. The Mac OS keeps it hidden because you don't use it directly.

desktop printer An icon on the desktop used to manage printer settings and current *print jobs.*

dialog box A window that displays options you can set or select.

digital signature Functions as a handwritten signature, identifying the person who vouches for the accuracy and authenticity of the signed document.

DIMM Dual in-line memory module.

disk cache Improves system performance by storing recently used information from disk in a dedicated part of memory. Accessing information in memory is much faster than accessing information on disk.

disk image A file that, when mounted using Disk Copy or a similar utility, appears on the desktop as if it were a removable disk.

DogCow Also known as Clarus, it is the official mascot of Mac hackers and is pictured in many Page Setup Options dialog boxes.

domain name The part of a *URL* that identifies the owner of an Internet location. A domain name has the form companyname.com, organizationname.net, schoolname.edu, militaryunitname.mil, governmentagencyname.gov, and so forth.

double-click speed The rate at which you have to click so that the Mac OS perceives two clicks in a row as a single event.

download The process of receiving software or other computer files from another computer, over a network, generally through a modem and telephone line.

dpi (dots-per-inch) A measure of how fine or coarse the dots are that make up a printed image. More dots-per-inch means smaller dots, and smaller dots mean finer (less coarse) printing.

drag To move the mouse while holding down the mouse button.

drag-and-drop editing To copy selected text, graphics, and other material by dragging it to another place in the same window, a different window, or the desktop. This capability works only with applications that are designed to take advantage of it, such as SimpleText, Stickies, Note Pad, the ScrapBook, and Finder.

drag-and-drop open To drag a document to a compatible application in Finder thereby highlighting the application, and then releasing the mouse button, causing the application to open the document.

drop box A shared folder in which network users may place items, but only the folder's owner can see them.

DSL (Digital Subscriber Line) An add-on for standard telephone service that enables you to maintain a constant, high-speed networking connection over a standard telephone line.

dynamic RAM allocation An operating system technology that allows the operating system to respond to an application's request for more or less memory, as needed.

easy installation Installs all of the software components that are recommended for your computer model.

edition A file that contains a live copy of the material in a *publisher*. When the publisher changes, the edition is updated. *Subscribers* contain copies of editions.

enclosing folder The folder that contains another folder.

encryption The process of making messages or files unrecognizable, for example to keep someone from reading a sensitive document.

Ethernet A high-speed standard for connecting computers and other devices in a network. Ethernet ports are built into many newer Mac OS computer and Laser-Writer printer models. Its connectors and cabling cost more than *LocalTalk* equivalents.

EtherTalk A type of network that uses *AppleTalk* software and communications protocols over *Ethernet* cabling.

extension A software module that is loaded during startup and adds features or capabilities to the Mac OS. See also *file name extension*.

fair use Defines the criteria that must be considered before using another person's copyrighted work (printed or recorded materials).

Favorites Often-accessed items. Aliases can be added to the Favorites folder in the System Folder, which then appear on the Favorites menu in the Apple Menu and in Navigation Services dialog boxes.

file ID number The number that the Mac OS uses internally to identify the original item to which an alias is attached even if you have renamed or moved that original item.

file mapping The technique used by the Mac OS of treating a program file as part of *virtual memory* so that fragments of a program are only loaded into memory as needed.

filename extension The last part of a filename that follows a period and indicates the kind of file on the Internet and a DOS or Windows computer (along with some other computer systems). Also referred to as a filename suffix.

file server A computer running a program that makes files centrally available for other computers on a network.

file sharing Enables you to share files, folders, and disks with people whose computers are connected to yours in a network.

file spec (specification) Tells the Mac OS exactly where to find a file or folder.

firewall A special program or programs on a local area network (LAN) whose purpose is to prevent Internet users from getting into the local network and to stop local network users from sending sensitive information out.

fixed-size font Contains exact pictures of every letter, digit, and symbol for one size of a font. Fixed-size fonts often are called *bitmap fonts* because each picture precisely maps the dots, or *bits*, to be displayed or printed for one character.

folder-action script An AppleScript script that is attached to a folder so that it can watch and respond to user interaction with that folder in the Finder.

font A set of *characters* that have a common and consistent design.

font family A collection of differently styled variations (such as bold, italic, and plain) of a single *font*. Many *fixed-size*, *TrueType*, and *PostScript* fonts come in the four basic styles: plain, bold, italic, and bold italic. Some PostScript font families include 20 or more styled versions.

Fonts folder Located in the System Folder, this folder includes all *fixed-size*, *PostScript*, and *TrueType* fonts.

font suitcase A folderlike container specifically for *fixed-size* and *TrueType* fonts. You can create a new font-suitcase file by duplicating an existing font-suitcase file, opening the duplicate, and dragging its contents to the Trash.

fork Part of a Mac OS file. Many Mac OS files include a data fork and a resource fork where different types of information are stored.

fps (frames-per-second) Measures how smoothly a motion picture plays. More frames-per-second means smoother playback. This measurement is used when discussing the *frame rate* of time-based media.

fragmented memory See *memory fragmentation*.

frame One still image that is part of a series of still images, which, when shown in sequence, produce the illusion of movement.

frame rate The number of frames displayed in one second. The TV frame rate is 30 fps in the United States and other countries that use the NTSC broadcasting standard; 25 fps in countries that use the PAL or SEACAM standard. The standard movie frame rate is 24 fps. (See also *fps*.)

freeware Free software distributed through user groups and online information services. Most freeware is copyrighted by the person who created it; few freeware programs are in the public domain.

FTP (File Transfer Protocol) The data communications *protocol* used by the Internet and other TCP/IP networks to transfer files between computers.

FTP site A collection of files on an FTP server available for downloading.

full motion Video displayed at frame rates of 24 to 30 fps. The human eye perceives fairly smooth motion at frame rates of 12 to 18 fps. (See also *fps* and *frame rate*.)

gamma correction A method the computer's video circuitry uses to balance color on a monitor. Color balancing is necessary because the intensity of color on a monitor does not correspond uniformly to the intensity of the video signal that generates the picture on the monitor.

glyph A distinct visual representation of one character (such as a lowercase *z*), multiple characters treated as one (such as the ligature æ), or a nonprinting character (such as a space).

grid fitting The process of modifying characters at small point sizes so they fit the grid of dots on the relatively coarse display screen. The font designer provides a set of instructions (also known as *hints*) for a *TrueType* or *PostScript* font that tells the Mac OS how to modify character outlines to fit the grid.

group A collection of individual, registered users. You can grant specific access privileges for a shared item to a group instead of to a single user.

guest A network user who is not identified by a registered name and password. Also, a user who does not specifically have a Multiple Users account.

hack A programming effort that accomplishes something ingenious or unconventional.

hacker A person who likes to tinker with computers, and especially with computer software code. Some hackers create new software, but many hackers use programs such as ResEdit to make unauthorized changes to existing software.

handler A named set of *script* commands that you can execute by naming the handler elsewhere in the same script. Instead of repeating a set of commands several times in different parts of a script, you can make the set of commands a handler and invoke the handler each place you would have repeated the set of commands. This is also sometimes called a subroutine.

helper application A program that handles a particular kind of data encountered on the Internet.

home page The page that a Web browser displays when you first open it. This term is also often used to refer to the main page of a personal Web site.

hot spots Places in a QuickTime VR panorama that you can click to go to another scene in the panorama or to a QuickTime VR object.

hyperlink Underlined text or an image on a *Web page* that, when you click it, takes you to another page on the same or a different Web site.

icon A small picture that represents an entity such as a program, document, folder, or disk.

initialization A process that creates a blank disk directory, whose effect is the same as erasing the disk. Initialization actually wipes out the means of accessing the existing files on the disk without actually touching the content of files.

insertion point A blinking vertical bar that indicates where text will be inserted if you start typing.

installation Places a new or updated version of software on your disk.

interapplication communication (IAC) The technology that enables programs to send each other messages requesting action and receiving the results of requested actions. In the Mac OS, IAC is called *Apple events* and is the basis of *AppleScript*.

Internet A worldwide network that provides e-mail, Web pages, news, file storage and retrieval, and other services and information.

Internet Service Provider (ISP) A company that gives you access to the Internet via your modem.

ISDN (Integrated Services Digital Technology) A special telephone technology that allows for higher-speed network transmissions over long distances.

kerning Adjusting the space between pairs of letters so the spacing within the word looks consistent.

keychain Technology in Mac OS 9 that enables a user to store password and passphrases for network connections and encrypted files. The keychain file is the document in which the user's passwords are stored.

label A means of categorizing files, folders, and disks. Each label has its own color and text, which you can change with the Labels control panel.

LAN See *local area network*.

language script system Software that enables the Mac OS to use an additional natural language, such as Japanese. Multiple languages can use one language script system (for example, the Roman script is used for English, French, Italian, Spanish, and German).

launch The opening of a program that you want to use.

ligature A glyph composed of two merged characters. For example, *f* and *l* can be merged to form *fl*.

link See *hyperlink*.

local area network (LAN) A system of computers that are interconnected for sharing information and services and are located in proximity such as in an office, home, school, or campus.

localization The development of software whose dialog-box messages, screens, menus, and other screen elements use the language spoken in the region in which the software is sold.

LocalTalk A relatively low-speed standard for connecting computers, printers, and other devices to create an *AppleTalk* network. LocalTalk uses the built-in serial "printer" ports of Mac OS computers (or specialized adapters for Macs that don't include a serial port) and the LocalTalk ports of many LaserWriter printers.

location file A file that, when opened, takes you to a location on the Internet or a local area network.

login A prompt to enter a username and password to access a secured resource (such as a network connection or a user profile in Mac OS 9). Also, the name of the application that enables multiple users to access a single Macintosh in Mac OS 9.

lossless A type of compression algorithm that regenerates exactly the same data as the uncompressed original.

MacBinary A scheme for encoding the special information in a Macintosh file's data and resource forks into a file format appropriate for transmission over the Internet.

memory fragmentation The condition wherein available memory has become divided into multiple disjointed blocks, with each block separated by an open program. The Mac OS cannot automatically consolidate fragmented memory nor open a program in multiple blocks. You can fix memory fragmentation by quitting all open programs.

memory management unit (MMU) A part of the PowerPC processor chip, the MMU is required for virtual memory.

memory partition The block of memory dedicated to the code, resources, and data that a program or process has for its exclusive use while it is open.

memory protection An operating system technology that makes it impossible for one active application to read and write data from another active application's storage space in RAM. Memory protection helps applications run with fewer crashes.

memory size The amount of memory allocated to a program when you open it. You can change a program's minimum and preferred memory sizes with the Get Info command.

microkernel The central module of some operating systems that provides essential services and management to other parts of the operating system and applications.

modem A device that connects a computer to telephone lines. It converts digital information from the computer into sounds for transmission over phone lines and converts sounds from phone lines to digital information for the computer. (The term *modem* is a shortened form of *modulator-demodulator*.) This term is also used informally for devices that connect computers using other technologies, such as TV cable, DSL, and ISDN connections.

modem script Software consisting of the modem commands necessary to start and stop a remote access connection for a particular type of modem.

movie Any time-related data, such as video, sound, animation, and graphs, that change over time; Apple's format for organizing, storing, and exchanging time-related data.

mount To make a disk's contents available to the computer. In the case of hard disks, this happens every time you start up the computer. You can also use the Drive Setup utility program or a similar disk utility to mount disks.

multimedia A presentation combining text or graphics with video, animation, or sound, and presented on a computer.

multitasking The capability to have multiple programs open and executing concurrently.

multithreading An operating system technology that allows tasks in an application to share processor time.

navigate Opening of disks and folders until you have opened the one that contains the item you need; to go from one *Web page* to another.

network A collection of interconnected, individually controlled computers, printers, and other devices together with the hardware, software, and protocols used to connect them. A network lets connected devices exchange messages and information.

network administrator Someone who sets up and/or maintains a centralized file server and other network services. The network administrator does not control access to folders and files on the server's disks; that is the responsibility of each person who puts items on the disks.

network interface card (NIC) An internal adapter card that provides a network port.

network location A type of file that opens a particular file server in the Network Browser.

network time servers Computers on a network or the Internet that keep accurate time.

networking protocol A set of rules for exchanging data over a *network*.

newsgroup A subject on the Internet's *Usenet*. It is a collection of people and messages pertaining to that particular subject.

nonblocking alert box An alert box from a background application that appears in a floating window so that the current application's activities are not halted.

object A kind of information, such as words, paragraphs, and characters, that an application knows how to work with. An application's *AppleScript* dictionary lists the kinds of objects it can work with under script control.

online information service A source that provides discussion groups, shareware, and freeware directly to your computer through telephone lines and modems. Examples include America Online (800-827-6364), CompuServe (800-292-3900), and various *Internet* sites. Except for the Internet, online information services charge access fees.

operating system Software that controls the basic activities of a computer system. Also known as *system software*.

original item A file, folder, or disk to which an *alias* points, and which opens when you open its alias.

orphaned alias An *alias* that has lost its link with its original item (and, therefore, the Mac OS cannot find it).

outline font A font whose *glyphs* are outlined by curves and straight lines that can be smoothly enlarged or reduced to any size and then filled with dots.

owner A registered user or group that can assign access privileges to a shared folder; the person who can access all disks and folders (even those not explicitly shared with the Sharing command). This latter owner's name and password are set in the File Sharing or Sharing Setup control panel.

package A logical grouping of system files that are related, such as all of the items that make up fax software, or all of the parts of QuickTime.

palette A window that contains controls or tools or displays auxiliary information for the application program that you're currently using.

partition To divide a hard drive into several smaller volumes, each of which the computer treats as a separate disk. Also, another name for any of the volumes created by dividing a hard drive. See also *memory partition*.

passphrase Like a password, but generally consisting of more than one word. (The larger a password or passphrase, the more difficult it is to guess or otherwise discover.)

password A combination of letters, digits, and symbols that must be typed accurately to gain access to information or services on the Internet or a *local area network*.

peer-to-peer file sharing The process of sharing folders, disks, and their contents with other people's computers — not a central file server — on a network.

PhoneNet An inexpensive LocalTalk cabling system for connecting computers, printers, and other devices to an *AppleTalk* network.

pixel Short for picture element, a pixel is the smallest dot that the computer and monitor can display.

pixel depth The number of memory bits used to store each pixel of a displayed image. The number of colors available depends on the number of bits. For example, 256 colors require 8 bits per pixel, and thousands of colors require 16 bits per pixel.

plug-ins Software that works with existing applications to extend their capabilities. For instance, plug-ins exist for the Sherlock 2 application that enable it to search additional Internet sites.

point of presence (POP) An entry point to the Internet. Also, a telephone number that gains access to the Internet through an Internet service provider.

pop-up menu A menu that is not in the menu bar, but that is marked with an arrowhead and pops open when you click it.

PostScript font An outline font that conforms to the specifications of the PostScript programming language. PostScript fonts can be smoothly scaled to any size, rotated, and made to follow a curved path. Originally designed for printing on LaserWriters and other PostScript output devices, the Adobe Type Manager (ATM) software makes PostScript fonts work equally well onscreen and with non-PostScript printers. (Compare *TrueType*.)

PostScript printers Printers that interpret PostScript commands to create printable images.

PPD (PostScript Printer Description) A file that contains the optional features of a PostScript printer such as its resolution and paper tray configuration.

PRAM (parameter RAM) A small amount of battery-powered memory that stores system settings such as time, date, mouse tracking speed, speaker volume, and choice of startup disk.

preemptive multitasking A scheme for multitasking applications where the operating system has control over how much processor time each application can use.

Preferences folder Holds files that contain the settings you make in control panels and with the Preferences commands of application programs.

primary script The *language script system* used by system dialog boxes and menus. If you are working on a computer that is set up for English, Roman is your primary script; your secondary script can be any other installed language script, such as Japanese.

printer driver Software that prepares pages for, and communicates with, a particular type of printer. This software resides in the Extensions folder inside the System Folder.

print job A file of page descriptions that is sent to a particular type of printer. Also called a *print request* or *spool file*.

print request See *print job*.

print server A computer or a program on a computer that manages one or more shared printers on a network.

program A set of coded instructions that direct a computer in performing a specific task.

program linking The process of sharing programs by sending and receiving *Apple events* across a network. You must turn on program linking in the File Sharing or Sharing Setup control panel. You can use Finder's Sharing command to enable or prevent linking to individual programs.

protocol See *networking protocol*.

publisher A section of a document, a copy of which has been saved as an *edition* for other documents to subscribe to.

RAM Random-access memory, which is physical memory built into the computer in the form of electronic chips or small circuit boards called DIMMs or SIMMs. (Some PowerBooks have special memory boards that are unique to each model.)

RAM disk Memory that is set aside to be used as if it were a very fast hard disk.

registered user Network users who must enter their names and any passwords that you've assigned them before they can connect to your computer to share files or programs.

repeat loop An arrangement of *AppleScript* commands that begins with a Repeat command and ends with an End Repeat command. AppleScript executes the commands between the Repeat and End Repeat commands for the number of times specified in the Repeat command.

resolution The perceived smoothness of a displayed or printed image. Printed resolution is measured in dots-per-inch (*dpi*). A high-resolution printed image has more dots-per-inch than a low-resolution printed image. When referring to computer monitors, the resolution determines the number of *pixels* that appear on the screen, which determines the size of the overall screen image.

resolve an alias What the Mac OS does to find the original item that is represented by an *alias*.

resources Information such as text, menus, icons, pictures, or patterns used by the Mac OS, an application, or other software.

ROM Read-only memory.

root level The main level of a disk, which is what you see when you open the disk icon.

script A collection of *AppleScript* commands that perform a specific task. Also, short for *language script system*, which is software that defines a method of writing (vertical or horizontal, left-to-right, or right-to-left). A script also provides rules for text sorting, word breaking, and the formatting of dates, times, and numbers.

script applet *AppleScript* scripts saved as applets or small applications.

scripting additions Files that add commands to the *AppleScript* language, much as plug-in filters add menu commands to Photoshop or the contents of the Word Commands folder add various features to Microsoft Word. Scripting additions reside in a folder called Scripting Additions, which is in the System Folder.

script recording A process in which *AppleScript* watches as you work with an application and automatically writes a corresponding *script*.

selection rectangle A dotted-line box that you drag around items to select them all.

server A program that provides information or services to clients on demand.

shareware Low-cost software distributed through user groups and online information services. Shareware depends on the honor and honesty of people who use it. You're expected to pay the author a small fee if you plan to use the software.

Shift+click Holding down the Shift key while clicking the mouse to select multiple items or a range of items.

SIMMs Single in-line memory modules.

smoothing See *antialias*.

software One or more programs that consist of coded instructions that direct a computer in performing a task.

sound track A set of related sounds that may accompany various actions you perform with menus, windows, controls, and icons. Also, an audible part of a movie.

spool file See *print job*.

spooling A printer-driver operation in which the driver saves page descriptions in a file (called a *spool file*) for later printing.

standard installation This type of installation installs basic modules such as the Mac OS and QuickTime plus any additional modules you select.

startup disk A disk with the Finder and System files in its System Folder, and which enables the computer to begin operation.

Startup Items folder Items placed here are opened automatically when your Mac is started.

stationery pad A template document that contains preset format and contents.

streaming media Movies designed to be played over the Internet as they are downloaded.

stuffed file A file (or group of files) that has been compressed and archived using the StuffIt file format from Aladdin Systems.

subdirectories The equivalent in other operating systems to folders in the Mac OS.

submenu A secondary menu that pops out from the side of another menu. A submenu appears when you place the pointer on a menu item that has an arrowhead at the right side of the menu. These are sometimes referred to as hierarchical menus.

subscriber A copy of an *edition* that has been placed in a document and that can be updated automatically when the edition is updated by its *publisher*.

suite In *AppleScript*, a group of related commands and other items.

symmetrical multiprocessing An operating system technology that allows the operating system and applications to take advantage of two or more processors installed in the computer.

system enabler A plug-in software component that modifies the Mac OS to work with a particular computer model.

system extension See *extension*.

System file Contains sounds, keyboard layouts, and language script systems, as well as the basic Mac OS software.

System Folder Stores the essential software (including Finder, the System file, control panels, and extensions) that gives the Mac OS its unique appearance and behavior.

system software Software that controls the basic activities of a computer system. Also known as the operating system.

theme A group of all the settings in the Appearance control panel.

thread A string of messages about the same subject in a newsgroup. Also, a single task being executed within a (possibly multithreaded) program.

track One channel of a QuickTime movie, containing video, sound, closed-captioned text, MIDI data, time codes, or other time-related data.

tracking The overall spacing between letters in an entire document or text selection. Text with loose tracking has extra space between the characters in words. Text with tight tracking has characters squeezed close together.

tracking speed The rate at which the pointer moves as you drag the mouse.

transceiver A connector box that converts a general AAUI Ethernet port, which is built into many Mac models, to the specific kind of port needed for a particular type of Ethernet cable in a network.

translator A program that translates your documents from one file format to another file format, such as a PICT graphic to a GIF graphic.

Trojan horse Destructive software that masquerades as something useful, such as a utility program or game.

TrueType The outline font technology built into the Mac OS (and Microsoft Windows). TrueType fonts can be smoothly scaled to any size onscreen or to any type of printer.

Type 1 font A PostScript font that includes instructions for grid fitting so that the font can be scaled to small sizes and low printer resolutions with good results.

universal installation Yields a version of the Mac OS that can be used by any compatible Mac model.

UNIX A complex and powerful operating system whose TCP/IP networking protocol is the basis of the Internet.

unmount To remove a disk's icon from the desktop and make the disk's contents unavailable without deleting the items in that disk permanently.

Unshielded twisted-pair (UTP) The type of cable used in a 10Base-T or 100Base-T Ethernet network.

upload The process of sending files from your computer to another computer.

URL (Uniform Resource Locator) An *Internet* address. This can be the address of a *Web page*, a file on an *FTP* site, or anything else that you can access on the Internet.

Usenet A worldwide *Internet* bulletin board system that enables people to post messages and join discussions about subjects that interest them.

user group An organization that provides information to people who use computers. Many user groups, such as BMUG (510-549-2684), have extensive libraries of *shareware* and *freeware*, which they distribute on floppy disk for a nominal fee. For the names and phone numbers of user groups near you, call Apple's referral line (800-538-9696).

variable A container for information in a *script*. You can place data in a variable and then use it elsewhere in the script.

virtual memory Additional memory made available by the Mac OS treating part of a hard disk as if it were built-in memory.

virus Software designed to spread itself by illicitly attaching copies of itself to legitimate software. Some viruses perform malicious actions, such as erasing your hard drive. Even seemingly innocuous viruses can interfere with the normal functioning of your computer. Not the same as a *bug*.

volume A disk or a part of a disk that the computer treats as a separate storage device. Each volume has a disk icon on the desktop.

Web browser A program that displays *Web pages* from the Internet.

Web page A basic unit that the World Wide Web uses to display information (including text, pictures, animation, audio, and video clips). A Web page can also contain *hyperlinks* to the same page or to other Web pages (on the same or a different Web server).

Web server A computer or a program running on a computer that provides information to a Web browser program.

worm Software that replicates like a virus but without attaching itself to other software. It may be benign or malicious.

write protect The process of locking a disk so that it cannot be erased, have its name changed, have files copied to it or duplicated from it, or have files or folders it contains moved to the desktop or trash.

Zip disk A removable storage disk made to work with removable drives manufactured or licensed by Iomega Corporation.

zipped file A file (or group of files) that has been compressed and archived using the PKZip or WinZip format. Also, a file compressed using the UNIX gzip standard.

Index

Continued

Continued

Continued

Continued

Continued

my2cents.idgbooks.com